Offal: Rejected and Reclaimed Food
Proceedings of the Oxford Symposium on Food and Cookery 2016

Offal: Rejected and Reclaimed Food

Proceedings of the Oxford Symposium on Food and Cookery 2016

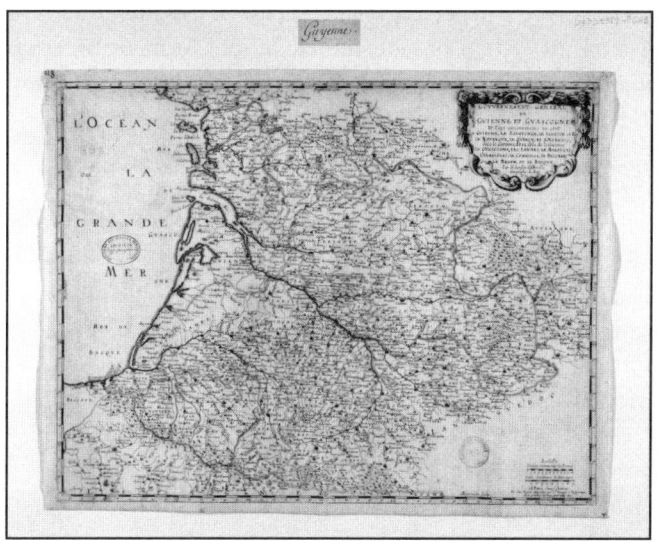

Edited by Mark McWilliams

Prospect Books
2017

First published in Great Britain in 2017 by Prospect Books, 26 Parke Road, London SW13 9NG.

© 2017 as a collection Prospect Books.
© 2017 in individual articles rests with the authors.

The authors assert their moral right to be identified as authors in accordance with the Copyright, Designs & Patents Act 1988. No part of this publication may be reproduced, stored in a retrieval system or transmitted in any form or by any means, electronic, mechanical, photocopying, recording or otherwise, without the prior permission of the copyright holders.

ISBN 978-1-909-248-55-7

The front cover illustration is by Kent Monkman, *Les Castors Du Roi*, 2011, acrylic on canvas from the collection of the Montreal Museum of Fine Arts.
Image courtesy of Kent Monkman.

The back cover shows *Lodge* (2009) by David Diviny.

Design and typesetting in Gill Sans and Adobe Garamond by Catheryn Kilgarriff and Rebecca Gillieron.

Printed and bound in Great Britain.

Contents

Foreword
Mark McWilliams ... 9

Plenary Papers

Marginalized Meats? Contextualizing Offal Consumption in 1940s Spain
Suzanne Dunai ... 11

It's All Edible: Four Views of Offal
Peter Hertzmann ... 21

The Ends of Offal: Reflections on Laboratory-Grown Meat
Ben Wurgaft ... 40

Symposium Papers

'Vulgarly Termed Lights': The Curious History of Lung Cookery
Ken Albala ... 49

Şırdan: The Pornographic Dish of a Conservative Land
Nilhan Aras ... 56

Offal and the Master Cook: Nose-to-Tail Eating in Late Medieval Germany
Volker Bach ... 64

Foie Gras: The Quantum Offal
Guillemette Barthouil ... 72

Leverpostej – More than Just a Danish Way of Eating Offal
Nina Bauer ... 84

An Internal Crisis: The Shifting Value of Offal in the UK Meat Industry
Barley Blyton, Polly Russell and Tessa Tricks ... 94

'Un Vrai Jambalaya – 'A Real Mess': The Complex Western Mediterranean Origins of Louisiana's Famous Dish
Anthony F. Buccini ... 105

Offal: Rejected and Reclaimed Food

The Three Great 'Rare Tastes' in Japanese Culinary History: Sea Cucumber Entrails, Sea Urchin Gonads and Mullet Roe
Voltaire Cang — *121*

A Woman Holding a Liver
Amanda Couch — *134*

Hog's Puddings, White Puddings, Liverings and Andolians: The Rise and Fall of England's Offal Puddings c.1500-c.1800
Jan Davison — *148*

Liver for Cats and Kids: The Fall of Offal in Istanbul Cuisine
Pelin Dumanlı — *157*

A Waste of Flavour
Thom Eagle — *166*

A Knife and an Onion: Reclaiming Food and Skills in Central London
Anastasia Edwards — *172*

The Search for Lost Blood: Why the Blood Has Run Dry in British Black Pudding
Jessica Fagin — *182*

Fish Heads, Tapioca and Sweet-Potato Leaves: The Ingredients of Survival in Occupied Malaya during World War II
Laura Fan — *192*

Beaver as Offal: The Presence and Absence of Beavers in Canadian Cuisine
L. Sasha Gora — *200*

'Starbuggs?': Natural Dyes, Disgusting Drinks and the Controversy over Cochineal Use at Starbucks
Amy Butler Greenfield — *211*

The Case of Missing Brains, a Long Way from Rome
Alexandra Grigorieva — *220*

Gut Feelings: Tripe in American Poetries
Naomi Guttman — *224*

Offal: Rejected and Reclaimed Food

Copying and Copyright: The Recipe Text as Offal
Heidi Hakimi-Hood, Amanda Milian and Carrie Helms Tippen — *229*

Waste against Waste: Medicinal Offal Products, 'Artificial Digestion' and the Nineteenth-Century Thrift Movement
Lisa Haushofer — *239*

Offal People: Resurrecting Chicken Feet on the Streets of Cape Town
Arundhatie Biswas Kundal — *252*

The Good, the Bad and the Ugly: The Allure of Offal Cuisine in Japan
Christopher Laurent — *263*

Food Waste: Attitudes, Behaviors and Perceptions at Hamilton College
Eunice Lee — *271*

Pig, Pork, Prep, Print: Cochon555 and Whole Animal Cookery Discourse
Robert McKeown — *281*

Blood, Not So Simple
Jennifer McLagan — *294*

Frikandel, the Most Popular Dutch Snack: Wasteful or Sustainable?
Lenno Munnikes — *302*

Offal and Extremities in Art
Gillian Riley — *310*

'A Sentimental Passion of a Vegetable Fashion': How American Culture, Politics and Commercial Agriculture Reflect and Influence Shifting Opinions of Fruit and Vegetable Offal
Charity Robey — *316*

Gone and Forgotten: Hooksteaks, Trashbags and Other Vanished Icelandic Offal Dishes
Nanna Rögnvaldardóttir — *329*

Outlaw Offal: The Curious Cases of *Tête De Veau* and *Foie Gras*
Richard Shepro — *339*

Offal: Rejected and Reclaimed Food

Mocotó Jam: Children's Food
Marcella Sulis and Myriam Melchior   *353*

The Tradition of Offal in the Greek World: From Classical Antiquity to (post-) Byzantine Time
Stephanos Tanis   *362*

Axolotl: Pre-Hispanic Delicacy, Rejected Monster and Reclaimed Wonder of Science and Literature
Fernando Valerio-Holguín   *374*

Abjecting Crab Brain: Offal Eating and Ethnic Identity in The Joy Luck Club
Jiachen Zhang   *384*

The Lore of Tripe: Middle East and Beyond
Sami Zubaida   *394*

Foreword

At the conclusion of each year's Oxford Symposium on Food and Cookery, symposiasts gather to wrap up the fascinating discussions of the preceding three days. The business of that final session, though, is to choose the theme for the symposium that will follow three years later. The symposium alternates between general and specific topics, and in 2013 attendees were tasked with finding a focused subject for 2016. Raucous conversation filled St. Catherine's lecture hall as symposiasts yelled out individual favourites, but that year a consensus emerged much more quickly than usual: offal. Some of the organizers – myself included – seemed worried that this topic might be too narrow, but the growing enthusiasm in the room suggested interest and energy that developed into one of the most rewarding symposiums in memory.

What those excited symposiasts knew was not just the cultish popularity of offal, spurred in the West by the nose-to-tail movement (re)popularized by Fergus Henderson and others, but also that the term itself has a more flexible meaning than often assumed. Noting the word's origin in the Middle Dutch *afval* and the German *abfall*, the *OED* does include what seems the common use: 'The edible parts collectively which are cut off in preparing the carcass of an animal for food.' But even that seemingly concrete definition immediately suggests the role of culture: 'In early use applied mainly to the entrails; later extended to include the head, tail, and internal organs such as the heart, liver, etc.' What counts as offal, it seems, is open for negotiation; what counts changes as needs and tastes change. The nature of those changes is suggested in the next definition: 'The parts of a slaughtered or dead animal considered unfit for human consumption.' The key words there are 'considered unfit': unlike something that is simply unsafe, here we have a cultural choice: what is 'fit' for us to eat. At once implied is culinary affiliation and differentiation (because they eat some food does not make it fit for us), and that cuts both ways: offal can be both the subsistence fare of the brutish poor or the rare delicacy of the cultured elite – and sometimes both at once!

Over three lovely summer days in Oxford, symposiasts worked through the shifting meanings of offal and the changes in what foods might be considered in that category in different times and places. As might be expected, presenters expressed much nostalgia over what has been lost and perhaps more delight over what has been rediscovered; both emotions seemed fueled by growing concerns about waste and sustainability. The flexibility of the term itself combined with the usual quirkiness of the symposium to produce the fascinating papers included in this volume, but even this wide-ranging collection cannot hope to include the wonderful conversations that occurred over endless tea and coffee and what must surely have been some of the finest meals in symposium history. For joining me in those conversations and for their help in preparing this volume, I particularly thank Bee Wilson, Ursula Heinzelmann, Cathy Kaufman, Elisabeth Luard, Catheryn Kilgarriff and, of course, the many authors who made the symposium such a memorable success.

Mark McWilliams
Editor, Oxford Symposium on Food and Cookery

Marginalized Meats? Contextualizing Offal Consumption in 1940s Spain

Suzanne Dunai

After a brutal civil war, the dictatorship of Francisco Franco in Spain (1939-1975) consolidated power through policies of repression and coercion that included the effort to control food and its everyday consumption. Spain's foodways were a useful way to manage a demobilizing population and to achieve Franco's ideal of a 'New State' (*Nuevo Estado*). The regime tightly regulated the movement of goods throughout the country and redistributed food according to the state's prioritization of provisioning. Economically, the regime's bureaucracy adopted a policy of autarky, which consisted of extreme state control and the theory of 'self-sufficiency'. Autarky regulated every aspect of food consumption through production control, price setting and consumer rationing. It forced Spaniards to consume only what they could produce as a nationalistic sacrifice to the *patria*. In terms of gender, the regime required that all Spanish women between the ages of eighteen and thirty-five complete a six-month 'feminine training' that included twenty-four hours of cooking classes, ensuring that women cooked Spain's national dishes in a uniform manner.[1] Through the Catholic Church, Spaniards were forced to adhere to a religious calendar of fasting and feast days.[2] Food traversed public and private spheres, facilitating the regime's access to both the streets and the home through restaurants and home cooking. Franco passed legislation that required all restaurants to serve lunch before 2:30 p.m. and dinner before 9:30 p.m., regulating when Spaniards were allowed to eat in public.[3] In private life, Franco intervened to implement a 'family-style' rationing system from 1939 to 1943 that allocated 100% of a ration for adult males, while women received 80% of a ration and children received 60%, thus replicating a patriarchal hierarchy with every meal.[4] While these are only examples of some of the food-related policies, they reinforce the argument that the Franco regime went to great lengths to control comestibles and the Spanish population.

Because autarky coincided with widespread deprivation, often known as the 'years of hunger', many scholars of everyday life have argued that the regime fostered a culture of scarcity and have portrayed Spaniards as victims of totalitarian policies. Rafael Abella has claimed that the food situation in postwar Spain was so desperate that traditional non-foods such as orange peels were incorporated into the Spanish diet.[5] Michael Richards goes so far as to claim that Franco used his control of the food supply as a weapon against the working classes to force them into submission to Francoist culture.[6] And the most recent literature on the period provides details of how ordinary Spaniards struggled to survive within a foodscape of scarcity.[7] Social historians have emphasized the political apathy of the Spanish population in their struggle to survive, while cultural historians have chronicled the gastronomic stagnation caused by food shortages. Yet this paper will challenge some of these previous assertions by exploring the consumption of one particular foodstuff in Spanish cuisine and diet: offal. Spaniards living in the postwar period formed strong opinions of offal, and an investigation into the interaction between public opinion and the regime in regard to offal demonstrates how Spaniards made active choices in their consumer habits, and in doing so, engaged the authoritarian political culture of the Francoist state.

Food carried particular political potential in the authoritarian politics of the Franco regime because it was consumed by all Spaniards. Food was an opportune vehicle for transmitting aspects of the regime's ideology as it possessed the capacity to reinforce political and social symbolism. As Carol Helstosky has found in the case of Mussolini's Italy, autarky was a way to force citizens to consume a nationalized diet and assume a national, Fascist identity.[8] When Franco came to power, he modelled his food policy after that of the Italian Fascist state with the hope of achieving a similar nationalization process in Spain.[9] Through an authoritarian diet that carefully monitored ingredients, quantities and feeding times, the dictatorship sought to maximize its control over the population in their everyday public and private life. Yet, this article will demonstrate that Franco's food policy faced obstructions in its implementation and was often resisted in the practice of everyday life.

Offal (*despojos*) is a useful case study to elucidate the complex relationship between the Francoist state and consumers because public opinion of the foodstuff was so strong. Offal, which I define as the non-muscular parts of slaughtered animals such as organs, hooves, tails, heads, ears, blood and bones, came under the purview of the Francoist state and was highly politicized according to the ideology of the regime. However, similar to other consumer goods of the time, it was haphazardly regulated so that occasionally Spaniards could enjoy their favourite dishes free from the watchful eye of the state. For example, the day after the official end of the Civil War, on 2 April 1939, the regime declared that beef, pork and lamb offal would be sold without state intervention in the prices or rationing.[10] Yet Spaniards' freedom to buy offal without regulation did not last long. By the end of that year, Franco reversed his policy and offal became incorporated within the rationing system. Offal policy changed once again in a decree issued 16 September 1941 that declared that ranchers could determine their own price when selling offal to meat vendors. But this freedom faced restrictions in a decree issued 31 October 1941 which limited the sale of offal to active members of the Offal Union (*sindicato de despojos*).[11] These laws only applied to some types of offal because by 1942 the price for bones was regulated to 3.10 pesetas per kilo with stomachs and brains allowed to sell for 1.15 and 0.15 pesetas respectively.[12] Preserved offal was subjected to different regulations in that the regime outlawed all forms of meat preservation on 6 October 1939. The prohibition of preserved offal was enacted

Contextualizing Offal Consumption in 1940s Spain

as an effort to curb hoarding, but the regime amended its policy in a subsequent decree issued on 15 July 1940 to allow for stomach and livers to undergo preservation treatments.[13] The regime's policy on offal changed often, and such inconsistency created venues for Spaniards to practice non-conformity to the dictatorship through their habitual consumption of food.

This article will analyze popular perceptions of offal and how consumers interacted with the state in their everyday life through three sub-questions of exploration: Was offal a common or unusual consumer good in postwar society? Was it cheap or expensive to buy? And was offal nutritious, or did it pose health risks to the Spaniards? Spanish responses to these questions and how they acted on them through consumer choice reveal how offal acted as a conduit of political participation in Spain's postwar society. And although the Franco regime attempted to regulate the consumption of offal – sometimes incentivizing consumption and other times prohibiting it – Spaniards maintained many of their habitual patterns, demonstrating the limitations of the state and the spectrum of consensus and non-conformity that occurred in the food culture of the postwar period.

I. Was It Normal?

Some Spaniards of the postwar period would answer this question with a resounding 'no', while many others would answer it with a determined 'of course'! The period of rationing in Spain is remembered in history as the 'years of hunger', and several oral histories collected by scholars provide accounts of Spaniards having to eat cat, nettles and even rocks to fill their hungry bellies.[14] These shocking stories of survival chronicle shifts in edibility, and offal often has been lumped within foods on the edge of edibility. These oral histories suggest that the consumption of offal was often seen as a 'last resort' or the only means of survival for many families. In the aftermath of the destruction of the civil war, some Spaniards complained because their consumer choice was reduced to offal. They held up the food item as a critique of the culture of scarcity imposed by the Franco regime that forced inedible foods into their diets, limiting their food choices. But the culinary literature and the government records that contain references to offal tell a different story. Many cookbooks championed offal as an integral part of Spanish cuisine, and the sale of offal throughout cities greatly expanded in the 1940s. Even before the imposition of a culture of austerity during the civil war and the Franco dictatorship, offal recipes filled cookbooks and offal stores (*casqueros*) peppered the Spanish cityscape. During the years of hunger, many Spaniards expressed a hunger for offal. It gained new prestige in Spanish taste partly due to government regulation and partly to satisfy Spaniards' taste for the food.

On one hand, offal functioned as a scapegoated foodstuff to symbolize Spain's economic problems in the postwar period. Pre-Civil War Spain saw the rise of a national Spanish cuisine that corresponded with the growth of the middle classes, and the consumption of meat was seen as a status symbol of this emerging class.[15] The war and the Franco regime threatened the financial security of the middle classes, and as a result, many Spaniards begrudgingly resorted to eating offal in order to maintain their appearance as middle class. But these Spaniards complained and grumbled about their limited food options under autarky, and they used offal as a way to express their discontent. Complaints about eating offal were a way that Spain's middle classes directed their disgust at the regime that failed to provide them with better food options.

For example, the University Student Union of the Falange (*Sindicato estudiantes universitarios*) complained to the regime regarding the poor quality of food that they received from the university dining halls.[16] Their condemnation included an incident where students refused to eat the beef hearts that the university provided for their meal. These upper and middle class students enjoyed the economic means to attend university and had enough financial and social confidence to refuse the food, a luxury not available to many Spaniards during the time. Their complaints were directed to the food provisioning headquarters and demanded that they receive better food from the state. In this case of students being served hearts, offal was rejected by wealthy Spaniards as a mark of poverty. The Francoist state attempted to impose a uniform, nationalized culinary culture that included offal, but some elites refused to modify their diet to food that they considered as socially inferior.

On the other hand, despite this one case of expressed audacity at consuming offal and refusal to subscribe to the nationalized diet of the regime, other Spaniards acquiesced to Spain's new foodscape through their consumption of offal either for nutritional or economic reasons. Madrid's city records show that not only did many offal vendors maintain their business in the aftermath of the war, but many new vendors eagerly applied for permits to become sellers of animal leftovers.[17] The state used Spanish desire to consume meat to its benefit, and the regulation of meat and its consumption became a way to regulate Spaniards. All meat sold within the city had to pass through the municipal butcher where the quality, cuts and prices were carefully regulated.[18] Offal vendors (*casqueros*) in Madrid had to prove membership in the Madrid Federation for Meat Industries in order to receive their offal-vending license.[19] Standalone offal stores had to be 150 m from any other offal vendors and offal stalls within markets had to be at least 50 m apart. Thus, the regime was able to control the movement of people within the city as ordinary housewives travelled within the foodscape to acquire provisions for their families. The regime was eager to approve new offal vendor permits after the war due to the desire of municipal officials to curb the excessive length of market lines.[20] Yet the lines for meat persisted, meaning that Spaniards participated within the confines of Francoism to acquire the food that they wanted.

Likewise, culinary literature of the time incorporated offal into their indices of recipes for all occasions, without complaint or stigmatization. One Barcelona cookbook, *Cocina Familiar* (*Family Cooking*) written under the pseudonym 'María del Carmen' and published in the postwar period, dedicated an entire section to offal.[21] The recipes instructed housewives to cook using tongues, hooves, brains, kidneys and livers as the star of the menu. With over sixty offal recipes included in the book, Spanish housewives had plenty of meal ideas for incorporating offal into their family diets. This was not exceptional, as the best-selling cookbook of the postwar period, María Mestayer de Echague's *Cocina Completa*, contains no less than twenty-two recipes for brains alone, and countless additional recipes that call for livers and kidneys.[22] If Spanish women wanted to cook with offal, there was no shortage of literature that encouraged the normalization of this sometimes marginalized animal product.

Overall, despite the occasional protest against the consumption of offal – usually by middle-class Spaniards who lamented their downward mobility more than the taste of the animal organs – it was normal for Spaniards to consume tongues, tails, livers, kidneys, brains, intestines and hooves. Some sources from the time attempted to exoticize the habitual consumption of offal, but this underscores the sheer demand for the food, as it was expressed in the increase in offal vendor permits and its prevalence in cookbooks of the time. Likewise, cookbooks unapologetically incorporated offal recipes as standard dishes in Spanish gastronomy. Despite the attempt of some Spaniards to use offal as a platform of critique for the dictatorship, most Spaniards viewed offal as normal and an integral part of their food habits.

II. Was It Cheap?

However, to say that offal was ordinary oversimplifies the cultural value assigned to offal. The sale of offal was a lucrative business in the postwar period, and some Spaniards took advantage of the economic opportunity to open new offal stores in Barcelona and Madrid. In general, most cuts of offal were cheaper than the prime cuts of meat, but some offal parts were more expensive. Those who valued offal highly paid the premium to enjoy their favourite part of the animal: not steak or roast, but *foie gras*, beef kidneys and oxtail. Other parts – such as blood and bones – were the only animal protein that many Spaniards could afford, and so their diminished purchasing power reduced their enjoyment to less culturally-valued parts of the animal. Likewise, with the government attempting to control the economy of offal through price setting and its geographic availability, intervention clashed with preconceived values assigned to offal. A closer look at the monetary value of offal reveals its cultural value and more broadly elucidates the relationship between the government's intervention in the sale of offal and Spanish consumption of it.

Proof of the financial value of offal is seen in its level of importation. Although the Francoist economic system of autarky rejected the notion of importing goods and the ideology assumed that Spain should be self-sufficient, the regime made an exception for meat. After the civil war, Franco formed an agreement with Argentina's leader Peron and by the mid-1940s Spain was receiving a regular supply of frozen meat to satisfy Spaniards' hunger. In 1944, Spain imported 85,452,000 pesetas gold of meat from Argentina, of which 6,187,000 pesetas gold (7% of the cost) was paid for offal.[23] This was not enough offal for Spaniards. *La Carne* (*Meat*), a magazine circulated among members of a meat vendor's union, published a joke about the lack of offal among the shipments of meat received from Argentina: 'We appreciate the cuts, but would appreciate it more if you could cut less!'.²⁴ The meat vendors who received meat from Argentina had difficulty selling it because the cuts lacked the usual bones, skins and gristle that Spanish housewives were accustomed to using in their recipes. This joke indicates how the normalization of offal translated to regular demand for the product. Meat vendors risked losing business for their inability to supply sufficient quantity of offal and the meat products demanded for their hungry clients. Offal, although sometimes cheap, was quite lucrative to Spanish businesses.

This paradox of economically cheap yet highly culturally-valued offal was negotiated in the market controlled by Franco and in the market where ordinary Spanish housewives shopped. Great price variation among types of offal was not unique to the 1940s, as anthropologists Nicalau-Nous and Pujol-Andreu have observed. They have found that offal had the greatest price-variation among consumer goods in Spain in the early twentieth century, and a similar price-variation can be observed in the postwar period as well.²⁵ In 1946 for example, the city of Madrid had an average price regulation of 15.20 pesetas for the top cut of boneless beef. Beef kidneys had an average value of 19 pesetas, while beef tallow was priced at 5.70 pesetas and the bones only cost a typical Madrid housewife 0.93 pesetas.²⁶ Offal could fit any budget and so was in high demand across many different income levels. Some types of offal – such as blood, hooves, heads, tripe, lungs and hearts – were not regulated and so their prices were not tracked by the Francoist state.

The fact that it cost more to buy kidneys than to buy beefsteak reveals the extent to which the Franco regime assigned value to particular types of offal, and how much the regime thought Spaniards should value and pay for the meat cuts. The low price of tallow and bones reflect the opposite – they contained little value to the regime and so were assigned a lower market price. More interesting still is the offal that was overlooked by the state and priced by individual vendors. The lack of price regulation meant that it did not have an assigned value by the regime, leaving Spaniards to interpret its worth freely. Rather than taking a uniform approach to offal, there were several inconsistencies in government policies pertaining to offal. These inconsistencies provided Spaniards with some consumer choice and purchasing power, autonomous from the coercion of the state.

Offal was in such high demand that the Franco regime broke with its policy of autarky to import offal from Argentina, and still that was not enough offal to satisfy the Spanish appetite. Spaniards simultaneously belittled the value of offal while demanding more of the product, fostering paradoxes within Francoist policy towards the foodstuff. The price of various types of offal varied greatly and the Franco regime struggled to control Spanish views of the products. Within this ambiguity, the practice of everyday life and the habitual consumption of offal existed beyond the control of Francoism.

III. Was It Healthy?

Part of the cultural demand for offal stemmed from new discoveries in nutrition. Some Spanish food experts praised offal for its rich content in proteins and fats while others warned the public to avoid the health dangers of eating animal organs. Nutritionists waged an offal debate in the 1940s, leaving Spaniards to make their own food choices according to their understanding of the dissemination of health information into the home. Meat rationing for Spaniards was set at 100 g per adult male per day, but actual availability of meat within neighbourhoods or throughout the week varied widely.[27] Scholarly reconstructions of the 1940s Spanish diet calculate that Spaniards only consumed an average of 13.37 g of pork a day, 0.72 g of goat and lamb meat, 9.99 g of beef, 1.16 g of fowl, 5.61 g of wild game and 4.16 g of consumable offal for a total of 35.01 g per person per day.[28] Medical prescriptions for or against meat consumption generated a debate in food provisioning for Spaniards, and the competition between ideals bled into discussions of Francoism and visions for the Spanish body.

Many of the major proponents of offal consumption were advocates for more protein in the Mediterranean diet. Internationally-renowned doctors Richet and Marañón claimed that humans needed 200g to 300g of animal protein a day.[29] They actively rejected the claims of vegetarians, arguing that humans cannot survive without the frequent consumption of animal protein. Their calculations for the amount of animal protein needed by Spaniards were double to triple the amount of what the Francoist rationing system allocated. Their interpretation of nutrition strongly critiqued the Spanish diet imposed by the Franco regime and insinuated that the government's rations were insufficient for the needs of the Spanish body. The authors did not directly criticize Francoism or the rationing system, but justified through science that the state's food provisioning program was inadequate, creating an indirect critique of the regime.

Advances in nutritional science spread into popular culture and into cookbooks of the time. Cookbook series author Carmen Sanahuja de Sans had the following praise for offal:

> Offal consists of a diversity of meats and internal parts of cattle that are greatly appreciated for their substantial nutritional value. Beef head alone is highly nutritious. Brains are good prepared in a number of styles but are best as meat pies. [...] In the fanciest tables veal liver is served for its exquisite taste and high nutritional value. More modest tables serve beef liver.[30]

Sanahuja de Sans praised the nutritional value of offal and assigned great worth to it within Spanish cuisine. Her summary of offal mirrored the arguments of nutritionists, but she framed the information in a way that made offal desirable to middle class housewives – a tasty, popular and luxurious food choice. Cookbook authors, magazine writers and cooking instructors disseminated their perspectives on the health of offal consumption through their networks that transcended economic levels and reached beyond cities to reach a wider Spanish audience.

On the other side of the debate, vegetarian doctors were very vocal against the consumption of meat, and especially targeted offal as an unhealthy or immoral food choice. Vegetarianism, or the set of beliefs that supports the purposeful abstinence of meat from the diet, gained popularity in Europe in the early twentieth century as part of the naturalist movement.[31] While vegetarianism was more common among anarchists and therefore largely repressed during the Franco dictatorship, some factions of the Catholic Church were advocates of vegetarianism and were tolerated if not encouraged.[32] The coalescence of postwar religious fervour and diet is best exemplified through the work of Dr Joaquin Garcia Roca who was a medical doctor, presbyter and vegetarian advocate. His publication, *La Alimentación natural de hombre* (*Man's Natural Diet*) equated spiritual purity with cooking purity, advocating for a raw-food diet among his followers. He went further to propose that Natural Law discouraged cooking food and that diseases were caused from the sin of eating unnatural foods, including meat.[33] For Garcia Roca, one of the most heinous offenses to a person's physical and moral health was the consumption of meat. For vegetarians of the time, their ideology was in direct opposition to the ideology of Francoism that provisioned meat to every Spaniard with the expectation of a uniform, nationalized diet.

Thus, health informed how Spaniards viewed certain foods and influenced how Spaniards and the Franco regime assigned cultural value to offal. Since medical doctors advocated for eating more meat, it exposed the failure of the Franco regime to supply sufficient quantities of meat to meet the nutritional standards needed by the population. At the same time, vegetarianism, an ideology independent of Francoism, became more difficult to defend due to the ideological censorship of the regime, but was not difficult to practice due to the meat shortages observed on a daily basis. As the topic of health demonstrates, Spaniard's view of offal was far from uniform. Despite the regime's efforts to carefully regulate meat, the health debate exemplifies how Francoism could not control how Spaniards perceived meat and its value to their families.

IV. The Offal of Everyday Life

Offal was paramount to public discourse in 1940s Spain, and an analysis of its meaning for different groups of Spaniards exemplifies how food choice provided some manoeuvrability in everyday life. Despite the repression imposed by the Franco regime through food restrictions, some consumer choice remained, and how Spaniards formed assumptions on certain foods, such as offal, reflect how Spaniards negotiated the political landscape of the dictatorship. Offal was not accessible to all Spaniards, but its occasional deregulation and affordability allowed Spain's middle classes to enjoy eating meat products, even if they consumed the offal begrudgingly. Most doctors praised the health benefits of offal and encouraged Spaniards to eat organs when they could, but some doctors who subscribed to vegetarianism warned against the dangers of offal consumption. Within popular opinion, there was no taboo regarding the consumption of tongues, ears, hooves, tails and organs as many offal vendors lined the streets of

Contextualizing Offal Consumption in 1940s Spain

Spain's most populous cities, and cookbooks printed endless recipes for housewives to prepare the food for their families. Still, offal was rejected by some Spaniards based on their preconceived beliefs, that offal was a lower-class food, was unhealthy or was immoral to consume. Yet overall, offal consumption was normalized into everyday life in the 1940s and remains a lasting hallmark of the period.

As food was politicized during the dictatorship, historians can observe variations to the diet propagated by the Franco regime. Although the authoritarian state attempted to control every aspect of public and private life through food, a closer look at the culinary culture of the time provides glimpses of non-conformity and oversight in the practice of everyday life.

Notes

1. Delegación Nacional de la Sección Femenina de FET y de las JONS, *Programas para escuelas de hogar de la Sección Femenina* (Madrid: Delegación Nacional de la Sección Femenina de FET y de las JONS, 1959), pp. 3,7.; María Jesús Dueñas Cepeda, 'La Construcción de las relaciones de género en la ideología de la Sección Femenina, 1934-1977' in *Encuadramiento Femenino, Socialización y cultura en el Franquismo*, ed. by Lucía Prieto-Borrega (Málaga: Centro de Ediciones de la Diputación de Málaga, 2010), pp. 23-73.
2. 'Cocina de Cuaresma,' *Medina*, 25 March 1945, p. 28.; Gonzalo Bosch Bierge, *Cocina de vigilia* (Barcelona: Editorial Hogar, 1940).
3. Tomás Espuny Gómez, *Legislación de abastos: Exposición metódica de las principales disposiciones vigentes* (Tarragona: Imprenta de José Pijoan, 1942), pp. 376-77.; Miguel Mínguez de Rico, *Reglamento de trabajo para la industria de Hotelería, Cafés, Bares y similares: Disposiciones vigentes obligatorias saber 'El Plato único', precios de hospedajes, sanciones y régimen de comidas en el Nuevo Estado* (Madrid: Editorial Ibérica, 1939), p. 51.
4. Antonio Giráldez Lomba, *Sobrevivir en los Anos del hambre en Vigo* (Vigo: Instituto de Estudios Vigueses, 2002), pp. 61, 64.
5. Rafael Abella, *La Vida Cotidiana Bajo el Régimen de Franco* (Madrid: Ediciones Temas de Hoy, 1996), p. 71.; Isaías Lafuente, *Tiempos de hambre: Viaje a la España de posguerra* (Madrid: Temas de Hoy, 1999).
6. Michael Richards, *A Time of Silence: Civil War and the Culture of Repression 1936-1945* (Cambridge: Cambridge University Press, 1998).
7. Encarnación Barranquero Texeira and Lucía Prieto Borrego, *Así Sobrevivimos al Hambre: Estrategias de supervivencia de las mujeres en la postguerra española* (Málaga: Servicio de Publicaciones, Centro de Ediciones de la Diputación de Málaga, 2003).; Antonio Cazorla Sanchez, *Fear and Progress: Ordinary Lives in Franco's Spain, 1939-1975* (Malden: Wiley-Blackwell, 2010).
8. Carol Helstosky, *Garlic and Oil: Politics and Food in Italy* (Oxford: Berg Press, 2004), p. 4.
9. Ana Cabana and Alba Diaz Geada, 'Exploring Modernization: Agrarian Fascism in Rural Spain, 1936-1951' in *Agriculture in the Age of Fascism: Authoritarian technocracy and rural modernization, 1922-1945*, ed. by Lourenzo Fernandez Prieto, Juan Pan Montojo and Miguel Cabo (Tournhout: Brepols publishers, 2014), p. 197.
10. 'Han desparecido las colas de pan: Sobraron millares de kilos y el vecindario pudo adquirirlos sin limitación' *Arriba*, 2 April 1939, p. 3.
11. Espuny Gómez, p. 241.
12. Espuny Gómez, p. 447.
13. Espuny Gómez, p. 445.

14. Abella, p. 71.
15. Roser Nicalau-Nous and Josep Pujol-Andreu, 'El Consumo de proteínas animales en Barcelona entre las décadas 1830 y 1930: evolución y factores condicionales' in *Investigaciones de Historia Económica* 2005, otoño número 3, 101-34.
16. 'Madrid, 12 de junio de 1944. Camarada Jefe del Departamento Central de Abastecimiento', Fondo Auxilio Social, *Caja* 3 (122) 1658. Archivo General de Administración.
17. *La Carne*, 1 March 1945, 'Licencias de apertura' Archivo de Villa, Inventario General, Tomo 110, Folio 1 (micro). *Negociado de cartillas, 1936-1942*. Ayuntamiento de Madrid, 1947.
18. C. Sanz Egaña, *La carne como alimento* (Madrid: Ediciones Pegaso, 1944), p. 72.
19. *La Carne*, 1 March 1945; 'Licencias de apertura' Archivo de Villa, Inventario General, Tomo 110, Folio 1 (micro). *Negociado de cartillas, 1936-1942*. Ayuntamiento de Madrid, 1947.
20. Giráldez Lomba, *Sobrevivir en los años del hambre*, p. 208.
21. María del Carmen, *Cocina Familiar* (Barcelona: Tipografía La Académica de Serra y Russell, 1940?).
22. Lara Anderson, *Cooking up the Nation: Spanish Culinary Texts and Culinary Nationalization in the Late Nineteenth and Early Twentieth Century Spain* (Rochester: Tamesis, 2013), p. 91; María Mestayer de Echague (Marquesa de Parabere), *Enciclopedia culinaria: La cocina completa*, 6 ed. (Madrid: Espasa-Calpe, 1949), p. 899.
23. Instituto Nacional de Estadística, *Anuario estadístico de España, 1945-1946*, Edición manual (Madrid: Presidencia del Gobierno, Instituto Nacional de Estadística, 1946), p. 851. Archivo Central de Cruz Roja Española (DCCRE).
24. *La Carne* Año III número 62: 15 September 1947, 2.
25. Roser Nicalau-Nous and Josep Pujol-Andreu, 'Variaciones regionales de los precios de consumo y de las dietas en España, en los inicios de la transición demográfica' in *Revista de historia económica*, 24.3 (January 2006), 526.
26. Delegación Provincial de Abastecimientos y transportes de Madrid, *Memoria del ejercicio 1946* (Madrid: Delegación Provincial de Abastecimientos y transportes de Madrid, 1947).
27. Espuny Gómez, p. 241.
28. A. Graciani Pérez-Rand, F. Rodriguez Artalejo, J.R. Banegas Banegas, R. Hernández Vecino and J. del Rey Calero, *Consumo de alimentos en España en el periodo 1940-1988* (Madrid: UA Ediciones, 1996), pp. 89, 95, 83, 105, 109, 116.
29. Ch. Richet and G. Marañón, *Alimentación y regímenes alimentarios*, (Madrid: Espasa-Calpe, 1942), p. 131.
30. Carmen Sanhuja de Sans, *El Libro de cocina para ti*, 3 ed. (Barcelona: Editorial Sintes, 1951), p.19.
31. Josep María Rosello, *La vuelta a la naturaleza: El pensamiento naturista hispano (1890-2000): naturismo libertario, trofología, vegetarismo naturista, vegetarismo social y librecultura* (Bilbao: Virus Memoria, 2003), p. 27.
32. Rosello, p. 235.
33. Joaquín García Roca, *La Alimentación natural de hombre* (Barcelona: Editorial Sanatorium, 1949), p. 14.

It's All Edible: Four Views of Offal

Peter Hertzmann

After walking up the north side of Pacific Street from Grant Avenue and ushering my charges first across Stockton Street and then, turning left, to the south side of Pacific Street, I took a long deep breath and gathered everyone on the corner. For the next three blocks, my group of about twelve tourists would be pressing their way down the most heavily packed sidewalk on the busiest day of the week at the worst time of the day in the most densely populated district of San Francisco.[1] These three blocks on the west side of Stockton Street in the late-1970s were chock-a-block with fishmongers, butchers, vegetable vendors, bakeries, and restaurants. The street was wall-to-wall shoppers, and any gawking tourists hindered the locals' efficient shopping.

Saturdays also meant that a worn pick-up truck stacked twelve-feet high with cages would be parked in the first block selling live poultry. Where there was space between the open storefronts, the occasional unlicensed vendor would set up a small table to sell one or two vegetables or some small item from China.

The foot traffic tacked mostly from north to south, but it was possible to walk upstream if you stayed close to the curb or walked in the street. Periodically, a truck would park along the curb, blocking those impatient folks walking in the street. The deliveryman would make a pile of boxes on the sidewalk near the curb. Then, the driver would steer a box-loaded hand truck through the stream of bodies. This temporary annoyance did little to stem the flow of shoppers, each one intent on completing the task at hand.

Before I let my group enjoin the battle, I instructed them to go at their own pace and walk no further than the corner of Clay Street, three blocks distant. By the time I had moved to the second or third store, as was typical, only four or so people stayed within listening distance. When we stopped in front of a grocery store, I discussed the vegetable varieties that were unfamiliar from their personal shopping. In front of a bakery, I chatted about the differences between steamed or deep-fried versus baked pastries. At a fish store, I identified the various live species including the frogs and turtles. In front of the butcher shops, I pointed out the pig and chicken feet and the whole chickens and ducks with their heads still attached to their bodies.

No matter what my group observed in the fresh-food stores, it was always the hotel pans of cooked food in the restaurant windows that raised the most eyebrows, and maybe turned a few stomachs. Along with the cooked-vegetable and meat dishes common to each restaurant and the roast ducks, roast chickens, roast pork and roast ribs hanging in the window, there would be pans with cooked pig's ear, pig's snout, pig's intestines, chicken feet and duck's tongues. These were the standard items. Certain restaurants would sometimes feature roast pig's kidneys or chicken livers. As I described each item and discussed the concept of eating a food for its texture rather than taste, some of my group drew closer to learn more while others drifted away. For many, it was their first contact with offal, although I rarely used the term since few of my charges knew what it meant.

Terminology

Prior to the rise of nose-to-tail dining in the United States and Britain, the average diner didn't think of offal, or at least the word. Sometimes you'd hear the terms 'organ meats' or 'variety meats', but it was more common to hear a portion of meat referred to by a specific name, whether its true morphologic name, like 'liver', or market name, like 'sweetbreads'.[2] In random questioning of people I meet, I find that most older people have a concept of offal that falls into either the 'organ camp' or the 'guts camp', and that most younger people have no concept of offal since they claim to have never heard the term.

I've been in many cooking classes in the last fifty years where an instructor has informed the class that the term 'offal' is derived from the two words 'fall' and 'off' indicating that these were the parts of the animal that fell to the ground during the dressing of the carcass. This concept is even used in the etymology portion of many online dictionaries.[3] Anyone who has ever witnessed a hot carcass from a recently slaughtered animal being dressed can attest to the fact that nothing in the pleural cavity, primarily the heart and lungs, falls off because everything is captured by the combination of the ribcage and the diaphragm. A similar effect is true for the digestive system, which is attached at both the oesophagus and anus along with various collagenous attachments to the wall of the peritoneal cavity. There may be some bulging of the intestines or the stomach, but these will not fall to the ground until they are detached. Thus the concept of 'falling off' may make for interesting imagery but is strictly fantasy.[4]

The goal of this paper is to clarify one of the principal meanings of offal: 'The edible parts collectively which are cut off in preparing the carcass of an animal for food'.[5] The *OED* definition continues to read: 'In early use applied mainly to the entrails; later extended to include the head, tail, and internal organs such as the heart, liver, etc.' In this discussion, I propose modifying the definition to include all parts of an animal which do not consist primarily of skeletal muscle and are used raw or minimally processed as an ingredient of a prepared product. This is essentially saying the same as 'the edible parts collectively which are cut off in preparing the carcass of an animal for food', but since most people are unaware of what parts are harvested during the dressing of a carcass, some clarification is helpful. Also, not all carcasses are dressed by every producer the same way. The list of items removed during dressing will vary, and some offal, such as tendons, can only be harvested from a dressed carcass. Checking the list below, there are some items like tongue, skirt and cheek that are primarily skeletal meat, but are still considered offal because they are not part of a dressed carcass.

I suggest that 'offal' only applies to raw or minimally processed food items. Thus back fat is offal. When it is rendered as lard it may still be, but when cured to make *lardo,* it ceases being offal. Beef tripe is offal because it is one of the four chambers of the stomach that has been minimally processed and will be used as an ingredient in a completed dish. It will not be eaten as it is provided by a butcher without further processing.

The *OED* implies, in its third edition, with the statement, 'edible parts collectively which are cut off', that offal is a collective noun. It may be better to describe 'offal' as a mass noun.[6] Thus we can refer to offal as being either singular or plural in English, but we cannot use the word with a count term proceeding it.

Looking at the frequency of usage in Google's Ngram Viewer, the noun form of 'offal', in all meanings, peaks around 1865 with a frequency of about one in 1.2 million words and has one nadir since then in 1985 with a frequency of about one in 4 million words.[7] In the 120 years between the peak and the nadir, usage of the term was reduced by about seventy per cent. Unfortunately, this data lacks the granularity to give an idea of how common it is to find offal referred to in food related books.

There are also probably regional differences in the use of the word offal that we need to account for when looking at frequency. In the nineteenth century, John Farmer wrote: 'Offal. – This term is far more colloquial in Western America than in England. It is applied to the same parts of the carcases of animals; but whereas in England no one would think of speaking of calf's heart, pig's fry, sheep's kidneys, etc., as dishes of *offal,* in the States such phraseology is not unusual.'[8] Even though Farmer observed this more than a century ago, I think those regional differences still exist.

Up until now, I have made no distinction made between offal in different species of animals. For the remainder of this paper, only offal from the domesticated bovine, porcine, ovine and caprine models will be considered. Although poultry, game and seafood have harvestable, edible offal, they will not be part of this discussion.

Identification

Any list of the specific items referred to as offal will have issues. Completeness is the first potential problem. Is there any single item missing? Fabrication is another potential problem. The United Nations' *Standard for Edible Meat Co-products* differentiates between four different ways of fabricating a tongue and provides a specification for certain muscles that may be removed in certain fabrications.[9] Other lists are not that specific. Animal age can be a problem since some offal is only harvestable during certain periods of an animal's life. The animal's sex can be an issue due to differences in genitalia. Parts that are harvestable on one species may not exist or be edible on a different species.

There are many categorization systems that can be used to make edible offal easier to comprehend. The following list follows the functional systems of the four mammals being discussed in this paper.[10] The specific items in the list are derived primarily from the UN *Standard*, the most complete listing currently available.[11]

NERVOUS SYSTEM

BRAIN

Provided whole (including the cerebellum, the lobes, the thalamus and the annular protuberance) or peeled (meninges removed) except for a porcine brain where it is only provided whole. Sales of brains are limited in some countries based on species and age and prohibited in others.

VASCULAR SYSTEM

HEART

Provided whole with the blood vessels trimmed close to the body of the organ. The ossa cordis is removed on a bovine heart. Buyer must specify if auricles, aorta and pulmonary truncus are removed; fat cover retained or removed at the base; or heart left untrimmed. May be provided as part of the pluck, consisting of the liver, heart, lungs, trachea and a portion of the diaphragm, and sometimes with the thick skirt, spleen and thymus gland attached (not bovine), or just combined with the lungs.

SPLEEN

Provided with the splenic blood vessels removed. In ruminants, the spleen is attached to the rumen and all connecting tissue must be removed. The spleen is not saleable for human consumption in some countries.

DIGESTIVE SYSTEM

TONGUE

Long cut: The tongue with its root, most of the hyoid bones, larynx, epiglottis, and first three rings of trachea still attached. Buyer must specify approximate fat depth retained and if the lymph and salivary glands are present. Bovine tongues require a colour (white, black or spotted) specification. The long cut is not saleable in all countries.

Short cut: Similar to the long cut without the larynx, epiglottis, and trachea. Buyer must specify approximate fat depth retained and if the lymph and salivary glands are present. Bovine tongues require a colour (white, black or spotted) specification

Swiss cut: What remains after all of the hyoid bones and most of the attached fat have been removed from a short cut. The muscular part of the root and the base are removed. This cut consists solely of the body of the muscle. Bovine tongues require a colour (white, black or spotted) specification.

Root trim: Produced from the meat trimmed when producing a short cut. Sometimes referred to as throat trimmings (bovine and porcine only).

Root fillet: Derived from the tongue root by removing the muscles from each side (bovine only).

SALIVARY GLAND

The whole parotid gland provided with the interior lining of the cheek attached (bovine and porcine only).

OESPHAGUS

Provided as a whole tube from the pharynx to the bovine rumen or porcine stomach. Also available as weasand, the fleshy part around the oesophagus (bovine only).

STOMACH

In ruminants, the stomach consists of four compartments or chambers named the rumen (paunch), reticulum (honeycomb), omasum (book, bible) and abomasum (reed). Each part is also referred to as tripe.

Rumen: Provided raw and washed with the dark membrane retained, and the external surface trimmed free of fat deposits. May be supplied with the reticulum removed or attached, the dark inner layer removed, and blanched and bleached.

Rumen pillars: Sometimes called mountain-chain tripe. Removed as one piece from rumen and supplied raw (bovine only).

Reticulum: Provided raw and washed. May be supplied split or it its natural shape and blanched and bleached (bovine only).

Omasum: Provided raw and washed. May be supplied blanched and bleached (bovine only).

Abomasum: Provided raw and washed (bovine only).

The non-ruminant stomach is similar to the abomasum.

Stomach: Provided washed only. May be supplied inside out, cleaned, trimmed, and scalded. May also be supplied bleached and stiffened (porcine only).

Stomach lining: Provided washed only (porcine only).

LIVER

Provided whole including the Spiegel lobe and the capsule. May be supplied with the lymph nodes retained or removed, vena cava removed and ligament removed. Colour may be specified and the liver supplied peeled (bovine only).

PANCREAS

Provided as the whole gland. Sometimes sold, incorrectly, as sweetbreads (porcine only).

INTESTINE

Provided as the whole tube that extends between the duodenum, the exit of the stomach, and the anus. The intestines, or parts of the intestines, are not saleable for human consumption in some countries. The intestines may be supplied in parts (see following), with the fat removed or retained, by length, and with the mucous membrane (lining) removed.

Small intestine: Extends from the duodenum to the ileum. May be supplied with the fat removed or retained, by length, and with the mucous membrane removed.

Large intestine: Extends from the ileum to the rectum and includes the colon and caecum (sometimes referred to as the bung). May be sold whole with the rectum attached or as individual sections. May be supplied with the fat removed or retained and with the mucous membrane removed (bovine, ovine and caprine).

Large intestine: Extends from the ileum to the rectum and includes the colon and caecum. May be sold intact or in pieces representing the caecum, upper colon and the robe, referring to the dorsal-lumbar part of the colon (porcine only). Sometimes referred to as the chitterling.

Rectum: The termination of the intestines, ends with the anus (bovine and porcine only).

Sometimes referred to as the bung (porcine only). Anus may be sold separately.

RESPIRATORY SYSTEM

LUNG

Provided as the whole organ. May be supplied with the trachea removed, lobes separated or just the diaphragmatic lobe only. Colour may be specified (bovine only). May be supplied as part of the pluck, consisting of the liver, heart, lungs, trachea and a portion of the diaphragm, and sometimes with the thick skirt, spleen and thymus attached (not bovine), or just combined with the heart. The lungs are not saleable for human consumption in some countries.

TRACHEA

Provided as a whole tube from the base of the larynx to the lungs.

URO-GENITAL SYSTEM

KIDNEY

Provided as the whole organ with the blood vessels, urethra and capsule removed. May be provided with external fat retained or removed, and with renal hilus and internal fat retained or removed.

TESTIS

Provided as the whole gland. May be provided with the capsule intact or removed.

PENIS

Also called a pizzel. Provided as the whole organ with the skin removed. The penis may be provided with the root attachment material retained or removed and the tip retained or removed (bovine only).

MAMMARY GLANDS

Also called the udders. Provided as the whole glands. The mammary glands may be provided with the fat retained or removed, and raw or cooked (bovine only).

BLADDER

Provided as the whole organ (porcine only).

UTERUS

Provided as the whole organ (porcine only).

OVARY

Provided as the whole gland (porcine only).

SKIN AND MEMBRANES

SKIN

Provided as large sheets of skin with essentially no fat attached (porcine only).

MASK

Provided as single piece of skin removed from the skull (porcine only).

EARS

Provided as the entire pinna with the auricular cartilage and muscle attached and hair removed (bovine only). Provided whole or cut square.

SNOUT

Provided as the skin around the nose with or without the nasal cartilage attached (porcine only).

LIPS

Provided as the skin around the mouth (porcine only).

MEMBRANE

Miscellaneous sheaths of connective tissue stripped from muscle cuts during the butchering process (bovine only).

MUSCLES AND FAT

DIAPHRAGM

Whole diaphragm: Includes the peripheral muscle, called the skirt (porcine only). Provided with fat and connective tissue retained or removed.

Thick (outside) skirt: Connects the diaphragm to the plate (porcine only, provided as standard meat cut in the bovine model). Provided with or without the connective tissue.

Thin (inside) skirt: Connects the diaphragm to the plate and the flank (porcine only, provided as standard meat cut in the bovine model). Provided with or without the connective tissue.

Diaphragm membrane: The fascia covering of the diaphragm. May include small amounts of red meat (bovine only).

Skirt Sinew: The connective tissue removed from the skirt meat. May include small amounts of muscle and fat (bovine and porcine only).

Skirt membrane: The peritoneal lining attached to the thick skirt. May include small amounts of muscle and fat (bovine only).

CAUL FAT

Provided as sheets of transparent membrane with a netting of fat (porcine only).

CLEAR PLATE

Provided as a layer of fat from the loin section of the carcass, with or without skin attached, commonly called back fat (porcine only).

ABDOMINAL FAT

Provided as uneven sheets of fat (bovine and porcine only). Sometimes referred to as leaf fat. Also referred to as suet (bovine only).

FLANK FAT

Provided as uneven sheets of fat (bovine and porcine only).

MESENTRY

Provided whole or in large pieces (porcine only).

MARROW BONES

Provided as sawn shaft sections of the femur and humerus bones containing the marrow, which is primarily fat in mature animals (bovine and porcine only).

MISCELLANEOUS

HEAD

Provided as the whole head detached between the occipital joint and the first cervical vertebrae. In ruminants, the hide is removed.

Cheek: The muscle that covers the external portions of the upper and lower jaws, extending between the lips and the parotid gland, which may or may not be attached. May be provided with the papillae removed (bovine only).

Papillae: Provided as a separate item from cheek (bovine only).

Cheek meat: Provided as just the musculature of the cheek with no portions of lymph nodes, glands or connective tissue (bovine only).

Head meat: General classification for all musculature trimmed from the head with no portions of lymph nodes, glands or connective tissue and no trim pieces derived from the tongue or the neck (bovine, ovine only).

Temple muscles: Provided with skin removed (porcine only).

NECK BONES

Provided as the seven cervical vertebrae and attached meat remaining after trimming. May have up to four thoracic vertebrae and rib heads attached (porcine only).

FOOT

Foot: Provided separated through the long pastern bone, skinned or scalded and plucked. May be provided sawn or not (bovine only).

Fore foot (trotter): Provided separated from the fore leg at the carpel joint, with the skin either intact or removed (porcine only).

Hind foot (hind trotter): Provided separated from the hind leg at the tarsal joint, with the skin either intact or removed (porcine only).

TAIL

The bovine tail is separated from carcass between the sacral and coccygeal vertebrae. Provided with excess fat cover trimmed and as a specific number of vertebrae.

The porcine tail is separated from the carcass between the second and third coccygeal vertebrae and trimmed of excess fat and skin near the transection. Provided with coccygeal cartilage and connective tissue trimmed or retained.

TENDONS

Provided as any of the superficial and deep tendons and surrounding tissue of the hind legs (bovine, ovine and caprine only).

Provided as the superficial and deep flexor tendons and surrounding tissue of the fore legs (bovine only).

Provided as the superficial and deep Achilles tendons and surrounding tissue of the hind legs (bovine only).

LIGAMENTS

Provided whole or in portions of the ligamentum nuchae (paddywhack or back strap) from the neck and thoracic region of the carcass (bovine only). Probably edible, but usually processed into a dog chew.

BLOOD

Provided in a stabilized form, fibrin removed, and as blood serum or blood plasma, either cooled or frozen.

THYMUS GLAND

Provided as the whole gland with the surrounding fat and connective tissue either retained or removed. Sometimes referred to as the sweetbreads.

Morphology

The list of offal provided above represents many different types and combinations of tissue. Understanding the differences in tissue is helpful if one's goal is to cook and eat offal.

There are five types of tissue found in cattle, sheep, goats and pigs: muscle tissue, connective tissue, nervous tissue, epithelial tissue and mineralized tissue.[12] Bone is mineralized tissue. Since bone is not considered edible, it will be ignored in the following discussion.

Muscle tissue

There are three types of muscle tissue: skeletal (or striated), cardiac and smooth.[13] In older texts, these muscle types were referred to as red, heart and white muscles.[14]

Skeletal muscle is the muscle of most meat. It's the muscle that an animal voluntarily contracts and relaxes when it decides to walk, run, swat a fly or chew. Skeletal muscle is also referred to as striated muscle because it contains repeating functional units called sarcomeres, which give skeletal muscle its striated appearance.[15] To our eyes, skeletal muscle appears to be made up of parallel, red-coloured fibres, what is sometimes referred to in recipe instructions as the meat's grain.[16] Among the different types of offal, the muscles of the head and tail are skeletal muscle. They also contain a relatively high amount of collagen. Exposing these muscles to heat to convert the collagen to gelatine makes them readily edible.[17] These muscles, when trimmed, are an exception to my definition of offal being not primarily skeletal muscle. Tongue is another example of skeletal muscle that is also offal.[18]

Heart muscle is an involuntary muscle. It contracts and relaxes in a continuous rhythm from before an animal's birth until a short while after it dies. It is also striated muscle. The heart is lined with epithelium, which renders the heart waterproof.[19] Cartilaginous valves open and close as blood is pumped from one chamber to the next by the involuntary muscle contractions. In preparing a heart for cooking, the organ must be opened, and any blood clots found must be washed out. It is usually wise to strip off any connective tissue bound to the heart's exterior and do the same on the interior. Depending on the preparation, the fat of the outer surface may be removed or left in place. Although the muscle in a heart is well used and theoretically tough as shoe leather, there are quick techniques that produce tasty results without a long braise.[20]

Smooth muscle is involuntary and non-striated. In animals, it is sometimes referred to as white muscle because it resembles connective tissue and may even be found covered in the same.[21] It is white and somewhat bland in flavour because smooth muscle is poorly supplied with blood.[22] Its movement is slow but determined. It is slow muscle that moves food in its various digested states from the entry to past the exit. Tripe is produced by scalding and bleaching a rumen, reticulum or omasum of a ruminant and stripping it of its mucosal lining leaving mostly smooth muscle.[23]

Connective tissue
Connective tissue consists of three main components: fibres, ground substance and cells.[24] The fibres can be divided as elastic, reticular and collagenous. In one simplistic view, connective tissue binds and supports the body together.[25] In the case of tendons, it's collagenous fibres that attach muscles to bone. In the case of adipose tissue, or fat, its reticular fibres that keeps it all together. Dense connective tissue can be found all over the body. It's the tissue that wraps the skirts and overlaps the muscle's connection to the diaphragm and the peritoneal wall. It's mostly what makes up the capsule that covers a testis or the thymus gland.

Nervous tissue
Nervous tissue enables a response to stimuli and coordinates bodily functions. It is consumed in the form of brains. From an eating standpoint, brains are similar to the edible glands, but physiologically, glands derive from epithelial cells whereas brains are more complex. Both may be presented for sale with a connective tissue covering, or they may be sold already peeled. Fresh brains are particularly perishable, especially when compared to skeletal muscle.[26]

Epithelial tissue
Epithelial tissue covers the exterior body as skin and lines interior surfaces such as the

peritoneal cavity as the peritoneum.[27] All glands form from an ingrowth of an epithelial surface.[28] Animal skin posses problems for the cook because of the need to remove hair from the slaughtered animal. Pigskin is edible, but it requires special handling in the slaughterhouse to remove the bristles. Skin from hides is generally considered inedible.

Practicalities

The availability of offal to the consumer is a near perfect model of supply and demand. The model, in this case, is modified by ethnic shrinking, marketplace changes, fads, government regulations, slaughterhouse practicalities, restaurant and butcher practicalities and non-edible competition.

Ethnic Shrinking

Ethnic shrinking is the concept that as first-generation immigrants decrease in population and are replaced as consumers by the second generation, the demand for food items from the motherland decreases. The first generation, although they may accept certain food items of their adopted land, still has a desire for products from the group's origin. The desire is greater with adults then it may be with children, where memories of the homeland are also stronger.

Twenty years ago, I could walk into one of the butcher shops in my area that catered to the local Latino community, the majority of which were from the Mexican state of Michoacán, and find a whole, fresh pig's head in the meat case. Ten years ago, the meat case no longer held a pig's head, but the butcher had many in the freezer. Today, if I want a pig's head, I must special order it. The demand that was present when there were more first-generation immigrants is no longer there now that their children are buying the groceries.

My paternal grandparents emigrated from Germany in their late teens. My grandmother couldn't cook. I never saw them eat German food. My maternal grandparents came to America from Germany as sponsored refugees. My grandfather was sixty years old, and my grandmother was seven years younger. She was an excellent, trained cook. Whenever I was left with her as a child, I ate German food. My mother, who emigrated at the age of twenty, was not as good of a cook as her mother, but we still ate the offal common to her native Munich. Brains, sweetbreads, liver and tongue, along with sausages made with natural pork casings, were all common on the dinner table when I was growing up. By the time I completed college in the mid-seventies, grocery stores had become supermarkets and independent butchers were difficult to find in my mother's neighbourhood. The markets in suburbia had moved away from offal, and so had my mother.

Marketplace Changes

The concept of a grocery store has changed dramatically since Piggly Wiggly became the first self-service grocery store in 1916.[29] The first supermarket, a store with separate product departments, was started in 1930.[30] In 1967, Iowa Beef Packers introduced boxed meat, and supermarket chains started replacing concessionaire butcher shops with in-house staff that opened the boxes, performed some minor cutting and trimming and repackaged the meat on plastic trays with the store's labelling.[31] Where in the past it was possible to obtain offal from a butcher, butchers became scarce, and, along with them, offal became scarce.

Even though the average supermarket carries more than forty-two thousand items, offal may be hard to find.[32] I can find canned escargot at my local hypermarket, but no fresh offal. The only offal available frozen is pre-sliced beef liver. If I head to a nearby stand-alone butcher that sources boxed primals, then some fresh liver is available, but I'm lucky to live near a number of butcher shops. Most people don't.

A different form of marketplace change occurs in locations such as rural America where traditions are forgotten or modernized.[33] As succeeding generations continue to move away from their parents' or grandparents' way of eating, and fast food continues to influence eating habits, old food customs are lost.

Just as the local market for offal is fading from view, export sales of offal are increasing. A trend that started in the 1970s with the United States exporting a majority of the offal harvested has continued to this day.[34] A similar situation is true for the United Kingdom.[35]

Fads

Whether the current phase of nose-to-tail dining started with Fergus Henderson or some lesser-known chef, this excuse for whole-animal dining became popular in the mid-1990s and has continued to sporadically appear on the worldwide dining scene.[36] Its biggest single effect, twenty years later as most whole-animal restaurants have moved onto a different theme, is the wide inclusion of pork belly on modern menus. Pork belly is not offal, but people previously shied away from it, unless it was called bacon, because of its high fat content. Chefs love to prepare pork belly because of its high profit margin.

Government Regulations

In the United States and many countries, the national government regulates the slaughtering of animals and the harvesting of their meat.[37] Slaughterhouse operators must work within the limits set forth in these regulations or risk being shut down. With respect to offal, this means that when the carcass is eviscerated, the viscera intended for human consumption must be keep aligned with the carcass until the latter is inspected and passed. A similar case is true for non-visceral items such as feet or the mammary glands. Some offal may require additional inspection.[38]

In the United States, all meat intended for interstate sales must be federally inspected. State inspection is allowed as long as the meat isn't transported across state lines with the exception of slaughterhouses where the state employees are certified to act as agents for the USDA's Food Safety Inspection Service.[39] There are also custom-exempt slaughterhouses that process animals only for the animal's owner. Technically, the meat and by-products cannot be sold and their use is limited to the owner's household and non-paying guests and employees.[40]

United States regulations also prohibit the selling of certain offal for human consumption. Prohibited items include thyroid glands, laryngeal muscle tissue and lungs.[41]

Slaughterhouse Practicalities
The ability of a specific slaughterhouse to fabricate individual offal items is often a function of scale. Each animal has a fixed number of harvestable parts, and a case of any unique part may be more than a small facility produces in a single day. Once a carcass is passed by the inspector, the slaughterhouse must either quickly process all the offal, or pass it along to a renderer who may in turn pass it along to an aggregator for processing. This is especially common with intestines. These are usually processed by a third party into sausage casings.

In-house processing requires each item to be trimmed to a saleable condition and then packaged and frozen. Some items, such as stomachs intended for the tripe market, may need to be cleaned, scalded and bleached.[42] Special equipment is required to perform this process in any substantial volume.

Items such as blood require special collection and processing equipment.[43] To harvest pork skin, the slaughterhouse must have the ability to scald the hog carcass before eviscerating the animal. Small slaughterhouses often lack the special equipment required for this.

The output from a slaughterhouse will never perfectly match demand. At times, the offal output will exceed orders. The processed offal, since it more perishable than skeletal muscle, must be frozen and stored until it can be sold. This requires freezer storage space, which in addition to its initial building cost has significant energy requirements. The longer the offal is in storage, the more it costs to keep it frozen.

Restaurant and Butcher Practicalities
The issues for restaurants and butcher shops are similar. They both need to be able to obtain sufficient product to sell while at the same time ensuring that they sell it before it spoils. In an ethic neighbourhood, that shouldn't be a problem for the offal associated with that ethnic group. In other neighbourhoods, selling out a complete purchase may be problematic.

Chefs and butchers sourcing whole carcasses have a separate issue with offal. Although the carcass is purchased directly from a farmer, the slaughtering is usually performed by a third party. The abattoir charges a fee based on returning just a dressed carcass to the farmer. The abattoir keeps the offal and resells it to a renderer, who in turn sells it to an aggregator who processes the offal for wholesale distribution.[44] If the abattoir processes enough animals each week, and has the processing capabilities, they may process and sell the offal themselves. If the chef or butcher pays, by way of the farmer, for the kidneys, heart and liver, he will get those items, but there will be no guarantee that the organs came from the specific carcass they purchased. This all assumes that the butcher is in a locale where customers purchase offal, which is unlikely if the butcher doesn't have ethic clientele. Similarly, the chef must have adventuresome customers, or else the offal will become expensive staff meals.

When chef and butchers purchase offal from the wholesale market, they are often required by suppliers to purchase in case lots. If less than case quantities are available, they may have to pay a substantially higher unit price for the same item. Assume that the chef or butcher wishes to buy a whole beef liver. These weigh about 4.5 kilograms (10 pounds) each before peeling and deveining, and they are often only available frozen. One liver will yield about forty portions. Liver spoils rapidly. Any thawed portions need to be sold in a day or two, or turned into a cooked value-added product, such as a *pâté* or luncheon meat. Selling liver in the retail market is probably easier than selling beef hearts, lamb kidneys, and pig ears.

Non-edible Competition
The dressed carcass from the typical steer, before chilling, will weigh about sixty per cent of the live animal weight.[45] The forty per cent that is not part of the carcass does not go to waste. In all but the smallest of slaughterhouses, all of the remainder is sold for use as offal, pet food or non-food applications. So many animal parts are components of other products that people seriously wanting to avoid using animal products have to look at the ingredients going into dietary supplements, pharmaceutical drugs, cosmetics, household cleaning products, clothing, footwear and many other items in common use.[46] Some of the uses, such as those for hides, trace back for millennia. Others such as extracting oestrogens and progesterone from bovine ovaries are more recent.[47] Some of the non-food uses are so profitable that for some large processors, there is more income to be made from by-products than from skeletal muscle.

Conclusion
In the thirty-five years that have transpired since I traipsed through San Francisco's Chinatown with tourists in tow, a large, first-generation Chinese community has developed closer to my home. Now when I am in need of pig's ear, snout, or intestines, or chicken feet, or duck tongues or gizzards, I drive a few miles to a supermarket where all the offal I desire is available on plastic-film-covered Styrofoam trays. When I walked those three blocks in San Francisco a few months back, most of the food items I found in the past were still there although many of the shops had changed, the live-poultry truck was gone, and a different first-generation group of Chinese-speaking immigrants were walking the streets.

It's All Edible: Four Views of Offal

Acknowledgements

Although much of the information presented in this paper came from printed or online sources, significant information was obtained by discussing the subject matter with the following individuals, all of whom are much more familiar with the topic than I am:

Joshua Applestone, Owner, The Applestone Meat Company, Accord, NY
Camas Davis, Owner, Portland Meat Collective, Portland, OR
Chris Fuller, Manager, U.S. Foods Meat Production Facility, San Diego, CA
Greg Gunthorp, Farmer, Gunthorp Farms, LaGrange, IN
Brandon Harpster, Executive Chef at Single Barrel Restaurant and Chef Instructor at Southeast Community College, Lincoln, NE
Dana Means, Manager of Offal Sales, Harris Ranch Beef Company, Selma, CA
Kathryn Quanbeck, Program Manager, Niche Meat Processor Assistance Network, Corvallis, OR
Gregg Rentfrow, Beef Scientist, Food Systems Innovation Center, University of Kentucky, Lexington, KY
Charlie Thieriot, Owner, Llano Seco Meats, Chico, CA

Notes

1. This time period was before the 1989 Loma Prieta Earthquake struck the San Francisco Bay Area. Saturdays were particularly busy because whole families living outside the city would come to Chinatown to shop and then have lunch at one of the two principal dim-sum restaurants. The earthquake damaged the only freeway leading into Chinatown, and after it was closed, the Saturday-morning foot traffic decreased significantly.
2. Other euphemisms for offal include: 'odd bits' (Jennifer McLagan, *Odd Bits: How to Cook the Rest of the Animal* (Berkeley: Ten Speed Press, 2011), p. 139); 'edible meat co-products' (*UNECE Standard for Edible Meat Co-Products* (New York: United Nations, 2008), p. 14); 'by-products' (*Weekly National Carlot Meat Report* (Des Moines: Livestock, Poultry & Grain Market News, Agricultural Marketing Service, United States Department of Agriculture, 19 March 2016).
3. 'Offal', *Merriam-Webster.com*. Merriam-Webster < http://www.merriam-webster.com/dictionary/offal> [accessed 23 March 2016]; 'offal' *Dictionary.com*, Random House, Inc. <http://www.dictionary.com/browse/offal> [accessed 23 March 2016]; 'offal' *Oxford Dictionaries*, Oxford University Press <http://www.oxforddictionaries.com/us/definition/english/offal> [accessed 23 March 2016]
4. The concept of 'falling off' is inline with the first definition listed in the Oxford English Dictionary, which uses as an example 'as husks from milling grain'. 'offal, n. and adj.' *OED Online*. Oxford University Press, March 2016 [accessed 23 March 2016]
5. 'offal, n. and adj.'; Of the seven separate definitions given in the 2004 edition of the *OED*, only one refers to edible animal parts. The other six definitions relate to some form of waste. The Trustees of the Oxford Symposium on Food and Cookery, for their 2016 meeting, chose to expand the subject to 'rejected and reclaimed foods' to allow papers to address a wider range of subjects than would be addressed by strict interpretation of the term.
6. Although the *OED Online* claims that 'offal' may occasionally be used as a count noun, in cookery, it is

unlikely to be so non-specific as to call for 'a piece of offal' in a recipe.
7. Google Books Ngram Viewer <https://books.google.com/ngrams> [accessed 23 March 2016]. For a discussion of *N*-grams, see Jean-Baptiste Michel and others, 'Quantitative Analysis of Culture Using Millions of Digitized Books', *Science* 331.6014 (13 Jan 2011), pp. 176-82.
8. John S Farmer, *Americanisms – Old & New* (London: Thomas Poulter & Sons, 1889), p. 397.
9. *UNECE Standard for Edible Meat Co-Products*.
10. Roderick MacGregor, *The Structure of the Meat Animals* (London: The Technical Press Ltd., 1952).
11. *UNECE Standard for Edible Meat Co-Products*.
12. Wikipedia contributors, 'Tissue (biology)', *Wikipedia, The Free Encyclopedia*, 19 March 2016, 04:52 UTC, <https://en.wikipedia.org/w/index.php?title=Tissue_(biology)&oldid=710810789> [accessed 1 April 2016].
13. Wikipedia contributors, 'Muscle', *Wikipedia, The Free Encyclopedia*, 31 March 2016, 09:29 UTC, <https://en.wikipedia.org/w/index.php?title=Muscle&oldid=712826350> [accessed 30 March 2106].
14. MacGregor, pp. 50-51.
15. Wikipedia contributors, 'Striated muscle tissue', *Wikipedia, The Free Encyclopedia*, 17 March 2016, 13:06 UTC, <https://en.wikipedia.org/w/index.php?title=Striated_muscle_tissue&oldid=710523885> [accessed 31 March 2016]; Wikipedia contributors, 'Sarcomere', *Wikipedia, The Free Encyclopedia*, 11 February 2016, 01:28 UTC, <https://en.wikipedia.org/w/index.php?title=Sarcomere&oldid=704347262> [accessed 31 March 2016].
16. Thomas J. Murrey, *Practical Carving* (New York: Frederick A. Stokes, 1887), p. 14.
17. Helen Charley, *Food Science* (New York: John Wiley & Sons, 1970), p. 385.
18. *Institutional Meat Purchase Specifications for Variety Meats and Edible By-Products* (Washington, DC: Agricultural Marketing Service, United States Department of Agriculture, 1993), pp. 3, 8.
19. MacGregor, p. 90.
20. McLagen, p. 121.
21. MacGregor, p. 90.
22. John C. Forrest and others, *Principles of Meat Science* (San Francisco: W.H. Freeman and Company, 1975), p. 45.
23. Frank G. Ashbrook, *Butchering, Processing and Preservation of Meat* (New York: Van Nostrand Reinholt Company, 1955), p. 104.
24. Wikipedia contributors, 'Connective tissue', *Wikipedia, The Free Encyclopedia*, 18 March 2016, 01:55 UTC, <https://en.wikipedia.org/w/index.php?title=Connective_tissue&oldid=710622762> [accessed 1 April 2016].
25. 'Classification of Tissue Types', IvyRose Holistic <http://www.ivyroses.com/HumanBody/Tissue/Tissue_4-Tissue-Types.php> [accessed 1 April 2016].
26. McLagen, p. 39; *2002 ASHRAE Handbook: Refrigeration* (Atlanta: American Society of Heating, Refrigerating and Air-Conditioning Engineers, Inc., 2002), p 10.9.
27. Wikipedia contributors, 'Peritoneum', *Wikipedia, The Free Encyclopedia*, 10 February 2016, 11:50 UTC, <https://en.wikipedia.org/w/index.php?title=Peritoneum&oldid=704239141> [accessed 1 April 2016].
28. Wikipedia contributors, 'Gland', *Wikipedia, The Free Encyclopedia*, 23 March 2016, 02:18 UTC, <https://en.wikipedia.org/w/index.php?title=Gland&oldid=711472166> [accessed 1 April 2016].
29. 'About Us', Piggly Wiggly <http://www.pigglywiggly.com/about-us> [accessed 2 April 2016].
30. 'About King Kullen Supermarkets', King Kullen Grocery Co., Inc. <http://www.kingkullen.com/about-us/> [accessed 2 April 2016].
31. Eric Schlosser, *Fast Food Nation* (New York: HarperCollins Books, 2002), p. 154.
32 'Supermarket Facts', Food Marketing Institute <http://www.fmi.org/research-resources/supermarket-facts> [accessed 2 April 2016].
33. Regina Sexton, '"I'd ate it like chocolate!": The Disappearing Offal Food Traditions of Cork City', in *Disappearing Foods, Studies in Foods and Dishes at Risk*, ed. by Harlan Walker (Totnes, Devon: Prospect Books, 1995), pp. 172-88.

34. Ralph Bean, 'Beef Tongues to Pork Maws, Foreign Markets Hunger for Variety Meats', *AgExporter* 8.5 (June-July 1996), p. 12.
35. 'Growing Global Market For Offal', The Cattle Site, 26 September 2010 <http://www.thecattlesite.com/articles/2521/growing-global-market-for-offal/> [accessed 3 April 2016].
36. 'Welcome to St. John', St. John Restaurant <https://www.stjohngroup.uk.com/about_us/> [accessed 2 April 2016].
37. 'Humane Slaughter of Livestock', United States Regulation 9 CFR §313; 'Federal Meat Inspection Act', United States Code 21 U.S.C. 12.
38. 'Inspection of Mammary Glands', United States Regulation 9 CFR §310.17.
39. Racheal J. Johnson, Daniel L. Marti and Lauren Gwin, 'Slaughter and Processing Options and Issues for Locally Sourced Meat', *Outlook, A Report from the USDA Economic Research Service,* June 2012.
40. 'Slaughtering, Cutting, and Processing', Cornell University <http://smallfarms.cornell.edu/2012/07/07/slaughtering-cutting-and-processing/> [accessed 3 April 2016].
41. 'Disposition of Thyroid Glands and Laryngeal Muscle Tissue', United States Regulation 9 CFR §310.15; 'Disposition of Lungs', United States Regulation 9 CFR §310.16.
42. 'Alternative Techniques for the Hygienic Processing of Offal', *Meat Technology Update,* No. 01/5, October 2001.
43. John Sjöberg, *Animal Blood Recovery for Edible Purposes* (Malmö, Sweden: Anitec, [n.d.]).
44. The rendering service may be provided at no charge to the processor, or in the case of small processors, for a fee. In some cases the renderers buys the offal from the processor. Each circumstance is different.
45. Rob Holland and others, *How Much Meat to Expect from a Beef Carcass* (Knoxville, TN: University of Tennessee Institute of Agriculture, [n.d.]).
46. Reuben Proctor and Lars Thomsen, *A Comprehensive Guide to Identifying and Avoiding Ingredients of Animal Origin in Everyday Products* (New York: The Experiment, 2013) Adobe Digital Edition.
47. Forrest, pp. 366-68.

The Ends of Offal: Reflections on Laboratory-Grown Meat[1]

Benjamin Aldes Wurgaft

'Corpse reclamation'. 'A foreign fart'. 'Soylent green'. 'Syrup of soot'. 'I wish the people pushing this garbage had to eat it at every meal for the rest of their lives'. These are statements that have been made about two novel foods introduced to English audiences, either as a consumable or as an idea, several hundred years apart. One of them is very important in our day-to-day existence, and the other could, in theory, become very important. One of them is coffee, introduced via the coffee-houses of London but first at Oxford in 1650 – just where, in the city of Oxford, is a matter of some dispute. The other is laboratory-grown meat, otherwise known as 'vat meat', 'shmeat', 'frankenmeat' and, what almost became the official term, 'cultured meat'. I say 'almost' because, as of 2017, a new term, 'clean meat', is being championed by certain players in the world of laboratory-grown meat, who deem 'clean' semantically superior to 'cultured'. For anyone interested in the role of disgust in reactions to laboratory-grown meat, this effort to create a semantic shift is fascinating: it writes laboratory-grown meat directly into anthropology's well-known categories of the clean and unclean, almost seeming to do anthropologists' work for them. To be clear, laboratory-grown meat, whether it is called cultured or clean, is not yet on the market as a foodstuff.

Some historians surmise that seventeenth-century London consumers found coffee disgusting not only because of its flavour, but because it represented a novel and unfamiliar category of beverage, something hot, bitter and non-alcoholic. That revulsion was obviously, and for many of us happily, overcome, and we now drink coffee (or tea, which is also a hot and often bitter beverage) every day. Some promoters of cultured meat love to cite such cases of generational change. In the course of the ethnographic work I have conducted within the cultured meat movement, I am often asked to provide historical case studies that prove that humans are adaptive creatures, receptive towards new foods. My interlocutors often hope that history will turn out to be a repository of promising precedents, giving us reason to think that we might soon redefine the category of 'meat' to include animal protein grown in a lab rather than produced through conventional methods of breeding, raising and slaughtering livestock. As they know, however, the history of meat's modernization shows precisely the opposite tendency, namely the restriction, rather than the expansion, of the Western sense of what counts as meat. This is a striking counterpoint to the other ways in which Western tastes have diversified as we gain access to new foods. As we try them, we shift some of those foods from the category of 'disgusting' to the categories of 'edible', or even 'desirable'.

The history of food can be seen as a history of edibility-formation, certainly, but also as a history of foods dropping out of edibility. Harold McGee has limned meat's modernization as a shift from a 'rural style' of raising, killing and eating animals, to an 'urban style', a shift which, to be sure, was not sudden, nor steadily progressive, nor universal, but nevertheless maps on to the progress of urbanization.[2] The newer urban style of carnivory was then greatly magnified in every sense – scope, geographic range and audience – by industrialization. All this matters for edibility, because the consumption of a wide variety of types of meat, including offal, gradually dropped out of the picture in Western Europe and North America. Exceptions abound, of course, but they are just that, exceptions, and the point of this admittedly potted narrative is the gradual diminishment of the types of domesticated animals considered to be sources of meat, and a diminishment of the number of the parts of their bodies considered to be edible.

Promoting cultured meat is not my task in this talk, but neither is signalling smug agreement with its critics, who consider it simply disgusting to eat meat produced in laboratories through cell culture techniques, and who question cultured meat's status as food. These are objections we should be curious about, having put offal on our own tables, literally or figuratively, in the face of widespread prejudice against it. For me, criticisms of laboratory-grown meat are most interesting as ethnographic data. When critics draw a hard line between the laboratory and the farm, or when they invoke what the bioethicist Leon Kass has called the 'wisdom of repugnance', they're on weak footing, historically and argumentatively.[3] But they tell us much about how certain categories of consumers establish edibility, uncleanliness or even abjection. And it matters that public criticisms of laboratory-grown meat, and discussions of its edibility, are well in advance of actual opportunities to eat it. While cultured meat has been eaten in public on several staged and well-documented occasions – effectively media events – what has been served and eaten are tiny amounts of laboriously and expensively produced animal protein, essentially proofs-of-concept establishing that cell culture techniques can be used to produce something edible. Even within the cultured meat movement, debates flare up over the ultimate viability of cultured meat, especially as a foodstuff produced and sold at 'scale', that is, to the point where it becomes competitive with conventional meat.

Researchers in both industrial and university laboratories are still trying to surmount the many technical challenges of tissue-engineering meat, from perfecting a comparatively simple form of meat like hamburger to producing more complex forms of meat such as steak, which depends on a complex structure for its characteristic texture and flavour, and must be made in three dimensions, thereby requiring vascularization systems that are very difficult to work out. These technical challenges are very similar to those faced by researchers in regenerative medicine, who seek to use tissue engineering to repair, re-grow or replace diseased or damaged human body parts. In fact, cultured meat is a technology based on work in regenerative medicine and medical tissue engineering more broadly. It seeks to repurpose work done in those fields, towards the production of food. Part of this case of 'technology transfer', however, is a shift in scale: whereas tissue grown for medical transplant is comparatively small in size, and immensely valuable from the standpoint of the medical work it is meant to do, tissue grown for consumption as food must ultimately be massive in size, and relatively cheap, if it is meant to be consumed in the way we consume hamburger meat.

As of 2017, cultured meat research is still small in scale. In my several years of ethnographic work, only a handful of companies have been operating, and a similarly small number of academic researchers are conducting research directly intended to lead to meat production. One important advocacy and research-funding institution, the non-profit New Harvest, works to encourage research into cultured meat, which they consider one variation of the practice of 'cellular agriculture', the use of cell culture techniques to grow products that would otherwise be taken from animal bodies.

Several other organizations take a very active interest, including the Good Food Institute, which pushes for the label, 'clean meat'. There are annual scientific conferences, and cultured meat promoters and practitioners speak at major technology conferences such as TED (Technology, Entertainment, Design) and Austin's South by Southwest, but cultured meat is not yet an industry. Many bemoan the fact that the conversation surrounding the practice of growing meat in labs has grown far faster than the technology itself. In that conversation, the themes of rejection, reclamation and the reconsideration of the meaning of meat itself, all loom large. In other words, even before it becomes a food product, cultured meat has come to have a distinctive relationship, or a set of relationships, with the category of 'offal'.

One great irony of laboratory-grown meat is that this novel food-of-the-future has already been treated like a kind of science-fiction offal: something that might only exist in a particular version of the future, but that you might not want to eat, preferring a more familiar kind of meat. And yet in the vision of the future held dear by the cultured meat movement, there would be no more offal, or at least not much of it, for anyone to eat, because animal bodies would not be born, raised and killed in an industrial agricultural setting. Offal and laboratory-grown meat thus stand to illuminate each other; each prompts a reconsideration of meat itself, both in the definitional sense, and in the sense of how we eat it and why and in what amounts. Both are 'negative space' around high-value cuts of meat. Offal performs this function in an obvious way indicated by the word's etymology – offal comes from *ab-fall*, or 'that which falls away in the butchering process' – and cultured meat does so, or at least it aspires to do so, by duplicating high-value cuts by means other than large-scale, industrial animal agriculture, the system that optimizes for high-value cuts.

The distinctive case of cultured meat, and the much more diffuse and historically long-running practices of consuming and rejecting offal, both point to a surprising trait that meat possesses. Meat displays a combination of semiotic stability and instability, or, if you prefer, it tends signify powerfully, as compared to other foods, while its actual definition shimmers, shifts, wobbles and shakes. It has an intense, but uncertain, meaning. This particular quality of signification is linked, by some writers, to meat's symbolic representation of our mastery over nature. Others link to the human mortality of which non-human animal bodies remind us. Such changeability echoes the history of meat consumption, which in Europe and North America only began to resemble our contemporary patterns in the mid-nineteenth century, part of a broader dietary change linked to agricultural productivity, urbanization and industrialization.

The shaking of meat's meanings, within the discourse around laboratory-grown meat, opens onto a series of important philosophical problems. The one that preoccupies me the most could be called the problem of organisms and artefacts. The German intellectual historian Hans Blumenberg articulated it this way, in the late 1950s. For Blumenberg, modern thought is shaped by the tension between organisms and artefacts, between things that grow and things that we make.[4] This yields a persistent question at the boundary of psychology and philosophy, namely whether the artificial world we have made for ourselves can be experienced as deeply legitimate in the same sense that we experience our given environment as legitimate. Laboratory-grown meat does not have to make it to the supermarkets to prompt this kind of philosophical reflection, or to prompt pressing reflections on the ethical and environmental damage caused by industrial animal agriculture. It can do this work even in its current state, as a kind of technological promise.

As of 2017, such promises have been circulating for a short time from the standpoint of history, but for an irritatingly long time from the standpoint of individual, impatient, technology-watchers. For about fifteen years, scientists, engineers, entrepreneurs, futurists and others have been trying to promote the creation of pieces of muscle tissue, based on biopsies taken from domesticated animals. The result, displayed most famously in an August 2013 hamburger demonstration in London, is meat for which no animal body was born, raised, slaughtered or butchered. Not only did no animal need to suffer for that 2013 burger, no butchering of a carcass was necessary. This is celebrated, by those who celebrate such things, as a way of minimizing waste and suffering at once: *there is no full animal to eat*, and thus there is no waste; there is not even wasteful suffering, as the tissue produced lacks nerves, much less a central nervous system within which an animal might experience pain. In the promotional literature surrounding cultured meat it is almost mandatory to quote a kind of promise Winston Churchill made in 1932: 'We shall escape the absurdity of growing a whole chicken in order to eat the breast or wing, by growing these parts separately under a suitable medium.'[5] Notably, Churchill did not imagine growing other parts like the feet or the gizzard. A literary echo of Churchill's vision arrived in the early 1950s, in the American science fiction writers Fredrik Pohl and C.M. Kornbluth's *The Space Merchants*. In that novel's dystopian rather than utopian future tense, an entire factory of workers are fed each day by a single organism, something called Chicken Little, a quivering, rubbery grey hemisphere of chicken meat. Pohl and Kornbluth don't specify the 'part', but that seems to be beside the point – pieces of Chicken Little are 'harvested', apparently painlessly, with a sword, and they all have the same flavour and consistency.[6] Chicken Little is a caricature of the way people eat meat in affluent countries. 'She' is just a debased version of higher-value cuts and nothing else, or in McGee's terms, this is the urban style of meat-eating, presumably on steroids and antibiotics.

The dark side of abundance is precisely what cultured meat's advocates want to repair, and their sense of impending crisis seems licensed by the state of industrial meat production. The scale at which we produce, and consume, meat and the pace at which production and consumption are growing have ruinous effects from many standpoints. Some numbers: at present, animal agriculture, and perhaps especially Concentrated Animal Feeding Operations or CAFOs, are thought to contribute about 18% of our greenhouse gas emissions each year. They also occupy a large percentage of our available farmland, and create breeding grounds for viral agents affecting both non-human and human animals. As of the late 1990s, some 40% of grain production was fed to animals, much of that going to meat animals, an important detail since, as we know, it is more calorically efficient to grow plants and feed them to humans than to use animals as meaty intermediaries along the trophic scale between plants and humans. And as soon as we think about grain production, we naturally also have to think of water; making meat is an incredibly water-intensive process. To feed more meat-eaters by conventional means means much more than just breeding and slaughtering more animals. It entails a large number of costs that may appear external from the standpoint of the meat consumer, but that have serious environmental consequences, that are unevenly spread between rich and poor countries. Indeed, and in striking resonance with the theme of offal, the limiting factor for animal production in many countries is not feed, or water, or land, but waste, its management and disposal.

And, almost needless to say, industrial animal agriculture also produces what many see as the unnecessarily cruel treatment of food animals. In examining harm to animals, proponents of cultured meat, especially ones who come from the world of vegan activism, often cite Jeremy Bentham's 1789 insistence that, when it comes to considerations of the rights of animals, the question is not whether they can reason but, rather, whether they can suffer, and they obviously can and do.[7] That the cultured meat movement tends to select utilitarianism as its preferred variant of moral philosophy is hardly accidental; many within the animal rights community have read Peter Singer's 1975 *Animal Liberation*, which extended utilitarianism's focus on the 'greatest good' to non-human animals.[8] While utilitarianism dominates within the cultured meat movement, it is not alone; there are also those whose views come closer to the 'deontic'; that is, they're concerned not with effects or the promotion of the greatest possible happiness, but with the moral character of our actions, with their inherent rightness or wrongness. Some who take this view have questioned whether or not cultured meat would just be a 'moral crutch' – and questioned whether it would actually constitute the moral advance that others claim it would. There are, as you might imagine, vastly more dimensions to the cultured meat movement than I can describe in this talk, but one worth mentioning is the broadly shared, albeit strikingly old-fashioned, notion that civilization goes through stages of moral progress, and that technological and moral progress tend to march together, the former aiding the latter. In other words, ideas about the moral advantages of growing meat in laboratories are often connected to ideas about the progressive character of techno-civilization.

In my research I also ask what it means, in a cultural rather than a purely philosophical sense, when environmental damage, health risk and the moral problem of cruelty to food animals become not local and limited but general and infrastructural. For industrial animal agriculture does form a bio-infrastructure underlying our civilization; dairy and meat mammals are, numerically speaking, the 'dominant' vertebrates on Earth, constituting the bulk of our zoomass – in the year 2000 it was estimated that their number was around 4.3 billion. And the infrastructure of animal agriculture grows as the meat industry struggles to meet rising demands for their products. That demand is especially on the rise in China and India, and many demographers expect it to increase in those centres both of population growth and, significantly, of a growing middle class: the story of rising meat consumption is also the story of the spread of the Western Diet, by some reckonings about four-times as land-intensive as largely vegetarian non-Western diets. Most broadly, we have to ask if the mid-twenty-first century's growth in meat consumption will sustain late twentieth-century trends. Between 1960 and 2000, global meat production increased about threefold: a replication of such growth would be disastrous, but even a slower rate of increase could have dire consequences, especially against a background of climate change and the loss of farmland.

The process of producing cultured meat, as conducted for the famous 2013 hamburger, is laborious, shifting the work of growing muscle from the cow to the laboratory bench. Dr Mark Post, a professor of medicine at Maastricht University, working with his staff, used cell culture and tissue engineering techniques to produce muscle strands that were formed into the shape of a hamburger. They began with a sample of muscle cells taken from the hindquarters of a Blanc Bleu Belge, a breed that is itself a more traditional form of 'biotechnology', bred to emphasize a myostatin mutation that causes it to produce extra muscle mass. Isolated skeletal muscle cells were then encouraged to proliferate in a growth medium. The cells merged, forming 'myotubes' roughly .3 mm in length, and Post's team then placed the myotubes together in a circular configuration around a 'hub' made of gel. These configurations of myotubes began to display muscle's natural tendency to contract; the team 'exercised' them, by mechanical means (electrical means are also possible), and they accordingly bulked up. The result was a small ring of muscle tissue, which was cut up into strands, and this whole process was then repeated until a great, great many strands were combined to form the burger. In 2013, Mark Post's narration of the process emphasized the growth potential of the cell: a single one could become a trillion, and 'a few cells from a single cow could turn into ten tons of meat'. Mark was transparent about the amount of time and money it took to create the burger – several months of his lab technicians' time, and over $300,000 dollars, as widely reported in the media.[9] The expectation was never for the cost to remain high, but for it to plummet as the technology scales up, eventually reaching or going below the cost of conventional hamburger. Needless to say, no bones, no skin, no organs were grown. There was nothing to throw away, or to describe as offal, and indeed, as challenging as it is to make muscle tissue, making functional organ tissue is often harder still. The cultured burger made from the cells of the blanc bleu belge could be imagined as the continuation, through new technical means, of the anthropocentric tendency literally embodied by that animal: nonhuman animals turned into technologies driven by the human desire for particular types of animal flesh.

While I've stressed the obvious parallels between cultured meat and offal, which have to do with their joint existence (pun intended) on the fringes of modern Western meat consumption, their relation is more properly ambiguous. If truly scaled up in the way that Mark Post and other promoters of cultured meat suggest, the production of these kinds of hamburgers – not to mention chicken breasts, meatballs, pork loins and even steaks – could aid and abet the gradual elimination of industrial animal agriculture, and thus the millions of tons of less desired parts that are not simply 'wasted' but are turned into a wide range of other things, including not only 'variety meats' but ingredients for pharmaceuticals, cosmetics and household and industrial products, according to one United States Department of Agriculture Report. The discarded portions of animal carcasses have afterlives that tie industrial meat production to other industries. The effects of transforming our meat infrastructure through cultured meat would thus extend far beyond the food system. The repercussions of cultured meat would include their own form of figurative 'offal', in the sense of side effects on other forms of enterprise, some of which are difficult to anticipate. This could be rephrased as a counterfactual: what is the world like without domesticated food animal carcasses?

But even as artists and designers, excited by the idea of cultured meat, have tried to imagine what new, carcass-free forms it might take, offal, that sign of unavoidable animality, has crept back in. In August 2014, at a party held one year after the unveiling of his burger, Mark Post was presented with a book called the *In Vitro Meat Cookbook*, produced by the Dutch design consortium Next Nature. A vast range of forms of meat were included in that book, from the very untraditional – such as 'meat paint' children could use like finger paint and then consume – to traditional meat forms like steak. This range could be usefully recast: it runs between the 'mimetic' to the 'nonmimetic', from laboratory-grown muscle tissue designed to appeal to our existing tastes, to tissue designed to expand those tastes or to respond to the presumably transformed appetites of the future. But whereas one popular type of cultured meat fantasy promotes pieces of meat as if they developed on an animal, but with no trace of the rest of the body, Next Nature presumed that a mimetic future for cultured meat would include everything from bones and marrow broth to sweetbreads and lungs. We must assume that, in the imagined future that Next Nature's cookbook describes, residual tastes for organs have caused scientists to create cultured organs for consumption as variety meats – and yet this would not only be a dazzlingly wasteful application of medical tissue engineering, something plausible only in a Star Trek-like future of cornucopian abundance; it would also be bizarre, in symbolic terms. Of course this is all fantasy, but it matters enormously that even as we fantasize about a future of cultured meat, offal follows, shadowing the very technology that tries to make it unnecessary.

Once more on the relationship between cultured meat and offal: when we began to think of growing meat in laboratories, we also began to introduce new instabilities to an already-unstable object, namely meat. Those new instabilities derived from the fact that culturing meat means both imitating nature and not imitating it, or to put the point differently, it means replicating the natural by a painstaking method, making something happen by human intention that happens in the wild without intention – effectively, to introduce human will where it was not before, and to try to do so seamlessly. Hans Blumenberg proposed that, for two thousand years, the question of the meaning of all art or fabrication had been answered by Aristotle, who called art 'the imitation of nature', here meaning both *natura naturans* and *natura naturata*: both nature as a 'productive principle' and nature as a 'produced form'. This epoch ends in modernity, however, through the will to rebel against our inherited 'imitative' version of art, as though copying and responding to the world we are given is not enough. Blumenberg was trying to name the modern condition of alienation, of course, which is a very typical thing for an historian or philosopher of the modern West to do, but he also went further, and his writings are much more fine-grained about the relationship between making and the legitimation crises we often experience: Blumenberg asserts that, in modernity, the need to create, and to know ourselves through creation, tangles up in our sense that doing so constitutes a transgression against the given, and against the given's endowment with bedrock meaning. Thus, Blumenberg says, 'the sum of modern intellectual history constitutes the antagonism between the mechanical and the organic, art and nature, the will to form and the givenness of forms, between labor and rest.'[10] To make meat in laboratories produces a sense of unease because it shifts us, in Blumenberg's terms, from rest to labour, from the organic to the mechanical. We are, here, contemplating eating meat that never had parents.

Blumenberg is not suggesting that we restrict human creation, of course, and it is not towards that end that I invoke him. Rather, he is useful because the project of creating cultured meat raises enormous, and perhaps unanswerable, questions about 'ends'. For Blumenberg's version of Aristotle, 'ends' mean a sense of purposefulness that living things possess. Notably, offal has the symbolic power to remind us that our meat was once a self-contained creature with its own purposes. And purposefulness can be understood as something else, which Blumenberg glosses in Heideggerian language, as 'the identity of Being and nature'.[11] Human ends have a different quality: they are less knowable, less certain and always subject to philosophical questions. To try to abandon offal by moving meat away from the bodies of animals might be to fully embrace the openness of ends, to sustain a kind of questioning that causes the very unease Blumenberg wants to map. And as I've tried to show, even as the pioneers of cultured meat contemplate new futures for flesh, offal travels along with them. To a reader of Freud this looks suspiciously like the repressed always finding a way to return.

Notes

1. The text of this plenary address has been lightly revised to address changes in the world of laboratory-grown meat since the talk was given in July, 2016.
2. Harold McGee, *On Food and Cooking: The Science and Lore of the Kitchen* (New York: Scribner, 2004), p. 135.
3. Leon R. Kass, 'The Wisdom of Repugnance', *The New Republic*, 2 June 1997, pp. 17-26.
4. Hans Blumenberg, 'Imitation of Nature: Towards a Prehistory of the Idea of the Creative Being', trans. by Anna Wertz, *Qui Parle*, 12.1 (Spring/Summer 2000), 17-54.
5. Winston Churchill, 'Fifty Years Hence', *Popular Mechanics*, March 1932, p. 396 <http://rolandanderson.se/Winston_Churchill/Fifty_Years_Hence.php>.
6. Frederik Pohl and C.M. Kornbluth, *The Space Merchants* (New York: Ballantine, 1953)
7. Jeremy Bentham, *An Introduction to the Principles of Morals and Legislation*, *The Collected Works of Jeremy Bentham*, ed. by J. H. Burns and H.L.A. Hart (Oxford: Oxford University Press, 1970), p. 283.
8. Peter Singer, *Animal Liberation: The Definitive Classic of the Animal Movement* (New York: Harper Perennial, 2009).
9. Mark Post, 'Meet the New Meat', TEDxHaarlem, *TEDBlog*, 6 August 2013 <http://blog.ted.com/meet-the-new-meat-a-tedx-talk-to-pair-with-the-first-lab-grown-hamburger/>.
10. Blumenberg, p. 23.
11. Blumenberg, p. 47.

'Vulgarly Termed Lights': The Curious History of Lung Cookery

Ken Albala

All foods have a history, not merely a record of when they are introduced and how they have been used, but a story of attitudes toward them, which shifts oftentimes due to completely exogenous factors that may derive from science, religion, economic and social change or merely random chance. A food beloved in one generation may be forgotten by the next. A recipe that serves as a marker of elite social class in one century may be demoted as common and ordinary in another. An ingredient scarcely eaten one decade may become a miracle food, a sacred food, a hip popular item on restaurant menus and equally capriciously disappear thereafter. This is what happened to lungs. This paper recounts the story of lungs from a popular dish many centuries ago, to a barely considered marginal species of offal, to a food associated with poverty in the industrial era, to a forbidden food sought out by intrepid gastronomes for its rarity, and finally to a marker of ethnic identity. These changes in fortune and their various triggers provide an excellent example of how a food's social and cultural meaning can shift for totally random reasons.

To start, medieval recipes rarely name lungs alone in a dish. There were many euphemisms, but, more importantly, lungs were often cooked with other viscera such as heart, trachea, and liver. So in English we find words like pluck or lights. When these are mentioned there is no particular stigma against them, reflecting not a need to be frugal but rather a general familiarity and appreciation for organ meats. For example, in the medieval Catalan *Libre de Sent Sovi* these are called *Freixures*. These are first boiled, then sliced and fried with onions before the broth is added back along with typical medieval flavourings like spices, vinegar and bread crumbs to thicken. Interestingly the author tells us that four lungs to one liver is the right proportion.[1] Similarly the *Menagier de Paris* instructs his young bride that when a cow is butchered, the organs can be found at the tripe shop, where you can purchase the belly, stomach, spleen, lungs, liver and feet for eight sols.[2] These organ meats are referred to as nomblez or numbles in English, or ombles whence is said to derive the term humble pie. But there is no indication that these were in any way disprized, and they are called for in several recipes. Numbles are also found in the *Forme of Cury*, a cookbook associated with the court of Richard II, where they are likewise parboiled, diced and mixed with broth, bread vinegar, wine, onions, blood to colour and a spice mixture known as 'powdor fort'.[3]

The German sources are also rich with lung recipes, often in sausages with liver, but also on their own. In the sixteenth century, Sabina Welserin offers a simple dish:

'To make a spoon dish of lungs: Boil the lung, chop it small, fry it in fat, break eggs into it, add spices and meat broth, then it is done.'[4] Italian authors are a little more inventive. The *coratella* (lungs and windpipe) of a pig, for example, in Scappi is boiled then mixed with grated cheese, herbs, spices, raisins, eggs and stuffed into caul fat and then roasted on a spit or grilled.[5] This was a dish deemed appropriate to serve at the papal court in the sixteenth century. Writing in the early seventeenth century, Antonio Frugoli confers, 'The lungs of all quadrupeds are good to eat, and easier to digest than liver, but it's cold and bad for phlegmatics and will offer little nutrition. The best are of pork, veal and kid, and even of diverse other animals as long as it's young, fat and served with good herbs and enough spices included.'[6]

Interestingly, the medical authorities of the period are usually explicit about the social meaning of food, specifying which foods are fit for elites and which for labouring men, but lungs are not stigmatized as such in the dietary literature. In fact their evaluation is fairly consistent, though opinion varies to the extent in which they nourish the body.

Alessandro Petronio in the *Victu Romanorum et sanitate tuenda* says, 'Lungs, because something like a sponge, if eaten copiously, remarkably inflate the stomach: and truly they contain very little nourishing juice, thus offer the body little aliment.' He contends, along with Galen, that it is difficult to digest, because of its lightness unless well mixed with other ingredients, it descends slowly through the digestive passage and generates crude humours in the stomach.[7]

In *Diaeteticon*, Ludovicus Nonnius says, 'Lungs are truly more easy to digest [than other organ meats] because of its light texture, and it is spongy, however it is a pituitous aliment and its ability to nourish inferior to liver.'[8]

Thomas Moffett says, 'Lungs of Beasts are softer than the Heart, Liver, Kidneys and Spleen, easier therefor of Concoction' by which he means digestion in the stomach. But he also warns they are therefore phlegmatic and appropriate for those with hot and dry dispositions, those that suffer from hot agues. However, the texture suggests that it is not fit for labouring men whose powerful stomachs would cause it to putrefy before it offered any viable nutritional value.[9]

Tobias Venner says, 'The lights are of light digestion, of little nourishment, and the same not good but phlegmatic.'[10] Louis Lemery writing in the early eighteenth century says lungs 'are soft in consistency, moist, succulent and light, easy to digest and fairly nourishing. In sum, they can serve as a good aliment'.[11]

The Industrial Era

At some point in the nineteenth century, however, the attitude toward lungs as food begins to shift, in ways that I think are due to its price and more powerful associations with the working classes. An intimation of this is already found early in the century. In *Le cuisinier econome*, M. Archambault writes that *mou de veau* 'is among all parts of the veal that of which one makes the least usage, nonetheless there are those who find it agreeable.' The recipe *au blanc* includes cutting into small pieces, sautéing with flour, adding bouillon and mushrooms, degreasing and then adding egg yolks and a little vinegar.[12] About the same time an Italian recipe appeared in *La Nuova cucina economica* by Vicenzo Agnoletti that involves slicing the liver, heart and lungs into finger length batons, and frying with simple salt and pepper before serving with lemon juice.[13] The appearance in specifically frugal cookbooks signals not only the growing market for such literature but also that lungs were in fact considered an appropriate food for modest budgets.

The social meaning of lungs takes a decided turn in the industrial era, it seems, in part because of the greater demand for meat among the general populace, its greater availability due to improved transport in steam locomotives with refrigerated cars (at first with ice) and the need to dispose of what were considered for the first time less than desirable parts. Added to this of course was the growing level of poverty.

There is ample evidence that lungs and other appurtenances of sheep and pigs especially were considered the quintessentially frugal food by the mid-nineteenth century. Regarding lamb or sheep haslet (in the American and coincidentally original meaning of that word, entrails), also referred to as pluck, which includes the heart, liver and lights, Thomas de Voe, author of *The Market Assistant*, a guide to shopping in 1867, remarked that these were 'Sold at Low Prices'. He also comments that in England pluck only refers to the lungs, as it did thirty years prior in the US.[14] Mrs Beeton was a little more specific about the price. She only includes lights in 'A Savoury and Economical Dish' of pig's liver with potatoes and bacon that costs only 1 shilling 6 pence and feeds six or seven people.[15] That equals about $6 in today's US currency.[16] Francatelli, writing specifically for the impoverished working classes, confers, 'Sheep's pluck [including heart, liver and lights], properly cooked, will furnish a meat dinner enough for twelve persons at a very moderate cost.' His recipe consists of strewing the sliced organs on onions, covering with breadcrumbs and baking. Pig's Fry is a similar mixture, floured and fried first then made into a kind of ragout.[17] Alexis Soyer says, 'Lambs Fry is sometimes to be had for a trifle; you can purchase it from about threepence or fourpence per pound.'[18] That's about 50 cents per pound in today's currency – and in fact cheaper than any organ meat that can be purchased today. Remarkably according to the USDA report for 2 June 2016, the value of a ½ pound beef lung was only 3 cents.[19] Of course that's only because it can no longer be sold for human consumption in the US; other organ meats fetch higher prices, and, thanks to decreasing demand, sometimes they can be quite expensive.

The larger point is that compared to 150 years ago, today there are no comparably cheap cuts of meat. Lungs would therefore have been a much greater marker of class, because extraordinarily cheap, and much more firmly associated with poverty. But the meaning of lungs has changed entirely once again in the latter twentieth century.

The Contemporary Scene in the United States and Elsewhere

For the past forty-five years the importation and retail of lungs for human consumption has been banned in the United States.[20] The logic behind the ruling was not fear of tuberculosis, which cast suspicion on lung consumption early in the twentieth century, but apparently the danger of accidental contamination with stomach fluids in the process of butchering. The stomach itself, it seems, can be easily cleaned so there was no such fear over eating tripe and intestines, but, composed of many tiny alveoli designed for oxygen transport, lungs proved too difficult to render safe and were thereafter relegated to the production of pet food. Unlike other organ meats, lungs were virtually unknown to an entire generation of Americans.

This ruling obviously outraged expatriate Scots and those of Scottish descent for whom a proper haggis including lungs was requisite for occasions such as Robbie Burns' Birthday. Burns penned a celebrated poem about haggis, 'chieftain o' the pudding race', and thereafter became forever associated with this dish, composed of lungs along with other organ meats and oats stuffed into a sheep's stomach and boiled.[21] Despite several fleeting proposals to lift the ban, most recently a few years ago, lungs remain a forbidden and therefore alluringly illicit 'strange' food, eaten as much to display machismo and daring while abroad for adventurous foodie travellers as it is a marker of Scottish identity. A highland dinner for tourists is not complete without Scotch whisky and a piper marching in the haggis, which is ceremoniously opened by the master of ceremonies and delved out to those willing to partake of true Scottishness, with a side of neeps and tatties.

For example the Highlands restaurant declares itself 'An award winning contemporary authentic gastro pub located in the heart of the West Village in downtown New York. Owned and operated by Scots. HIGHLANDS is a true Authentic Experience of Modern Scotland today'.[22] The haggis they serve is of course not the real thing, as it includes no lungs.

In the US there was in fact a black market for authentic Haggis, and a true dyed-in-the-wool Scots colleague of mine bought one surreptitiously every year on the streets of Berkeley where it was handed off by a renegade butcher in exchange for an envelope of unmarked bills. For the unScottish and for most Americans who had never tasted a real Haggis, eating it is a moment of personal pride, a species of culinary accomplishment, precisely because it is illegal and potentially dangerous, at least according to the USDA. Only those intrepid gastronomes with the 'guts' to down the haggis could enjoy bragging rights among their sheepish friends. Interestingly, few other foods have retained such a powerful ability to inspire revulsion among Americans, which only adds to its allure.

There is a small subgenre of haggis jokes, like the man who wins a Robbie Burns contest, the third prize for which is a haggis dinner for two. He then reveals that the second prize was a haggis dinner for one, and first prize meant you didn't have to eat it at all.

The irony of these decidedly American jokes is that haggis and the lungs included in it are not particularly strongly flavoured. If anything, it is the dark colour and spongy texture of lung on its own that turns off the American palate, and no doubt simple unfamiliarity for most. A generation ago this was not the case. My mother recalled that as a child she was regularly fed lungs, and, although it was one of the cheaper meats available during the depression, there was a market for it. But the meaning of lungs for Americans has changed entirely since then.

Nowadays eating offal and lungs also confers the opportunity for bravado for those daring enough to try them. The weirder the food, the more adventuresome the eater is considered to be and the more cultural capital one amasses from collecting such experiences, even at the expense of appropriating a supposedly foreign and exotic cuisine for one's personal benefit. I believe this has played some role in the persistence of lung cookery on menus in Europe. It is not merely the nose to tail ethic, but what Lisa Heldke calls 'the quest for novelty' and authenticity – a constant game of one-upmanship among gastronomic elites.[23] On some level, I think restaurant menus, to some extent catering to tourists, offer lungs precisely because they allure intrepid eaters who can boast about it later.

Lungs never went off the menu completely in Europe, but there seems to be a kind of revival catering to tourists, or at least noticed by guidebooks and companies offering tours. Last spring I went in search of an authentic Viennese restaurant and was led to a charming hole in the wall called the Walfviertlerhof by an expatriate friend who assured me that they spoke no English and that I could find real Viennese dishes there. On the menu there was *beuschel* (or more precisely *kalbsrahmbeuscherl mit serviettenknödel* – which is a bread dumpling cooked in a napkin and sliced), the very mention of which had my friend regret he had ever brought me. I ate it nonetheless and it was glorious. But thinking I had scored an original authentic find, I was later disappointed to find the dish recommended in an online tourist travel guide about how to eat like a local in Vienna. In any case, the dish remains a culinary score in a sense, because it can't be found in the US or replicated. Its value is a cultural capital, an experience that can't be easily found without hunting down the right restaurant abroad.

Lungs with artichokes (*Coratella d'abbacchio con i carciofi*) can also be found in Rome's Jewish Ghetto, and I took a class of food history students from Boston University there with the expressed intention of offering them a strange and unique gastronomic adventure. Jewish restaurants there do serve the local populace, but it seems a large part of their business comes from tourists seeking out an authentic and slightly frightening experience. Tour guides boast the fact that they take people to restaurants serving the 'quinto quarto' – cuts like lung, tripe and other organ meats, of which Romans are so fond. The implication is that to get the full experience to the place you need to at least taste the lung dishes. A *Huffington Post* article about '17 Classic Italian Street Foods That Everyone Should Try At Least Once' includes the Sicilian '*pani ca meusa*, or chopped veal's spleen and lung steamed in lard and then stuffed in a sandwich. Trust the Italians: this tastes *way* better than it sounds'.[24] As with the Scottish and Austrian examples, this is largely a matter of gastronomic adventure.

Although I have not been able to cover the rich Asian literature on the topic, it appears that a similar story can be told for the traditional Sichuan dish called husband and wife lung slices. Today it is more often made with tripe and brisket, even in China, much to the chagrin of those who travel there to find it.

The meaning of these lung recipes is of course very different for someone within the culture. Interestingly some have been revived as an integral part of culinary identity. Many people embrace them precisely because they are traditional and unusual and reflect native foodways, insisting that lungs should not be lost as the Western threshold of repugnance rises and as industrial mass-produced food infantilizes the common palate, relegating such 'specialty meats' to the abattoir floor. Lung recipes do stubbornly survive, and they exemplify the persistence of foods widely considered disgusting, eaten precisely because they are reminders of national, regional or ethnic identity. But here the food may mean one thing for the person within the culture and something very different for the outsider.

Modern European cookbooks which purport to reteach traditional recipes often contain lungs. For example *La cucina Fiorentina: storie e ricette* by Aldo Santini includes a recipe for *coratella* – the heart liver lung and spleen of lamb, cooked in a casserole with porcini, garlic and sage, and finished with broth and tomato. It is presented as *casalingo* – a traditional homey dish that should not be lost.[25]

A similar book called *Recettes de cuisine traditionelle de viande de veau* includes '*Mou de veau*' and claims that 'today the consumption of veal lung has fallen into desuetude'. But the editor decides to remove nothing from the original text drawn from Escoffier and thus offers one version *en civet* and another *a la Provençal* with onion, white wine, tomatoes and parsley.[26] The books intention is to reclaim heritage, to revitalize it and perhaps inspire people to serve such dishes again as an integral part of their gastronomic history.

These are merely two examples of not only how a food can be strange and adventurous to one person while traditional and a marker of identity for another. The larger lesson to be learned from the history of lungs is that foods do change meaning over time: they are avoided or relished or designated for people of a particular social class for reasons that have nothing inherent in the product itself.

Notes

1. *The Book of Sent Soví,* ed. by Joan Santanach, trans. by Robin M. Vogelzang (Barcelona: Barcino-Tamesis, 2008), pp. 118-19.
2. *The Good Wife's Guide,* trans. by Gina L. Greco and Christine M. Rose (Ithaca: Cornell University Press, 2009), p. 274.
3. *Curye on Inglysch*, ed. by Constance B. Heiatt and Sharon Butler (London: Oxford University Press, 1985), p. 100. According to Heiatt's concordance, there are another seven recipes for numbles in the medieval English cookbooks, including one for porpoise (*Concordance of English Recipes* (Tempe, AZ: ACMRS, 2006), p. 62).
4. Sabina Welserin, recipe 45 in Volker Bach, *The German Reformation Kitchen* (Lanham, MD: Rowman

and Littlefield, 2016).
5. *The Opera of Bartolomeo Scappi*, trans. by Terence Scully (Toronto: University of Toronto Press, 2008), p. 188 (p. 47 in original ed. of 1570).
6. Antonio Frugoli, *Practica e Scalcheria* (Rome: Cavalli, 1631), p. 101.
7. Alessandro Petronio, *Victu Romanorum et sanitate tuenda* (Rome: Aedibus Populi Romani, 1586), p. 152.
8. Ludovicus Nonnius, *Diaeteticon* (Antwerp: Petri Belleri, 1645), p. 201.
9. Thomas Moffett, *Health's Improvement,* composed late sixteenth century (London: T. Osborne, 1746), p. 200.
10. Tobias Venner, *Via recta ad vitam longam* (London: T.S., 1622), p. 91.
11. Louis Lemery, *Traité des aliments* (Paris: Pierre Witte, 1705), p. 224.
12. M. Archambault, *Le cuisinier econome*, 3rd ed. (Paris: Renard, 1825), p. 100. These recipes appear to be simplified adaptations of an earlier book: M. Viard, *Le Cuisinier Royal ou l'art de Fair la cuisine…pour tout les fortunes,* 10th ed. (Paris: Barba, 1820), p. 142.
13. Vicenzo Agnoletti, *La Nuova Cucina economica* (Milan: Agnelli, 1819), p. 158.
14. Thomas deVoe, *The Market Assistant* (New York: Hurd and Houghton, 1867), p. 93.
15. Isabella Beeton, *Dictionary of Everyday Cookery* (London: S.O. Beeton, 1865), p. 251.
16. Lawrence H. Officer and Samuel H. Williamson, 'Computing "Real Value" Over Time with a Conversion between U.K. Pounds and U.S. Dollars, 1774 to Present', *MeasuringWorth*, 2017 <http://www.measuringworth.com/exchange/>.
17. Charles Elmé Francatelli, *A Plain Cookery Book for the Working Classes* (London: Bosworth and Harrison, 1861), pp. 40-42.
18. Alexis Soyer, *Soyer's Shilling Cookery for the People* (London Routledge, 1860), p. 61.
19. 'USDA BY-PRODUCT DROP VALUE (STEER) FOB CENTRAL U.S.', United States Department of Agriculture <http://www.ams.usda.gov/mnreports/nw_ls441.txt>.
20. '§ 310.16Disposition of lungs. (a) Livestock lungs shall not be saved for use as human food. (b) Lungs found to be affected with disease or pathology and lungs found to be adulterated with chemical or biological residue shall be condemned and identified as 'U.S. Inspected and Condemned.' Condemned lungs may not be saved for pet food or other nonhuman food purposes. They shall be maintained under inspectional control and disposed of in accordance with §§ 314.1 and 314.3 of this subchapter. (c) Lungs not condemned under paragraph (b) of this section may be used in the preparation of pet food or for other nonhuman food purposes at the official establishment, provided they are handled in the manner prescribed in § 318.12 of this subchapter, or they may be distributed from the establishment in commerce, or otherwise, in accordance with the conditions prescribed in § 325.8 of this subchapter for nonhuman food purposes or they may be so distributed to pharmaceutical manufacturers for pharmaceutical use in accordance with §§ 314.9 and 325.19(b) of this subchapter, if they are labeled as "Inedible [SPECIES] Lungs—for Pharmaceutical Use Only." Otherwise, they shall be disposed of at the official establishment, in accordance with §§ 314.1 and 314.3 of this subchapter' (United States Code of Federal Regulations, 36 FR 11639, 17 June 1971 <http://www.gpo.gov/fdsys/pkg/CFR-2012-title9-vol2/xml/CFR-2012-title9-vol2-part310.xml>).
21. 'To a Haggis', in Robert Burns, *Robert Burns: Selected Poems and Songs,* ed. by Robert P. Irvine (Oxford: Oxford University Press, 2013), p. 134
22. 'Highlands NYC', Highlands NYC, 2015 <http://www.highlands-nyc.com/>.
23. Lisa Heldke, *Exotic Appetites* (New York: Routledge, 2003). Amusingly, Heldke's prime example of the adventuresome eater is the Symposium's own Paul Levi.
24. '17 Classic Italian Street Foods That Everyone Should Try At Least Once', *The Huffington Post*, 19 November 2013 <http://www.huffingtonpost.com/2015/11/06/italian-street-foods-everyone-should-try_n_8280680.html>.
25. Aldo Santini, *La cucina Fiorentina: storie e ricette* (Florence: Tarka, 2014), n.p. (Google ebook).
26. Auguste Escoffier and Pierre-Emmanuel Malissin, *Recettes de Cuisine Traditionnelle de Viande de Veau* (Paris: Syllabaire, 2013).

Şırdan: The Pornographic Dish of a Conservative Land

Nilhan Aras

Anatolia is conservative, prioritizing family life and patriarchal control, but in the case of food this conservatism can quickly be replaced by wild adventurism. Some savoury dishes and desserts have quite offensive or provocative words as names; such words would be off-limits in daily life, but somehow they are allowed in the case of food, whether due to innocent folk naiveté or to the unstoppable resurfacing of repressed emotions. Beyond provocative names, there are many dishes that include aphrodisiac ingredients or are even considered aphrodisiacs themselves. Dishes and desserts with erotic connotations and suggestive visual appearance include *Kadınbudu Köfte* [Woman's Buttocks Meatballs], *Dilberdudağı* [Lips of the Gorgeous], *Vezir Parmağı* [Vizier's Fingers], *Hanım Göbeği* [The Lady's Navel], *İncir Dolması* [Stuffed Figs], and beyond the erotic evocations of their names, the bombastic, amorous appearance of these dishes are almost erotic adventures in themselves. And there are other dishes with names that seem destined to become topics of sociology theses, like the *Kerhane Tatlısı* [Bordello Dessert] or *Şıllık Tatlısı* [Dessert of the Bitch] that are well-known in southern Turkey, but very much loved all across the country.

While such examples may be found all over Anatolia, in southern Turkey, in the Anatolian lands surrounded by the Mediterranean Sea, there are two savoury offal dishes that push the boundaries of provocation even further in visual terms. One of them is *şırdan*, made from the abomasum (the fourth and final stomach compartment in ruminants); the other is *mumbar*, prepared from the large intestines of the animal. This article focuses on şırdan, which has a unique place in the cuisine of the southernmost city of Adana.

The shape of the abomasum makes it ideal to be stuffed. It is laborious to prepare; so at home, it is cooked only for special occasions. Only professional cooks and street vendors prepare şırdan on a daily basis. The dish requires a pilaf cooked by using yellow rice in the husk, minced meat made from ribs, lard and/or suede and pepper paste; this stuffing is filled into sheep or lamb's şırdan and the split sides of the organ are then knit before the stuffed şırdan pieces are boiled. The dish is served with lots of ground cumin sprinkled on top to add flavour and ease the digestion.

Adana

Adana is a city located in southern Turkey, adjacent to the Mediterranean Sea. It is the sixth biggest city of Turkey with a population of more than two million people. Although Adana has a very hot climate even during the winter, the natives of the town are known with their love for meat; their cuisine lovingly treasures every part of the animal. Adana folk love meat and prefer it to fish dishes. The population of the city consists mostly of Arabs, Kurds, the nomadic local population called Yörük and Turkish people; all these ethnic groups have culinary cultures that predominantly rely on meat dishes, as well as all sorts of heavy and fatty food.

Adana is not a conservative, hermetically sealed society, but the town is deeply patriarchal, and women's behaviour is carefully monitored. This macho approach restraints the free movement and freedom of action of the women – at least to an extent. There are specific things deemed 'unsuitable' for women, especially in a crowded places. Modernity has clearly changed a lot of things, but questions about what is appropriate for women was remains a concern for society. For example, it was regarded as totally 'normal' that women went out for meals with their families, but up until recent years it raised eyebrows if a woman went out alone to eat and drink, or if she dined at a restaurant with female friends. It was even more unthinkable for women to eat something on the street, casually feasting alone or with a friend.

Despite such patriarchal attitudes, the women of Adana are very influential and authoritative domestically, and that includes their position in the kitchen. In Adana society, food is one of the most important rituals of daily life. Families in Adana often plan dinner for the next day while they are having breakfast. (If possible, food seems even more central in the neighbouring town of Gaziantep, where natives are said to plan dinner for the next week during breakfast). Subsequent meals are always a source of inspiration and imagination for natives of Adana, and lunches and dinners are always planned well ahead.

Regardless of their ethnic background, people in Adana cherish all sorts of offal. Nonetheless, the place of *şırdan* and *Mumbar* are special. As a reminder, şırdan is made out of abomasum (the fourth and final stomach compartment in ruminants); and *mumbar* is prepared from the large intestines of the animal. Both offal dishes are stuffed with rice and cooked like *dolma* – other stuffed dishes. Şırdan is so much loved by Adana's natives that raw abomasums feature as one of the top imports to Adana from other cities.

Şırdan/Şirden

Şırdan is made from the abomasum, the last part of the digestive system of the herbivorous ruminant animals' stomachs that have multiple chambers. The fourth stomach of ruminants, the abomasum links the small intestine to the rumen and the rest of the system. The herbs chewed by the animals are digested here once more by gastric juices. The digested food passes onto the intestines. When the ruminant is born, this part of its stomach grows first, but the other three parts soon develop to similar maturity. Because of this, the şırdan used in cooking is taken from newborns.

Due to the creased, wrinkled texture of its walls and membranes, in some Turkish dialects *şırdan* is also called *kırk dilim* [forty layers], *kırk yaprak* [forty leaves] and *kırk ambar* [forty barns]. In the Uzbek language, *şırdan*'s name is *şirdon*; in Chuvashi, it is *şartan* and *şarttan*. The etymological dictionaries, such as Turkish sources dating from the year 1500s, like *Câmi-ül Fürs* (the oldest source that mentions *şırdan*) and *Müntehab-ı Şifa* [*Seçilmiş Şifalar* or *Selected Cures*], written in old Anatolian Turkish, point out that these parts of the animal 'thicken the blood'. Evliya Çelebi, one of the greatest travellers of the seventeenth century, mentions *şırdan* three times in his seminal work *Seyahatname* [*Travelogue*]. The etymology of *şırdan* denotes that the word passed into Turkish from Farsi from the word, *şīrdān/şīrdan*. In Farsi, *şīr* means 'milk' and *dān* means 'cup, bearer'. Nevertheless, şırdan is referred to as '*mentu*' in the poem '*Kenzü'l-İştihâ*' by the Iranian poet Mevlânâ Ebû İshak Hallâc-ı Şirâzî's (died 1423 or 1427).[1]

Şırdan refers to both the dish and the organ, the abomasum. The milk consumed by the calf is flows directly into the *şırdan*, due to the special qualities of the digestive system of ruminants. Consequently, the *şırdan* from newborns contains rennet, the most natural starter for cheese. *Şırdan* was used as a starter for cheese, a very common practice in dairy production, up until about fifty years ago in Anatolia, and şırdan is still sometimes used this way in rural areas, in places where nomadic or semi-nomadic people resist the pressures of modernization and still continue the old ways.

To use *şırdan* as a starter, the *şırdan* of a lamb or a newborn goat is taken from an animal that has not be weaned, that is still consuming only the mother's milk. The *şırdan* should be washed and salted, and then left to dry in the open air for up to a month. The dried *şırdan* is then left to soak in a jar filled with water. In some places, chickpeas, figs or grapes are put inside the jar to speed up the fermentation process. The jar is sealed and left to rest for a week (sometimes ten days, or even longer in some parts of Anatolia). Once the starter is ready, the *şırdan* is taken out of the jar, and the watery mixture is reserved for other use.

Figure 1.
Stuffed şırdan in the pot.

Şırdan: The Pornographic Dish of a Conservative Land

Şırdan/Şirden Dolması/Stuffed *Şırdan/Şirden*

During the Ottoman Empire, *Şırdan Dolması* [Stuffed *Şırdan*] was a palace dish made according to the following recipe: lungs and heart of a lamb or goat were cooked with rice and spices (mostly salt and cinnamon), and that mixture was stuffed inside *şirden* (the old spelling of *şırdan*) before being cooked in pure, crystalline water. The *şirden* that are cooked are taken off from the pot and laid in a tray to cool down. The *şirden* pieces were then sliced thinly, dipped in an egg batter and fried in ghee. Outside of the palace, most of the Ottoman people ate Stuffed *Şirden* and *Mumbar* [Stuffed Intestines] as festive dishes.

The nineteenth-century Ottoman cookbook *Melceü't Tabbahin* [*Sanctuary of the Cooks*] includes the following recipe:

> *Mumba*r and *Şirden*: Their preparation: Required amount of *mumbar* and *şirden* are taken and cleaned with knives as they should be, by scraping them off. Otherwise, they are soaked overnight into salty water, and washed off by flapping them until their foams cease to come out. It is better to use this second way. In whatever manner, get them prepared. Then take adequate amount of lungs and few hearts, and mince them finely with onions as they should be, add some rice that is washed off, salts and pepper and cinnamon and knead them all very well, add some water and knead as if you are kneading the dough of *lokma* [a desert] and tie up one side of the *mumbar* and fill in this mixture from the other with the help of a funnel, tie the other side as well, and pierce all over the *mumbar* or şirden all over and put them inside water while it is boiling and take the *şirden* and *mumbar* out once they are cooked and place the *mumbar* over a tray by rolling them into a spiral. Once cooled down, fry them in sizzling butter. Slice the şirden off thinly and dip them inside battered eggs and fry them in butter and it will be exquisite. The *mumbar* may also be filled with just minced meat and rice, or onion, minced meat and rice that are cooked together beforehand; all these latter recipes result in different tastes.[2]

Today, Stuffed *Şırdan* is cooked in a similar manner, although nowadays, with the frequent use of tomato paste to Turkish cuisine, Stuffed *Şırdan* are often cooked in water mixed with tomato paste. The primary difference between the past and now is that Stuffed *Şırdan* are served just after cooking, but in the past they were then dipped in egg and fried.

Şırdan vendor Ali Tunç, known as the '*Şırdancı Ali Baba*' throughout Adana, told me about a decade ago that the best Stuffed *Şırdan* was made from Eastern Anatolian lambs, ideally males lambs below one year of age. He told me:

> *Şırdan* is the upper part of the lambs' stomach. The best comes from sheep or lambs that are at or below one year of age; this is because these are more tender and tasty. And also, they must be from the Eastern sheep. You first wash *Şırdan*

with cold water. Then you soak them for 5-10 minutes in hot water. In this way, their texture gets better. They become really clean, almost transparent. The rice must be the yellow husk one; it is the best. If you cannot find it, then Baldo type from Thracian part of Turkey would also do. I then have the minced meat made out of the ribs, and cook it with butter. I then add up the rice to the minced meat and the pepper paste, and mix all up and fill it all up the Şırdan. The Stuffed Şırdan cooks inside clear water. For three hours. The original of the pots used are copper, but nowadays they are cooked in chrome or steel pots. Şırdan is cooked usually at night, because it is consumed after alcohol and because nights are cooler. I have seen a lot of people who were falling off their chairs as they were so drunk and then after eating two Stuffed Şırdan, they get up on their feet totally sober. Şırdan is also ideal for those who want to gain weight.

It might be thought that, due to its physical location, this organ might harbour bacteria. But the Food Engineers Chamber's Adana branch diligently inspected *şırdan* within the framework of the European Union candidacy process. The whole procedure of slaughtering of the animal, removing the *şırdan* and preparing the şırdan dish itself, including its stuffing and cooking, were closely observed for a period of five months. At the end of the inspection, Işıl Var, the Head of the Adana branch, declared that they had not come across 'any bacteria or harmful organisms that may endanger human lives', and that the dish of Stuffed *Şırdan* may be consumed safely after being cooked well and under hygienic circumstances.

Adana Townsfolk's Relationship with Stuffed *Şırdan*

Even though *şırdan* is a heavy, fatty dish, it is eaten in all seasons, at all times of the day. *Şırdan* is consumed most on mild winter nights, but it may even be found as street food year round, often eaten on the sidewalk during lunch breaks. The street vendors selling *şırdan* prepare the dish by boiling it throughout the night, and keep the *şırdan* simmering over cauldrons placed over small gas stoves on the street. When lunchtime arrives, this curious food is then consumed by the city's *crème de la crème* and working classes alike, making for a gastronomical ritual shared by the whole of city.

But there is a surprising aspect to şırdan eaten on the street. Stuffed *Şırdan* is not an ordinary dish, and Adana's patriarchal, male dominated society does not allow open relationships between men and women. Considering this restrictive environment, it is a real sight to come across chic women, dressed in well-tailored suits, bending over the cauldrons of *şırdan* vendors, eyeing all the Stuffed *Şırdan* pieces one by one, selecting the ones they like the most, pointing their prized pieces out to the street vendor and eventually heartily biting the *şırdan* in public. Given its appearance, şırdan is morphologically beyond the boundaries of eroticism, delving right into the realm of pornography. Aside from *şırdan*'s interesting appearance, it is difficult to eat out on the street. The top part points upward, erect, and fatty juices of the dish ooze out

Şırdan: The Pornographic Dish of a Conservative Land

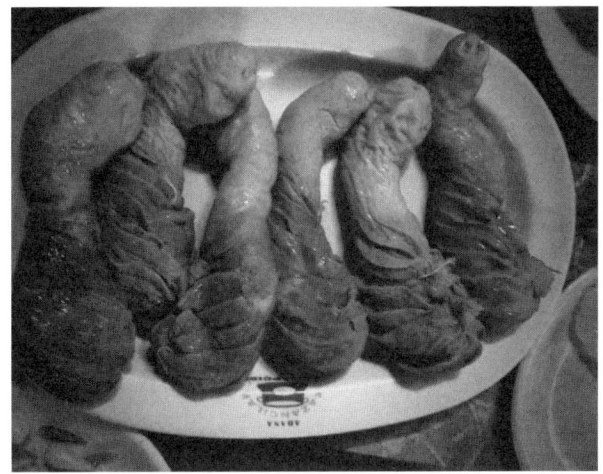

Figure 2.
Şırdan on display at a restaurant.

Figure 3.
Şırdan with its distinctive spice mixture.

with every bite. With tactful bites, the fatty juices do not drip on the chic dresses, but they do leak down from the side of the lips, gliding down the neck and even making their way to the *décolletage*. Chirping with laughter, upper crust ladies warn each other about the dripping juices. Most important of all, the ladies are most often either alone or with their female friends surrounding them. Yes, they may sometimes have male colleagues, dressed sharply for business, with them, but rarely do their husbands accompany them for these lunch escapades enamoured with şırdan.

These steamy food affairs hint that Adana's extraordinary infatuation with

Offal: Rejected and Reclaimed Food

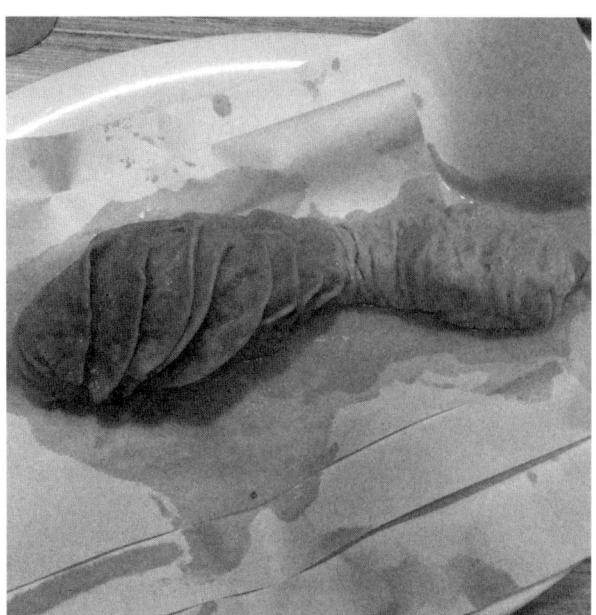

*Figure 4.
A juicy şırdan!*

şırdan may be more that innocent appetite. Certainly appearances suggest some subliminal message concerning this phallic dish with its long, thick stem topped with a round head and its skin-like outer texture, filled fully with tasty rice, complete with dark, globular knobs at its end. Adana's townsfolk love to consume hot food, and spices are common, whether inside their dishes or sprinkled over the food. Once you settle at a table at a restaurant in Adana, you are served many types of greens and salads. Most of these said to possess aphrodisiac qualities, part of 'Eastern culture', and at least conceptually they feed and support the libido. The natives of Adana, who have a real zest for life, for entertainment and for love affairs, consume aphrodisiac foods in great quantity at every meal of the day. This is the context for the popularity of this provocatively shaped stuffed dish that is eaten freely out on the street despite the patriarchal rules that might be expected to restrict its open consumption. In the end, *şırdan* is just offal stuffed with rice. But, when I say, 'Let's have some rice for lunch' to Adana folk, I receive replies without enthusiasm. But when somebody says, 'Let's go for a *şırdan*', the eyes of Adana's natives light up in ways that imply a reason beyond mere desire for the taste of the dish. It's almost enough to demand psychological or sociological study.

In any case, it is certainly a challenge to taste *şırdan* for the first time. According to observations of *şırdan* addicts, nine out of ten of those who come across the dish opt out of trying it. One of the reasons for such negative initial reactions is the dish's pungent smell. But those who taste it once cannot give up *şırdan*.

Nevertheless, *şırdan* is beneficial in other ways: the dish is believed to cancel out the negative effects of alcohol and intoxication. Hence, the dish is much sought after long nights out in Adana, whose population does have a penchant for Turkey's local alcoholic drink, anise-flavoured *rakı*. The post-midnight vendors of *şırdan* line up nearby nightclubs and along the narrow alleys of the side streets. Indeed, it may well be the coupling of *rakı* and *şırdan* that have made the latter a staple of Adana's folk culture in the first place.

In Anatolian culture, it was not customary to dine out, but the practice has become much more common in recent years. Until recently, it was thought, 'the women of the household did not cook well, and this is the reason a family dined out'. While this perception has started to change, it still lingers in the mentality of some people in Anatolia – especially the women. Luckily, with the ascendancy of the culinary sector, many more people, especially men, are eating out. In case of Adana, dining out also means having drinks out – and that was the habit in the old days too, unlike in much of Anatolia. The şırdan vendors have taken advantage of increased sales to expand their businesses. In addition to setting up their cauldrons on the streets, some have opened up small shops selling *şırdan*. There are now *şırdan* shops in all parts of the city, from the most prestigious districts to less frequented alleys. Moreover, it is not just the local people that circle the cauldrons or sit at tables eating *şırdan*; there are many tourists who do so, as well. All over the city, you catch glimpses of *şırdan*.

In Lieu of a Conclusion...

This is the story of *şırdan* in a nutshell, of this dish known for its tastiness in southern Anatolia and for its infamous appearance throughout the rest of the country. But there are many other surprising aspects concerning this bizarre dish, just as there are for the other provocatively named or shaped foods of conservative Anatolia. In case of *şırdan*, an Anatolian pun is especially true; 'Two types feel sorry about this dish; the ones who have tasted it, and those who have not' – because it is a challenge to begin eating it, and once having tasted, a bigger challenge to give up craving for *şırdan*.

Notes

1. On etymology, see Ahmed Cavid, *Tercüme-i Kenzü'l-İştihâ - 15. Yüzyıldan Bir Mutfak Sözlüğü*, ed. by Seyit Ali Kahraman and Priscilla Mary Işın (Istanbul: Kitap Yayınevi, 2006) and Priscilla Mary Işın, *Osmanlı Mutfak Sözlüğü* (Istanbul: Kitap Yayınevi, 2010). On beliefs about medicinal value, see Celalüddin Hızır (Hacı Paşa), *Müntahab-ı Şifa I-II*, ed. by Zafer Önler (Istanbul: Simurg Yayınları, 1999).
2. Mehmet Kamil, *Melceü't Tabbahin: Ascilarin siginagi*, ed. by Cüneyt Kut (Istanbul: Turkiye Yazma Eserler Kurumu Baskanligi, 2015); translated from Old Ottoman by the author.

Image Credits

Photographs appear by permission of Sinan Hamamsarılar, Mehmet Ali Sağbili, Tangör Tan and Can Ünal.

Offal and the Master Cook: Nose-to-Tail Eating in Late Medieval Germany

Volker Bach

Meat, Staple and Luxury

Germany, like all of Europe, had suffered a significant population loss through recurrent plague epidemics after 1348. It is impossible to say exactly how great the decline was, but estimates range as high as half of the total, with some areas hit even worse. This loss led to economic dislocation and a dearth of labour. Rising wages met a reduced demand for food, and much land that had been used to grow grain and vegetables was given over to animal husbandry requiring less labour and yielding higher-value products. As a result, the people who survived the epidemics ate a diet that was more varied and richer in animal products than previously or later. As with population figures, estimates of how much meat was eaten range widely, and it is safe to assume that the image of a golden age of gluttony is wrong. Nonetheless, meat was part of the daily diet for almost everyone in some form or other. The sixteenth-century poet Hans Sachs describes the general expectations of different diets by social class in the *Ständebuch* (book of estates): 'Rice, pepper sauce, other good side dishes, poultry, fish, galantines sweet and savoury, and for the peasant and artisan millet, barley, lentils, peas and beans, blood puddings, sausages, soups, root vegetables and potherbs so they may also fill their bellies.'[1]

In the course of the late fifteenth and sixteenth centuries, population growth led to rising food prices and a reversion to intensive grain farming, putting meat out of reach for an ever growing number of people. This trend, too, was present all over Europe, interrupted only briefly by regional wars and epidemics, and continued until the agricultural and transport revolutions of the nineteenth century. The expectation of meat as a daily part of a complete diet prevailed in popular culture, echoed in Grimm's fairy tales through the phrase *'Gesottenes und Gebratenes'* (boiled and roast meat) used to signify a generous table. In this world, any meat would sell, and being able to supply enough could make you wealthy.

Butchers and Cooks

In late medieval Germany, animal husbandry was a decentralized business. Feudal lords and substantial farmers occasionally raised large herds of cattle, pigs and sheep, but the majority of domestic animals were kept by urban and rural smallholders. Oxen and cows were part of any larger farm; pigs, often fed on waste, were a fixture of urban and rural households alike; cottagers kept goats for milk and meat; and almost every

Offal and the Master Cook

home that could spare the space and labour had chickens. The nexus at which the meat supply concentrated and profits could be maximized was in processing, which was mainly in the hands of professional butchers. While they also slaughtered animals for pay on behalf of their owners, urban butchers made most of their money through guilds monopolizing the sale of meat in their town or city. This could be an extremely lucrative business for people with the skill to fatten up and efficiently process animals. In some larger cities, master butchers went over entirely to the commercial side of the business, leaving the actual processing to subordinates. Since the meat supply of the cities was an emotionally significant issue for governments, it was heavily regulated and is therefore documented much better than the work of itinerant rural butchers.

One place for which we have good surviving documentation is Lübeck, a rich and powerful trading city on the Baltic shore. Sited within easy reach of the ox road from Jutland and surrounded by excellent pastures, its meat market was well supplied and its master butchers wealthy. They hired *küter* – skilled craftsmen who did not qualify for mastership – to do the actual butchering while they concentrated on purchasing and fattening animals. Their position was defended – outsiders were limited in what meat they could bring to the city – but also circumscribed for the benefit of private citizens, who had the right of first purchase for any livestock brought in. All animals slaughtered for sale had to be brought to a designated slaughterhouse, the *küterhaus*, and driven across a bridge in public view to show they could walk on their own. Slaughter for private consumption could take place at home or at the *küterhaus*.

Once the animal had been killed and processed, the butcher would pay the *küter* a specified fee and hand over the intestines (*kaldunen*), tallow and other pieces of lower quality. The *küter*, in turn, paid the butcher a small sum for the offal he had received. Our sources are silent on what happened to these pieces next. Like much food of low status, they went into the undocumented ecosystem of small retail, the world where pre-soaked salt fish were sold by the piece and bacon by the portion. Meanwhile, the finer parts were cut according to regulation – reference measures were kept to ensure this was done correctly – and brought to the stalls of the master butchers.[2]

There is a reference to offal being sold on the market in the Lübeck butchers' roll, but it is likely that at least some of it was also cooked.[3] Anyone who professionally butchered animals would have learned how, since perishable parts, especially organ meats, had to be prepared immediately. A further indication that *küter* cooked is found in the neighbouring city of Hamburg. The system of paying *küter* for meat processing in money and offal was similar here, though it is far less well documented.[4] Here, the authorities imposed a guild ordinance on butchers and cooks for hire in 1538 to define their rights vis-à-vis the master butchers and cookshop owners.[5] It stipulated that all members had to be able to cook and preserve meat, and that they would provide cooks to accompany the city's military forces on campaign.

While working for master butchers gave these people a regular income, a significant part of their money was earned working for private customers. Pigs were raised in many homes, and it was not uncommon for wealthier households to buy cattle in season. Larger institutions – noble households, military garrisons, hospitals or courts – also circumvented meat markets, buying their day-to-day supply on the hoof. Turning livestock into food, preserved meat and saleable commodities, required expert skill. The process included removing and processing organs that could not be preserved, making sausages and black pudding, rendering fats and breaking open bones to extract marrow. Many of the products had to be consumed immediately, and it was customary for householders to share these with their neighbours. In effect, every private slaughter also included cooking a feast, and the butcher also acted as cook. This was not the same in institutional contexts, where the meat was distributed fresh, but unless a butcher was permanently retained on the staff, the person in charge would still have needed the requisite skills for other clients. Butchers were always cooks.

The Art of the Master Cook: Nose-to-Tail in Practice

When we look at offal cookery in the context of medieval recipe collections, the foremost aspect in our mind is usually dearth. The late Ernst Schubert, peerless expert on the realities of medieval life, pointed out that no modern gastronome would seek inspiration in the practice of eating chicken lungs.[6] No doubt most people above all sought to make the most of a precious and scarce resource, but doing so involved professional skill that we would imagine its practitioners took pride in. Fortunately, we do not need to imagine; we have a surviving source to bear witness to this.

In 1460, an unknown scribe copied a recipe collection ascribed to one Master Hans (*Maister Hannsen*), self-identified as a cook to the house of Wurttemberg. The collection, now held in Basel, may indeed go back to a personal cook of Count Ulrich V of Wurttemberg.[7] It contains a wide variety of recipes, from plain dishes to showy display food, as well as anecdotes, jokes and doggerel verse. A translation into English would be a great asset for medieval food scholars. Master Hans, whatever his real identity, took great pride in his professional skill. He uses the longest passage in the book to show off, describing how a good kitchen team can turn a single calf into a spread of varied dishes fit for a nobleman using every part of the animal. The rambling style switching between first and third person narrative and imperative recipe style contrasts with the otherwise traditional recipes that are often part of a longer written tradition. The story may have been dictated by an author unused to the medium.

If you have nothing but veal:

> We came to a place where we found nothing but veal, and my lord had many guests, so he bought the calf. Then he came and took hot wine and stabbed the calf completely [to death] and cut off its head completely, high on the neck. He split the head down the middle and took out the brain and washed the rest nicely and cooked it cleanly and mades a head dish from it. Then he takes the feet, chops off the knees and makes a galantine.

Offal and the Master Cook

Now he takes the innards of it and washes it nicely and makes it nice and takes bacon and fine white bread that he cuts into cubes. Take as many eggs as you wish and mix the eggs and bacon into it and fill the neck and the wämlein [one of the stomachs] and let it boil nicely and cook it separately, that way it stays white. When it is boiled, boil the wampen [belly, or another of the stomachs] and the magen [one of the stomachs] in slices, and put them into a bowl when you wish to serve them. Place the innards on top and that makes a nice dish.

Then take the liver of the calf, chop it up raw, and then take fine white bread and bacon. Cube the bacon and grate the bread and season it with spices, and take eggs and mix it all together with each other. Put fat into a pan and put the liver and all these things together into it. Stir it well over the fire so that it does not burn. Then take the net (caul) and put it on the table and when it hardens, wrap it in the net and place it on a griddle, and put two or three pieces of wood onto it to turn it over with. That way it does not break apart when it is roasted. Cut it into seven pieces in a bowl, and what you cut off, grind up and pass it through a cloth with good spices and good wine. That way it turns out good. Then take the brain and place it on a cloth, tie it together and boil it with the cloth or inside it, and when it is boiled, take a pound of almonds and grind them up small with good broth or soup. Pass it through a cloth with fine white wheat bread and pass the brain through with the other things, and take clean fat, and boil it. Also take a good wine and the blood of the calf, but not too much of the blood. Then take good dry *lebkuchen*, not too little, grind it up small and put it in. If you don't have sugar, use honey instead and clean fat, that way it turns out smooth. Season it with good spices and take that in right measure, a good sprinkling of spices on top.[8]

Take the lung of a calf and wash it nicely, and boil it in a pot and chop it small. Take good broth or soup and twelve egg yolks and cook that together, that is a good spoon dish.

Take the head of the calf, wash it nicely, pick it off cleanly and cut it into small patches, and cook it with good spices and saffron and parsley.

Take the breast and a roastable meat of what animal you find or may get and chop it small, and take the blood, and don't make it too black once it is done. Then take rye bread and grate it small. Take the blood and sixty-three eggs, beat them with it, and also add the grated bread, and chop it small and add good spices and cook it nicely with cloves, and of the bread take half or more, you make the roast with it.

Also take a small kettle and put in broth or soup and place it over a burning fire, then take the roasting meat and put it in there and let it boil until it is done. When it is well ready, take it out and let it cool, then take bacon, cut it up small, lard the roast with that and also stick it with whole cloves. Then take good wine with it, and good spices, and sugar, and prepare a soup to go with the roast.

Of the roast: take the long [probably filet strips cut along the kidney roast] together and place it in hot broth and let it boil till it is done. Do not let it overcook, and when it is done, place it on the table if you wish, and let it cool. Now you may cut it as you wish. Afterwards, make a bound pepper sauce of it, and take onions and an apple with it, chop it up into that, and take fat from the meat and the blood into a pan and add it, make it cleanly, with good spices. That way it is [like] venison.

And the breast you cut lengthwise, that is served as a meat [dish]. And you shall take the legs that still have meat on them and chop them into small pieces and take a soup or broth of the meat, with vinegar added, and the blood of the calf should also be added, and boil it in there. And put in chopped meat with good bacon, and season it with good spices. That makes a good *fürhess*.[9]

We can get descriptions of several dishes from this account, many including or made entirely from what modern cooks would consider offal. It is important to recall that medieval ideas need not have agreed with this. Some organ meats were prized rather than rejected until very recently. Others would always have required skill and effort to render acceptable. A systematic analysis would be interesting, but is not possible here. Instead, we will look at some of the dishes and the techniques described.

The first clearly identifiable dish is a bread pudding cooked inside a stomach. This probably served as much to diversify the number of dishes that could be cooked in a single pot as to render stomachs palatable. A Low German cookery source mentions it as something travelling cooks can do when they have limited equipment, noting that root vegetables, onions or 'many things, whatever you wish' can be prepared this way.[10] The technique was still common by the early twentieth century, and no doubt still is used wherever circumstances call for it.[11] Other recipe collections include instructions for filling stomachs with meat or meat mixtures for boiling. Bread was commonly used as a cooking ingredient at the time, and this may be nothing more than an artful riff on the kind of bread porridge made with fresh meat broth that the Eulenspiegel collection of short stories describes as a customary gift to children on slaughter days in the mid-sixteenth century.[12] The remaining stomachs and intestines are simply boiled and arranged on a platter, no doubt a common way of serving them.

The liver is used for another dish reminiscent of Roman *isicia*, caul-wrapped roasted meat mixtures that enjoyed great popularity. The fifteenth-century Innsbruck recipe collection lists a similar dish among a range of options for preparing liver:

If you want to make stuffed calf's liver, chop the liver small and add eggs to it and season it, and take the caul and put it in and let it cook or fry it in a pan, or make a sauce for it or make it thin and serve it as a spoon dish (*müez*).[13]

The recipe also suggests that the roasted liver is served in a sauce made from cut-off pieces, another common use for liver that is described in more detail in a fifteenth-century recipe collection from Mondsee monastery. The recipe begins with roasting a beef liver in slices, then continues:

> Grind one of the pieces in a mortar and add pepper, ginger and anise. Mill it finely with vinegar. Let it boil, so that it thickens. Then let it cool, put in the [roasted] liver and serve it as [though it was] a deer's liver. Liver of wild boar can also be cooked this way, with good broth.[14]

Like the liver, the brain is frequently mentioned in surviving recipe collections as an ingredient in high-class foods. Here, it is prepared in a laborious process in keeping with medieval traditions of luxury food: Boiled, mashed, passed through with almond milk and white breadcrumbs, and cooked again to make a white spoon dish. The white colour was likely the main attraction here. *Hirnmus*, a brain-based spoon dish, is mentioned in several recipe collections. The Viennese Dorotheenkloster collection gives us more detailed instructions regarding the process:

> Put a veal brain in a cloth and cook it in that cloth. When it is cooked, take half a pound of almonds, pound them and grind them fine, take good broth and pass it through with them. [Take] wheat flour, bread, and the brain and pass it through together and add clean lard to it, then it becomes smooth, and season it with spices, take of these to the right measure, and strew it well with sugar and spices.[15]

The same collection also described how a skilful cook could prepare the brain of a calf inside the opened skull by pouring hot fat over it while the entire head was being roasted.[16] Clearly, flashiness was part of the trade.

What is made with the rest of the head is less clear. The description of a head dish (*haubt essen*) is inconclusive. The two sections of the text include slightly different wording, suggesting the meat was picked off, cooked and seasoned with saffron and parsley. The mention of galantine (*sullcz*) in the same paragraph may suggest that this is a variant of the still popular *Kopfsülze*. Galantines were often made with saffron and herbs. It is equally possible, though, that the boiled feet were served in jelly and the proximity is accidental. We have few contemporary recipes to guide us, but contemporary sources suggest that preparing the head inventively was an important part of a cook's skill.

Going by surviving recipes, lungs were not a popular meat. Here, they are turned into an egg-bound spoon dish that we have corroborating evidence for in several recipe collections. Other methods of preparing lung included adding it to sausage, making it into meatballs and using it as an ingredient in a filling for fritters. In contrast to the way liver and brains were treated, there is no evidence that the flavour or texture were in any way relevant. Lung, it seems, was eaten so as not to waste it. Two such recipes may serve to illustrate:

If you want to make good fried calf's lung chop the lung finely and add a little cooked bacon (*gesotes specks*) and two or three egg yolks, season it and make little balls. Make a good fritter batter, draw the balls through it and fry them, and do not oversalt it etc.[17]

If you want to make a *bubenpfulben*, take the tongue and the lung of a calf, cut it up small, cut bacon into it and chop it finely. Break eggs into it and season with saffron and pepper. Then make thin sheets of egg dough and wrap it in them. Brush the ends with egg and fry them in fat.[18]

The description of blood being used in no fewer than three dishes raises the question whether a single calf would have provided enough. Other recipes from the period suggest blood was a popular and coveted ingredient fit for fine dining. Here, it is used in two sauces and a pan dish referred to as a *fürhess*. The name is etymologically derived from the forequarter of a hare, though by the fifteenth century *fürhess* could be made from any kind of meat. It involved frying meat scraps in a pan, often with other ingredients, and adding blood that would boil and clot, producing a thick, spoonable mass. The dish probably has its origins in a method of using the blood and less desirable parts of smaller animals and domestic fowl. Another recipe in the Master Hans collection describes the process in more detail: 'To make a *fürhes* from the blood of a calf: Item, take the blood of the calf, add wine and mix it. Set it by the fire and let it boil well. If you have no sugar, take honey and gingerbread (*leczelltn*) instead, and add fat. That way, the spoon dish turns out fine. Also, chop the lung into it, and this must be well boiled. You must not forget the salt, and also add good spices.'[19]

Blood-thickened sauces are also mentioned in several other sources, though the addition of eggs in such quantity – sixty-three – is not something I have seen documented elsewhere.

Conclusions

The great majority of offal recipes in our sources are not common fare. Reconstructing the scene Meister Hans describes makes it clear that producing them depended on a wealth of equipment: Knives and choppers, pans and pots, mortars, cloth and string as well as the hands to use, clean and transport them. The ingredients also bear out this interpretation. Saffron, honey, sugar, spices, wine, white bread and almonds, even bacon, eggs and butter or lard were status markers in their own right, foods that were beyond most people's financial reach. Clearly, the people who had offal prepared this way could just as easily have afforded not to eat it, but chose to. Speculating about their motivation is as diverting as it is fruitless. The practicalities of slaughtering in the home – in itself a mark of distinction – may have dictated it: the moral economy of a meat-poor environment may have militated against any form of waste, or tradition may have demanded it. Perhaps they simply liked the taste. What we can say is that in order to raise offal to the dignity of the lordly table, they depended on two familiar methods: the addition of high-status ingredients and the skilled labour of professional cooks who took great pride in their abilities. The latter aspect is too often forgotten when focusing on the role of exotic foodstuffs in conveying status.

Notes

1. Jost Amman, *Das Ständebuch*, ed. and trans. by Ursula Schulze (Cologne: Anaconda Verlag, 2006), p. 85, figure 39.
2. *Die älteren lübeckischen Zunftrollen*, ed. by C. Wehrmann (Lübeck: Ferdinand Grauthoff, 1872) pp. 259 ff.
3. '…unde moghen de kaldunen zellen uppe de neghesten lede boven en' (Wehrmann, p. 268).
4. Otto Rüdiger, *Die ältesten hamburgischen Zunftrollen und Brüderschaftsstatuten* (Hamburg: Lucas Gräfe, 1874), document 28b, concession of 1361.
5. Rüdiger, doc. 20a.
6. Ernst Schubert, *Essen und Trinken im Mittelalter* (Darmstadt: WBG 2006), p. 107.
7. *Maister Hannsen des von wirtenberg koch…*, ed. and trans. by Trude Ehlert (Frankfurt: Tupperware Verlag 1996).
8. *Maister Hannsen*, recipe 190.
9. *Maister Hannsen*, recipe 191.
10. 'Ein mittelniederdeutsches Kochbuch des 15. Jahrhunderts', ed. by Hans Wiswe, in *Braunschweigisches Jahrbuch* 37 (1956), 19-55, recipe 27.
11. Dorothy Hartley, *Food in England* (London: Little, Brown & Co. 1999), p. 36 ff.
12. Hermann Bote, *Ein kurzweiliges Buch von Till Eulenspiegel aus dem Lande Braunschweig. Wie er sein Leben vollbracht hat. Sechsundneunzig seiner Geschichten. Herausgegeben, in die Sprache unserer Zeit übertragen und mit Anmerkungen versehen von Siegfried H. Sichtermann* (Frankfurt: Insel Verlag, 1978), p. 39.
13. Doris Aichholzer, '*Wildu machen ain guet essen…*', in *Drei mittelhochdeutsche Kochbücher: Erstedition, Übersetzung, Kommentar* (Berne: Peter Lang, 1999), p. 211, Innsbruck MS 61.
14. Aichholzer, p. 163, Mondsee MS 129.
15.. Aichholzer, p. 315, Dorotheenkloster MS 129.
16. Aichholzer, p. 261, Dorotheenkloster MS 17.
17. Aichholzer, p. 225, Dorotheenkloster MS 102.
18. *Rheinfränkisches Kochbuch um 1445, Text, Übersetzung, Anmerkungen und Glossar,* ed. and trans. by Thomas Gloning (Frankfurt: Tupperware Verlag 1998), recipe 40.
19. *Maister Hannsen*, p. 309, recipe 244.

Foie Gras: The Quantum Offal

Guillemette Barthouil

Introduction
Foie gras is currently defined as 'coming from an animal specially fattened with force-feeding, and weighing a minimum of 300g for duck *foie gras* and 400g for goose *foie gras*. Its colour should be light and uniform'.[1] The technical term for this condition of the liver is *steatosis hepatis*, mainly caused by providing the animals with large quantities of corn during the ten to fifteen days of *gavage*. Corn (*Zea mays*) has become the main feed for producing *foie gras*, for a few reasons: its high levels of carbohydrates provide the primary material for lipid synthesis in the liver; it is rich in biotin (vitamin B7), which is necessary for achieving a high degree of lipid synthesis; and finally, it has low levels of lipotropic compounds (compounds that break down fats), which facilitates lipid accumulation in the liver. *Gavage* and corn are two essential elements to the production of *foie gras* as we now know it – and, though they have a quite recent history in the Southwest of France, the region now produces more than half of the world's production as of 2010. What series of cultural and economic transformations led to the development of *foie gras* from fatty livers? And what implications does this history have for the offal category in general? I have structured this essay into two parts to address each question in turn.

I. A Brief History of Fatty Livers
Foie gras culture has been traced back to the Egyptians and Romans fattening geese. These practices were then spread across Europe by Jews observing the laws of Kashrut who did not use the fat of the pig, and were 'passed down from generation to generation in the French countryside' (CIFOG 2014). Yet it is unlikely that these practices existed in the same way across time and place. Olivier de Serres in *Le théâtre de l'agriculture* describes two distinct fattening techniques existing simultaneously in France at the end of the sixteenth century. He differentiates between the general technique of hand-feeding geese and ducks balls of cooked flour, honey and figs to obtain whiter flesh and 'le grand foie' and the specific 'practice of Gascony' based on letting animals eat whole grains in profusion to produce fat. As argued by Duhart (2009), *foie gras* in the Southwest of France is an internal innovation and does not seem to emerge from Roman and Egyptian tradition.

The Culture of Fat in Southwest France
But with less mystery one fattens geese, according to the practice of Gascony, where it

is familiar husbandry. In mid-October, geese destined for fattening are slightly plucked between legs and thighs, then locked in a narrow place: in which, as prisoners, they cannot walk much; and for which reason also, a dark place is chosen in which they are forced to stay all day. Lacking a dark place, one pricks their eyes: geese, despite blindness, do not get bored of eating and gain weight by themselves; provided that they could get used to the place before, once or twice only. Furthermore, the place should be warm, without wind and coldness coming in their home, which work strongly against geese taking fat, as does dirt, which one thus cleans often. To fatten their meat takes only millet, or oats boiled in water. They want always to have food and beverage in abundance. Provided that the weather favours this husbandry, as cold and dry are desired, in fifteen days or three weeks, geese fatten to perfection.[2]

In Olivier De Serres's description of the fattening tradition specific to the Southwest of France, we find no mention of livers of any kind. Current theoretical and practical knowledge tells us that some enlarged livers might have been produced by these fattening techniques, as livers of fattened *poulardes* and capons can be today. The fact that they are not mentioned, however, strongly suggests that they were not the aim of

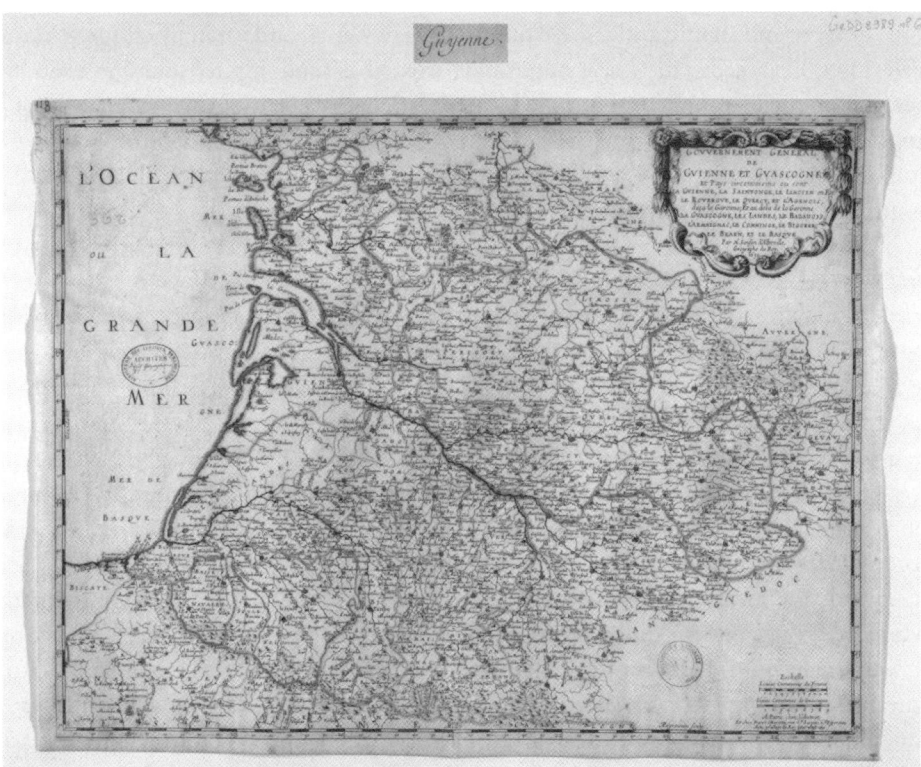

Figure 1. Gascony in 1650. Bibliothèque national de France

the production at the time and were perhaps not even valued gastronomically as in other parts of France and Europe (Scappi 1570). In sixteenth-century rural Gascony, at least, the main aim of fattening geese and ducks was to produce fat.

Geese and ducks were found on almost every farm and were essential for poorer farmers that could not afford to rear their own pigs. After slaughter, the goose or duck fat was rendered and preserved in stoneware pots, and 'could keep its colour and good taste for two years' (Joigneau 1863: 973). Meat was salted to be preserved throughout the year (De Serres 2001). Despite the sixteenth-century dietary discourse classifying animal fats as substances difficult to digest and therefore not appropriate for more 'delicate' (i.e. wealthy) human beings, doctors would recommend to use it as a *fond de sauce*, or a base of a sauce, instead of as an ingredient (Duhart 2009: 194). Goose and duck fats had a good reputation. They were recognized to be soft, fine, and better and 'more delicate than pork fat' (Flandrin 1983: 383). These evaluations are reflected in the high retail price of duck fat at Bayonne's market in 1790 (Dulaurens 1790). The culture of fat of the Southwest was not only based on goose and duck fat, but also made use of pork fat (Duhart 2009: 196) – it was the former, however, that seemed most important to the region's identity. They are what characterized the territory from the outsider's point of view, and significantly, these products were valued and eaten by all social classes (Valeri 1977). Though fatty livers might have existed as food, my research has found no mention of them in Gascony up until the seventeenth century. And while absence of proof does not equal proof of absence, it is highly unlikely that such a strong culture of fat would also have valued a good such as the fatty liver and leave virtually no record of its production and consumption.

New World–Old World Assimilation

While the culture of fat was predominant in the sixteenth century, some elements of change had already been introduced. Corn (*Zea mays*) was first brought back to Europe by Christopher Columbus in 1493 or 1496 and is first mentioned being grown in Bayonne in 1523 (Gay 1984). The humid and temperate climate of the Southwest of France favoured its cultivation, though it was not an integral part of the local food culture until the eighteenth century. It was first named '*milhoc*', meaning big millet in the vernacular idiom *gascon*, named after the cereal for fattening poultry that it came to replace (Carraretto 2005: 56). As corn was untaxed, peasants began cultivating it in their yards for their own consumption, in a fashion 'dissimulated and almost furtive' (Montanari 1995: 141). The home garden is the space were maize met another protagonist of *foie gras* history: *Cairina moschata*, the Muscovy duck. Brought back from Central America, its strong similarity with old-world ducks enabled it to be quickly integrated into the farmyard. Muscovy duck did not replace any other breed, but differentiated itself by being dumb, black and having a huge appetite (Belon 1555: 174).

The Muscovy duck and maize both brought from Central America were associated for the first time in the Southwest of France for the sake of making fat. This assimilation set the stage for a slow revolution: from a culture of fat to a culture of *foie gras*.

Corn as Food and Feed
A food crisis for both humans and their animals facilitated the birth of a corn culture in the Southwest of France. 'Poor consumers opened their doors to' this secondary cereal mainly grown for domestic consumption (Braudel 1979: 178). First a food of famine, corn had by the end of the seventeenth century become a food of everyday life, as the main ingredient in the ubiquitous porridge of the Southwest, called *milhàs* or *cruchade*. Yet at a symbolic level, corn did not replace wheat's status as the 'cereal of civilization' (Braudel 1979), and in fact even helped to increase its commercialization (Frêche 1971:520-23). Peasants would sell wheat and keep corn for themselves, preferring the latter's yield and nutritional value to those of millet: 'Our farmers do not nourish themselves with meslin, nor barley, nor rye, accustomed to so substantial bread made with corn. Any other would not suit nor support them and for the same price, we have seen the trade one grain against another, because a corn seed provides their food as much as two half seed of wheat.'[3] From the second half of the seventeenth century onward, corn became essential for farmers' daily diet, as much as preserved fat and meat. A delicate equilibrium had to be found with corn between food and feed.

Around the same time, the innovation of preserving meat in its own fat, leading to *confit*, is thought to have emerged (Duhart 2009: 205). The history of confit remains very blurry, and, though no historical documents are yet known to support this hypothesis, from a technical point of view it is possible that the higher fat content of geese and ducks, because they were fed corn during the fattening period, facilitated this development. At the time, fattening geese and ducks for making confit happened from mid-October to February, after the corn harvest and when the stocks were still high. Balancing corn for birds and corn for humans was a delicate equilibrium in the late seventeenth and early eighteenth centuries, when yields were around four quintal (a French quintal corresponds to 48.951 kg) per hectare (Lescaret 1983:17): such low yields would suggest limiting poultry's corn consumption.[4] In this context, *foie gras* production, which in the late eighteenth century required twenty-five litres (Heuze 1868:157) of corn per ducks, would certainly not be a peasant's priority. If fatty livers occurred it was likely more by chance than by will: 'Before obtaining *foie gras* became the primary objective of overfeeding palmipeds, it was primarily motivated by a desire to produce fat and preserved meat' (Duhart 2009).[5]

From Fatty Livers to Foie Gras
As in the rest the French kingdom at the beginning of the eighteenth century, multiple kinds of fatty livers were used as food in the Southwest. Fatty livers of duck and goose were placed in the same category as those of 'chickens, capon, and young pigs' (Lemery 1702). Menon in his *Nouveau traité de cuisine* (1739) gives a recipe for '*Pâté of Périgueux*: take two pounds of truffle, twelve *foie gras*, three pounds of lard, parsley, chive, chopped

mushroom …'.⁶ Mentioning twelve foies gras in such a context suggests they were quite small. Indeed, the typicality of this recipe appears to be more in the use of truffle than of fatty livers.

During the second half of the eighteenth century, however, an internal innovation in the Southwest greatly changed regional poultry husbandry. Augustin Parmentier's work on corn and new agricultural techniques dramatically increased yields, making corn much more available for feed. Furthermore, the first form of *gorgeage* used in the region, first mentioned in 1780, was to introduce whole corn into the mouth of ducks by hand, in a culture 'already used to manually feeding turkeys with acorns' (Rozier 1805). Too dangerous with geese's toothed beak, this technique was very much adapted to the Mulard duck: a sterile hybrid, very much appreciated for its ability to 'take' fat, that cohabited in peasants' courtyards with its progenitors, a Muscovy male and a Pekin or colvert female (*Anas platyrynchos*). By the end of the eighteenth century, the use of a tin funnel, *embuc*, made this work much less hazardous for ducks and geese.⁷ *L'embuc* spread quickly throughout Gascony, and 'at the end of the eighteenth century, *embucare* was the rule in Gersoise Gascony' (Dralet 1801: 254).

Thus, the three following developments allowed for the later emergence of *foie gras* production in the Southwest of France:
- Corn was available, and its higher starch rate, higher biotin rate and lower choline rate favoured accumulation of lipids in the liver⁸
- The Mulard duck was selected for its high fat production and its faculty of *steatosis hepatis*⁹
- *Embucare* was a widespread technique.

The interaction of these innovations within the cultural and economical context of nineteenth-century France led to the rise of an endemic *foie gras* culture in Gascony. Valorization of *foie gras* by the flourishing of French gastronomy in the nineteenth century created a market for this good, raw or processed into prestigious pâtés of Toulouse and Périgueux. For the Parisian cook, the issue of supply arose. In fact, trade was limited and highly inconsistent at the beginning of the nineteenth century (Servanti 1993), but it eventually stabilized under the Second Empire (1852-1860), and when Armand Husson reviewed its consumption in *Les consommations de Paris,* he estimated its volume to be 'four thousand *foie gras* from the high-Garonne, Lot, Tarn, Tarn-et-Garonne, Gers and Southwest' (Servanti 1993). Railways made the product available throughout the country, and chefs began to change its gastronomic status. Antonin Carême, father of the *grande cuisine classique*, gave *foie gras* a new place in the menu set. The *gros pâtés de foie gras* switched from entremets to entrée as the product become central to French gastronomy. Parisian gastronomes like Grimod de la Reynière began to differentiate the Southwest culture of *foie gras* from the one of Alsace by the type of animal: 'Our poet is too well-informed not to know that if *pâtés de Strasbourg* are goose liver, those of Toulouse, Auch, and Agen are livers of ducks.'¹⁰

Industrialization

With Nicolas Appert's revolutionary canning technique, an airtight way of food preservation using tin cans, spreading through the French countryside during the second half of the nineteenth century, a *foie gras* industry began to emerge. Producers of pâtés and terrines diversified their products with tin cans, *conserves*, with *foie gras* becoming the main ingredient. The technique allowed producers to make preparations that could last for many years, to transport *foie gras* easily and even to improve it with time, and thus the product became quickly adopted by gastronomes especially in the capital. Escoffier himself confessed that 'it [was] difficult to obtain better results than the manufacturer' for a *parfait de foie gras* (Escoffier 1921 (2009): 649).

From November to March, *conserveurs* would go to *marché au gras* to either buy *foie gras* alone – when farmers would keep the rest of the animal for their own consumption as confit – or purchase the whole duck or goose. During the first half of the twentieth century 'gavage [was] considered by corn producers as a active source of complementary revenue that they could sell on local markets' (Mognard 2011). *Foie gras* was seldom enjoyed by those who produced it in rural Southwest France, from the nineteenth century up to 1960. Even in 1960, only 15% of *foie gras* produced in the Southwest was bought by local *conserveries* while the remaining 85% was sent to Paris, Strasbourg and Périgord (Larat 1963:335). The product was mostly enjoyed outside its production area. While the cultures of *gras* and *foie gras* cohabited across different social classes and spaces in Gascony for more than a century, after the 1960s this coexistence changed dramatically.

Around this time (1959), André Daguin, the chef-owner of l'Hôtel de France in Auch, influenced by the Nouvelle Cuisine, put a grilled *magret*, duck breast, on his menu. What may seem a trivial decision actually represents a first culinary step away from the culture of fat, a small revolution in the Southwest of France where *magret* had always been confit. Non-existent before, a market of raw force-fed duck meat emerges, at first geared towards chefs. This new way of cooking replaced confit in a few decades, as the culture of fat gradually decreased.

In rural areas, the introduction of hybrid corn alongside the Green Revolution hastened the end of the self-sufficient agrarian system of the Southwest of France. Corn became a commercial grain, and consequently a market structure developed around emerging cereal cooperatives. First built as communal storage facilities, cooperatives became a vector of the Green Revolution by providing hybrid seeds, chemicals and tractors to its members. Corn quickly became the main commercial grain of the Southwest, thanks both to its climate and to the guaranteed prices of the EU Common Agricultural Policy (CAP) first implemented in 1962.

The CAP reform of 1992, however, pushed cooperatives to change their investment strategy (Vincent 2001: 8). The guaranteed price policy for corn stopped and EU subsidies began to be calculated on land area and yield – but the regional landscape did not allow for indefinite field expansion as it might have in other parts of France.

Local members' remuneration dropped. Willing to diversify their revenue streams and add value to their corn, cooperatives invested in the growing *foie gras* industry. Up until the 1990s the *foie gras* market had gradually increased, but a couple of innovations then substantially enhanced its productivity: artificial insemination dropped duckling prices, breeding and force-feeding became two different jobs, centralized slaughterhouses were built, and *gavage à la pâtée* was invented.[11] The two main barriers to industrialization were broken: time constraints and harsh working conditions.

Cooperatives became the primary link between corn and *foie gras*. First involved in production, providing corn, feed, consulting and materials, they soon bought leading local *conserveries*, and came to hold 80% of the French market (CIFOG 2010).[12] *Foie gras* thus became the single aim of an entire industry.

II. Fatty Livers, *Foie Gras*, and the Offal Category

Foie gras as we now know it emerged from the interaction of agricultural practices in the Southwest and the gastronomic context of nineteenth-century France. Before then, '*foie gras*' as such did not exist – there were only, as it were, 'fatty livers'. Though the phrases are literal translations of each other, historical analysis reveals the fact that they represent two different products, with different methods and purposes of production and fundamentally different understandings of the organ and its use as food. Studying *foie gras* thus brings us into the permeable boundaries of the offal category, some of which I will investigate below.

Offal as Organ Meat

Foie gras is liver, liver is an organ – therefore *foie gras* is an organ. According to the Oxford English Dictionary online, offal refers to 'the entrails and internal organs of an animal used as food'. By definition, therefore, *foie gras* is offal.

Yet this semantic game becomes complicated when its subject is situated in historical context. Throughout time ducks and geese have been fed and force-fed with greater and greater intention to transform their livers. This historical perspective can question the seemingly simple affirmation that '*foie gras* is liver'.

The nineteenth-century cultural shift from fatty livers to *foie gras* is critical. Gastronomically speaking, fatty livers were used as a kind of liver that had become more fat than the average. It was a fattier and richer liver preferred by cooks for its delicacy; however in the kitchen it was still used as belonging to the liver category, as the 1739 recipe for *Pâté de Périgueux* shows. This characteristic was also shared with the livers of many other kinds of poultry. Fatty livers become *foie gras* when animals are force-fed with the deliberate purpose to change the organ's physical composition, texture, and taste. At this point, gastronomically speaking, *foie gras* becomes its own category, separate from livers. At the beginning of the nineteenth century, the first moments of this cultural and culinary shift, it was still mainly used in pâté. It gradually became more and more valued on its own, canned or cooked in a restaurant. Culinary approaches specific to *foie gras* emerged, and with it a different culinary culture.

Though from a gastronomical point of view, *foie gras* can hardly be considered part of the liver category, it is, being a liver, still involved the metabolic processes of ducks and geese. Is an organ's involvement in metabolic process thus a sufficient condition for being a member of the offal set?

Offal as By-Product or Off-Cut
In the Southwest of France, fatty livers were a by-product of the culture of fat up until the nineteenth century. The aim of fattening ducks and geese was to produce enough fat for the year's provision. Enlarged livers could occur, but their occurrence was unpredictable. When *foie gras* became an gastronomical end, confit meat was the provision aim. For more than a century-and-a-half, from the beginning of the nineteenth century to the second half of the twentieth, both products were neither off-cuts nor the singular goal: they were valued in different spaces. The culture of fat, with confit, continued to live in the rural territory of the Southwest, while the culture of *foie gras* emerged in urban areas – first in Paris, followed by other French cities. Yet these two spaces certainly interacted, as *foie gras* was emerged out of the culture of fat. Farmers would sell all the foies gras and keep the rest of the animal for themselves.

With industrialization, *foie gras* has become the primary goal of a whole industry – an industry ruled by corn cooperatives, running all aspects of production from corn seed to *foie gras* brands. The *foie gras* market developed into a way of creating added value and making a stable market for the existing corn industry of Southwest France. Most offal tend to be seen and used as a kind of by-product or off-cut; can an offal also be the ultimate goal of a whole industry?

Offal as Cheap, Waste
As a result of industrial breeding of ducks to favour production of *foie gras*, the muscle and adipose tissues have now become the waste. Ducks have been bred to produce larger livers and smaller breast and legs in a shorter time. Today, breeds like HYTOP 95 are promoted to produce livers of 610g and magret of 380g in 84 days.[13] By comparison, a local breed called Kriaxera, still used by a few farmers in the French Basque country, give an average *foie gras* of 550g and magret of 450g in 120 days. Depending on its quality, raw *foie gras* is sold from 30 to 50€/kg, while magret fetches 10 to 15€/kg, leg 4€/kg and rendered fat 4€/kg. What used to be crucial products for local economies and household provisions, meat and fat are discounted to shift the stock. About 3kg of meat is produced for 600g of *foie gras*. Producers have innovated to find new ways of selling the huge amount of meat left over from *foie gras* production. By the end of the twentieth century, duck breast prosciutto, duck sausage, duck carpaccio and minced duck meat had been created – food for daily use.

Foie gras, by contrast, despite its industrialization, has not been banalized into a quotidian foodstuff. It still symbolizes French gastronomy, a delicacy served in special occasions with a certain Southwest authenticity (Poulain 1988). It is an image that has become accessible to everyone, with prices always going down. The liver has made the rest of the animal become the 'waste', and it itself has become the most expensive piece of the duck or goose by far – the anti-offal.

Offal as Rejected, Maligned
The historical and technical shift from fatty livers to *foie gras* has led to a strong rejection of the food by a growing part of the population. It is mainly the gavage technique, which allows for consistent production of *foie gras*, that is deemed unacceptable from an ethical point of view. In *Le grand dictionnaire de cuisine,* Alexandre Dumas confesses 'to get there [to the point where *foie gras* occurs], these animals are subjected to untold troubles, which were not even deployed on the first Christians' (Dumas 1873: 252).[14] Similar arguments against torture and employing certain strains of anthropomorphism are used nowadays by the 'Stop Gavage' campaign. Would *foie gras* sans gavage be less maligned? Could there be such a thing as a 'natural' *foie gras*, a product that would not be wrought and wrested from ducks and geese by humans for their own hedonism?

The flagship example of the 'natural *foie gras*' movement is found in Spain, where a farmer named Eduardo Sousa aims to create a system that would allow geese to produce *foie gras* without force-feeding, using their 'natural' gorging ability.[15] Dan Barber, chef and co-owner of restaurant Blue Hill in New York State, describes his first degustation: 'I took a bite. The smell was what got to me first, because as I chewed I was struck by the smell of meat. I most especially smelled liver. *Foie gras*, as a rule, is never described as delicious liver – you wouldn't describe white truffles as perfumed fungus, either – but here I was, unmistakably tasting liver. And not metallic, muddy-tasting liver, but sweet, deeply flavoured, livery liver.'[16] The scheme reminds one of the pre-nineteenth-century fatty livers, when enlarged livers occasionally occurred as by-products of the culture of fat. In this current practice, 400g livers can occur, but most obtained are between 150 and 300g. '*Foie gras*', however, remains the aim of the husbandry, neither a by-product nor cheap – as if reclaiming the gastronomical and ethical 'offal'ness of *foie gras* would make it less maligned.[17]

Foie Gras as Offal
Foie gras has perhaps become such a charged symbol because it embodies a delicious tension between the anatomical expectation of the liver category and the disruption of the very same category. It is the liver that aims to transcend the organ meats, even the flesh in general. It is the ur-offal and anti-offal simultaneously: the quantum offal.

Notes

1. Quotation translated from French by the author: '*Un foie gras cru provient d'un animal spécialement engraissé par gavage et pèse au minimum 300 g pour le foie gras de canard et 400 g pour le foie gras d'oie. La couleur doit être claire et uniforme*' (Ministère de l'économie des finances et de l'emploi, *Préparation de viande, produits à base de viandes de volaille et de lapin, foies gras de volaille*, 2008 http://www.economie.gouv.fr/files/directions_services/daj/marches_publics/oeap/gem/preparations_de_viandes/preparations_de_viandes.pdf).
2. De Serres, 2001: 550-1. Quotation translated from the sixteenth-century French by the author. The original is reproduced below: '*Mais avec moins de mystère engraisse-on les oyes, selon la pratique de Gascogne, ou ce mesnage est familier. A la mi-octobre, les oyes destinées à engraisser, sont légèrement esplumées entre les jambes et les cuisses, puis enfermées en lieu étroit: auquel comme prisonnières, elle ne puissent beaucoup cheminer: pour laquelle cause aussi, sera t-il choisi obscur, dont seront-elles contraintes séjourner tous-jours en un mesme lieu. A faute de lieu obscur, l'on crève les yeux aux oyes: lesquelles, quoi qu'aveugles, ne laissent de manger et prendre d'elles-même la viande ; pourveu que ce soit en endroit qu'auparavant elles ayent accoustumé, une fois ou deux seulement. Davantage, sera le lieu chaud, estans les vents et froidures entrans leur logis, fort contraires aux oyes, pour prendre graisse, comme aussi la saleté, par quoi le nettoyera-on souvent. Leur viande à engraisser est le seul millet, ou avoine bouilli dans l'eau. Veulent avoir toujours de la viande et du bruvage abondamment. Pourveu que le temps favorise ce mesnage, qu'à cela l'on le désire froid et sec, dans quinze jours ou trois semaine, les oyes deviendront grasses en perfection.*'
3. Quotation translated from the French by the author: '*Nos paysans ne se nourrissent ni de méteil, ni d'orge, ni de seigle, accoutumés au pain si substantiel fait avec le mais. Tout autre ne serait leur convenir, ni les soutenir et à prix égal, nous les avons vus troquer en nourriture un grain contre l'autre, ce parce que une conque de maïs leur fournit en nourriture autant que deux conques et demie de froment*' (Archives Départementales des Pyrénées-Atlantiques, C281, Mémoires des magistrat de la ville de Bayonne, 1771).
4. Nowadays yields are around 100 quintal per hectare.
5. Quotation translated by the author: '*Avant que l'obtention du foie gras ne devînt l'objectif premier de la suralimentation des palmipèdes, celle-ci fût principalement motivée par une volonté de produire de la graisse et de la viande de conserve.*'
6. Quotation translated by the author: '*Pâté de Périgueux*': '*prenez deux livres de truffes, douze foies gras, trois livres de panne, persil, ciboule, champignons haché…*'.
7. Gallet, a farmer living close to Carcassonne, is thought to have invented the tool (Servanti 1997).
8. Maisadour, *Foie gras et qualité du maïs*, 2009 <http://www.maisadour-semences.fr/semences-varietes-mais-grain-dossiers-alimentation-carard-oie.php>.
9. Baeza and others, *La stéatose hépathique chez les palmipèdes*, INRA Production Animale 26 (5): 403-14 <http://www6.inra.fr/productions-animales/2013-Volume-26/Numero-5-pp.-385-454/La-steatose-hepatique-chez-les-palmipedes>.
10. Quotation translated from the French by the author: '*Notre poète est trop bien instruit pour ignorer que si les pâtés de strasbourg sont foie d'oies, ceux de Toulouse, d'auch, d'Agen sont des foies de canards*' (Grimod 1804: 308).
11. *Gavage à la pâtée* is opposed to the traditional gavage with whole grain. Ducks are fed with a corn porridge composed of 98% of corn. This 'innovation' could in fact also be seen as a re-introduction of the older eastern tradition of feeding geese and ducks with balls of cooked flour.
12. Maisadour owns Delpeyrat, Comtesse du barry, Excel, Canard du midi and Sarrade; Euralis owns Rougié et Montfort; Lur Berri owns Labeyrie.
13. Accouvoir Grimaud et frères.
14. Quotation translated from the French by the author: '*Pour en arriver là, on soumet ces animaux à des tourments inouïs, qui n'ont même pas été déployés sur les premiers chrétiens.*'
15. 'La Pateria de Sousa', Spanish Organic Farm SL, 2015 <http://lapateria.eu/>.
16. Dan Barber, 'The Farmer Who Makes Ethical *Foie Gras*', The Guardian, 18 January 2015 <http://www.

theguardian.com/world/2015/jan/18/the-farmer-who-makes-ethical-foie-gras>.
17. The price of Pateria de sousa *foie gras* entier mi-cuit is 1105,55€/kg, compared to the price of artisanal kriaxera *foie gras* entier mi-cuit of 105 €/kg.

Bibliography

Armengaud, Françoise, '*Anthropomorphisme: vraie question ou faux débat?*', *Les animaux d'élevage ont-ils droit au bien-être?*(Paris: INRA, 2001), pp. 165-87.

Bages, Robert, '*Permanences et innovations dans l'alimentation paysanne: du repas quotidien au menu de fête*', *Voyage en alimentation* (Paris: ARF, 1995), pp. 113-27.

Barthouil, Guillemette, '*Le rôle du maïs dans la diffusion du foie gras dans le Sud-Ouest de la France – Etude de cas sur le bassin de l'Adour-*' (Unpublished master's thesis, Université Paris-Sorbonne, 2012).

Braudel, Fernand, '*Les structures du quotidien: le possible et l'impossible*', *Civilisation matérielle, économie et capitalisme, XV-XVIIIe siècle* (Paris: Armand Collin, 1979).

Belon, Pierre, *L'histoire de la nature des Oyseaux* (Paris: Gilles Corrozt, 1555).

Bizac, A., *La production et le développement des conserves de foie gras au cours du XX siècle* (Paris: ITAVI, 2003).

Carraretto, Maryse, *Histoire de maïs. D'une divinité amérindienne à ses avatars transgéniques* (Paris: CHTS, 2005).

Caro, Mark, *The Foie Gras War, How a 5000 Year Old Delivery Inspired the World's Fiercest Food Fight* (New York: Simon and Schuster, 2009).

CIFOG (Comité Interprofessionnel des Palmipèdes à *Foie Gras*), 'History', *Foie Gras – Facts and Truth*, 2015 <http://foiegras-factsandtruth.com/heritage/history>.

Descola, Pierre, *Par-delà nature et culture* (Paris: Gallimard, 2005).

De Serres, Olivier, *Le théâtre de l'agriculture* (Paris: Actes Sud, 2001).

Duhart, Frédéric, *De confit en foie gras, Une histoire des oies et des canards du Sud-Ouest (*Bayonne: Elkar, 2009).

Dulaurens, Edouard, *Inventaire sommaire des archives communales antérieures à 1790* (Bayonne: Lamaignère, 1894).

Dumas, Alexandre, *Le grand dictionnaire de cuisine* (Paris: Edition Pierre Grobel, 1873).

Duby, George and Armand Wallon, *Histoire de la France rurale*, 4 vols (Paris: Seuil, 1981).

Escoffier, Auguste, *Le guide culinaire* (Paris: Flammarion, 1921 (2009)).

Faucher, D., '*Le maïs en France*', *Annales de Géographie*, 224 (1931): 113-121.

Flandrin, Jean-Louis, '*Le goût et la nécessité: sur l'usage des graisses dans les cuisines d'Europe Occidentales* (XIV – XVIII siècle)', *Annales ESC*, 38 (1983).

Grimod de la Reynière, Alexandre B., *Almanach des gourmands*, 8 vols (Paris: Maradan, 1804-1812).

Heuze, Gustave, *La france agricole. Région sud-ouest ou région du maïs* (Paris: Hachette, 1868).

Joigneau, Pierre, *Le livre de la ferme et des maisons de campagnes* (Paris: Masson, 1863).

Lemery, Louis, *Traité des aliments* (Paris: Pierre Vitte, 1702).

Lescaret, Jean-Pierre, *L'introduction et la propagantion du maïs dans le département des landes* (Dax: 1983).

Litt, J., G. Guy, A. Jentzer, and F. Guerder, *Principales évolutions des résultats techniques et des performances économiques dans les ateliers d'élevage et de gavage de palmipèdes à foie gras en filière longue entre 1987 et 2006* (Mont-de-Marsan: ITAVI, 2006).

Mognard, Elise, 'Les trois traditions du *foie gras* dans la gastronomie française', Anthropology of Food, 8 (2011) <http://aof.revues.org/6789>.

Philippe, Nicolas, 'Emergence, développement et rôle des coopératives agricoles en France. Aperçu sur une histoire séculaire', *Economie rurale*, 184 (1988): 116-22.

Poulain, Jean-Pierre et Neirink, Edmond, *Histoire de la cuisine et des cuisiniers: techniques culinaires et pratiques de table, en France, du Moyen-âge à nos jours* (Paris: Lanore, 2009).

Rouch, E., 'L'agriculture pauvre du Sud-Ouest devant la croissance économique française', *Economie rurale*, 48 (1961): 3-25.

Scappi, Bartolomeo, *The Opera of Bartolomeo Scappi (1570), l'arte e prudenzo d'un maestro cuoco*, ed. Luigi Ballerini, trans. Terrence Scully (Toronto: University of Toronto Press, 2008).

Servanti, Silvano *La grande histoire du foie gras*, (Paris: Flammarion, 1993).

Valeri, Renée, *Le confit et son rôle dans l'alimentation traditionnelle du Sud-Ouest de la France* (Lund: Liberlaromedel, 1977).

Leverpostej – More than Just a Danish Way of Eating Offal

Nina Bauer

In Denmark it is impossible to talk about offal without giving *leverpostej* its due. It is an almost unavoidable part of Danish daily meals and the most widely eaten item at lunch. While once pig's liver only entered the kitchen in the butchering season, it became a staple of the Danish table year round due to changes in the food industry, in the structure of meals and in the technology of kitchenware. Over a century, *leverpostej* became so inherently Danish that it seems as if it had always been that way. As a journalist described it in 2010, 'If something has been the fuel and molecular building blocks for dairy men, shot putters, nuclear physicists, kayakers, windmill producers, filmmakers, soccer players, and all other Danes who have raised the red and white flag high in the world, it is the minced mix of pig's liver, speck, onions, anchovies and spices.'[1] The interesting thing about offal as part of a national cuisine is that its way into the kitchen is rarely as straightforward as one might believe. As food historian Else Marie Boyhus says, 'Offal demands a special effort.'[2] Offal challenges the way we think about our food. There have been and still are many arguments for and against eating offal based on nutrition, health concerns, political and economic considerations and cultural values. The history of eating *leverpostej* can therefore help further our understanding of the structures and mechanisms that, with or without our knowledge, regulate what we put on our tables.

Leverpostej as a Dish

The Danish reference work *Gastronomisk leksikon* defines *leverpostej* as a mixture of ground liver, most often pork liver, and lard baked with either a roux or thickening.[3] It is often flavoured with things like onion or anchovies and spices like pepper and allspice. The biggest difference between French pâté and *leverpostej* is the consistency. *Leverpostej* has a much softer consistency than the typical pâté and is meant to be spread onto rye bread and eaten as an open sandwich. Sometimes it is garnished with things like sliced cucumber or pickled beetroot.

At the Danish Christmas lunch, *leverpostej* occupies a special place on the table. Here it is most often served hot instead of cold and garnished with bacon and mushrooms. *Leverpostej* is thus for both festive and everyday consumption, and it is the object of many debates about the most correct or delicious way of serving it.

Before discussing the dish further, it is necessary to look closer at the name itself.

Leverpostej – More than Just a Danish Way of Eating Offal

'What's in a name? That which we call a rose by any other name would smell as sweet,' wrote Shakespeare, and the notion that a name does not always adequately define and embrace all aspects of the thing it names seems relevant to the academic pursuit of the meaning of *leverpostej*.[4]

In most translations, *leverpostej* is called 'liver pâté' or 'liver paste', drawing on the terms used in French cuisine. *Leverpostej* is sort of a weird amalgam of the two in its texture and how it is cooked. It is not usually as firm as a typical French pâté but still firmer than the more mousse-like liver pastes that you see in other countries. Baking it sets it apart from the typical paste.

A literal translation of the Danish word would actually be something like 'liver pie', which reveals that the precursor to *leverpostej* may have originated in the *postejpande*, an ancestor of the famous Dutch oven.[5] It is clear, though, that *leverpostej* is not a pie in a traditional sense since the minced liver is not encased in dough; in this respect it is more like a terrine. So why does the name *leverpostej* and its translations suggest it is something it is not? The answer may have something to do with the baking of the minced liver mix. Curiously, for the longest time *leverpostej* was in the same category as savoury pies and therefore kept the name even though there is no pastry involved.[6]

In the beginning *leverpostej* was a delicacy not available to everyone. In his memoirs, written in 1873, about his life as a young man in Copenhagen, the priest Johannes Plenge mentions a *leverpostej* in a specific charcuterie as quite the attraction for those who could afford it.[7] Liver was not easy to come by, especially pig's liver; it was expensive unless you raised livestock yourself. In the 1860s 500 g of *leverpostej* was sold for two marks, the equivalent of half a day's wages for a worker.[8]

In fine dining, though, it became customary to serve *leverpostej* spread very thinly over a piece of bread, and it was considered bad manners to gorge on it or to eat it without the bread.[9] However, in the late 1800s, an agricultural crisis and a golden opportunity for export made *leverpostej* available if not for everybody then at least for all but the lower working class.

The Bacon and Liver Bonanza of the Danish Meat Packing Industry

The industrialization of the meat packing industry had a tremendous effect on the Danish meal. In the 1870s and 1880s, grain prices dropped drastically, causing many Danish farmers to shift from grains to livestock. This shift was facilitated by growing exports to England of meat and dairy, especially bacon and butter. In 1898 Denmark was second only to the United States when it came to providing bacon to the English market.[10]

As a result, pigs became very popular for Danish farmers. Where it had been common earlier for farms to keep a few pigs themselves, keeping the offal for their own use (in sausages among other things) and sending the carcasses to be sold in market towns, now the whole animal was delivered to the newly established specialized slaughterhouses that dealt only with pigs. The focus on bacon in the Danish meat packing industry prompted Welsh journalist and advocator of protectionism Ernest Edwin Williams to rename the Danish slaughterhouses 'co-operative Bacon-Curing Factories'.[11]

Exporting bacon to the English market fundamentally changed the way offal was used in Denmark. Offal from the slaughterhouses was sold domestically in large quantities, especially after Germany stopped all import of both slaughtered and live pigs from Denmark in December 1895. As pig's livers flooded the home market, it became clear that large scale industry would be required instead of just the shopkeepers, butchers and pedlars with small productions. To illustrate the sheer scale of operations, the number of pigs slaughtered in 1900, from both private and co-operative slaughterhouses, was about 1.1 million, which would have amounted to something like 1500 tons of liver.[12]

The scene was set for specialized factories to take over production of *leverpostej*. Development was most explosive in and around Copenhagen. In 1906, two factories were mentioned in the Copenhagen directory, but just two years later, in 1908, the number had risen to twelve.[13]

The sudden boom in factories making *leverpostej* shaped the industry. In a 1913 book about the meat industry and its economy, a sausage maker named H. F. Schneekloth commented that 'no country could measure up to the Danish production of *leverpostej*'.[14] As Denmark was and still is the only country that makes *leverpostej* in the first place, that may seem a foregone conclusion, but the amount of *leverpostej* produced in Denmark today is truly staggering for such a small country and a for such a specialized product.

From the beginning, most factories were very specialized, making only *leverpostej*, but a few did branch out into other charcuterie products. The most notable of these started in 1916 when Lars Pedersen sold his renowned factory to Jens Steffensen, a sausage maker who already had his own sausage factory. Steffensen continued to produce both sausages and *leverpostej*, and later other charcuterie products, until 1966 when the company merged with S. Houlberg A/S to become an industry giant under the name Steff-Houlberg. It still produced *leverpostej*, but by then it was just one product among many.[15]

However, some factories remained dedicated to *leverpostej*. The biggest producer today, Stryhn's Leverpostej A/S, had its beginnings in 1941, when Henry Stryhn quit his job as chauffeur and salesman for Steffensen and started his own one-man business selling *leverpostej* from his freight bicycle. In 1945 he partnered with a *leverpostej* factory in Copenhagen; in 1956 the factory moved to Himmelev outside Roskilde as it needed more space for increased production.[16] The number of *leverpostej* made by the factory has continued to grow: in a 2006 interview, the CEO of Stryhn's estimated the daily production of *leverpostej* at about 85,000 trays of 500 g each.[17]

Leverpostej came to the Danes' table came through the food industry, but export to England is only part of the explanation for its breakthrough. While export made pig's livers available in large quantities, technological advances were needed too: the invention of the meat grinder and the kitchen stove made mincing and baking *leverpostej* possible on a larger scale than before. This scale, in turn, lowered the price of *leverpostej* so significantly that it became a staple of Danish cuisine.

The meat grinder and the stove were both introduced in the middle of the nineteenth century. Grinders made mincing meat and offal possible on a large scale, and when they became available for home use later in the century, housewives too could make dishes that had been either impossible or overly difficult before. Around the same period, the invention of the kitchen stove revolutionized the cooking of offal in Denmark, but its introduction into Danish homes happened only gradually. Since a very important part of preparing *leverpostej* is its baking, a steady and controllable heat source is needed, which required much skill when baking could only be done by placing baking tins or trays directly on the hearth or by using a baker's oven. The new kitchen stoves, equipped with ovens, brought easier baking into smaller households.

Many of the early recipes for *leverpostej* that emerged in cookbooks in the second half of the nineteenth century were so complicated and demanded such specialized kitchen tools that few middle or working class housewives would be able to follow them in their own kitchens. As Halvor Petersen comments in his book about *leverpostej*, 'These recipes seem primarily to have been developed for lunches and dinners held by the well-to-do part of the bourgeoisie.'[18] Without command of a fully staffed kitchen and the means to procure fresh livers, average Danes bought their *leverpostej* at charcuteries or as part of packed lunches pedlars sold by workplaces.

The Danish Packed Lunch

The packed lunch is a fundamental part of the Danish meal structure and as such an important part of Danish society. You cannot, at least not without Herculean effort and a lot of money (eating out is quite expensive in Denmark) avoid having to bring your own lunch at some point or another. According to a book on the history of the packed lunch in Denmark, the introduction of open sandwiches as a full meal in the middle of the day was the biggest change in Danish eating habits in modern times.[19]

This change in meal structure began with the working class but spread to most corners of society over the course of the twentieth century. The working class was affected first because the change was prompted by developments in working conditions in large-scale agriculture and industry. René Bühlmann and Stig Püschl summarize this shift from a hot midday meal to a cold packed lunch as 'a class phenomenon that emerged among the farm workers and was completed by the workers in the cities, and it was not indicative of "haute cuisine" but rather of a pure and simple need'.[20]

Farm workers had been used to bringing some sort of sustenance with them when they went to work in the fields, something to keep the hunger at bay between the main meals. In the cities, workers usually went home to eat their lunch and then returned to work, but with decreases in working hours from the 1880s onwards significantly shortening the midday break and increases in transportation time in an industrialized society, many people could no longer make it home for lunch. As a result, workers had to bring their own cold lunch with them and postpone the hot meal of the day until evening. The packed lunch thus became a necessity just as *leverpostej* became available to low income households.

The impact of *leverpostej* on the Danish packed lunch cannot be underestimated and it has been characterized as 'The *piéce de résistance* of the packed lunch'.[21] Workers quickly discovered that an easy thing to make was bread with butter, lard, cold cuts, and *leverpostej* packed in old newspaper and later in lunchboxes. The variety of the food depended on what you could afford. Soon *leverpostej* became the ideal sandwich spread since housewives did not even need to butter the bread beforehand and since *leverpostej* offered much more in the way of taste and nutrition than butter or lard.

While housewives in larger households and among the rural population began to make their own *leverpostej*, helped by the availability of meat grinders made for home use and increasingly advanced ovens, the majority still bought their *leverpostej* readymade. As *leverpostej* does not keep for long, especially without proper means to keep it cool, a lot of people were dependent on being able to buy their *leverpostej* from pedlars or charcuteries, who, in turn, either got it from a factory or made it themselves. This created a curious phenomenon in advertising for *leverpostej*. If it was made by the shopkeeper, the ads repeatedly stressed that it was 'homemade' as opposed to 'factory-made', even though homemade might have been a bit of a stretch seeing as it was made in the back of a shop.[22]

Leverpostej arrived to the shops straight from the factories still ensconced in big enamel trays. The *leverpostej* was then turned out of the tray, which in turn was washed and sent back to the factory. The shopkeeper then garnished the *leverpostej*, sometimes with *sky* and speck in decorative patterns.[23]

Customers would then come in and buy one or two slices of *leverpostej*. They seldom bought more than that since *leverpostej* did not keep for more than a couple of days in these pre-refrigerator times. A family with the adults working and the children going to school had a lot of lunchboxes to fill during the week, and the visit to the charcuterie would be an almost daily occurrence for most working class families.

School and *leverpostej* are irrevocably associated with one another in the minds of most Danes. There seems to be a mutual memory linked to the smell of *leverpostej* permeating the air in the classroom after the lunch break (in most Danish schools the pupils eat in their classroom). These memories are shared across generations and social strata considering that about 92% of Danes eat *leverpostej* and 26% eat it daily.[24]

It is interesting that the contents of school lunchboxes have not changed very much in the last hundred or so years. Children still pull slices of rye bread with *leverpostej* out of their lunchboxes, even though now it may be accompanied by more exotic foods as well. According to Stryhn's factory, earlier they could follow the school year at the factory by looking at the sales figures. During school holidays, sales dropped because *leverpostej* was not needed for the children's lunchboxes.[25]

The National Lunch Dish

During the German occupation of Denmark from 1940 to 1945, shortages quickly made substitute goods become a reality, though the conditions in Denmark never became as severe as in other occupied countries like Holland or France. Despite the Danish government imposing price controls and rationing early on, it became difficult for many housewives to make ends meet when it came to feeding their families adequately. At the same time, a growing awareness of the intricacies of proper nutrition, of vitamins and their importance in the diet, prompted nutritionists to raise concerns about the negative impact austerity measures would have on public health.

As public nutrition information flourished during the war, *leverpostej* came to play important rhetorical and nutritional roles. Danish cookbooks and nutritional literature were subject to censure just like other publications during the five-year occupation, and any patriotic or wartime sentiments had to be carefully considered. Writers therefore found new ways to express national identity by focusing on the food and dishes that were inherently Danish and shrouding them in veiled references to Danish culture and the hardiness of the Danes.[26]

In this context, *Leverpostej* was heralded as the national lunchmeat both by the private sector, including doctors and cookbook writers, and by the government, through state nutritionists. One author in particular was not humble in her praise of *leverpostej*: 'The *leverpostej* – our national spread – must not be despised, as it has a considerable vitamin content that we, especially in the winter, have a hard time getting any other way. So let us be faithful to it.'[27]

At the time, *leverpostej* was still a relatively cheap source of vitamins and minerals and, as such, an ideal food in times of crisis. Families without the means to adequately feed their children could get their children enrolled in a meal programme where they would get free lunches at school. This was called '*sikringskost*', literally translated as 'security diet', and was meant to ensure that its recipients got at least one nutritionally sound meal a day. *Leverpostej* was unavoidable in this diet but not always a favourite, since some schools tried to use it to boost the children's vitamin intake by mixing in drops of cod liver oil.[28]

Nevertheless, liver also became scarce as the war wore on. Both factories and shopkeepers were hard pressed to make enough good quality *leverpostej* with the liver available to them, and so strange liver substitutions started to emerge. *Leverpostej* was made with lungs, udders, other entrails and, in some harrowing examples, waste products from the fishing industry and decoctions from mussel processing plants. Add to that a more liberal use of flour or the inclusion of more water or stock to increase the volume and mask the missing liver, and the *leverpostej* became practically unrecognizable. In her cookbook, Dr Johanne Christiansen warned her readers that 'One ought to make one's *leverpostej* from scratch, since it happens, that the factories use other pieces of offal, margarine and flour'.[29]

This practice of substituting liver with lesser kinds of offal in *leverpostej* became so widespread that the government had to step in. In October 1941, the Ministry of Trade presented a series of strict guidelines that should ensure that *leverpostej* produced in Denmark met a certain standard. Among other things, these guidelines stated that a product could not bear the name *leverpostej* unless it contained at least 20% liver and no more than 35% milk or stock. The goal of the standardization was not to raise the bar but rather to eliminate the worst adulterations.[30]

The resulting standardized *leverpostej* very quickly became popularly known as '*folkeleverpostej*' (something like 'the people's *leverpostej*' in English), a name playing on its commonness and supposed popular appeal. However, the standardized *leverpostej* was not embraced by the Danes. It was continuously ridiculed in both satirical magazines and regular newspapers. In some ways it could be called the Danish equivalent of the English National Loaf.

The Second World War firmly established the position of *leverpostej* as an important part of Danish cuisine and of the cultural identity of the Danes, and from then on *leverpostej* was embraced as something uniquely Danish, something that foreigners visiting Denmark did not eat with quite the same gusto when presented with rye bread and *leverpostej*. Maybe visiting tourists were simply unable to properly appreciate it since they were not brought up eating it.

A Colour, a Metaphor and a Symbol of Mediocrity

More than any other Danish dish, *leverpostej* has transcended the boundaries of the kitchen and the table to become a true national symbol, and it has come to be used as a metaphor for anything stereotypically Danish. The most interesting part of this development is that *leverpostej* now embodies both the unique and the mediocre in Danish culture. So ingrained is this association in the Danish language that it is not even considered slang to use *leverpostej* as a metaphorical description of some aspect of Danish culture, society or even someone's hair colour.

A friend of mine once characterized the colour of *leverpostej* as 'a special pink variant of grey', and, as such, a colour completely unachievable by anything other than *leverpostej* itself. However, if you study it closely, you will see that *leverpostej* does not just have one colour. There is the browned, sometimes slightly burned top and the paler innards whose colour can vary quite a lot from sandy to grey and brown. And sometimes *leverpostej* can also have, I must admit to my friend's delight, a sort of pale pinkish sheen.

Nevertheless, when taking about something being the colour of *leverpostej*, most often the colour referred to is one that does not even seem like a real colour but more like a forgettable mixture of light and dark greys and browns. When spoken in connection the colour of someone's hair, *leverpostej* usually refers to some sort of dark blonde: something that is not quite blonde and not quite brown and as such perhaps *leverpostej* really is an appropriate name for a colour. Still I have yet to meet a person who feels delighted to have his or her hair described as *leverpostej*.

Leverpostej – More than Just a Danish Way of Eating Offal

It is fascinating how a product that is so widespread and enjoyed all over Denmark is talked about at the same time as being the most pedestrian thing you can think about. Perhaps the answer lies in the very popularity of *leverpostej*. One might say that it has become victim of its own success. With so many people eating it on a daily basis, *leverpostej* has come to be the most common thing to eat, and this commonness becomes transferred to the rhetorical imagery of *leverpostej*. In some ways, this use of *leverpostej* is equivalent to the way in which the word 'beige' is sometimes used in English: something or someone normal to the point of blandness.

In older rhetorical and metaphorical uses of *leverpostej*, the focus was primarily on the physical attributes of the dish, most notably the consistency. People with greasy and messy hair were said to have 'combed their hair with *leverpostej*', while people who missed observing something directly in front of them had 'polished their glasses with *leverpostej*'.[31] These examples originated as part of the workplace jargon in the interwar period; it was the workers, probably inspired by the content of their own lunchboxes, that made *leverpostej* a part of the Danish language far outside the sphere of the meal.

Later uses of *leverpostej* in both spoken and written language seem to have more or less abandoned the physical characteristics, except for the colour, and instead focus on the ubiquity of *leverpostej*. However, it is only *leverpostej* as an everyday food that has made the transition into a metaphor. *Leverpostej*'s place on the table at the celebratory lunches at Christmas and sometimes also Easter remains something special, but that celebratory aspect seems to be forgotten at any other part of the year.

Newspaper headlines very often reference *leverpostej* this way, and there is no limit to the range of subjects that can be debated under a reference to the national dish. For example, the headline '*Leverpostej* as an Asiatic Trump Card' covers an article about architecture, and the headline 'The World Economy Is still *leverpostej* and Overcast Weather' covers a story that does not mention anything about the food industry.[32]

As a cultural metaphor, the role of *leverpostej* in Denmark is thus dominated by largely negative connotations, but that has not seemed to influence its gastronomic popularity at all.

Conclusion

Leverpostej has become such an inescapable part of the Danish foodscape that it may seem as if it has always been that way. But as shown in this article, *leverpostej* has undergone some fundamental changes in the way it is viewed and in the scope of its influence on how Danes view themselves and their culture.

Even halal butchers now sell *leverpostej*, though since they use calf's liver or even chicken livers instead of pig's liver the finished products may in fact be much closer to a French liver pâté than *leverpostej*. However, it is still sold under the name *leverpostej*, because to be part of Danish culture you will have to understand the Danish affinity for *leverpostej*, even if you don't enjoy it yourself.

The origin of *leverpostej* is not shrouded in romantic tales or nostalgic ideas about nineteenth-century rural life. Rather, it was a result of the industrialization. It became a clever use of a by-product from the slaughterhouses, since bacon curing was the main focus of the meat packing industry. Nevertheless, *leverpostej* itself became romanticized during the Second World War when it was put forward as the quintessential Danish lunch item and became something uniquely tied to Danish culture. This idea still persists today, even though *leverpostej* simultaneously has entered the language as a metaphor for the bland and mediocre. As such *leverpostej* continues to baffle anyone who was not been brought up eating it.

Notes

1. Stig Olesen, '*Leverståhej*', *Ud og se med DSB*, April 2010, 8. All translations by the author unless otherwise indicated.
2. Else-Marie Boyhus, *Grisen – en køkkenhistorie* (Copenhagen: Gyldendal, 1998), p. 62.
3. *Gastronomisk leksikon*, eds. Carl Pedersen and others (Copenhagen: Nyt Nordisk Forlag, 2010), p. 188.
4. William Shakespeare, *Romeo and Juliet*, 2.2.43-44.
5. An advanced form of pie tin on three legs with a special lid, it was placed on the hearth with hot embers heaped on top of it to cook the pie from the top and bottom simultaneously. It was widely used until the invention of the kitchen stove made it obsolete. For more on the history of Danish pies, see Else-Marie Boyhus, *Postejer og tærter- Historisk kogebog* (Højbjerg: Womianum, 1987).
6. Halvor Petersen, *Et stykke med leverpostej – Danmarks nationalpålæg* (Roskilde: Roskilde Museums Forlag, 1997), p. 15.
7. Johannes Christian Ludvig Plenge, *Nogle Træk af Livet i Kjøbenhavn for en Menneskealder siden* (Copenhagen: 1873), p. 19. *Charcuterie* is the nearest approximation to the Danish *viktualieforretning* and *Pålægsforretning*. These shops primarily sold cold cooked meats but also things like eggs, butter, beer and brandy. From the 1900s on salads also became part of the product range.
8. Petersen, p. 40.
9. Charles Kjerulf, *Erindringer. 1. del. Grøn Ungdom 1858-1880* (Copenhagen: 1915), p. 78.
10. H. Hertel, '*Udførselen af Landbrugets Produkter*', *Nationaløkonomisk Tidsskrift*, 6.4 (1898), p. 264.
11. Ernest Edwin Williams, *The Foreigner in the Farmyard* (London: William Heinemann, 1897), p. 44.
12. Petersen, p. 40.
13. Peterson, pp. 41-42.
14. H.F. Schneekloth, *Økonomisk Vejleder for Kød-Industrien* (Copenhagen: 1913), p. 133.
15. Petersen, pp. 61-81.
16. Annemette Løkke Jacobsen, '*Danmarks postejliste – historien om en lokal virksomhed i Roskilde*', *ROMU – Årskrift fra Roskilde Museum* (Roskilde: Roskilde Museums Forlag, 1993), pp. 69-71.
17. Steen Jespersen, 'Den danske leverpostej skal fremtidssikres', *Berlingske Business*, 25 February 2006 <http://www.business.dk/diverse/den-danske-leverpostej-skal-fremtidssikres>.
18. Petersen, p. 30.
19. *Madpakken – Træk af spisevanernes historie*, eds. René Bühlmann and others (Copenhagen: Forlaget Fremad, 1992), p.19.
20. *Madpakken*, p. 19.
21. *Madpakken*, p. 29.
22. Petersen, p. 35.
23. *Sky* is a clear, savoury aspic jelly used to garnish cold dishes and open sandwiches.
24. Anne Pihl Rasmussen, '*Kun en dansker spiser leverpostej*', *Avisen.dk*, 30 September 2007 <http://www.avisen.dk/kun-en-dansker-spiser-leverpostej_62816.aspx>.

25. Jacobsen, p. 72.
26. Nina Bauer, *Tiden Løsen – Ingen Sløsen – En undersøgelse af ernæringsopdragelsen I Danmark under besættelsen 1940-1945* (Unpublished master thesis, Københavns Universitet 2012), pp. 5-32 and 95-102.
27. Susanne Palsbo, *Opfindsomhed i en Krisetid – En Haandfuld Rationeringsopskrifter og aktuelle Husholdningsraad* (Copenhagen: Nationaltidendes Bibliotek, 1943), p. 107.
28. Else Svensgaard, '*Madpakken i dag og dengang*', *Dansk Madhistorie – fra fortid til nutid* (Auning: Dansk Landbrugsmuseum, 2012), p. 69.
29. Johanne Christiansen, *Rationel Sparekogebog – Beskyttende Kost – Vinterpart* (Copenhagen: 1940), p. 85.
30. Petersen, pp. 87-92.
31. Petersen, p. 85.
32. Both examples are my translations of Danish headlines.

An Internal Crisis: The Shifting Value of Offal in the UK Meat Industry

Barley Blyton, Polly Russell and Tessa Tricks

Offal in the Archive

> Vic was doing the tripes – a tripe is about as big as a wheelbarrow which goes on the floor, first you skim the fat off, then you cut it open to get all the cud out, which he did, but once you cut it it spews a little bit bigger. Anyway, so Vic leans over the tripe trying to get a hold of it – and this is filled with blood and cud and everything – and his false teeth fall out right in the middle. Anyway pretty quickly Vic leans in and scoops 'em out, wipes 'em on his apron and pops 'em back in. And my father says: 'teeth a bit loose today Vic?' and Vic says 'ye, couldn't find mine today. These are mother in law's' – Extract from a British Library National Life Story food interview with butcher David Swain (2002:3A).

At *The Fifth Quarter: Go Green for More Profit* conference (2010), food waste campaigner Tristram Stuart called for an offal marketing drive to revitalize UK consumption figures. In his book *Waste: Uncovering the Global Food Scandal*, Stuart stated that we now waste a half to a third of each animal killed due to changing customs and because 'anything that is not fed back to animals has to be sent for specialist rendering, incineration or other processing at a punitive cost' (2009: 145). Speaking on behalf of the industry, Dr Phil Hadley – Senior Regional Manager for EBLEX – identified the loss of both processor skills and infrastructure to handle offal as the reason that 'offal has become a disposal issue, rather than a value issue' (Johnston, 2010).[1]

Suffice to say, offal is largely undervalued and off the menu in the UK in 2016.[2] Within living memory the economic value of offal has diminished and most consumers regard it with disgust rather than delectation. But under which circumstances did the offal business once thrive and what has changed in the intervening sixty years?

Answers to this question can be found among a series of oral history interviews collected and housed by the British Library Sound Archive. In 1998, responding to the huge changes in UK food production and consumption that have occurred within living memory, National Life Stories (NLS), a charity residing at the British Library Sound Archive, initiated a wide-ranging oral history project focused on the food industry. Championing a 'life story' methodology the NLS project *Food: from Source to Salespoint* (FSS) recorded interviews with individuals across a broad range of food sectors.

The 'life story' method attempts to situate individuals associated with a particular industry within the broader context of their personal lives. Recordings include details about childhood, education, beliefs and relationships as well as descriptions of economic life. FSS currently holds more than 250 food producer recordings and is still growing. There are interviews with farmers, restaurateurs, retailers, food writers and with a cross-section of employees working for large-scale manufacturers and retailers such as Tesco or Northern Foods.

In particular, this paper focuses on a collection of fifteen NLS recordings conducted with men involved in UK meat production from the 1930s to the millennium. It traces offal in the food chain from slaughter to sale to consumption. The interviewees include slaughterhouse workers and owners, butchers and meat dealers, many of whom entered the trade between 1920 and 1940 and were recorded between 1999 and 2003. Containing numerous references to offal, these lengthy, biographical accounts offer evidence of how offal was valued, managed and understood within the meat trade for much of the twentieth century.

Within the industry offal was referred to as 'the fifth quarter'. Rather than referring to a cut, this term hints at the transformation of the animal into more than a sum of its parts. The fifth quarter relied upon maximizing the value of by-products and wasting nothing. The fifth quarter had to be made, and making it required skill, business acumen and effective social relations.

Further interviews with technologists and category managers working in the meat departments of a large British retailer suggest how the industry conceptualizes the modern consumer as 'squeamish' and reluctant to engage with the animal origins of meat. These recordings document how in the late twentieth century increased levels of technology, a growing distance between animal, producer and consumer, a notion of convenience and a decline in former social networks – which profited from the distribution of the whole animal – have combined to take the value out of offal.

Slaughter and Sale, Usage and Waste 1920-1950

Historically, it was partly the management of offal in the middle ages that elevated butchery to a recognized trade. As Sussex butcher Ron Stedman explained, it was only once butchers were officially sanctioned to deal with by-products and waste that butchers were recognized as a livery company:

> The butchers had a hall outside Aldersgate (London) in 989! It is the only hall in history that goes back as far as that. The butchers had a hall! But the butchers were [not then] recognized as being a livery company because of the way it was run. You must remember that butchers killed in the street, blood and offal ran in the gutters, so inhabitants of the City thought little of them [....] It wasn't until a Lord Mayor gave the Butchers Company a way of getting rid of their waste and offal into the Thames that we began to be thought of as a guild or a livery (2003:2B).

Until recent crises in food production and the transformation of consumer tastes, the successful management of waste and useable offal was inextricably linked with notions of professionalism as well as being integral to business viability.³

Britain is currently home to approximately 285 registered abattoirs licensed to slaughter livestock (AHDB Pork, 2016). Outside of the industry, few people today have visited or are aware of slaughterhouses, despite the largest processing tens of thousands of animals per year (Defra, 2015).4 Located in secluded areas and with high security, contemporary slaughterhouses remain hidden. The invisibility of animal slaughter is a relatively recent phenomenon; as late as the 1970s the slaughterhouse was a feature of most villages and towns, with village butchers often having an abattoir attached.5

Many of the interviewees' memories of the profession begin with the slaughtering practices of their childhood. For many, the slaughterhouse was their introduction to the meat trade. Bob Dixon, a third-generation butcher from Sunderland described how managing offal was integral to the slaughtering process:

> In the slaughterhouse the beast would be divided. You'd take all the offal out – your lungs, your liver, your heart and then you'd wash 'em' (1999:2A). A number of recordings attested to the fact that in the slaughterhouse 'nothing used to get thrown away […] and everything was made use of. (Swain, 2002:3A; Baker, 1999: 1A; Herbert, 1999: 3B; Cramer, 1999 4A)

While slaughterhouse workers derived their fifth-quarter profit by dividing up the whole animal, butchers made their fifth-quarter profit from processes of transformation: making sausages, faggots, jellies and brawns, and in some cases, soap (Collimore, 2001:1B).

The interviews detail the various ways in which profit might be generated from offal on a day to day basis. Hides would be graded and sent to auction, hooves were used to make Neat's Foot Oil (conditioning oil for leather) and the intestines of sheep and pigs were sold for sausage skin. Trotters were boiled-down for jelly and pig's heads were used to make brawn and sausages. Fat was collected in a bin – along with waste bones and hooves – to be processed into soap by manufacturers like John Knights, or alternatively composted for fertilizer (see Stedman, 2002:3B; Cramer, 1999:2A). Before the use of oil became widespread, fat was 'valuable for lubricating all the wagons and carts' (Hewitt, 1999:3A). Chicken heads and feet were collected by 'the gut man' and reportedly went back into animal feed (Stone, 2001:7A). What happened to eyes was less clear, but certainly they had little value and often feature in pranks recounted by interviewees.

The distribution of some by-products was dependent upon the scale of the slaughter. In the larger slaughterhouses blood would frequently go down the drain (Baker, 2002:4A), but with small operations blood was used for black pudding or fetched by locals to feed their tomatoes. Intestines also 'went back on the land' (Swain, 2002:2A) or were fed to the pigs: 'Pigs were never fed very much because we used to throw all the inedible offal from the slaughterhouse out. That's what they lived on. It did stink [....] Wonderful fertilizer though [....] Grass didn't half grow' (Nicholson, 1999:3A).

Fifth-quarter profit in the slaughterhouse depended, in part, on knife skills. Roger Baker, a slaughterhouse owner, explained that the first skill of a slaughter man is knife sharpening and the first task is to skin the head: 'You didn't start with the hide because if you cut the skin of the hide you very easily devalued it – then you'd get a class-2 hide and lose 10 shillings!' (2002:3A). Talking of the 1950s, Helmsley butcher Geoff Nicholson remembers claims that 'hides alone would pay for the slaughtering' (1999:3A). It is no wonder then that interviewees emphasized the expertise required to remove hides undamaged and could recall the names of talented colleagues (see, for instance, Brewster 2000: 5B).

Certainly the monetary value of offal explains why interviewees repeatedly commented on cutting skills and chastised the wasteful. In addition though, offal provided a way for those in the meat trade to earn respect and establish their butchery credentials. David Swain, who took over his family's butchers shop and bacon business in Eastbourne, recalled how his father, a talented butcher, earned the admiration of his peers and customers by giving cutting demonstrations at country shows (2002: 4A).

As with slaughter workers, butchers posed waste as a non-issue because 'waste seemed to have a value' (Cramer, 1999:3B). Paul Langley who started out as a butcher's boy at Phillip Cramer's shop in London in the early 1960s, recounted: 'You used to get paid for your fat and bones, like a lot of money then, you know, I can remember, you'd get five pounds a week, which don't seem like a lot of money but it probably was for waste' (Langley, 1999:2B). Professions built upon the management of offal thrived within this system and were often lucrative:

> The fat and bone man would come round, old Albert, crafty as a sack of weasels he was, he'd try everything to bolt you up [...] but now you have to pay to have it taken away [...] he used to come by in an old truck, [...] with a load of old grey hessian sacks and he'd have your bins, you'd keep the fat and bones separate cos the fat was worth so much more because they'd render it down for dripping and things like that and he'd weigh it up, but as I say, he was crafty. I remember him cos he always had loads and loads of money on him, big pocket full of money (1999:2B).

Langley's recording includes an anecdote about how the 'bone man' was able to pay for his house out of his cash-in-hand collections and his savings were a pile of unopened wage-packets on top of the wardrobe.

Different parts of offal could fluctuate in value depending on demand, but all together they were relied on to provide a profitable fifth quarter for slaughterhouse workers, butchers and the other various trades that depended upon the non-edible offal. On the basis of these interviewees the meat trade was a potentially lucrative industry. Many of those interviewed were members of the Worshipful Company of Butchers and had prosperous careers; several went on to become the Masters of the Guild, while others were prominent liverymen with directorships in meat and livestock associations and businesses in slaughter or sale.[6]

Sale

When many of the interviewees started in the meat industry, Smithfield had double the trading hours it does today. The market traded in whole carcasses and had to sell out daily as refrigeration facilities were absent or limited (Stone 2001:6B): 'We never thought about cutting things off [....] There was always the problem, if you buy the breast what are we going to do with the legs? The market in portioning grew up in the 60s' (Stedman, 2002:10B). Following slaughter day the butcher would receive an entire carcass complete with edible offal: 'Monday was slaughter day, on Tuesday and Wednesday [customers] would buy stewing and cheaper cuts – offal or sausages. Thursday, Friday, Saturday would be the roasting cuts. That was the pattern all the way through no matter where you went' (Mallion, 1999:5B). This pattern of eating adopted by most customers allowed butchers to predict sales and to utilize and sell offal while fresh, therefore avoiding waste.

By making space for tangents and stories, the archives are full of encounters between butchers, meat and offal that manage to capture some of the viscerality of everyday experience. For instance, Swain recalls, 'Shop workers would put liquid fat in their mouths, and then blow it all over the hanging skinned lambs carcasses so it looked all nice and speckled…if there was anyone artistic, father was very good at this, he'd get some newly congealed blood and paint roses on it' (2004:4A). According to interviews, butchers handled offal with ease, but the recordings suggest that customer attitudes have transformed in the last few decades.

For the first half of the twentieth century, for instance, butchers would still 'hang quarters of beef outside, with great kidney knobs coming out' (Swain, 2002:4A). This practice dwindled as traffic increased, but there is no suggestion from interviewees that customers would have preferred the living origins of their meat to be any less explicit. Swain, in fact, describes an item known as a 'belly-set'. An eighteen inch stick with a spike on one end and a hook on the other, this was the ultimate implement for informing customers on the provenance of their offal: 'When the carcass was hanging up, you would draw half way down the diaphragm and open the carcass up then pull the 'belly-set' [referring to internal organs] up and over the head like an apron. The heads were always left on' (2004:4A). The fact that customers did not recoil from the visibility of butchered animals suggests how consumer attitudes have changed. The notion that meat is preferable when abstracted and divorced from its living origins – described as 'sarcophagan' logic by Noilie Vialles – is an increasing characteristic of contemporary meat consumption (1994:127-8).

NLS recordings conducted with the employees working in the meat and poultry division of a large British retailer would seem to bear this out. In explaining the rationale behind portioned, packaged and often skinless and boneless meat products, Technologists, Product Developers and Buyers alluded to customer 'squeamishness' and a resistance to encountering the 'animalness' of meat. As one Meat Buyer, interviewed in 2004, explained:

> We've moved [...] so away from a rural environment [...] the majority of the population live in a town. You know, they don't really see a live chicken on a day to day basis any more and therefore they've become squeamish about dealing with the consequences of that and they've become disassociated with it and you know, they all say Britain's a nation of animal lovers and things like that. Well maybe we are [...] but people really don't want to know and when they think about it, they're put off eating it (Name Withheld, 2004).

In short, the capacity to manage and make profit from offal relied upon a combination of related factors including regulated patterns of trade, butchers' willingness to handle and manipulate offal and customers' lack of squeamishness about animal products.

A Lot to Digest: Changing Pace, Changing Tastes

The trade in offal in the early part of the twentieth century was reliant upon small networks of slaughterhouses, butchers and associated suppliers. Management of food production by the Government during the Second World War meant increasingly centralized organization, distribution and control. These developments had a significant impact on small-scale UK slaughterhouses and on the wider farming community. Baker described the rise in large-scale slaughterhouses and the consequent closure of smaller abattoirs throughout the late 1950s and 1960s (2002: 5B).

According to Baker, during the post-war period the retailer became instrumental in shaping and managing the supply chain. As a supplier to the British retailer Sainsbury, he recalled how his order from them rose from 100 to 500 lambs a week over a fortnight (2002:3B). As well as presenting logistical challenges, Baker explained that by taking on supermarket clients he risked alienating smaller butcher clients: 'We had to keep quiet that we were selling to Sainsbury's, we had to refer to it as Jo's ... didn't want the small butchers to know what we were doing' (Baker, 2002:3B).

In 1966, having survived the closures endured by smaller slaughterhouses, Baker built a large, modern slaughterhouse with a cutting room attached in order to supply the supermarkets. It included the most up to date machinery, including a 'pig scraper that [would] take the hair out' (2002:3B). Supplying food manufacturers such as Findus and Birdseye as well as rapidly expanding retailers meant that by 1968 Baker could no longer manage to supply the local butchers who had once been the mainstay of his livelihood. By switching to cattle-only slaughter for large-scale customers he was able to process the same numbers in an hour that had previously been slaughtered over a week (2002:3B).

Despite complaining about ever increasing hygiene regulations in the 1960s and 1970s, and the difficulty of deriving profit from the fifth quarter, the slaughter workers conceded that the concentration of slaughterhouses and improved technology such as automated cutting machines made economic sense for those that were able to keep up (Stone, 2001:8B; Cramer, 1999:9B). Davies noted that physical labour in the slaughterhouse was replaced by mental stress as inter-trade competition became increasingly fierce. What had formerly been phrased as 'camaraderie' was now phrased as 'survival of the fittest' (Davies, 2001:12B).

Recordings with butchers describing trade during this period and throughout the 1970s state that they began to buy pre-cut meat and less offal as they 'modernized' their stock to keep up with the supermarkets (Hewitt: 1999:3A). At the same time, there was a disruptive new player on the scene. Poultry had been a rare luxury when the interviewees were first starting out in the trade (Nicholson, 1999: 1A). In the early 1950s, however, co-operation between an entrepreneurial group of farmers and innovative food retailers – notably, Sainsbury's – put an end to poultry's rarity. Using innovations in animal selection, disease control and new technologies in slaughter, processing and storage, they set the UK poultry industry into action. Poultry sales soared from one million in 1950 to 200 million a decade later (Godley and Williams, 2009:47).

The poultry industry's smart marketing spoke to decreasing family sizes and shifts in women's working hours, reinventing a luxury item as a staple (Mackenzie, 2004; Godley and Williams, 2009). Many of those interviewed commented on changing consumer needs. As Stedman mentions, his female customers were now 'a different kettle of fish to what they were then' (1999:9A). Frequent assertions claimed that the modern housewife no longer knew how to cook and had little concern about the provenance of her meat (Breading 1999: 3A; Brewster, 2000; Kley, 2003)[7].

Increasing their monopoly throughout the 1970s, supermarkets were able to negotiate to carry only the premium cuts. 'You can't blame them', explained slaughterhouse worker Brian Hewitt, 'that's business, but they are not doing the job of the general butchers … using the whole carcass' (1999:5B).

Since the offal that had formerly been sent to butchers along with the carcass was no longer required by supermarkets, slaughterhouses were forced to find new markets (Baker, 2003:7A). Whereas in discussions of earlier practices the slaughter men had gone to lengths to detail possible outlets, Hewitt and Nicholson simply noted that after the slaughterhouses had been 'modernized' offal would be sent for 'processing' (1999:3B; 1999:6A). Those who did elaborate stated that by-products continued to be used for fertilizer, pharmaceuticals and cosmetics and were collected from the slaughterhouse by manufacturers. Offal still had a place in the consumable sector but only in the guise of burgers and other processed meats (Dixon, 1999:2B).

Making up the fifth quarter became increasingly difficult as 'packaging and production costs became higher and the by-product price became less and less'

An Internal Crisis: The Shifting Value of Offal in the UK

(Brewster, 2000:6B). Baker noted that in 1984 his company started making dog food in order to utilize offal (2002:7B). Other interviewees described how offal was increasingly transformed into low-value animal feed as consumers lost the taste for it (Baker, 2002:5B).

One Track Mind?

If the steep decline in butcher's shops and slaughterhouses and a transformation in consumer taste and expectations initiated a slow decline of offal consumption in the UK, the BSE crisis accelerated the process dramatically. Following an extended period of research into the disease, the UK government confirmed a link between BSE and Creutzfeldt-Jakob Disease. The EU banned exports of British beef from March 1996, and offal cuts such as brain, spinal-cord, spleen, thymus, tonsils and intestines had to be stained and disposed of. According to Hewitt, it cost the industry £22 million that year to get rid of this offal (Hewitt, 1999:2B; Atkinson, ND).

A number of interviewees reported going out of business or faced severe financial struggles as a result of the ban. Brewster described the BSE crisis as the 'worst disaster' ever to hit the industry: 'It was nearly impossible for us to accept the existence of this disease' (2000:1A). He recalls claiming in a radio interview that it was not too serious but he knew in his 'heart of hearts' that the sterilization process involved in animal feed had become insufficient during a process of regulatory changes in the 1980s (2000:12 A).

Reflecting on the origin of the BSE crisis, Hewitt identified lax standards, deskilling and a lack of informal accountability between industry workers as contributing factors that had crept into the industry:

> In the old days the spinal cord was removed and cleaned and sent to butchers for their sausages. There would have been a Dickens of a row if you didn't trim the spinal cord off, make it all clean and trim all the glands off. Then things went lapse, reusing them, it can't have been good (1999:2B).

The suggestion that there would have been a 'row' harks back to the workers' former notion that 'you could abuse the system, but if you did you wouldn't be in business very long' (Baker, 2002:3B). Changes in the social network of the industry also meant that the former, albeit informal mechanisms of trade accountability which had kept the industry in check broke down, along with the absence of formal accountability via regulation. This combined with the long-standing imperative, and pride in, making the fifth quarter contributed to what were disastrous consequences for the industry and a further demise in the circulation of offal.

Conclusion: Offal, Camaraderie and Masculinity

If the successful management of offal ensured profit and pride, it also played a role in determining the shared values of the meat trade community and in reproducing masculine identity at work. With its close association with waste, its historically low value and its capacity to deteriorate quickly in comparison with meat, offal carries connotations of risk, disgust, pollution and dirt. Handling and managing offal on a daily basis allowed meat trade professionals to re-appropriate and re-work offal, not only as a product, but as a symbol.

Offal often played a part in initiation rituals. Interviewees variously described their hats being filled with eyeballs, being tipped into a bucket of turkey guts or finding their shoes replaced with bones (Swain, 2002; Langley, 1999; Stedman, 1999). In this capacity offal was the means through which butchers demonstrated a shared sense of raucous humour and a capacity to stomach what to most would be disgusting.

Recordings suggest that the visceral, embodied and physical nature of the profession contributed to create a separate world with its own traditions, values and modes of communication. Interviewees documented with relish the use of 'back-slang', a 'secret' language used in front of customers. Phrases like *Batcha calla namow* ('look at that woman') were part of daily life (Stedman, 2002:6B).

The appeal of joining a community of butchers was described by Langley, a working class lad from London: 'The butcher's shop, it was knives and blood and all that, it must have been hard to work in a butcher's shop. It always had that kind of image, didn't it? It was always fun, it was always a laugh. If there's noise in the high street where's it coming from? The butcher's shop' (1999:1A). Later in the recording Langley explicitly makes the connection between working as a butcher and a form of masculinity recognizable and appealing to women:

> All the tearaways wanted to work in the butchers, and they did, like I say, the ones I worked with they were, Mr Cramer's staff like Billy, he was a boxer, Garry, they were all that sort of type of, you know, not, oh I don't know if I can say that, not poofy types, you know, more, the manly type weren't they the butchers …. All the girls used to like the butchers, that's why we all always wanted to work in the butchers, especially our shop, Cramer's […] all the girls used to flock around the shop and that was it (1999:1A).

As described by Langley and others, being part of the meat trade meant belonging to and performing as part of a clearly identified masculine community.

Interviewees described their work in terms of hard, physical labour – carrying huge carcasses, delivering heavy baskets of meat to customers, moving large volumes of waste. By contrast, women, usually described as 'the housewife', wanted something easy to cook, ideally already prepared on a tray. Butchers are closely identified in the recordings with red meat, especially beef, but women are alleged to have a preference for chicken (see Brewster, 2000:13b for example). Meat trade professionals described a world governed by a system of informal conduct, personal relations, unwritten rules and alternative language. The supermarket, with it formalized structures and systems, by contrast is described as appealing to housewives. Offal in the recordings became a vehicle through which a nostalgic account of the trade was told. It was used to describe

An Internal Crisis: The Shifting Value of Offal in the UK

a culture of lost traditions, relations and rituals, forgotten skills, abandoned notions of taste and diminished forms of masculine identity. Women were invoked to explain how and why the trade had been forced to modernize (Hewitt, 1999:1B).

Oral history recordings provide an account of economic production as grounded in social life. The voices of meat trade workers from the archive attest to the fact that offal's decline in economic and cultural value was lost in line with a decline in informal networks, a new notion of convenience, transformed supply chains and the anxieties resulting from BSE. These various changes arose in tandem with the imposition of increased levels of technology and distance between the producer and the consumer – and the producer and the animal. This new notion of convenience catered to the modern individual rather than the former pre-war practices and social networks which supported and profited from the distribution of the whole animal; attributing value to hide, hoof, tail and tripe.

Notes

1. EBLEX is the organisation for beef and lamb levy payers in England, which exists to enhance the profitability and sustainability of the English beef and lamb sector.
2. Chefs such as Fergus Henderson have championed nose-to-tail eating and contributed greatly to a growing trend around offal, but offal consumption more broadly remains limited.
3. The BSE crisis (1990) and Foot and Mouth crisis (2001) precipitated changes in laws relating to meat processing and prohibited the sale and consumption of certain meat organs.
4. The NLS *Food: from Source to Salespoint* project collected 290 recordings with food producers. These are available to listen to, sometimes with full transcripts, at the British Library. In May 2016 the British Library also made 120 of these recordings equating to 940 hours of interviews available online <http://sounds.bl.uk/Oral-history/Food>.
5. Pierce's in Chew Magna outside Bristol remains an example of a butcher premises with slaughtering facilities attached.
6. The seventh oldest livery company of the City of London.
7. Contrastingly, many butchers spoke of their intimate knowledge of meat claiming that they 'could tell where it had grown up. Who dressed it. Had [the beast] been castrated' (Brewster 2000:5B), just by sight. Nostalgia for their mothers' culinary skills, especially when it came to cooking with offal was often detailed, including mention of faggots, brawn and brains.

References

AHDB Pork, 'English Abattoir Numbers' (2016) <http://pork.ahdb.org.uk/prices-stats/industry-structure/england-abattoir-numbers/> [accessed 21 May 2016].

Atkinson, N. 'The Impact of BSE on the UK economy' (No Date) <http://www.veterinaria.org/revistas/vetenfinf/bse/14Atkinson.html> [accessed 21 May 2016].

DEFRA, *UK Weekly Numbers of Livestock Slaughtered January 1973 to 2015* (2016) <https://data.gov.uk/dataset/slaughter_statistics/resource/67278d3f-6435-4244-8584-156bc7a1cdd0> [accessed 21 May 2016].

Godley, A. and Williams, B. 'The Chicken, the Factory Farm and the Supermarket' in *Food Chains: From Farmyard to Shopping Cart*, ed. by R. Horowitz and W. Berlasco (Philadelphia: University of Pennsylvania Press, 2009), pp. 47-61.

Johnston, C. 'Opportunities For UK Offal', *The Meat Site* (2010) <http://www.themeatsite.com/articles/1037/opportunities-for-uk-offal> [accessed 21 May 2016].

Mintz, S. *Sweetness and Power: The Place of Sugar in Modern History* (New York: Viking, 1985).

Stuart, T. *Waste: Uncovering the Global Food Scandal* (London: Penguin, 2009).

Vialles, N. *Animal to Edible* (Cambridge: Cambridge University Press, 1994).

Audio References

All audio references: *Food: from Sources to Salespoint*, 1998 – 2013. British Library Sound & Moving Image Catalogue reference: C821 <http//sami.bl.uk>.

Baker, Roger. 2002-3. C821/97
Breading, John. 1999. C821/16
Brewster, John. 2000. C821/34
Collimore, Colin. 2001. C821/41
Cramer, Phillip. 1999. C821/27
Davis, Eric. 2001. C821/214
Dixon, Robert. 1999. C821/22
Herbert, Trevor. 1999. C821/19
Hewitt, Brian, 1999. C821/20
Kley, Audrey, 2003. C821/109
Langley, Paul, 1999. C821/24
Mackenzie, Andrew, 2004. C821/135
Mallion, Fred. 1999. C821/21
Meat Buyer (Name Withheld until 2035), 2004.
Nicholson, Geoff. 1999. C821/25
Stedman, Ronald. 1999- 2000. C821/30
Stone, John. 2001. C821/93
Swain, David. 2002. C821/91

Un Vrai Jambalaya – 'A Real Mess': The Southern French Origins of Louisiana's Famous Dish

Anthony F. Buccini

Kan to fe en janmbalaya, to me to zepi e to touf en pe to lavyann e to me diri. Se kofèr ye pèl sa janmbalaya. To gen tou sa melanje ansanm.[1]

1. Introduction

That the culinary culture of modern Louisiana derives in large measure from France is obvious, with many food products (such as *andouille*), composed dishes (such as *étouffée*) and foodways (*la boucherie*) that not only bear French names but also 'make sense' in terms of traditional French regional cookery: the connections are sufficiently numerous that there was a tendency for casual observers to assume that the gastronomy of New Orleans and southern Louisiana was essentially all of French origin, albeit with substantial adaptations to the local environment's offerings. In recent decades, however, as an increasing appreciation of the role played by African Americans in the formation of American culture has developed, that view has had to be modified. In terms of the culinary culture of Louisiana, there is indisputable evidence of African influence, which seems obvious now that we understand so much better the general demographic and sociocultural impact of African Americans from early colonial times. But with this very much necessary correction to the Euro-centric view there has come – perhaps inevitably – a sort of overreaction, a tendency with regard to Louisiana's foodways to attribute all popular influences not just to African Americans but to give them explicitly African origins. In some cases, this reasoning is justified with facts linguistic, culinary and historical, but in other cases the argumentation is weak, based on false and anachronistic assumptions and a disregard for the role played by the marginal, poor French colonists and with that a real misunderstanding of the creolization process (Buccini 2016a). Louisiana's popular cuisine, like Louisiana's colonial French dialect and its French Creole language, is the product of a complex evolution through which non-elite French and African influences gave rise to a new cultural form with a distinct 'culinary grammar' (Buccini 2016b) and limited number of more or less direct surface inheritances from both France and Africa.

In this paper I argue that the famous Louisianan dish jambalaya was in origin a southern French peasant stew featuring *abatis* (giblets, neck, wings, feet) which was often eaten as a *soupo courto*, that is, a stretched dish to which water was added and then a starch requiring cooking, namely, either pasta or rice. Moreover, both the dish and the name jambalaya are related to the family of messy peasant stews investigated in Buccini (2006) (*ciambotta*, *xamfaina*, etc.). In Louisiana, where there was a relatively great abundance of poultry and game birds, jambalaya came to feature the meat of the fowl, rather than just the *abatis*, and was stretched through the addition of cornmeal or rice (pasta was unavailable). In the course of the eighteenth century, the name jambalaya came to be applied in Louisiana to a style of stretched stew made with any core ingredients, especially poultry/fowl but also other meats and seafood, and stretched specifically with rice.²

2. Two Widely-held Views on the Origins of Jambalaya

A single dish cannot stand for an entire cuisine, but with jambalaya we have a case that illustrates issues of more general application in the study of Louisiana's culinary culture. Jambalaya is an emblematic dish for the region and is clearly associated with the broader French and French Creole cultural milieu of the Gulf Coast. Unattested in any text from Louisiana's French and Spanish colonial period (ending with the Louisiana Purchase of 1803), it is described in anecdotes and recipes starting in the mid-nineteenth century in connection with Mobile, Alabama, the original capital of '*la Louisiane*', as well as New Orleans and the rest of French-influenced southern Louisiana; elsewhere, it is mentioned in a nineteenth century Provençal dictionary. Though now known throughout the world, there is no other older evidence for jambalaya having been known in northern France or Saint-Domingue or the other French colonies, nor is the word found in other Atlantic World areas (West Africa, the Spanish-speaking Americas, etc.).

Jambalaya is a stew made from meat and/or seafood and some vegetables to which is added stock and then rice, all cooked in one pot, in essence an archetypical peasant dish, whatever its origins may be. Nowadays, while the combinations of meat and seafood vary considerably, the rest of the ingredients and the basic cooking method has become rather set. The flavourings consist of the so-called Louisiana French 'Trinity' of bell pepper, onion and celery, as well as garlic, and also typical now is the addition of hot sauce and Worcestershire sauce, with bay leaves also usually included. Tomatoes are a very common addition, but so made the dish is said to be 'Creole jambalaya'; without tomatoes, the dish is called 'brown' or 'Cajun jambalaya'. Regarding the choice of proteins, a pork product is normal, with andouille sausage being very popular but ham, tasso ham and salt pork are also considered 'authentic' additions. Of other meats, chicken is the most common, though all manner of game birds and many game meats are also used, whereas beef and veal are not. Shrimp is the most common seafood, though again, considerable variation in the choice of crustaceans, shellfish and, less often, finfish is accepted.

Received opinion regarding the origins of jambalaya among both popular food writers and scholars is nearly unanimous in seeing the dish as not being of French provenance, but divided on whence it came between two camps. The older position, offered in the *Penguin Companion to Food* (Davidson 2002: 146), sees it as a Spanish dish, deriving from *paella*. The newer and clearly ascendant position is that it is of West African origin and should be seen as a variant of *Jollof* rice or some other, roughly similar one-pot composition with rice. There are two main reasons for seeking the origins of jambalaya outside French culinary traditions: 1) there seems to be no corresponding rice dish in France's modern regional cuisines and, indeed, in the view of most food writers, rice is a marginal element in traditional French cookery; 2) the name of the dish has no obvious French source and seems at least superficially altogether outlandish in that regard.

The historical justification for the derivation of jambalaya from paella is, of course, the Spanish ownership of Louisiana from 1763 to 1800. From a culinary standpoint, the two dishes are clearly similar in a general sense – meat and/or seafood with aromatic vegetables and rice added to the cooking vessel – though there are certainly differences with regard to the cooking procedure, the rice being sautéed and then boiled in paella and simply boiled in jambalaya, and the vessels used; the paella pan is unknown in traditional Louisianan cookery. Much then rides on the strength of the etymology, mentioned already by Hess (1992: 66) as the standard one and repeated by many others since. It is claimed that 'jambalaya' is a contracted compound of Spanish *jamón* or French *jambon* and the Catalan word *paella*. From a linguist's perspective, the derivation is wanting on several points and ultimately seems absurd: First, though ham or some other pork product is regularly included in jambalaya, it is normally a secondary, seasoning ingredient rather than the primary and featured ingredient. Second, the phonological development from *jambon* + *paella* to *jambalaya* is odd and warrants explanation if it is to be accepted. Third, the syntax of the compound is fine for English but totally alien to both Spanish and French, where one would expect '*paella de jambon*'. The weakness of the etymology calls into question the merits of the historical justification. The Spanish demographic presence and impact on popular culture in Louisiana was quite limited, and the only abiding Spanish settlement was a small group of Canary Islanders (Dessens 2005: 246). While paella is today a national dish of Spain and surely eaten in the Canaries, in the eighteenth century it was a regional dish of Valencia, and there is evidence neither for a noteworthy Valencian presence in Louisiana nor for the consumption of paella in the Canaries during the relevant period.

Historical justification for a possible West African source for jambalaya is far stronger, as already in the early decades of the colony, hundreds of West African slaves were brought over, including many from sub-regions where rice was cultivated and regularly consumed (Hall 1992). Indeed, there is good evidence that the French made a point of importing some slaves from such areas precisely to exploit their familiarity with the production of rice. From a culinary standpoint, our lack of detailed knowledge of West African cookery in the eighteenth century makes it impossible to identify any specific dish that jambalaya could be derived from, but one-pot combinations of meat and seafood with rice are certain to have existed in West Africa. Again, an etymological connection between the name 'jambalaya' and some African source would greatly strengthen an otherwise vague relationship, and a number have been offered, though some are linguistically extremely farfetched, such as those of Read (relating it to 'Congo *cimbolo, zimbolo* "biscuit"'; 1933: 371) and Dessens (deriving it from Bambara *niame-niame* 'food', 2005: 258). The most commonly cited African-based etymology for 'jambalaya' is only partly so: again, it is claimed that the core element is the French word for ham which was combined with an African word, cited as *yaya* or *ya* meaning 'rice' (Fertel 2008: 325) – alas, food writers fail to mention any specific African source language, but I have found *ya* meaning 'cooked rice' in the western dialect of the West African Dan language (Mande family) (Erman & Loh 2008: 190). Thus 'jambalaya' is sometimes claimed to be a contraction of an unattested *jambon à la ya*. While it is possible that there were some western Dan speakers among the slaves of Louisiana, this etymology remains quite unconvincing, given that it again is wrongly based on the idea that ham is the principal ingredient with the alleged French phrase 'ham with rice', seemingly incorporating an independent loanword for 'rice' which is found neither in Louisiana French nor Louisiana French Creole (*diri* 'rice'). In the end, it appears this is not so much an etymology as an invention devised to lend support to a pre-existing assumption.

Recently a thoroughly African and specifically Wolof etymology has been proposed by anthropologist E.N. Anderson (2009), who suggests 'jambalaya' is derived from a putative compound of *jamba* 'to mix' and *laax* (x = voiceless velar fricative) 'porridge from a cereal'; Anderson offers no explanation of the phonological development to 'jambalaya'. He seems not to be a native speaker of Wolof himself, and so whether this particular compound conforms to the rules of word formation in this language remains something for an expert to determine. Be that as it may, the compound is one of Anderson's own invention, not one attested in Wolof, and one wonders: if this dish is to be connected to the Wolof – well-known cultivators and consumers of rice who were well represented in Louisiana's slave population – precisely for its putative central use of rice, why does the compound not have as an element the Wolof word for that grain (*ceeb*), as in the famous dish *ceebu jën* ('rice + fish')?

3. The French Connection

What seems remarkable is that these amateur etymologies have been widely embraced despite the fact that it has long been known that the word 'jambalaya' is attested from southern France shortly after the first attestations of it were recorded in the United States: Mistral's (1879-1886) entry in his Provençal dictionary for 'jambalaya' was noted already in the 1930s (Read 1933: 24). Proponents of the Spanish and West African theories generally ignore this point, while Anderson (2009) explicitly dismisses the significance of Mistral's entry with an unsubstantiated claim and a misunderstanding of the nature of the Provençal corpus: 'But in fact it occurs in Provence only in writings of people who had travelled to New Orleans. They must have picked it up there. Surely the enormous volume of Provençal literature would have included it if it had been around earlier.[3]

Hess (1992: 64ff.) is the first food scholar to consider in some detail the possible links between Louisiana's jambalaya and Provençal cookery, though her primary focus is on South Carolina's Low Country cooking and the history of *pelaus* ('pilafs'); her main concern is to demonstrate a connection of Provençal uses of rice to Arab and Persian traditions, and her suggested partial Arabic etymology for 'jambalaya' (*-laia* < Ar. *alya* 'sheep-tail fat' (p. 67) is not credible.

The most insightful study of the origins of jambalaya is Sigal (2007), based as it is on a broad body of textual evidence and careful analysis without recourse to fanciful etymological speculation; a number of his observations are echoed here. Sigal believes the name 'jambalaya' to be of Provençal origin, though he cannot fully demonstrate that conclusion, and ultimately is cautiously noncommittal with regard to the genealogy of the dish (p. 115).

4. The Big Easy – A One-Pot Dish

Before turning to my own etymology of 'jambalaya' I would like to consider briefly the attestations of the dish and recipes for it from the United States from the first mention in 1849 to the 1930's, listed and summarized in Table 1 (overleaf):

First, all these recipes are associated with the Gulf Coast and especially New Orleans and Mobile, Alabama. Second, with regard to the name, there is little variation of the form beyond the orthographic level, though deviant forms are attested from Alabama and Mississippi/Missouri. Third, with regard to the dish itself, it is clear that a degree of variation of ingredients exists, but there is a clear core set of ingredients: chicken or some other fowl (the central ingredient in a preponderance of the recipes), ham or some other pork product and rice; seafood variants are mentioned in several sources. The modern day inclusion of the so-called 'Trinity' of vegetables (bell pepper, onion, celery) is conspicuously absent, with onion or garlic being used for flavouring. Tomato seems to be a facultative addition with no clear evidence in the references cited in Table 1 for the alleged Cajun/Creole split mentioned above. In another text I have found (Whitehead 1889: 350), however, we possibly see the beginnings of that distinction: Whitehead lists three varieties of jambalaya, one which is perhaps indirectly referred to as 'creole' (chicken, onion, tomatoes and rice); a second referred to as 'the American planter's way' (ham, onion, red pepper and rice without tomato); a third referred to as 'Florida Spanish' (fish, ham, onion, tomato and rice).

The overall picture is clear: ham is a common secondary ingredient, occasionally the featured one, but most of the early descriptions of the dish present chicken or some other fowl as the base of the unmarked version, with other, and especially seafood versions, thought of as common variants. If we are going to seek the origins of jambalaya, we cannot take as our starting point the modern dish in which vegetables are a more prominent element and render the dish much more like Louisiana's gumbo and the putative West African ancestors. Certainly, the old recipes are particularly true to the modern Louisianan sense of the dish as one that is simple and easy to make.

Table 1. Jambalaya: attestations from the US (see Sigal 2008)

i) "jambalaya" Alabama 1849 (Solon Robinson, *American Agriculturalist*). Recipe: chicken, onions, rice (no tomatoes, no pork).
ii) "jambalaya" New Orleans 1872 (New Orleans *Times*). No recipe.
iii) "jam-ba-la-yah" New Orleans 1875 (New Orleans *Times*). Recipe: rice, red beans, smoked sausages, ham, red peppers, chicken, oysters (no tomatoes).
iv) "jombalyeeyah" New Orleans 1875 (*New Orleans Co-operative News*, cited in *The Cultivator and Country Gentleman* (Albany NY)). Recipe: rice, fat pickled pork, various meats (bear, venison, ham, turtle, owl, duck, squirrel, catfish), garlic, onion (no tomatoes). [Intended as a joke?]
v) "jam bolayah" Mobile 1878 (*Gulf City Cook Book*). Recipe: chicken giblets, neck, wing tips, feet, oysters; onion, tomato, rice, lard.
vi) "jumberlie" Alabama (presumably) 1881 (*What Mrs. Fisher Knows About Old Southern Cooking…*). Recipe: chicken, rice, tomatoes, ham.
vii) "jumballya" New Orleans 1885 (*Creole Cookery Book*). Recipe: chicken or turkey, rice, ham, lard (also seafood options), (no tomatoes).
viii) "jambalaya" New Orleans 1885 (*La Cuisine Creole*, Lafcadio Hearn). Recipe: fowl, rice, ham (no tomatoes).
ix) "jambolaya" New Orleans 1893 (*Favorite Dishes*, A Columbian Autograph Souvenir). Recipe: chicken or turkey, rice, lard, onion, tomato.
x) "jambalaya" Laurel, MS 1900 (*Laurel Cook Book*). Recipe: chicken or turkey, rice, ham, lard, onion, tomatoes, oysters.
xi) "jambalaya" New Orleans 1901 (*Mme. Begue and Her Recipes*). Recipe: chicken, ham, lard, onion, tomato, rice; recipe for a variant: shrimp, lard, onion, rice (no tomatoes).
xii) "jambalaya" New Orleans 1901 (*Picayune's Creole Cook Book*). Recipe: pork, sausage, ham, onion, garlic, rice (no tomatoes); recipes for other versions given: crab; shrimp; jambalaya au congris.
xiii) "jambalaya" Lake Charles, LA 1902 (*Southern Pacific Rice Cook Book*). Recipe: pork, onion, ham, sausage, rice (no tomatoes); variants (all with tomatoes): crab, shrimp, oyster, crawfish.
xiv) "jumballaya" New Orleans 1903 (*Cooking in Old Creole Days*, Celestine Eustis). Recipe: chicken, rice. Optional: tomatoes, peas, okra.
xv) "jambolin" Gulfport, MS & St Louis MO 1937 (*Tried and True Recipes*). Recipe: ham or bacon, tomatoes, onion, rice.

5. French Connection II

In 2004/2005, while researching vegetable stews of the western Mediterranean, I concluded primarily on the basis of Mistral's entry that 'jambalaya' was related to the group of names I was studying but due to time and word-count constraints, left the issue out of my article of 2006. When I returned to the topic several years later and encountered Sigal's piece, I knew that was the case in light of the nineteenth century American material he presented.

In addition to Mistral, Sigal (2007: 103-05) discusses two other nineteenth century Provençal texts which use the word (cited by Mistral):

> 1837, in a poem by Chailan: *jambaraia* (in the sense of 'rabble' or 'mishmash')
> 1865, in a poem by Peise: *jambalaia* (in the sense of 'rabble')
> 1878, Mistral's Provençal dictionary: *jambalaia, jabalaia, jambaraia* (*mot arabe*) s.m. *Ragoût de riz avec une volaille, macédoine, meli-mélo, cohue, v. mescladisso, pelau*. Sigal's translation: "(Arab word) Stew of rice with fowl, mixed vegetables, mish-mash, rabble, see *melange, pilau*."

The first two poetic texts do not use the word in a culinary sense but rather figuratively in the sense of 'rabble' or 'mishmash'. The third attestation, in Mistral's dictionary, gives those figurative senses but also two culinary senses: the first of these, 'a stew of rice with fowl' is clearly directly relatable to Louisiana's famous dish, while the second meaning is a '*macédoine*', glossed elsewhere as a mix of vegetables. Given the late date of Mistral's mention of the rice and fowl preparation, it could represent an import from Louisiana to southern France in the nineteenth century, a possibility that Sigal suggests. A broader consideration of the problem, however, shows that explanation not to be straightforward.

In this regard, let us consider some more recent attestations of a culinary use of this word in Provençal dialects in the twentieth century.

> 1940, Toulon (Provence): *jambalaio* (vegetable stew, of cianfotta/ratatouille type?)
> 1967, Nice (Provence): *jambalaia* (included in a list of words denoting meat dishes)
> 1995, Menton (Provence): *giambalaia* (vegetable stew of cianfotta/ratatouille type) [4]

Two of the three probably reflect Mistral's vague definition of a '*macédoine*' and are apparently local names for the famous summer vegetable stew that in Nice is known as *ratatouille*. In Compan's lexicon of Niçois, however, the word 'jambalaia' appears in a list of meat dishes but down amongst those which clearly feature 'variety cuts' of meat, and one is tempted to wonder if the offal involved is *abatis* – giblets, wings, feet and neck of a fowl, the central ingredients in one of the earliest American recipes (Table 1:v) from Mobile.[5]

The use of 'jambalaia' in Nice perhaps links up with another, obviously related word attested in Mistral and other earlier Provençal dictionaries, the first of which was published in 1785.

> 1785 (Achard's dictionary of Provence and le Comté-Venaissin: »**jambinetto**, s.f. *Fricasée, ragoût, sorte d'étuvée faite avec de petits oiseaux au nids, & cuits dans un pot avec du lard.*«
>
> 1847 (Honnorat's Provençal dictionary): *jambineta s.f. Fricasée, ragoût, sorte d'étuvée faite avec de jeunes oiseaux. Éty. de jambineta, dit pour petite jambe, ragoût de petits pieds*«
>
> 1879-1886 (Mistral's Provençal dictionary): *jambineto s.f. Sorte d'étuvée, de fricassée, faite avec des oisillons.*«

The word in question, *jambineta (-o)*, appears to have the same root as 'jambalaia' but a different complex suffix and in all three attestations the meaning is the same: a wet cooked dish comprised of cured pork and very small birds, in a sense, another offal dish.

Finally, in a dictionary for the Occitan dialect of Languedoc immediately to the west of Provence published in 1756 (de Sauvages: 256), we find another related word, *jhimbëlôto*, again with the same root but a different complex suffix, which is defined as '*une Blanquete, sorte de ragoût q'on fait des blanquetes d'Agneau & d'un reste de gigot coupé en petites tranches auxquelles on fait une sausse*' ['a kind of ragout, that one makes from fresh slices of lamb and the leftovers of a lamb roast sliced thin, for which one makes a sauce'].[6] This form also appears in Azaïs (1876: 337) as *gimbeloto* and is there described briefly as a stew of hare or rabbit pieces. Thus, in the mid eighteenth century, words clearly related to 'jambalaya' were current in different parts of southern France with meanings related in a general way to the sense that eventually emerges in the later attestations from Louisiana and Alabama.

6. More 'Peasant Slop': Western Mediterranean Offal Stews

In Buccini 2006, I argue that the many western Mediterranean summer vegetable stews, of which the Provençal *ratatouia/ratatoulha* (Fr. *ratatouille*) is the most famous, are in fact historically related in complex ways and, further, that one of the families of names for the dish, and possibly the dish itself, originated in the region of Campania in southern Italy. There we find two forms of the name, *cianfotta* and *ciambotta*. The linguistic evidence points to the first of these variants being the source for the Catalan word denoting such a vegetable stew, *xamfaina*, with adaptation of the initial consonant and replacement of the Neapolitan suffix *otta* with one that is specific to the dialects of north-eastern Iberia, *aina*. On the basis of relictal evidence from southern Italian dialects where words related to *cianfotta* indicate offal stews and the fact that Catalan *xamfaina* was further borrowed into Spanish (and Portuguese) where it (*chanfaina*) indicates only offal or meat preparations, I also argue that *cianfotta/ciambotta* most likely were originally designations of peasant offal stews before the introduction of the

Un Vrai Jambalaya – 'A Real Mess'

American vegetables allowed for the creation of the ratatouille-like dishes (141).

While it was the Neapolitan *cianfotta* variant that was borrowed into mainland Catalan dialects, it was the other variant, *ciambotta*, that was borrowed into the Catalan of the Balearic Islands, where we find a related vegetable dish under the name *tombet*, with a different choice in adapting the Neapolitan initial *ci-* (ch-sound) to the Catalan sound system. And there is every reason to believe that Neapolitan *ciambotta* is similarly the source for the Occitan/Provençal stew names discussed above.

Table 2. Diffusion and Adaptation of Peasant Stew Names.

Np. cianf-otta   ⇒ Ct. xamf-aina, samf-aina ⇒ Sp. chanfaina, etc.

Np. ciamb-otta   ⇒ BCt. tomb-et
                              ⇒ Oc./Pr. *jamb-al-alha/*jamb-in-eta/*jamb-el-ota

---

The initial voiceless affricate of Neapolitan was in southern France adapted to the near equivalent in the sound system, namely *j-*. As in Catalan, the Neapolitan suffix was replaced but in this case with different sets of complex suffixes. In the case of *jhimbëloto*, the double suffix was **el-ota*, perhaps with diminutive force; in the case of *jambineto*, it was **in-eta*, surely with diminutive force, given the dish was based around the use of tiny birds. In the case of Louisiana's 'jambalaya', the original Occitan/Provençal form must go back to an unattested **jambalalha*, again with a double suffix composed of the semantically neutral *al* and the widely used suffix *alha*; the palatal *l* (spelt traditionally »lh«) is rendered in many dialects of Occitan/Provençal, as well as in the cognates in French, as *y*. This suffix has two semantic functions (Adams 1913: 70ff.): it denotes collectives, thus very appropriate for a stew bringing together different but related items, and a pejorative, which is appropriate for a peasant stew and corresponds perfectly with the etymological evidence for the Neapolitan *ciambotta*, etc. discussed in my 2006 paper.

Table 3. Derived Forms with jamb- from Neapolitan ciamb-otta.

jamb-al-aya   *jamb-al-alha
jamb-in-eto   *jamb-in-eta
jhimb-ël-oto   *jamb-el-ota

It is important to note that while 'jambalaya' is not attested in Provençal texts of the eighteenth century or earlier, its diminutive correlate is, and it stands to reason that these two stews, based on birds, need to be viewed together, with the diminutive following from the stew using the offal (or meat) of full-grown birds: the diminutive implies the existence of a base form. It is also surely no coincidence that we find evidence in southern France of the same semantic shift, from offal (or meat) stew to summer vegetable stew, that took place both in southern Italy and the Catalan-speaking lands, i.e. in three regions with strong cultural and specifically culinary ties dating back to the Middle Ages (cf. Buccini 2013, 2015 on the spread of pasta): Mistral indicates 'jambalaya' denotes both kinds of stews, while the twentieth century dialect evidence from Provence shows Nice apparently with the offal/meat sense and Toulon and Menton with the vegetable sense.

In the end, one must conclude that this kind of formal and semantic embedding in Occitan/Provençal of peasant stew names with a root *jamb-* fitted with double suffixes, together with the strong links of that group of names and dishes to etymologically related forms and their referents in Italy and Iberia, renders it certain that Louisiana's 'jambalaya' – the dish and the name – hail from the south of France.

7. *Soupo courto:* Making Ends Meet

One question remains, however: is the addition of rice to the stew a feature contributed to the Louisianan dish by the Spanish or, more plausibly, West Africans? Such a development cannot be ruled out, but I believe that there is very strong evidence that it was the French settlers themselves who included rice in the dish and that some of them were accustomed to doing so already before emigrating to the Gulf Coast.

Most food historians work on the assumption that rice was seldom eaten in France in the Early Modern period, with only a few of the writers, notably Hess and Sigal, who have studied jambalaya acknowledging that the composed dishes known as *pelaus* (pilafs) were very much a part of the cuisine of the middle and upper classes of southern France; yet both Hess (1992: 71) and Sigal (2007: 114) reject the idea that rice was broadly consumed across social classes. Judging from the etymological evidence, however, there is no reason to connect 'jambalaia' with the more well-to-do classes: jambalaia and jambineta are non-elite or specifically peasant dishes and that class association would account for their extremely marginal representation in texts, where they appear almost exclusively in dialect dictionaries.

A careful examination of the evidence for rice consumption shows common opinion to be wrong. It is certainly true that in northern France, rice was seldom consumed except in the form of *riz au lait*, that is, rice pudding, but somewhat surprisingly rice was a food that was associated with hardship and poverty, for it was used as an emergency ration for the poor in times of famine, when wheat and other widely produced grains were in short supply.[7] It was also a secondary ration for both the French navy and, at times, the French army, the members of which were hardly considered worthy of being offered luxuries. Rice could be and was purchased in bulk from abroad, especially from Spain and northern Italy, but since rice was a useful crop with a very high yield, the French also established fairly extensive rice fields in the far south, both in Provence and Languedoc, and this endeavour was quite successful from the sixteenth century until the mid-eighteenth century, when the central government realized that rice fields were also breeding grounds for malaria and a strain on water resources.[8]

It is then not surprising that, during this period, not only did the more well-to-do enjoy their *pelaus* but the lower classes also consumed rice to a degree, the self-same people who likely enjoyed jambalaia and jambineta. One use of rice that we know lower classes enjoyed was in a kind of dish called in Provençal and Occitan a *soupo courto*, described in texts from the twentieth century but also attested already in the seventeenth century. A *soupo courto* was simply a stew or ragout that was stretched either through the addition of pasta or rice.[9] In an Occitan text of 1636 we are explicitly told of a *rougnounado,* a stew of lamb and lamb kidney, cooked with rice and, of specific relevance here, is the mention in a Provençal dictionary from 1723 of a *soupo courto* in which the stretching element was pasta but the stew was one of *abatis*, the giblets and trimmings of a bird and one that likely was called 'jambalaia'.[10] The association between bird offal stew being stretched with rice seems to have been so common that *soupo courto* came to refer to the combination and perhaps this helped in the gradual marginalization of the word 'jambalaia' in Provençal. Southern French meat stews of the sort known as *carbounado* were also stretched with rice, and this is attested as well from the eighteenth century (Achard 1785: 155). In other words, in the south of France, whence must come the name and the stew of fowl and cured pork known as 'jambalaya', there was already in the period before and during the settlement of Louisiana a custom of stretching such stews with either rice or pasta among the lower ranks of society.

There remains one further issue to address, namely the question of the regional provenance of the settlers. It is well known that a large majority of the settlers in Louisiana and other French colonies came from the north and the west of France, areas where rice consumption was surely not high and 'jambalaia' was unknown or foreign. There are two counterpoints to be made here. First, a large portion of male settlers in Louisiana were former soldiers and sailors and they surely were well acquainted with rice as a food. We might further wonder whether the southern French word 'jambalaia' was part of military jargon for a stew of fowl, just as later another word of Provençal origin, 'ratatouille', spread throughout France as military slang for a bad stew.

A specifically military source for the introduction of the word to Louisiana is, however, not necessary. Though the bulk of the French population was from the north and west of France, there were noteworthy numbers of settlers from Occitania and at least some from Provence. But here we must call to mind a concept from sociolinguistics, that of the 'founder principle' (Mufwene 1996). In the study of the development of colonial varieties and creole languages, it has been noted that the linguistic composition of the original population of a colony typically has an amplified influence on the linguistic developments – in effect, they establish a colonial norm to which newcomers tend to adjust. In the case of Louisiana, it is noteworthy that in the very first few years of the colony, when the population was extremely small, of 111 artisans recruited for service there, 89 of them came not from the west or the north but from the south, from Languedoc and Provence (Brasseaux 2005: 11-12). In all likelihood, they brought with them a taste for stews of fowl and cured pork, stretched with rice.

8. Swept Away: The Fate of 'Jambalaya' in France

Though settlers from Languedoc and Provence were never the dominant demographic group in the Louisiana colony, they did form a noteworthy minority there at least in the early years. In an environment in which fowl of all sorts – domestic and wild – were relatively easily obtained, it is in no way surprising that one of their favoured preparations became established as a local dish, nor is it surprising that with greater availability of the meat of the birds, the tendency was for the dish to be 'upgraded' from one of offal and trimmings to one of meat. Given the scarcity of wheat flour and the demand for bread, it is also not surprising that pasta as a stretching element for the stew known as 'jambalaya' was not an option in Louisiana for rendering it a '*soupo courto*'. On the other hand, the availability of rice, which increased over time as the colony developed, was both a familiar and practical choice for the colonists, starting with those from southern France who originally introduced the dish. But there are unsurprisingly some indications that less well-off people commonly consumed their jambalaya stretched with corn mush when rice was too expensive (Sigal 2008 citing Buchanan), a practice which calls to mind the flexibility of the southern French peasants who stretched their traditional stews with a variety of starchy foods, from turnips to pasta and rice and on to potatoes, when they became an available and accepted resource.

While it is clear that the name 'jambalaya' survived in the twentieth century at best only marginally in Provence, be it as a name for a vegetable stew (Toulon, Menton) or apparently as a name for some manner of offal preparation (Nice), a dish very much resembling our reconstructed *ur*-jambalaya, as a stew of *abatis* with cured pork, survives quite robustly in Languedoc, albeit under another name. Here we refer to the regionally still popular *ragoût d'escoubilles*, which permits a considerable degree of variation with regard to the principal and secondary ingredients but can be characterized first and foremost as a stew made of bird trimmings (wings, tail and giblets of chicken, turkey or goose), flavoured with pork products (e.g. *lard fumé* or sausages) and aromatic vegetables (onion and often also celery and carrots and some tomato concentrate) and reinforced with turnips and/or potatoes.[11] It is tempting to believe that this name *ragoût d'escoubilles* at some point replaced completely the older *jambalaya* in Languedoc and the origin of the application of the term *escoubilles* – in Occitan, literally 'sweepings' and more generally 'garbage', a derivative of the verb *escoubà* 'to sweep' – may have been inspired by a folk etymological reinterpretation of the opaque 'jambalaya': perhaps Occitan-speakers reanalysed 'jambalaya' as *jam + balaya* through association of the latter part with the French verb *balayer* 'to sweep' and its derivative *balayures* 'sweepings'; translated into Occitan, one arrives at a colourful and very local name for a humble food associated with local identity.

Supporting the possibility of this particular folk etymological reanalysis and reinterpretation is an old 'just-so' story that has long circulated to explain the origin of the name 'jambalaya' in a specifically Louisianan context (e.g. Wikipedia: 'Jambalaya'). According to this story, a late-arriving guest at an inn in New Orleans was informed that the inn's offerings were all sold out, so the guest said 'John, sweep something together!' – in French *Jean, balayez!* – and the guest bestowed this phrase on the chef's improvised dish as its name. The story is clearly historically false but demonstrates precisely the folksy poetics at work that likely gave rise to the Occitan name *ragoût d'escoubilles*. In effect, the *abatis* stew of present-day Languedoc represents a continuation of the same dish that was brought to Lower Louisiana in the early eighteenth century and its name almost certainly an indirect continuation of 'jambalaya' that arose through folk-etymological reanalysis and calquing into Occitan.

9. Con de Manon: Les Sources!

In this article we have demonstrated that the name of Louisiana's emblematic dish has a clear, linguistically coherent etymology in the Provençal/Occitan language of southern France and also that that word is itself part of a family of related names of dishes in that region. That these words are, moreover, clearly related in complex but, under close inspection, obvious ways to culinary terms attested in southern Italy and the Catalan-speaking lands only strengthens further the case for 'jambalaya' being an import to Louisiana from southern France. Demographic data on the founding colonial population on the Gulf Coast lends yet more support to our argument. The degree to which the more purely culinary evidence lends further weight to the linguistic evidence is striking. We have shown that there is overwhelming circumstantial evidence for the existence of a stew of fowl (and more specifically of *abatis*) in Provence and likely Languedoc as well in the period preceding and contemporaneous with France's colonial efforts in Lower Louisiana. Further evidence has been adduced indicating that the consumption of rice in southern France among the non-elite levels of society was common during this time and that, in fact, throughout most of this period, rice was a local product in both Languedoc and Provence. We have then demonstrated specifically that stews of various types, including ones made of *abatis*, were regularly stretched with both pasta and rice; in Louisiana, where pasta was unavailable but rice was usually on hand, the semantic shift of 'jambalaya' from a stew of fowl or fowl offal to a stew cooked together with rice was a natural development, but the unmarked version of this dish on the Gulf Coast has always remained fowl-based. The origins of Louisiana's dish would, of course, not have been a problem in culinary history, had the dish and its name lived on robustly in direct association in southern France but in this regard too, the evidence of the marginal survival of the name in parts of Provence indicating conceptually related dishes (peasant summer vegetable stews and some manner of offal stew) and of a closely related dish in Languedoc with a different name that itself appears to be a folk reinterpretation of the old word *jambalaia* completes the picture: Louisiana's jambalaya, both the dish and its name, are undeniably southern French in origin.

Notes

1. 'When you make a jambalaya, you put your *zepi* (onions and garlic) and you stew a bit your meat and you put in rice. That's why they call that jambalaya. You have all that mixed together' (Louisiana French Creole informant, Valdman 1998: 202). In Louisiana French, 'jambalaya' has the figurative meanings of 'mixture', 'muddle' and 'mess'. Many thanks to Amy Dahlstrom.
2. This article is envisioned as the first part of a longer consideration of certain key aspects of culinary culture not only within the Louisiana colony but also with regard to its relationship to the culinary cultures of the Anglophone southeast of the United States, the French colony of Saint-Domingue, and additionally to metropolitan France. The seemingly Eurocentric starting point presented here will be shown in this further work to be a part of the basis of a reassessment and re-appreciation of the crucial role played by Africans and African Americans in the genesis of the new Atlantic World cuisines of the American South and the Caribbean region.
3. Provençal is amply attested from the Middle Ages on but the corpus has its limitations and no European language is so strongly attested as to ensure the recording of all words, especially not ones belonging to the lowest registers; in addition, one notes that Provençal came under strong pressure from French as a written language already in the sixteenth/seventeenth century. Finally, demonstrably old names of peasant dishes in more robustly attested languages often remained unrecorded until the nineteenth or twentieth century. Regarding the travels of Mistral and the two poets he cites, neither Mistral nor Chailan ever travelled to the Americas; in the case of Peise (born/died Toulon, 1820-1878) I can find no detailed biography. That said, the possibility of 'jambalaya' being re-introduced to Provence from Louisiana remains but I will treat that question in detail elsewhere.
4. For the dialect of Toulon, see Arnoux 1940; for Nice, see Compan 1967: 125; for Menton, see Andrews 1995. Another relatively recent reference to 'jambalaia' from Provence is in Jouveau (1990: 140), a work focussing on the traditional cookery of the region, but it is difficult to assess the status of the word in the author's personal knowledge of Provençal: he offers a traditional recipe with chicken that is without doubt closely related to Louisiana's dish but he sets the name off in quotation marks, indicating it is Provençal, but it is not clear whether this particular name for the dish was retrieved, as it were, from Mistral. Nonetheless, the traditional recipe he gives, in the context of our general discussion, is suggestive.
5. Compan's work is a thematic word list, not a dictionary, and details given are few, but in the case of *jambalaia*, he adds parenthetically and rather cryptically '*(la ratatouille frite)*'. Given the context, it seems clear he is not referring to the summer vegetable stew here but rather uses the word 'ratatouille' in its old pejorative sense of a bad stew, a stew of leftovers or offal.
6. It is not wholly clear why the initial vowel in this form appears as *i* rather than *a*: it may be the result of a purely lexical influence/reanalysis or it may be the result of a minor phonological change. More study of the dialect is required but one notes that in the same dictionary, the name of a ring-shaped pastry appears as *jhimbëlêto* from It. *ciambella* (cf. Prov. *gimbeleto, jambeleto*, Fr. *gimblette*). The complex suffix has as first element a variant of the one in 'jamb**a**laya', namely *el*; the second suffix, *ot-*, is common, typically with diminutive force. Note that in Occitan/Provençal, many but not all dialects have undergone a regular sound change of unstressed final *a > o*; some orthographical systems reflect this change, others do not, hence the variation in forms cited here. Noteworthy is the inclusion here

of leftover meat (ambiguously as addition or alternative) which puts this dish in the category of a 'bad stew' (commonly also referred to in old sources as *ratatouia/ratatouille*).
7. For example, Bloch 1900: 21, in reference to famine in the mid-eighteenth century: 'À *défaut de pain, c'est avec du riz qu'on assure la subsistance des habitants*.'
8. Heller 1996: 73: 'Grain yields normally did not exceed 5 or 6:1 anywhere in France. Because rice culture can produce yields of up to 40:1, the cultivation of rice was increasing rapidly in Provence according to Quiqueran de Beaujeu [writing in 1551].' Buc'hoz (1770: 158) comments on the current cultivation of rice in Languedoc and Provence, but shortly thereafter, Bouche (1785: 5) laments the French government's elimination of Provence's rice fields, 'more beautiful than those of Piemonte' and the former source of 'considerable commerce'.
9. Literally 'short soup', with 'short' referring to the lack of liquid in the final product. Chanot-Bullier 1988: 74: '*La soupo courto n'es pas uno soupo, mai un fricot*' ['a *soupo courto* is not a soup but a stew']; the recipe offered there is stretched with pasta.
10. The 1770 poetic text refers fondly to '*rougnounado en de ris*' (Le Sage 1636: 16). *Soupo courto* is glossed as '*terme de pasticie* [involving pasta] *Potage d'Abatis*' by Pellas 1723: 65. Achard's (1785), Azaïs's (1876) and Mistral's (1879-1866) dictionaries also gloss *soupo courto* as a dish of *abatis*.
11. Many recipes demonstrating the range of ingredients used are available online in French. A readily available recipe in English can be found in Conran 2012: 201; her version uses chicken wings and giblets and is a fairly typical one, though it does not include any pork products.

References

Achard, Claude-François. 1785. *Dictionnaire de la Provence et du Comté-Vanaissin* (Marseille: Mossy).
Adams, Edward L. 1913. *Word-Formation in Provençal* (New York: Macmillan).
Anderson, E.N. 2009. 'African Influences on Maya Foods', Society for Economic Botany annual conference, Charleston, SC <http://www.krazykioti.com/articles/maya-ethnobotany-four-studies/> [accessed 15 May 2016].
Andrews, Colman. 1995. 'Please, Hold the Jerusalem Artichokes', *Los Angeles Times* <http://articles.latimes.com/1995-10-05/food/fo-53381_1_jerusalem-artichoke> [accessed 15 May 2016].
Arnoux, Carle. 1940. *Breviàri dóu gènt parla prouvençau* (Toulon) <http://www.cieldoc.com/libre/integral/libro347.pdf> [accessed 15 May 2016].
Azaïs, Gabriel. 1876. *Dictionnaire des idiomes romans du midi de la France, Vol 2* (Paris: Maisonneuve).
Bloch, Camille. 1900. *Études sur l'histoire économique de la France (1760-1789)* (Paris: Picard).
Bouche, Charles-François. 1785. *Essai sur l'histoire de Provence* (Marseille: Mossy).
Brasseaux, Carl A. 2005. *French, Cajun, Creole, Houma. A Primer on Francophone Louisiana* (Baton Rouge: Louisiana State University Press).
Buccini, Anthony F. 2006. 'Western Mediterranean Vegetable Stews and the Integration of Culinary Exotica', in Richard Hosking (ed.), *Authenticity in the Kitchen. Proceedings of the Oxford Symposium on Food and Cookery 2005*, 132-145 (Totnes, Devon: Prospect).
_____. 2013. 'Lasagna: A Layered History', in Mark McWilliams (ed.), *Stuffed and Wrapped: Proceedings of the Oxford Symposium on Food and Cookery 2012*, 94-104 (Totnes, Devon: Prospect).
_____. 2015. 'The Merchants of Genoa and the Diffusion of Pasta Culture in Southern Europe', in Mark McWilliams (ed.), *Food and Markets: Proceedings of the Oxford Symposium on Food and Cookery 2014*, 54-64 (Totnes, Devon: Prospect).
_____. 2016a. 'From *Kongri* to *Diri ak Djondjon*: Slavery, Creolisation and Culinary Genesis in Saint-Domingue and Independent Haiti', Dublin Gastronomy Symposium, May, 2016 <http://arrow.dit.ie/dgs/2016/May31/20/>.
_____. 2016b. 'Defining "Cuisine": Communication, Culinary Grammar, and the Typology of Cuisine',

in Mark McWilliams (ed.), *Food and Communication: Proceedings of the Oxford Symposium 2015*, 105-121 (Totnes, Devon: Prospect).
Buc'hoz, Pierre-Joseph. 1770. *Dictionnaire universel des plantes, arbres et arbustes de la France, Vol. 3* (Paris: Lacombe).
Chanot-Bullier, Calixtine. 1988 [1966]. *Vieilles recettes de cuisine provençale* (Marseille: Tacussel).
Compan, André. 1967. *Glossaire raisonné de la langue niçoise* (Nice: Tiranty).
Conran, Caroline. 2012. *Sud de France: The Food and Cooking of Languedoc* (Totnes, Devon: Prospect).
Davidson, Alan. 2002. *The Penguin Companion to Food* (Harmondsworth: Penguin).
de Sauvages, Pierre Augustin Boissier. 1756. *Dictionnaire languedocien-françois, Vol. 2* (Nimes: Michel Gaude).
Dessens, Nathalie. 2005. 'From Saint Domingue to Louisiana', in Bradley G. Bond (ed.), *French Colonial Louisiana and the Atlantic World*, 244-264 (Baton Rouge: Louisiana State University Press).
Erman, Anna and Japhet Kahouye Loh, (eds.). 2008. *Dictionnaire Dan-Français (Dan de l'Ouest)* (N.P.: MeaBooks).
Fertel, Rien. 2007. 'Jambalaya', in Andrew F. Smith (ed.), *The Oxford Companion to American Food and Drink*, 325 (Oxford: Oxford University Press).
Hall, Gwendolyn Midlo. 1992. *Africans in Colonial Louisiana: The Development of Afro-Creole Culture in the Eighteenth Century* (Baton Rouge: Louisiana State University Press).
Heller, Henry. 1996. *Labour, science and technology in France, 1500-1620* (Cambridge: Cambridge University Press).
Hess, Karen. 1992. *The Carolina Rice Kitchen: The African Connection* (Columbia, S.C.: University of South Carolina Press).
Honnorat, Simon-Jude. 1846-1847. *Dictionnaire Provençal-Français* (3 vol.) (Digne: Repos).
Jouveau, René. 1990. *La cuisine provençale de tradition populaire* (Aix: Paul Roubaud).
Le Sage, Daniel. 1636. *Les Folies du Sieur Le Sage*. Montpellier: Jean Pech.
Mistral, Frédéric. 1979 [1879-1886]. *Lou trésor dóu Felibrige ou dictionnaire provençal-francais (vol. 2, G-Z)* (Barcelona: Marcel Petit).
Mufwene, Salikoko S. 1996. 'The Founder Principle in Creole Genesis', *Diachronica* 13: 83-134.
Pellas, Sauveur-André. 1723. *Dictionnaire provençal et françois* (Avignon: Offray).
Read, William A. 1933. Review of Jay Ditchy, *Les Acadiens Louisianais et Leur Parler. Zeitschrift für französische Sprache und Literatur* 57: 365-75.
Sigal, Andrew. 2007. 'Jambalaya by Any Other Name', *Petits Propos Culinaires* 84: 101-19.
_____. 2008. 'Jambalaya: History, Origins and Etymology, <http://www.sigal.org/culinaryhistory/jambalaya/jambalaya.htm> [accessed 20 April 2016]:.
Valdman, Albert and others (eds.). 1998. *Dictionary of Louisiana Creole* (Bloomington: Indiana University Press).
Whitehead, Jessup. 1889. *The Steward's Handbook and Guide to Party Catering* (Chicago).
Wikipedia contributors. 'Jambalaya', *Wikipedia* <https://en.wikipedia.org/wiki/Jambalaya> [accessed 31 July 2016].

The Three Great 'Rare Tastes' in Japanese Culinary History: Sea Cucumber Entrails, Sea Urchin Gonads and Mullet Roe

Voltaire Cang

Throughout its history, Japan has had the tradition of designating the 'three great' or 'three best' representatives of certain categories of people, places, events and things, including food. Among the better known are its 'three great heroes', the warrior lords Oda Nobunaga, Toyotomi Hideyoshi and Tokugawa Ieyasu, and the 'three great cities' of Tokyo, Osaka and Nagoya.[1] Many of the designations, however, are arbitrary and lack scientific support, and only a few are backed by historical evidence or official authority. The food categories especially are subject to disagreement and controversy, such as the 'three best ramen dishes' consisting of Sapporo ramen (Hokkaido), Hakata ramen (Fukuoka), and Kitakata ramen (Fukushima) or the 'three great *wagyū* [Japanese beef]' from Kobe, Matsuzaka, and Omi. Nonetheless, the 'three great rare tastes' [*sandai-chinmi*] comprising sea cucumber entrails [*konowata*], sea urchin gonads [*uni*], and mullet roe [*karasumi*] have been lodged in their positions for centuries and are widely accepted.[2] Aside from being public knowledge from at least the Edo Period (from 1603 to 1868), the triumvirate of rare tastes currently enjoys official recognition from Japan's Ministry of Agriculture, Forestry and Fisheries (MAFF).[3]

The 'three great rare tastes' in Japan form the main theme of this paper. Particular focus is paid to *konowata* and *uni*, not only because of their status as marine 'offal' that is relevant to the current context, but also because of the relatively scarce amount of information and research in English available on the culinary history of these two food items, especially *konowata*.

Konowata: Origins
The Japanese language term *konowata* literally translates into 'entrails [*wata*] of [*no*] the sea cucumber [*ko*]'. The sea cucumber itself is commonly called *namako* [*nama*=fresh/raw], whether in its raw, cooked or dried form, although the proper term for dried sea cucumbers is *iriko* [*iri*=desiccated]. Until recently and still in some fishing communities in Japan, the sea cucumber is simply referred to as *ko*. There are two main theses on the etymology: first, *ko* means 'small' in Japanese, and could refer to the sea cucumber's tendency to shrink considerably after processing into food or medicine. Second, *ko* could also have come from the crunching sound (*kori-kori*) made when chewing the cartilage-like sea cucumber.[4]

Offal: Rejected and Reclaimed Food

The sea cucumber is an ancient marine animal that has been utilized for traditional medicine and consumed in diets mainly in the Asia-Pacific region for more than a millennium, particularly in China. In Japan, the sea cucumber is accorded an anecdote in the *Kojiki* [Record of Ancient Matters] (c. 711), the nation's oldest extant chronicle of history and mythology: the goddess-deity of the dawn and mirth, *Ame-no-Uzume-no-Mikoto*, displeased because the sea cucumber does not reply to her command for all sea creatures to become her subjects, is prompted to cut off its mouth with her sword, resulting in its ridged, nearly invisible mouth today.[5] In more mundane historical records of the same era, the sea cucumber appears simply as food: dried sea cucumber is listed among the delicacies that were regularly offered to the court in Nara as tributes from Noto Province (now part of Ishikawa Prefecture along the Sea of Japan), beginning from the year 732 in the Nara Period (from 710 to 794).[6] *Iriko* or dried sea cucumber is also cited in the *Izumi Fūdoki*, a gazette completed circa 733 that describes Izumi Province (presently Shimane Prefecture) and also lists several sea cucumber food processing communities located in the region.[7]

Sea cucumber entrails, that is, *konowata*, would appear in historical records more than a century later, during the Heian Period (from 794 to 1192) after the capital was moved from Nara to Kyoto. Like the dried sea cucumber, *konowata* came to be listed among the tributes or taxes specified by the imperial government to be exacted from Noto Province, first appearing in the *Engishiki* [Procedures of the Engi Era], the compilation of laws and regulations completed in 927.[8] In these ancient regulations, Noto Province was designated as the sole official source for *konowata* tributes to the court.

Ishikawa Prefecture, particularly its northern Noto Peninsula region, is still a major producer of *konowata* today. Indeed, *konowata* is considered a valuable, top-quality specialty of the prefecture, although there are many who dispute Noto's status as the 'best' producer of the entrails.[9] Perhaps the strongest dissenters are from Aichi Prefecture who have formed a 'rare tastes' [*chinmi*] cooperative and often cite a scholarly guide to local seafood published in 1831, *Uo kagami*, that declares *konowata* from Mikawa Province (presently the eastern half of Aichi Prefecture) as the best of all. Other sources including academic articles cite references that describe Aichi Prefecture's western half, the former Owari Province, as producers of *konowata* that are the 'finest under heaven'.[10] Government authority, however, defers from directly identifying the producers of the 'best' *konowata*. In its description of Japan's 'three great rare tastes', although MAFF specifically identifies the best sea urchin (from Echizen in Fukui Prefecture in the west) and declares Nagasaki Prefecture alone as the prime producer of mullet roe in the country, it divides the honour for sea cucumber entrails, referring to Noto (Ishikawa Prefecture) and Owari and Mikawa (both in Aichi Prefecture) as 'historically important centres' for *konowata* production.[11]

In any case, by the seventeenth century in Japan, as dried sea cucumber had already become a valuable export commodity to the Asian continent, many fishing communities from Kyushu in the south to Hokkaido in the north were already actively engaged in sea cucumber fishing and processing.[12] High-quality *konowata* was readily available in many of these areas, though these were processed solely for domestic consumption and enjoyed almost exclusively by the aristocratic and political elite.

Nonetheless, *konowata* has long been identified with Noto Province since ancient times. It was indeed a vital food product for the governing authorities, not simply for economic or even nutritional sustenance, but more so for its political utility. *Konowata* was already an officially regulated form of tribute from the province to the imperial rulers in Kyoto from at least the tenth century, and it became even more important in the years when Noto was governed by the Hatakeyama clan from 1408 to 1577. The clan largely depended on *konowata* gifts to the imperial court in return for the court's patronage and protection; at the same time, *konowata* helped sustain the lives of many communities in the province.

Historical records of tributes paid to Kyoto from Noto, wherever available, indicate large amounts of *konowata* offered to the imperial court during critical periods in Noto's history. For example, in the years immediately after the Onin War, the bitterly fought civil war that involved the shogunate in Kyoto and several provincial lords in the nation, more than twenty times the usual volume of *konowata* was offered to the shogunate by then lord Hatakeyama Yoshimune. Yoshimune had recently been installed as the third-generation lord of Noto despite some members of his clan having fought alongside the opponents of the Kyoto government. To regain the shogun's favour and obtain forgiveness, Yoshimune exclusively gifted him with large amounts of *konowata* beginning in the year 1477 when the Onin War ended and then almost every year thereafter. Invariably included among his annual offering of the entrails was the 'first harvest of *konowata*' [*hatsu konowata*], the most symbolic and, therefore, valuable from the season's produce.[13]

Succeeding lords of the Hatakeyama clan continued to pay *konowata* tributes to the rulers in Kyoto as it had already become a favoured delicacy among the aristocratic and political elite for its rarity and distinctive taste. The Hatakeyama clan's control of *konowata* production in Noto was efficiently channelled into shogunate patronage, allowing the clan to establish and consolidate authority over the province for nearly two centuries. It was also able to promote development in Noto, so that by the mid-sixteenth century and into the seventh generation of Hatakeyama lordship, Noto Province, notably its *konowata*-producing areas, was frequently described as rich and thriving and with a continually growing population.[14]

Konowata: Production

The author recently conducted a research-survey on the production process of sea cucumber entrails in Ishikawa Prefecture, formerly Noto Province. The survey entailed a visit to the city of Nanao, the old provincial capital and one of the most historically important sea cucumber fishing and production centres in early modern Japan. Nanao is still known as a major producer of *konowata*, and its production methods

Offal: Rejected and Reclaimed Food

from fishing all the way to final product packaging have not changed much over the centuries. Results of the survey are summarized briefly below. (All data in the following section are from the survey unless otherwise indicated.)

Under the law, sea cucumber commercial fishing in Ishikawa Prefecture is limited to the winter season, officially from November to March in the next year. Sea cucumbers thrive in both deep and shallow waters and generally live on the seafloor, subsisting on whatever they manage to scavenge in the sand. They are found in great numbers in the shallow waters of the Noto Peninsula, where they are caught by dredge nets and occasionally by deep-sea women divers [*ama*]. In Nanao, the total daily catch amounts to two metric tons (2000 kilograms) on average (Figure 1).

Figure 1
The port in Nanao; sea cucumber fishing boats are docked for the day.

Figure 2
Net enclosures for harvested sea cucumbers.

Figure 3
Removing the innards.

Caught sea cucumbers are moved to a net enclosure located near the shore dock where they remain for one to three days as they purge scavenged debris from inside their systems (Figure 2). After they have cleaned themselves, the creatures are then brought to the auction house for purchase by the commercial producers, then transferred to factories for processing. Most of the factories are located in the same dock area where the fishing boats are moored and the daily auctions take place.

Konowata processing is all done manually. The only tool is a short knife, which is used to make a small incision (about one centimetre) in the underside of the sea cucumber close to its mouth, from which seawater is drained and the innards extracted by hand (Figure 3). The emptied sea cucumbers are dried and processed into *iriko* for export, mostly to China (Figure 4). The innards are then examined and sorted according to their quality and final use: *konowata* (entrails proper), *ni-ban wata* ['number two' entrails] (second-class *konowata*), gonads, and extraneous internal organs and debris (Figure 5).

Figure 4
Sea cucumbers before (left) and after (right, deflated) processing.

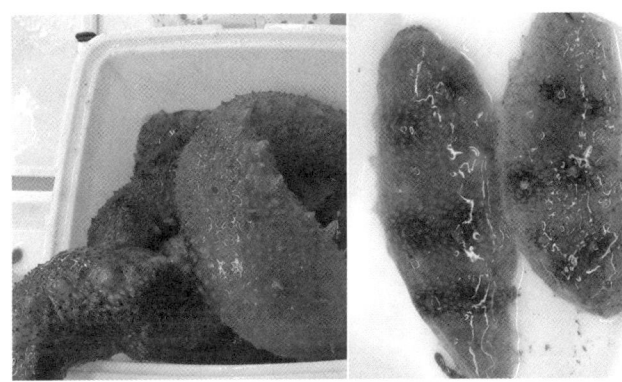

Figure 5
Sorting the innards.

Figure 6
Kuchiko drying in the sun.

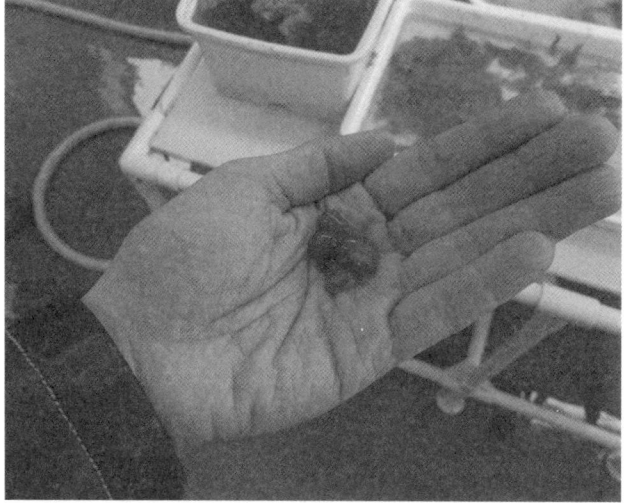

Figure 7
Sea cucumber entrails.

The gonads are processed into *kuchiko*, another type of *chinmi* 'rare taste' from sea cucumber. *Kuchiko* amount to a very small percentage of the harvest, with only 100 grams of dried gonads produced per ton of sea cucumber. Dried *kuchiko* are easily recognizable for their shape (little inverted triangles, said to come from the form of traditional *shamisen* guitar picks) and colour (a deep orange that is the result of drying for about three weeks in the sun) (Figure 6).[15] At present, a 12-gram morsel of *kuchiko* sells for 2000 Japanese yen (£15) retail, corresponding to about 170 yen (£1.25) per gram (as of July 2016).

The Three Great 'Rare Tastes' in Japanese Culinary History

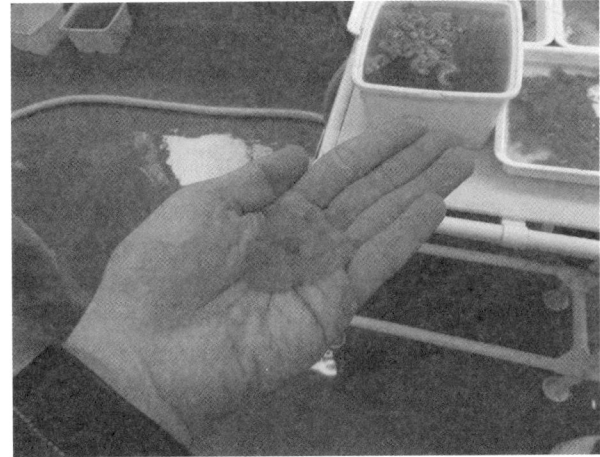

Figure 8
Sea cucumber gonads.

Figure 9
Konowata ready to eat.

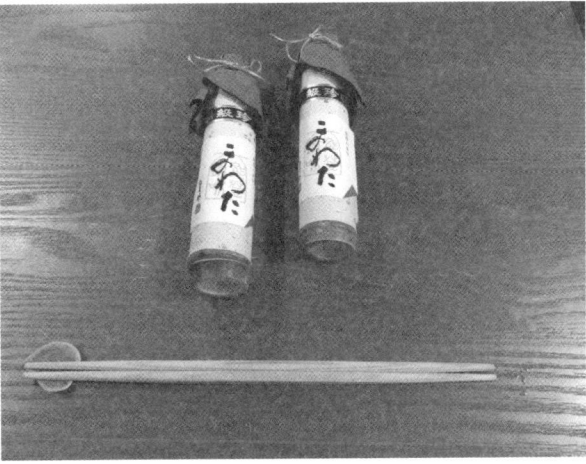

Figure 10
Bamboo tubes containing konowata.

Although from the same insides of the sea cucumber, *konowata* has a less appetizing colour – green-grey with a yellow-orange hue – and an even less desirable appearance than *kuchiko*, both pre- and post-processing (Figures 7, 8, and 9). After the entrails are sorted from other innards, they are washed, drained and then fermented in sea salt for three days on average. They turn into a slightly brighter colour during fermentation, after which they are packed into green bamboo tubes, the traditional containers for *konowata*, or small glass jars, a late twentieth-century novelty (Figure 10). *Konowata* are sometimes sold in small pail-shaped wooden containers; though traditional, these are no longer as common as bamboo or glass.

About 100 grams of entrails are extracted from five kilograms of sea cucumbers on average, which amounts to 200 times more than the volume of *kuchiko* that may be processed from gonads.[16] There is more intestine than gonad in sea cucumbers, needless to say, and because the entrails are not dried, *konowata* do not lose as much volume during processing. *Konowata* have a very brief shelf life, however – three days with refrigeration or up to six months frozen. (Like most food products, freezing considerably diminishes the taste of *konowata*, and producers prefer to sell them refrigerated.) The short shelf life is the prime reason for *konowata*'s rarity and high price: 25 grams – a tablespoon's worth – retail for about 1000 yen (£7.50), approximately 40 yen (£0.30) per gram in the current market (July 2016).

Konowata as Food in Japan

Konowata is the least consumed among the three 'great rare tastes'. In Japan, the sea urchin [*uni*] is a familiar form of sushi, while mullet roe [*karasumi*] is eaten regularly – relatively, that is – as appetizers or used as an ingredient in pasta dishes served in restaurants as well as in the home. Japan's largest and most popular recipe website lists 284 recipes for mullet roe, 179 alone for mullet roe pasta. *Uni* merits 572 different recipes. *Konowata*, however, is found in only one recipe, in which the entrails are not even used for the dish, but mentioned as a by-product obtained through the preparation of fresh sea cucumbers.[17] The big disparity in recipe numbers reflect the variety of ways mullet roe and *uni* are actually consumed, in contrast to *konowata* which is almost always eaten in one manner only – as is, raw though slightly fermented. The three rare tastes also differ greatly in terms of availability: whereas both *uni* and mullet roe are easily preserved and are regularly imported in big quantities so that they are found in many retail supermarkets and specialty shops all over Japan, very little *konowata* is produced – and may only be produced – domestically and only in the winter season, with most of it bought directly from producers for immediate consumption.

As food, *konowata* is often categorized as a type of *shiokara*, defined as 'preserved foodstuff made from fish, crustacean, squid, shellfish or sometimes fowl meat into which salt amounting to about thirty per cent of its volume has been added and which is stored for a long period in a watertight container'.[18] Most *shiokara* include the viscera of the marine animal that is fermented together with its meat; the most common variety in Japan is squid [*ika-no-shiokara*]. Today, *shiokara* is consumed frequently as an accompaniment to alcohol, especially *sake*, and is sometimes used as flavouring for fresh salads, noodles, cooked vegetables and other foods. Until the mid-twentieth century in Japan *shiokara* was considered a dish by itself that was convenient for the meal table: it did not require cooking and tiny portions were enough to accompany big servings of rice and other grains that made for a filling meal.[19]

Konowata is also consumed like other *shiokara*, that is, as a *sake* accompaniment, but it is unique from most *shiokara* that are actually stored for many months or even years. In this sense *konowata* is not 'preserved foodstuff' per se. *Konowata* is also unique from other *shiokara* for its singular role in Japanese culinary history: aside from having been a beloved delicacy among the aristocratic and warrior elite for centuries, *konowata* was an important component in the meals of Sen Rikyu (from 1522 to 1591), the historical figure who is widely acknowledged to have revolutionized Japanese eating habits through his innovation of *kaiseki*, the Japanese meal form and concept that is considered 'the defining feature of culinary "Japaneseness"'.[20]

Rikyu is better known as the man who established the Way of Tea tradition (i.e. 'tea ceremony'), and during his lifetime he held hundreds of tea gatherings where meals were offered before the ritualized tea service. Details of his gatherings including menus were noted down in diaries and published several decades after his death as records called *chakaiki* [literally, 'records of tea gatherings']. One such record, the *Matsuya kaiki*, is the oldest of its kind and contains meal menus served by Rikyu and other hosts in a series of tea gatherings. The record details gatherings held during a period spanning almost 120 years, from 1533 to 1650.[21]

Sixteen menus by Rikyu are recorded in the *Matsuya kaiki*. The following menu, served on the nineteenth day of the first month (around mid-February in the current calendar) of 1583, has been called the most 'representative' of his meals and is cited by different food authors as *kaiseki* in its most fundamental form:

Soup	Vegetables and quail
Dish 1	Sea bream
Dish 2	*Konowata*
Dish 3	*Dengaku* [Vegetable, fish or tofu, with sweetened miso]

(After-meal sweets for tea)[22]

The menu is of the 'one-soup-and-three-side-dishes' pattern [*ichi-jū-san-sai*] that constitutes the basic structure of *kaiseki*.[23] It is spare for one important reason: Rikyu is reported to have wanted to break with the increasingly lavish feasting practices of his time, thereby creating a 'revolution in Japanese cuisine' that also 'changed the course of culinary history'.[24] This early and simple composition of *kaiseki* is considered one of the primary meal patterns, if not the most basic structure of the meal itself, in Japanese food culture.²⁵

Though Rikyu is often acknowledged as the chief proponent of simple *kaiseki*, the form did not derive from him; the same meal structure appeared much earlier and was sometimes illustrated in scroll paintings that depict the lifestyles of ancient Japanese. One such illustration is found in the *Yamaisōshi* [Scroll of Diseases and Deformities] (c. mid-twelfth century), in a mealtime scene where a man is opening his mouth wide to show his rotting teeth to a woman, presumably his wife. The man's meal has been placed in front of him but is still uneaten; it clearly shows a bowl of rice served with one soup and three side dishes.²⁶

In Rikyu's prototype meal above, *konowata* constitutes one proper course which alone would already have fully complemented the rice and soup. Compared to the other two main dishes, *konowata* would not have required any cooking or any other kind of preparation, either – it would have been served as is, tasting thoroughly of the sea. *Konowata* is a very simple yet complete dish that not only symbolizes emphatically the simplicity in meals that Rikyu was said to have aspired after, it also illustrates two other cardinal rules for his *kaiseki* and all *kaiseki* meals in the centuries thereafter: one, that the elements of the meal must be appropriate to the season and, two, that the meal be flavoured naturally, that is, subtly and simply. Indeed, these two rules are cardinal to the idea of Japanese cooking and food service in general.²⁷

(It bears noting that this particular *kaiseki* meal was served in midwinter, which is the season when *konowata* is exclusively processed and is at its best. In Japanese literature, the term *namako* or sea cucumber is a literary metaphor, called a 'seasonal term' in Japanese prose and poetry tradition, that is used to signify the winter season.)

Kaiseki in present-day Japan, however, has since been transformed into an elaborate eating style that no longer retains the simplicity of Rikyu's prototype.²⁸ Rikyu nonetheless remains a legitimizing force in the Japanese tea tradition as well as in the nation's culinary history, so that many influential chefs and proponents of *kaiseki* continue to trace the origins of their cooking style and food service to Rikyu despite its transformation into an extravagant cuisine at the opposite end of the style endorsed by its 'founding father'.²⁹ Many *kaiseki* chefs and restaurateurs continue to include *konowata* in their menus as well: aside from being a rare and conveniently expensive addition to the restaurant course meal, *konowata* functions as a legitimizing link to Rikyu's prototype *kaiseki*.

Uni: A Brief Discussion

Uni is frequently translated as sea urchin roe; the English term is very common and is always used in restaurant menus and found in scholarly literature as well. More properly – scientifically, that is – *uni* are sea urchin gonads. Sushi diners know *uni* and are familiar with their yellow-orange colour and rich taste, but not many are likely aware that these are actually the sea animal's 'ovaries and testes with immature germ cells'.³⁰

Uni has been consumed as food in Japan since prehistoric times, and shell mounds

The Three Great 'Rare Tastes' in Japanese Culinary History

from the Jomon Era (from c. 12000 to 300 BCE) have yielded large deposits of fossilized *uni* shells from various archaeological sites in the country, mostly in the northern Tohoku and Hokkaido regions.[31] *Uni* has also been written about in ancient texts: the earliest mention of the sea urchin as food is found in the annotated version of the Yōro Code of laws (promulgated in 757) called the *Ryō-no-gige* (dated 833), which includes it in the list of tributary offerings designated for the imperial court.[32] A recipe for *uni* has also been discovered in similar court documents from the same period: it calls for slices of abalone to be mixed with *uni* and flavoured with sea salt, then stored for a few days before serving.[33] (Incidentally, sea urchins and sea cucumbers belong to the same phylum of marine animals called echinoderms, which also include starfish and sea lilies.)

Although *uni* has been consumed for several thousand years in Japan, it became a popular food only in the decades after World War II. *Uni* had been harvested in many areas of the country, but it was difficult to transport the products fast and fresh, and the demand, whether for the fresh or the salt-preserved kind, always far outstripped the domestic supply. Until the mid-twentieth century, most of the Japanese populace ate *uni* only on special occasions and almost always in its preserved form; they were also offered as (expensive) gifts during such occasions.[34]

It was only in the 1950s when Japan's economic rise allowed it to import *uni* in huge volumes that it became more readily available in markets and sushi restaurants. The 1950s also coincides with the period when *kaiten-zushi* ['conveyor belt' sushi] shops began operating in Japan, with *uni* becoming a regular component in the menus of such shops from the early years. Aside from sushi, *uni* is eaten as a topping for rice (*uni-don*, or *uni* on rice in a bowl, is a perennial favourite) or in vegetable and other seafood dishes. It is also eaten as *shiokara*, the aforementioned preserved foodstuff that accompanies *sake*. Presently, the Japanese are the world's biggest *uni* consumers, gobbling up more than eighty per cent of the world's production. (The French are a far second.)[35]

Uni was named one of the 'three great rare tastes' during the Edo Period under the Tokugawa shogunate. Together with the other two delicacies, it was highly valued not only for its taste, but more so because it was produced in very small quantities, so that the best – and frequently almost all the harvest – was regularly offered to the shoguns as tributes and gifts. Since sea urchin from Echizen Province (now Fukui Prefecture) was particularly rare, the Tokugawa shoguns proclaimed Echizen *uni* as one of the 'three great rare tastes under heaven', alongside the equally rare *konowata* from Owari and *karasumi* [mullet roe] from Nagasaki.[36] Echizen *uni* is still rare today: twenty other prefectures in Japan produce more *uni* than Fukui, and the total harvest (21 tons) amounts to less than one per cent to that of the top producer, Hokkaido (6,541).[37] Rare taste, indeed.

Conclusion

Exactly when and how the 'three great rare tastes' came to be is unclear; there is no existing scholarly work on the subject, and almost none even for the more general food category that is *chinmi* ['rare tastes']. Nonetheless, *chinmi* is a popular topic in hundreds of books and websites on Japanese food, with many acknowledging the *konowata-uni-karasumi* triumvirate as the 'greatest' of all rare tastes. The three are also recognized by public authority, including the Ministry of Agriculture, Forestry and Fisheries as indicated earlier, as well as by the Japan Food Industry Association. Although most books and websites on *chinmi* point to the ruling Tokugawa shogunate and sometimes the Japanese public in the Edo Period as the first proponents of the idea of the 'three great rare tastes', none cite supporting sources; this may be a starting point of inquiry for further study.

This paper has attempted to provide a prolegomenon to research on the three 'great' *chinmi*, although it has limited the discussion to sea cucumber entrails and, briefly, to sea urchin gonads in light of the current symposium context on offal. The fact that all 'three great rare tastes' happen to be marine products indicate the importance of seafood to the Japanese diet. The roles played especially by the two marine 'offal' – *konowata* and *uni* – in Japanese food culture further emphasize such importance, as well as the great influence they have exerted in Japanese history, culinary and otherwise.

Notes

1. All Japanese personal names in the main text are written in the conventional order, that is, surname (Oda) first, followed by the given name (Nobunaga).
2. *San*三=three; *dai*大=great; *chin*珍=rare; *mi*味=taste. *Chinmi*, literally 'rare taste', is officially defined as 'a food product usually from a marine animal that has been specially processed to bring out its particular taste' by the National Business Federation of *Chinmi* Industries, or Zenchinren, in Japan. See Akira Shimizu, '*Chinmi* (Lecture)', *Science of Cookery*, 4.1 (1971), pp. 32-38 (in Japanese).
3. See <http://www.maff.go.jp/j/heya/sodan/1601/01.html> (in Japanese).
4. *Nihon kokugo daijiten* [Comprehensive Dictionary of the Japanese National Language], ed. by *Nihon daijiten kankokai* [Japan comprehensive dictionary publishing association] (Tokyo: Shogakukan, 1974), vol. 7, p. 376.
5. Yoshiyuki Tsurumi, *Namako* [Sea Cucumber], ed. H. Nakamura (Tokyo: Misuzu Shobo, 1999), p. 248.
6. Kojiro Kakiuchi and Yukei Kigoshi, '*Noto no namako seisan to shokuyō bunkashi no kenkyū* [Research on Sea Cucumber Production in Noto and Its Cultural History as Food]', *Archaeological Bulletin Kanazawa University*, 33 (2012), pp. 63-82, p. 71.
7. Tsurumi, *Namako*, p. 248.
8. The National Institute of Japanese Literature database, <http://base1.nijl.ac.jp/~kojiruien/inshokubu/frame/f000946.html> (in Japanese).
9. Matsunosuke Nishiyama (ed.), *Tabemono no nihonshi sōran* [Comprehensive History of Food in Japan] (Tokyo: Shinjinbutsu Oraisha, 1994).
10. See <http://www.chinmi.net/pages/museum/history/history10.html#6-1>(in Japanese).
11. See <http://www.maff.go.jp/j/heya/sodan/1601/01.html> (in Japanese).
12. Jun Akamine, 'The Status of the Sea Cucumber Fisheries and Trade in Japan: Past and Present', in A. Lovatelli, C. Conand, S. Purcell, S. Uthicke, J. F. Hamel, and A. Mercier (eds.), *Advances in Sea Cucumber Aquaculture and Management* (FAO fisheries and aquaculture technical paper no. 463) (Rome: FAO, 2004).
13. Kakiuchi and Kigoshi, p. 75.
14. Kakiuchi and Kigoshi, p. 77.

15. *Kuchi* means mouth in Japanese. The gonads are removed from the opening near the mouth of the sea cucumber [*ko*], hence the name *kuchiko*.
16. Figures are the industry average.
17. *Cookpad*, <http://cookpad.com/recipe/245597> (in Japanese).
18. Naomichi Ishige, *Nihon no shokubunkashi* [History of Japanese Food Culture] (Tokyo: Iwanami Shoten, 2015), p. 35. An English translation of this work, *The History and Culture of Japanese Food* (London: Kegan Paul, 2001) was published earlier, which has since been protested by Ishige. In the preface to his recent work in Japanese (the former volume), Ishige asserts that the English edition was published without his corrections or approval and that he has not received royalties as its original author. The definition of *shiokara* in this paper was translated by this author from the Japanese language work and is slightly different from the translation given in the English volume.
19. Ishige, p. 44.
20. Katarzyna Cwiertka, *Modern Japanese Cuisine: Food, Power and National Identity* (London: Reaktion Books, 2006), p. 109. Rikyu is also transcribed as Rikyū in some texts. (This paper avoids the use of macrons representing long vowel sounds for proper names.) There is some dispute concerning Rikyu's actual role in establishing *kaiseki*. See Eric C. Rath, 'Reevaluating Rikyū: Kaiseki and the Origins of Japanese Cuisine', *Journal of Japanese Studies*, 39.1 (2013), pp. 67-96.
21. Soshitsu Sen (ed.), *Matsuya kaiki*, *Chadō koten zenshū* [Complete Anthology of Ancient Texts in the Way of Tea], vol. 9 (Kyoto: Tankosha, 1958).
22. Hiroichi Tsutsui, *Kaiseki no kenkyū* [Research on *kaiseki*] (Kyoto: Tankosha, 2002), pp. 98-99.
23. Nobuo Harada, *Washoku to nihon bunka* [Japanese Food and Japanese Culture] (Tokyo: Shogakukan, 2005), pp. 93-94.
24. Isao Kumakura, 'Tea and Japan's Culinary Revolution', *Japan Echo*, 26.2 (1999), pp. 43-62, p. 43.
25. Isao Kumakura, *Nihon ryōri no rekishi* [History of Japanese Cuisine] (Tokyo: Yoshikawa Kobunkan, 2007), p. 29.
26. Kumakura, *Nihon ryōri no rekishi*, pp. 27-30. This specific illustration is viewable online at the digital archives of the Kyoto National Museum: <http://www.kyohaku.go.jp/jp/syuzou/meihin/emaki/item04.html>.
27. Shizuo Tsuji, *Japanese Cooking: A Simple Art* (Tokyo: Kodansha International, 2012).
28. Yoshihiro Murata, *Kaiseki: The Exquisite Cuisine of Kyoto's Kikunoi Restaurant* (Tokyo: Kodansha International, 2006).
29. Cwiertka, p. 110.
30. Yukio Yokota, 'Fishery and Consumption of the Sea Urchin in Japan', in Yukio Yokota, Valeria Matranga and Zuzana Smolenicka (eds.), *The Sea Urchin: From Basic Biology to Aquaculture* (Lisse, The Netherlands: A. A. Balkema, 2002), pp. 129-138, p. 129.
31. Ryuzaburo Takahashi, Takeji Toizumi and Yasushi Kojo, 'Archaeological Studies of Japan: Current studies of the Jomon Archaeology', *Journal of the Japanese Archaeological Association* 5 (1998), pp. 47-72.
32. Kazuhiro Kawamura, '*Hokkaido ni okeru uni gyogyō to shigen kanri* [Sea Urchin Fisheries and Resource Management in Hokkaido], *Journal of the Hokkaido Fisheries Scientific Institution* 26 (1969), pp. 608–637.
33. Yokota, p. 129.
34. Yokota, p. 130.
35. N. L. Andrew and others, 'Status and Management of World Sea Urchin Fisheries', *Oceanography and Marine Biology: An Annual Review* 40 (2002), pp. 343-425, p. 344.
36. Japan Food Industry Association, '*Echizen uni* (Report on regional food product branding)', from <http://www.shokusan.or.jp/sys/upload/726pdf6.pdf> (in Japanese).
37. Andrew and others, p. 354.

A Woman Holding a Liver

Amanda Couch

For the Oxford Symposium of Food and Cookery's theme *Offal*, I presented a performance-lecture, *A Woman Holding a Liver*, which contextually and artistically explored the practice and history of *haruspicy*, or liver divination, followed by the divination of a lamb's liver.

A Woman Holding a Liver began with an outline of the ancient practice of *haruspicy*. I showed examples of liver divination represented in art and material culture, and contextualized it from my personal and artistic perspectives, as well as in relation to chance strategies in art history. I outlined my methods for performing an examination of a liver, drawn from a wealth of classical scholarship, before undertaking an inspection of a lamb's liver, divining in response to a question that was collectively decided by the audience-participants.

Haruspicy: A Brief History

According to Patrick Curry, philosopher and specialist in Religious Studies, it is now widely accepted that divination is universal. Evidence of its existence can be found throughout human history and amongst most societies.[1] Peter Struck, Professor and Chair of Classical Studies at the University of Pennsylvania, writes that divination was neither 'exotic or marginal. The inclinations of the gods, like the weather, were simply a part of the ancient atmosphere'.[2] Furthermore Ulla Susanne Koch, specialist in Mesopotamian science and religion, contends that the practice of *extispicy*, divination using the entrails, which includes liver divination, was one of the most pervasive and successful of the Mesopotamian divinatory practices, transmitting its influence across the ancient world.[3]

Despite the prevalence of *haruspicy*, the evidence of actual 'representations of livers from antiquity is rare', as are images of liver divination itself.[4] Some examples include the thirty-two models of livers from the palace of Mari, in modern-day Syria in the Musée du Louvre, Paris, dated between 1800 BC and 1700 BC, exquisite little forms that would fit in the palm of your hand (Figure 1).[5] Each represents a specific malformation of what is thought to have been an actual liver, accompanied by a cuneiform inscription detailing the associated prediction. In the British Museum, there is a liver tablet from Sippar in southern Mesopotamia and dated from between 1900 BC and 1600 BC (Figure 2): about 15 cm by 15 cm, its surface grid of fifty-five sections has been described as a 'handbook for the interpretation of any or all perforations' unlike any other known specimen.[6] There is also an Etruscan diagram known as the Piacenza Liver: in bronze from the late second century BC, it was found at Decima di Gossolengo.[7]

As far as Greece is concerned, there appear to be no models of livers, but there are a few representations of *haruspicy* or, as it was termed in Greece, *hepatoscopy*. The most

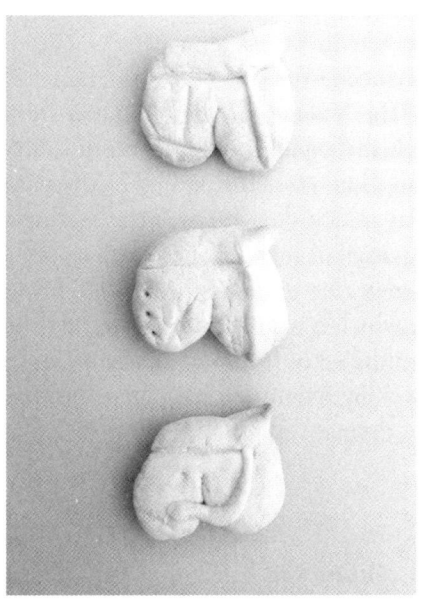

Figure 1
Amanda Couch, Extispicy Biscuits: The Louvre Livers 2016, each approx. 8.5 × 7 cm. Representations in baked shortbread dough of AO19833, AO19829, and AO19839, three of the thirty-two liver models found at Mari from 1800 - 1700 BC. Originals in clay, approx. each around 8 × 6cm, Musée du Louvre, Paris.

Figure 2
Amanda Couch, Extispicy Biscuits: The Liver Tablet from Sippar 2016, 15 × 16 cm. Baked shortbread dough representation of the Liver Tablet from Sippar, 1900 - 1600 BC. Original in clay, 14.6 × 14.6 cm, British Museum, London.

common examples show a warrior apparently examining a sacrificial victim and/or its organs. In Greece, as in many ancient cultures, divination was often employed at the battlefield before the commencement of a campaign. Such examples on ceramic vessels show a warrior, facing left, towards a male, who is presenting a liver for inspection, and there is also sometimes a gesturing older man standing behind. In ancient Mesopotamia and in Etruria liver diviners were highborn men, but in Greece anyone was able to become a *mantis/manteis*. The title of my performance-lecture references the name of the 2002 essay by classicist Annette Hupfloher, 'The Woman Holding a Liver from Mantineia: Female Manteis and Beyond', in which she explores the fifth century life-size marble relief sculpture from Arcadian Mantineia known as the *Stele of Diotima*, in the National Archaeological Museum of Greece, Athens.[8] It depicts a woman holding a liver, and is thought to be the only representation, visual or literary, of a female *manteis* or liver diviner in existence.[9] In his book *The Seer in Ancient Greece*, Michael Flower proposes that 'We can easily imagine a context in which a woman might interpret the entrails of a sacrificial animal within a domestic setting – for instance, on the occasion of her client leaving home for war or travel or seeking whether a particular business venture or marriage was advantageous'.[10]

The Liver and Chance

Rather than offal, the subject of this symposium, described as a rejected, wasted or overlooked part of an animal, the liver in ancient cultures was believed to be 'the seat of the soul'.[11] At the moment of a sacrifice, it was supposed that the gods merged with the animal, inscribing their communication on the *exta*, the entrails. The liver was perceived as a 'divine text in which the will of the gods was written', and this 'tablet' was translated by the *bārû*, or seer, and the message portrayed to the enquirer.[12] Today, the concept of the soul is a contested and problematic idea, which is not the focus of my interests, and a realm in which I do not want to venture into in this paper. Rather my frame is contemporary art practice: through my lens as a fine artist, I am making connections between divination and chance, a key strategy in artists' investigations throughout the twentieth century, as well as the contemporary. Chance is the idea of indeterminacy and contingency employed in the creation of and/or at the point of 'reception' of an artwork.[13]

Dada was memorably one of the early adopters of chance as a strategy. Dadaist Hans Richter wrote of its 'secret way', which was:

> To restore the work of art its primeval magic power, and to find the way back to the immediacy it had lost through contact with people like Lessing, Winckelmann and Goethe. [...] Absolute acceptance of chance brought us into the realm of magic, conjurations, oracles, and divination from the entrails of lambs and birds.[14]

A Woman Holding a Liver

One hundred years on from the birth of Dada, strategies of chance remain an important method in art practice for artists who employ chance to introduce uncertainty and contingency in the making: who set a 'process [...] in motion that has unpredictable results'.[15]

Today, we understand the importance of the liver, the largest organ within the body, which if it starts to fail, can lead to death within a few days. However, the liver is able to regenerate, which new stem cell research is just beginning to comprehend.[16] Historically, it was also considered to be generative, having the ability to inspire reflection. According to Plato, it was 'an organ from which thoughts proceeding from the mind are "reflected as in a mirror" to the other belly organs'.[17]

The liver looms large over my own personal history. As a child in the mid-1980s, I witnessed my father becoming ill with a mysterious disease. At the time, he was given transfusions of donated blood to support his body whilst the doctors tried to diagnose what was ailing him, but which, it turned out, was contaminated with the yet undiscovered Hepatitis C. In my late teens, I travelled to India and contracted Hepatitis A, which might explain why recently a reflexologist diagnosed me with a 'sluggish liver'. So perhaps this may be why I have undertaken these studies to become a *haruspex*, to discover knowledge of my own liver.

In her essay, 'Memoir as Method, or "What the Devil was I up to anyway?"', anthropologist Laura S. Grillo explores her problematic encounters with West African diviners. Originating as an academic research project, the study quickly turns personal, which she failed to foresee. Grillo was once married to a native West African whose family still resides in Abidjan, Côte d'Ivoire. Returning to the family, she engaged in a series of interviews with diviners in the community, all of whom stipulated they must first consult for her, in order to show their techniques and to 'convince [her] of divination's efficacy'.[18] But because of her personal troubles she writes, 'each consultation implicated me more and more as the subject of research'.[19]

Grillo is troubled, yet excited by the methodological and ethical implications of such a research project, and its repercussions on the work, her academic reputation and career. For me as an artist, first and foremost, my academic identity has developed out of, and because of, my art practice, so I am less concerned by an academic integrity designed by the sciences, and more interested in how such exploration can be utilized as material for artistic investigation. Grillo's discovery of not just the reflective capacities of divination but also how studying it complicates and muddies the water of academic research chimes with my motivations. Because of these challenges, she turns to more creative methods, such as fiction and memoir. She confesses:

> Divination engenders a reflexive move that turns the inquirer back on herself; [it] is the process of puzzling out one's own meanings and motivations. In investigating divination, I had naturally become the object of my own inquiry. Subject and object were blurred. [...] I felt that no academic discourse could

convey the startling accuracy of the diviners' readings of my past and present situation. […] They made me wonder what I believed and made me rethink what I was there to achieve.[20]

Having recently turned forty, I find myself at a reflective point in my life. Discovering the practice of liver divination has offered me the opportunity to engage with old and new knowledges, to play with the personal and professional, to embrace marginalized discourses, as well as disciplines beyond fine art, such as the classics, archaeology and philosophy.

Haruspex Studies

So I began my studies to become a *manteis,* beginning with the anatomy of the liver. In addition to examining the various liver models and diagrams discussed before along with contemporary biomedical illustrations and the examples of Classical archaeological scholarship by Ulla Susanna Koch, Ulla Jeyes and Morris Jastrow, to name but a few referenced throughout this paper, I have also inspected, photographed and printed actual lamb's livers to aid this understanding.

The liver is seen as a landscape, which is reflected in much of the language describing its features. The area around each constituent is known as its 'land', and similar terminology is used to name specific areas, such as the Palace Gate, and the Path.[21]

The liver is structured in relation to the left and right lobes, which in ancient Mesopotamia were the exact opposite to modern anatomy's left and right lobes. The Babylonian right (modern anatomy's left or *lobus sinister*) pertains to *pars familiaris*, the enquirer, i.e. to us, and the Babylonian left (modern anatomy's right or *lobus dexter*) is *pars hostilis*, the 'enemy' or the other.

Each area in ancient Mesopotamian practice was also structured left and right, which was extremely complex.[22] As the practice moved west, the Greeks, for example, performed a much more simplified system. In my studies, I have used the Mesopotamian schema as a basis, and like both I take into account the liver's overall appearance, shape and colour, but am also governed by the specific features of the liver, in line with the near Eastern model. However, I have chosen to simplify the schema assigning a single charge (negative or positive) to each feature. As long as I maintain a consistency in my activities, the readings should be reliable and dependable.

Each feature represents a part of human life. The size, shape, position, orientation and intensity of a feature signify a particular meaning, and each holds a negative or positive value. The association of such significance, as Jeyes notes, '[s]trike[s] a note in human psychology of perception. Thus the normal, whole, sound, bright, big, straight, long, broad etc. was seen as favourable, and in contrast to the abnormal, broken, infected, dull, small, crooked, short, narrow etc., which was deemed unfavourable'.[23]

A bad or negative sign, 'depression or deficiency […] would cause an unfavourable omen result when it appeared on [the] right side and a favourable one on a left side'.[24]

Figure 3
Gabriel Orozco, Yielding Stone, 1992, Plasticine, 35.6 × 43.2 × 43.2 cm. Collection of the artist. Image courtesy of the artist and Marian Goodman Gallery.

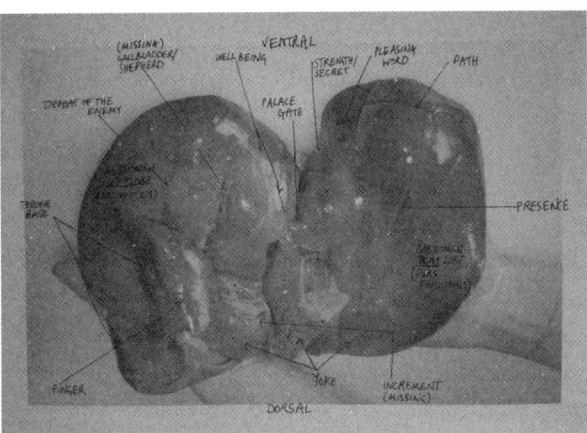

Figure 4
Diagram showing the twelve features on the Front of the Pouch.

And a good or positive sign found on the right would be deemed favourable, and occurring on the left, unfavourable.

Many of the features are known as 'drawings', grooves or impressions made by the proximity of other organs. Akin to Mexican contemporary artist Gabriel Orozco's 1992 *Yielding Stone* (Figure 3) – a Plasticine ball that is pushed through New York 'to represent a body in action', its form moulded by chance, its 'amorphous shape' 'inscribed' by the streets – the liver is 'inscribed' by its anatomical neighbours in the belly cavity, as well as the creature's wider environment, which appear as 'signs' on the organ to be read.[25]

In Mesopotamian ritual, an inspection encompassed twelve main features on the visceral surface of the liver, known as Front of the Pouch. The placement and meanings of some of the terms and features of the liver are still contested, despite much research and publication.[26] However, it is generally agreed that an examination is conducted in a particular order, which is what I always follow in my examinations (Figure 4). Beginning on the Babylonian right lobe and, working left, starting with:

The Presence: A 'drawing', a vertical groove on the Babylonian right lobe, formed by the impression of the abomasum, the fourth stomach. Its presence is a sign that the examination can go ahead, and is therefore favourable.

The Path: Another 'drawing', a horizontal groove on the Babylonian right, also formed by the impression of the abomasum. It refers to a military campaign, a journey to be taken, and/or the course of human life. The appearance of the path is always favourable.

The Pleasing Word: A horizontal groove on the Babylonian right lobe. It symbolizes oral matters: words or news from man (or god). Its presence is favourable.

The Strength: A ligament or vertical groove (drawing) inside the Palace Gate on the right. Also known as the Secret, its meanings refer to this term. Damage or its absence is unfavourable.

The Palace Gate: The umbilical fissure dividing the Babylonian right lobe from the left. It signifies the palace, administration, income. If it is long on the right and short on the left, it is positive, and if it is long on the left and short on the right it is negative.

The Well-Being: The vertical drawing on the Babylonian left lobe, referring to safety, health and prosperity, as well as general health and well-being. The groove is not always present, so if it is, it is extra favourable.

The Gall Bladder/Shepherd: It would have been present on the Babylonian left lobe, representing the king or throne. In my context with the livers coming from butchers there are no gallbladders, so we observe the direction it may have been pointing evident in the marks left behind in its removal. To the Babylonian right would be unfavourable, and to left would be favourable.

The Defeat of the Enemy Army: A vertical groove on the Babylonian left to the left of the gallbladder. It is similar to the Path and, like its name suggests, is connected to military campaigns. Its meanings mirror those of the Path.

The Throne Base: An impression (drawing) made by the right kidney. It signified the king's most private life and immediate circle of family and courtiers, dreams and bedchamber. Today it could be translated as the private life of the enquirer: love, family and close friends.

The Finger: The Caudate Lobe/*processus pyramidalis*. In Greek divination, it was the most important feature, the 'head' of the liver. It is about leadership in general. Its shape was of critical importance. If it was missing, then king or country would suffer misfortune.

The Yoke: Another 'drawing' made by the impression of the omasum, the third stomach, connecting the left and right lobes. It meant the city, diplomacy, boundaries, invasion or infiltration of pests or unwanted guests.

The Increment or Increase: It is part of the Caudate Lobe, the *processus papillaris*, referring to crops, markets, the harvest and economy. 'If [the Finger] was abnormally small and the [Increment] abnormally large, [this] pointed to a reversal in natural order', i.e. a negative sign.[27] If there are two Increases, there will be a proliferation in wealth.

A range of other features and considerations are also inspected, such as weapons, crosses, and jokers. The numbers of markings or features have a general system: one and two examples of a marking follow the rule of that particular feature, three or more reverses the prediction, and is an example of a joker. The drawings should appear as a 'normal' length, which is approximately three finger widths, otherwise they also act as jokers.

By employing chance, through the abattoir and butcher rather than a sacrifice, my livers have been acquired from animals reared for human consumption and will always be healthy. I am therefore unlikely to observe any morphological changes due to disease or parasites. Other types of morphology or contusions may occur as a result of butchery and transport as well as through the individual indeterminate ways the animal has developed.

Haruspicy is 'a binary system, yielding a "yes" or "no" answer to a question posed'.[28]

Amanda Couch: **A Woman Holding a Liver 2016** Observation Chart

Question

Will the UK invoke Article 50?

	Name/feature	Favourable	Unfavourable	Anomalies
1.	*manzazu* or *naplastu* **(divine) PRESENCE STATION or VIEW** DRAWING	✓		✓
2.	*padanu* **PATH** DRAWING	✓		
3.	*pû ṭābu* **PLEASING WORD** DRAWING		✓	
4.	*danānu* **STRENGTH / SECRET** DRAWING	✓✓		
5.	*bab ekalli* **PALACE GATE** FLESH		✓	
6.	*šulmu* **WELLBEING** Including *padān imitti marti* **PATH TO THE RIGHT OF THE GALL-BLADDER** DRAWING		✓	
7.	*martu* **THE GALL-BLADDER/ SHEPHERD** FLESH		✓	
8.	*mihis pan umman nakrin* **DEFEAT OF THE ENEMY (ARMY)** (Also known as The Path to the Left of the Gallbladder) DRAWING	✓		
9.	*niddi kussî* **THRONE BASE** DRAWING		✓	
10.	*ubānu / šumma* **FINGER** FLESH	✓		
11.	*nīru* **YOKE** DRAWING		✓	
12.	*ṣibtu* **INCREASE/INCREMENT** FLESH	✓		

Figure 5
Page one of the observation chart given out to symposiasts.

The interpretation for each aspect with its metaphorical meaning was not taken literally but simply assigned a 'good' or 'bad' label. For example, if a feature states that the enemy army will suffer, the meaning is deemed favourable to the enquirer. This allows for a number of observations to be gleaned from any given liver, and the interpretations – good, bad, or confused – noted, which the diviner then totals, summarizing the results in relation to the original question (Figure 5). The *extispicy* could be indeterminate, which would require another attempt.[29] But one must be careful, for to do too much *extispicy*, the Babylonians believed, a *baru* would 'die the death of transgression'.[30]

The liver was seen as a mirror of the larger world. The idea of interconnectivity was at the very centre of Babylonian divination; as Koch states, 'All branches of divination [...] shared the same fundamental idea: events in the universe are related to one another; if one occurs, its correlate may be expected. [It] appears from the very beginning to have been a detailed application of this basic idea.'[31]

With this in mind, before I report on the examination that occurred at the symposium, I will briefly return to Orozco's *Yielding Stone,* which, like the liver, speaks as much about the future as it does the past. Art historian Rye Dag Holmboe proposes that when 'reading' *Yielding Stone,* 'The impressions of the past form only a part of the story. What seems of greater importance is that the work does not so much summon up the primordial or the archaic as what is yet to be. [...] [It] is in a perpetual process of becoming.'[32]

As *Yielding Stone* sits in the gallery or packaging crate, it is also informed by its environment, by the weight of gravity, the falling of dust, which 'mark[s], every moment, by the sensation of time'.[33] The liver is similarly in a state of becoming: through the death of its host, the writing of the gods, its removal from the body and the butchering process, and through the summoning of a future during the process of inspection, intuiting the message of what is to come. For us, it is an organ, but for the ancients, 'it provided a bridge between what is and what is yet to unfold from the spiritual realm into the sphere of human destiny'.[34]

The Examination

The after dinner slot on the Saturday night of the symposium, with a heady mixture of wine, conviviality and excitement, meant that the posing of a question that would elicit a 'yes' or 'no' answer was a highly emotive affair. Discussions bounced from Brexit, across the water to Trump, and back again. And, as it was just a fortnight after the referendum on Britain's place in Europe, the UK's vote to leave the EU was on many a symposiast's heart and mind, and the question, 'Will the UK invoke Article 50?', was agreed.

A small clear bag of two livers acquired from my local butcher, William Rose on Lordship Lane, East Dulwich, London was put on the table. I stated my system in acquiring them, undertaking the same steps every time I prepare for a divination. I leave my house at nine a.m., and by bike, with a small backpack, cycle to the butchers, which takes about seven minutes. I ask for two whole lamb's livers, and request that no further trimming be done. Once I return home, I then leave the bag in the fridge, on the glass shelf, so as to prevent impressions etching into the organ from the wire shelves, until the divination is to take place. These livers then travelled from London to Oxford, carefully packed in a cool bag, and placed in a fridge on site until the evening's event. I then opened the bag and pulled out one liver at random. Handouts of a diagram displaying the features that make up the Front of the Pouch were distributed, as well a sheet containing a table of these features for symposiasts to tally the favourable and unfavourable markings, if they wished (Figure 5).

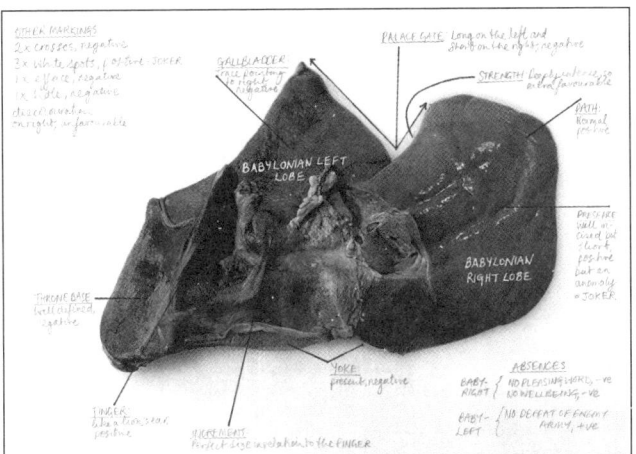

Figure 6
Diagram with a photograph of the liver divined at the symposium showing the features of the inspection.

The Babylonian Right
Beginning with the Babylonian right, the liver revealed a Presence. It was a little short, but was well incised and present, which allowed the examination to go ahead. As it was shorter than three finger lengths, which is considered the 'normal' length, it was marked down as an anomaly. The 'drawing' of the Path was normal and therefore favourable, but there was no Pleasing Word, which is unfavourable. The Strength or Secret was found and was deeply intense, and so extra favourable. The Palace Gate was long on the left and short on the right, which is considered a bad omen, and there was no Wellbeing, also unfavourable.

The Babylonian Left
On the Babylonian left, the Gallbladder or Shepherd was not present, as is usual with all my livers, but its trace pointed in the Babylonian right, which was therefore unfavourable. The drawing, the Defeat of the Enemy Army, which isn't always obvious, was absent (see fig 7.). It follows similar rules to the Path, but as it is to be found on the Babylonian left it has the opposite meaning, and so its absence is considered favourable. The Throne Base was well defined, and therefore unfavourable.

Figure 7 Documentation of the performance divination at the Oxford Symposium of Food and Cooker, 9 July 2016: Locating the Secret inside the Palace Gate. Image courtesy of Joshua Evans.

Area of Appendages

Appendages are not affected by their position on the right or left sides of the liver, and are read according to their presence, shape and size. Therefore, the Finger was a good shape, like a lion's ear, which is favourable, and was an appropriate size in relation to the Increment, i.e. the finger being much bigger than the Increment. The Yoke was present and therefore unfavourable. The Increment or Increase was present and the correct scale to the Finger, and was therefore favourable.

Other Markings and Colouring

There were no unfavourable weapons, clubs or pegs. There were two crosses, which are always unfavourable, and three white spots. White spots are generally unfavourable but as there were three, the rule is reversed. There was no splitting, fissures or tears, and no foot, but there was one efface and one hole. There was discolouration on the right, which is considered unfavourable.

The emotional investment in the examination was such that anxious cries and concerns were constantly voiced when a feature, or absence of a feature, was interpreted as unfavourable. At one point a keen audience member, who was a researcher herself, reminded the group that they should not be concerned with individual features at that stage, that it was the accumulation of the features, good and bad, which would result in a concluding positive or negative answer to the question, and that the process of the examination was an exercise in data collection with which to form the final analysis.

examination was an exercise in data collection with which to form the final analysis.

In total we had ten favourable signs and eleven unfavourable signs, which would ordinarily give us a 'no' answer. However, as we had three spots, they triggered the role of the *Niphu* jokers, i.e. a triple occurrence of a particular feature which reverses the outcome of the inspection, resulting here, in a 'yes' answer. Conversely, we had the anomaly of the Presence being shorter than the normal three finger lengths, which is also considered a *Niphu* joker, reversing the outcome once more. Hence, on the night of Saturday 9 July 2016, our liver's answer to the question, 'Will the UK invoke Article 50?', resulted in a 'no'.

This conclusion was not surprisingly received with great joy and relief, and the audience-participants, who were genuinely invested in the divination process, left the lecture theatre happy and excited, heading to the bar annexe of St Catherine's College for a celebratory drink and some folk singing, reassured of the UK's place in Europe, at least for that night.

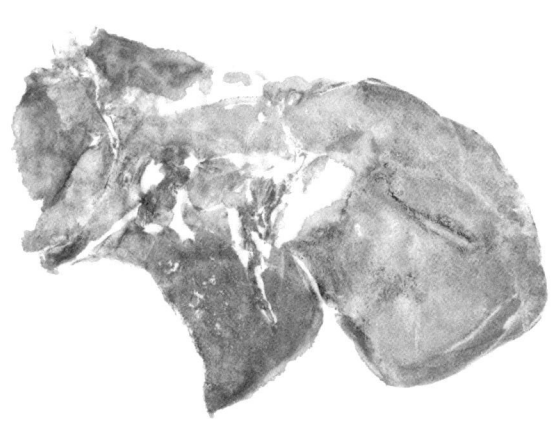

Figure 8
Amanda Couch, monotype print of the liver divined at the symposium, part of The Liver Models series 2016 – ongoing, ink on Chinese rice paper, 30 cm by 22 cm.

Notes

1. Patrick Curry, 'Introduction', in *Divination: Perspectives for a New Millennium,* ed. by Patrick Curry (Farnham: Ashgate, 2013), pp.1-9 (p.1) <https://ebookcentral.proquest.com/lib/ucreative-ebooks/detail.action?docID=581328> [accessed 19 January 2017].
2. Peter T. Struck, 'A World Full of Signs: Understanding Divination In Ancient Stoicism', in *Seeing with Different Eyes: Essays in Astrology and Divination,* ed. by Patrick Curry and Angela Voss (Newcastle upon Tyne: Cambridge Scholars Publishing, 2007), pp. 3-20 (p.3).
3. Ulla Susanne Koch, 'Three Strikes and You are Out! A View on Cognitive Theory and the First-Millennium Extispicy Ritual', *Divination and Interpretation of Signs in the Ancient World*, ed. by Amar Annus (Chicago: Oriental Institute of the University of Chicago), 6 (2010), 43-60 (45). <http://oi.uchicago.edu/pdf/ois6.pdf> [accessed 19 January 2017].
4. Annette Hupfloher, 'The Woman Holding a Liver from Mantineia: Female Manteis and Beyond', *Papers from the Third International Seminar on Ancient Arcadia* (Athens: Norwegian Institute, 2002)

<https://digitalt.uib.no/bitstream/handle/1956.2/2930/Hupfloher_The%20Woman%20Holding%20a%20Liver%5b...%5d.pdf?sequence=1> [accessed 19 January 2017].

5. Thirty-two liver models from Mari, 1800-1700 BC, clay, approx. each 8cm by 6 cm, Musée du Louvre, Paris.
6. The Liver Tablet from Sippar, 1900-1600 BC, clay, 14.6 cm by 14.6 cm, British Museum, London <http://www.britishmuseum.org/research/collection_online/collection_object_details.aspx?objectId=361996&partId=1> [accessed 26 January 2017]; B. Landsberger and H. Tadmor, 'Fragments of Clay Liver Models from Hazor', *Israel Exploration Journal* 14 (1964), 201-18 (p. 202).
7. Liver of Piacenza, found near Gossolengo, late 2nd century BC, bronze, 12.6 cm by 7.6 cm by 6 cm, Musei civici, Palazzo Farnese, Piacenza.
8. Hupfloher; The Stele of Diotima from Mantineia, c. 425-400 BC, marble, 148 cm by 80 cm, the National Archaeological Museum of Greece, Athens <http://www.perseus.tufts.edu/hopper/artifact?name=Athens%2C+NM+226&object=Sculpture> [accessed 26 January 2017].
9. Michael Attyah Flower, *The Seer in Ancient Greece* (Berkeley: University of California Press, 2008), p. 212.
10. Flower, p. 212-14.
11. Morris Jastrow, *Aspects of Religious Belief and Practice in Babylonia and Assyria* (New York: G.P. Putnam's Sons, 1911), p.196 <https://archive.org/details/aspectsofreligio00jast> [accessed 19 January 2017].
12. Eckart Frahm, 'Reading The Tablet, The Exta, and The Body: The Hermeneutics of Cuneiform Signs in Babylonian and Assyrian Text Commentaries and Divinatory Texts', *Divination and Interpretation of Signs in the Ancient World*, ed. by Amar Annus (Chicago: Oriental Institute of the University of Chicago), 6 (2010), 43-60 (45). <http://oi.uchicago.edu/pdf/ois6.pdf> [accessed 19 January 2017].
13. Margaret Iversen, 'Introduction: The Aesthetics of Chance', in *Documents of Contemporary Art. Chance*, ed. by Margaret Iversen (Cambridge: MIT Press, 2010), pp.12-27, where she defines the difference between artists who employ chance at the 'moment of composition' and those at the point of 'reception' (p. 16).
14. Hans Richter, *Dada. Art and Anti-Art* (London: Thames and Hudson, 1965), pp. 61, 59-60.
15. Iversen, p. 19.
16. See the research of MRC Centre for Regenerative Medicine (CRM) at the University of Edinburgh <http://www.crm.ed.ac.uk/research/group/liver-stem-cells-and-regeneration> and Euro Stem Cell <http://www.eurostemcell.org/factsheet/chronic-liver-disease-how-could-regenerative-medicine-help> [accessed 19 January 2017].
21. Plato's *Timeaus* 3.38; Jan Purnis, 'Digestive Tracts: Early Modern Discourses of Digestion' (unpublished doctoral thesis, University of Toronto, 2010), p. 80 <https://tspace.library.utoronto.ca/bitstream/1807/33822/1/Purnis_Jan_K_201011_PhD_thesis.pdf> [accessed 9 December 2016].
18. Laura S. Grillo, 'Memoir as Method, or "What the Devil Was I up to anyway?"', in *Divination,* ed. by Patrick Curry (Farnham: Ashgate, 2013), pp. 39-46 (p. 39).
19. Grillo, p. 39.
20. Grillo, p. 40-41.
21. Ulla Jeyes, 'The "Palace Gate" of the Liver: A Study of Terminology and Methods in Babylonian Extispicy', *Journal of Cuneiform Studies* 30 (1978), 209-33 (209).
22. Ulla Jeyes, 'Divination As A Science In Ancient Mesopotamia', in *Jaarbericht "Ex Oriente Lux"* 32 (1991–1992), 23-41 (35) <http://www.michaelsheiser.com/PaleoBabble/DivinationScienceMesopotamia.pdf> [accessed 19 January 2017].
23. Ulla Jeyes, *Old Babylonian Extispicy: Omen Texts in the British Museum*, (Istanbul: Nederlands Historisch-Archaeologisch Instituut te İstanbul, 1989), p. 51.
24. Jeyes, 'The "Palace Gate"', p. 209.
25. Gabriel Orozco, *Yielding Stone*, 1992, Plasticine, 36.8 cm by 39.4 cm by 40.6 cm, Collection of the artist; The Museum of Modern Art, Multimedia, 'Gabriel Orozco, Yielding Stone, 1992' (2016) <https://www.moma.org/explore/multimedia/audios/174/1915> [accessed 19 January 2017]; Rye Dag Holmboe, 'Gabriel Orozco: Cosmic Matter and Other Leftovers', in *The White Review* (2011) <http://www.

thewhitereview.org/art/gabriel-orozco-cosmic-matter-and-other-leftovers/> [accessed 19 January 2017].
26. Ulla Susanne Koch-Westenholz, *Babylonian Liver Omens: The Chapters Manzāzu, Padānu and Pān tākalti of the Babylonian Extispicy Series mainly from Aššurbanipal's Library* (Copenhagen: Museum Tusculanum Press, 2000), p. 44.
27. Morris Jastrow, 'Omen', in *Encyclopaedia Britannica*, 11th edn, 20 (1910), pp. 102-03 (p. 103).
28. Derek Collins, 'Mapping the Entrails: The Practice of Greek Hepatoscopy', *American Journal of Philology*, 129.3 (2008), 319-45, (319) <https://muse.jhu.edu/article/247052> [accessed 19 January 2017].
29. Collins, p. 336.
30. H. Zimmern, 'Beiträge zur Kenntnis der Babylonischen Religion: Die Beschwörungstafe' *Šurpu, Ritualtafeln für den Wahrsager, Beschwörer und Sänger,* (Leipzig: Hinrichs, 1910), pp. 18-19, in Ulla Susanne Koch, 'Sheep and Sky: Systems of Divinatory Interpretation', in *The Oxford Handbook of Cuneiform Culture,* ed. by Karen Radner and Eleanor Robson (Oxford: Oxford University Press, 2011), pp. 447-69 (p. 465).
31. Koch-Westenholz, *Babylonian Liver Omens*, p. 11.
32. Holmboe.
33. Holmboe.
34. Jeremy Naydler, *The Future of the Ancient World: Essays on the History of Human Consciousness* (Rochester, Vermont: Inner Traditions, 2009), p. 155.

Hog's Puddings, Black Puddings, White Puddings, Liverings and Andolians: The Rise and Fall of England's Offal Puddings c.1500-c.1800

Jan Davison

Andrew Boorde's *Dyetary of Health* (1542) pulled no punches on the consequences of consuming offal: 'All the inwards of beestes and of fowles, as the herte, the lyver, the lunges, and trypes, and trylybubbes, wyth all the entrayles, is harde of dygestyon, and doth increase grose humoures.' [1] Yet the risks to well-being went unheeded in many quarters. Thomas Dawson, author of *The Good Huswifes Jewell* (1597), one of the earliest English cookbooks, provides recipes for black puddings of sheep's blood, a hog's pudding of liver, white puddings prepared from liver and lights (lungs) or kidney and marrow and others made with calves' chaldron – the entrails.[2] There were few parts of a pig or calf that could not be chopped small, combined with suet, cereal, eggs and cream, stuffed into a length of gut or sheep's stomach, and boiled up as a pudding.

The sixteenth to the mid-eighteenth century was the golden age of offal puddings. They were considered an essential part of the English table and were made in countless variations. A rifle through the cookery books of this period reveals the range of puddings prepared: white, black, ising, liver, liveridge, marrow, pith (the spinal marrow or cord), hog's, heifer's udder, cow's heel, haggis, and *andouilles* and *andolians* of calf or pig's intestines prepared in the French style (see below). The following recipe for liver puddings comes from the personal collection of the seventeenth scholar and diarist John Evelyn:

> Take hogges liver, parboil it, grate it and take as much grated Bread as liver, sweeten with sugar & spice all sorts (except pepper) to your liking, sweet Creame and egges, more yolkes than whites, reasonably full of Currance, a spoonefull or two of sack [fortified wine, similar to medium sweet sherry], beefe suet and marrow, maqueroons and [Naples] biscuits [sponge fingers]...a little musk, mix these together and so fill the Gutts.[3]

Evelyn's recipe is typical of many offal puddings from this period. Cooked offal, usually from the pig, was mixed with bread or other filler, enriched with plenty of eggs and cream, flavoured with spices and sweetened with sugar. Looking at this recipe today, the combination of sweet with savoury is what first strikes us as out of the ordinary. But for the time, the ingredients point to another surprise. The spices and flavourings Evelyn lists, cinnamon, cloves, mace, sugar and musk, an exclusive scent obtained from the male musk deer of Southern Asia, were the height of fashion: they were coveted and expensive and available only to the nobility, landed gentry and wealthy merchants. The fact that they were used to flavour offal puddings suggests the puddings had status. Offal puddings were seen not as food for paupers, but as puddings to be enjoyed by the privileged.

Paradoxically, for much of this period, the consumption of offal, now considered a lowly food, was largely confined to the elite. For most of the population deprived of land on which to farm, to feed livestock or to forage, consumption of meat of any kind, even offal, was limited, if any was consumed at all. This situation only changed towards the mid-eighteenth century when the keeping of a cottage pig became commonplace within the rural population; a significant development made possible by the introduction of potatoes which proved an ideal foodstuff for fattening them.

Early English cookbooks, such as Thomas Dawson's with which we began, reflect dishes served at court. They open a window onto the kitchens of the great households noisy with the chopping and pounding of ingredients, the air tingling with spices. Of the myriad offal pudding recipes proffered, those prepared from liver or blood appear most widely. *A Book of Cookrye,* published in 1584, provides us with two of the first recorded recipes for liver puddings. In the first, for 'liverings of a swine' the cooked and pounded liver is combined with egg yolks and beef suet and seasoned with salt, pepper, cloves and mace to produce a soft, richly liver-flavoured savoury pudding. The second version, described as a 'white pudding' is more typical of the period: the pounded liver is combined with cream, grated halfpenny loaf (the best white bread enriched with eggs), dried fruit – dates and raisins, saffron and sugar.[4] Liver puddings of this latter style continued to be enjoyed through the seventeenth century with one important addition: rosewater. This reflected a new culinary trend of using perfumes to add exoticism and status to a dish. Hence John Evelyn's liver puddings flavoured with musk. Offal puddings perfectly mirrored changing fashions in foods and flavours.

Robert May, chef to some of the wealthiest households, provides a recipe for a 'leveredge' pudding that is extravagant in its use of both rosewater and sugar: used together these defined the taste for much of the seventeenth century. Sugar, which seduced with its sweetness, was considered the pinnacle of culinary desire and pleasure as well as a display of affluence.

> Boil a hogs liver very dry, and when it is cold grate it and take as much grated manchet [high quality white bread] as liver, sift them through a cullender and season them with cloves, mace and cinamon, as much of all the other spices, half a pound of sugar, a pound and a half of currans [currants], half a pint of rose-water, three pound of beef suet minced small, eight eggs [yolks] and but four whites.[5]

Robert May's recipe is helpful in that it provides quantities for the ingredients, enabling a modern cook to replicate the puddings. Testing the recipe was instructive, not least because the result was unexpected. There was no sense that the pudding contained liver: the other principal ingredients, the bread, suet, sugar and fruit, dominate. The rosewater, which I anticipated might be overwhelming, added an exotic but subtle flavour. I could see the appeal. John Evelyn's recipe, made using May's as a guide, produced very similar results, the macaroons and sponge fingers adding to the pudding's sweetness and belying its liver base. The soft bready texture, fruited and spiced, closely resembles what the English today call bread pudding.[6] We may assume that the intention was not to conceal the flavour of the liver but to ensure the pudding accorded with the pervading tastes of the day. For variety, May advises that liver puddings can also be flavoured with sweet herbs and fennel seed, caraway seed or similar, although he cannot resist serving them with beaten butter and sugar.[7]

Other offal puddings were prepared from the hog's 'humbles' – the liver, lungs and heart – which were boiled, chopped small, pounded and melded with cream, eggs, fruit, grated bread, hog's fat or beef suet and suitably spiced.[8] Joseph Cooper, self-proclaimed 'chiefe cook to the late King' (Charles I), provides a recipe for a pudding of swine's lights (lungs) with currants, which appears in a number of cookery books around this time: 'Parboyl the Lights [lungs], and mince them very small with Suet, and mix it with grated bread, Cream, Currans, Eggs, nutmeg, Salt and Rosewater, and fill them in skins.'[9] So where would these fruited and sweet offal puddings, with, to modern tastes, contrary ingredients and flavours, appear in the course of a meal? Up until the early- to mid-eighteenth century, ingredients did not determine the position of dishes on the menu; and no distinction was made between sweet and savoury. As one dish among many, puddings such as these were included as part of the first course as a useful means of adding bulk to the meal and steadying the appetite; they were also provided as 'out-works', meaning small free-standing plates of food set on the table for diners to consume through the meal as they chose.

Finely chopped intestines, typically those of a calf, also found their way into puddings. In 1750, Hertfordshire farmer and writer William Ellis emphasizes the labour involved in preparing the entrails, scouring them with salt over several days until 'clean and sweet', observing: 'the preparation of chitterlins will prove the cleanliness or sluttishness of a housewife, as much as any meat whatsoever will.'[10] Thomas Dawson includes a recipe for what he describes as 'haggas'. The calf's entrails are boiled and shredded small and mixed with the familiar offal pudding ingredients: beef suet, bread, egg yolks and whites, cream, mace and nutmeg, 'a good deal of sugar', rosewater and various herbs: winter savoury, parsley, thyme and pennyroyal mint. Joseph Cooper offers almost the same recipe as Dawson, adding currants and specifying thick cream.[11] Gervase Markham in his *Country Contentments* (1623) prepares 'Pudding of a Calves Mugget' (entrails) with similar ingredients to Dawson, adding a 'pretty quantitie' of assorted bitter herbs – strawberry leaves, sorrel, endive and chicory, currants and dates, and a 'good store' of butter, while Sir Kenelm Digby, whose personal recipe collection (1669) reflects the dishes enjoyed by his courtly circle, notes a meatier version, combining the 'whitest and finest' of veal intestines with fresh pork.[12]

Alongside these rich chitterling puddings, the French *andouille,* prepared from the pig's large intestine and stomach, made a brief appearance on the English table. *Andouilles* were introduced to Britain by the Normans and an early reference appears in the late twelfth century, but they are notably absent from English cookery books until the late seventeenth century.[13] Robert May and his contemporary, William Rabisha, another professional chef, include recipes for 'Andolians' in their respective cookbooks.[14] They also appear in the influential cookery manual of the French chef François Massialot (1702) and that of the cook to the Earl of Chesterfield, Vincent La Chapelle (1733). To make *andouilles,* which in contrast to English chitterling puddings contained no eggs or cream, lengths of the small intestine were taken and stuffed with bundles of the large intestine, which had been thoroughly cleaned, cooked, cut into lengths and seasoned with herbs and spices. The *andouilles* were tied and poached in water and then grilled or fried.[15] Rabisha advises they are sliced and eaten with mustard; Massialot recommends serving them on bread moistened with mutton gravy and lemon juice. Despite a fashion for all things French, the English it seems had little appetite for the gutsy *andouille,* its taste betraying its contents, and even with a move to simpler fare, for which it was ideally suited, it failed to gain wide appeal.

Black (blood) puddings were highly regarded through this period, even considered a delicacy, and as with other offal puddings they were presented as a side dish.[16] Among the earliest published recipes for black puddings we discover one using the blood of a swan which, as now, was a bird whose consumption was exclusive to the monarch (a medieval recipe uses the blood of porpoise, also the preserve of royalty). The swan's blood was combined with minced suet and fine oatmeal steeped in milk and seasoned with nutmeg, pepper, sweet herbs, coriander seeds, finely chopped lemon peel and the eminently fashionable rosewater. This mixture was stuffed into the neck of the swan, sewn in securely and poached. As a mundane alternative, the blood of a goose was substituted for swan. The recipe, set down by John Murrell in his *New Booke of Cookerie* (1615), was widely copied and was one of several exotic black puddings to appear in print; others use the blood of a chicken, calf or fawn.[17] Sir Kenelm Digby's recipe for 'Black Puddings' (1669) prepared with 'two or three spoonfuls (or more) of Chicken's blood' is notable for the wealth of other ingredients that go to make the puddings: cream flavoured with cinnamon and nutmeg, ground almonds, grated bread, marrow, eggs, sugar, salt, rosewater and to cap it all, scent of musk or ambergris – a sweet musk-scented secretion from the intestine of the sperm whale.[18]

More conventional black pudding recipes using pig's blood, and occasionally ox or sheep's blood, are remarkably consistent in ingredients and method of making. Cooks use groats (husked oats), oatmeal or bread, soaked in milk, blood or broth, to give substance to the puddings.[19] The cereal is stirred into the blood along with cream, occasionally eggs, and beef suet or pork leaf fat.[20] With respect to flavouring, recurring favourites include cloves, mace and nutmeg, along with the herbs, thyme, fennel seed and mint, often the species known as pennyroyal. Pennyroyal, the smallest and most pungent of the mints, grew wild and abundantly at this time. It was also known as 'pudding grass' – grass meaning 'herb', reflecting its important culinary role. Patrick Lamb, master cook to five monarchs, provides a typical recipe:

> Take a Quart or Chopin of whole Oatmeal, boil it over the Fire in a Quart of milk, and let it stand till next morning to swell; then put to it a Pound and half of Beef-Sewet, shred; season it moderately with Pepper and Salt, take a small Handful of Penny-royal, a small Handful of Parsley, and a little Thyme, wash and mince all these very fine, and put them to your Oatmeal, with three Pints of Hogs or Sheeps Blood, and a Pint of Cream; mix all these Ingredients together, and warm them a little over the Fire, that they may fill the easier into the Guts; tie them up…and boil and fry them the same Way before you serve them.[21]

Cream and eggs are not used in contemporary English black puddings. One might assume that their inclusion produces a richer and softer pudding. Having tested Lamb's recipe, and others of the period, my conclusion is that in the quantities used they do not.[22] The puddings are remarkably similar to those made today. With respect to the inclusion of egg, it has the same protein structure as blood and cooks in the same way. However, replacing conventional groats with breadcrumbs, as in the following recipe from Robert May, produces a soft black pudding, with a texture similar to a smooth pâté – quite delicious. If there is one historic English black pudding recipe to resurrect, this would be my first choice: 'Take blood and strain it, put in three pints of the blood, and two of cream, three penny manchets [loaves] grated, and beef suet cut square like small dice or hogs flakes, yolks of eight eggs, salt, sweet herbs, nutmeg, cloves, mace and pepper.'[23]

Interest in offal puddings of all kinds began to wane through the eighteenth century. This was brought about through a combination of technological innovation, which had begun some time before, and a change in fashion, which saw the gradual divergence of sweet and savoury flavours. John Murrell writing in 1615 is the first to cite the new invention which revolutionized pudding making – the pudding cloth.[24] Up until this time the making of puddings was closely associated with the pig: its intestines were the primary receptacle in which to hold the pudding mixture. A length of gut would be stuffed with the mixture and tied at both ends, giving rise to the proverb, 'Everything hath an end, and a pudding hath two.'[25] As pig's intestines were only available at the time of slaughter, puddings, although on occasion made of other ingredients, were closely associated with the pig and utilizing what it had to offer. The pudding cloth, by contrast, enabled boiled puddings to be prepared year-round, not just in the winter months when most pigs were killed. This ease of making led, through the course of the seventeenth century, to a proliferation of styles of pudding, one or more steps removed from their original porcine offal origins. This experimentation and diversification marked the beginning of the end of offal puddings, though they retained their popularity through the seventeenth century.

The real death knell for offal puddings arose in the early-eighteenth century, with a change in taste and a move to separate sweet and savoury flavours. This notion, first advanced by court cooks, filtered down through the social classes through the course of the century. It also coincided with another culinary change, a move to simpler dishes with fewer ingredients. Elaborate offal puddings – fruited, spiced, sweet and perfumed – were out of date. Simply by removing the offal in offal puddings, the remaining ingredients – breadcrumbs, flour, rice, oatmeal, ground almonds, eggs, cream, dried fruit, sugar and suet – readily formed the basis of England's boiled and steamed sweet puddings; a development already underway with the advent of the pudding cloth.

Eliza Smith in *The Compleat Housewife* reflects these new fashions in her recipe for liver puddings. She takes grated hog's liver and bread, suet, salt, chopped herbs, 'some spice', eggs and a little cream. Gone are the sugar and the dried fruits of earlier recipes, the spices are pared down and replaced by herbs, while eggs and cream are used more sparingly:

> To half a pound of grated bread, put half a pound of hog's liver, boiled cold and grated; a pound and half of suet finely shred, a handful of salt, a handful of sweet-herbs chopp'd small, some spice. Mix all these together, with six eggs, well beaten, and a little thick cream; fill your guts and boil them; when cold, cut them in round slices an inch thick; fry them in butter; and garnish your fowls, hash or fricasy.[26]

I have made Eliza Smith's liver puddings. They are very good. As she suggests, sliced thickly and fried, the slices crisp nicely and are a savoury satisfying titbit, worthy of a place alongside roast poultry; they would also be a novel addition to a much later development, the English breakfast. Unfortunately, the liver pudding in its new eighteenth century savoury incarnation did not last. Smith's pared down recipe is not only one of the first to appear, but also one of the last.

By the second half of the eighteenth century, stripped of the comforting ingredients – the bread, eggs, fruits and cream – that had made them so popular in the preceding centuries, English puddings of organs and entrails foundered: they disappear from the cookery books and from the tables of the well-to-do. By this time haggis had become firmly associated with Scotland. Hannah Glasse's 1758 edition of *Art of Cookery* includes instructions, 'To make a Scotch Haggass'. The pudding has been modified from that prepared by English cooks a century earlier to include the lights, heart and chitterlings of a calf combined with suet and oatmeal seasoned with salt and pepper. Although Glasse notes, 'some add a pint of good thick Cream and put in a little beaten Mace, Clove or Nutmeg'.[27]

Yet this was not quite the end of England's offal puddings. By happenstance, with the introduction of the cottager's pig around this time, simple puddings of the pig's humbles, cooked and combined with plenty of groats became, along with black puddings, an essential food of the rural poor, made when the pig was slaughtered. Eliza Smith provides one of the few recipes published from this time that records these frugal puddings, describing them as 'White Puddings for the Family'. She cooks the hog's harslet (offal) in water until tender, and uses the hot stock to steep the groats for several hours. The offal is chopped 'very small' and mixed with the groats, some flour, a good deal of shredded sage, salt and (too costly for most peasants) cloves and mace.[28] The dietary value of white puddings or hog's puddings as they were also known was noted by William Cobbett in 1822: 'The innards [of the pig] are next taken out, and if the wife be not a sluttern, here in the mere offal, in the mere garbage, there is food, and delicate food too, for a large family for a week; and hogs' puddings for the children, and some of the neighbours' children, who come to play with them; for these things are by no means to be overlooked.'[29]

Ingredients for hog's pudding varied by locality, some were mainly offal, others included scraps of fatty meat or large quantities of fat, and some were sweetened with fruit and spices; yet there was one constant, the high proportion of cereal, whether groats, oatmeal or flour, which ensured the puddings went a long way. Hog's and groats puddings are still made in Devon and Cornwall, though now devoid of offal, and typically made from fatty pork combined with bread, rusk or groats, and spices, particularly black pepper.

A plainer black pudding, without the eggs and cream of the courtly style, also became commonplace in the eighteenth century. Eliza Smith and Hannah Glasse provide similar recipes. They take groats boiled in offal stock (or in Hannah Glasse's case, water) and combine them with blood, diced pork fat, assorted herbs, including thyme and pennyroyal, salt, cloves and mace.[30] William Ellis in *The Country Housewife's Family Companion* (1750) sets out his way of preparing black hog's puddings 'in the very best housewiferly manner for cheapness, and yet good enough for a farmer's family or for sale.' He soaks whole oatmeal (groats) overnight in hot water and salt. The following morning he instructs:

> mix as much blood with the oatmeal as will colour it, and add to it some crumbled bread, pennyroyal, and onion cut small, with some chopt bits of hogs hard fat. These being all well mixed together, begin to fill a gut a yard long… and when it is about three parts filled, and squeezed all of a thickness, tie each gut so filled at each end with thrum-thread; and while water is boiling, put these puddings into it, and boil them till they become dark colour'd and tender, which will be in about an hour's time; then take them out the water, and while they are hot, twist them into links, ready to be dressed, by either broiling or frying them.[31]

The Rise and Fall of England's Offal Puddings

Ellis's recipe is noteworthy for the inclusion of onion, which from the early twentieth century became an essential ingredient in English black puddings. Indeed modern black puddings continue to be made in much the same way as Ellis describes. Today, England's black puddings and the West Country's hog's and groats puddings are mere vestiges of a complex and diverse culinary tradition that fed the English predilection for offal cooked in pig's guts.

Notes

1. Andrew Boorde, *Dyetary of Health* (London: Robert Wyer, for John Gowghe, 1542), p. 276.
2. Thomas Dawson, *The Good Huswifes Jewell*, 2nd edn, 2 parts (London: Edward White, 1596-1597), Part I (1596), p. 10; Part II (1597), pp. 51-56.
3. *John Evelyn, Cook: The Manuscript Receipt Book of John Evelyn 1620-1706*, ed. Christopher Driver (Totnes: Prospect Books, 1977), p. 56.
4. A.W., *A Book of Cookrye Very Necessary for All Such as Delight Therin* (London: the author, 1584), p. 12-13.
5. Robert May, *The Accomplisht Cook*, 1685 edn (London: Nath. Brooke, 1685; repr. Totnes: Prospect Books, 2000), p. 184.
6. A traditional English baked pudding of stale bread combined with fat, sugar and dried fruit.
7. May, p. 26.
8. Beef suet was commonly used for making puddings and sausages in this period. There were two reasons: first, pigs were small and scrubby, still bearing a resemblance to wild swine, and did not fatten readily (improved breeds were a product of the late-eighteenth century); and second, pork fat was highly valued for cooking and was often reserved for this purpose.
9. Jos. Cooper, *The Art of Cookery refin'd and augmented* (London: R. Lowndes, 1654), p. 147.
10. William Ellis, *The Country Housewife's Family Companion* (London: the author, 1750; repr. Totnes: Prospect Books, 2000), pp. 145-46.
11. Dawson, Part II, p. 53; Cooper, p. 139. It is apparent from these recipes that many of the haggis puddings made at this time were very different from the sheep's offal and oatmeal version that is made today, although according to the *Oxford English Dictionary*, the first record of 'hagws of a schepe' appears in 1430: 'c. 1430 *Two Cookery-bks.* 39, Hagws of a schepe. Take þe Roppis with þe talowe, & parboyle hem; þan hakke hem smal.'
12. Gervase Markham, *Country Contentments or the English House-Wife*, 1623 edn (London: the author, 1623), p. 70; Kenelm Digby, Sir, *The Closet of the Eminently Learned Sir Kenelme Digbie Opened*, (London: H. Brome, 1669), pp. 198-99.
13. Alexander Neckham, *De Utensilibus* (*The Treatise de Utensibilus*), in *A Volume of Vocabularies, illustrating the condition and manners of our forefathers...from the tenth century to the fifteenth*, ed. by Thomas Wright (1857), Vol. I, p. 104, in *A Library of National Antiquities* ed. by J. Mayer (Liverpool: the author, 1857).
14. May, pp. 22-23; William Rabisha, *The Whole Body of Cookery dissected, taught and fully manifested...*, 1682 edn (London: Giles Calvert, 1682), p. 86.
15. Vincent La Chapelle, *The Modern Cook*, (London: the author, 1733), pp. 321-28; François Massialot, *The Court and Country Cook*, trans. J.K. (London: A. & J. Churchill, M. Gillyflower, 1702), pp. 55-57.
16. Black puddings did not make an appearance on the English breakfast table until the twentieth century.
17. John Murrell, *A New Booke of Cookerie* (London; John Browne, 1615; repr. New York: Da Capo Press, 1972), p. 37-38.
18. Digby, p. 205.
19. Groats: grain that has had the husks removed. The term usually applies to oats and is the first stage of

processing before the oats are rolled or ground into a meal, although it can sometimes refer to wheat, barley or maize.
20. Leaf fat is found inside the pig and is highly regarded for its flavour.
21. Patrick Lamb, *Royal Cookery*, 3rd edn (London: E. and R. Nutt, and A. Roper, 1726), p. 204. Lamb served King Charles II, King James II, King William and Queen Mary (joint monarchs), and Queen Anne.
22. Others tested: Dawson, 'To make blacke puddings', Part I, p. 10; Markham, 'A Blood Pudding', pp. 70-71; May, 'Other Blood Puddings', 'To make Puddings of Blood after the Italian fashion' and 'To make Black Puddings of Beefers Blood', pp. 23, 26, 126-27; Eliza Smith, 'To make black Hogs Puddings', *The Complete Housewife,* 9th edn (London: J. and J. Pemberton, 1739); Mrs Rundell, 'To make Black-Puddings – Another Way', *A New System of Domestic Cookery*, 1816 edn (London: Murray, 1816; repr. London: Persephone Books, 2009).
23. May, p. 23.
24. In the recipe 'A Cambridge Pudding', Murrell instructs the pudding is 'tyed in a faire cloth' (p. 37).
25. Sixteenth-century proverb, Linda and Roger Flavell, *Dictionary of Proverbs and their Origins*, (London: Kyle Cathie, 1993), pp. 199-200.
26. Smith, pp. 110-11.
27. Hannah Glasse, *The Art of Cookery Made Plain and Easy,* 6th edn (London: the author, 1758), p. 376. For the history of haggis see Adam Balic, 'The Haggis', *Wrapped and Stuffed Foods, Proceedings of the Oxford Symposium on Food and Cookery 2012,* ed. Mark McWilliams (Totnes: Prospect Books, 2013), pp. 82-93.
28. Smith, p. 111.
29. William Cobbett, *Cottage Economy* (London: E. Clement, 1822), paragraph 147.
30. Smith, p. 111; Glasse, *The Art of Cookery Made Plain and Easy* (London: the author, 1747), p. 126.
31 Ellis, p. 139.

Liver for Cats and Kids: The Fall of Offal in Istanbul

Pelin Dumanlı

History of Istanbul Cuisine and Offal Culture

The roots of our culinary traditions, an important part of our daily lives, often come from very ancient times. In Istanbul, the city where I live, home to the tastes that formed my palate, the cuisine has been influenced by many cultures. Some of these traditions come from the Byzantines, others from the Ottomans or Central Asian Turks. Each culture's offal repertory has contributed much to Istanbul's cuisine. However, these traditions have somehow been forgotten or updated beyond recognition in today's fast-changing times.

Istanbul's cuisine has been continuously renewing itself since it was developed from the civilizations that reigned in and around the city. Istanbul grew near both trade routes and fertile soils for animal husbandry and farming. As a result, the wide cultural structure of Istanbul's cuisine is built from the traditions of Byzantium, the Ottoman Empire, Anatolian civilizations such as the Hittites and Seljuk, the Central Asian Turks and three major religions.

As a foodstuff, offal has been affected by all this history. It survives to this day developed by the distinct food culture of each ancient civilization and blended with modern ingredients and traditions.

In Turkey, especially in Istanbul, offal has been eaten since ancient times. It is assumed that offal's widespread consumption comes from the region's nomadic past. During the Ottoman era, offal was a regular food in the diet of the public as well as the military and palace elite.[1] Offal has a history of specialized production and sale in Istanbul. In the slaughterhouses, *sakatatçılar* are responsible for the process of taking organs out of the animal, and *bağırsakçılar* clean and wash intestines. Offal was sold not just by street vendors, who used to sell liver dishes and head pilaf, but also in dedicated shops, named *ciğerci*, instead of in butcher shops. There is a long history of tripe and trotter shops in Istanbul.

While the amount of offal eaten in the city declined as the country modernized, the tradition of offal eating continued until the 1990s when the chicken-processing sector in Turkey suddenly emerged. At the same time, offal sellers faced a health scare when doctors claimed that offal caused high cholesterol. With a new alternative readily available, prejudices towards offal intensified. Offal sellers had to close their businesses or change their names by adding chicken to their offerings. As habits started to change, many of the animal parts that used to be revered lost their former value. Some parts became more popular, while others became less common.

Offal: Rejected and Reclaimed Food

Yet in spite of these obstacles, there has always been a group of people who are fond of offal and never gave it up. They cook offal in their homes to enjoy its taste. My family is one of them. Offal was one of the leading components on my grandmother's dinner table. If nothing else, there would be a pot of livers boiling for the cats. My mother learned these customs from her own family elders, and she made an effort to pass them on to us by feeding us in the same way. This family heritage is most likely the reason I developed an interest in offal at such an early age. I feel as lucky as those cats that savoured my grandmother's livers. Unfortunately, few of my friends share this love. Offal's appearance does not help either, so the squeamish attitude we are all familiar with continues.

About Offal: Meaning, Etymology and Consumption

Offal, variety meat or the fifth quarter, are the internal organs and external parts of the animal that are removed before the carcass is cut up.In the Turkish Food Codex, *et* [meat] is defined as the edible parts taken from bovine and ovine animals such as cattle, sheep and goats; domesticated winged animals such as chicken, turkey; and rabbit and pig. Offal is defined as the following parts taken from the animals listed in the definition of meat above, excluding poultry: 'liver, kidney, brain, spleen, testes, heart, tongue, external red muscle meat of oesophagus, muscle of diaphragm, tripe, intestine, trotters, head, organ and organ parts'.[2]

The word for offal in Turkish, *sakatat*, comes from Arabic, meaning low quality food product. In the 1545 dictionary by Ahterı-i Kebir, *sakatat* refers to the useless or fallen part of every object and the inedible parts of the animal. However, in Turkish cuisine, offal was never considered as a waste or an undesired part; on the contrary it was always fed to small children, hopefully giving them the much-desired strength and growth of 'blood'. Adults ate it too: depending on the cultural context, offal might be considered both as food for the poor or as a delicacy that commands a high price.

Beside Turks, offal is also prevalent in the rest of world. The term 'Fifth Quarter' (*il quinto quarto*), which Anissa Helou chose as the title of her offal cookbook, is used for offal in Italian.[3] French butchers also use the fifth quarter to describe the parts that do not belong to the four quarters of the carcass. In Turkish there is another phrase, *çeyrekçi* (quarterer) that was used for the street butchers in the Ottoman period. It can be assumed that the word 'quarter' is used because the carcass gets separated into four main parts after the animal is slaughtered.

In Istanbul we usually buy offal from a special shop named *ciğerci* [liver shop]. Since the Ottoman period, many offal shops were opened by Albanians who had worked at the slaughterhouse in the Sütlüce region. The offal sellers have come a long way, from street vendors carrying their goods on a stick to independent shops to the recent moves to sell chicken in addition to offal.

There are also some special restaurants that only sell offal specialities like different kinds of soup and offal kebabs. They used to be very popular, and each neighbourhood had their own. Nowadays, though, they are struggling to exist. Those that survive have had to change their style and add new dishes to the menu, but there is a beautiful tradition being left behind; tripe soup cooks used to prepare the offal on a counter near the entrance of the shop. It makes me sad that it is no longer possible to hear the regular rhythm of the cleaver chopping at the tripe when I have never even heard it for myself. It was such a joy for me to hear stories about that sound that I am bitter not to have been able to experience it myself.

Offal in Cookbooks

Cookbooks are didactic sources that may lead people to cook at home. While many buy cookbooks aspirationally, we can still use them to obtain hints of consumption patterns. Examining cookbooks published in Istanbul helps us understand patterns of domestic offal consumption and cooking technique. Before we examine the cookbooks published from 1928 until today, let's take a look what was written in the early periods, which will help us make comparisons with later years.

Turgut Kut, who completed an important bibliographical study on this subject, generated a chronological list of old manuscripts and printed works:

> The first Turkish cookbook *Melceü't- Tabbâhîn* [Refuge of Cooks] was printed by lithography in Istanbul in 1844. This work of Mehmed Kâmil, a lecturer at the medical school, was published nine times during the years 1844-88. Türabi Efendi's book *A Manual of Turkish Cookery* is simply an English translation of *Melceü't-Tabbâhîn*. Then in 1880-81 *Yeni Yemek Kitabı* [*New Cookbook*] came out. This work was republished in 1924 and 1927 under the new title *Yeni Usül Yemek Kitabı* [*The New Style Cookbook*] by Muammer Mihri, who tried to appropriate it to his own authorship. In 1882, Ayşe Fahriye's book *Ev Kadını* [*Housewife*] made some additions to Istanbul cuisine. While these two last books reveal the European habits and innovations that were popular among the elite in the late nineteenth century; they also reflect Istanbul's traditional cuisine. Mahmud Nedim's book *Aşçıbaşı* [*The Head Chef*] published in 1900 includes also regional recipes reflecting the author's military memories of some rural locations in Anatolia. This book does not include many European recipes compared to *Housewife* and *A New Cookbook*.[4]

When we look at the early cookbooks we see that the offal culture that was inherited from Central Asian and Ottoman culinary traditions still survived in the recipes. In the nineteenth century, the Ottoman Empire's developing culinary culture incorporated cooking techniques from Europe, especially France, and offal adapted itself to new cooking techniques. We can find examples of the new versions of offal in the cookbooks written in the nineteenth and twentieth centuries. This *alafranga* [European] effect shows itself in the recipes of the twentieth century cookbooks, such as Milanese pan-fried brain and omelette with kidneys.

Özge Samancı studied nineteenth-century cookbooks to reveal European dishes that were introduced to Istanbul cuisine, but she also gives the percentage of each basic dish category in cookbooks, including offal. According to this analysis, offal dishes constitute 2% of 267 recipes in *Melce-ut Tabbahin* (1844), 1.3% of 802 recipes in *Ev Kadını* (1882), 4% of 164 recipes in *Yeni Yemek Kitabı* (1882-83) and lastly 3% of 304 recipes in *Aşçıbaşı* (1900).[5]

Some of the offal types mentioned in these recipes, such as *şirden* (the final stomach of the cud-chewing animals/ abomasum) are not popular in Istanbul today. We come across *şirden* in *Melceu'ut Tabbahin* (1844) and *Yeni Yemek Kitabı* (1882-83), but it is almost forgotten in Istanbul's cuisine today. While few in Istanbul are familiar with *şirden*, it is known among families from the Adana region and available in some tripe restaurants.

In *Ev Kadını*, we learn that there used to be different kinds of tripe dishes in nineteenth-century Istanbul cuisine. Tripe soup, tripe stew and a tripe dish prepared with eggs are all mentioned in the book. Ayşe Fahriye suggests that there should be three different cutting boards in the kitchen; one for meat, one for vegetables and the last one for chopping up the tripe. At the end of the book, she lists kitchen utensils needed in a proper kitchen; there should be one funnel for *bumbar dolması* [stuffed intestine] and one for *sucuk* [spiced sausage]. All parts of tripe and the intestines were used in cooking in Istanbul households.[6]

The letter reform of 1928, which established the current Turkish alphabet, offers a useful starting point to compare the Turkish-script cookbooks that began to be printed then. I tried to choose one of the most-printed cookbooks for each decade.

Title, author, publication date
Ev Kadınının Yemek Kitabı Alaturka ve Alafranga Mükemmel Yemek, Tatlı ve Pastalar Kitabı, Fahriye Nedim, 1933
Alaturka ve Alafranga Yemek Öğretimi, Ekrem Muhittin Yeğen, 1946
500 Yemek ve Tatlı Reçeteleri, Bahri Özdeniz, 1961
Türk Mutfak Sanatı, Necip Usta (Ertürk), 1978
Ağız Tadı, Sevim Tanör, 1985
Kolay ve Ekonomik Yemekler, Leman Cılızoğlu Eryılmaz, 1992
İşyerimiz Mutfak, Mesleğimiz Aşçılık, Sanatımız pişirmek, Aydın Yılmaz, 2000
Mutfak Keyfi, Oktay Usta, 2012

Table 1: Chronological list of Turkey's most-printed cookbooks since 1928.

The Fall of Offal in Istanbul

It would be appropriate to start with the cookbook published by Fahriye Nedim, which first appeared in 1933.[7] This book was reprinted over a hundred times and remains in print today. The book offers 935 recipes. including fifty for offal. The purpose of the book is to present both *alaturka* [traditional] and *alafranga* [European] recipes to housewives. In her preface, Nedim claims that she aimed to help housewives who want to make their family and friends happy. She proposes a list of dishes suitable for every season; offal is usually suggested in the winter. Her fifty offal recipes are given under several categories such as cattle meat, veal meat, sheep meat, , pilaf, pasta and *tirit*.[8] There is no separate category for offal; these dishes included with meat dishes, given the impression that offal had the same value as meat. The remarkable recipes are for *tirit* with marrow, trotter, liver, tripe and tongue. Other recipes that stand out include a special dish of wrapped intestine (*bağırsak sarması*), a pastry stuffing from trotter (*paça böreği içi*) and Edirne-style tongue recipes. assoiated with the city of Edirne.

Another bestselling Turkish cookbook is Ekrem Muhittin Yeğen's, which was often included in the hope chests of engaged girls in the 1950s and 60s.[9] The book was also used as a textbook in girls' schools. The book includes 27 offal recipes in a total of 339. Among them are traditional offal recipes such as tripe soup (as served in the diners around the market), tripe with chickpea; remarkable European-style recipes include suckling lamb's head cooked in parchment paper, Venetian tripe, Milanese pan-fried brain and omelette with kidneys.

Bahri Özdeniz's *500 Yemek ve Tatlı Reçeteleri* [Main Course and Dessert Recipes], written in 1943 and reprinted in the 1950s, 60s and 70s, provides important information about offal.[10] After a brief consideration of Turkish culinary culture, the preface includes a philosophical discussion of appetite. Özdeniz then compares European and Turkish culinary cultures and offers some examples of fusion recipes: trotter *tirit*, trotter *pelte* (a kind of gelled dish) and fried sheep intestines stand out among the offal recipes, and *tirit* reappears later in the book. This book also does not separate offal either: the recipes are categorized in terms of animal type and cooking technique, such as boiled sheep innards and sautéed sheep innards. Another outstanding recipe is stuffed trotter (*paça dolması*): the muscles of the boiled trotter are cut out, the remaining soft meat is chopped up, cooked with onions and spices and then stuffed into trotter meat. This dish existed during the Ottoman period, and the book's trotter *dolma* recipe is the same one mentioned in *Ev Kadını*, published in 1881. The reappearance of the recipe after seven decades shows that old recipes continued to persist in Istanbul's culinary culture.

In 1978, the famous Turkish chef Necip Usta published *Türk Mutfak Sanatı* [The Art of Turkish Cuisine].[11] This cookbook reflects the author's experiences cooking in five-star hotels abroad and his deep knowledge about Turkish cuisine. There are 34 offal dishes among the book's 1034 recipes. *Alafranga* style dishes dominate the book; however, the offal recipes represent Turkish culture. Antakya-style *cartlak kebap* [throat kebab], sautéed Trakya sweetbreads and *terbiyeli* [seasoned] Beykoz trotter are some of them. The *bağırsak sarması* [wrapped intestine] recipe is very detailed compared to earlier versions; there is even a detailed picture. In a significant change from earlier cookbooks, 25 of the 34 offal recipes are categorized as offal; unlike earlier books where offal appeared among other cuts of meat. That the titles including the expressions '*alaturka* and *alafranga* recipes' give us the biggest clue about the change in the cuisine; this expression was used in many cookbooks until through 1980s. We encounter both solely *alafranga* recipes and a synthesis of *alafranga* and *alaturka* recipes in the books of the period. Brain with Mornay sauce, cattle tongue roast and Italian-style mushrooms and liver on skewers are some examples of *alafranga* style dishes.

1985's *Ağız Tadı* includes only 20 offal recipes among a total of 442.[12] The author, Sevim Tanör, is a teacher of nutrition and home economics, and her intended audience included students, culinary enthusiasts and young housewives. While there aren't many offal recipes, its continued presence in the 1980s suggests that offal still preserves its importance, especially in various dishes such as soup and pilaf and in main course dishes. While lamb liver soup and tripe soup represent *alaturka* recipes in the book, Italian style tripe soup is an example of a *alafranga* recipe. Another outstanding recipe we come across for the first time in these cookbooks is brain soup. This dish seem as if it was derived from a synthesis of both Turkish and European cuisines, but when we search foreign sources we find dishes like pork brain soup, so it may have a European origin. The cooking technique involves adding gravy and chopped brain, with the membrane taken out, to a classic soup base thickened with flour and butter. The final step, adding scrambled egg yolk and lemon for extra taste and thickening, suggests that this recipe might come from the Istanbul tradition. The book's brain recipes do not consist of only soups: there is also brain with spinach and purée, soufflé with brain, pan-fried brain, brain au gratin, *beyin lokması* [fried brain dumplings prepared with a yeasty batter], potato balls with brain and brain salad with purée. Indeed, it is interesting that almost half the offal recipes involve brain. It is obvious that techniques such as soufflé and gratin come from the *alafranga* cooking style, but the remaining brain recipes seem to be examples of the traditional style. Besides brain dishes, this book has two other recipes, liver roast and liver pudding, featured for the first time in a Turkish cookbook.

The 1990s seem to mark a sharp change. *Kolay ve Ekonomik Yemekler* [*Easy and Affordable Dishes*], first published in 1992, reflects the decrease of offal recipes in cookbooks.[13] In fact, offal is replaced in the soup category by *yalancı işkembe* [faux tripe soup], prepared using chicken skin instead of tripe. I assume that cholesterol and other health issues, which my family experienced, led to offal being preferred less starting in the 1990s. I have found no new offal recipes introduced since then, and traditional offal recipes diminish as we come closer to today.

Indeed, it was a challenge for me to find a cookbook from the 2000s that includes traditional recipes. Globalization made international cuisines more desirable, and cookbooks published in Turkey also reflected this fact. I chose *İşyerimiz Mutfak, Mesleğimiz Aşçılık, Sanatımız Pişirmek* [*Our Office is the Kitchen, Our Profession is Cookery, Our Art is to Cook*] written by Aydın Yılmaz, a cook from the famous Bolu

The Fall of Offal in Istanbul

region.[14] Although it was published in 2000, it seems more like a product of what he learned since the 1950s. Yılmaz includes 11 offal recipes (out of 415 total), his knowledge about offal is extensive, and three pages are devoted to discussing offal.

In the 2010s, cookbooks seem to be becoming more concept oriented, often locally adapted versions of popular books that were written abroad, rather than written directly to depict Istanbul's cuisine or to meet Turkish tastes. For example, Oktay (Usta) Aymelek, a cook with television shows and many followers, features offal recipes on his television show and website, but his cookbooks from this period, like 2012's *Mutfak Keyfi* [*Kitchen Pleasure*], do not include offal.[15] While demand for offal seems to have diminished, I hope that offal will find its place in cookbooks again with new developments in gastronomy and even new recipes (see Table 2 overleaf).

While European style cooking techniques have enriched the cuisine of İstanbul, some flavours and dishes have disappeared. *Tirit* is the best example to this change. Versions of this dish, prepared by soaking old bread in meat stock, that use liver, tripe or trotter seem to have been completely forgotten in Istanbul today. Other offal dishes, like trotter soup, chickpea and tripe stew and tripe soup, have successfully survived in Istanbul. Still other dishes survive but have changed: many rice dishes that had been made with a variety of offal are, since the 1980s, made only with liver. The list of offal that have disappeared from the cookbooks include parts that were once popular: şirden, lungs, sweetbreads, and oxtail.

Offal held a considerable place in recipes from the early Republic era until the 1950s. However, the publication of offal recipes began to decrease in kind and number in the 1950s. a process that accelerated from 1980 on. Over the same period, the offal shop, once an inseparable part of Istanbul neighbourhoods, is getting more and more scarce. In a sad way, both the tradition of cooking offal at home and the trade of offal butchery are slowly dying. Home cooking of offal is in danger of being forgotten in Istanbul's cuisine; sad for the cats, but more so for the young generations to come.

Author's name Publication date		Ekrem	Bahri	Necip Ertürk, 1978		Leman Cılızoğlu	Aydın Yılmaz, 2000	Oktay Aymelek, 2012
Total recipes	935	339	500	1034	442	406	415	201
Offal recipes	50	27	24	34	20	7	11	0
Tripe	5	4	1	5	3		3	
Brain	7	6	3	5	9	2	3	
Trotter	7	6	7	2	2	2	2	
Liver	13	4	6	7	6	1	2	
Kidney	3	3	2	6		2	1	
Tongue	3	2	1	2				
Head	5	1	2	1			1	
Heart	1		2					
Intestine	3	1	1	1				
Marrow bone	2							
Ram's testicles	1		1					
Sweetbreads				4				

Table 2: Numbers of the offal dishes in the most printed cookbooks since the letter reform in Turkish Republic in 1928 to today

Notes

1. Özge Samancı, 'The Culinary Culture of the Ottoman Palace & İstanbul during the Last Period of theEmpire', in *Turkish Cuisine*, ed. by Arif Bilgin, Özge Samancı, trans. and ed. by Cumhur Orancı (Ankara: Ministry of Culture and Tourism, 2008), pp. 199-217.
2. Turgut Kut, 'A Bibliography of Turkish Cookery Books up to 1927', in *Turkish Cuisine*, ed. by Arif Bilgin, Özge Samancı, trans. and ed. by Cumhur Orancı (Ankara: Ministry of Culture and Tourism, 2008), pp. 329-37.
3. Anisa Helou, *The Fifth Quarter: An Offal Cookbook*, (London: Absolute Press, 2011), p. 10.
4. Turgut Kut, *Açıklamalı Yemek Kitapları Bibliyografisi (Eski Harfli Yazma ve Basma Eserler)* (Ankara: Kültür ve Turizm Bakanlığı Milli Folklor Araştırma Dairesi Yayınları, 1985).
5. Özge Samancı '*19. Yy İstanbul Mutfağında Yeni Lezzetler*', *Yemek ve Kültür*, 6 (2008), 86-96.
6. Ayşe Fahriye. *Ev Kadını* (Istanbul: Mahmud Bey Matbaası, 1882-83).
7. Fahriye Nedim, *Alaturka ve Alafranga Mükemmel Yemek ve Tatlı Kitabı* (Istanbul: İnkılap Kitabevi, 1933).
8. *Tirit* is a name of both the dish and cooking technique, which is prepared with stale bread chunks soaked in broth. It has different versions either with or without offal such as tripe, trotter, minced meat lamb or chicken.

9. Ekrem Muhittin Yeğen, *Alaturka ve Alafranga Yemek Öğretimi* (Istanbul: Güler Basımevi, 1946).
10. Bahri Özdeniz, *Alaturka Alafranga 500 Yemek ve Tatlı Reçeteleri* (Istanbul: İkbal Yayıncılık:1961).
11. Necip Usta (Ertürk), *Türk Mutfak Sanatı* (Istanbul: Kıral Matbaası, 1978).
12. Sevim Tanör, *Ağız Tadı* (Istanbul: Sistem Yayıncılık, 1985).
13. Leman Cılızoğlu Eryılmaz, *Kolay ve Ekonomik Yemekler* (Istanbul: Remzi Kitabevi, 2011).
14. Aydın Yılmaz, *Aşçının El Kitabı: İşyerimiz Mutfak, Mesleğimiz Aşçılık, Sanatımız Pişirmek* (Istanbul: Öztiryakiler Endüstriyel Mutfak Kültürü Yayınları, 2000).
15. Oktay Aymelek, *Oktay Usta ile Mutfak Keyfi* (Istanbul: Yakamoz Yayıncılık, 2012).

A Waste of Flavour

Thom Eagle

We all know that we need to waste less food, at both a personal and an industrial level. Magazines and television show us how to marshal and corral leftovers, how to cook once and eat for the week, while campaigns such as the War On Waste show us the apparent futility of these endeavours; we fret over a bag of liquefying salad while tons of unwanted roots or brassicas rot in the fields. We are encouraged to see each item of food as a precious commodity, the product of a unique animal life or of a year's careful farming, when it is clear that supermarkets and the farms which supply them see only a continuous cycle of disposable stock, with waste the inevitable consequence of our need for convenience, availability and consistency. Somewhere between these two extremes sits the restaurant kitchen. My first job was in a university canteen, doling out food to the summer schools and language classes that populated it during the vacation, and the amount of waste involved was quite phenomenal. We would spend the lunch service handing over neatly small portions of lasagne or pie, explaining carefully to the baffled Italians that, sorry, they could only have one bread roll each – and then sling trayfuls into the gobbler. There was a salad bar, the upkeep and decoration of which occupied the entirety of one chef's working hours; he would spend every day carving tomato roses, fanning strawberries, arranging neat tangles of julienned carrots around his plates of quiche, cold cuts and coleslaws, only to see the whole thing demolished in the first half-hour of lunch. Then he'd pick up the pieces, throw away the detritus and start all over again.

This kitchen, which occupied a space as big as the dining area, was an operation of volume, where little if any attention was paid to the actual quality of the food served; in such an environment, ingredients can be very cheap indeed, and are, perhaps understandably, treated as disposable, less important than the time required to prepare them and the space required to store the finished product. Most businesses do not run like that, but a degree of wastage is always expected. In the case of meat and fish especially, you have only a short window of time in which to sell each raw piece, say three days; after that, you can cook it and buy yourself another three days, and that's that. Hopefully you feed it to yourself or to your staff, but it is of no further use to the kitchen. A menu is a balancing act between choice and frugality; it needs to be of a big enough size to satisfy the majority of your customers, but not so big as to leave your fridges groaning with uneaten, uncooked and unwanted food. This is especially true, I think, in the early years of a restaurant, when you are still finding your clientele and are not necessarily busy all of the time; it is, at any rate, manageable. Short or entirely set menus, as well as allowing a tight focusing of the kitchen's skill, are a way of minimizing this sort of wastage.

Imagine, then, that your restaurant only offers a set menu, that it only takes bookings; barring no-shows, who you will publicly shame and perhaps blacklist, you need never throw away another piece of protein! This is ideal, you might think, both economically and ecologically – but mainly the former. Your food costs might be perfectly balanced, you might sell every piece of prepared food that comes out of your kitchen, but it still generates a huge amount of waste. More, in fact, than most lower-end restaurants. Broadly speaking, the higher the quality of food, the greater the quantity of raw materials that a kitchen deals with. A decent pub might cut their own chips; a gastropub makes their own ketchup to go with their own chips. A really good one makes their own salt to go on their own chips, and maybe bypasses the ketchup. Almost anything can be got peeled, portioned and packaged, industrially produced for poky, time-poor kitchens; conversely, at the other end of the market, anything which can be got in its raw unprocessed state, from potatoes to whole fish and sides of meat, generally is. This is a good thing. You get a fresher product (or at least have more of an idea of how fresh it is), and you get more control over it. (Fishmongers, for example, tend to prepare fillets of mackerel by cutting out the flesh around the bones, while I like to pin-bone them properly with tweezers.) However, you also end up with a huge amount of rubbish. A lot can go in the stockpot, but you are still left with potato, garlic and carrot peelings, radish or turnip tops, the stalks and excess leaves of cabbages, kohlrabi, cauliflowers and kale, cephalopod guts, mollusc and crustacean shells, the heads and entrails of oily fish, excess fat or trim from almost any animal; then the waste from the restaurant itself, ends of wine and milk and bread, coffee grounds and tea leaves, unfit for their original purpose but still, often, useful. I work at a plant nursery with a kitchen garden, so a lot of the vegetable matter can go straight onto the groaning compost heaps; even with this luxury, there is still a lot to throw away. This, it strikes me, is a very modern problem. We're lucky, in fact, that this is a case of ethics rather than mere survival.

The history of cuisine – broadly coincident with the histories of agriculture and of human civilization – is, by and large, an account of what can be salvaged, by salting, brewing, burying or hanging, in the face of decay and death. Long distant hunter-gatherers could enjoy their occasional feasts, stuffing themselves with meat and with offal and throwing what they could not eat to their dogs, knowing that tomorrow would mean a return to nuts, berries and wild greens; but settlements and fields meant kitchens, larders and storehouses, and with them, the techniques required to husband resources against the times of scarcity. Many of these techniques are still in use today, in professional and amateur kitchens alike; although dropping off since the advent of refrigeration, they have recently remerged, albeit excused with descriptors such as 'artisan' and 'home-made', and associated warmly with the so-called 'peasant' cuisines of the world. In fact, of course, such techniques were once universal, and gave rise to much of what we call 'cuisine'. What was revolutionary about refrigeration was not that it allowed us to store food for long periods – humanity has always found ways of doing that – but that it allowed us to do so in a state of stasis. While this is undoubtedly convenient, it is also less interesting and often less delicious. The fact that we can keep milk as milk, and enjoy it for breakfast every morning, means we don't have to make it into butter, or yoghurt, or cheese, as our ancestors would. Of course, we can still go and buy those things, but they, too, are static products, where once our food was in a constant state of change.

Milk, at any rate, is nutritious and tasty, and it's not surprising that we would try to preserve it; of more interest to me are the ingredients that we felt the need to coax gently into palatability, through a long process, often, of fermentation. Who first ate an olive? In their fresh state they are inedibly bitter, hard and unpleasant; their taste, far from being 'as old as cold water', is a product, rather, of human intervention and ingenuity.[1] While such early food processes are often glossed as happy accidents, it's hard to see how these acrid fruit were first left in a bath of lye or salt to develop their complex, divisive flavour. Chef Stevie Parle does a similar thing with sloes, turning them into a kind of British olive; an excellent idea, but there is less of a leap from the raw sloe, which responds well to cooking and sweetening, than there is from the raw olive. The olive must have seemed a kind of waste product of nature, a fruit which, though not poisonous, could not be eaten – if even this could be rendered edible, what could be done with other waste products?

A brief glance through the cookbook of Apicius, which collates recipes from a few hundred years of Roman civilization, will show you the absolute ubiquity of *garum* within that cuisine, from the very highest tables and down; in fact, several different grades, comparable to those which govern olive oil, were available, to suit usage and salary.[2] Although often translated as anchovy sauce, this substance could have been made from a ferment of any small pelagic fish or mollusc and would have given the dockyards of the Empire a quite unbelievable stench. This was the waste of the fishing industry rather than the kitchen. Both fish too small to bother eating and the guts and trim from larger ones could be pressed into service as a sauce which seems to have been a sort of universal seasoning in classical Rome, much as the (very similar) *nước mắm* is in Vietnam, or as sriracha has become for a certain kind of ramen enthusiast. Now, if *garum* was made of fish offal alone, its ubiquity would be entirely understandable. The deep umami taste of fermented, salty protein is hugely addictive, and to create it entirely from waste is quite remarkable. The fact is, though, that its production also involves quite large amounts of salt, which, if not a luxury item in the ancient world (it was too important for that), was at least expensive; its profligate use, economically necessary in, say curing the choice parts of the family pig for the winter, seems a little excessive for a flavouring – but still it was made. This combination of the epicurean and the economical points to a use for waste in our own kitchens. Salt, happily, is now freely available, and if we can use it to extract such a depth of flavour from rubbish, why wouldn't we?

Traditionally a nation of vinegar pickles, Britain now has a lot of chefs (myself included), influenced by the cuisines of South East Asia, Eastern Europe, and North America, who are discovering the possibilities of the widespread pickling method of lacto-fermentation, which relies on bacteria to do most of the work for you; kimchi, originally Korean, is a very popular style. The process is very simple. Vegetables, often cabbage or other brassicas, are rubbed with salt and perhaps sugar, and left overnight; the next day, they are drained and combined with a thick, spicy paste, then packed into jars, barrels or pits, and left to ferment for days, weeks, or months. When you bottle something in vinegar, you are, after the initial period of pickling, keeping it essentially static; the salt and the acid combine to kill off all microbial life, and the pickles themselves remain stable, with a slow move, perhaps, towards an unwanted mushiness. A lactic ferment, by contrast, is a living thing. It will keep changing every day it is alive, and the vegetables in it will undergo a process almost like cooking. We are familiar, I suppose, with the so-called cooking which a fish *ceviche* undergoes, bathed in its curing acid; the long ferment of kimchi allows something almost like stewing to occur, breaking down tough vegetable fibres into something chewable, digestible, delicious. Enter, then, my kitchen waste.

The amount of kale that a relatively small garden can produce over the course of a winter is really quite astonishing, and the percentage of that which is tough, barely edible stalk can be disheartening; when the pile for compost is twice as big as the pile for blanching, you start to wonder what to do with it. The answer, of course, is kimchi. The thick stalks of *cavolo nero*, finely chopped into little squares and massaged with coarse salt, become juicy and richly green; fermented with chilli, garlic and herbs, they soften and mellow, and their strong cabbage flavour deepens to an almost truffle-like pungency. Here, as with *garum*, we find that waste plus salt equals dense flavour. Michael Pollan and others have noted the almost fanatical fear of microbes which has taken root over the past fifty years or so.[3] Once you rid yourself of that, though, fermentation turns out to be easy and almost intuitive, watching the bubbling development of your pickles almost like a pet. Kimchi (or sauerkraut, which uses a similar dry-salting style) is an excellent way to deal with harder vegetables; for softer ones I turn to the Ukrainian chef Olia Hercules' recipe for fermented tomatoes in her book *Mamushka*[4]. When I came across this it was, happily, the height of summer, with a huge glut of tomatoes coming in from our kitchen garden, all of them very rich and flavoursome, but the recipe works almost as well with imported Dutch tomatoes in the middle of winter. Pour a simple brine, 35g of salt and sugar to a litre of water, over your tomatoes; leave to ferment. That's it. It works just as well for mixed pickles, little squash, young carrots, radishes and so on; for some reason, my cucumbers always fail, but I'm working on it.

Although this style of ferment demands a better quality of raw material, it leaves you with a waste product of its own – the excess brine. This, especially in the case of tomatoes, is no hardship. The combination of umami-rich, deeply savoury tomato with the added punch of fermentation is a powerful one, and I found myself fermenting tomatoes that were over- or under-ripe, scarred or woolly or just a bit dull, purely for the sake of the brine, which I used as a dressing, as a cooking medium (I'd recommend it for shellfish), and most importantly, as a starter for other ferments. Sweet, salty and already teeming with lactic acid bacteria, it gives body and heft to the more watery vegetables, and allows you to start a ferment with greater peace of mind. Other bacteria, yeasts and moulds are much less likely to take root where there is already an established community. Most of the time, I have a fairly cavalier attitude towards this; most pickles will happily get started by themselves, and will tell you, by smell or by sight, when they have gone bad. I take pH readings for peace of mind, and if a ferment sits for too long without going sour, out it goes. Fermenting protein – especially animal protein – requires a little more care.

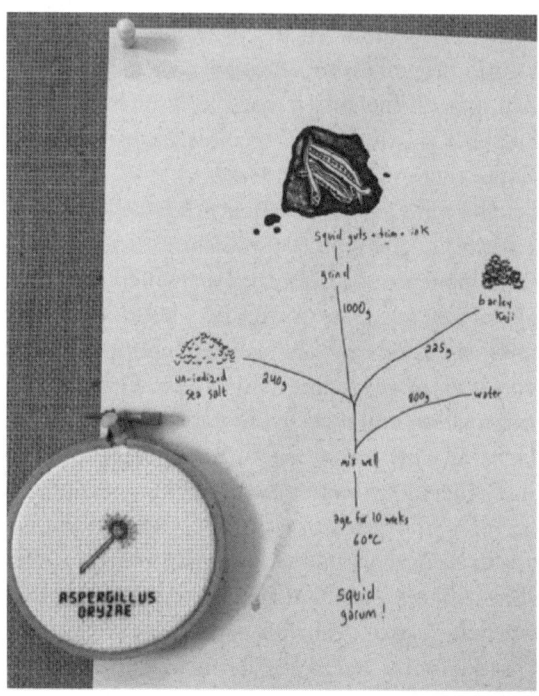

Figure 1
Rene Redzepi on Twitter (@ReneRedzepiNoma, 5 September 2015)

We sell a fair amount of squid in the restaurant, which, you'll know if you have ever prepared a whole one, come with quite a lot of built-in waste. Guts, skin, ink-sacks, those two extra-long tentacles, the baby gurnard or sole they always seem to have just eaten, the often tough wings, trim; added together, a third or even a half of the weight of these cephalopods can be thrown away, a waste of landfill space, of the restaurant's money, and of the quotas, stowage and time of our beleaguered fishing industry. Given this, and my vague researches in classical cuisines, I was extremely interested when I came across a Rene Redzepi recipe for squid *garum* (Figure 1). Up to this point, I had never considered making such a thing; now, with the tools and ingredients at my disposal, here was a recipe. Meat or fish are, justifiably, the source of some of our greatest fears about bacteria and illness. No one wants to get botulism, or worse, cause an outbreak through a restaurant kitchen; there are, though, fairly easy ways to avoid it. Large amounts of salt or smaller ones of saltpetre, sufficient acidity, and inoculation with 'friendly' microbes are all ways to avoid poisoning; Redzepi's recipe uses a lot of salt and barley *koji,* a steamed grain covered with a sweet mould, used in the production of miso. I didn't have any of that, so I soured the mixture with my tomato brine, bringing the pH down to four and adding, I hoped, sufficient lactic acid bacteria to combat anything more menacing. After leaving the lot at 60° for 10 weeks (one of many reasons not to try this at home) I was left with an extremely dark and complex fish sauce; I've used it ever since, as an anchovy substitute, and nobody has got ill yet.[5]

Churning on-the-turn cream into butter, dry-curing meat and cheeses, fermenting guts and roots and bones: these are all ancient skills, fundamental to the development of our cultural and culinary identities, which have been supplanted in the modern kitchen by the tin can, the freezer and the refrigerator, but these modern methods can only keep fresh things fresh, preserving a static ideal of what good food should look like. Food doesn't have to be complicated, we're told – just buy the best you can, at the height of its season, and enjoy it at its freshest. This is all well and good, and if it keeps us from flavourless, air-freighted or intensively grown produce, then all the better; but such a prescriptive, subtly competitive model of cooking gives us nowhere to go if we 'fail', if our vegetables aren't the freshest or if we leave that tomato one day past its ideal ripeness. I don't know (and I don't know if you could possibly work out) if my efforts to preserve and adapt, to salvage flavour from rubbish, can possibly count against the huge wastefulness – of water, gas and packaging, as well as of food – which plagues the restaurant industry. It is good, though, I think, to develop and rediscover these ancient skills: to try and find a third way between the convenience of cheap, industrialized food and the beatific elitism of some of the farm-to-fork movement; to make the best of the materials and resources we have to hand; and to learn that frugality and care need not be merely puritanical. We can, if we like, create pure flavour out of bones, out of guts and out of waste. I invite you, at least, to try.

Notes

1. Lawrence Durrell, Prospero's Cell (London: Penguin, 1978), p. 96.
2. Apicius, *The Roman Cookery Book : A Critical Translation of The Art Of Cooking, trans. Barbara Flower and Elisabeth Rosenbaum* (London: Harrap, 1974), passim.
3. See Michael Pollan, Cooked: A Natural History of Transformation (London: Penguin, 2014).
4. Olia Hercules, Mamushka (London: Mitchell Beazley, 2015), p. 157.
5. As well as Redzepi's recipe, I'm indebted to Robert I. Curtis, 'Umami and the Foods of Classical Antiquity', The American Journal of Culinary Nutrition 90 (2005), pp. 712-18.

A Knife and an Onion: Reclaiming Food and Skills in Central London

Anastasia Edwards

Introduction

London is a food-rich city: one can find ingredients for almost any international dish and sample almost any type of cuisine. For many people, however, this gastronomic wealth is out of reach. Because they are on low incomes, or have lost jobs, or are on small pensions, or are living in isolation, many Londoners increasingly find it a challenge to eat a healthy and varied diet. Hovering between hunger and food security, they must sometimes appeal to charitable organizations for help. Food poverty is hard to document precisely, but the use of foodbanks provides a reliable barometer. Figures recently published by the Trussell Trust show that in the 2015/2016 financial year, 110,364 food parcels (including 42,503 for children) were distributed by the Trussell Trust in London, a five per cent increase on the previous financial year (the population of Greater London is around 8.6 million people).

This paper looks at three charities operating in Central London that, in different ways, aim to feed people in need and to help them to change their relationship to food and cooking. (The first two charities are branches of national organizations.) The first, the Waterloo Foodbank, helps people at times of food crisis; the second, Eat Well Spend Less, aims to give people the skills to cook affordable yet balanced meals; and the third, In-Deep, provides meals and comfort to people over fifty. While the Waterloo Foodbank is just south of the River Thames and In-Deep is just north, both are within a fifteen-minute walk of the Houses of Parliament. They therefore offer, on many levels, insights into food poverty in the heart of London.

Focussing on the 'social initiatives' aspect of this year's Symposium theme, this paper considers some of the cheapest and simplest food available: the bargain tins and no-brand supermarket items that many food-lovers and cooks might reject as unworthy of a healthy, interesting meal, let alone a feast. Yet, among the food poor in central London, these basic foodstuffs can, depending on the context in which they are prepared and eaten, assume a positive significance greater than their mere energetic and nutritional value.

The focus of this paper has been to record as much about the workings of these charities as possible in the space provided, while providing some remarks on the ways in which the food that they distribute changes in significance. The paper does not aim to be definitive or even comprehensive, as food poverty is a hugely complex issue, but rather seeks to record in a small way that even the cheapest 'rejected and reclaimed' foodstuffs can carry complex meaning. The research is almost solely based on numerous interviews. While I had hoped, at the outset, to interview more of the charities' recipients, direct access can prove tricky, as the charities that minister to vulnerable people are understandably protective of them. For this reason, I have prioritized quotations by charity workers that relate stories about individual recipients.

The Waterloo Foodbank

The Waterloo Foodbank is a collaboration between the Trussell Trust, a United Kingdom-wide network of 424 foodbanks, and Oasis, an evangelical Christian church and social activist movement under the leadership of its founder Steve Chalke. Oasis runs a primary and secondary school and many other ventures dedicated to helping the poor who live within a 500-meter radius of its spire in Lambeth North.

The Trussell Trust model is one shared by many other foodbanks worldwide: people who find themselves unable to afford food approach welfare agencies, which refer them to a foodbank and give them vouchers for a three-day food parcel. The Waterloo Foodbank works with around 140 welfare agencies, and food cannot be obtained on a walk-in basis without referral from one of these organizations. The food in the parcel consists of a standard allocation of food items that varies only according to the size of the recipient family (see Figure 1 on p. 181 for the typical contents of a Waterloo Foodbank parcel designated for a household of three to four people). The food in the parcels has to be non-perishable, both because it needs to be stored, often for several months, and also because, although it is meant to last for three days, people often try to stretch it out for longer. Although some food items are in packets, such as pasta and sugar, most of the food, including meat and vegetables, are in tins.

Nathan Jones, an employee of Oasis who runs the foodbank as well as many of Oasis's other projects, explains the genesis of the foodbank, which started five years ago:

> 'We run a primary school and realized that some of the families in the primary school couldn't afford to eat over Christmas. And that's not putting a nice roast turkey dinner on the table: it's a fortnight school holiday and the parents can't afford to feed the kids for a fortnight. So we decided to get some parcels together for the families concerned and the response was so popular that we decided we had to do something more.'

Contrary to some media reports, the people who come to foodbanks are far from opportunistic. 'I've hardly ever met anybody who I genuinely didn't think needed support,' says Jones:

> I think that's the thing we want to get across to people. These are people who

are so desperate they literally cannot put food on their family's table. I've stood outside here with people and put my arm around them and walked them through the door because they were so embarrassed, so ashamed at being at a foodbank. And that's the kind of people you get. You don't get people who are trying to steal free food off people.

According to Jones, the primary reason why sixty per cent of people come to the foodbank is because of benefit sanctions or benefit delays, which 'has been a massive issue' in recent years. The other issue is just that the cost of living in Central London is 'insane'. 'The living wage isn't anywhere near a living wage, and zero-hours contracts have a massive impact on some of the people who come here,' he explains. 'Even the people who are working still have to come to a foodbank. That is an incredible thing to be able to say in the sixth-richest city in the world. So those kinds of thing are a real issue: cost of living and security around employment and sanctions and benefit delays. They are the big ones for us.'

Ninety per cent of the food is donated, much of it by shoppers in a nearby Tesco, who are asked by foodbank volunteers to add an item of two to their own food shop, and to place these items in a large container once they have paid for it. Since the Trussel Trust established a more formal national link with Tesco, the supermarket weighs the donated food, ascribes a monetary value to each kilogram and donates thirty per cent of that value in cash to the foodbank, which, says Jones, 'funds a lot of what we do'.

Nonetheless, Jones felt it was too risky to be solely dependent on one source of food, and he has sought other channels of food donations. One especially successful partnership has come through the Waterloo Business Improvement District (WBID). Some twenty-odd businesses in the district have agreed to collect food, and supply boxes into which their employees can deposit food on an on-going basis. The logistical challenges of obtaining and distributing even donated food are significant, though, and perhaps the most welcome aspect of this arrangement is that distribution is taken care of: four times per year, a catering company that is part of the WBID uses one of its vans to drive to all the donor companies to collect the contents of the boxes and then bring the food right to the foodbank's 'front door'. 'That is a dream for us,' says Jones. 'Logistically it's not too complicated, as there is a guy from the catering company who manages a lot of it, and then it's not resource for us.'

Jones also developed a link with the nearby world-famous Borough Market after he and his wife took the challenge of living off a food parcel for three days as part of a 2015 sponsorship appeal to raise money for the foodbank. The food in the parcels aims to be nutritionally balanced, but Jones said that by the end of three days they 'craved vegetables'. Vegetables and fruit, essential to health, are relatively expensive compared to other more energy-rich foods, such as pasta, and the foodbank staff were finding that many clients were only eating one portion of the government-recommended 'five-a-day'. Jones thus approached two vendors at Borough Market, Ted's Veg and Bread

Ahead, and asked them to donate food they could no longer sell. 'This is not stuff that's on its last legs,' explains Jones. 'This is all stuff that's top of the range but, because it's Borough Market, as soon as it starts to look like it's anything but perfect they can't sell it.' Again, distribution is a challenge: the foodbank, which does not own a van, must hire a Zip Car twice a week, at a cost of about £14 per trip. This expense, which works out at more than £100 per month, is often unaffordable for what is, in the realm of privation, considered a luxury.

One irony is that this fresh food cannot be officially placed in a parcel, as it is perishable and could present a liability for the Trussell Trust should a client feel that something might have gone off and made them ill. In future, once a source of funding for the collection from Borough Market becomes secure, Jones hopes to use the fresh produce and bread in another Trussell Trust scheme he has to helped to implement in central London: Eat Well Spend Less.

Eat Well Spend Less

Eat Well Spend Less (EWSL) is a six-week cookery course that teaches people on low-incomes, many of whom are in debt and caught up in a cycle of buying expensive ready meals, how to reduce their food bills and to cook more healthily. First developed in Salisbury in 2004, the course is now taught at sixty-one foodbanks around the UK. The course typically meets one morning per week, and is followed by a meal at which the eight participants and two volunteers sit down to eat what they have cooked. While the cooking is taking place, the volunteers, a couple of whom are themselves graduates of the course, talk informally about the ways in which the participants can save money and the pitfalls they can avoid while shopping in supermarkets (see Figures 2 and 3 overleaf for some of their handouts)

EWSL's chief developer was Alex Howell, whose research in focus groups led him to some staggering facts. 'I was really shocked by demographics,' he explained:

> 'Many people had never knowingly eaten an onion. In a lot of households cooking has not been the norm for a generation, and when that knowledge has gone it has gone. In other countries food is still a priority, but not here, since the seventies. I began by asking them, "If all barriers were removed what kind of food would you like to be eating?" For many people the answer was, "Instead of Tesco Yorkshire pudding it would be Aunt Betty's Yorkshire Pudding". And if I asked them what they would buy if they had £1 to spend, it was often a portion of chips.'

Howell realized that many people, having no idea where to begin to cook, were spending far too much of their income on expensive supermarket ready meals and takeaways. Many people were terrified of touching fresh food and picking up a knife. He realized that rather than presenting them with a revolutionary change to their lives,

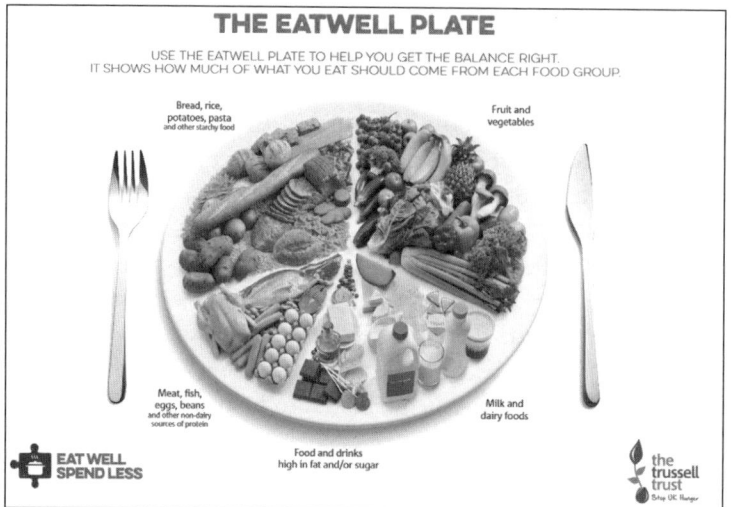

Figure 2

The Eatwell Plate from Eat Well Spend Less.

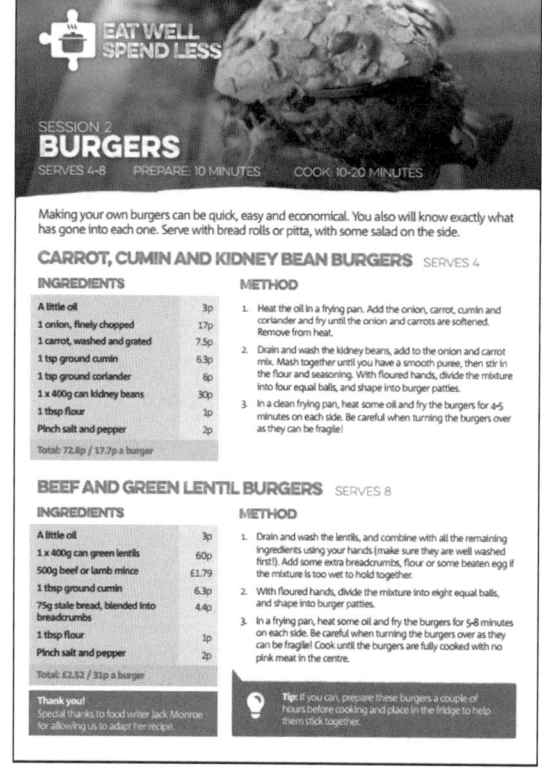

Figure 3

Recipes from Eat Well Spend Less.

EWSL would have more of a chance of success if it worked with the familiar. A lot of the EWSL recipes are thus for healthy versions of meals that people were already eating: curry, pizza and cereal bars. Howell remembers how one participant, who had spent £12 on Domino's pizza the night before, was amazed and empowered by learning to cook pizza for less than £1.

'Confidence is key: there is no substitute for a knife and an onion,' he explains. 'Once people realize how easy it is…. Brands perpetuate a myth that cooking is hard. It is a complicated picture: supermarkets are not always a safe place.' Part of the EWSL mission is also to encourage people to set a routine of breakfast, lunch and dinner, which is grounding and which also helps them to think about budgeting for meals.

Rachel Smith, a student who coordinates EWSL as part of her course work, has worked very closely with many of the participants of courses in Waterloo. She describes the impact the course can have:

> People are like, 'Wow I didn't realise that I could make a tomato sauce from scratch that tastes better than one from a tin, that's cheaper than one from a tin, that's healthier than one from a tin.' They are amazed by that, and amazed by how quickly and easily you can cook things from scratch. We've had people sending us photos saying, 'Look! This is what I cook at home now and I never would have done that before.' Having that reduction in their food bills after coming on the course really makes a massive difference, and having that sense of freedom of having a bit more disposable income and not having that fear of getting into debt. Even freeing up £5 per week can make a big difference. We help them create menu plans and suggest how they might go about shopping a bit more wisely, go round to different places or maybe go to the markets where they can get cheap access to fruit and vegetables. We discuss some of the traps that you can fall into when buying food and sometimes it's a real eye opener for people and they say, 'I didn't realise that supermarkets are trying to make me buy all these deals that I don't really need, and that they put all the branded stuff at eye level.' All those little things, it's just raising people's awareness.

While the course ostensibly focuses on cookery skills, it is fundamentally a home economics course, a distinction that Nathan Jones, of Oasis's Waterloo Foodbank, believes is crucial. Ultimately, it seems, the goal of EWSL and Oasis's related debt-management courses is to make foodbanks redundant. This goal can only be achieved by getting to know people, recognizing their anxieties, and understanding the particular challenges they face. The decision to come to a foodbank, an often emotionally drastic step for people who might never have appealed to a charity before, is a culmination of an often-intricate web of challenges, habits, and reversals of circumstance.

'We see it as part of wider project,' Jones explains:

> We started the food bank because you're catching people at their lowest point of need: they can't afford to put food on the table. So we talk a lot about raising the safety net. For a lot of people, we give them a cup of tea; we sit down and

chat with them. The presenting idea is that "you've got no food", but what's the actual issue? Hopefully we can catch them at money management, and hopefully you can catch them at interview skills. Hopefully they won't need debt advice and hopefully they won't need foodbanks. That's why the cup of tea is important.

In-Deep

Colin Chapman would agree about the paramount importance and wider project of offering someone a cup of tea. In 2001 he founded In-Deep, a charity that addresses the isolation experienced by over fifty-years-olds in South Westminster. The chief method is to offer communal meals: one lunch and one breakfast per week, and one three-course dinner once a month. The charity also distributes some 400 food hampers across London at Christmas, and it had recently begun to offer meals in adjacent neighbourhoods.

Fifteen years ago, Chapman had a good job at the National Film Theatre in London. During a period of recession, he lost his job and found himself homeless and dependent on drugs and alcohol. While he had grown up in relative affluence in Oval in London, just across the river from Westminster, he was too ashamed to stay near his family, and so he slept in doorways and in the gardens of housing estates in South Westminster. A turning point came when an old man took pity on him and invited Chapman up to his flat to sleep. "'Pop, you don't even know me,'" Chapman recalls saying. 'He was a guy who used to light lanterns in churches.… I went in and noticed how filthy and disgusting his place was, so I said to him, "Let's go out and have a cup of tea and after I'm going to clean your flat."'

Soon Chapman acquired a reputation, among the older people of the neighbourhood, as a window cleaner, and they often asked him to help clean their windows and do odd jobs, often in exchange for cups of tea, a drink he cherishes to this day. While getting to know these older people, he realized the profound isolation that afflicted many of them, especially those who were living on limited incomes, many of whom didn't see their families very often and many of whom had ailments that made venturing too far afield a physical challenge. He was especially distressed at the poverty of their nutrition, which often had as much to do with the cost of the energy needed to cook a meal as with the ingredients themselves.

One day during that period, he collapsed and was brought to hospital. In an extraordinary coincidence, his estranged father happened to be in the same hospital at the same time – in the next bed. Chapman technically died more than once that night, but, to the astonishment of the seasoned consultant who treated him, he not only survived, but was able to be dismissed a few days later. Chapman, who had not been brought up going to church and who had not up to that point been religious in any sense, came to feel that he had been saved by the Holy Spirit in a miraculous act of conversion. Furthermore, he has since felt that the Holy Spirit intended him to fall so dramatically through the cracks so that he could understand the need of the elderly. Part of the Holy Spirit's plan was local: according to Chapman, it was not coincidence that he had been homeless in Westminster, and that every time he left the area 'something happened' to bring him back.

Soon after his conversion, he founded the charity In-Deep, so called because 'its roots run deep into the community'. Around that time he also met his wife Emma, a trained nurse, who is in charge of fundraising and accounts, while Colin focuses more on logistics and day-to-day operations. From the outset, the format of the charity's work was clear: it would provide one baked potato lunch on a Wednesday, one Full English Breakfast on a Friday, and one three-course roast dinner once a month on a Saturday to anyone over fifty who wanted to come. On Fridays there would also be manicurists and pedicurists, as Chapman, in getting to know elderly people, realized how neglected their feet and hands were, and how poor care of these could lead to all sorts of other problems. The meals are all held in a hall, which has a kitchen, on a housing estate in South Westminster.

Colin and Emma Chapman bemoan the way the elderly feed themselves. Emma notes, 'Often, they will be only eating a biscuit for breakfast, and then maybe a porkpie for dinner.' Colin notes that it is much easier to eat egg and beans on toast on a regular basis, which just involves quick cooking on the hob, than to use an oven. Many elderly have to budget carefully, and sometimes the food budget gets sacrificed to a meagre entertainment budget.

The Wednesday baked potato meal was thus designed to give people a nutritious, energy-rich boost, but in a context where a shared meal also provides less tangible social and emotional nourishment. Nutritionists have visited and approved the meal, whose menu has not wavered from the charity's inception. Chapman roasts several chickens the day before, and makes up some coleslaw and salad and tuna salad. There are also beetroot and baked beans and cheese on offer, and real butter (rather than cheaper substitutes). The suggested donation is £2, which just about covers the cost of the ingredients, and on average about thirty diners come per week.

Another feature of the Wednesday lunch is that food and cleaning products donated by charities are displayed on tables around the hall for the guests to buy. On a recent visit these donations included many kinds of pasta, biscuits, tuna, vegetables, chocolates and tinned rice pudding, and collectively evoked a well-stocked convenience store. This initiative allows the diners to fill gaps in their weekly food shop, empowers them to feel that they are contributing to the charity (the donations genuinely help) and also empowers them with a sense that they can exercise some choice in lives that often offer few options. Chapman describes a woman who buys large jars of instant coffee from In-Deep, jars that would typically cost £7 in a supermarket:

> 'I am really pleased,' she said to me, 'because if I come to you to buy the bits I need that are expensive, I can buy something else. If I go there [to a supermarket] it means I can't have my little bit of this.' So it helps us to raise some money and it helps them.'

The impetus for the roast beef dinner came when an elderly woman confided in him that it had been fifteen years since she had had 'a little bit of beef', as her budget only permitted buying frozen pre-packaged meals from the budget supermarket Iceland. Chapman recalls:

> 'I couldn't believe she had to buy that shite! No one has a real roast dinner, because it costs too much, you know, so that was one the things we were going to do when we set up: we were going to do a roast dinner and we've never wavered from that…. Many times we have tried to maybe change it a bit, but, nope, they want to stick to tradition. Once I changed it and no one turned up, no one turned up…. I put roast dinners back on.'

At all In-Deep meals the mood is more akin to a lunch party than a merely functional meal, and that is intentional. Diners' food choices are honoured: one woman wants only a potato and beetroot, another just beans and cheese, yet another a bit of everything. One woman requests her tea from a particular glass mug, kept aside specially for her, and it is common knowledge that there are seating preferences: people save seats for their particular friends, in a spirit of inclusion that celebrates their ability, in this context, to have some choice and control in their lives.

The logistical challenges for In-Deep are significant, although the charity is lucky to have been given the means to buy a van. The operating budget is £45,000 per year, which is raised from a mixture of donations and grants. Apart from the manicurists and pedicurists, no one, including Colin and Emma, is on the payroll. By far the largest outgoing is rent, for both the hall in which the meals are served and the office space that the serves as the charity's headquarters. Rent hikes, extremely common in London across all sectors, are a constant worry.

Shopping for meals remains a challenge. The day before each meal, Chapman visits at least four supermarkets to ensure he catches the best of the fluctuating weekly deals offered at each. As a small charity, In-Deep has found it impossible to receive any help from the major supermarkets, although Chapman patronizes them regularly. 'Not Sainsbury's or anything,' he says. 'We can't get nothing out of them. We seem to do so much in the communities, and you get nothing. The bigger you are, the more they like to donate to them, for publicity and everything. Can you imagine what we could do if we had that sort of backing?'

Conclusion

Although In-Deep, Eat Well Spend Less, and the Waterloo Foodbank have somewhat different constituencies, they have much in common. All are run by people who, in one way or another, feel a spiritual mandate to help poor people (although it is not mixed with proselytizing). In all three charities the resource of time is as much of a challenge as raising money: they rely on volunteers to carry out most of the many tasks involved in running them. All are run by people who not only have an in-depth knowledge of the neighbourhoods to which they minster, but they also live in those neighbourhoods. And they have been recognized for their work: Oasis founder Steven Chalke holds an MBE, and Colin Chapman was awarded an MBE in the Queen's Birthday honours in 2012 for founding In-Deep, as well as a Queen's Award For Voluntary Service in 2013 (one of only seventeen charities out of 240 nominated to receive the award). Justly lauded by the establishment, they are all are filling gaps increasingly ignored by the state.

Food Allocation Form: Three-Four Persons

Volunteer:	Voucher No:	Date:

Item	Allocation	Amount given
Cereal	1 large	
Soup (can/packet)	4 standard	
Beans/spaghetti in sauce	4 standard	
Tomatoes/pasta sauce	4 standard	
Vegetables	4 standard	
Meat	3 standard	
Or Vegetarian	2 standard	
Fish	4 standard	
Fruit	2 standard	
Rice pudding/custard	2 standard	
Sponge pudding	1 standard	
Biscuits	1 large packet	
Sugar	1kg	
Pasta/rice/noodles	1.5 kg	
Instant Mash	1 packet	
Tea or coffee	160 bags/medium jar	
Long-life juice	1 litre	
Milk UHT	2 litres	

Extra items when available

Snacks	1	
Sauces	1 jar/packet	
Chocolate	1 medium bar	
Jam	1 standard	
Powdered Milk	300-500g	

Client signature to confirm food received:	

Figure 1 Typical contents of a Waterloo Foodbank parcel for three to four people.

The Search for Lost Blood: Why the Blood Has Run Dry in British Black Pudding

Jessica Fagin

Introduction

'I want our children to grow up enjoying the taste of British apples as well as Cornish sardines, Norfolk turkey, Melton Mowbray pork pies, Wensleydale cheese, Herefordshire pears and, of course, black pudding,' pledged Elizabeth Truss, then Secretary of State for Environment, Food and Rural Affairs in her opening speech to the Anglia Farmers Association conference.[1] Tapping into ideals of nationalism through locally sourced traditional food, black pudding was elevated as a symbol of time-honoured Britishness. Black pudding, a blood sausage that in the UK has many regional varieties, from Lancashire to the Outer Hebrides, uses blood from slaughter, most commonly from pigs, mixed with local grain, fat, herbs and spices. Truss's wish may have been granted. Producers claim sales of this once poverty food have increased by 25%, it is featured on the menus of Michelin starred restaurants and Stornoway black pudding has received EU Protection of Geographical Indication (PGI) certification. Despite the rhetoric of tradition, almost all black pudding made in the UK uses industrially produced dried pig's blood imported from intensive slaughter operations in Europe. Simultaneously, blood is being structurally removed from local food chains as abattoirs treat it as waste bound for incineration plants.

I explore this central paradox through the social, political and economic forces that influence decisions to use dried or fresh blood: processes of industrialization and commodification as well as anxieties over health and safety. Ethnographically positioned through the experiences of black pudding makers and abattoir workers, alongside the oral histories of butchers and abattoir workers recorded for the British Library Source to Salespoint sound archives, this paper is grounded at the sites and with the actors of production. Theoretically, Kopytoff's 'cultural biography of things', which suggests that 'commodities must be not only produced materially as things, but also culturally marked as being a certain kind of thing', is used as a framework to consider blood as a material and a culturally constructed substance in the food chain which flows, congeals and infects.[2] Key to my analysis is an appraisal of how the commodity value of blood comes into and out of status; this substance with a specific liquid materiality captured under the category offal reconsiders the rejected or inedible as a temporary, fluid state. This ambiguity is further complicated by the PGI accreditation awarded to Stornoway black pudding, which has rewritten the use of industrialized dried blood back into narratives of traditional subsistence production in an on-going cultural biography which moves value even further away from material pragmatism. At the intersection of production, legislation and tradition, blood's shifting materiality reveals the dispersal of power and constructions of value in the British meat industry.

Shifting Values: Making and Unmaking Blood as a Commodity

'Everything went straight down the drain, you wouldn't be able to do it now.'

Roger Barker, abattoir owner

Though a source of vital nutrition, animal blood has been both valued as a commodity derived from the process of slaughter and considered a waste product; its value has not followed a linear path from subsistence to industrialized food systems. Blood has been affected by social, political and economic contingencies that have created shifts in value: issues of access for black pudding producers and edibility for consumers. Roger Barker's recollection of pig slaughter in the 1960s at his family abattoir – that 'you cut it down the throat, bleed it where it fell. You didn't move it, the blood would drain down into the effluent works, everything went straight down the drain – you wouldn't be able to do that now' – is a tidy vignette to begin a focus on time and value.[3] A Marxist perspective might question if blood is a commodity or not, but for Barker it was waste: meat was the commodity. Waste is a measured value of production, alongside embodied labour, the nurture of the animal and the cutting of its throat. Removing blood was part of a commodifying process: blood transferred its value onto something it was once part of, rendering it 'devil's dust', the bits that fall off, offal.[4] Barker, however, moves on from situating blood as waste. Sometimes blood did have an exchange value and was sold to local butchers to make black pudding. Blood's value was changeable, discretionary, dependent on the proximity of his customers and his relations with them. Indeed, abattoir owners recalling the 1960s – at the start of the supermarket boom, when production incentives were focussed on increasing the output of flesh – have had to be pushed to elaborate on what happened to the blood after slaughter, even more than the organ offal which provided additional 'fifth quarter' income. Whether stirred immediately to defibrinate before it congealed to use as an ingredient for black pudding (made on-site to create value-added products at more modernized abattoirs), used by local butchers or kept for fertilizer, blood had a use value, an exchange value – or it was a waste product. Blood's value was fluid and ambiguous.

British abattoirs have been victim to constant change affecting their location, function and size. Up until the 1930s, there were over 12,000 abattoirs in England and Wales, and, up until the 1970s, they were as a rule relatively small, owned by butchers and located close to urban centres.[5] A century of government policy reform and changing ownership, including the wartime Ministry of Food, diminished numbers.

Offal: Rejected and Reclaimed Food

This shift was exacerbated by UK participation in the European Common Agricultural Policy and the subsequent reduction in national grants and, most saliently, by the rise of the supermarket as abattoirs' foremost customer. These factors forced a concentration in the size and location of abattoirs on a national level. Whilst these changing geographies limited the local availability of offal in general, Broadway's analysis suggests that the control asserted through supermarkets' buying power had a greater effect.[6] All abattoir owners cited the growth of supermarkets as their primary customer as integral to the devaluation of offal and blood, through being unable to maintain relationships with local butchers because of demands to direct their production towards packaged cuts of flesh. Offal was once integral to profits: as one abattoir owner shares, 'all products were produced in the 1960s as a range, to add value. Today it's become much more specialist, the capital you need to invest is so prohibitive that you couldn't do it on one site even if you wanted to.'[7] The specialization towards producing flesh, especially for those with existing offal production facilities on site, diminished the practice of making pies, sausages or black pudding to add value to flesh with offal and blood. Businesses shifted focus from social relations, proximity and adding value to speed, singularity and competition. There are now less than 400 approved abattoirs in the UK.[8] Pig slaughter has become concentrated in East Anglia, accounting for over two thirds of all slaughtered pigs.[9] In this uneven terrain, access to fresh blood is severely limited.

Slaughter waste, of which blood is the largest component by volume, has become a highly political issue, exacerbated by the BSE crisis between 1987 and 1996 which, after much speculation, identified the source as prions ingested through animal feed made from animal by-products.[10] The use of animal by-products in the food system, which includes blood and offal, is now heavily monitored and has subsequently increased slaughter waste, alongside a loss in profits from the potential sale of offal. Waste is either incinerated or sent to landfill or rendering plants at a cost to the abattoir. Sustainable food advocacy calls for consuming offal to cut slaughter waste.[11] Stuart specifically proposes eating black pudding but herein lies the problem: British abattoirs are not collecting blood as an edible product. Urgent calls to find revenue in waste have promoted investment in technologies to process waste whether into biofuel through anaerobic digestion or into rendered, patented blood products to use as enhancers, such as meat stretchers and glues for processed meat products, of which dried blood is one.[12] The production sites for dried blood are based in Holland and Belgium, operated by multinational food corporations that hold patents to the specific processing technologies and have the scale of killing to legitimize their economic viability. At present, only three British abattoirs hold a license to sell their blood for processing into edible products, and BPEX, the British pig trade body, makes no mention of blood as a separate trade product at all. Precautions over health and safety have structurally removed fresh blood from the food chain.

Dried blood is a highly technical industrialized product and, for some, a positive approach to internalizing waste within the food system, even if that food system is uneven and extends from a local to a continental scale. In the UK, it has enabled black pudding makers to continue to produce blood sausages in the deficit of fresh blood. The owner of Bury Black Pudding, one of the largest producers in the county, has been explicit about his use of dried blood: 'supplying 12 tons to supermarkets per week? It would be impossible' without it.[13] Blood has emerged with a commodity value only at a distance from its consumer. Its journey into the food chain is through division and intensive technological rendering, transforming an informal substance to a specialized product. The adoption of dried blood removes black pudding from direct supply by abattoirs and into a market of highly processed, internationally traded products. It knocks what was once a subsistence food out of kilter from local food systems encompassing ever broader territories.

Blood? It's a Grey Area: Interpreting Legalities for Small Producers and Abattoirs

Is using fresh blood as an edible ingredient legal? When this question was asked to those working along the meat commodity chain, no one shared interpretations, yet most believe that using fresh blood is illegal or impossible. Neither the abattoir workers nor the black pudding producers nor the manufacturer of a dried blood product are in agreement. Responses range from 'you can't, but I don't know what law relates to it, I think it's BSE regulations' to 'only if you make black pudding in the slaughterhouse' to 'you can, but I can't sell it and I can't give it away' to 'it's a grey area'. With the almost ubiquitous use of dried blood by both large- and small-scale producers, the incentive to interrogate regulations, complicated by their frequently changing stipulations, has developed into myth making, which one producer identified as 'old wives tales'. On both micro and macro levels, politics is pushing producers' knowledge and practices away from the use of fresh blood.

The BSE crisis instigated an intensive restructuring of regulatory bodies towards more transparent distribution of power, rather than concentrating policymaking informed by influential players in the meat industry.[14] A key change was the implementation of European Community regulations outlining specific rules for categorizing non-edible by-products (EC 1774/2002) and regulations for safe hygiene around food from animal origin (EC 853/2004). Whether any part of the animal is categorized as meat, as waste or as by-product – ultimately edible or inedible, for human or animal – must be decided before slaughter, with all animal parts kept separate and identifiable after slaughter to be certified as edible. Vets legitimize an animal as safe for consumption through its internal organs, so regulations were articulated in terms of contact and contamination between these internal and external animal parts. Using fresh blood in this regulatory context is potentially legal, depending on the circumstances of how it is harvested. In response to these binary regulations, and with their focus squarely pointed towards an output of safe flesh, abattoirs developed spatially-zoned practices isolating each species and separating the treatments of the interiors and exteriors of animal bodies; they provided corridors for access by different species, washrooms for workers between zones and separate baths to sanitize used knives. Pigs are first stunned and hung, then killed with a cut to the throat. Blood makes contact with the uncleaned or unskinned exterior of the body as it falls to the floor and channels into drains, where the blood of multiple animals blends into an unidentifiable mass. Before the animal is eviscerated, it is cleaned and de-haired in boiling baths, allowing abattoir workers to access the interior without risk of contamination from the exterior.

Under current regulations, the process of killing marks blood as inedible the moment it is let from the animal, but actual practice complicates this seemingly clear distinction. I visited a small, independent abattoir, one of the remaining few that service an adjacent butcher. Based on proximity, it should be an ideal spatial scenario to produce black pudding from a ready supply of fresh blood. Yet the butcher shop buys black pudding from Stornoway and elsewhere, whilst the abattoir disposes of the blood from slaughter. One morning, the slaughterman had just killed and bled a pig, his arms splattered with fresh blood. A colleague from the butcher shop came in with a tray of hot sausage rolls to share with the workers. The slaughterman nonchalantly wiped his bloody hands on the fabric of his outerwear and proceeded to eat his snack. For him, this unregulated, unchecked liquid didn't evoke anxiety. He could see the animals he had killed were healthy. When he came to dispose of the blood collected in drainage buckets from the morning's kills, he threw it in a designated industrial waste bin, and sprayed the contents blue, intentionally contaminating it to remove it from the food chain. Workers wear more protective clothing to prevent ingesting or being stained by the blue dye than they do to protect themselves from contact with an animal carcass or blood. The overarching discourse of blood as contaminating or contaminated is constructed through regulation rather than because of innate, certain danger. Whilst the taxonomy of safe and unsafe foods increases, the onus is on the individual abattoir to invest in safe technologies to collect, store, transport or dispose of blood, paradoxically resulting in its intentional contamination and inedibility.

Apart from the larger producers on Stornoway and in Bury, most black pudding makers are often small scale; they own their own pigs and produce black pudding alongside a range of artisanal pork products, such as hams, sausages and bacon. They maintain direct relationships with the remaining smaller legacy abattoirs, which kill fewer animals and work on request. For producers, the disposal of fresh blood at the abattoir has created a blind spot, so now even those on the frontline of meat production no longer know whether they can access blood. There is no exposure or demand, and without demand there is no incentive for producers to question regulations.

Their own myths take shape amidst a complicated discourse warning them of the potential dangers of blood. One producer articulates this dislocation:

> I was told originally that it was illegal and we've got an abattoir just up the road and he said, bring a bucket and you can have it, it's fresh blood, but it's not our

blood, I'm guessing it's not, they'll just bleed a pig and catch it in a bucket, right underneath. I don't know, I'm not sure about it, so if you think about the logic of it, did a vet inspect it? So we've just said no, we're not going to go down that road.

This doubt exists despite taking pigs every week to a trusted abattoir, where he knows they are inspected by a vet. The discourse of contamination is too off-putting for him. He can identify his pig when it is returned as a carcass, but he cannot identify the origin of a bucket of blood.

Butchers frequently express the abject pain and financial loss suffered during the BSE and Foot and Mouth crises. The risk of diseased meat is deeply feared, and the liquid nature of blood makes it uniquely suspicious in a regulated environment. One producer determined to use fresh blood only received clarity about its legal status by interrogating DEFRA, because the published regulations, which focus on singular, easily contained parts, left a grey area in his understanding between slaughter and supply. After acquiring a slaughter license, he arranged with the abattoir to stand under his pig to collect the blood, waiting for the vet to approve the animal's health, before rushing it back to his kitchen six miles away to make black pudding. He nurtures a relationship with the foreman to ensure he is allowed to intercept the blood from the slaughter line. His presence, although an anomaly, assures him of the safety of the blood; as he stated, 'I am my own quality control.' However, his tactic is untenable for many small-scale producers because of its use of valuable time and dependence on a privileged location. In such a highly regulated environment, making black pudding requires producers either to rearticulate relationships with the abattoir, returning to close relation-based exchanges and finding loopholes in the regulations of fresh blood, or to avoid acquiring fresh blood from abattoirs all together.

Dried-up Traditions

In 2006, the only four butcher shops in the town of Stornoway on the remote, sparsely populated Isle of Lewis in the Outer Hebrides joined forces to apply for PGI accreditation for their black pudding, known locally in Gaelic as *marag-dhubh*. Stornoway black pudding had developed a reputation as a chef's favourite, exported to hotels, delicatessens and supermarkets in large quantities. Word of imitation Stornoway-style puddings being produced and sold on the mainland called the butchers into action to protect the authenticity of their product. PGI offers producers legal protection against imitation foods which make false or appropriated claims of geographical production. Like the *appellation d'origine contrôlée* French system before it, this European Union scheme was borne of existing commercial competition. PGI accreditation formalizes stipulations that producers must adhere to in certifying a product as authentically made within a particular region. (Protection of Geographical Origin accreditation (PGO) stipulates instead that ingredients need to be grown and produced in a specific area.) Under EU legislation, Stornoway black pudding must be made within a circumscribed area and can include only beef suet, onions, oatmeal, salt, pepper, casings (natural or synthetic) and blood. The blood can be sheep, pig or cow. It can be either dried or fresh.[17]

Stornoway black pudding displays the stark contrast between the historical food scarcity of the crofting system and the gourmandization experienced through food trends, PGI accreditation and mass production. The current producers are third- or fourth-generation butchers who remember their fathers working in their shops to make puddings not with pig's blood, which has little to no presence or history on the island, but with ox and sheep blood from the local abattoir. Despite the profitable businesses that have flourished through the reputation and increased production of Stornoway black pudding, the butchers still refer to it as a 'poverty food'. Their knowledge of its origins extends further back to crofters, who used only sheep blood and sheep's intestines, softened in sea water and filled to make the puddings. During my visit, islanders often shared stories of these sheep blood puddings, which they had not tasted for many years. I was told by one butcher, 'It's a very basic product. It's what you'd expect of a product that came from where it came from, the croft, using up the bits. You have oatmeal as base, fat or suet, salt and pepper and blood. Five ingredients and that's all.'

In the subsistence crofting system, neither blood nor meat fit easily as a commodity. People owned their own labour and livestock, and the exchange of blood or puddings would have been informal. Black pudding was a pragmatic way of using all the parts of the kill to add essential nutritional sustenance to the crofters' simple diet. Despite its recent fame and accreditation, the local history museum on Lewis had no ephemera on this now praised local delicacy. 'It just was', I was told. 'It wasn't anything special.' The response indicated historical status; traditionally black pudding was outside of recorded history and acknowledged ritual. Capturing and legitimizing the tradition is a contemporary phenomenon instigated through protection and commerciality. The promotional campaign for accreditation reproduced narratives of tradition and authenticity. It claimed that because the traditional crofting puddings were part of recent history, no Stornoway producer would make one that wasn't 'close enough to the quality and purity of the original.'[16] By placing producers in a moment of history which in fact was not theirs and positioning them as protectors of tradition, the campaign could claim that it was their memory, skill and judgement that ensured the pudding's authenticity. Of the three accredited producers on the island, two use only dried blood, which along with the oatmeal, fat, seasoning and synthetic casings are bought wholesale from the mainland. The Stornoway abattoir was one of the casualties of centralized meat production. Diminished local crofting did not offer enough business to keep it open permanently. It now opens for two weeks a year, to serve the few remaining crofters who are heavily subsidized by EU grants. Only one butcher on the island sells meat from the abattoir when available, but for the rest of the year, all meat on the island is purchased from a mainland wholesaler. With the current increased demand for black puddings, it would be impossible for the abattoir to supply enough blood. All blood from the abattoir currently goes to landfill.

Rather than propose that Stornoway black pudding is itself an imitation, too far removed from the sheep blood sausages once produced on the croft, I would suggest, following Weiss, that it is the concept of authenticity which needs reframing. Authenticity for Weiss is an on-going state rather than a captured moment. Authenticity is dialogic, dynamic and ambiguous.[17] The butchers are reproducing an island tradition, making puddings within a viable material economy. The black puddings that their fathers made had already shifted from the crofting tradition, in dialogue with their own moment in time. In this context, of an all-but-closed abattoir and diminished agriculture and animal husbandry, the current practice is perhaps the most authentic way they can be commercial. The ways of survival have shifted with time, and a resuscitation of traditional sheep blood puddings would now be artificial. However, paradox remains: to produce a consistent tradition, to create the genuine article as required by PGI accreditation, producers have become dependent on buying blood as a commodity. To meet the increased market for Stornoway black pudding as a statement of authenticity captured in a regulated product and brand, producers are increasingly dependent on consistency, enabled by a reliable commodity they can buy: dried blood. Though PGI accreditation, industrialized blood has been written into narratives of the continuing reproduction of an island tradition.

The final butcher I met on Stornoway, I was told beforehand by enthused locals, used fresh ox blood. Knowing the temporality of the local abattoir, and having yet to encounter an abattoir which harvested edible, transportable blood, I assumed I was being told a local yarn to charm me. I shared my scepticism with him when we met at his shop. 'Come in', he said, 'I'll show you it, have a glass.' I didn't take him up on the offer, but the stories were true. In the cold store, nestled under hanging sides of pork, sat a churn with the label, 'Blood for human consumption.' He was using fresh ox blood, sourced from an abattoir on the mainland that supplies all the other island butchers with their meat. The missing ingredient? An anticoagulant preservative – along with the use of a hollow knife attached to a rubber hose enabling the abattoir to collect the blood without risk of contamination.

The availability of fresh blood was omitted from the other producers' stories. Despite the binary classifications of edible and inedible blood, the producers were not all following the same path in how they mediate the use of fresh or dried blood, or how they communicate how production is incentivized by demand, be it ethical or commercial. The producers on Stornoway who use dried blood articulate the need for consistency as the driving factor. They don't have to deal with the tricky issues of edibility and inedibility. They have a safe material that allows them to produce on mass and without pause. The producer who used fresh blood was willing to trade consistency of supply for the ability to use the fresh ox blood that was more traditional to his butcher shop. Whilst I have outlined the structural, historical and political reasons which make the access and use of fresh blood complicated, unclear and unappealing, its use is also mediated through anxiety, instrumentalism, trust relations and, most importantly, agency. Legislation and accreditation offer not just rules, but narratives for producers to appropriate if they do not want to deal with the perceived difficulties of using fresh blood. The very few butchers who do use fresh blood do so aware that they cannot produce in large volumes, despite the fact that the UK is sending huge volumes of blood to landfill every day. Black pudding production on Stornoway has always been a story of survival, and this perhaps is the consistent tradition. These three butchers on this small island, in their own interpretations, continue their trade through their adaptability to survive.

Conclusion

> In the homogenized world of commodities, an eventful story of a thing becomes the story of various singularizations of it, of classifications and reclassifications in an uncertain world of categories whose importance shifts with every minor change in context. As with persons, the drama here lies in the uncertainties of valuation and identity.
>
> Kopytoff[18]

Throughout its cultural biography, blood in the British meat industry comes into and out of commodity status, each shift instigated by uncertainty about its value, its risk, its authenticity. For butchers and abattoirs in the early twentieth century, or for crofters in Stornoway, blood wasn't a commodity at all, but in keeping with the old butcher's adage of 'it's not what you sell, it's what you throw away', rather a way of using everything when an animal was killed for meat. The industrialization of the abattoirs and their focus on packaged cuts of meat no doubt relegated the use of blood to processed animal feed, fertilizer or waste, whilst discourses of risk and contamination that emerged following the BSE crisis have led to persistent uncertainties of how to value and identify fresh blood. Blood has become extraneous and feared in equal measure so that even butchers don't know how or if they can legally source it. It is both morally and economically rejected. The liquid nature of blood poses specific issues in a regulated and risk-obsessed environment. The confusion between abattoirs and butchers is met by the ambiguity of regulating a spurting, liquid substance. The commodity status of blood, as a dried product, masks a history of dislocation, industrialization, waste and risk. Yet its availability is also the means through which most producers can consider making black pudding at all. In the most recent event in blood's cultural biography, narratives of tradition and authenticity are woven into structural and economic contingencies. This shift again re-evaluates the status of blood, and of offal in general. At this heightened manifestation of cultural construction and technological rendering, can blood even continue to be considered as offal at all?

Notes

1. Elizabeth Truss, 'Speech to the Norfolk Farming Conference', *GOV.UK*, 12 February 2015 <https://www.gov.uk/government/speeches/elizabeth-truss-speech-to-the-norfolk-farming-conference, 2015> [accessed 1 April 2015].
2. Igor Kopytoff, 'The Cultural Biography of Things: Commoditization as Process', in *The Social Life of Things: Commodities in Cultural Perspective*, ed. by Arjun Appadurai (Cambridge: Cambridge University Press, 1986), pp. 64-94 (p. 9).
3. Roger Baker, Steve Hussey (interviewer) and Eva Simmons (interviewer), *Food: From Source to Salespoint* (British Library Sound Archives 2002-2003), F12099-F12102, F15129-F15131 .
4. Karl Marx, *Capital Volume One* (London: New Left Review), p. 313
5. Michael Broadway, 'The British Slaughtering Industry: A Dying Business?', *Geography* 87.3, 268-80.
6. Broadway.
7. Colin Jay and Linda Sandino (interviewer), *Food: From Source to Salespoint* (British Library Sound Archives 2003), F13765-F13768.
8. Food Standards Agency, 'Approved red, poultry, and game meat establishments', *Food Standards Agency* <https://www.food.gov.uk/enforcement/sectorrules/meatplantsprems/meatpremlicence> [accessed 31 March 2015].
9. Broadway.
10. Ioannis S. Arvanitoyannis and Demetrios Ladas, 'Meat Waste Treatment Methods and Potential Uses', *International Journal of Food Science and Technology* 43 (2008) 543-59.
11. Tristram Stuart, *Waste: Uncovering the Global Food Scandal* (London: Penguin, 2008); Joyce D'Silva, and John Webster, *The Meat Crisis* (London: Earthscan, 2010).
12. Food Standards Agency, 'The Future of Abattoirs', *Food Standards Agency* <http://www.food.gov.uk/multimedia/pdfs/board/fsa080504a2.pdf , 2015> [accessed 31 April 2015]; Clara S.F. Bah, Alaa El-Din A. Bekhit, Alan Carne and Michelle A. McConnell, 'Slaughterhouse Blood: An Emerging Source of Bioactive Compounds', *Comprehensive Reviews in Food Science & Food Safety* 12.3 (May 2013), 314-31.
13. 'Black Pudding v Boudin Noir', *Food Programme*, BBC Radio 4, 23 April 2013 <http://www.bbc.co.uk/programmes/b01s395f> [accessed 7 March 2015].
14. Erik Millstone and Patrick van Ewanenberg, 'The Evolution of Food Policy-Making Institutions in UK, EU and Codex Alimentarius', *Social Policy and Administration* 36.6, 593-609.
15. Department for Environment, Food & Rural Affairs, 'Specification: Stornoway Black Pudding', *GOV.UK* <https://www.gov.uk/government/uploads/system/uploads/attachment_data/file/271307/pfn-stornoway-black-pudding-pgi.pdf> [accessed 31 Oct. 2016].
16. Seumus Macinnes, *Stornoway Black Pudding Bible* (Edinburgh: Birlinn, 2010).
17. Allen S. Weiss, 'Authenticity', *Gastronomica* 11.4 (2011), 74-77.
18. Kopytoff, p. 90.

Fish Heads, Tapioca and Sweet-Potato Leaves: The Ingredients of Survival in Occupied Malaya during World War II

Laura Fan

The most important ingredient for surviving World War II in Malaya and Singapore was the right attitude. The Japanese Occupation lasted for three years and eight months, from February 1942 to September 1945. Mental flexibility, creative problem-solving skills and quick-thinking responses could make the difference between life and death – and the first step was finding enough food.

The creative use of previously marginal foodstuffs such as fish heads, tapioca, sweet-potato leaves, frogs and snails reduced the risk of a protracted and uncomfortable death caused by malnutrition and the infections and organ failure that follow in its wake.[1]

Bulk calories were initially provided by the minimal rice rations issued by the Japanese.[2] Later, when the rice began to run out, this diet was supplemented with the tapioca and sweet potatoes people grew. As with root vegetables, green vegetables were not difficult to grow, as long as you had access to land. Sources of protein were the hardest to find. Beans and peanuts were not difficult to acquire, but you had to eat a lot of them to feel full. Fish heads, if you could get them, proved extremely popular and remain so today.

Access, social as well as geographical, mattered more than money in finding sufficient protein. The royal families from Kedah, a northern state with an extensive shoreline, had fish. Meanwhile the royal family from Negeri Sembilan, an inland state, only ate fish irregularly.[3] Individuals who had access to the seaside or rivers fished surreptitiously, out of sight from Japanese or local authorities. While they and their families ate what they caught, the regulations controlling commercial fishing and lack of transport meant that very little could be sold in the cities.

Excessive regulation strangled the fishing industry. Commercial fishermen were required to obtain a license from the authorities every six months, to fly the Japanese flag and to sell to designated vendors.[4] Only the sorts of fish the Japanese didn't want were released for sale at controlled prices that were much lower than black market prices.[5] Even if you had fish to sell, transport was another problem as the Japanese had requisitioned functioning motor transport. The tremendous demand for fish meant that only the wealthy, cunning and lucky managed to obtain them.

A man who later became an important Singaporean public figure, Tommy Koh, caught eels at night from nearby rainwater drains.[6] One family lived in a gracious Malayan town in the hills and obtained their protein from 'whatever was available:

frogs, biawak (monitor lizards) and snails'.⁷ Many people had no fish for the entire period; their protein came mainly from beans, peanuts and the odd egg.

Before the war, households did not compose a meal around fish heads, which were regarded as offal to be discarded. Under Occupation, the Japanese took the fish, leaving the rejected portion for the local population. In Singapore, the fish vendors threw fish offal into a bamboo basket. People would come and take the number of fish heads that corresponded with the number of people in their families and compose meals from that.⁸

During the war, fish heads were cooked in myriad ways: stewed in curries with okra, braised in claypots with soy sauce, used to flavour rice porridges and added to soup with tofu and pickled vegetables. The range of recipes attests to the adaptability of fish heads. They have protein, collagen and calcium, allowing them to be fried, boiled, grilled, steamed or sautéed, yielding dishes both delicious and nutritious. Fish heads also possess different textures, from the softness of the cheek to the gelatinous quality of the lips, providing textural variety to mitigate dietary monotony. Wartime experience resulted in a host of recipes that are now much loved and cherished. Today, fish heads enjoy a firm place in Malaysian cuisine and are high on the nostalgic wish list for Malaysians returning home.

Many successful fish head restaurants have carried on for generations and continue to arouse strong loyalty. However, not everyone likes fish heads. For one thing, they take skill to eat as the meat has to be teased out from the bones. Then there's the squeamishness that comes from finding a fish eye staring from your plate. For these reasons, although almost all Malaysians profess to enjoy eating fish heads, it has been surprisingly difficult recently to find people who would eat these dishes with me.

Fish head curry, especially, should be eaten communally. To enjoy a classic Indian-style garoupa fish head curry, it's wise to organize eight to ten people to ensure that justice is done to the dish. Chinese variants of the Indian fish head curry cater to smaller numbers, but it's still not a dish to be eaten on your own.

Each fish head restaurant jealously guards its methods for cooking fish heads. When asked how it was prepared, the proprietors often smile and say, 'It's a family secret.' These family secrets have translated into business ventures that have lasted for generations.

Few fish head restaurants accept credit cards. There is one post-war Singapore restaurant producing a silky, collagen-rich fish head noodle soup without a single bone that has a clientele of hedge fund managers and advertising executives, but the area recently gentrified, and was previously populated by petty traders.⁹ Generally, most fish head restaurants are located in marginal areas: ports, railway depots, across from markets and behind prisons. The offal nourishes workers who need protein but lack cash. Fish head provides a delicious and affordable way to nourish the body, today as it did during the Japanese Occupation.

One well established Singapore fish head restaurant, Nan Hwa Chong Fish Head

Steamboat Corner, has been in business since 1927. Unlike other restaurants, their way with fish head is remarkably simple. The process involves putting sliced fish heads in a charcoal-fired hotpot with a boiling stock seasoned with salted fish, pickled vegetables and some dried seaweed. Various raw vegetables can be added to the hotpot. Bowls of steamed white rice round out the meal. It doesn't sound very good, but it is fresh, tasty and affordable. The décor is tired, with charcoal burns on most tables, but they're packed every night. The family behind the restaurant has remained united. They have reinvested their profits into real estate over ninety years and now own four prime shoplots worth a small fortune. Long after wartime restrictions have been lifted, some fish head restaurants remain enduringly popular.

By comparison, plain tapioca and sweet-potato leaves now evoke memories of deprivation and feelings of aversion in the elderly, although not among the younger generations. Tapioca tubers and sweet potato leaves are both easy to grow so they formed a major part of the diet during the Occupation. These two plants provided the calories and vitamins that kept the people of Malaya and Singapore alive.

Before the war, tapioca was known as a famine food. During the Occupation, people turned to tapioca again. The tuber filled the stomachs of everyone, from the Chinese widow and her young children to the guerrilla soldier hiding out in the jungle to the British POW.[10] *Manihot esculenta* can kill you if eaten raw but is satisfying to eat if cooked properly. Tapioca dishes can also be cooked in several different ways, and its bland gentle flavour takes seasonings well. It's possible not to recognize it from one dish to the next. Tapioca can be fried, boiled, steamed, deep-fried, grated and heated with palm sugar and topped with coconut cream or roasted whole in embers to be eaten the next morning.[11] If dried and ground, it can be made into flour for noodles, or into tiny translucent balls, used worldwide in instant puddings. Limited only by the knowledge of the cook, the tapioca plant can take on a variety of flavours and textures, a godsend in a time of limited ingredients.

Why was such a useful ingredient so disliked by those who survived the war? This may be due to the treatment of tapioca as a rice substitute. The rice ration given by the Japanese dwindled as the war ground on; to provide more food, cooks would cube tapioca and add it to the rice. This method doesn't completely remove the naturally occurring hydrogen cyanide from the tuber. Everyone that I interviewed who disliked tapioca had eaten it in this manner, boiled up in a gooey mass with rice. Additionally, tapioca is less calorific than white rice. To obtain the same number of calories, more than double the volume of tapioca has to be consumed. Without a variety of accompanying dishes, eating all of that tapioca must have felt unending.

There are two types of tapioca, bitter and sweet. The sweet type, which has substantially less hydrogen cyanide, is the one largely consumed in Malaysia, then and now. Both the tubers and the shoots of the tapioca plant contain hydrogen cyanide, with the shoots having four times as much of the fatal toxin.[12] Traditional methods of preparing tapioca involve grating and boiling the tuber and discarding the cooking water. These actions disperse the toxin and make the tuber safe to eat.

Hydrogen cyanide has its uses though. Anyone can plant a cutting of tapioca and come back in ten months to find something worth eating. There is no need to secure the tapioca plot from anything but man. Animals that tend to raid crops locally include wild boar and monkeys. Both stay far away from the bitter toxin found in the tapioca plant. Even insects ignore its leaves. The Malays have a saying about tapioca, one can merely '*tanam, tinggal, tuai*' [plant, leave, harvest].[13] Moreover, the tubers can keep in the ground for up to three years, providing an invisible store of food, an important benefit in a time of food confiscations and petty theft.

Removed from wartime sugar restrictions, however, tapioca is the base for many favourite local sweets. Grated fresh and squeezed of excess liquid, tapioca is the invisible starch that mixes beautifully with coconut milk and palm sugar. Baked or steamed and tinted in layers and rolled in freshly shredded coconut, tapioca sweetmeats ornament the Malaysian tea table in pretty colours and shapes.

Oddly enough, it is the sweet potato leaf that garners the most opprobrium. Three elderly gentlemen declared vehemently to this interviewer that they hated sweet potato leaves and would never willingly eat them again. Today, sweet potato leaves feature regularly in casual dining. However, before the war, it was regarded as food to feed pigs, not people. The urgency surrounding growing food during the Occupation meant that the ease of growing sweet potato leaves ensured their popular consumption.

The leaves grow from cuttings, and harvest is possible within two-and-a-half weeks of planting. Stir-fried with garlic, dried shrimp, chilli, and plenty of oil, they make a nice accompaniment to a meal, pleasant although not particularly distinctive. However, when cooked without oil, they have a dry, astringent quality. Given the limited availability of oil in wartime, this may account for the powerful animosity of the octogenarians.

Sweet potatoes themselves are ready for harvest within four to five months after planting. But don't wait too long before eating them. Unlike commercially cultivated orange or purple sweet potatoes, these red-skinned, buff-fleshed sweet potatoes don't keep well. If eaten within a week from harvesting, they're an absolute delight. After boiling whole, a few turns of the wooden spoon results in a fluffy mound of creamy goodness, even without the addition of butter. However, if kept for a few weeks, the skin develops dark patches, and when sliced the exposed flesh turns a mouldy green within seconds.

While it is inspiring to see how creative and resourceful people had been with these extreme food restrictions, it is also important to look at how the situation became so dire in the first place. How was it that an affluent, industrious colony, successful in exporting tin and rubber, located in the tropics, could suddenly find itself existing on offal, famine starches and vegetables previously used to feed livestock?

The punitive and administrative choices made by the Japanese military government destroyed the supply chain of essential foodstuffs. Confiscating food supplies to feed the occupying military forces, destroying existing transportation systems and ignoring local patterns of food production and distribution resulted in the catastrophic breakdown of food networks in Malaya and Singapore.

Before the war, the Malayan peninsula and Singapore depended on food imports particularly for rice, the main source of calories for the local population. In 1939, two-thirds of the rice consumed in British Malaya was imported.[14] During the first two years of the war, rice was still being imported from Thailand and Burma. However, from 1944 the Allied naval blockade significantly disrupted shipments of rice to Malaya and Singapore. Moreover, Britain's retaking of Burma meant that Burmese rice was no longer available. Food shortages started to become a desperate problem.

The Japanese policy response to food shortages was to initiate a 'Grow More Food' campaign that saw golf courses, front lawns, cricket pitches and rubber plantations dug up to grow vegetables. If you didn't grow food, your land could be confiscated.[15] Although approximately four times as much land was dedicated to cultivate root crops (acreage under cultivation grew from 63,000 acres before the war to 245,000 acres by the end of 1945), all of that effort only doubled the root crop harvest because of the depleted fertility of the soil.[16]

The rice shortage was exacerbated by Sook Ching, the Japanese massacre of the Chinese in the first phase of the Occupation. Among the dead were the traders who had handled the domestic processing and foreign importation of rice and all of the transport that this entailed. For example, the types of ground transport used to collect padi included bicycles, ox carts, trains and appropriately sized lorries. For regional rice distribution, ships such as small boats, barges, lighters and steamships were used.[17] This entire network was destroyed. In its place, the Mitsubishi Trading Co. was put in charge of the distribution of rice and other grains, and the Mitsui Trading Co. controlled the distribution of sugar and salt.[18] The Japanese imposed a top-down, centralized system of collection, milling and distribution without understanding the complexity of the system it had replaced.[19]

In addition, disastrous price controls and out of control seizures of padi by the local agents of the Japanese trading companies made it increasingly uneconomical for the Malay padi farmers to grow more rice.[20] At the end of the war, the rice supplies in Malaya were only 17% of what they had been at the beginning of the Occupation.[21] By 1944 it was clear that their system was not working, and that the prospect of mass starvation loomed. The Japanese administration decided they had to find a way to work with the local community to restore food supplies.[22]

Additional strain on the food supply came from the need to feed the occupying Japanese forces. The Japanese government did not supply any food to their military forces overseas.[23] *Bushido* or warrior spirit was meant to fuel their bodies: invading troops were told that they 'should live off the land' and take local supplies.[24] For the Japanese nation, this policy decision was tragic. By the end of World War II, it was found that more Japanese military deaths had been caused by starvation than from combat.²⁵ The policy also did not endear the occupiers to local populations. Crops and stores were seized without warning, and the Japanese regulations ensured that the best meat, fish and vegetables went to the occupiers. It was clear to the local population that their food policies were governed by the principle that the 'indigenous population in the empire should go hungry before the Japanese'.²⁶

The people of Malaya and Singapore had to work together to ensure their survival. Only by cooperation could they obtain a sufficient quantity and variety of nutrients to maintain reasonable health. For example, rice rations were provided for resident males over the age of twelve who worked for the Japanese administration or businesses. Sharing rice supplies with family members, and mixing the rice with tapioca grown in the villages, might provide sufficient calories for a family. Young boys in Singapore and Kuala Lumpur who lived near markets were sent before dawn to queue so that their mothers could come later and buy any vegetables available that day.²⁷ Young women in both suburbs and countryside were growing sweet-potato leaves and four-angle beans. Boys were slipping into drains to catch eels, diving surreptitiously from houses backing the sea to net shrimp and grabbing frogs to put into the soup pot. In those families that survived, everyone helped to put something on the table.

Wartime topics remain sensitive for many, but Malaysians and Singaporeans love to talk about food. Food is an essential shared interest, bridging the fracture lines of race, class, religion and politics. It has proven invaluable as an entry point to discussion of the Japanese Occupation: the simple question 'What did you eat…?' has unlocked fascinating reminiscences. We have only a few more years to record personal accounts from that era. Meanwhile, recent research is shedding new light from a variety of local and Japanese perspectives.

Marginal foods enabled survival, and fish head curry has become a regional speciality. In the current era of double-digit food inflation in many Asian countries, tales of resilience and ingenuity are inspiring a new generation of cooks to rediscover the ingredients, gardening skills and cooking practices that helped Malaya survive the war.

Notes

1. Lizzie Collingham provides a clear and precise discussion of the stages in which the body breaks down under nutritional dystrophy. Her description accompanied with observations from a survivor of the Leningrad siege as well as a discussion of autopsy results of the victims (*The Taste of War: World War II and the Battle for Food* (New York: Penguin, 2012), p. 6).
2. The rice ration varied from state to state. The ration also represented an ideal amount rather than a guaranteed supply. If supplies fell short then they merely distributed what they had and that was that. Notably, farmers didn't receive a rice ration as they were assumed to be able to be able to grow their own food.
3. Interview between Sultan Abdul Halim of Kedah and his daughter Tunku Puteri Intan Safinaz, 1 March 2016, and interview between Tuanku Najihah, Tunku Shahariah and Tunku Puteri Intan Safinaz, 4 April 2016. The Japanese presence was much greater in the southern state of Negeri Sembilan. They

experienced more severe food shortages and an oppressive military presence.
4. Wong Hong Suen, *Wartime Kitchen: Food and Eating in Singapore 1942-1950* (Singapore: Edition Didier Millet Pte. Ltd. and National Museum Singapore, 2009), p. 72. Interviews with survivors of the Occupation relate that in northern Malaysia, a similar system ensured that the entire commercial hauls of fishing vessels were taken by authorities at the port (interview with Salmah Osman, 8 May 2016, Kuala Lumpur).
5. Wong, p. 72.
6. Russel Zehnder and Gozde Zehnder, *Eat to Live: Wartime Recipes Part 3, Fishing for Food* <https://www.youtube.com/watch?v=ZKataKrQFxQ8> [accessed 25 November 2015].
7. Interview with Tan Sri Abu Zarim on June 2014. The war disrupted his studies as he was meant to travel to Australia to take up engineering. During the Occupation, he worked as a Malay-to-English interpreter in the Supreme Court. The job was important not for the salary, which rampant inflation soon rendered negligible, but for the two sacks of rice that formed part of his monthly compensation. On weekends, he returned to his parent's home in Kuala Pilah, Negeri Sembilan. His father had worked as a schools inspector under the British, which meant that under the Japanese, it was prudent to keep a unobtrusive profile and remain in their ancestral village. Their family survived on what they grew and caught, and also on their son's rice ration.
8. Zehnder and Zehnder.
9. This is Swee Kee Fishhead Noodles located on Amoy Street, a gentrified row of shoplots that have been renovated to UNESCO standards.
10. Midge Gillies, *The Barbed-Wire University: The Real Lives of Allied Prisoners of War in the Second World War* (London: Aurum Press Limited, 2011), p. 127.
11. To' Puan Rosita bt. Abdullah, *Kulit Manis: A Taste of Terengganu's Heritage* (Kuala Lumpur: My Viscom Editions Sdn. Bhd, 2009), p. 82.
12. S.L. Tan, 'Cassava – Silently, the Tuber Fills', *UTAR Agriculture Science Journal*, 1:2 (April 2015), 12-23 (14-15).
13. Tan, p. 15.
14. Paul H. Krastoska, 'Introduction', in *Food Supplies and the Japanese Occupation in South-East Asia*, ed. by Paul H. Krastoska (London: Macmillan, 1998), p. 4.
15. Paul H. Krastoska, 'Malayan Food Shortages and the Kedah Rice Industry during the Japanese Occupation', in *Food Supplies and the Japanese Occupation in South-East Asia*, ed. by Paul H. Krastoska (London: Macmillan, 1998), p. 106.
16. Krastoska, 'Malayan Food Shortages', p. 107.
17. Krastoska, 'Introduction', p. 13. James Scott presents a fine-grained analysis of how Malay villagers and Chinese mill owners negotiated their needs in terms of labour and money, including a description of how rural padi farmers would pay young men to transport padi by bicycle to the end of the village's road for pick-up by the Chinese mill owners (*Weapons of the Weak: Everyday Forms of Peasant Resistance* (New Haven: Yale University Press, 1985), pp. 212-20).
18. Akashi Yoji, 'Colonel Watanabe Wataru: The Architect of the Malayan Military Administration, December 1941-March 1943', in *New Perspectives on the Japanese Occupation in Malaya and Singapore, 1941-1945*, ed. by Akashi Yoji and Yoshimura Mako (Singapore: NUS Press, 2008, reprint 2013), p. 54.
19. Aiko Kurasawa, 'Transportation and Rice Distribution in South-East Asia during the Second World War', in *Food Supplies and the Japanese Occupation in South-East Asia*, ed. by Paul H. Krastoska (London: Macmillan, 1998), p. 33.
20. Krastoska includes wonderfully wry observations from the Cambridge-educated Principal Agricultural Officer of Kedah, Tunku Yaacob, a prince and brother of the reigning Sultan of Kedah, about the disastrous padi collection policies implemented by the Japanese ('Malayan Food Shortages', p. 114).
21. Kurasawa, 'Transportation and Rice Distribution', p. 56.
22. Akashi, p. 5.
23. This policy of not supplying food caused 60% of the 1.74 million Japanese World War II military deaths,

deaths by starvation (Collingham, p. 10).
24. Collingham, pp. 10, 230.
25. Collingham, p. 10.
26. Collingham, p. 247.
27. Interview with Cheong Laitong on 28 February 2016.

Beaver as Offal: The Presence and Absence of Beavers in Canadian Cuisine

L. Sasha Gora

Figure 1
Still from video 'All for a Hat', as presented in Minnesota History Centre exhibit Then Now Wow. Courtesy The Minnesota Historical Society, Therese Scheller, illustrator.

Big teeth and an even bigger tail, a beaver looks ahead. 'All for a hat', spell out the words above, and so begins a video about the fur trade at the Minnesota History Centre (Figure 1). As a Canadian visiting the exhibition, my first thought was that it could be called Canadian history in a nutshell. As Glynnis Hood writes, the beaver is a 'furry rodent with an overbite and a history the size of a country'.[1] Is there an animal more significant to historical and contemporary imaginations of Canada than the beaver? Since 1975, it has been an official emblem of Canada.[2] As an emblem the beaver takes on the symbolism of an entire country, its values, histories and ideals. It becomes a marker of identity, a visual and material representation of an abstract idea. I argue that the symbolic and cultural value of the beaver in Canada overshadows the fact that it is also meat. Due to the history of the fur trade, the beaver was once over-trapped and the species was reduced to scant numbers. This is no longer the case; however, one is highly unlikely to see it on a restaurant menu in Canada.

As offal asks what parts of an animal are fit to eat, when and by whom, it also connects to the question of which animals are thought fit to eat at all. Why do we stop eating something? And why do we then eat it again? What cultural assumptions are behind which foods are rejected? What can be gleaned about meat, social hierarchies and changing tastes by studying the beaver as a rejected food, or as underrepresented food, in contemporary Canadian cuisine? This paper argues that both the fur trade and the contemporary cultural significance of the animal have rendered beaver meat as offal. Because it is illegal to buy and sell wild game in most of Canada, if one wants to eat beaver one has to trap it oneself. This essay is structured based on how one would do so. The first section is about beaver spotting, which beavers do we see and how do we see them. The second section is about the cultural practices and rules and regulations of hunting, and the third is about beaver as food.

Beaver Spotting

Nearly identical in appearance, there are two distinct species of beavers that are indigenous to both North American and Europe. The Eurasian beaver (*Castor fiber*) once lived in temperate forests from Britain to Russia to Mongolia.[3] From the Pacific to the Atlantic and from Alaska to the Gulf Coast, the North American beaver (*Castor canadensis*) is just as wide ranging.[4] The similarities between the two are so pronounced that they were once considered the same species until chromosome analysis identified them as distinct. However, even in captivity, they do not interbreed.[5]

Although the beaver looms large in Canada's history and thriving populations once again live across the country, its presence in the country's culinary history is less apparent. Rachel Poliquin suggests something similar about the animal itself. She begins *Beaver* by pointing out that despite the visual traces beavers leave behind the beaver itself is difficult to spot.[6] This argument comes alive in an installation. Sculptor David Diviney exhibited *Lodge* at Dalhousie Art Gallery, Halifax, in 2010 (see Figure 2 overleaf), but had first presented the work in a reflecting pool at a bus station in Kitchener, Ontario (see Figure 3 overleaf). Masses of skinny logs that are rather uniform in width make the sculpture appear life-like. One can almost imagine a beaver swimming out from underneath, but only from a distance. The logs are not actually logs at all; Diviney fashioned PVC pipe with construction adhesive to resemble wood. He tells Portia Priegert: 'It draws attention to both the site, this pool, and this form that's gleaned from the natural world – proposing a transition between the natural and the built environment.'[7] The work plays with appearances and transforms upon closer inspection. What is wood turns to PVC, what is organic turns to synthetic. Additionally, it is representative of how it is much easier to spot traces of a beaver rather than the animal itself. What is *Lodge* trying to prompt viewers to see? Because the installation visualizes the contrast between how something looks and what it is, it

Figure 2
David Diviney, Lodge (2010), detail, Styrofoam coolers, PVC piping, caulk, construction adhesive, corks, paint, 113 cm by 232 cm by 225 cm, Photo: Steve Farmer; Courtesy of the artist.

Figure 3
David Diviney, Lodge (2009), Styrofoam coolers, PVC piping, caulk, construction adhesive, corks, paint, 113 cm by 232 cm by 225 cm, Photo: courtesy of the artist.

can be interpreted as engaging viewers to reflect on what is perceived as natural and what is not. *Lodge* draws attention to the geographical presence of 'nature' in urban spaces. It also relates to the idea of creating distance from nature. Moreover, actual beaver lodges are also points of tension. As beavers are able to manipulate their own environments, constructing dams and lodges from mud, sticks and stones, this also puts them in competition with humans as architects of their surroundings. From afar beavers can appear as cute, desirable neighbours, but up close they can also be the source of conflict for landowners, executing conflicting ideas of how to engineer the local environment.

Beaver Trapping

Hunting can be a sign of status. Depending on the context and period, hunting can either indicate wealth and nobility, or poverty. Regarding Canada, John Ralston Saul writes, 'Until well into the nineteenth century, hunting was a central source of wealth. Farming, a theoretically more advanced undertaking, was a recipe for poverty.'[8] This no longer is the case as hunting for profit is illegal in Canada, and yet hunting is still connected to social status and issues related to rights regarding land ownership and land use.

Specific cultural practices of hunting can influence perspectives on animals and what parts count as edible. How an animal is hunted or trapped reveals how an animal is valued. During the fur trade's peak, 100,000 pelts a year were sent to Europe.[9] Driven by the fashion trend in seventeenth-century Europe for felt hats, the quest for beaver led to settlement further and further west across North America. Many hats later, the species was nearing extinction by the mid-1800s.[10] Travel narratives and natural histories describe how beavers were trapped and killed during this period. Such accounts also reveal how these techniques changed. One traditional method that was associated with Aboriginals up until the late eighteenth century was 'breaking open dams, then netting or spearing the fleeing beavers'. Other methods include breaking dams 'to lure the beavers out for repairs' and blocking the lodge entrance. In the late seventeenth century, steel traps replaced traditional methods.[11] To attract beavers, hunters baited them. As Poliquin writes: 'Once steel traps baited with castoreum came into common usage, North American beaver populations were systematically obliterated from the Atlantic to the Pacific coasts.'[12]

During the fur trade the beaver's pelt was valued more than its meat. What happened to the meat? It is not clear how much meat was being eaten, and by whom, and what happened to what did not become food. However, not even all of the pelts were making it into hats. There were simply too many. In the frenzy of the trade, 'supply doubled over demand, and skins often sat mouldering in warehouses in the hope of raising prices'.[13] The further north a beaver lives, the thicker its fur, which means a more desirable pelt. Yet, caught up in the frenzy, hunters were trapping beavers in warmer areas, which meant that 'millions of pelts rotted unused'.[14] If not all of the pelts were being used, surely it was the same for the beaver flesh. The fur trade rendered beaver meat as a type of offal as the fur was considered much more valuable than the meat.

The Toronto-based artist of Cree ancestry Kent Monkman tells a similar story of the destruction of over-hunting in his 2015 installation at the Gardiner Museum, Toronto (Figure 4). It consists of a buffalo jump (a cliff formation Native Americans used for hunting mass quantities of plains bison), a sculpture of the artist's alter ego, Miss Chief Eagle Testickle, two full-sized bison, and a pile of smashed ceramics that represent bone. According to the press release:

> *The Rise and Fall of Civilization* references the near extinction of the American bison in the 1800s when humans killed approximately 50 million, reducing their numbers to the hundreds. The settlers killed the bison for their pelts, wastefully leaving the meat to rot [...] . This compacted bone [...] tells the story of thousands of years of sustainable hunting, layer by layer, before the quick destruction of the bison by the European settlers.[15]

The installation contrasts two different approaches to hunting: a sustainable one in which the entire animal was used and a destructive one in which the animal was hunted for one part as a commodity and the rest was largely discarded, like offal. With both bison and beaver, the pelt was the object of desire, and the rest was rejected.

Monkman further alludes to the destruction of over-hunting in his 2011 painting *Le Roi de Castor* [*The Beaver King*] (Figure 5). The title does not tell which king, but it is most likely King Henry IV of France who encouraged the fur trade and seized it as an opportunity to solidify an empire in North America.[16] Nor does it quite prepare us for the massacre it depicts, one in which Europeans, Aboriginals and Catholics priests are all complicit. Painted in an historical style that looks much older than its production date suggests, it represents colonialism in the Americas as a bloody battle over beavers, one with both economic and symbolic stakes. It is an ironic story in the sense that killing beavers generated wealth and power, while also risking replenishing a steady supply of beavers on which that wealth and power was based. Monkman's painting critically offers a take on Canada's colonial history with the beaver as the main victim. Canada's animal emblem seems to be symbolic of the country's contradictory relationship to nature. As Glynnis Hood writes in *The Beaver Manifesto*, 'In many ways

Figure 4
Kent Monkman, The Rise and Fall of Civilization, Mixed Media Installation, 2015, Gardiner Museum, Photo: Jimmy Limit.

Canada is a country with a split personality, one that defines itself by the very wilderness it nearly destroyed.'[17]

Although traders valued pelts over meat for their commercial value, game meat was still important at times. Suman Roy and Brooke Ali briefly touch on this history in their cookbook *From Pemmican to Poutine: A Journey through Canada's Culinary History*. The authors identify game meat as one of the first available food sources to settlers. Beyond securing food, Roy and Ali argue this was also a way of expressing new rights to land:

> It was also a measure of the new freedom available in the New World. In the 1600s, game hunting was a leisure activity for the wealthy and the nobility and it was forbidden to anyone but the high echelons of society. Settlers in the New World, however, were given the right to hunt the local game; a privilege that would have meant one was on par with the elite in the old country.

Roy and Ali's claim implies that hunting became a practice of freedom and an indicator of a society in which more people had more freedom. Yet, this dwindled in popularity once settlers had larger homesteads with cattle. Here, the authors describe hunting differently. Although hunting was one of the first available food sources, the authors write that with more sufficient homesteads, the settlers 'no longer needed to rely on the often unreliable practice of hunting for their protein'. Hunting goes from something the settlers could rely on to something that was unreliable. Nonetheless, this does not necessarily imply a decrease in value. Roy and Ali write, 'Game then became a supplementary ingredient, added to the pantry to provide variety to the meal plan and for special occasions.'[18] However, James E. McWilliams suggests differently. Writing

Figure 5
Kent Monkman, Les Castors Du Roi, 96 x 84 inches, 2011, acrylic on canvas, collection of the Montreal Museum of Fine Arts. Image courtesy of Kent Monkman.

about colonial America, he argues that the British believed that civilized people relied on domesticated animals. Hunting was thus associated with frontier food; whereas, 'true and proper Englishmen domesticated rather than hunted their protein'.[19] Eating domesticated animals was considered more refined than having to hunt one's dinner.

Today hunting is about more than just food and subsistence. It is about the experience. In *A View to Death in the Morning*, the anthropologist Matt Cartmill writes, 'In short, hunting in the modern world is not to be understood as a practical means of latching onto some cheap protein. It is intelligible only as symbolic behaviour, like a game or a religious ceremony, and the emotions that the hunt arouses can be understood only in symbolic terms.'[20] Cartmill suggests that hunting is not about food. When it is not necessary to hunt, to do so becomes symbolic. He also mentions that emotions are attached to hunting. In a context in which animals and meat are normally two different things and the latter is available to buy in grocery stores in tidy cuts wrapped up neatly in plastic wrap, there is a disconnect between how an animal becomes meat. Hunting clearly connects the two.

Canada has strict wild meat regulations that differ in each province and territory. Newfoundland and Nova Scotia allow the buying and selling of wild game. In Nunavut one can purchase wild game in supermarkets. Under Ontario's Food Safety and Quality Act, hunted game that is not killed in a slaughterhouse is classified as 'inedible material'. In Ontario, and most of Canada, only meat that has been inspected and then slaughtered in a government-licensed facility is legal to sell. In Ontario, there are both hunting and trapping licenses. Residents of the province require an Outdoors Card and all applicable licenses and tags with the exception of Ontario resident hunter apprentices and members of Aboriginal communities with treaty hunting rights in Ontario. As the regulations state, 'These hunters are not required to be in possession of an Outdoors Card provided they are hunting for food, social or ceremonial purposes within their traditional or treaty area […] .'[21] This brings up food and cultural sovereignty and who has rights to which lands. Aboriginal peoples with treaty hunting rights can only hunt on their lands. To hunt in a different area would require a license.

The season for trapping beaver is October to the end of April or May. In order to get a trapping license one must complete the Fur Harvest, Fur Management and Conservation Course. It is a forty-hour class (thirty-two in the classroom and eight hours of hands-on pelt preparation and trap-setting). The regulations assume one is interested first and foremost in the pelt of the animal as they specify that 'the meat from beaver […] can be eaten'.[22] This statement suggests that the pelt is still valued over the meat, and that eating the beaver is an afterthought. The fur thus reduces the meat to offal, the less desired part of the animal.

Grab It by the Tail: Beaver as Food

Most people looking for beaver in the culinary realm in Canada today would first encounter BeaverTails. This is not the tail of an actual beaver, but a pastry. It is made from whole-wheat, yeasted dough that is stretched flat, fried in hot oil and topped with melted butter and sweet confections. Grant and Pam Hooker rebranded this fair staple as a Canadian treat in 1978 when they opened their first BeaverTails stall. Since then the chain has spread across the country and now has franchises in South Korea, the United States and the United Arab Emirates. The name of the both the chain and the pastry influences how beaver is seen as edible. *From Pemmican to Poutine: A Journey through Canada's Culinary History* does not have any recipes for beaver meat, but it does have one for BeaverTails pastries.

Who eats beaver meat? When beaver is identified as food in Canada, it is often considered 'country food', Aboriginal food. For example, beaver is not included in Health Canada's general Food Guide, but is in their Food Guide for first Nations, Inuit and Métis. Beaver appears in Indigenous cookbooks, such as *Gathering What the Great Nature Provided: Food Traditions of the Gitksan* (1980), *Pachamama: cuisine des Premières Nations* (2009) and *Feast for All Seasons: Traditional Native Peoples' Cuisine* (2010).[23] However, the history of beaver as food also crosses the Atlantic. The Catholic Church classified beavers as fish as they are primarily aquatic, which meant that Catholics could eat beaver on Fridays and during Lent. The authors of *The Eurasian Beaver* argue that this could have been influential in the overhunting of beavers in Europe as Lent coincides with when female beavers are either suckling young or highly pregnant.[24] This challenges the common narrative that it was the quest for beaver pelts that drove beavers nearly to extinction. Many questions remain. How common was it to eat beaver in Europe and in what regions? When did this become less common? Was this due to diminishing numbers of beavers, or other cultural reasons? Why does little of this history seem to live on in contemporary culinary memory on either side of the Atlantic?

Beaver does, however, appear in some Canadian cookbooks. One example is *The Northern Cookbook*, which was first published in 1967 by the Canadian Department of Indian Affairs and Northern Development. There is a recipe for 'Sweet Pickled Beaver'. As already mentioned, *From Pemmican to Poutine: A Journey through Canada's Culinary History* identifies beaver as edible, but does not include any recipes. Rose Murray's *A Taste of Canada* does the same. It is also absent from *Northern Bounty A Celebration of Canadian Cuisine* and *A Taste of History: The Origins of Québec's Gastronomy*, despite the latter containing recipes for other game meats and even a section on offal. Beaver is likely to be absent in most contemporary Canadian cookbooks.[25]

In 2015 Derek Dammann, co-owner with Jamie Oliver of Maison Publique in Montreal, published *True North: Canadian Cooking from Coast to Coast* with Chris Johnson. An article that reviews it is titled 'Eating Beaver in Search of Canadian Cuisine'. The title plays on stereotypes. It is much better at being catchy than it is at previewing the article's content: the complexities of defining a cuisine (or cuisines) in a geographically massive country with myriad cultural influences. The author nonetheless circles back to beavers in the article and quotes Dammann: 'The working title of the book was "How to Eat Beaver" [...], but it had a really sexual connotation so we were really doubting whether HarperCollins was going to fly with that one.'[26] The book does mention beaver as edible, but once again does not include a recipe. However, it does offer one chef's view on the politics of game. In introducing a recipe for Hare Ravioli, Dammann refers to 'the whole wild game thing in Canada' as 'pretty strange'.[27] He is critical that in Quebec, where he cooks, he is allowed to legally serve seal and hare, but not moose. That does not stop him from including recipes for 'Moose Tongue Smoked Meat' and 'Smoked Caribou Carpaccio'. This returns to the issue of hunting regulations, and to which animals are deemed fit to eat.

There is a recipe for beaver in one contemporary Canadian cookbook: chef Martin Picard's 2012 *Sugar Shack Au Pied de Cochon*. Picard has a reputation for being an extreme carnivore, which seems like a fitting source for a beaver recipe. His beaver dish is called 'Confederation Beaver' and, in addition to beaver tail and flesh, calls for maple-smoked ham, foie gras and pig's blood.[28] Both its name and ingredients are controversial. For a 2013 episode of *Parts Unknown*, Anthony Bourdain travelled to Quebec, where he ate beaver for the first time. It was Martin Picard who cooked it from him. Forgoing the foie gras, he cooked it in a chunky stew. Bourdain's verdict was 'Absolutely delicious'.[29]

Besides delicious, what does beaver taste like? Because I have never come across a restaurant that offers it and I do not hunt, I have to instead rely on the taste buds of others. In 1941, Marius Barbeau wrote that 'the meat was extensively consumed, and the tail was a delicacy – its flavour and appearance resemble those of the choicest bacon'.[30] One is left to wonder if this is his own description, or one that he had been given. Either way, bacon suggests a fatty meat. Poliquin quotes the French naturalist Pierre Belon's description of beaver tail tasting like 'nicely dressed eel'.[31] Dolly Jørgensen, an environmental historian specializing in Nordic flora and fauna who studies the history of beavers in the Nordic region, references historic texts, such as a 1757 Swedish treatise by Nils Gissler, describing beaver as tasting like pork. However, when Jørgensen had the chance to try beaver herself in 2014 at the Riga restaurant 1221, in a starter of smoked beaver served with pineapple vinaigrette and pine nuts, she rejected that description: 'I can tell you that it doesn't taste like pork.' She offers no details beyond saying that it was tasty and had a strong flavour.[32] In an article for the *Globe and Mail*, Les Perreaux describes beaver as tasting like very fatty lamb. He also quotes chef Picard: 'I can say beaver tastes a bit like chicken, but it is unique.'[33] Bacon, eel, pork, fatty lamb, chicken. The descriptions of the flavour of beaver cover the sea, land and sky.

When asked about beaver meat, David McMillian from the Montreal restaurant Joe Beef answered, 'It sucks. It's not good.' When asked how he would describe the taste of it, he pauses and says, 'Beaver sucks. Like dirty duck. You know. How can I say? Swampy, trouty duck. But then Martin said it tastes like scallops.'[34] It seems that beaver is an acquired taste, which brings up the question that if it were legal to serve wild game in provinces like Ontario and Quebec, would it be popular? Would diners order it?

Conclusion: Beaver as Offal

If offal asks what parts of an animal are fit to eat, when and for whom, it also connects to the question of which animals are fit to eat at all. If offal is understood as rejected, or even despised, then can beaver be understood as a type of offal? Surely during the fur trade, it was offal. The meat of the animal was often left to rot, as the fur was considered much more valuable. But why was it rejected as food? Perhaps as a product of modernization? Perhaps because of illusions of abundance? When they were on the brink of extinction, it was of course important that beavers stopped being food, but ironically when it would have been advantageous to eat them, no one had an appetite for beaver. The difficulties of imagining beaver as edible are not specific to Canada. Poliquin writes about how destruction caused by large beaver populations in South America led the governments of Chile and Argentina to encourage commercial trapping. Beaver even found its way onto the menus of some restaurants, but never gained popularity: 'No one was keen to eat beaver.'[35] The exception to this rule might be instances of 'extreme eating', where it is the objective to eat unusual things, and eating becomes a kind of competitive sport. Beaver as an everyday food is something else. We give many animals we eat, with the exception of poultry, different names. Cows become beef, pigs become pork, sheep becomes lamb or mutton, deer become venison. But beaver is beaver. The symbolic and cultural value of Canada's animal mascot overshadows the fact that it is also meat. The idea of the beaver as food in a contemporary Canadian context is a taboo, and one with a long history of cultural transformations. Many questions remain about just how popular beaver meat was and for whom historically, but considering why in Canada the beaver is more often imagined as an emblem and less as meat provides an interesting example of the hierarchies and histories of eating animals.

Notes

1. Glynnis Hood, *The Beaver Manifesto* (Toronto: Rocky Mountain Books, 2011), p. IX.
2. Rudy Boonstra, 'Beaver', *The Canadian Encyclopaedia*, Historica Canada, 2015 <http://www.thecanadianencyclopedia.ca/en/article/beaver/≥> [accessed 4 February 2016].
3. Guy Musser, 'Beaver', *Encyclopaedia Britannica*, 2016 <http://www.britannica.com/animal/beaver≥> [accessed 25 January 2016].
4. Dietland Muller-Schwarze, *The Beaver: Its Life and Impact* (Ithaca, NY: Cornell University Press, 2011), p. 13.
5. Muller-Schwarze, p. 17.
6. Rachel Poliquin, *Beaver* (London: Reaktion Books, 2015), p. 7.
7. Portia Priegert, 'The Do-It-Yourself Deconstructions of David Diviney', *gallerieswest*, 31 December 2008 <http://www.gallerieswest.ca/artists/profiles/david-diviney/≥> [accessed 21 January 2016].
8. John Ralston Saul, *A Fair Country: Telling Truths About Canada* (Toronto: Penguin, 2008), p. 46.
9. Government of Canada, 'Official Symbols of Canada', *Canada.ca*, 2016 <http://canada.pch.gc.ca/eng/1444070816842> [accessed 20 January 2016].
10. Boonstra.
11. Poliquin, p. 76.

12. Poliquin, p. 79.
13. Poliquin, p. 106.
14. Poliquin, p. 105.
15. Gardiner Museum, 'Kent Monkman: The Rise and Fall of Civilization', *Gardiner Museum* 2016 <http://www.gardinermuseum.on.ca/exhibition/kent-monkman-the-rise-and-fall-of-civilization> [accessed 3 February 2016].
16. Government of Canada.
17. Hood, p. 40.
18. Suman Roy and Brooke Ali, *From Pemmican to Poutine: A Journey through Canada's Culinary History* (Toronto: The Key Publishing House Inc., 2010), p. 43.
19. James E. McWilliams, *A Revolution in Eating: How the Quest for Food Shaped America* (New York: Columbia University Press, 2005), p. 8.
20. Matt Cartmill, *A View to Death in the Morning: Hunting and Nature Through History* (Cambridge: Harvard University Press, 1996), p. 29.
21. Government of Ontario, 'Food Safety and Quality Act, 2001, S.O. 2001, c. 20', *Ontario Regulations*, 1 July 2014 <https://www.ontario.ca/laws/regulation/050031> [accessed 27 January 2016]
22. Government of Ontario.
23. People of 'Ksan, *Gathering What the Great Nature Provided: Food Traditions of the Gitksan* (Vancouver: Douglas and McIntyre, 1980), Manuel Kak'wa Kurtness *Pachamama: cuisine des Premières Nations* (Montreal: Boréal, 2009) and Andrew George, *Feast for All Seasons: Traditional Native Peoples' Cuisine* (Vancouver: Arsenal Pulp Press, 2010).
24. Róisín Campbell-Palmer and others, *The Eurasian Beaver* (Exeter: Pelagic, 2015), p. 24.
25. Eleanor A. Ellis, *The Northern Cookbook* (Ottawa: Canadian Department of Indian Affairs and Northern Development, 1967); Rose Murray, *A Taste of Canada: A Culinary Journey* (Vancouver, Whitecap, 2010); *Northern Bounty A Celebration of Canadian Cuisine*, ed. by Jo Marie Powers and Anita Stewart (Toronto: Random House, 1995); Mark Lafrance and Yvon Desloges, *A Taste of History: The Origins of Québec's Gastronomy* (Quebec: Chenelière, 1989).
26. Nick Rose, 'Eating Beaver in Search of Canadian Cuisine', *MUNCHIES*, 17 November 2015 <https://munchies.vice.com/en/articles/eating-beaver-in-search-of-canadian-cuisine> [accessed 13 March 2016].
27. Derek Dammann and Chris Johns, *True North. Canadian Cooking from Coast to Coast* (Toronto: HarperCollins, 2015), p. 49.
28. Martin Picard, *Sugar Shack Au Pied de Cochon* (Montreal: Restaurant Au Pied de Cochon, 2012), pp. 360-65.
29. 'Canada', *Anthony Bourdain: Parts Unknown*, CNN, 5 May 2013 (season 1, episode 4).
30. Marius Barbeau, 'The Beaver in Canadian Art', *Beaver* 272 (September 1941), 14-18 (14).
31. Poliquin, p. 22.
32. Dolly Jørgensen, 'Beaver for Lent', *The Return of Native Nordic Fauna*, 19 April 2014 <http://dolly.jorgensenweb.net/nordicnature/?p=1568> [accessed 22 March 2016].
33. Les Perreau. 'Quebec Lets Select Restaurants Put Hunted Wild Game on Menu', *Globe and Mail*, 24 February 2014 <http://www.theglobeandmail.com/news/national/quebec-puts-wild-game-back-on-menu/article1707677/> [accessed 3 February 2016].
34. Phone call with David McMillian, 1 July 2016.
35. Poliquin, p. 195.

'Starbuggs?': Natural Dyes, Disgusting Drinks and the Controversy over Cochineal Use at Starbucks

Amy Butler Greenfield

Early in 2012, a Starbucks barista in the Midwestern United States noticed an odd ingredient in the company's Strawberries and Crème Frappuccino. In addition to strawberries, the drink was coloured with cochineal, a natural red food dye derived from the tiny scale insect *Dactylopius coccus*. Like many food and drink companies, the Starbucks coffee chain had turned to cochineal and other natural dyes in an effort to attract health-conscious consumers. As Starbucks was about to discover, however, not all aspects of nature are pleasing to everyone, and some provoke outright disgust.[1]

The barista took a snapshot of the ingredient list and emailed it to Daelyn Fortney, a vegan blogger, who posted the photo on her blog, *This Dish Is Veg*. Soon cochineal was at the centre of an Internet storm, an object of international outrage and revulsion – as was Starbucks, for using 'bugs' in its drinks. The storm died down only when Starbucks pledged to seek alternative red dyes for its products.[2]

Other foods have faced a sudden decline in popularity, but cochineal's fall from grace was unusually dramatic and swift. Why? What can this controversy tell us about the way that food disgust operates in a modern media age?

Because the Internet was central to cochineal's fall, the process is extremely well documented. By examining the way the original blog post was reframed and how the media reacted, we can trace the development of the controversy day by day, and sometimes hour by hour. Why was cochineal deemed acceptable in the first place? How and why was the original Starbucks story reframed? What role did Internet dynamics and economics play in creating and amplifying the controversy? Were there were really bug parts in Starbucks drinks – and does it matter if there were? Finally, what effect did the Starbucks controversy have on cochineal markets and producers?

Cochineal in the Kitchen

Insects are natural, but for many people eating them is not. In Western cultures, the very idea of eating a bug often evokes what the psychologist Paul Rozin calls 'core disgust'. This reaction goes well beyond mere physical distaste for a bitter substance (although some insects, including cochineal, do indeed taste bitter); it involves revulsion at the mere prospect of eating the offensive substance. With few exceptions, Western cuisines have shunned insects, perhaps because we link them so strongly with contamination, filth, bodily violation and death.[3]

Given this deep-seated horror of eating insects, it is not surprising that cochineal evoked widespread disgust in 2012. What is surprising is that cochineal wasn't widely rejected on those grounds long before. Yet the historical record shows that for centuries cochineal has been not just accepted, but even highly prized.

Originating in ancient Mexico, cochineal has a long history as a dye for food, textiles, cosmetics and medicines. Dried and ground, the insects were used to colour tamales and other foodstuffs in the ancient Americas. After cochineal reached Europe, the dye became highly valued there as well, eventually becoming a common kitchen item in many Western countries. Used particularly in the making of confections, jellies, icings and baked goods, it was employed by a multitude of cooks, including Elizabeth Raffald, Antonin Carême and Isabella Beeton.[4]

Was it general ignorance of cochineal's true nature that allowed it to become so popular in the West? On balance, the evidence suggests otherwise. Although very few Europeans in the sixteenth and seventeenth centuries knew exactly what cochineal was, many theorized that it might be a 'worm' of some sort – a zoological category that at the time included many insects. This did not in the least discourage them from consuming it. In 1685, when the Dutch microscope pioneer Antoni van Leeuwenhoek proved that cochineal was indeed a bug, he was not bothered by this discovery, and neither were his correspondents. By the late 1700s, the knowledge that cochineal was an insect had permeated through to most educated Europeans, who do not appear to have been revolted, either. On the contrary, the use of cochineal in European recipes was on the increase, and the liqueur alkermes – made from cochineal – was at the apex of its reputation as a miracle cure. Even at the start of the twentieth century, people were not squeamish about cochineal. Indeed, one can read hundreds of mentions of cochineal from the 1520s to the 1930s and not find a single expression of disgust.[5]

Why wasn't cochineal shunned? No doubt it helped that dried cochineal looked like peppercorns. Only after 1685 was it possible – with an excellent microscope – to confirm that the 'peppercorns' were actually insects. Moreover, many consumers bought their cochineal already pulverized or in liquid form, further attenuating the visual link. It probably also helped that cochineal was an expensive luxury; anyone lucky enough to obtain it was unlikely to cavil about its origins. Perhaps, too, people were less inclined to fuss about a pinch of dried insect powder because they lived in a world where more conspicuous live insects were everywhere, from flies at the butcher to mealworms in the flour.[6]

By the 1800s, sanitation standards were rising, yet the market for cochineal continued to increase. This was partly because many consumers were worried about the potential toxicity of artificial red dyes, as well as adulterants such as red lead. Cochineal, by contrast, was widely regarded as safe. What finally took cochineal off the table wasn't fear or disgust, but price competition: in the early twentieth century, production of cochineal virtually collapsed as cheaper artificial red dyes saturated the market. Farmers abandoned cochineal as a marketable crop until the 1960s, when the growing interest in natural foods sparked a cochineal revival.⁷

Stealth Revival

Modern cochineal is highly filtered, in addition to being pasteurized and checked for contaminants. It is essentially free of bug parts. The dye has never been safer, more sanitary or farther removed from its insect origins. Why, then, did cochineal suddenly become revolting in 2012?⁸

The answer is complex, but part of what set the stage for the Starbucks incident is this: cochineal's revival happened by stealth. Manufacturers were allowed to label the dye as 'natural coloring' in the United States and as E120 in the European Union. The upshot was that most people had no idea that they were eating an insect-derived substance. This helped account for the success of the dye even in an age when many Western and Westernized societies were growing ever more sanitation-conscious and bug-phobic.⁹

And cochineal was indeed a success. In the 1970s, demand for cochineal continued to increase, particularly after the United States Food and Drug Administration (FDA) banned artificial dye Red No. 2 because research suggested it was a carcinogen. Later the FDA would restrict the use of artificial dye Red No. 3 on similar grounds. By the early 2000s, food manufacturers were purchasing around two million pounds of cochineal a year, and the dye could be found in a host of foods, including yogurt, sausages, candy, juice, pudding, ice cream, cheese and various beverages.¹⁰

Among food manufacturers, cochineal was considered an ideal dye: it remained light- and heat-stable over a long shelf life, had no known safety issues and could be blended with other ingredients to produce a range of red, pinks, oranges and purples. For Starbucks, it must have been a straightforward choice to rely on cochineal, which they used not only in strawberry drinks but also in several baked goods.¹¹

Unfortunately, the increasing presence of cochineal created problems for certain consumers: vegans, vegetarians, those who kept kosher and halal diets and the handful of people who reported anaphylactic reactions to the dye. Their protests led the FDA to require clear labelling of cochineal in ingredients lists from 2011. Drinks made on the spot – like the Frappuccino – were excepted, but not the cartons used to make them.¹²

It was this behind-the-counter labelling that alerted the Starbucks barista to the presence of cochineal in the strawberry Frappuccino in 2012.

An Internet Storm

When the barista took her snapshot, she had no plans to start a campaign to ban cochineal from Starbucks. Instead, her goals were much more modest: to warn vegans away from the Strawberries and Crème Frappuccino. While Starbucks had not advertised the Frappuccino as a vegan drink, it had made much of the fact that it could be made dairy-free with soy milk; this had led vegans and strict vegetarians to conclude that soy Frappuccinos were vegan.¹³

As the barista wrote to blogger Daelyn Fortney, 'I was hoping you guys could help get the word out there so that no veg*ns end up drinking this formerly vegan Frappuccino by mistake!' Echoing this approach, Fortney initially framed her post as a warning to vegans about incorrect labelling: 'So vegans, beware,' she wrote on 14 March 2012. 'It just goes to show, even if we get the thumbs up on supposed vegan products, it's always good to double check packaging, if possible. You never know when something new will be slipped in.'[14]

Over the next two days, Fortney's post failed to get any traction. It was not picked up by other bloggers, still less by any news media. On 16 March, Fortney edited her original post. After emailing Starbucks directly about the issue, she copied in their response, which made it clear that no change in policy was forthcoming: '"At Starbucks, we strive to carry products that meet a variety of dietary lifestyles and needs [...]. While the strawberry base isn't a vegan product, it helps us move away from artificial dyes."'[15]

This updated blog post also failed to turn heads. That week only one other blogger – Red Hot Vegans of Austin, Texas – linked to the post.[16] Three days later, Fortney's original post was picked up by Consumerist.com, which had a wide readership, but again the issue failed to ignite. Notably, however, the article's headline finished with a hot-button phrase about bugs in food: 'Strawberry Frappuccinos No Longer Vegan, Contain Ground-Up Bugs'.[17]

Meeting with so little interest, Fortney changed her own language – and her tactics. On the fast-growing social-action platform Change.org, she started a petition titled 'Starbucks: stop using bugs to color your strawberry drinks.' In the petition itself, Fortney shared the barista's photo and explained that cochineal extract was 'simply stated... bugs.' She suggested alternative vegan dyes, then finished, 'Please let Starbucks know, you don't want crushed bugs in your drink!'[18]

Reframed as an issue of bugs in food, Fortney's protest finally attracted attention. On 26 March, the cascade of stories began. 'Starbuggs? Strawberry Frappuccino Colored by Insects' was the headline at the ABC News website. The UK's *Daily Mail* demanded, 'One tall Strawberry Frappuccino – extra insects please!' The story ran on a Portland, Oregon newscast, with the anchors expressing disgust and warning that viewers 'may find some of this video disturbing'. The *Seattle Post-Intelligencer*, an online-only newspaper, ran the story that night: 'Starbugs? Bug Extract behind Strawberry Frappuccino's Pink Hue'.[19]

On 27 March, the story went even wider, appearing in the *International Business Times*, the *Boston Globe*, CBS News and on blogs and websites as far away as Indonesia. The following day, even more news agencies, bloggers and websites were covering the Starbucks saga, including powerful players such as CNN, *Time*, *USA Today*, MSNBC and the *Huffington Post*. Soon NPR would be asking, 'Is That a Crushed Bug in Your Frothy Starbucks Drink?' The reach of those stories was further extended by social media. The *Huffington Post* article, for instance, would be shared over 2000 times.[20]

Starbucks was in trouble.

Natural Dyes, Disgusting Drinks and Cochineal at Starbucks

Disgust and Clickability

Why did the Starbucks story go viral?

Fortney's reframing of the issue was critical. Before the Starbucks incident, vegans and strict vegetarians had sometimes used the Internet to alert others to cochineal's presence in a particular food or drink, but they had attracted little notice outside their own circles. Fortney's initial post followed this typical track, but her change in tactics and language modified the trajectory.

Of the two, it was the change in language, more than the use of Change.org, that proved newsworthy. The petition tended to be mentioned late in news stories, if it was mentioned at all, while the key phrases Fortney used – 'bugs', 'crushed bugs', 'bugs in your drink' (or close variations) – were almost always in the headline or the lead paragraph.

The other word that featured prominently in both the petition and in news stories was 'Starbucks'. Fortney's protest was newsworthy in part because it focused on Starbucks, an iconic company with an international reach and a carefully cultivated reputation for hipness and healthiness.

What really made the story spread so widely and so quickly, however, were the dynamics of the Internet. By 2012, a story in a local newspaper could be shared across the world, and the next day people who read it could blog about it, sharing a link so that others could see exactly what they were talking about. Along with this expanded reach, however, the economics of the Internet brought new pressures to bear. It was becoming clear that stories featuring strong emotions such as disgust and outrage were very effective at garnering views and shares on the Internet, thereby increasing the status and importance – and sometimes income – of the website and writer. This helps explain why many journalists and bloggers played up the disgusting nature of cochineal. Their headlines were meant to turn the reader's stomach, and the stories themselves used language like 'disgusting', 'gross', and 'creepy crawlies' to underscore the point. Websites even linked the Starbucks story to other items on revolting foods, such as '11 Disgusting Ingredients You Eat Every Day'.[21]

Images were another way to amplify disgust. Many photo montages showed magnified insects in close proximity to a Starbucks Frappuccino, although often the insects were not cochineal. The image favoured by bloggers was a big beetle that was unrelated to cochineal and bore no resemblance to it. It was shown alive, whole, hairy and enlarged, engineered to attract attention and induce outrage.[22]

Journalists who took a broader view of the issues sometimes succumbed to the impulse to amplify disgust, too. In a news story broadcast by CNN on March 28th, Brian Todd interviewed Starbucks customers (who were unfazed upon learning that cochineal was in their drinks), then cut to a video clip of Bear Grylls eating a live rhino beetle grub – a sight almost guaranteed to make viewers feel disgust.[23]

Reality check

Starbucks could have argued that these words and images were an unfair representation of modern-day filtered cochineal. It also could have pointed out that there are bug parts in many foods. Under FDA regulations, chocolate can have up to 59 insect fragments per 100 grams, and up to 10% of coffee beans can be insect-infested. This opens up the interesting possibility that there might be more bug parts in a cup of coffee or hot chocolate than in a Frappuccino.[24]

Understandably, this was not an argument Starbucks wanted to make. Yet the company had to do something. Over 2000 people had signed Fortney's petition by 29 March, and 'Starbuggs' stories continued to be broadcast to millions. 'Starbucks Puts Dead Beetles in Frappuccinos' ran one headline that day, while the *Washington Post* asked, 'The New Pink Slime?' and *Gawker* talked about 'beetle juice'. Experts commented on the Starbucks 'PR crisis'.[25]

Later that day, Starbucks CEO Cliff Burrows announced that the company was 'reviewing alternative natural ingredients'. Starbucks intended to remove cochineal from all its foods, not just vegan ones. On 18 April, Burrows gave a further update: Starbucks would use lycopene, a tomato derivative, in its Frappuccino and other strawberry drinks. By early July, Starbucks food and drink were free of cochineal.[26]

Impact

During the Starbucks storm, little was said about the people who produced its cochineal. More than 85% of the world's cochineal is produced in Peru, mostly by poor rural families in the scrublands of the Andean highlands, where cochineal can be an economic lifeline. What were the repercussions for those families when cochineal was portrayed as an object of disgust and repudiated by Starbucks?[27]

Cochineal markets had been volatile for centuries, and in 2012 the price of cochineal was already falling steeply, after being sky-high for several years. This makes it difficult to estimate exactly how much the Starbucks incident contributed to the price fall, although it certainly cost farmers something.[28]

If more companies had abandoned cochineal in the wake of the Starbuck incident, it could have been devastating. After Starbucks's announcement, however, coverage of the incident changed. While some praised Starbucks for being responsive to consumers, others questioned whether the company had given in too easily to Internet pressure. Even the comments on Starbucks's own blog posts about the issue were strongly divided, with many people writing that they were not bothered by cochineal.[29]

In July 2013, a similar incident involving Dannon yogurt turned out very differently. When a campaign group launched a petition calling on the company to stop using cochineal, Dannon immediately defended its use of the dye, saying it was safe, FDA approved and clearly labelled. 'Any of our products that contain carmine clearly list it as an ingredient,' Dannon's spokesperson said. 'Anyone who wishes to avoid it can.' After reporting on Dannon's statement, mainstream news sources dropped the issue, as did most bloggers. There was no repeat of the sustained coverage of the Starbucks incident.[30]

Since then, the market for cochineal has remained healthy. Nevertheless, suppliers of other natural red food dyes maintain that companies using cochineal are vulnerable to public outcry. The Starbucks incident remains a cautionary tale, an example of how swiftly a campaign based on disgust can spread in the Internet age.[31]

Notes

1. Lisa Baertlein, 'Starbucks Revamps Bakery Food Ingredients', *Reuters*, 3 June 2009 <http://uk.reuters.com/article/us-starbucks-idUSTRE55175Y20090602> [accessed 11 April 2016].
2. Daelyn Fortney, 'Beware: Starbucks' Soy Strawberries & Creme Frappuccino Is NOT Vegan', *This Dish Is Veg*, 14 March 2012 <http://www.thisdishisvegetarian.com/2012/03/beware-starbucks-soy-strawberries-creme.html> [accessed 14 January 2016].
3. P. Rozin and A.E. Fallon, 'A Perspective on Disgust', *Psychological Review*, 94 (1987), 23-41; Jeffrey Lockwood, *The Infested Mind: Why Humans Fear, Loathe, and Love Insects* (Oxford: Oxford University Press, 2013), pp. 60-64, 110, 160.
4. Amy Greenfield, *A Perfect Red: Empire, Espionage, and the Quest for the Color of Desire* (New York: HarperCollins, 2005), pp. 40, 84, 233; Kate Colquhoun, *Taste: The Story of Britain through its Cooking* (London: Bloomsbury, 2008), p. 231; Marie-Antonin Carême, *Le cuisinier parisien*, (Paris, 1842), p. 244; Isabella Beeton, *Mrs Beeton's Dictionary of Every-Day Cookery* (London, 1865), p. 166.
5. Greenfield, *Perfect Red*, pp. 126-27, 134-35, 150, 154-56, 163-64, 233-34; Amy Butler Greenfield, 'Alkermes: "A Liqueur of Prodigious Strength"', *Gastronomica* 7 (2007), 25-30; Friedrich Johann Bertuch, *Bilderbuch für Kinder*, 6 (1807): Engraving LXXV.
6. Greenfield, *Perfect Red*, p. 150. On the importance of appearance in provoking insect disgust reactions, see Ophelia Deroy, Ben Reade and Charles Spence, 'The Insectivore's Dilemma, and How to Take the West Out of It', *Food Quality and Preference*, 44 (2015), 44-55.
7. Greenfield, *Perfect Red*, pp. 232-34, 242-43; Bee Wilson, *Swindled: The Dark History of Food Fraud, from Poisoned Candy to Counterfeit Coffee* (Princeton, NJ: Princeton University Press, 2008), pp. 3-4, 28-30, 113, 135-36, 141.
8. See Arr Oh, 'Cochineal Dye Bugs Starbucks Customers', *Scientific American*, 5 April 2012 <http://blogs.scientificamerican.com/guest-blog/cochineal-dye-bugs-starbucks-customers/> [accessed 14 January 2016]; 'Carmine' http://www.colormaker.com/natural-ingredients_carmine.html> [accessed 18 April 2016].
9. Greenfield, *Perfect Red*, p. 243; Associated Press, 'F.D.A. Limits Red Dye No. 3', New York Times, 30 January 1990 <http://www.nytimes.com/1990/01/30/science/fda-limits-red-dye-no-3.html> [accessed 27 April 2016]
10. Greenfield, *Perfect Red*, p. 243. Red No. 2 was also known as amaranth and Natural Red 4 in the United States, and as E123 in Europe.
11. Greenfield, *Perfect Red*, p. 244; Cliff Burrows, 'Update Regarding Cochineal Extract', *My Starbucks Idea*, Starbucks.com, 29 March 2012 <http://blogs.starbucks.com/blogs/customer/archive/2012/03/29/update-regarding-cochineal-extract.aspx> [accessed 12 April 2016].
12. Greenfield, *Perfect Red*, pp. 245-246; U.S. Food and Drug Administration, *Federal Register* Doc E9-5286, 11 March 2009 <http://www.fda.gov/ohrms/dockets/98fr/E9-5286.htm> [accessed 12 April 2016].
13. Lindsay S., 'How Do You Customize Your Frappuccino Blended Beverage?', *Starbucks*, Starbucks.com, 4 June 2011 <http://www.starbucks.com/blog/how-do-you-customize-your-frappuccino174-blended-beverage/1031> [accessed 27 April 2016]; Abby Bean, 'Review of Starbucks' New (Secretly Vegan)

Frappuccinos', *A (Soy) Bean*, 11 May 2010 < http://a-soy-bean.blogspot.co.uk/2010/05/review-of-starbucks-new-secretly-vegan.html> [accessed 27 April 2016]
14. Fortney, 'Beware'.
15. Fortney, 'Beware',16 March 2012 update [accessed 14 January 2016].
16. Marie Dadap, 'Vegan Week in Review', *Red Hot Vegan*, 12 March 2012 <http://www.redhotvegans.com/2012/03/vegan-week-in-review-2/> [accessed 12 April 2016].
17. Laura Northrup, 'Strawberry Frappuccinos No Longer Vegan, Contain Ground-Up Bugs', *Consumerist*, 23 March 2012 <https://consumerist.com/2012/03/23/strawberry-frappuccinos-no-longer-vegan-contain-bug-extract/> [accessed 12 April 2016].
18. Daelyn Fortney, 'Starbucks: stop Using Bugs to Color Your Strawberry Drinks', *Change.org*, <https://www.change.org/p/starbucks-stop-using-bugs-to-color-your-strawberry-flavored-drinks#petition-letter>; Fortney, 'Beware', 26 March 2012 update [accessed 14 January 2016].
19. Alan Farnham, 'Starbuggs? Strawberry Frappuccino Colored by Insects', ABC News, 26 March 2012 <http://abcnews.go.com/blogs/business/2012/03/starbuggs-strawberry-frappuccino-colored-by-insects/> [accessed 14 January 2016]; Kristie Lau, 'One Tall Strawberry Frappuccino – Extra Insects Please!', *The Daily Mail*, 26 March 2012 <http://www.dailymail.co.uk/femail/article-2120796/Starbucks-admits-Strawberry-Frappuccino-contains-crushed-bugs.html> [accessed 14 January 2016]; KOIN 6 (Portland, Oregon), 'Starbucks reveals Frappuccino additive', Nexstar Broadcasting, 26 March 2012 <https://www.youtube.com/watch?v=h4O5A5pAFg8> [accessed 14 April 2016]; KOMO-TV (Seattle, Washington), 'Starbugs? Bug Extract behind Strawberry Frappuccino's Pink Hue', Hearst Broadcasting, 26 March 2012 <http://www.seattlepi.com/local/komo/article/Starbugs-Bug-extract-behind-Strawberry-3436254.php> [accessed 15 January 2016].
20. Ryan Jaslow, 'Starbucks Strawberry Frappuccinos Dyed with Crushed Up Cochineal Bugs, Report Says', *CBS News*, 27 March 2012 <http://www.cbsnews.com/news/starbucks-strawberry-frappuccinos-dyed-with-crushed-up-cochineal-bugs-report-says/> [accessed 14 April 2016]; Anila Alexander, 'Starbucks Strawberry Frappuccino Flavoring Contains Crushed Bug Extract', *International Business Times*, 27 March 2012 <http://www.ibtimes.com/starbucks-strawberry-frappuccino-flavoring-contains-crushed-bug-extract-can-causes-asthma-allergic> [accessed 14 April 2016]; Deborah Kotz, 'Starbucks Flavoring Contains Bug Extracts', *Boston Globe*, 27 March 2012 <https://www.bostonglobe.com/lifestyle/health-wellness/2012/03/27/starbucks-flavoring-contains-bug-extracts/qawKH7J8AVgmlg5uxylL9M/story.html> [accessed 14 April 2016]; Afriza Hanifa, 'Starbucks Gunakan Serangga Sebagai Pewarna Makanan?', *Republika*, 27 March 2012 <http://internasional.republika.co.id/berita/internasional/global/12/03/27/m1i698-starbucks-gunakan-serangga-sebagai-pewarna-makanan> [accessed 15 April 2016]; Fortney, 'Beware', 29 March 2012 update; Nancy Shute, 'Is That a Crushed Bug in Your Frothy Starbucks Drink?', *The Salt*, National Public Radio, 30 March 2012 <http://www.npr.org/sections/thesalt/2012/03/30/149700341/food-coloring-made-from-insects-irks-some-starbucks-patrons> [accessed 14 April 2016]; Tara Kelly, 'Starbucks Beetle Extract', *Huffington Post*, 28 March 2012 <http://www.huffingtonpost.com/2012/03/28/starbucks-beetle-bug-extract_n_1385521.html> [accessed 14 April 2016].
21. Jonah Berger and Katherine L. Milkman, 'What Makes Online Content Viral?', *Journal of Marketing Research*, 49 (2012), 192-205; Laura Stampler, '11 Disgusting Ingredients You Eat Every Day That Food Companies Don't Talk About', *Business Insider*, 29 March 2012 <http://www.businessinsider.com/11-disgusting-ingredients-that-arent-advertised-in-food-2012-3?IR=T,> [accessed 18 April 2016].
22. Examples of insect images include: Anthony De La Cruz, 'Excuse Me I Think There's a Cochineal Insect in My Frapp', *It's Not You It's Me*, 27 March 2012 <http://itsnotyouitsmesite.blogspot.co.uk/2012/03/excuse-me-i-think-theres-cochineal.html> [accessed April 2016]; Roy Hollister, 'Excuse me, barista?', *Deemable Tech*, 28 March 2012 <http://deemable.com/2012/03/excuse-me-barista-theres-a-bug-in-my-strawberry-frappuccino-debunkable/> [accessed 20 April 2016]; Lisa Mason Lee, 'Starbucks Caught Using Bugs in Products', *Thecount.com*, 29 March 2012 <https://www.youtube.com/watch?v=1UIqAQOXFs0> [accessed 25 April 2016].
23. 'Starbucks Uses Bugs to Color Drink', *CNN*, 28 March 2012 <https://www.youtube.com/

watch?v=FizXPrbOxGo≥] [accessed 13 April 2016]; 'Man vs. Wild – Eating Giant Larva', *Man vs. Wild*, Discovery Channel, 29 April 2008 <https://www.youtube.com/watch?v=QuB3kr3ckYE≥> [accessed 19 April 2016].

24. U.S. Food and Drug Administration, 'Defects Level Handbook', U.S. Department of Health and Human Services, 2016 <http://www.fda.gov/food/guidanceregulation/guidancedocumentsregulatoryinformation/ucm056174.htm≥> [accessed 11 April 2016].

25. Eksith Rodrigo, 'Dear Starbucks', This Page Intentionally Left Ugly, 29 March 2012 <https://eksith.wordpress.com/2012/03/29/dear-starbucks-i-want-more-cochineal-extract-in-my-drink/> [accessed 20 April 2016]; Elizabeth Flock, 'The New Pink Slime?', *Washington Post*, 29 March 2012 <https://www.washingtonpost.com/blogs/blogpost/post/the-new-pink-slime-beetles-in-starbucks-frappuccinos-anger-consumers/2012/03/29/gIQAMr6NjS_blog.html≥> [accessed 13 January 2016]; Leah Beckmann, 'That's Beetle Juice in Your Vegan Frappuccino', *Gawker*, 29 March 2012 <http://gawker.com/5897463/thats-beetle-juice-in-your-vegan-frappuccino> [accessed 20 April 2016]; Bruce Horowitz, 'Vegans Bash Starbucks for Beetle Coloring in Frappuccinos', *USA Today*, 28 March 2012 <http://usatoday30.usatoday.com/money/industries/food/story/2012-03-28/starbucks-strawberry-frappuccino-beetle-juice/53839006/1≥> [accessed 13 January 2012].

26. Burrows, 'Update Regarding Cochineal Extract'; Burrows, 'Cochineal Extract Update', *My Starbucks Idea*, Starbucks.com, 18 April 2012 <http://blogs.starbucks.com/blogs/customer/archive/2012/04/18/cochineal-extract-update.aspx≥> [accessed 12 January 2016]; Fortney, 'Consumers Rejoice: Starbucks' Strawberries & Creme Frappuccino Is Bug-free', *This Dish Is Veg*, 7 September 2012 <http://www.thisdishisvegetarian.com/2012/07/grossed-out-consumers-rejoice-starbucks.html> [accessed 13 January 2016].

27. Greenfield, *Perfect Red*, p. 245; Luis Carlos Rodríguez, 'Land Clearance and Social Capital in Mountain Agro-Ecosystems: The Case of Opuntia Scrubland in Ayacucho, Peru', *Ecological Economics* 49.2 (June 2004), 243-42.

28. 'The Economics of a Color', *Maiwa*, Maiwa Handprints Ltd., 1 August 2010 <http://maiwahandprints.blogspot.co.uk/2010/08/economics-of-colour.html> [accessed 19 April 2016]; Luisa Fuster Cabeza (Peruvian Embassy, London), correspondence with the author, 10 June 2014.

29. A few of the articles and blogs that questioned the change were: Rodrigo, 'Dear Starbucks'; Gwen Pearson, 'Waiter? There's an Insect in my Frappucino', *Bug Gwen*, 30 March 2012 <https://membracid.wordpress.com/2012/03/30/waiter-theres-an-insect-in-my-frappuccino/> [accessed 15 January 2016]; Daniel Stone, 'Forget the Starbucks Backlash – We Should Be Eating More Bugs', *The Daily Beast*, 24 April 2012 <http://www.thedailybeast.com/articles/2012/04/24/forget-the-starbucks-backlash-we-should-be-eating-more-bugs.html> [accessed 25 April 2016]; 'Waiter, There's a Bug in my Frappuccino', *Skepchick*, 30 March 2012 <https://skepchick.org/2012/03/waiter-theres-a-bug-in-my-frappuccino/> [accessed 25 April 2016].

30. Jeff Cronin and Ariana Stone, 'Berries Over Bugs!', *Center for Science in the Public Interest*, 24 July 2013 <http://www.cspinet.org/new/201307241.html≥> [accessed 12 April 2016]; Rachel Tepper, 'Dannon Under Fire For Use Of Carmine, Insect-Based Color Additive', *Huffington Post*, 24 July 2013 <http://www.huffingtonpost.com/2013/07/24/dannon-carmine_n_3645757.html?>, [accessed 12 April 2016].

31. Catey Hill (reporter, *Wall Street Journal*), correspondence with the author, 18 June 2014; Fuster Cabeza 10 June 2014; Guido de Jager, 'Price Volatility and Consumer Demands Continue to Drive Carmine Replacement', *GNT*, GNT Group, 31 March 2016 <http://gnt-group.com/us-us/node/3216≥> [accessed 18 April 2016].

The Case of Missing Brains, a Long Way from Rome

Alexandra Grigorieva

If we look for brains at the largest recipe website in the world, Allrecipes.com – with forty million users and ninety-five recipes consulted per second – we will find exactly one recipe that describes cooking actual brains, as opposed to Halloween Brain Dip (hollowed out cauliflower filled with 'yucky' guacamole) or Pink Brain Shooter (peach jello and evaporated milk in a 'scary' brain mould).[1] Majorcan Style Brains ('braised with vinegar and chicken stock, then baked in an egg cream') was submitted to Allrecipes.com more than ten years ago and represents the exotic – Spanish cuisine.[2] Five people claim to have cooked the recipe over the years, and the same five have reviewed it in very positively.

The absence of brain recipes seems especially bizarre because the American South still has a strong tradition of eating brains. In the US, one can even purchase canned brains in milk gravy from Amazon, although canned brains were panned in a scathing *New York* magazine article by Paul Lukas back in 1996.[3] Amazon buyers undeterredly posted rave reviews of the product, a flavour of nostalgia for some, a health product for others, pure delight for the unconventional few amid some predictable expressions of disgust and references to zombie apocalypse, Creutzfeldt-Jakob disease and high cholesterol:

> 'My father used to make Pork Brains & Eggs for breakfast. With toast and apple butter.'

> 'We ordered this pig brain to eat with eggs for breakfast because my mom has Multiple Sclerosis. According to some research eating pig brain can restore some of the damage that MS does to your brain.'

> 'I like to eat these like cereal for breakfast, in a bowl with cold milk. You can also heat them up and add some cinnamon and it is more like oatmeal. If you have a child who won't eat much meat, these are very high in protein but don't have a meaty flavor, so you can puree this in the blender until smooth and then add a flavor your child likes (Hershey's chocolate sauce, or some strawberry jam) and then pour into popsicle molds and freeze for very healthy popsicles.'

> 'OMG this is so delicious, served inside of a peanut butter and jelly sandwich (preferably Peter Pan and homemade grape jelly). Literally put it in the sandwich. Always serve with a side of Cool Ranch Doritos and an orange Fanta!'[4]

The Case of Missing Brains, a Long Way from Rome

These are just some examples of the positive Amazon feedback, and no, the last two persons are not trolling: they have lots of reviewed products on Amazon described much in the same style.

So why are brains missing from Allrecipes and other US-centred recipe websites like Epicurious?[5] By contrast, there are many recipes for brains on European recipe websites, such as the German language Chefkoch.de, the biggest European recipe website with almost 2.5 million members and 275,000 recipes, and Marmiton.org, the most popular French-language recipe website with more than 67,000 recipes.[6] There may be some fancy Halloween creations, but in general these recipes offer different ways to use real brains.

With two notable exceptions. First, both websites have recipes of everyday dishes that contain no brains but are called 'brains', such as the French *'cervelle de canut'* ['brains of Lyon factory weaver', herby fromage blanc spread] and the German *'falsches Gehirn'* and *'verkehrtes Gehirn'* ['fake' or 'wrong/muddled brains', scrambled eggs with tomatoes].

Second, many recipes on both websites refer to 'brain sausages': *'cervelas'* on Marmiton.org, and *'Gehirnwurst/Hirnwurst'* and *'Bregenwurst/Brägenwurst'* on Chefkoch.de. Now this is really interesting. In their ground-breaking German Dictionary, the Brothers Grimm defined BREGENWURST in 1854 as *hirnwurst*, accompanying it with Italian and French parallels: *it. cervellata, franz. cervelas* (DWB 2.2). However, in a later volume that appeared in 1873, HIRNWURST is not explained as BREGENWURST, but as *'eine art feiner wurst, deren hauptteil das gehirn des schweines bildet'* ['a kind of fine sausage, that is mostly formed out of pork brain'] (DWB 10.7). Modern *Hirnwurst* (also called *Herrnwurst* [lord's sausage] and *Gelbwurst* [yellow sausage]) have diverged even further, referring to both a cooked sausage often used as a cold cut in Southern Germany and *Bregenwurst*, a raw sausage used for cooking in Northern Germany, particularly Saxony. Both of them lost their brains along the way.

However, back in 1857 German words *Hirnwurst* and *Bregenwurst* were interchangeable and made of pork mixed with brains as testified by Bernhardine Westing's *Die Wangereger Küche : Nebst einem Anhange, enthaltend feine und gewöhnliche Speisen für alle Jahreszeiten, sowie das einsetzen der Früchte, auch rohes Gemüse luftleer in Büchsen und Flaschen einzukochen* published in Oldenburg in the same year. Moreover, other brain sausages were popular in some regions of Europe as late as in 1901, as in the Russian recipe *'sosiski iz mozgov'*, an exquisite affair of calf brains, dinner rolls soaked in cream, butter, plenty of egg yolks, salt, pepper, nutmeg, all stuffed in casings, poached in milk halved with water and then browned in butter.[7] There could still be other brain sausages lurking in European culinary history and waiting to be rediscovered.

As for the *cervelas*, ultimately from Latin *cerebellata* [unattested 'brain sausage'], by the the nineteenth century, we could no longer expect brains in its recipes. British journalist E. S. Dallas made an apropos astringent observation in his 1877 *Kettner's Book of the Table: A Manual of Cookery: Practical, Theoretical, Historical* on 'things which [...] retain names no longer their own – cervelas without brains, [...]

cheesecakes without curds'.[8] So French *cervelas* popular in Alsace and Lyon region and first mentioned by Rabelais in 1552 as *cervelat* no longer contain brains.[9] Nor does the ubiquitous neighbouring *cervelat*, the national sausage of Switzerland, a cooked smoked sausage that has been made there without brains since at least 1749, according to a cookbook from Bern.[10] Although etymological dictionaries tend to derive French *cervelas* and Swiss *cervelat* from zervellada cheese and pork sausage (dialect of Milan), I don't think that there's any need for it. Renaissance Italian cookbooks have quite a few examples of *cervellata* and *cervellate* without a need for Northern dialect, and still with no brains.[11] Unless we draw a parallel between cheese as an eventual replacement for brains as it is supposedly in *cervelle de canut* [brains of weaver cheese spread] dish from Lyon, but this might be too far-fetched.

Basically *The Oxford Companion to Food* is correct in stating that these 'names [...] must have had a past connection with [...] "brain" but the connection has been lost; for no recent or modern recipes for cervelas call for brains as an ingredient'.[12] However, if we go back in time, we will find sausages made with brains in ancient Roman cuisine, only without a proper name for them yet. Apicius's Latin recipes collection (first to fourth century AD) has a section on sausages stuffed into casing called *FARCIMINA*, and the first recipe there describes a brain sausage: 'You grind eggs and brains, pine-nuts, black pepper, fish sauce and a bit of asafetida, fill casing with this, boil it, then brown on a grill and serve.'[13]

On a different, non-savoury note there is a modern Croatian milky dessert pudding from Dalmatia called *rožata* that now contains no brains whatsoever. It looks like it hails back to a sweet luscious Roman concoction of brains and rose petals that is not only present in one of the most precise recipes of Apicius ('*patina de rosis*'), but also described in full in the *Deipnosophists* of Athenaeus, when a fictional chef presents it to his master's dinner guests, making it also one of the very few recipes that we actually do have in Ancient Greek.[14]

Back in Ancient Rome, chefs seemed to have used brains much like the French chefs of the nineteeth and twentieth century used *foie gras*. Out of almost five hundred Latin recipes in Apicius, twenty-five especially lavish ones call for brains. There were not only sausages with brains, but also elaborate puddings with brains, a cucumber dish with brains, rich pulses and grain dishes with brains, various kinds of complex stuffing with brains to be used for chicken, kid, pig, hare and even cuttlefish.[15] It is as if the rule of thumb was that anything with brains would taste better. It probably did too. Not to mention that Celsus, Pliny, Quintus Serenus Sammonicus and other Roman writers on medical topics thought assorted brains (even camel, dog etc.) to be very beneficial for one's health.

So why are brains on the wane now, especially in the US? A combination of prudish offal disgust, overly disturbing graphic horror images and health scares seems to be responsible for that.

But it is a pity that we are mostly missing our brains now.

The Case of Missing Brains, a Long Way from Rome

Notes

1. The social network Allrecipes.com now has eighteen versions in twelve languages; I am speaking about the main US English version of the site (Stan Pavlovsky, 'Our Story', *allrecipes.com* <http://press.allrecipes.com/> [accessed 26 May 2016].
2. Penny, 'Majorcan Style Brains', *allrecipes.com* <http://allrecipes.com/recipe/19640/majorcan-style-brains/> [accessed 26 May 2016].
3. Paul Lukas, 'Mulling Brains', *New York*, 11 March 1996, p. 60.
4. 'Rose Pork Brains with Milk Gravy', *Amazon.com* <https://www.amazon.com/Rose-Pork-Brains-Gravy-Ounce/dp/B00FHIAIIE> [accessed 26 May 2016].
5. Interestingly not Food.com, where a few brain recipes are present, including son of a gun stew, from the American southwest, that is made of everything offal (Olha, 'Son of a Gun Stew (Cowboy Stew)', *Food.com* <http://www.food.com/recipe/son-of-a-gun-stew-cowboy-stew-152362> [accessed 26 May 2016].
6. 'Chefkock.de', *Wikipedia* <https://de.wikipedia.org/wiki/Chefkoch.de> [accessed 26 May 2016].
7. Elena Molokhovets, 'Brain Sausages (Sosiki iz mozgov)', *Classic Russian Cooking: Elena Molokhovets' A Gift to Young Housewives*, trans. by Joyce Toomre (Bloomington, IN: Indiana University Press, 1992), p. 225.
8. E.S. Dallas, *Kettner's Book of the Table: A Manual of Cookery: Practical, Theoretical, Historical* (London: Dalau, 1877), p. 48.
9. François Rabelais, *Le quart livre de Pantagruel, éd. Marty-Laveaux* (Paris: A. Lemerre, 1868), p. 414.
10. '*Das älteste Schweizer Rezept eines Cervelats ist im Bernerischen Koch-Büchlein aus dem Jahr 1749: "Nimme gebutzte Rinderdärm, mit nachfolgendem gefüllt, und zu Würsten gemacht: nimm Speck und Schweinefleisch, oder wann du willst Schaaf- oder anders Fleisch, hacke es wohl, nimm Salz, Pfefferpulver, weissen Wein, Nägelipulver, Majoran, Lauch oder Zwiebelen, nimme dann auch ein wenig frisches schweinigs Blut, knette alles wohl untereinander, thue es in die Därme Wursts-Weise, hernach räuche sie im Camin etwelche Tage, koche sie im Wasser, thu zuletzt ein wenig Wein daran: Sie behalten sich ein Monat lang gut, wann sie schon gekocht sind*' (Association Patrimoine Culinaire Suisse, '*Cervelat / Cervelas*', *Kulinarisches Erbe der Schweiz*, <http://www.patrimoineculinaire.ch/Produit/Cervelat-Cervelas/182> [accessed 26 May 2016].
11. On *cervellata*, see Anonimo Meridionale, 'affare cervellata', Libro di cucina B, cap. LXX (*c*. fourteenth to fifteenth century); for *cervellate*, Maestro Martino's *Libro de Arte Coquinaria* (*c*. 1450) includes a version with plenty of cheese mixed with sausage stuffing and also expensive golden saffron colouring, which reminds us of the future German *gelbwurst*.
12. Alan Davidson, 'Cervelas and Cervalat', *The Oxford Companion to Food*, ed. by Tom Jaine (Oxford: Oxford University Press, 2014), p. 159.
13. '*Ova et cerebella teres, nucleos pineos, piper, liquamen, laser modicum, et his intestinum implebis. elixas, postea assas et infers*' (Apicius 2.5.1). There is also a brain sausage without casing, *isicium* (Apicius 2.1.5).
14. Such sweet mixtures recall the brain popsicles with strawberry jam or chocolate from the Amazon reviews: bear in mind that a pudding is some kind of sausage, so savoury sausage easily morphs into sweetish pudding and vice versa, like Portuguese or Italian chocolate and cookie sausage. Apicus's recipe for '*patina de rosis*': '*Accipies rosas et exfoliabis, album tolles, mittes in mortarium, suffundes liquamen, fricabis. Postea mittes liquaminis ciatum unum semis et sucum por colum colabis. Accipies cerebella IV, enervabis et teres piperis scripulos VIII, suffunes ex suco, fricabis. Postea ova VIII frangis, vini ciatum unum semis et passi ciatum I, olei modicum. Postea patinam perunges et eam impones cineri calido, et sic inpensam supra scriptam mittes. Cum cocta fuerit in termospodio, piperis pulverem super asparges et inferes*' (Apicius 4.2.9); in Athenaeus, see 403d.
15. The practice of stuffing shellfish with brains still exists in modern Catalonia ('*Calamars farcits amb mandonguilles de gambes*', *Cuines* <http://www.ccma.cat/tv3/cuines/recepta/calamars-farcits-amb-mandonguilles-de-gambes/2512/> [accessed 26 May 2016]). It is also reflected in Athenaeus (4b), when one of the deipnosophists addresses the stuffed squid served at the banquet – 'you are wise, wise!' – he means that it is stuffed with brains.

Gut Feelings: Tripe in American Poetries

Naomi Guttman

For many, the word tripe is synonymous with garbage, food for animals. For others, it is the basis of nourishing soups and stews that hold within them the manifestation of ethnicity and nationality in the strange new world of America. This paper examines the role of tripe dishes, specifically 'tripe', 'chitlins' and 'menudo' in the poetry of several American poets who grew up in African American families or immigrant families from Mexico, Philippines and Italy. In poems by Kevin Young, R.A. Villanueva, Ray Gonzalez, Gary Soto and Lucia Perillo, we see a focus on metaphorical hungers engendered by tribal and personal homesickness. While at times this hunger suggests that tripe recipes are a means of dramatizing domestic and intergenerational conflict, in focusing the animal's gut, these poems remind us that our own guts transform what we eat: the organ that carries food through us also breaks down nutrients to be absorbed, creating and replacing our cells, our bodies. In this way, poetry is transformative as, like menudo, it takes the humble offal of life and creates something of value.

Though the word nostalgia has come to mean a 'wistful desire to return in thought or fact to a former time in one's life', the word's roots come from a combination of 'home' and 'pain', and originally connote 'acute homesickness'.[1] Wistfulness certainly plays a role in Gary Soto's children's poem 'Papi's Menudo' and in Ray Gonzalez's 'Praise the Tortilla, Praise Menudo, Praise Chorizo'.[2] Each poem presents homesickness in the sense we normally use it: the smells, tastes and texture of tripe cooked in the traditional ways are recalled with pride and tenderness and provide a trigger for memories of home, culture and family.

In Soto's poem, written for children, the child speaker marvels at the power of the father for whom the traditional tripe dish *menudo* is prepared for Sunday breakfast:

> It comes in
> A yellow pot,
> A curl of steam
> Unraveling
> When you lift
> The lid and look in:
> *Tripas* wagging
> Like tongues (11-18)

The child describes the stew with simplicity and wonder, but it's no accident that the tripe reminds him of wagging tongues: the dish not only brings comfort in the sense of literal sustenance, but calls to mind the language of home and homeland. Sunday is the day when the family turns on 'the Mexican/ Station is/ Starting up/ Its eight violins' (25-28), a sound that could make his father 'cry' (29). Tripe becomes the father's 'Medicine on Sunday', a cure for the homesickness of exile and of a life of manual labour (59). The sensory pleasure he takes in preparing for his meal is evident in the description of the flavourings he mixes into his bowl: along with a squeeze of lemon, the father

> [...] sprinkles
> His *menudo* with onion
> And runs oregano
> Between his lucky palms
> He roars, *Que rico!* (45-49)

The father's roar and his animal-like pleasure in the menudo kindle the child's hunger, and the child imitates the father: 'When/ He slurps,/ I slurp' (66-68). Interestingly, the father and child slurping together '[a]wake the whiskers/ Of my cat, Hambre' (69-70). The cat, whose name translates as 'Hunger', is then both real and metaphorical – the father's ancestral hungers are awakened by the ritual of Sunday menudo, and the child follows, finding delicious what his father does, perhaps because his father does.

In his poem, 'Praise the Tortilla, Praise Menudo, Praise Chorizo', Ray Gonzalez writes a memorial to foods of his childhood that give us a taste of his background as a Chicano kid growing up in Texas. The central stanza, devoted to *menudo*, demonstrates how Gonzalez takes for granted readers' familiarity with Spanish and with Mexican foods. Here *tripas* are connected to ancestry as well as poetry:

> I praise the menudo as visionary food that it is,
> the *tripas y posole* tight flashes of color
> we see as the red *caldo* smears across our notebooks
> like a vision we have not had in years,
> our lives going down like the empty bowls
> of menudo exploding in our stomachs
> with the *chili piquin* of our poetic dreams. (10-16)

The poet's stance toward the menudo's 'explosions' is slightly equivocal, given the image of 'our lives going down like the empty bowls' (14), but the connection between the 'visionary' sustenance of tripe and poetry is clear. The soup (*caldo*) 'smears across [...] notebooks' in which poets write, and the menudo, along with the heavy spices of 'poetic dreams', detonates in the eaters' guts (12, 16).

This connection between tripe and poetic inspiration – or poetic labour – is made even more clear in two R.A. Villanueva poems, 'Fish Heads' and 'Despedida'.[3] In Rigoberto Gonzalez's interview of Villanueva, he suggests that in 'Fish Heads' Villanueva celebrates his mother's food ethos of using every edible part of an animal and thereby creates an 'ars poetica' with a similar credo: the poet's task is to reclaim memories which would otherwise be forgotten or deemed unusable.⁴ As Villanueva puts it, the mother's 'warning' not to

> [...] *waste what should be eaten.* Reminds me
> of every delicate gift we have thrown away: tilapia stomach
> best soured with vinegar, milkfish liver to melt
> against the dome of the mouth. (9-12).

This ethos of using all animal parts and Villanueva's own exploration of the 'the viscera of memory and story' continues in another of Villanueva's poems, 'Despedida', which means farewell. In this poem, the speaker recounts a goodbye party for his family as they prepare to return to the United States after a visit to his parents' village in the Philippines. After the speaker's father and his friends have slaughtered a suckling pig for the traditional roast, the Lechón, they toast each other with a morning beer and watch the pig 'bleed out'. This blood is not wasted, however, but saved:

> for our farewell
> dinner, for the stew of innards and vinegar
> my brother, my sister, and I will feed to the dogs
> instead of tasting. (6-9)

Though the father participated in the pig's slaughter, the poem suggests his slight alienation from the local men when he does not join them in their 'first morning cigarette' (10). This could signify that the father may be slightly torn in his national allegiance; the children, however, seem to be firmly Americanized, with American palates that reject even a taste of the stew that will be made in their honour. In 'Fish Heads' this difference is underscored when the poem's speaker admits that he and his siblings 'wished gone/ [their mother's] tripe steamed with beef bouillon and onion broth' (16-17). Though as a child, Villanueva appreciated neither the value of a traditional farewell dinner nor the eating of offal as a special delicacy, the adult Villanueva looks back on these childhood food memories – emblems of his cultural identity as a Filipino-American – as means of recuperating his ancestral home and keeping alive a source of poetry that memorializes that which might be wasted.

The tradition of chitterlings, or chitlins, among African Americans can go two ways, as Linda Williams Nelson reminds us in her essay '"Hands in the Chit'lins": Notes on Native Anthropological Research among African American Woman'. Some African Americans reject chitlins as a dish redolent of the history of slavery and oppression, when their ancestors were forced by necessity to eat that which the master gave them – namely the parts '*low on the hog* (that is, chitlins, hogmaws, pig's feet)'. By contrast, other African Americans celebrate their history of strength and survival against great odds and their ingenuity in making 'palatable' that which is otherwise inedible. Often, foods such as this, what are in fact called soul foods, are served at important holidays, such as New Year's Day, when chitlins signify 'the hope for a prosperous new year'.⁵

The speaker of Kevin Young's 'Ode to Chitlins' falls securely into the latter category, celebrating the gritty road of the hog's entrails as it leads him back to honour his relatives and eulogize his father.[6] Addressing the chitlins as a 'wrinkled wise man', he makes the point that he would not trust people outside his own family to 'help with' their proper cleaning and cooking (7,10). At the same time, the speaker 'claims' chitlins as 'kin', comparing them to 'the uncle/ I one day learnt/ wasn't really' (24, 8, 19-21). Chitlins, then, are members of the speaker's family, his personal history, and form part of his spiritual and corporal sustenance. He writes: 'You fed me/ when I would have withered/ without you' (24-26). The medicine for the soul is especially important at the worst of times, such as in the period of grief after the speaker's father dies. When an uncle attempts to soothe him over the phone with prayer, all the speaker wants is to eat that uncle's 'best/ brisket, smoked slow' (34-35). Like that uncle's brisket, chitlins are 'family': 'Sweetbread's/ sister, tripe's long/ lost cousin' (17-19) as well as 'Pork loin's poor brother' (36), and so they link the speaker to the hog itself: that which he has ingested becomes family, becomes him.

By contrast, Lucia Perillo's poem 'Tripe', paints a picture of the domestic as a realm not saturated with the tender nostalgia we have encountered in the works discussed above, all of which are written by men and focus on men as the consumers of meals.[7] Villanueva's 'Fish Heads' may be the exception to this pattern, but even there the poet does not imaginatively occupy his mother's mind in the way Perillo does in 'Tripe'. Here, Perillo serves up a different kind of 'homesickness': that of the beleaguered woman strained by the constant work of housekeeping. Written in two large thick stanzas, the poem replicates a sonnet structure writ large, with the first eleven lines of the poem focused on the family and on tripe as a dish that signals the mother's desperation. After a stanza break, the poem continues for another fifteen lines that compares the tripe itself to the mother's prison, 'a sack inside of which she was boxing shadows' (13). The rest of this stanza goes on to muse about the larger rhetorical and metaphorical implications of eating an animal's stomach, 'a master alchemist: grass and slops and the green dirt/ transformed into other cuts of bloody, marbled beef' (16-17). The mother's efforts to create order out of chaos in the home contrast with her frustration at the regularity of housework, its repetition of reliable meats: 'chops and roasts/ and the parched breasts of chickens' (3-4), all of which serve to engender the home-sickness of female restlessness. Thus it is, muses Perillo's speaker, that the mother chooses tripe as an act of 'rebellion' against the regular menu (7). In her description, Perillo makes tripe's look and consistency, 'its pallor, its refusal/ to tear or shred when chawed […]/ until finally the wad must be swallowed whole', into a symbol of the mother's suffering, from which there is no escape (8-11).

That said, like the mother, the stomach – tripe – is a magician, a medium of transformation. One could say that like Gonzalez, Perillo manages to create of tripe a metaphor for art itself, that which creates something rich and strange out of the 'slops' of life. The mysterious innards that translate an herbivore's fodder into muscle, that which we love to eat, is only available to us because of the digestive system, as smelly as it may be. The longing her mother feels for liberation from her life, for transformation, is what the adult Perillo attaches to the smell of the tripe 'stewing, a ghastly sweet/ that drove us underneath the beds' (19-20). The poem ends with the image of the mother labouring over the steaming pot that 'billowed/ its sugary haze like the sweat of a hired man' (25-26). The conversion of 'sweet' into 'sweat' is a telling transformation: a hired man's sweat becomes a 'sugary haze', a phrase redolent of romantic and sexual longing.

Perhaps it is the drudgery of mothers turning the stomach into something delicious that is itself the inspiration for their children who become poets by mining their own and their mothers' styles of homesickness. The model of transforming the digestive system of one animal into a nourishing repast for another becomes that which sustains artists in the struggle to create out of their own specific 'hungers'.

Notes

1. 'Nostalgia', *English: Oxford Living Dictionaries*, Oxford University Press <https://en.oxforddictionaries.com/definition/nostalgia> [accessed 15 May 2016].
2. Gary Soto, 'Papi's Menudo', *Canto Familiar* (New York: Harcourt, 1995), pp.1-3; Ray Gonzalez, 'Praise the Tortilla, Praise Menudo, Praise Chorizo', *The Heat of Arrivals* (Brockport, NY: BOA Editions, 1996), p. 85.
3. R.A. Villanueva, 'Fish Heads', *Reliquaria* (Lincoln: University of Nebraska Press, 2014), p. 16; 'Despedida', *Reliquaria*, p. 28.
4. R.A. Villanueva, 'Small Press Spotlight: R.A. Villanueva' (Interview by Rigoberto Gonzalez), *Critical Mass: The Blog of the National Book Critics Circle Award Board of Directors* <http://bookcritics.org/blog/archive/small-press-spotlight-r.a.-villanueva> [accessed 15 May 2016].
5. Linda Williamson Nelson, '"Hands in the Chit'lins": Notes on Native Anthropological Research among African American Woman', *Unrelated Kin: Race and Gender in Women's Personal Narratives*, ed. by Gwendolyn Etter-Lewis and Michele Foster (New York: Routledge, 1996), pp. 183-99 (185-86).
6. Kevin Young, 'Ode to Chitlins', *Dear Darkness* (New York: Knopf, 2013), pp. 100-02.
7. Lucia Perillo, 'Tripe', *The Body Mutinies* (West Lafayette, IN: Purdue University Press, 1996), p. 15.

Copying and Copyright: The Recipe Text as Offal

Heidi Hakimi-Hood, Amanda Milian and Carrie Helms Tippen

This symposium and its proceedings offered a multitude of opportunities for defining, redefining, reclaiming and revalorizing offal. In taking our turn, we approach offal in this instance as an analogy that illustrates an arbitrary hierarchy of values. As Stephen Mennell argues in *All Manners of Food,* '[o]ffal is a good example of the changeability of objects of repugnance, and the interaction of "moral" and social grounds for food avoidance.'[1] Though any eater would readily acknowledge that chicken breasts and chicken livers are parts of the same chicken, the arbitrary value of white meat over organ meat, as Mennell illustrates, is the result of the complex triangulation of factors, specific to a particular time and place, played out in the ritual dramas of the daily meal. The 'changeability' of offal reveals that values have histories.

We broaden our approach to offal by describing the cookbook as a kind of offal to literature and composition. If poetry and prose are the choice dishes of literary publishing and study (the creative work of individual authors with rights to be one-of-a-kind), then recipes are utilitarian organ meats at best, and infinitely reproducible and anonymous castoffs at worst. Just as attitudes towards carving meats are culturally and historically situated, so too are attitudes toward the value of composition practices.

Though recipes have not typically been thought of as 'objects of repugnance', they have been historically undervalued by literary study and under-protected by intellectual property laws because they are often seen as derivative rather than original, as single-authored literary texts are thought to be. In most creative arts, copying as composition is taboo. A forgery is an object of repugnance because copying and its many synonyms (plagiarizing, pirating, thieving, stealing), in certain Western cultures, are constructed as moral wrongs, violence against property and owner's rights. Those moral values have been codified into intellectual property law and reinforced by social and cultural norms. However, as Martha Woodmansee and Peter Jaszi claim in *The Construction of Authorship*, the superior position of the single-authored, original text as the moral and legal gold standard of composition is arbitrary. Cultural works like recipes, 'improvised works', 'folklore', 'items of cultural heritage' and 'works of the oral tradition' operate under a very different set of values than those protected by copyright; these collaboratively authored and community-owned products 'are valued chiefly for their fidelity to tradition rather than their deviations from it'.[2] Put simply, the practices that inform recipe writing (collaboration, exchange, imitation) are generally marked as lesser forms of composition. However, just as chicken livers are favoured for their distinctive taste, recipes are made valuable by the very processes that mark them as inferior.

This essay explores the notion of cookbooks and recipes as a type of offal of intellectual property and composition that reveals the artificial construction of textual hierarchies. Because recipes are undervalued and under-protected by law, they are vulnerable to exploitation through piracy; however, as texts in the public domain, they are also available for creative remixing that may open up new possibilities for cultural identity. We argue that just as what counts as offal is a cultural construction of arbitrary tastes, so too what counts as legitimate composition and intellectual property is a cultural construction with a variable history.

Brief History

We contextualize a cookbook as offal by examining the history and narrative of a single set of recipes in three evolutions that span the nineteenth and twentieth centuries. Maria Eliza Ketelby Rundell's *A New System of Domestic Cookery* was published in London in 1806, with the author identified only as 'A Lady'. Rundell filed a legal injunction against her publisher, John Murray, an action that led to the court's suggestion that recipe collections were under-protected texts, an inferior kind of writing: useful, but not original. When she sought the rights to publish her work, Rundell faced the challenge of proving her work was an original, single-authored composition instead of a collaborative work compiled by her and her publisher. If Rundell could not prove original authorship of the recipes, the court maintained they did not deserve copyright protection. Almost immediately upon its publication in London, pirated American versions of *Domestic Cookery* appeared in Philadelphia and Boston. For roughly forty years, American publishers exploited the recipes' legal vulnerability, demonstrating taboo composition mixing theft, imitation, and (some) original composition. However, those pirated versions allowed *Domestic Cookery* to be widely available in the US so that more than a century after the book's initial publication, a strikingly similar, if not identical, recipe collection was printed by S. Thomas Bivins under the title *The Southern Cookbook: A Manual of Cooking and List of Menus Including Recipes Used by Noted Colored Cooks and Prominent Caterers* (1912). The three co-authors for this paper each describe how the text's bibliographic history marks recipe text as literary offal: valuable as a commodified text that sells, but devalued as the creative work of a legally recognized, rights-bearing author.

Theoretical Context: Cookery Books, Offal and Rubbish Theory

Our understanding of literary offal chimes readily with what Michael Thompson refers to as Rubbish Theory. As an instance, in *Rubbish Theory: The Creation and Destruction of Value*, Thompson examines the cultural value for items such as Victorian antiques, and he finds that these objects, over time, experience categorical shifts in their worth or desirability. In simplest terms, Rubbish Theory suggests that a once valued item may experience a transient phase in which it begins to decrease in value. From the transient phase, an item may be categorized as rubbish, or something that has no value. From the rubbish phase, an object can become durable and experience an increase in value.[3] Jonathan Rose extends Thompson's work by observing how Rubbish Theory mirrors the creation and destruction of cultural value in the literary market place. As an instance, Rose notes, '[f]irst edition books in nineteenth-century Britain could be very expensive, but eventually they would pass out of vogue and end up in the 2d. bookstalls. A generation or two later they would become collectors' items, and bibliophiles would bid up their price.'[4] Literary study, in turn, also emphasizes how popularity devalues a work. Usefulness has been seen as a weakness of the recipe text, a thing that makes it less valuable as a literary text. However, the recipe's political and social uses make it valuable for literary study. Jane Tompkins argues that 'twentieth-century literary criticism' has 'taught generations of students to equate popularity with debasement, emotionality with ineffectiveness, religiosity with fakery, domesticity with triviality, and all of these, implicitly, with womanly inferiority'.[5] This study of Rundell's recipe text has the potential to subvert this hierarchy and reclaim understandings of the authorship and popularity of *Domestic Cookery*.

Recipe as Offal of Intellectual Property

Without a doubt, Rundell's *Domestic Cookery* was valued by the book's publisher, Murray publishing house. This recipe text became a profitable publication and 'one of Murray's best properties'.[6] *Academy*, a British literary review, reported that *Domestic Cookery*, Walter Scott's *Marmion* and the *Quarterly Review*, were publications that 'formed the security' for John Murray II's 1813 purchase of the iconic Murray publishing house on Albemarle Street.[7] Elizabeth Lee suggests how *Domestic Cookery* originated:

Mrs Rundell began collecting recipes and household tips for her daughters. She sent the manuscript to the publisher John Murray, of whose family she was an old friend, and it was published in 1806 under the title of *Domestic Cookery*; a second amplified edition was completed at Ambleside where Mrs Rundell was living with her married daughter. The book had an immediate success, 5,000-10,000 copies were printed annually, and succeeding editions were enlarged and embellished by engravings.[8]

Given *Domestic Cookery*'s lucrative nature and large readership potential, how might a publication that garnered notoriety for one of London's prominent publishers be considered an undervalued kind of writing in the eyes of the law? In other words, how might we position *Domestic Cookery* as the offal of intellectual property?

To answer these questions, we first acknowledge that *Domestic Cookery* was viewed as Murray's property that Rundell sought to reclaim. In a move that was arguably subversive for her time and place as a widowed woman, Rundell pursued legal action against Murray; she endeavoured to make *Domestic Cookery* her copyright-protected property. After she filed a legal injunction to stop Murray from publishing *Domestic Cookery*, Rundell attempted to publish another version of the book with Longman in 1821.⁹ Murray then filed an injunction to prohibit Rundell from publishing the book with any of his contributions. Murray had provided a table of contents, added engravings and recipes, and suggested a carving essay.¹⁰ The lord chancellor eventually 'dissolved the injunction against Murray, but gave right to neither party, declaring that a court of law and not a court of equity must decide between them'.¹¹ Because she acknowledged that Murray's publishing of the book recognized *Domestic Cookery* as its property and not her work, we argue that Rundell wished to reclaim her rights to this property that brought her publisher prosperity. However, copyright law did not necessarily support Rundell's claim as the author of an original, creative composition. Indeed, Rundell offered her recipe manuscript to Murray, contributing to the court's understanding of who rightfully deserved copyright protection and claim to *Domestic Cookery*. As Edward Jacob documented in *Reports of Cases Argued and Determined in the High Court of Chancery*, the lord chancellor reported that '[w]e are not apprised of the circumstances under which this manuscript was given. If the Plaintiff had composed these receipts, or embodied and arranged them in a book, she would have a copyright in it, but if she had only collected them, and handed them over to Mr. Murray, I do not apprehend that they would be the subject of copyright'.¹² To be granted copyright for *Domestic Cookery*, Rundell would have to prove that the recipes were not merely a compilation of collected writings. If Rundell could have demonstrated that she had composed the recipes as her original work, then she would have been in a stronger position to argue for copyright. In short, the court questioned the originality of Rundell's contributions to *Domestic Cookery* and declared that a collection of recipes, whose author was technically unknown, did not merit copyright protection.

Even though she did file for legal protection for *Domestic Cookery*, Rundell initially did not request monetary compensation for this text. For example, '[i]n 1808 Murray presented Mrs Rundell with £150. She replied, "I never had the smallest idea of any return for what I considered a free gift to one whom I had long regarded as my friend."'¹³ Additionally, 'In acknowledging a copy of the second edition, Mrs Rundell begged Murray not to think of remunerating her further, and in the preface to the edition of 1810 she expressly stated that she would receive 'no emolument'.¹⁴ While her assertion that she receive no payment is likely a response to nineteenth-century societal expectations for women, Rundell sought to protect her rights to her book. Rundell's actions reflect the spirit of the recipe text itself. Since the word *recipe* derives from the Latin *recipere*, a term expressing 'both to give and to receive', the notion of exchange is implicit in understanding the recipe text as literary offal.¹⁵ Just as individuals redeem cast-off offal in exchange for sustenance, Rundell aimed to reclaim rights for the recipes she offered to Murray so that she might send them to another publisher. However, her legal action against Murray did not result in her obtaining copyright. Eventually, Rundell did agree to receive financial compensation from Murray, and, '[a]fter long delay, Mrs Rundell accepted Murray's offer of £2000 in full discharge of all her claims.'¹⁶

Rundell's legal actions highlight how she sought to reclaim authorship of her own text and obtain copyright protection for her work. We maintain that a seemingly innocuous cookbook caused a legal stir for a reputable British publishing house. Clearly, this work is more than a recipe collection that transforms into various meals. This recipe text is 'an embedded discourse, and like other embedded discourses, it can have a variety of relationships with its frame, or its bed'.[17] In this instance, the recipe became part of the discourse of British copyright history. According to the *Bookseller*, Rundell and Murray's court case 'is still one governing certain points in the law of copyright'.[18] Although she did not win her case, Rundell was empowered to reclaim what the court implied was a by-product of intellectual property.

Cookbooks as Offal in the United States

American publication of Rundell's *Domestic Cookery* began in 1807. On the one hand, Rundell's cookbook served the growing commercial market for cookery books in the young nation. On the other hand, its publication reflected the devaluation of cookbook authors as creators of items deemed as intellectual offal. In the US, as in England at the time, printed cookbooks defied the rules governing other printed material in terms of ownership and originality and reinforced a gendered division of power. Recipes could not be owned individually, but were communally shared, and thus, could not fall under individual copyright. Likewise, the popularity of cookbooks often did not rely on their originality, unlike other texts, but on their longevity. The only 'original', or newly created, item in a cookbook was often the preface, and in many cases, the preface likely came from the publisher and not the author. This feature of cookbooks demonstrated the gendered valuation of intellectual property in the early nineteenth century by demonstrating how men retained power over written language and its value.

Governmental views of intellectual property also reflected the devaluation of cookbooks. The United States government sought to establish protocols for its print material by creating the Copyright Act of 1790. Congress chose an important distinction between foreign and domestic publications in its Copyright Act, stating, 'Nothing in this act shall be construed to extend to prohibit the importation or vending, reprinting or publishing within the United States, of any [...] books, written, printed, or published by any person not a citizen of the United States.' The addition of this clause encouraged the practice of pirating English cookbooks in the nineteenth century.[19] Historian John Tebbel contended, 'the publishing business, in general, was actually opposed to international copyright, and its opposition was all an apathetic Congress needed to delay and postpone it until the end of the century.'[20] As demonstrated in Rundell's case against the Murray publishing house, the owner of the copyright, and the one who maintained the legal rights to print or reprint material, was often the publisher and not the author. Such practices were not limited to works produced outside of the US. Amelia Simmons's 1796 cookbook lacked protection, and in many cases publishers pirated her work without noting the origin.[21] This method of reproduction proved to be representative, not an exception. Publishers, and the broad American public, placed little value on the compilation of recipes as original work. All of these factors led to the process of viewing cookbook authors and the works themselves as literary offal and contributed to the undervaluation of works created by women.

Using the 1807 Philadelphia edition of Rundell's cookbook as a case study, we will argue in this section how pirating European cookbooks in America in the early nineteenth century demonstrated the devaluing of recipes as intellectual property and the exploitation of culinary authors by publishers. Printers and publishers were predominantly men, and, increasingly, in the nineteenth century, cookbook authors were women. Because cookbooks were viewed as offal, no strong protection existed to prevent imitation or plagiarism. Publishers could write a few lines in the preface explaining their purpose for publishing the cookbook and thus reclaim the text as their own. Barbara Ketchum Wheaton has demonstrated how cookbooks were often more collaborative pieces with 'a preface by one person, an introduction by another'.[22] The 1807 Philadelphia printing of Rundell's *Domestic Cookery* lists the author as 'a lady', the publisher as Benjamin Buzby, and the printer as R. Bailey. The collaborative nature of authorship in nineteenth-century cookbooks separated such works from the favoured literary works. The content of the American versions did not differ greatly if at all from the Rundell's initial publication of *Domestic Cookery*. If the perception of published recipes was that they were 'common', or literary offal, then they were unquestionably available for use by authors, publishers or anyone else, and did not require change. The recipe text was intellectually discardable and undervalued; leaving it open for exploitation by publishers and consumption by readers. Such works seemed to lack originality and, therefore, intellectual property rights in the nineteenth-century value system.

Rundell's book saturated the markets in the United States and became relatively popular, reaching at least thirty-seven editions.[23] The multiple reproductions of Rundell's cookbook between 1807 and 1844 suggests its value to American publishers, despite such undervaluing of its worth as intellectual property. A second edition went into publication the same year as the first and spread to booksellers in the major metropolitan areas, Philadelphia, Boston and New York, and in smaller nearby cities.[24] In 1823, Rundell's cookbook received an American edition with a new title, *The American Domestic Cookery*, but the original cookbook continued to be reproduced under the original title well into the 1840s.[25] *The American Domestic Cookery* maintained the same basic table of contents, but gained nine engravings and expanded text. Part of *Domestic Cookery*'s prolific publication record resulted from the absence of international copyright law that included cookbooks and recipes as a form of intellectual property. Despite rampant copying and reprinting, *Domestic Cookery* must have remained popular enough in Europe to keep Murray's profits high and his concern over American piracy low. While copyright law represented a major setback for cookbook authors and devalued their texts, the popularity of the book and its immense reach, in terms of the number of editions produced over multiple decades, made Rundell's cookery book more accessible. Rundell's cookbook thus achieved its height of popularity before mid-century and then began its decline into obscurity, or textual rubbish with little monetary value.

Copying as Offal of Composition

S. Thomas Bivins's 1912 *The Southern Cookbook* contains nearly seven hundred recipes evidently copied from Rundell's *Domestic Cookery*. The cookbook was prepared by Bivins and an assistant as a manual for African-American students of the Chester Domestic Training Institute, the normal school where Bivins was principal. Except for the original prefatory materials, all of the framing text also appears in *Domestic Cookery*, including passages like 'Observations on Dressing Fish', 'Directions to Servants', and many instructions for cleaning and removing stains.[26] Because there are many editions of *Domestic Cookery*, authorized and unauthorized, it is difficult to establish which particular edition served as Bivins's source in order to determine definitively which recipes, if any, are original or might be collected from another source. However, it is clear from a comparison to at least one digitized version of Rundell (London, 1814) that the text of many of the recipes is verbatim, though they appear at times to be copied in reverse order.[27] It is difficult to establish whether differences in Bivins's edition are changes that Bivins or his assistant made, that another American publisher made in a pirated edition, or that Rundell or Murray made in later authorized editions. Still, it is clear that Bivins is relying primarily on Rundell as his source text for the recipes in *The Southern Cookbook*.

Bivins and his text are often cited by scholars of Southern foodways as one of the earliest cookbooks formally published by an African-American author. In our estimation, that claim remains true and significant, regardless of the source of Bivins's recipes. The arbitrary hierarchy that values original authorship over copying categorizes *The Southern Cookbook* as offal, thereby minimizing the text's literary value. However, we argue that while knowing the source of the recipes is vital to a proper interpretation of the text, the 'asterisk' that marks these recipes as 'copied' does not diminish the text's value. Indeed, the book may be more important because of this intertextuality, as it can reveal how Bivins purposefully exploited the recipe's vulnerability as the offal of intellectual property in order to gain valuable capital.

Bivins broke no copyright laws in appropriating Rundell's recipes for his own use. At the time of the publication of *The Southern Cookbook* in 1912, copyright law in America had recently been updated in the 1909 Copyright Act. The new act did not extend to recipes (Section 5), to works published before 1909 (Section 1), or 'to the works of a foreign author' (Section 7).[28] Therefore, Rundell's recipes were in the public domain and legally available for creative reuse. Bivins is the copyright holder of the collection titled *The Southern Cookbook* under federal law because of the copyright notice following the title page: 'Entered according to Act of Congress, in the year 1912, by S. THOMAS BIVINS, In the Office of the Librarian of Congress at Washington'. I have used the words 'copied' and 'appropriated' above to describe Bivins's use of Rundell's text, but under Section 6 of the 1909 US Copyright Act, Bivins's text is best described as a 'compilation' of 'works in the public domain [… which] shall be regarded as new works subject to copyright'.[29] It is a compilation, and Bivins is a compiler, collector, curator, and editor.

In fact, Bivins makes no overt claims of originality. Bivins represents himself in the introduction as a compiler rather than author-inventor. The subtitle of the work makes clear that the recipes collected in this book are '*Used* By Noted Colored Cooks and Prominent Caterers' (emphasis ours); Bivins does not write *Created*. In the introduction, Bivins describes the practice of writing as 'construction'; he writes that he is 'supplying' and 'presenting' these recipes to the public. The only perhaps disingenuous claim Bivins makes is that these recipes have been collected after 'more than twenty years of experience and investigation', though evidence suggests that the recipes come from a single source.[30] Bivins's claims in the introduction do not suggest that he invented any of the recipes in this compilation. Instead, Bivins sells his book as a collection of tested and approved recipes. As future domestic workers and food service professionals, Bivins's readers would have valued a book of proven recipes certified as 'Southern' much more than a book of Bivins's original recipes.

Indeed, Bivins's offal compilation is most noteworthy for its inversion of power structures. Through fair use of public domain recipes, Bivins translates freely available resources into culinary and economic capital for himself and for his students. As a reference guide and textbook, *The Southern Cookbook* would provide time-tested information and a method for economic advancement through employment. Bivins makes clear that he does not see the domestic servant as an inferior or oppressed labourer. To the contrary, Bivins writes in the introduction: 'It is said that the mother who rocks the cradle controls the nation, but the domestic who faithfully and intelligently serves her who rocks the cradle is, in fact, the real ruler.'[31] The domestic servant is in a privileged position to direct the nation from the kitchen. The message of Bivins's cookbook is that cooking creatively in professional domestic employ is a means for acquiring power – economic, political and social.

Bivins's composition process mirrors this method of power acquisition. He takes his ingredients from the public domain and remixes them for his own use. Moreover, Bivins publishes and distributes these texts through alternate channels, segregated from traditional publishing because of race. Bivins's text is printed through the press of the Hampton Institute, a school for African and Native American students, and distributed to the guaranteed audience of his presumably African American students at the Chester Institute. Bivins takes his texts from dominant publishing, exploiting a weakness in law, in order to generate a text that is for the exclusive benefit of marginalized readers, published through marginalized channels, making both into a powerful centre. Just as narratives of African American foodways emphasize reclaiming offal as a key ingredient in soul food as a source of distinction and cultural pride, so too can reclaiming Bivins's text and its marginalized composition process be empowering. Bivins makes a bargain with the established hierarchy of texts, carving power and capital out of what had been marked by dominant power as a moral wrong, an object of repugnance, a marginalized press and a devalued text.

Conclusion

The story of this recipe collection is the story of the negotiation of subalterns against dominant structures and the strategic use of a political hierarchy's blind spots to eke power out of the margins. Elizabeth Rundell reclaimed her recipe writing with *Domestic Cookery*. Rundell as a woman author found that her authorial rights were not respected because of feminized composition (collaboration, collection and pastiche as woman-centred practices). Even though she did not receive full rights of legal ownership from her suit against Murray, more importantly, she secured her name as the rights-bearing author in the public record. This result insured that recipe texts would remain offal by law, freeing them for endless innovation as they circulated through feminized networks. Perceived as normative and lacking innovation, cookbooks written as guides for such mundane tasks as cooking reflected the commodification of women's roles in the nineteenth century. Though American publishers – largely male – exploited the weaknesses in international copyright law to earn profits for themselves without regard to the rights of a female author, they also managed to exert power as a new nation against their late colonial parent, making American distinction out of British raw materials. Bivins – this time marginalized by race rather than gender – similarly embraces the margins as a centre of power, taking advantage of devalued texts and segregated publishing and education to benefit himself and his students. The bibliographic history of *Domestic Cookery* and *The Southern Cookbook* demonstrates the recipe's status as textual offal, subversively composed, compiled, and distributed. Our act of narrating the arbitrariness of authorship hierarchy is also our act of reclaiming the offal recipe text – whether compiled, copied, or cribbed – as legitimate composition, useful for cultural innovation and identity formation.

Notes

1. Stephen Mennell, *All Manners of Food: Eating and Taste in England and France from the Middle Ages to the Present* (Oxford: Basil Blackwell, 1985), p. 310.
2. Martha Woodmansee and Peter Jaszi, *The Construction of Authorship: Textual Appropriation in Law and Literature* (Durham, NC: Duke University Press, 1994), p. 11.
3. Michael Thompson, *Rubbish Theory: The Creation and Destruction of Value* (Oxford: Oxford University Press, 1979), pp. 6-10.
4. Jonathan Rose, *The Intellectual Life of the British Working Classes* (London: Yale University Press, 2010), p. 121.
5. Jane Tompkins. *Sensational Designs: The Cultural Work of American Fiction, 1790-1860* (New York: Oxford University Press, 1985), p. 123.
6. 'A Publishing House One Hundred Years Ago', *Academy*, 10 November 1906, p. 471.

7. 'A Publishing House One Hundred Years Ago'.
8. Elizabeth Lee, 'Rundell, Maria Eliza (1745–1828)', rev. Anita McConnell, in *Oxford Dictionary of National Biography* <http://www.oxforddnb.com.ezproxy.tcu.edu/view/article/24278> [accessed 18 April 2016].
9. Lee.
10. 'Prosecutions and Miscellaneous Cases', *Edinburgh Annual Register*, January 1821, p. 83.
11. 'Prosecutions and Miscellaneous Cases'.
12. Edward Jacob, 'Rundell v. Murray', in *Reports of Cases Argued and Determined in the High Court of Chancery: During the Time of Lord Chancellor Eldon* (London: Joseph Butterworth and Son, 1828), pp. 311-16 <https://books.google.com/books?id=b20DAAAAQAAJ&pg=PR1#v=onepage&q&f=false> [accessed 11 May 2016] (p. 314).
13. Lee.
14. Lee.
15. Janet Floyd and Laurel Foster, 'The Recipe in its Cultural Contexts', in *The Recipe Reader: Narratives, Contexts, Traditions*, ed. by Floyd and Foster (Lincoln, NE: University of Nebraska Press, 2010), pp. 1-11 (p. 6).
16. Lee.
17. Susan J. Leonardi, 'Recipes for Reading: Summer Pasta, Lobster *a la Riseholme*, and Key Lime Pie', *PMLA* 104.3 (May 1989) pp. 340-47 (p. 340).
18. 'Memoir of John Murray', in *Bookseller*, 4 April 1891, 330-33 <https://books.google.com/books?id=4PMiAQAAMAAJ&lpg=PA332&ots=ZEpCiDG8Yi&dq=murray%20v%20rundell&pg=PA332#v=onepage&q=murray%20v%20rundell&f=false.> [accessed 11 May 2016] (p. 332).
19. Copyright Act 1790; John Tebbel, *A History of Book Publishing in the United States, Volume I: The Creation of an Industry, 1630-1865* (New York: R. R. Bowker, 1972), p. 141.
20. Tebbel, p. 561.
21. Karen Hess, *The Virginia House-wife by Mary Randolph* (Columbia, SC: University of South Carolina Press, 1984), p. xix.
22. Barbara Wheaton, 'Cookbooks as Social History Resources', in *Food in Time and Place: The American Historical Association Companion to Food History*, ed. Paul Freedman, Joyce E. Chaplin and Ken Albala (Oakland: University of California Press, 2014), p. 282.
23. Hess, p. xx.
24. A list of publishers came from a search on WorldCat and 'Online Books by Maria Eliza Ketelby Rundell (Rundell, Maria Eliza Ketelby, 1745-1828)', University of Pennsylvania Library <http://onlinebooks.library.upenn.edu/webbin/book/lookupname?key=Rundell%2c%20Maria%20Eliza%20Ketelby%2c%201745-1828> [accessed 11 March 2015].
25. Maria Eliza Ketelby Rundell, *American Domestic Cookery: Formed on Principles of Economy, for the Use of Private Families, By an Experienced Housekeeper* (New York: Evert Duyckinck, 1823) <https://books.google.com/books?id=p_MpAAAAYAAJ&pg=PA3#v=onepage&q&f=false> [accessed 20 May 2016].
26. S. Thomas Bivins, *The Southern Cookbook: A Manual of Cooking and List of Menus Including Recipes Used by Noted Colored Cooks and Prominent Caterers* (Hampton, VA: Press of the Hampton Institute, 1912) pp. 132-7.
27. Maria Rundell, *A New System of Domestic Cookery* (1807) (London: John Murray, 1814).
28. US Copyright Office, 'An Act to Amend and Consolidate the Acts Respecting Copyright (1909)' <http://copyright.gov/history/1909act.pdf> [accessed 1 March 2015].
29. US Copyright Office.
30. Bivins, p. 4.
31. Bivins, p. 5.

Waste against Waste: Medicinal Offal Products, 'Artificial Digestion' and the Nineteenth-Century Thrift Movement

Lisa Haushofer

The use of animal organs in medical therapy has lately received increasing attention, as transplant medicine is exploring the promise and potential of xenotransplantation. But animals have served as a reservoir for human therapeutics for centuries, and the use of animal organs in particular has been explored by historians of science studying such diverse medical therapies as organ transplantation, hormone replacement therapy and organotherapy.[1] A less well-known medical application of animal organs is that of the so-called digestive ferments (today referred to as enzymes) in late-nineteenth and early-twentieth century Britain and the United States, which is the subject of this essay. Digestive ferments were explored in the physiological laboratories of the nineteenth century amidst debates about the mechanism of digestion and the best scientific method of examining it. The paper will trace how the therapeutic potential of digestive ferments was negotiated against scientific and cultural notions of different animal organs. It will argue that their use took shape within a broader social and economic context concerned with waste utilization which legitimated their development, and which in turn was given credence through the economic utilization of otherwise wasted offal substances as digestive ferments. Concerns about waste also informed hopes to apply digestive ferments more broadly in a changing public health context. As reformers turned to the individual in an effort to economize the food supply through a focus on thrifty consumption, digestive ferment products were translated into wider use, and their primarily medicinal focus reconfigured for the culinary realm.

Artificial Digestion: The Scientific and Therapeutic Potential of Animal Stomachs

In November 1836, a German physiologist named Theodor Schwann took the third and fourth stomach of an ox, carefully separated the stomach wall from the rest of the organ, cut it into small pieces, added water and hydrochloric acid and left the whole to stand for twenty-four hours. The mixture was then filtered through canvas and paper, producing a murky, yellowish liquid. Schwann poured the liquid over small cubes of egg white, and observed that, with time, they dissolved. He concluded that the liquid obtained from the ox's digestive organ must contain an agent that was capable of performing digestion. In a series of tests, he managed to characterize that agent as a physiologically distinct substance, and he gave it the name 'Pepsin'.[2]

Schwann's research was part of a long probing for the mechanism of digestion that had intensified in the late eighteenth and early nineteenth centuries. Chemists, physiologists and natural philosophers debated whether digestion occurred as the result of mechanical, chemical or vital forces, or a mixture of the three.[3] At the end of the eighteenth century, physiologists added a new mode of inquiry to the more traditional methods of digestive research, such as examining the anatomical properties of the digestive tracts of different animals. This new method was called 'artificial digestion', and it initially consisted of obtaining gastric liquid from a live animal with a sponge, and then examining its effects on food outside the stomach.[4] Since the 1830s, artificial digestion had also been performed with artificial gastric juice, which was obtained by preparing extracts of animal organs. By the time Schwann prepared his solution from ox stomach in 1836, both mechanical and chemical forces had been acknowledged to play a role in the digestive process. But the exact nature of the chemical reaction was still a matter of debate. Some believed that digestion occurred as a result of the chemical properties of an acid that acted as a solvent on all foods. Others suspected that the different chemical constituents of foods acted on each other, after they had been made accessible through mechanical or chemical disintegration in the stomach. Schwann's experiments seemed to suggest, instead, that digestion was the result of specific physiological agents which could be extracted from the digestive organs of animals, and which had a transformative effect on food, without being themselves transformed in the process.[5] The mechanism of fermentation, among other known chemical reactions, provided a conceptual model for how such a chemical 'catalyst' might operate. Schwann therefore decided to refer to this new group of digestive agents that he had characterized as 'digestive ferments' (known today as digestive enzymes).[6]

The idea that digestive function could be located in physiological agents which could be found in animal organs, and which could therefore be isolated from the body, soon encouraged attempts to explore their therapeutic use. A German physician reported in 1841 that he had used Pepsin on himself and on a patient for a persistent 'weakness of the digestion after nervous fever'.[7] In France, French physician Lucien Corvisart, collaborating with a pharmacist named Pierre Charles Boudault, produced a pepsin he called '*poudre nutrimentive*' [nutritive powder] from the fourth stomachs of veal and mutton, and he accompanied this announcement with a series of case studies of its successful application.[8] By the time Pepsin entered the pharmacopoeias of the United States and Britain in 1883 and 1885, Pepsin was already a widely manufactured product in those countries, so that by 1861 the compiler of a new edition of a German drug compendium remarked that '[Pepsin] has been mass produced for a decade and consumed in great quantities in those places where people are least capable of cooking and eating sensibly – in England and in the United States'.[9]

From the Ox to the Ostrich: Chemistry, Comparative Anatomy and Commercialization

The question whether digestion was to be understood as a chemical, mechanical or physiological process was part of a larger debate about which method was best suited to the study of food and digestion, and which kinds of insights could be gained from such an inquiry. Comparative anatomists and naturalists investigated the morphological differences between the digestive organs of different animals, and compared them to the structures that allowed plants to transform matter. This research was cited by natural theologians as an example of the wisdom of the creator who had provided each creature in the world with the necessary apparatus to digest exactly those substances which had been provided in their particular zone of habitation. Digestion was an indicator of the kinds of foods that were naturally suited for each creature. Chemical investigations of food, in contrast, seemed to suggest that there was little difference between the foods consumed in near and distant parts of the world, since they all consisted of essentially interchangeable chemical elements.[10] Digestion, in this reading, was merely a mechanical or chemical disintegration of the component parts of composite foods; there was no difference between the constituents that made up food, and those that made up the body. This undermined the special role of digestion in effecting a qualitative change on food, a process in which substances of a lower degree of organization came to be made similar ('assimilated') to the consuming animal. The research on the agents of digestion performed by Schwann and others was in part a reassertion of the special role of physiological processes in the digestion of food matter; the transformation triggered by the newly described physiological agents of digestion could not be explained entirely with any known chemical reaction.

Amidst these changing approaches to food and digestion, comparative anatomical observations of digestive organs were increasingly mobilized as a rationale for digestive intervention in discussions of digestive ferment therapy. The place of humans in a hierarchy of creatures, ordered according to their digestive capacities, was no longer merely an indication of the kinds of substances that ought naturally to be incorporated, but an opportunity to utilize the digestive capacities of different animals to enhance the digestion of humans. Whereas the research of Schwann and Corvisart had been performed using the organs of herbivores, that is oxen, calves and muttons, therapeutic preparations of pepsin soon began to stress their provenance from the entrails of so-called omnivorous animals, mostly pigs. Partly, this was based on micro-anatomical and chemical observations of the mucous membrane of the pig, which showed similarities to the mucous membrane of humans and differed considerably from that of other animals.[11] Partly, the selection of pig organs was drawn from natural history and referenced the 'omnivorous' feeding patterns of the pig as compared to other animals. The 1862 International Exhibition in London, for instance, featured preparations of pepsin from the pig 'on the principle, that from the omnivorous nature of the pig, its stomach would secrete a juice better adapted to substitute the human digestive fluid than that of a purely herbivorous animal'.[12] Physiologists and pharmacists compared instead the quantities of meat or albumen digested by different animal organ extracts. Pharmacist Emil Scheffer, for instance, had observed that the same quantity of pepsin from the hog digested more albumen and beef than that of the calf.[13]

Claims about the digestive superiority of digestive ferments taken from omnivorous animals also resonated with popular representations of the pig as the ultimate lazy glutton. An 1867 sketch of the pig in the *British Farmer's Magazine*, for instance, portrayed the animal as an undiscriminating eater, which, like man, could:

> [...] eat vegetable or animal food [...], so when the trough is filled with potatoes and vegetables, it will make a very good dinner upon them; if the butcher chooses to throw some of the offal of the slaughter-house, the pig will eat the offal; if a thriftless housekeeper lets the pig have plum pudding and slices of roast beef, the most inveterate gormandizer [*sic*] could not attack them with greater zest than does his omnivorous companion.[14]

Pig pepsin, therefore, had the potential of allowing the digestion to adapt to the demands made upon it by the changing food landscape of the nineteenth century, at least for those who could afford it. A cartoon in the satirical magazine Punch reflected this imagined function of pig pepsin, suggesting that if such a substance really 'could impart the digestion of that animal to a human being, it should be an invaluable accessory to the convivialities of the Guildhall, the Mansion House, and the Halls of the great City Companies'.[15]

However, as chemical analyses of the digestive secretions gained more and more traction, the supposed differences between the digestive juices of carnivores and herbivores were increasingly questioned on chemical grounds. In 1867, Moritz Schiff compared the chemical composition of the digestive secretions of different animals, and concluded that there was no chemical difference between herbivores and carnivores concerning the composition and strength of their digestive juices.[16] This did not impede the use of claims about the characteristics of different animal organs among manufacturers in an increasingly competitive digestive ferment market, however. A striking example of this is the case of Ingluvin, a remedy supposedly made of the gizzards of chicken. It claimed to combine the intuition of the 'Chinese gastronomer' with the knowledge of the 'Caucasian chemist' by turning the Chinese culinary tradition of consuming poultry gizzards into a European remedy. Ingluvin's therapeutic rationale relied on the idea that grain-eating fowl, lacking a beak for crushing the hard shells of seed, relied solely on the mechanical and chemical powers of their digestive organs to break down their food. The digestive ferment gained from the extract of gizzards, therefore, was 'more efficient and potent' than the pepsin of the hog.[17] The hyperbolic character of Ingluvin's claims was not lost on contemporary commentators; in an article on supplementary rectal alimentation, physician Andrew Smith speculated that 'ere long we shall find upon our tables illuminated circulars in the highest style of decorative art announcing a new preparation fifty times as strong as ingluvin made from the gizzard of the ostrich'.[18]

'Nothing Is Useless': The Nineteenth-Century Waste Debate

The repurposing of animal organs as digestive aids in medical therapy took place amidst a broader debate about waste. Waste appeared as a unifying call to arms for a diverse set of problems and had broader political and moral connotations than our contemporary idea of 'refuse'. It was evoked in the context of resource management and optimization, as fears about the finite nature of resources in general, and about the food supply in particular, were met with a variety of economic, agricultural and scientific strategies to stretch them. The development of medicinal offal products informed these debates about waste, and was fed by them at the same time.

Concerns about waste were vocalized in particular by a network of educated professionals, entrepreneurs and scientists. This group, linked by similar educational paths at Britain's newly-formed non-conformist (non-Anglican) universities, believed that the nation's broad social problems could be addressed through technocratic expertise. They regularly exchanged ideas in the meetings of the Society for the Encouragement of Arts, Commerce and Manufacture, an institution founded in the eighteenth century that played a central role in the organization of several commercial exhibits, museums and lectures, including the Great Exhibition of 1851. Members discussed techniques for bringing into use a diverse set of 'wasted' resources, including uncultivated lands, unused manpower, inefficiently exploited time and hitherto unknown food sources.[19] In a speech to the Society, John Mechi, a regular attendant of the Society's proceedings and a juror in the Department of Arts and Science at the Great Exhibition, evoked the lingering Malthusian spectre of the mismatch between population and the food supply as a call to arms for bringing otherwise wasted natural resources into Britain's reach. These ideas included draining land that was otherwise not usable and making use of the waste matter of cities for the fertilization of the land.[20] One of the most prolific writers on the utilization of waste products was Peter Lund Simmonds, whose monograph *Waste Products and Undeveloped Substances* (1862) went through several editions, and who repeatedly addressed the Society of Arts on the topic of waste utilization.[21] Chemist and statesman Lyon Playfair, one of the key brains behind the idea and structure of the Great Exhibition, championed the ability of chemistry to optimize industrial processes by adding to human power, improving the economy of time, and devising 'methods of utilizing products apparently worthless, or of endowing bodies with properties which render them of increased value to industry'.[22] He later referred to these three kinds of interventions as the 'three conditions' for 'progress' in the arts of manufacture.[23]

Waste was also a favourite topic in popular literature. *Chambers' Magazine*, for example, printed a number of articles on waste and waste product utilization, often referring to the writings and speeches of Simmonds and Playfair.[24] A satirical poem in

Punch magazine suggested the current emphasis on making use of waste, such as in the utilization of sewage to the growth of food in fields, might be transferred to applying 'human waste', that is prisoners, to productive labour, rather than to 'send sewage to sea'.[25]

The theoretical debates and writings about the efficient utilization of waste products were materialized in the form of exhibitions and permanent museum collections illustrating the many uses to which otherwise wasted substances could be put to. The close kinship between waste, food and the utilization of natural and industrial by-products was reflected in the spatial proximity of these themes in the Bethnal Green Museum, a museum which housed the food collection and the animal products collection previously located at the South Kensington Museum together with the collection illustrating the utilization of waste products put together by Simmonds.[26] Both Simmonds and Playfair had contributed significantly to the development of the animal products collection, which dedicated one of its five classes to the 'Application of Waste Matters'.[27] Playfair also initially oversaw the Food Museum, which was originally suggested as part of an Economic Museum dedicated to the working classes, and which illustrated the uses of food in the body and the 'natural sources from which the various kinds of food have been obtained'.[28]

The discussions and practical applications of waste matter were accompanied by theoretical justifications of resource extraction. Edwin Lankester, a physician, medical officer and superintendent of the animal product and food collection at South Kensington, argued that 'the refuse of bone manufactures, the offal of slaughter-houses, and the refuse of our large towns', when studied closely, were 'not refuse' for practical as well as religious reasons. 'When we come to consider these things,' he wrote, 'we shall find that God has made no waste in the world at all. There is a maxim, "Waste not, want not;" and we have wasted, and do waste; and I shall call attention to this waste in many things, and show that many branches of industry have sprung up from the utilization of this waste.'[29] Using unused resources well was therefore not merely a commercial but a moral imperative. The efficient use of waste material was also heralded as a mark of civilization and progress. Lankester connected the cultivation of previously unused lands to an improvement of the climate in those regions, making them more inhabitable for human civilization.[30] And Playfair claimed that the efficient use of time, labour and resources was a mark of development, and separated highly civilized from less civilized nations. Drawing on biological analogies, he argued that the higher degree of economization could be observed for example in the number of digestive organs employed in the processing of food in animals – the higher animals had optimized the process by using only one stomach, whereas lower animals used several organs for the same process, making their labour more intensive and their results less efficient.[31]

This was the context in which new uses of offal as digestive aids were first conceived. Putting offal, the epitome of waste products, to good use by extracting the essences of animal organs for pharmaceutical purposes was an integral part of their development. The centralization of slaughterhouses all over Europe and the development of large packing-houses in the United States towards the end of the century further highlighted the economic potential of new uses for by-products.[32] The re-purposing of offal as digestive ferments was therefore often praised for its economy as much as for its therapeutic value. 'Pepsin, as everybody knows, is made from the stomach of the hog,' stated an article in the Bulletin of Pharmacy. 'The hog stomach has no value as an article of commerce except in this.'[33] Large slaughterhouses had begun to commence pepsin production themselves, rather than selling the offal to pharmacists and other pepsin manufacturers. 'The great pork-packing houses of America,' the article continued, 'have had either to throw away the stomachs or sell them to the pepsin makers, and this latter they have been doing time out of mind. But of late several of the largest of them have declined to sell, and have instead employed chemists to recover pepsin on their own account'. The Medical Bulletin of Philadelphia stressed the closeness of the site of production to the supply of raw materials, allowing for greater economy of time and avoiding losses due to decay during transit. The article described the Armour laboratory, which had the advantage of being

> situated close to where over a million and a half of hogs, over a million cattle, over six hundred thousand sheep, and a large number of calves are killed annually, assuring a large supply of very fresh raw materials [...]. The exceeding proneness of animal matter to decompose [...] renders imperative to avoid this loss during transit.[34]

While trade publications praised the economy of this development, and even suggested that it might allow manufacturers to sell their meat more cheaply, compensating from the gains made through the utilization of by-products, pharmacists expressed dismay at being deprived of a lucrative product. The packing-houses' 'unlimited capital and great commercial sagacity', it was feared, would allow them to completely take over the production of pepsin, while 'the manufacturing pharmacists, who have created the product and bled for it, will get the empty shell, while outsiders get the kernel'.[35]

Waste against Waste: Digestive Ferments, Thrift and The Kitchen

But digestive ferment products also had another connection to waste, which manifested as mid-century anxieties about the food supply shifted from a preoccupation with food production and procurement as a matter of political economy to concerns about food consumption at the level of the individual. Where the architects of the Great Exhibition, the Food Museum and the Waste Products Collection had focused on agricultural, scientific and economic measures to increase Britain's food supply, and called on institutions, manufacturers and administrators to prevent large-scale waste of resources, their late-nineteenth-century successors honed in on the use of food by consumers. England's food problem was relative, not absolute, claimed Benjamin

Ward Richardson, a physician and sanitary reformer, in a speech titled 'The Skeleton in the National Cupboard'. If England were to be invaded, he warned, there might not be immediate starvation, but the country 'would in a short time be convulsed politically, not from actual deficiency of supply, but from the difference of ability on the part of consumers to lay by stores of supply'.[36]

Health reformers of the 1870s and 1880s therefore set out to teach consumers how to consume, and they did so under the banner of thrift. Thrift reconfigured mid-century calls for un-wasteful institutional food production and procurement as admonitions to personal economy. Thrift was defined broadly by those advocating its spread. It was heralded as a panacea not only with regard to the food question but also in the realm of health more broadly, as well as in economic, religious and social matters. The thrift movement produced a remarkable literary output. Popular texts taught the application of thrift to personal savings, home-keeping, dress and spiritual living.[37] These books invariably contained sections about food and cooking which taught the basic principles of chemistry to allow housewives to make economic choices in their cooking, such as substituting meat for chemically equivalent vegetable substances. From 1874, women learned thriftful cooking at South Kensington's National Training School of Cookery.[38] Even a National Thrift Society was established in 1878, with its own journal (*Thrift*), much to the amusement of *Punch* magazine, which gleefully announced that one of its first orders of business had been to ask for money.[39]

But with the turn towards the individual as the locus of intervention to reduce waste and optimize the food supply came the preoccupation with a new variable for the efficient utilization of food inside the body: the process of digestion. No matter how abundant the food supply, and no matter how economically selected and prepared a home-cooked meal, an un-economic digestion could still produce large amounts of waste in the form of un-absorbed and therefore un-utilized food. In a speech titled 'On Thrift in Relation to Food', Richardson argued that the use of artificial digestion might bring the widespread use of cheaper but less digestible vegetable substances into reach by replacing the intermediate animal which made vegetables more easily assimilable for human digestion. '[T]here should be no difficulty,' Richardson believed, 'except the labour of research, in so modifying food taken from its prime source as to make it applicable to every necessity without the assistance of any intermediate animal at all.' That labour fell to the research endeavour of 'artificial digestion', in Richardson's mind.[40]

Richardson's hope of controlling the digestive process through the use of artificial digestion was shared by William Roberts, a physician and physiologist, who had dedicated much of his research to the digestive ferments. Roberts had clarified in particular the role of the ferments of the pancreas in the digestive process, and, together with a pharmaceutical chemist named Frederick Baden-Benger, he had developed a medicinal preparation of pancreas ferments called 'Liquor Pancreaticus'. The ferments of the pancreas transformed protein into peptone, in Roberts' opinion the end product of protein digestion. The progressive laboratory decoding of the digestive process led Roberts to believe that digestion could easily be controlled by substituting digestive ferments at every stage of food processing inside the body. In a speech given at a local meeting of the British Medical Association in 1879, Roberts boldly declared, '[t]he digestive processes are all of a purely chemical and mechanical nature; and they can be imitated successfully in the laboratory, and even in the sick room and nursery.' He produced a table of the digestive ferments that indicated the 'medicinal substitutes' or 'equivalents' for each ferment. The diastase of the saliva, for instance, could be substituted through '[v]arious preparations of malt; extracts of malt; malt flour; extract of pancreas'.[41] The result was a roadmap for imitating and intervening in the digestive process through the application of digestive ferments. Thrift of food had become located in the body.

But as the focus of food reformers shifted to individual consumption as a way to improve the availability of food, it became clear that artificial digestion had to be applied on a large scale in order to have an impact, and not be limited to the prescription of digestive ferment preparations through physicians responding to digestive complaints. '[H]owever useful preparations of this class may prove to be in a limited range of circumstances,' Roberts argued, 'it is pretty evident that, if artificially digested food is to be employed on the large scale, and among all classes, means must be found to bring the preparation of it within the range of culinary operations and the apparatus of the kitchen and sickroom.'[42] Digestive ferments, having found their way from the slaughterhouse into the laboratory, therefore took another turn into the kitchens of homes and hospitals in the form of so-called artificially digested foods. With his collaborator Benger, Roberts had himself developed a food product that had been enriched with digestive ferments of the pancreas. Once activated in the preparation process, the ferments would convert the food's proteins into the more digestible peptones, creating an artificially digested, or pre-digested, or 'peptonized' food – Benger's Food.

The move of digestive ferments into the kitchen was by no means self-evident, however, and considerable intellectual and material work went into naturalizing their use in domestic and convalescent settings. Roberts achieved this by stressing the naturalness of artificial digestion, and by emphasizing the artificiality of cooking and of some raw, natural foods. He suggested that digestion was merely an extension of the cooking process, and attempted to show through experiments that the changes produced by cooking facilitated the action of the digestive ferments. Cooking foods was a prerequisite for optimal digestive function, and the activity of digestive ferments observed in the laboratory continued and extended the work begun in the kitchen.[43] Roberts also drew on Claude Bernard's distinction between external digestion (the transformation of nutrients to be made absorbable into the bloodstream) and internal digestion (the transformation of nutrients in the blood into tissues of the body). The body was conceptualized as a kind of pipe, with an exterior and an interior surface, and adding digestive ferments to foodstuffs and pre-digesting them was essentially merely externalizing the already externally located part of digestion even more.[44] Finally, Roberts evoked culinary customs to suggest that ferments had already reached the dinner table. While cooking pre-empted and supported the work of ferments, the empirical selection of foods to be consumed in a raw state confirmed the importance of ferments for digestibility. Sugar, for instance, was consumed in a state in which it was already absorbable; it existed naturally in its digested state. Even more compelling was the case of the oyster, which, according to Roberts, was the only animal substance eaten raw. Its liver (dainty) consisted of glycogen, but separate from the liver, and it also contained the appropriate digestive ferment for glycogen, the hepatic diastase. The ferment was brought into contact with its substrate when it was crushed through chewing. Here was a case of a naturally occurring artificially digested food. 'The oyster in the uncooked state,' Roberts concluded, '[...] is, in fact, self-digestive.' Taken together, these reflections furbished Roberts with a justification for producing artificially digested foods. 'If we take all these considerations into account,' he concluded, 'it will appear, I think, not unnatural that we should try to help our invalids by administering their food in an already digested, or partially digested, condition. We should thereby only be adding one more to the numberless artificial contrivances with which our civilised life is surrounded.'[45]

Strengthened by this naturalizing rhetoric, digestive ferment products quickly entered the kitchens of hospitals and private households. Peptonizing was all the craze in hospital cooking, where nurses were instructed in preparing peptonized foods such as peptonized gruel or peptonized blancmanges with peptonizing liquids.[46] Popular cookbooks contained recipes for artificially digested foods such as peptonized or malted milks and jellies.[47] With these culinary and convalescent versions of peptonized products and recipes for their production, not only the medicinal organ essences themselves had reached the realm of the kitchen, but also the methods to which their study gave rise.

Conclusion

As medicinal offal products crossed multiple boundaries from the kitchen to the laboratory and back, their cultural and therapeutic significance was continuously renegotiated. They served as both markers for the digestive capacity of different species and as tools to increase that capacity. The powerful association of offal with waste facilitated their role as solutions to complex economic and social problems linked to inefficiency and wasteful food utilization, and conjured up visions of the thriftful and efficient eating and digesting body. The scale, intent and techniques of using animal organs for therapeutic purposes has no doubt changed since the nineteenth century, but the repurposing of living components of animal bodies remains complexly linked to scientific and cultural understandings of the body, as well as to economic considerations of scarcity.

Waste against Waste:

Notes

1. See for example, Thomas Schlich, *The Origins of Organ Transplantation: Surgery and Laboratory Science, 1880-1930* (Rochester: University of Rochester Press, 2010); Elizabeth Siegel Watkins, *The Estrogen Elixir: A History of Hormone Replacement Therapy in America* (Baltimore: The Johns Hopkins University Press, 2007); Bonnie Ellen Blustein, *Preserve Your Love for Science: Life of William A Hammond, American Neurologist* (Cambridge: Cambridge University Press, 2002), pp. 201-34; Merriley Borell, 'Organotherapy and the Emergence of Reproductive Endocrinology', *Journal of the History of Biology* 18.1 (1985), 1-30; Merriley Borell, 'Origins of the Hormone Concept: Internal Secretions and Physiological Research, 1889-1905' (unpublished doctoral thesis, Yale University, 1976).2007
2. Theodor Schwann, 'Ueber Das Wesen Des Verdauungsprocesses', *Archiv Für Anatomie, Physiologie Und Wissenschaftliche Medicin*, 1836, 90-138; Frederic L. Holmes, *Claude Bernard and Animal Chemistry: The Emergence of a Scientist* (Cambridge: Harvard University Press, 1974), pp. 163-72; Ohad Parnes, 'From Agents to Cells: Theodor Schann's Research Notes of the Years 1835-1838', in *Reworking the Bench: Research Notebooks in the History of Science*, ed. by F. L. Holmes, J. Renn, and Hans-Jörg Rheinberger (Dordrecht: Kluwer, 2003), pp. 119-39.
3. On pre-nineteenth-century theories of digestion, see, for example Holmes, pp. 141-59; Jessica Riskin, 'The Defecating Duck, Or, the Ambiguous Origins of Artificial Life', *Critical Inquiry* 29.4 (1 June 2003): 599-633; Emma Spary, *Eating the Enlightenment: Food and the Sciences in Paris* (Chicago: University of Chicago Press, 2012), pp. 17-50; Evan Ragland, 'Experimenting with Chemical Bodies: Science, Medicine and Philosophy in the Long History of Reiner de Graaf's Experiments on Digestion, from Harvey and Descartes to Claude Bernard' (unpublished doctoral thesis, Indiana University, 2012).
4. René Antoine Ferchault de Réaumur, 'Sur La Digestion Des Oiseaux', *Histoire de l'Académie Royale Des Sciences*, 1752, 266-307 and 461-96; Lazzaro Spallanzani, *Dissertations Relative to the Natural History of Animals and Vegetables*, vol. 1 (London: J. Murray, 1784); Holmes, pp. 143-44.
5. Parnes.
6. Schwann, p. 110.
7. 'Zeitung', *Haeser's Repertorium für die gesammte Medicin* 3.6 (1841), 308.
8. Lucien Corvisart, 'De L'emploi Des Poudres Nutrimentives (Pepsine Acidifiée), Ressources Qu'elles Offrent À La Médicine Pratique', *Bulletin Général de Thérapeutique Médicale, Chirurgicale, Obstétricale et Pharmaceutique* 47 (1854), 320-30.
9. H. M. Aschenbrenner, *Die neueren Arzneimittel und Arzneibereitungsformen* (Erlangen: Enke, 1861), p. 43.
10. The battle lines in these debates were not neatly drawn; for example, William Prout attempted to reconcile natural theology with the idea of chemical interchangeability of the core nutritional substances (*Chemistry, Meteorology, and the Function of Digestion: Considered with Reference to Natural Theology* (London: William Pickering, 1834), pp. 413-513), while William Flowers used a comparative anatomical approach purely on the basis of the mechanical properties of food, and argued for the chemical equivalence of various foods ('Lectures On the Comparative Anatomy of the Organs of Digestion of the Mammalia', *The Medical Times and Gazette* 1 (24 February 1872), 215-19).and argued for the chemical equivalence of various foods. William Prout, {\\i{}Chemistry, Meteorology, and the Function of Digestion: Considered with Reference to Natural Theology} (London: William Pickering, 1834
11. For example, Adolph Wasmann, 'Über die Verdauung', *Pharmaceutisches Central-Blatt* 10 (1839), 345-50, 353-58.
12. Edward Parrish, *A Treatise on Pharmacy* (Philadelphia: Henry C. Lea, 1867), p. 528.
13. Emil Scheffer, 'Liquid Pepsin and Saccharated Pepsin', *The Pharmaceutical Journal and Transactions* 30 (February 18, 1871), 666.
14. 'The Pig. His Characteristics, Usefulness, Etc.', *British Farmer's Magazine* 42.124 (1867), 21-22.
15. 'Aid to Digestion,' *Punch*, 23 February 1878.
16. Flower, p. 217; Maurice Schiff, *Leçons sur la physiologie de la digestion: faites au Muséum d'histoire*

naturelle de Florence, vol. 2 (Florence: Loescher, 1867), pp. 183-87.
17. 'Ingluvin,' *The Medical World* 13.4 (April 1895), xxi.
18. Andrew H. Smith, 'Supplementary Rectal Alimentation, and Especially by Defibrinated Blood, as Applicable to a Large Range of Cases in Which Nutritive Enemata Have Not Heretofore Been Employed', *Archives of Medicine* 1.2 (April 1879), p. 117.
19. On the early history of the Society, see Matthew Paskins, 'Sentimental Industry: The Society of Arts and the Encouragement of Public Useful Knowledge, 1754-1848' (unpublished doctoral thesis, University College London, 2014); Max Louis Kent, 'The British Enlightenment and the Spirit of the Industrial Revolution: The Society for the Encouragement of Arts, Manufactures and Commerce (1754-1815)' (unpublished doctoral thesis, University of California, 2007).
20. John Joseph Mechi, 'Fourth Paper on British Agriculture with Some Account of His Own Operations at Tiptree Hall Farm', *Journal of the Royal Society of Arts* 3.107 (8 December 1854), 49-58.
21. Peter Lund Simmonds, *Waste Products and Undeveloped Substances: Or, Hints for Enterprise in Neglected Fields* (London: R. Hardwicke, 1862); Peter Lund Simmonds, 'On the Useful Application of Waste Products and Undeveloped Substances', *Journal of the Royal Society of Arts* 17.846 (5 February 1869), 171-81; Peter Lund Simmonds, 'On the Utilization of Waste Substances', *Journal of the Royal Society of Arts* 7.325 (11 February 1859), 175-88; Peter Lund Simmonds, 'On Some Undeveloped and Unappreciated Articles of Raw Produce from Different Parts of the World', *Journal of the Society of Arts* 2.106 (1 December 1854), 33-42; for a succinct analysis of Simmonds and waste, see Timothy Cooper, 'Peter Lund Simmonds and the Political Ecology of "Waste Utilisation" in Victorian Britain', *Technology and Culture* 52.1 (January 2011), 21-44.
22. Lyon Playfair, 'The Chemical Principles Involved in the Manufactures of the Exhibition as Indicating the Necessity of Industrial Instruction', in *Lectures on the Results of the Great Exhibition of 1851* (London: G. Barclay, 1852), pp. 162-63.
23. Lyon Playfair, *Subjects of Social Welfare* (London: Casell, 1889), p. 249.
24. For example, 'Nothing Is Useless', *Chambers's Edinburgh Journal*, 11 July 1846; 'Waste Materials', *Chambers's Journal*, 13 June 1874; 'Wealth from Waste', *Chamber's Journal*, 4 April 1893.
25. 'Our Filth and Our Felons', *Punch*, 3 January 1855.
26. Ann Christie, '"Nothing of Intrinsic Value": The Scientific Collections at the Bethnal Green Museum', *V&A Online Journal*, no. 3 (Spring 2011); Pierre Desrochers, 'Promoting Corporate Environmental Sustainability in the Victorian Era: The Bethnal Green Museum Permanent Waste Exhibit (1875-1928)', *V&A Online Journal*, no. 3 (Spring 2011); Pierre Desrochers, 'Victorian Pioneers of Corporate Sustainability', *The Business History Review* 83.4 (2009), 703-29.
27. *Catalogue of the Collection of Animal Products* (London: Clowes and Sons, 1858), p. 1.
28. Edwin Lankester, *A Guide to the Food Collection in the South Kensington Museum* (London: Eyre and Spottiswoode, 1860), p. 1.
29. Edwin Lankester, *The Uses of Animals in Relation to Industry of Man: Being a Course of Lectures Delivered at the South Kensington Museum* (London: Hardwicke & Bogue, 1876), pp. 10-11.
30. Edwin Lankester, *Vegetable Substances Used for the Food of Man* (London: Charles Knight, 1832), p. 3.
31. Playfair, pp. 159-66.
32. On the development of slaughterhouses, see Dorothee Brantz, 'Slaughter in the City: The Establishment of Public Abattoirs in Paris and Berlin, 1780-1914' (unpublished doctoral thesis, University of Chicago, 2003), esp. pp. 130-32; William Cronon, *Nature's Metropolis: Chicago and the Great West* (London: W. W. Norton, 1991), pp. 207-62; Dorothee Brantz, 'Animal Bodies, Human Health, and the Reform of Slaughterhouses in Nineteenth-Century Berlin', *Food and History* 3.2 (1 January 2005), 193-215; Ian MacLachlan, 'A Bloody Offal Nuisance: The Persistence of Private Slaughter-Houses in Nineteenth-Century London', *Urban History* 34.2 (August 2007), 227-54; *Meat, Modernity, and the Rise of the Slaughterhouse*, ed. by Paula Young Lee (Durham, NH: University of New Hampshire Press, 2008).
33. 'The Digestive Ferment Market', *The Bulletin of Pharmacy* 5.9 (September 1891), 397.
34. 'The Digestive Ferments and Their Uses in Medicine and Surgery', *The Medical Bulletin: A Monthly*

Journal of Medicine and Surgery 16 (January 1894), 35.
35. 'Scientific Slaughtering', *Scientific American*, 20 January 1894, 37. This article appeared originally in *Drover's Magazine,* and was reprinted in trade journals such as *Ice and Refrigeration, Industrial Refrigeration* and *American Soap Journal and Manufacturing Chemist*; for pharmacists' fears of competition through the packinghouses, see 'The Digestive Ferment Market'.
36. Benjamin Ward Richardson, 'The Skeleton in the National Cupboard', *The Asclepiad* 3 (1886), 218.
37. For example, *Stepping-Stones to Thrift* (London: Warwick House, 1883); George Bartley, *Domestic Economy: Thrift in Every-Day Life* (London: Kegan Paul, 1878); Phebe Lankester, *The National Thrift Reader* (London: Allman and Son, 1880); *The Thrift Book: A Cyclopædia of Cottage Management* (London: Ward, Lock and Co., 1882); Samuel Smiles, *Thrift* (London: Murray, 1875); William Hoyle, *Wealth and Social Progress in Relation to Thrift, Temperance, and Trade* (Manchester: United Kingdom Alliance, 1887).'
38. On the National Training School of Cookery, see Yuriko Akiyama, *Feeding the Nation: Nutrition and Health in Britain before World War One* (London: Tauris Academic Studies, 2008).
39. 'Touching Thrift', *Punch*, 31 January 1880, Punch Historical Archive.
40. Benjamin Ward Richardson, 'On Thrift in Relation to Food', *Journal of the Society of Arts*, 19 March 1880, 383-85.
41. William Roberts, 'Observations on the Digestive Ferments and Their Therapeutical Uses', *British Medical Journal* 2.983 (1 November 1879), 683-85.
42. William Roberts, 'The Lumleian Lectures on the Digestive Ferments, and the Preparation and Use of Artificially Digested Food: Lecture III', *British Medical Journal* 1.1009 and 1010 (1880), 647.
43. Roberts, 'Lumleian Lectures III'.
44. William Roberts, 'The Lumleian Lectures on the Digestive Ferments, and the Preparation and Use of Artificially Digested Food: Lecture I', *British Medical Journal* 1.1006 (10 April 1880), 539; Roberts, 'Lumleian Lectures III', 647.
45. Roberts, 'Lumleian Lectures III', 647.
46. See for example, James Wallace Anderson, *Lectures on Medical Nursing: Delivered in the Royal Infirmary, Glasgow* (Glasgow: James Maclehose, 1883), pp. 83-84; Laurence Humphry, *A Manual of Nursing* (Philadelphia: P. Blakiston, Son, & Company, 1894), p. 242; E. M. Worsnop, *The Nurse's Handbook of Cookery: A Help in Sickness and Convalescence* (London: Black, 1897), pp. 96-100; James Kenneth Watson, *A Handbook for Nurses* (Philadelphia: W.B. Saunders, 1900), pp. 83-84.
47. See for example, Isabella Mary Beeton, *Mrs. Beeton's Everyday Cookery* (London: Ward, Lock, 1907), pp. 544-45; Margaret Johnes Mitchell, *The Fireless Cook Book* (New York: Doubleday, Page, 1911), pp. 199-200; *The New American Cook Book* (Springfield, OH: Mast, Crowell & Kirkpatrick, 1897), pp. 325-26, 330; *West Bend Cook Book* (Lake Mills, WI: Hattie E. Crump, 1915), p. 426.

Offal People: Resurrecting Chicken Feet on the Streets of South Africa

Arundhatie Biswas Kundal

> The pleasure of the table belongs to all ages, to all conditions, to all countries, and to all areas; it mingles with all other pleasures, and remains at last to console us.
>
> Jean Antheleme Brillant-Savarin

Introduction

While Southeast Asia remarkably touts its offal as one of its top tourist brand ambassadors, in South Africa 'chicken feet' chokes under a compelling cosmopolitan discrimination. *Braaied* (barbequed) chicken feet, popularly known as 'runaways', 'walkie-talkies', '*maotwana*' or in Xhosa '*amanqina enkukhu*', are gastronomical delights, the food-on-the-go of South African townships. These sprawling peri-urban settlements, a legacy of the country's decades of apartheid, are home to the majority of the country's poor black population, and many livelihoods depend on street food vending.

Poverty remains pervasive, especially in the global South as the triple burden of hunger, micronutrient deficiencies and obesity dominates food systems as epidemics of modern times. Traditional street food consumers are now increasingly being pushed toward 'aspirational eating', continuously seeking out globally diverse food rather than more nutritional diets. Far from lustrous televised cook-offs, food on the streets here is not just about eating but also about symbolically consuming identities, social bonding, and more importantly a survivalist strategy for many famished people. These are urban food struggles of our times, a lived reality enervated by the interplay of rapid urbanization, increasing dependency on purchasing food, limited accessibility of nutritional commodities and the rising monarchy of the Big Food industries. Food from the streets now faces an uncertain future, a crumbling tradition that the cityscape ignores, perhaps besotted with its celebrity as a tourist destination with squeaky clean streets. I argue in this paper that it is time to resurrect offal as a cultural niche in the urban food chain and restore the dignity of the women who sell it on the streets. Popularizing street food as a hygienic, affordable and sustainable cuisine could also maximize local resources, reduce waste and, perhaps most importantly, provide a livelihood, thereby improving food security.

Resurrecting Chicken Feet on the Streets of South Africa

Figure 1
Selling chicken feet in the Townships.

Walkie-talkie Towns

Cape Town's celebrated 'fifth- quarter' cuisine exists not on some celebrity chef's pricey table but rather is the kind of 'holy offal grail' that rises from its original homestead. The 'townships' that the Mother City cradles in its peripheries are the mecca of all 'variety meats'.[1] Walkie-talkies are variety meat with ligaments, cartilage, skin and tendons, which are not organs per say but still have a respectable place in the *quinto quarto* of township eating despite being rejected by most standards of public dining.

While trendy chefs in starry restaurants toil to upgrade the 'offal bits' to main courses, the townships and their offal survive as outcasts, as stark citadels of the apartheid legacy. Townships are the junkyards of colonialism, 'suburbs that are an enormous backyard of the whole white city, where categories and functions lose their ordination and logic' amidst the tinned shack-towns that that dot the Cape Flats.[2] Here humans and offal alike are segregated, disconnected from a city that has long been a melting pot of divergent cuisines. Philipi, Nyanga, Langa, Gugulethu, Crossroads and Khayelitsha are Cape Town's offal lands; home to the first residents, namely migrants who came from the former Ciskei and Transkei homelands, arriving in 1833.[3] These newcomers were 'carriers of tradition and nostalgia', connecting their new homes with their original homelands.[4] And offal certainly echoed in their food memories.

Offal as fringe street food and its exclusive availability in the black townships perhaps owes its censorship to apartheid policies, which not only aimed at racial division, but also restricted the movement and activities (including business) of the marginalized black community. A series of acts, such as the Native (Urban Areas) Act of 1923, restricted black people not just from residing in certain areas, but also from engaging in any economic activity except those allowed by their white employers.

Women could only get the right to reside in an urban area by virtue of a relationship with a man. A series of repressive laws followed – influx control, pass laws, the Group Areas Act and the 'white by night' policy.[5] Modified later, the 'move-laws' allowed natives to operate businesses only if they were mobile vendors able to move away swiftly before they became established in the neighbourhood landscape. After apartheid, deregulation measures had a meagre effect: Cape Town has fewer inner city traders and public space vendors than any other South African city. The city's by-laws include tedious registration processes, with expensive site allocations, operating charges and restricted permits owing to the limited number of trading bays in the central city. Today the townships remain underdeveloped communities spatially disconnected from urban centres, which offer better economic prospects; the townships teem with working-age people desperate for economic opportunity.

Black women comprise the majority of street traders in South Africa; they sell a wide range of commodities, including garments, fruit and vegetables, ready to eat foods and everyday knick-knacks. Of the half a million street traders across South Africa, seventy per cent are women selling food items.[6] Today, street food vending is probably the single largest employer in the informal sector and possibly one of the major contributors to the South African economy.[7] Offal, in particular chicken feet, is the predominant class of street food in the townships of Cape Town, with soaring demand because it is sold as a completely cooked, easy-on-the-wallet hot snack. This 'runaway' trade is uniquely spearheaded by women entrepreneurs who deal deftly with its procurement, preparation and sale. These are the little 'feet that feed' families, and this is their offal story.

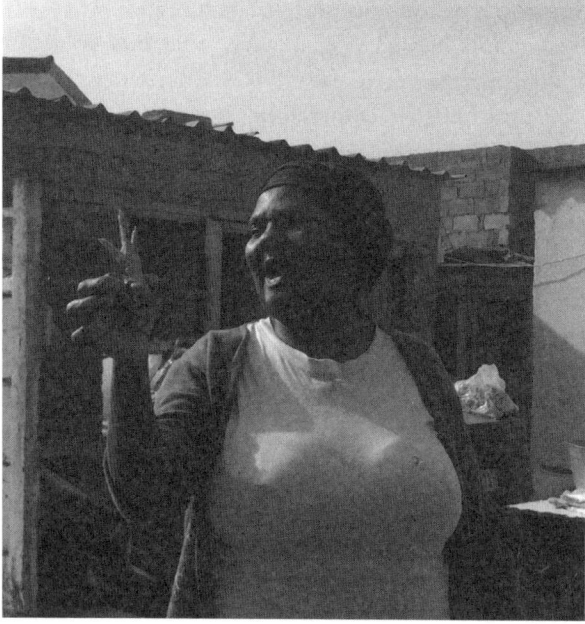

Figure 2
Selling chicken feet in the Townships.

Resurrecting Chicken Feet on the Streets of South Africa

Women with Chicken Feet

This very phrase risks conjuring an image of the villainous *Baba Yaga*, the witch from a Slavic childhood tale whose abode was embellished with spindly chicken feet. The sinister association when you hear the offal sellers, with their creased, sun-baked faces and deft hands weathered by the settling embers of the *braai*, tell their own tales. A stroll into the townships leads to smells of food, mingled with gospel music and the immutable clangour of urban sprawl, likely to dispel any prejudice against offal. *Braai* smoke, smouldering rows of chicken feet, bellows over a scattering landscape of satellite dishes stacked over tin box shacks. Thirty-six-year-old single mother Thobela Nkwinika sells walkie-talkies, or *amanqina enkukhu*, a trademark delicacy of the township. Her walkies sit on a makeshift grilling mesh, with the settling embers setting off an insatiable aroma. On a balmy Saturday afternoon, her kiosk is dwarfed by serpentine queues outside the Striker Meat Market in Phillipi on the eastern edge of Cape Town. Nearby an old camper van serves as a hair braiding parlour while a few people seeking the healing of traditional African medicine jostle outside a *sangoma*'s shack. Goats bleat around an overflowing rubbish heap in an attempt to ambush the *mealie* lady selling roasted corn; the constant tooting of cars drowns the rhythmic claps of little girls playing *mgusha*, a popular local game usually played by girls using old pantyhose knotted up in a long jump rope, while their parents hawk vegetables nearby. 'Wait until the crowds load their carts from the market' and 'the arsenal from my *braai* will do the trick' she tells me in Xhosa, a beautiful language enlivened with clicks that echo the beats of the street karaoke singer nearby.

As afternoon progresses, a couple people have already made a beeline for the feet. Going for seventy South African cents (approximately four cents US) apiece, she neatly packs the feet in old newspapers, handing them to customers who liberally douse them with chilli sauce from a recycled plastic bottle. Her clientele are largely fellow migrants looking for soul food, food that evokes a sense of belonging and identity. A woman hurtles in, carrying bags full of her weekend shopping, and orders a couple of 'feet'. After a minute of incessant prodding she tells me that the chicken feet take her back in time, evoking lingering memories of her childhood. She happily recalls mid-afternoon scuffles with mates at the chicken feet vendor's stall outside the school gates. Meanwhile two giggling teenagers tromp in, politely place their orders and quickly start digging in. They exclaim, 'Eating them is like popping sweets or eating wafers, but these are super cheap!' They munch crackling crisp roast chicken feet, popping them in their mouths with the toe first, deftly spitting the nails onto the ground while dexterously scraping skin and meat off with their teeth. The crunchy saga often culminates in determined chewing to the very last marrow. No one eats in silence here: the cacophony banter reinforces the fact that food is just not about eating and consuming. The food provides a space that facilitates socializing. Communal consumption here reinstates the power of a shared food system. As Arjun Appadurai notes, '[f]ood can be used to mark and create relations of equality, intimacy or solidarity or, instead, to uphold relations signalling rank, distance or segmentation.' Street food therefore also marks different types of class through its consumption.[8]

Wasted Little Feet

Churchill's famous remark that it was absurd to grow an entire chicken to eat only the breasts triggers muffled sniggers from Thobela. She refutes the common notion that the colonists propagated the use of offal as a sign of dominance, giving the nasty parts to the servants. 'In the countryside where I come from we don't waste anything, only the feathers are discarded,' she says. There are innumerable accounts of women who have resorted to selling chicken feet in front of local schools and markets for some extra income. Chicken feet also came to the rescue for many who lived in abject poverty. A poignant anecdote holds that Solomon Linda, the man behind the infectious song 'The Lion Sleeps Tonight', left behind a family in his village who lived by selling chicken feet.[9] Another beautifully intriguing play, Lara Foot Newton's *Marion and Solomon*, uses chicken feet as a metaphor for culture and poverty. Hence, Marion the aging, white, self-inflicted lonely-heart, invokes her own cultural mores when she rejects a couple of chicken feet. 'You could have smoked them for me, and marinated them in truffles and champagne for all I care. I still wouldn't have eaten them,' she admonishes Solomon, the black boy who has graciously offered her his grandmother's chicken feet. Shocked by how they look, Marion adds, 'we English are too conservative to do extremities. The middle of the chicken does very nicely, thank you.'[10]

It took a few decades until Fergus Henderson, the mogul of the nose-to-tail movement, began to overcome prejudices like Marion's. While many cultural traditions propagate the simple fact that, when it comes to food, you waste nothing, most modern diners find consuming innards and extremities close to bestial. It is interesting to note that the effort to return offal to American dining table took off during the Second World War when a team of leading social scientists were commissioned to address the looming meat shortage. When they found that patriotism alone wasn't enough incentive to encourage consumption of organ food, they cleverly urged people to insert offal into their meals for variety while media coverage promoted its nutritional value – and thus 'variety meats' were born.[11]

But offal's comeback was sadly short-lived because of the expansion of the industrialized food sector. With the quick fix magic of free glutamic acids, monosodium glutamate replaced chicken feet and other natural agents as the standard thickener and flavour enhancer of American soups, stews and gravies. Chicken feet contain glucosamine, chondroitin, collagen and trace minerals. Because these are all beneficial to the human body, some have made inflated health claims about chicken feet. A controversial American veterinarian, Harry Robertson, claimed that chicken feet had regenerative potential to improve arthritis and spinal-cord injuries – at least until his experiments were banned.[12] Another contentious torchbearer for offal is Cape Town's sport scientist Tim Noakes, whose Banting diet has attracted ardent followers and acerbic critics alike.[13] Noakes argues that offal is the healthiest food for humans, and his clinical experiments in Karoo involved poor labourers who given offal to 'replace the cheap rubbish they are eating'.[14] The Internet is also amusingly inundated with beauty products like BioCell Collagen, an American product that allegedly derives collagen peptide complex from chicken feet cartilage to promote younger looking skin and active joints.[15] You can even buy a voodoo chicken foot amulet to seek spiritual help![16] The sacred and profane are often enmeshed into local foodways as well. A voluntary South African graduation ceremony for *sangomas* known as the *'imfelo'* requires the sacrifice of a chicken, cutting up its head, feet and intestines while it is still alive.[17]

While some of these uses seem suspicious, there is no doubt that a well prepared *braaied* chicken foot is succulent, juicy and crunchy with the perfect balance of spices. Thobela carefully cleans and scrapes hers under a community water tap near her shack and then marinates them in an old pool chlorine bucket. But she no longer has grain-fed backyard chickens nor does she use fresh spices. Street vendors increasingly procure their ingredients from supermarket chains including seasoning sourced from distant wholesalers. Thobela is at the meat market well before its opening hours to pick up her frozen chicken feet; after thawing she has to then clean them and sometimes scrape off their sores before the chicken feet can be boiled and marinated in spices and a drizzle of oil and salt.

Street food now has to contend with the Big Food. McDonald's now lists South Africa as one of its most successful regions, with over two hundred outlets in all nine provinces. Fast food causes bellies to bloat along with sales; these establishments sate hunger with starchy, salted carbohydrate bombs washed down by sugar-packed drinks. Numerous studies documenting the impact of globalization have found that aspirational eating has pushed diets to become more globally diverse even while they remain less nutritional. Major food conglomerates entice consumers with budget meals, including KFC's plagiarized, hygienic street food aptly called the 'streetwise menu'.[18] A piece of chicken cooked to golden perfection with the regular pap (maize meal) and small gravy certainly seems more seductive than a sticky chicken foot.

South Africans consume about approximately 1.8 million tonnes of chicken a year, from flame-grilled drumsticks glossed with peri-peri sauce to 'walkie talkies'.[19] These are hard times as the onslaught of a relentless drought begins to take a toll on South African consumers, affecting anywhere between fifty-five and eighty per cent households.[20] Chicken is the main source of protein for poorer South Africans now. As demand grows, fuelled by a weak currency and escalating prices, more people are unable to meet their fundamental nutritional needs. Perhaps now is an apt time for a reality check on foodways as an intersecting cultural and social narrative. Is it wise to encourage high-end posh nosh or affordable indigenous food? The continued industrialization of food has compelled us to rethink 'food insecurity', which threatens to be a complex threat in perpetuity that limits the experiences of those most affected by it.

Whilst South Africa remains food secure at the national level, there is disturbing evidence that, at the household level, a greater hunger exists due to socio-economic factors in both urban and rural areas, coupled with continuing micronutrient deficiencies among children alongside increasing obesity in older children and adults. A few key statistics from the South African National Health and Nutrition Examination Survey (SANHANES-1) reveal that the largest percentage of participants experiencing hunger, a staggering 32.4 per cent, were from the urban informal localities.[21] South Africa faces a war on nutrition on two fronts: struggling against high rates of obesity and battling nutritional deficiency. Dinner is once again *mieliepap* (traditional porridge made from ground maize, a staple food of the Bantu) with *morogo* (wild or African spinach, an important part of the staple diet in rural communities) and a cheap cut of meat, poultry – chicken feet are a popular choice – or even *mopane* worms (actually caterpillars, a delicacy in some parts of Southern Africa and a bush food in others).

A severe shortage of employment opportunities related to the mechanization of dominant sectors (construction, transport and finance) are forcing men to enter the street vending trade, constricting women traders who once dominated the market. Research suggests that women enter street vending later their forties, later than men, who often start in their twenties.[22] Although this sector perhaps draws people because vending offers a means of livelihood with minimal skills and low start up costs, many studies have revealed that 'informal economic processes' in fact cross-cut the entire social structure. Smaller scale surveys suggest that women tend to dominate less lucrative segments of the informal economy in general, which is particularly the case among street traders.[23] Although cumulatively the informal sector contributes significantly to the gross domestic product, Statistics South Africa reveals that the informal sector has remained stagnant at about five per cent from 2001 to 2013.[24] Quandaries over the city's spatial and culinary divide spill over into this gendered space, affecting the most vulnerable and impoverished sections of a society marred by food insecurity. Evidence from recent research has indicated the pivotal role of informal trading to the economy of the country distributing more affordable and accessible goods. Yet the global Cape Town brand excludes its offal people. Why? Borrowing from Paul Rozin, perhaps the city invokes its 'core emotion of disgust' to the presence of offal on its manicured streets, an apparent violation of the 'body envelope of its infrastructural aesthetics'.[25] Chicken feet may remain revolting for most of us because 'we've gotten to the point where we only eat food that "has no semblance of having been a living creature"', says offal guru, chef Chris Cosentino.[26] Such attitudes shape national identities: 'like a language, food articulates notions of inclusion and exclusion, of national pride and xenophobia'.[27] Communities often ascertain 'which foods are social necessities and which are luxuries, and this distinction reflects the "social grammar" of a society, its moral and political make-up'.[28] The fading presence of offal on the streets offers visual proof of the country's changing dining climate.

The streets thus become a contested terrain for vendors who often end up waging a frustrating war with the economic, structural and political system. In the absence of an explicit national policy towards informal traders, women in the streets are facing now increasingly facing workplace insecurity, sexual harassment and evictions. Tedious licensing systems combine with a lack of micro-enterprising opportunities or unionization and systemic exclusion from the city's urban planning processes to leave the vendors with insufficient storage facilities and sanitation, lack of space to prepare meals and little access to clean water and sewage systems.

At the same time, the glass ceiling remains uncracked in chic food quarters as well: in the culinary media, cooking with offal has been vociferously recast as a masculine trait. So even home-grown celebrity women chefs like Siba play it safe by doing only occasional dressed up chicken feet far removed from what one finds in the street.[29] Masculinity and the politics of gender often combine to seize offal from a comestible space controlled by women in the kitchens. Recast as extreme, brutal and gross, offal is repeatedly portrayed as a masculine food in the media, with bulging, gym-honed bodies and butcher knives covered in blood. Interestingly, however, the townships still harbour a marginal group of women who slaughter and cook birds without sous vide machines or any well-powdered pout. Fact and fiction alike have reflected on the myriad ways gender, sex, class and race are produced through culinary negotiations. So while Anita Desai's *Feasting and Fasting* uncovers food as a trope to identify the patriarchal domination of women in the modern food capitalist era, Margaret Atwood's novel *The Edible Woman* describes the notion of being a consumed identity.[30] It is also encouraging to observe the focused efforts to use gender as an analytical tool, which is now an emergent field in food studies. Urban food politics further widens up its scope by tracing the centrality of gender and empowerment as enacted in food justice movements. Unfortunately gaps remain as too much academic literature still suffers from monotonous stories of despair and sorrow. These studies also tend to be technocratic and paternalistic, rarely relying on sex-disaggregated data.

Street-food surveys found that chicken feet sold in townships is often little more than skin and fat.[31] But chicken feet are meant to be consumed as a snack, the in-between comfort bite that is now being pushed to the dinner table. Case studies from the world over have proved that urban street food vendors can be instrumental in providing nutritious food 'on-the-go'. Globally, food safety workshops have successfully helped street vendors practice personal hygiene, sanitation and safe food preparation methods. Although the importance of street food as food security for the urban poor has been well documented in academic research, this new attentiveness to street food has now resulted in it being seen as 'smart food' and as a respectable means of livelihood. An estimated 2.5 billion people eat street food on an everyday basis, and in South Africa street food feeds a large proportion of impoverished black South Africans in the townships and in the urban informal settlements.[32] One example of this new attention is the World Street Food Congress, which not only attracts street food vendors every year but is also a serious attempt to showcase global street food as a strategic part of the food security dialogue. Platforms like this recognize the tremendous potential of street food around the world and encourage advocacy efforts to influence government policy makers.

Although popular, chicken feet are neither a panacea to end hunger nor a way to slow South Africa's rising obesity epidemic. With an increasing number of urban households falling victim to severe food insecurity coupled with fierce competition from the industrial food regimes, consuming the waste parts can contribute to food security. Examining food security as a larger urban social construct can deconstruct its binary characteristics of merely categorizing who is or is not food secure. Street food vending struggles as a largely unprotected and constrained sector in a country where unemployment rates stand at 25.7 per cent with women battling to fit in.[33] While there is plethora of anecdotal evidence on the abysmal conditions on street vendors' lives, street food studies have often cast offal as the charismatic lead with the potential to transform the livelihoods it sustains. Reclaiming this space for women offal vendors is therefore both imperative to the food justice movement and a progressive step to nurture culinary heritage. Because of the large number of women who sell chicken feet on the streets, simply formalizing this sector will perhaps not suffice. It will have to be steered beyond its survivalist nature and explored with a gendered lens as a context-specific and participatory process.

This pulsating underbelly of the city deploys offal to benefit, emancipate and empower a large number of penurious souls. But to survive it can no longer be seen as a kind of pariah. To make chicken feet equally accessible to curious tourists ticking-off their bucket lists and to natives alike, chicken feet will have to demand a space in inclusive urban planning. Chicken feet have the potential to offer a powerful alternative pathway towards a sustainable economy – a sharp contrast to the way the industrialized food system burdening us with dysfunctional food practices, sapping our health and eroding our environment. It is therefore time to support the offal women and their chicken feet before they stand only as monuments to lost food inheritance and as hapless victims of the politics of urban exclusion. This offal – people and food alike – must be reclaimed.

Notes

1. In the 1930s an unknown party wrote to the local newspaper claiming that Cape Town was the only city in South Africa that could truly call itself a metropolis. This description was popularly accepted, deriving from the Greek meter or metros meaning mother and polis meaning city, the mother city was born ('...Cape Town Mother City', *Cape Town Magazine* <http://www.capetownmagazine.com/whats-the-deal-with/cape-town-mother-city/125_22_10867> [accessed 3 March 2016]).
2. Nadine Godimer, *The Burger's Daughter* (London: Penguin Books, 1980), p.148.
3. Gerry Adlard, *An Introduction to Phillipi*, 14 July 2008 (unpublished but available on request).
4. Pablo Bose and Alisha Laramee, 'Taste of Home: Migration, Food and Belonging in a Changing Vermont', *Opportunities for Agriculture Working Paper Series*, 2.4 (2013), 1-7 (1).
5. Francie Lund, 'Women Street Traders in Urban South Africa: A synthesis of Selected Research Findings,

CSDS Research Report (School of Development Studies, University of Natal, Durban), 15 (1998), 1-41 (24).

6. International Labour Organization, 'Street Traders and their Organisations in South Africa', 2003, p.4 <http://www.inclusivecities.org/wp-content/uploads/2012/07/Budlender_ILO_SA_Street_Vendors_manual.pdf> [accessed 12 January 2016]
7. A.Von Holy and F.M. Makhoane, *International Journal of Food Microbiology* 111 (2006) pp. 89-92 (90).
8. Arjun Appadurai, 'Gastro-politics in Hindu South Asia.' *American Ethnologist* 8 (1981), 494-511 (496).
9. Sharon La Franiere, 'In the Jungle, the Unjust Jungle, a Small Victory,' *New York Times*, 22 March 2006 <http://www.nytimes.com/2006/03/22/world/africa/in-the-jungle-the-unjust-jungle-a-small-victory.html> [accessed 9th January 2016].
10. Lara Foot Newton, *Marion and Solomon* (London: Oberon Books, 2013), p. 22.
11. Newton, p. 22.
12. Cari Romm, 'The World War II Campaign to bring Organ Meats to the Dinner Table' *The Atlantic*, 25 September 2014 <https://www.theatlantic.com/health/archive/2014/09/the-world-war-ii-campaign-to-bring-organ-meats-to-the-dinner-table/380737/ [accessed 14 March 2016].
13. Banting diet is a low-carbohydrate, high-fat (LCHF) diet, named after its first consumer and made popular by Tim Noakes and others in their book *The Real Meal Revolution* (Waterfront, South Africa, 2013).
14. Chris Baron, 'Noaks Diet Has Devotees but Doctors, Scientists and Dieticians Aren't Sure', *The [Johannesburg] Times*, 23 July 2014, <http://www.timeslive.co.za/lifestyle/2014/07/23/Noakes-diet-has-devotees-but-doctors-scientists-and-dieticians-arent-so-sure> [accessed 13 December 2015].
15. Henry Weber, 'Incredible Powder Made from Chicken Feet Cures Everything', *Weekly World News* 19 December 1989, p. 28.
16. 'Chicken Foot Necklace New Orleans Louisiana Cajun Voodoo Magic' <https://www.amazon.com/Chicken-Necklace-Orleans-Louisianna-Voodoo/dp/B0067CILNI> [accessed 6 February 2016].
17. C.G. Ellis, 'A Case of Imfelo', *South African Family Practice*, March 1996, 122-23. <https://www.safpj.co.za/index.php/safpj/article/viewFile/2389/3003> [accessed 15th January 2016]
18. Kentucky Fried Chicken, 'Streetwise One Pap', *KFC*, 2016 <https://kfc.co.za/kfc-catalog/streetwise-meals/icm1031/> [accessed 10 February 2016].
19. Global Business and Business Center, *South Africa Investment and Business Guide, Volume I: Strategic and Practical Information* (Washington, DC: International Business Publications, 2015), p.184.
20. 'South Africa Spurns Free Trade to Protect Its Meat Market', *The Economist*, 17 November 2015 <http://www.economist.com/news/middle-east-and-africa/21678672-america-and-south-africa-are-beating-drumsticks-trade-war-playing-chicken> [accessed 10 February 2016].
21. Republic of South Africa Department of Health, *The South African National Health and Nutrition Examination Survey, 2012: SANHANNES-1* (Cape Town: HSRC Press, 2013) <http://www.hsrc.ac.za/en/research-outputs/ktree-doc/13850> [accessed 16th January 2016].
22. Lund, p. 24
23. Caroline Skinner, 'Street Trade In Africa: A Review', Working Paper No. 51, School of Developmental Studies, University of KwaZulu-Natal, April 2008, p. 1-31 (p. 9).
24. 'Informal Sector's Contribution to GDP Is Stagnant', *BusinessLive*, 15 August 2014 <https://www.businesslive.co.za/bd/companies/2014-08-15-informal-sectors-contribution-to-gdp-is-stagnant/> [accessed 24th January 2016].
25. Paul Rozin and April E. Fallon, 'A Perspective on Disgust', *Psychological Review* 94 (1987), 23-41.
26. Elena Ferretti, 'How to Eat Feet,' *Fox News*, 29 March 2011 <http://www.foxnews.com/food-drink/2011/03/29/how-to-eat-feet.html> [accessed 25th January 2016].
27. David Bell and Gill Valentine, *Consuming Geographies: We Are What We Eat* (London: Routledge, 1997), pp. 168-69.
28. C.J. Berry, *The Idea of Luxury: A Conceptual and Historical Investigation* (Cambridge: Cambridge University Press, 1994), pp. 41-42.

29. Drum Digital, 'Episode 10 DRUM presents Siba Cooking with Rebecca Malope', *Drum: The Beat Goes On*, 28 October 2011 <http://www.drum.co.za/uncategorized/episode-10-drum-presents-siba-cooking-with-rebecca-malope/≥ [accessed 28 February 2016].
30. Anita Desai, *Fasting and Feasting* (New York: Mariner,1999); Margaret Atwood, *The Edible Woman*, (Canada: McClelland and Stewart, 1969).
31. Ian Birrell, 'South Africa's Obesity Crisis: The Shape of Things to Come?', *Scroll.in*, 20 September 2014 <https://scroll.in/article/679568/south-africas-obesity-crisis-the-shape-of-things-to-come> [accessed 23 January 2016].
32. Peter Fellows and Martin Hilmi, *Selling Street and Snack Foods*, FAO Diversification Booklet 18, Rural Infrastructure and Agro-Industries Division, Food and Agriculture Organization of the United Nations, Rome: Food and Agriculture Organization of the United Nations, 2011) <http://www.fao.org/docrep/015/i2474e/i2474e00.pdf> [accessed 15 May 2016].
33. 'South Africa Unemployment Rate', *Trading Economics* <http://www.tradingeconomics.com/south-africa/unemployment-rate> [accessed 14 May 2016].

The Good, the Bad and the Ugly: The Allure of Offal Cuisine in Japan

Christopher Laurent

Out the window, sparsely populated luscious green mountains and valleys stream past in succession, making me forget I am still in Japan.

'You like meat?' asks Yasu the driver.

'I love meat. There isn't much I can't eat,' I boast remembering my breakfast of smelly *natto* fermented soybeans.

We soon arrive at a small shop in the countryside. I learn that the shop, a Japanese-owned Chinese restaurant, is famous for serving *Kubokawa* pork, a specialty of the region. We seat ourselves at a Japanese table so close to the ground I can barely fold my legs under it.

'Give us a full course and some of the raw as well,' orders Yasu.

The waitress comes back balancing a flat iron griddle on top of a portable gas burner. My mouth waters at the idea of eating grilled skewers, braised pork belly and thinly sliced loin. However, I can barely hide my distress when I see what comes out of the kitchen. The dark brown liver is sliced sashimi style and served with a salty citrus sauce. Honeycomb tripe is also served raw with a side of spicy sesame oil. On the griddle sizzles a sectioned heart, curly intestines and unidentifiable fat-coated organ meat.

In this paper, I examine why offal cuisine has become tasteful to so many Japanese people. My investigation is primarily based on ethnographic work on the island of Shikoku in the region of Kochi Japan. The region is famous for a cuisine that makes use of many foodstuffs that would be discarded elsewhere. Although the cuisine of the region is distinct in many ways from the rest of Japan, people's taste for these leftover bits exists nationwide. The prevailing attitude of Japanese people toward offal differs from other countries. Whereas offal is often regarded as an unwanted leftover that sells at a cheaper price in butcher shops, offal in Japan fetches a price that is sometimes comparable to steak. Unlike in the Western context where offal is often consumed by marginal groups like the poor, the rich and the adventurous, offal is now consumed by a significant portion of the population in Japan which in some cases include women and children. I argue that the love of, or disgust for, offal cuisine is not inherent or unchanging in people but is instead socially constructed within specific cultural contexts. Although offal cuisine emerged out of material limitations (i.e. poverty), it has come to signify something different in Japan where cuisine and culture have transformed these items that are rejected elsewhere into something people seek and desire. Simply put, offal is popular in Japan because it tastes good. The question that needs answering is what makes these dishes delectable to the Japanese palate?

Contextualizing Offal Eating

Broadly speaking, why are certain foods considered undesirable, or even inedible, to some, while the same foods are seen as delicious to others? It is certain that biology and evolution have shaped our taste preferences. Just as a newborn prefers sweet over bitter flavours, it is easy to imagine why people would prefer meat over offal. Yet these hierarchies that are assumed to be true for all are far from universal if we investigate different cultures. In this paper, I choose not to focus on the biological basis for our food choices but rather on what makes us enjoy vastly different food from one culture to another (Rozin and Vollmecke 1986). Anthropologists in particular have demonstrated a keen interest in explaining why cultural customs proscribe certain foods from being consumed (Douglas 2002; Harris 1998). Although disgust for offal bears some resemblance to the mechanisms that enforce food taboo, one can cite few examples of cultures where they are completely prohibited. Other studies have offered interesting models examining how the emotions that relate to food disgust are shaped through a process of acquisition of cultural values (Rozin and Fallon 1987). Although disgust and avoidance of certain foods has been the focus of much of the scholarly investigation, few studies have attempted to articulate the opposite (i.e. what makes food delicious). The boundary between what is good and what is bad is one that is socially constructed which means that it is regimented by culture (Cantarero and others 2009). I propose that what is socially constructed is not only the categories of good and bad but also the taste of this particular food or how the flavour is perceived on the palate.

In the specific case of offal, propensity to consume food that might be discarded elsewhere becomes a very personal choice nonetheless influenced by cultural values. These ingrained values collectively participate in shaping our palate – our preferences and how we discriminate between different tastes. For example, a person raised in Canada might not only acquire a preference for maple syrup, he or she will also be able to distinguish using taste alone imitation from real maple syrup. What shapes a taste for offal cuisine? Several authors have paid attention to how society's changing values affect people's desire to consume offal. According to Vialles (1988), people who consume offal are implicitly recognizing the animal provenance of meat, while people who do not consume them do it because they do not wish to be reminded that they are eating a living being. Other scholars have argued that offal consumption is driven by mechanisms of differentiation between social classes (Bourdieu 1984; Strong 2006; Lloyd 2012). In a more general sense, the appeal for this cuisine seems to manifest itself as the creature of evolving social norms where social connotations associated with non-meat animal parts are seen with desire or repugnance (Elias and Mennell 2000; Mennell 1995). Sudden changes in national political discourse seem to also play a role in transforming these unwanted leftovers into desirable food (Ducann 1986).

Yet, the appetite for offal has not been explored using the sense of taste, and how it is constructed in a different culture, as the focus of an investigation.

What is offal and how can we define such an imprecise category? For the purpose of this paper, the category of offal will not only include organ meat but other by-products of animal consumption. These leftovers will include non-muscle meat residue that are often considered waste. My definition of offal aims to be exhaustive, including not only viscera but also blood, tendon and cartilage. In addition to being considered garbage, blood, guts and bones elicit an almost immediate reaction of horror as the word gore itself signified filth in its old Germanic origin. It is important to remind the reader that the association of offal with trash parts is most relevant in the English languages as it carries a different meaning when translated into another language (Mennell 1995). Offal has no exact translatable equivalent in the Japanese language. In this paper, I will examine how this socially constructed category, whether it is considered disgusting or desirable, is difficult to superimpose onto the Japanese cultural context.

It is important to historically contextualize offal eating in Japan. Animal products have not always been part of the Japanese diet. Although outcast groups marginally consumed meat, it was long proscribed in Japan for religious reasons. After the Meiji restoration of 1868, the country's leadership actively promoted meat consumption in an attempt to emulate Western powers. Although meat was consumed in larger quantities after the modernization of Japan, offal was not considered a delicacy outright. In the late 1920s, Korean-imported labourers were opening the first offal cuisine (*horumon ryori*) restaurants in growing urban centres (Cwiertka 2007). Offal cuisine finds its roots among ethnic Korean colonial subjects in Japan. Through the culinary negotiation of a disenfranchised people, offal cuisine gained popularity as result of Post-World War II food shortages (Toshio 1999). Offal cuisine is part of the cultural heritage of Koreans in Japan as the community journal 'Offal Culture' (*horumon bunka*) attests (Chapman 2006). As offal cuisine gained popularity, it became dissociated with its modest immigrant origins. Dishes like grilled offal (*horumon yaki*) and offal hotpot (*motsunabe*), initially blue-collar male-centred fare, eventually became popular across genders and classes. These dishes are today associated with male drinking joints but enjoy remarkable success among women and even children.

Sampling Un/Desirable Food

In front of one of the many brightly lit restaurants of Osaka's *tsuruhashi* district, one can observe customers lining up to sample different cuts of grilled offal. Inside, these shops overwhelm the senses. An almost impenetrable smoke curtain hangs like a cloud over low tables encircled by calf-high stools. The sound of the smoke ventilators hovering above each table coupled with the numerous patrons squeezed together in loud conversation forces hungry customers to shout their orders out. The smell of grilled offal has impregnated the walls. The small orders are far from cheap but each has a different taste and texture. Honeycomb tripe (*hachinosu*) is chewy and tastes of its soy sauce and sesame oil marinade, while fatty intestine (*shiro*) is gummy and tastes of seared fat. In offal restaurants, variety always trumps ordering a large portion of one type of offal. Customers order many small plates of different kinds of offal in order to enjoy the many tastes and textures that this cuisine has to offer. The link between offal cuisine (*horumon*) and Korean permanent residents in Japan (*zainichi*) is still apparent in Osaka's Korean town. Gambling dens and offal restaurants in ghettoized parts of town are some of the limited recourse for a population that was never truly assimilated into Japanese society. In spite of this, Korean-style offal and grilled meat restaurants became popular across Japan.

In the region of Kochi, where I did my research, pork and boar offal are commonly consumed. During my research, I was offered the opportunity to observe the butchering of a freshly killed boar. The boar is first boiled to allow most of its hair to be pulled off. Then, it is given a clean shave before butchering because the skin should not go to waste. The meat is immediately served in thin raw slices with the skin on. The loin will be served *tataki* style seared on the outside and raw on the inside. The internal organs are removed through a ventral incision, and the liver is set aside to be grilled later. My host and his hunting companions remark that the boar looks eerily human, and, when I ask if it is an adult, they joke that it is of middle school age. Recognizing animal provenance, and even human likeness, is key in understanding why people would either object or delight in its consumption. In the mountains of Kochi, the wild boar population is a plague as it damages agricultural land. In this place, boar hunting and consumption has been practiced for generations. Today, the regional government subsidises the hunting and promotes the cuisine (*gibier ryori*). In the town of Kubokawa, local restaurants have turned the by-product of the pork industry into an enticing cuisine described in the first paragraph of this paper. What is remarkable is that raw pork offal dishes feature prominently in this cuisine, something unthinkable in any other cultural context.

At the Kochi cooking school, students sit quietly facing the instructor, a special guest from a famous establishment. Today's class is on *suppon ryori* or soft shell turtle cuisine. Our instructor pulls out a swarming creature from a box hidden beneath the table. He stabs the live softshell turtle in the neck and collects its blood in a bowl that he mixes with alcohol and hot water. He calls on tasting volunteers, but the classroom remains ghostly quiet. He points at me, the only foreigner in the classroom. I slowly walk up to the front of the class, look at the small cup with crimson liquid in it and down it in one gulp. Softshell turtle blood collected in this manner is usually the first dish of an elaborate stew. Drinking the blood is not only a delicacy; it is supposed to awaken a man's sexual drive. In Japan, there seems to be a link between offal eating, drinking and manliness. A popular item in grilled chicken skewer shops (*yakitoriya*) is chicken sternum and knee cartilage (*nankotsu*). The crunchy and charred snack is often accompanied by Japanese distilled liquor (*shochu*). Beef tendons braised in soy sauce (*gyusuji nikomi*) is another popular dish in Kochi drinking establishments. The tendons are cut into small pieces and cooked for hours so that they have a soft gelatinous texture. The saltiness of the soy sauce makes it a perfect drinking accompaniment. In this way, drinking establishments across Japan often offer menus centring on blood, cartilage and tripe.

Socially Constructed Tastes

In order to understand the success of offal cuisine in Japan, one must appreciate that, although the use of taste categories is universal, what determines good taste emerges out of a specific cultural context. Taste in Japan is as much a function of flavour as it is of texture. The Japanese language contains hundreds of words that describe texture, illustrating its nuanced importance within Japanese culture (Yoshikawa and others 1970). Culturally speaking, the Japanese palate is trained from an early age to be adventurous and to seek flavour, colour and textural diversity (Freedman 2015). Offal is an ideal ingredient as it adds a diversity of textures to a meal. In the Western context, texture is seldom included under the umbrella of taste, but it is evident that both are not mutually exclusive. For example, freshly baked bread is more palatable than bread that has been siting out all day in part because of the difference in texture. Recent studies also reveal that texture can affect the mechanics behind taste perception (Harker and others 2006). In Japan, offal cuisine is desirable in part because people seek these unique textures that are difficult to reproduce elsewhere. With offal dishes each bite is different as, for example, braised tendon and fried cartilage usually also carry bits of flesh and fat, which help contrast each bite. In a sense, offal is good because one can taste a wide array of textures ranging from chewy to crunchy.

In Japan, normally rejected foods are often endowed with health attributes. Offal is touted as helping to build physical and mental 'stamina'. Certain foods are particularly suited to relieving tiredness infusing new vigour (*sutamina*) in the person that consumes it. Most Western foods, and in particular meat, were adopted in Japan as part of the imperative to modernize and to increase the strength of the Japanese population and its army (Cwiertka 2007). Offal cuisine would later inherit these same characteristics, providing sustained levels of energy to the exhausted Japanese workforce. For this reason, offal cuisine was initially a popular food for blue-collar Japanese men. Most recently, products containing collagen have been extremely popular amongst Japanese women. Although the link between beauty and youth and collagen consumption has been undermined by scientific research, most Japanese consumers associate the elasticity of the skin with its consumption. In the region of Kochi, the traditional dish of broiled moray eel (*utsubo*) is sought out for its skin, which is purported to contain much collagen. Offal cuisine has attached itself to the recent popularity of collagen-rich foods becoming a favourite for young urban women. The Japanese media plays a large role in helping spread dubious information about the age defying and weight loss properties of these foods. For example, fermented soybeans (*natto*) was sold out in groceries stores following false news reports that its daily consumption made you lose weight. The media is tapping into the already widely held cultural belief that the most undesirable foods possess powerful health qualities that one can almost taste.

Offal cuisine in Japan arose less as a necessity than as a function of Japan's specific cultural views on waste. Unlike in Europe, where offal had been considered a poor man's food, Japan only adopted meat eating at the end of the nineteenth century and in smaller quantities so that a distinction between different cuts of meats never fully cemented itself. In the Japanese kitchen, a paramount rule is to never let any leftover food go to waste. Cross scoring the base of bamboo shoots to make them less tough or deep frying fish scales to use as toppings are two of the ways Japanese cuisine recycles unwanted parts because not to do so would be considered *mottainai*, a term used in Japanese to convey a sense a regret concerning wastefulness. For example, wasting time idling or throwing away leftover food is considered *mottainai*. The expression has its roots in the combination of religious beliefs of Buddhism and Shintoism that value the sacredness of all things material. Nowadays, *mottainai* has come to signify much more as it is believed to be a traditional cultural attitude unique to Japan. The *mottainai* attitude is firmly ingrained in Japanese culture and is relied upon to explain why Japanese people are better at recycling or eating every last grain of rice in a bowl. In Japan, discarding unwanted foods is not only wasteful, it is seen as irreverent. In a culture in which objects are believed to possess spirits, reclaimed food incorporates cultural values that one can taste. Offal cuisine not only fits the cultural expectation of parsimony, it tastes good precisely because it embodies respect for all things.

When my friend Yasu invited me to eat *Kubokawa* pork, he made a point to ask me if I ate meat. I noticed his puzzlement at my reaction of distress when I was presented with the various assorted cuts of offal. Why would someone who claims to love meat not be hungry for such a mouth-watering selection? I argue that the distinction between meat and organ meat is not as pronounced in Japan. Although in the Western context, attitudes toward offal have changed over time (Lloyd 2012; Mennell 1995), the separation between meat and non-meat remains clearly demarcated. This is not the case in Japan where meat and offal emerged out of a very different historical and cultural context. Until the modernization of the country, meat and offal was butchered and consumed by a social caste considered impure (*burakumin*). When animal consumption was introduced to the daily diet, it was consumed in such small amounts that a clear separation between meat and offal never fully materialized. In contemporary Japan, offal does not seem to suffer from lower status. For instance, grocery stores do not segregate offal from other meat on their shelves. In Kochi, it is quite common to find what looks like small orange grapes, in fact chicken ovaries (*chochin*), sold next to regular cuts of poultry. Unlike Western cuisine, Japanese offal cuisine does not attempt to transform offal into something different using elaborate sauces or preparation techniques. Instead offal are served in their simplest form, often grilled or in hot pots, with no attempt to camouflage its origins. Offal meats are therefore not seen as cheaper cuts that have to be tinkered with in order to make them palatable, but rather as delicious on their own.

Conclusion

Offal cuisine emerged in male working-class drinking establishments and to this day remains popular among this clientele. Although offal cuisine was developed in this specific social context, it has broadened its appeal to a larger spectrum of Japanese consumers. I have argued that offal eating in Japan is different from offal eating elsewhere. A hierarchy of animal cuts never fully cemented in the way it is socially stratified in Europe or America. The difference with Japan is precisely one of categorization. Foods that would be considered unfit for consumption in the Western context are deemed delicious in Japan. In this cultural setting, tripe, cartilage, skin and blood are not only considered edible, consumers value them. I argue that the Japanese consumer's desire to eat offal is not a result of social pressures but rather arises out of a genuine taste for it. This taste for offal can be better understood through the social construction of taste. Textures, health attributes, attitudes about waste and definitions of meat all play a role in explaining the popularity of offal cuisine in Japan. Offal cuisine is sought after because Japanese conceptions of taste are anchored in a web of ascribed values. Collectively, these elements manifest themselves in the form of a taste for offal cuisine, one that lives as much in the mind as on the tongue.

Bibliography

Bourdieu, Pierre. 1984. *Distinction: A Social Critique of the Judgement of Taste* (Cambridge, MA: Harvard University Press).

Cantarero, Louis, Jeremy MacClancy, C. Jeya Henry, Helen Macbeth, and others. 2009. 'From Edible to Inedible: Social Construction, Family Socialisation and Upbringing', in Jeremy MacClancy, C. Jeya Henry and Helen Macbeth (eds.), *Consuming the Inedible: Neglected Dimensions of Food Choice* (New York: Berghahn), pp. 205-14.

Chapman, David. 2006. 'Beyond the Colonised and the Colonisers: Intellectual Discourse and the Inclusion of Korean-Japanese Women's Voices'. *Japanese Studies*, 26.3: 353-63.

Cwiertka, Katarzyna. 2007. *Modern Japanese Cuisine: Food, Power and National Identity* (London: Reaktion Books).

Douglas, Mary. 2002. *Purity and Danger: An Analysis of Concepts of Pollution and Taboo* (London: Routledge).

Ducann, Charlotte. 1986. *Offal and the New Brutalism: A Book About Food* (London: David & Charles).

Elias, Norbert, Edmund Jephcott, Eric Dunning, Johan Goudsblom, and Stephen Mennell. 2000. *The Civilizing Process* (Oxford: Blackwell Publishers).

Freedman, Irith. 2015. 'Cultural Specificity in Food Choice – The Case of Ethnography in Japan', *Appetite*, September.

Harker, F. Roger, Rachel L. Amos, Gemma Echeverría, and F. Anne Gunson. 2006. 'Influence of Texture on Taste: Insights Gained During Studies of Hardness, Juiciness, and Sweetness of Apple Fruit', *Journal of Food Science* 71.2: S77-S82.

Harris, Marvin. 1998. *Good to Eat: Riddles of Food and Culture* (Long Grove, IL: Waveland Press).

Lloyd, Paul. 2012. 'The Changing Status of Offal'. *Food, Culture & Society* 15.1: 61-75.

Mennell, Stephen. 1995. *All Manners of Food: Eating and Taste in England and France from the Middle Ages to the Present* (Urbana: University of Illinois Press).

Rozin, Paul, and April E. Fallon. 1987. 'A Perspective on Disgust', *Psychological Review* 94.1: 23-41.

Rozin, Paul, and and T. A. Vollmecke. 1986. 'Food Likes and Dislikes', *Annual Review of Nutrition* 6 (1): 433-56.
Strong, Jeremy. 2006. 'The Modern Offal Eaters', *Gastronomica: The Journal of Food and Culture* 6.3: 30-39.
Toshio, Miyatsuka. 1999. 'Yakiniku–Savory Dish with Simple Origins', *Japan Quarterly* 46.4: 31.
Vialles, Noélie. 1988. '*La viande ou la bête*', *Terrain*, no. 10 (April): 86-96.
Yoshikawa, S., S. Nishimaru, T. Tashiro, and M. Yoshida. 1970. 'Collection and Classification of Words for Description of Food Texture', *Journal of Texture Studies* 1.4: 437-42.

Food Waste: Attitudes, Behaviours and Perceptions at Hamilton College

Eunice Lee

As my eyes scan the conveyor belt for a place to leave my empty plate, I take in the other dirty dishes steadily making their way back to the dish room. On one plate, I see a half-eaten pizza growing soggy in a pool of watery marinara sauce. On another, I see a quarter of a bagel sandwich sitting forlornly next to an unappetizing pile of scrambled eggs. I am astounded by how much uneaten food I see left behind. Unfortunately, the amount of waste I see here is not unique to this particular trip to the conveyor belt. In fact, the astonishing amount of plates that return to the kitchens of Hamilton College's two main dining halls still laden with food shows that our college community regularly discards edible food.

In the United States, nearly forty per cent of all available food is lost due to inefficiency along the supply chain.[1] Food waste is an on-going global dilemma that is just as ubiquitous on our small liberal arts campus in Clinton, New York. For members of the Hamilton community, this should be a huge concern, because wasting food also wastes the time, money and natural resources required to grow, harvest, transport and prepare our food. Furthermore, it contributes to climate change when food scraps decompose in landfills and emit methane gas.

Fortunately, our school has already taken a number of steps toward reducing this waste, or at least finding alternative uses for it, through food donations and composting. Student volunteer organizations, such as Hamilton Association for Volunteering, Outreach & Charity (HAVOC), The Harvest and Hamilton vs. Hunger, pack leftover dining hall food and donate up to a hundred meals each month to local senior centres and food banks. Meanwhile, the staff of Bon Appétit Management Company, the catering service employed by Hamilton, collects food scraps from the prep lines (mostly inedible pre-consumer waste) and dish rooms (mostly post- consumer leftover waste) of both Soper Commons Café and the Green Café at McEwen, the school's two main dining halls.[2] Employees of Physical Plant, the college's maintenance, grounds and operations body, then transport dumpsters filled with this waste to Ed Crane Farm, a neighbouring dairy farm, where it becomes composted as organic fertilizer. In recent years, Hamilton has been able to compost approximately 123.5 tonnes of food scraps annually.[3]

Nevertheless, many members of our college community remain unaware of not only these initiatives, but also the negative effects of wasting food. As an Environmental

Offal: Rejected and Reclaimed Food

Studies major attending Hamilton College, I attempt to understand the culture of waste that we live in and examine the ways we, as a campus community, consider wasted food by interviewing students, faculty and staff members across our community. By looking not at global trends of wasteful behaviour, but specifically at the attitudes of individuals on this particular campus, I come to realize how reducing food waste heavily depends on our personal ethics, motivation and interest in the matter.

Growing up, I was taught to eat everything on my plate. I didn't hear the 'there are starving children in Africa who are less fortunate than you are' line that guilted so many others into finishing their meals. Instead, my father told me in a very commanding tone that leaving food on my plate was wasteful. Anytime I left a few kernels of rice in my bowl or some uneaten vegetables in my soup, I was promptly scolded for my imprudence. The only time I was permitted to leave food on my plate was when I reached a point where I was forcing the last remaining bites into my mouth. If I had any leftovers, my dad would eat them.

As I grew older, my father became more lenient, allowing me to leave behind what I could not finish. This new tolerance might have come from our increasingly Americanized lifestyle, as our Korean heritage became less prominent in our lives in this land of 'plenty'. One sign of this change was in our dinners, which progressively featured more non-Korean dishes. My father, an immigrant to the United States, grew up in post-war 1970s South Korea. Until the end of the war, most Koreans lived poorly; the older generation, in particular, remembered how limited food was during both the Japanese occupation of the Korean peninsula and the Korean War. It makes sense then why my dad learned to eat everything that his mother served him, and why he has taught my sister and me to follow his practice.

All of this, though, I recognized in hindsight. When I was younger, aware of my dad's frugal character, I believed that his insistence on not wasting food was mostly due to his wanting to make the most of his money spent on groceries. I'm sure his personality has inevitably contributed to our family culture of not wasting food. It has certainly influenced my older sister, who admits that the main reason why she doesn't waste food is because she hates wasting her money. But, no matter how the three of us came to think this way, my family upbringing has impacted my perspective on food waste and created an impulse within me to end each meal with an empty plate both at home and at Hamilton.

Coming from a background different than most, I'm taken aback by the eating habits and culture of waste found at Hamilton College. How can people possibly think to throw away something that not only nourishes growth and survival, but also provides joy and comfort?

Food Waste:

In order to cater to the near two thousand people that circulate through the dining halls each day, the food served at Commons and McEwen seems to take on a form of seeming abundance. I say 'seeming' because the vegetables found in the salad bars, the meats served in the hot food lines and the bread located by the toasters are in fact limited resources that depend on our earth's ability to successfully produce the raw ingredients that make them up. This 'abundance' is represented by the buffets found in both cafeterias.

It becomes so easy to pile your plate with as much food as your eyes can see, whilst you navigate from the sandwich line, to the pizza counter, then to the dessert table. According to Derek Roy, Executive Chef of Bon Appétit at Hamilton, this buffet-style availability of food allows you to take more food than you can often finish. The all-you-can-eat setup of Commons and McEwen thus encourages us to try one dish after another. If we want more food, or if we don't like what we took, the possibility exists for us to take more food because it's made readily available. And whether we recognize it or not, the reassurance we might feel knowing that we can easily access food in the dining halls further perpetuates a sense of indifference toward campus food waste.

As students of Hamilton, we're obligated to participate in a meal plan, receiving seven, fourteen or twenty-eight meals a week, depending on which dormitory we live in. This system forces many of us to rely on dining hall food for sustenance, which in turn entails eating food that we may not always enjoy. More often than not, I hear students complain about how 'gross' the food is or how 'there's nothing good to eat'. As one friend says matter-of-factly, 'That's why I add hot sauce to everything'. But even with hot sauce, this friend, among other students, continues to leave food on her plate. Interestingly, two professors indicated that they find themselves clearing their plates more often at McEwen than at Commons because they prefer the food there. Faculty, I notice, don't often eat in the cafeterias, so they may have a rather skewed opinion about the food. Nevertheless, in addition to the vast availability of food options, taste preference is clearly another factor that influences wasteful behaviour at Hamilton.

As I begin paying more attention to my own and others' eating habits, I notice a third contributor of wastefulness: portion size. In some instances, we may be responsible for this waste by picking up too much food at once. One professor, for example, told me that she likes to take small samples from each food station, but doesn't finish everything on her plate. In other instances, how much food we get is out of our control. For example, a friend and I both received several spoonfuls of sautéed vegetables and rice, even when we asked for a 'little' of each. Then during lunch at McEwen one day, another friend showed me her plate and said, 'Look, I asked for a little spinach and they gave me so much. This *always* happens when I ask for just one dish,' she complained. 'I want to get other food from the salad bar or something, but they always think that I just want the dish that I asked for. It's so annoying, because now I can't finish it all.'

Perhaps it's not fair for my friend to judge the servers so harshly. After all, when there's a long line of hungry students waiting to get their food immediately served, it's difficult to scoop out regular portions. Even with less time pressure, it's just as challenging to dole out standard helpings. I myself discover this while packing containers of leftovers as a volunteer for HAVOC and The Harvest. Unless we vocalize more clearly how much we want, the servers will never know to give us more or less. But how hard would it be, really, to just say, 'That's enough'?

Through these interviews, I realized that it's not that people don't recognize food waste as problematic. It's more that people don't understand to what extent, or have difficulty articulating, why wasting food is bad. Moreover, they don't associate this issue with dining at Hamilton. For instance, one student never thought about the issue until I asked him about it. 'I don't really pay attention to what's on the conveyor belts,' he admitted, 'so I don't notice if people leave a lot of food on their plates.' Even some of the professors I spoke to believed that Hamilton didn't waste large amounts of food, adding that they also rarely pay attention to what's left on people's plates.

Of course, this does not imply that everyone wastes food and is completely naïve to the problem at Hamilton College. Two students even overemphasized, 'There's *so* much waste. It's terrible! *Every* plate is covered with uneaten food.' In truth, not every plate on the conveyor belts returns with leftovers. Yet this further illustrates how food waste is undoubtedly a concern that resonates more with certain individuals than others.

A variety of factors contribute to food waste, such as the dining hall buffets, taste preference, portioning and even the lack of time, which, while unmentioned above, is also relevant in student life. But, for those who feel indifferently towards food waste, how do we get them to start caring and increase their awareness of this issue? One way might be to conduct waste audits to physically demonstrate how much edible food we regularly toss out.

During one week in September 2014, Victoria Blumenfeld, a student member of Hamilton's chapter of Real Food Challenge, a collegiate network dedicated towards promoting sustainable foods, conducted a waste audit in Commons.[4] With a table set up by the conveyor belt leading into the dish room, Victoria had three separate bins to collect edible, inedible and miscellaneous waste. 'The miscellaneous one was really for napkins and other random trash, whereas the inedible one focused on bones and egg shells,' she explained. 'I had gloves and a big spoon so if people didn't want to do it themselves, I would separate their plate for them.'

For five consecutive days, Victoria patiently collected and weighed all of the waste returning to the conveyor belt during dinner service from 4:30 to 8:00 p.m. In total, 182 kilograms of food scraps were collected and 4667 people swiped their student cards to eat at Commons for dinner throughout this five-day period.[5] The results from this project alone are noteworthy. But, what's more remarkable is the range of reactions Victoria encountered while weighing people's waste.

'I'd say the responses were mainly split into three categories: supportive, neutral or no response and disgust,' she recounted. 'The people on the supportive end really appreciated the work and seemed genuinely interested in the project. A bunch of people would ask what I was doing and when I explained the idea behind it, they usually responded pretty positively. A couple of students would make a note of showing me their empty plate every day and excitedly saying something along the lines of "Clean Plate Club!" or "Look, no waste from me!"' In a different vein, 'the neutral people would just shove their waste in the bin without saying anything and didn't really seem interested,' she described.

What really struck me during our conversation, however, was the response she got from a minority of individuals 'that were truly grossed out by the whole thing and either ignored me or explicitly refused to participate'. During one dinner, in particular, two girls entered the dish room and one of them started walking over to Victoria with her plate. Suddenly, the second girl stopped her friend and said, 'No, what are you doing? We are *not* doing this. This is disgusting.' Both girls then proceeded to drop their plates on the rotating conveyor belt and walked away.

Hearing this, I was speechless. Was food waste truly so repulsing that it should incite such a reaction? Although it's reassuring to know that most students responded positively to Victoria's waste experiment, those that showed no interest or disgust should be encouraged to start caring about food waste, because this is a problem that requires collective attention and action both at and away from Hamilton College.

~

As global citizens, it's hard to deny that both helping those in need and inflicting as little harm as possible onto the environment we live in are good acts, morally just acts, in fact. So, why do we as a society not view wasting food as immoral? Why don't more of us consider carelessly throwing away edible food as potentially violating human and environmental ethics?

Philosophy professor Alexandra Plakias suggests three theories for why food waste might not be regarded as a moral problem. The first theory is supererogation, where a supererogatory act is a morally good act that goes beyond the call of action. In the case of food waste, and its associated social and environmental costs, donating leftover food and composting scraps can be seen as earning 'moral brownie points'. That is, they are actions that are morally good but not required for us to be considered morally upstanding citizens.

These acts are perhaps perceived as supererogatory because the negative effects of wasting food are less physically tangible than, say, seeing someone physically abuse an animal. 'We don't physically see any harm that would encourage or motivate us to reduce the harm produced from wasting food,' describes Professor Plakias. And the 'invisible' ways to reduce this harm are donating food, using natural resources more efficiently and reducing our contribution to methane gas emission.

A second theory is the socio-psychological phenomenon of moral licensing, where we do something positive (perhaps even morally right) to subconsciously discount any negative consequences that follow. 'For example, if we consume "right", by buying organically or humanely produced food,' Professor Plakias explains, 'We might feel that it's okay to waste our food because we already performed one "good" or "moral" act that day.'

We often forget that human exploitation of nature's resources impacts the health and sustainability of other living and non-living forms on this planet. Any harm that we directly or indirectly inflict onto our current environment will, in one way or another, negatively affect future generations. And if we believe that harming humans is morally wrong, then harming the environment ought to be considered just as unethical. Like with many of the environmental issues our current generation faces today, it's difficult to see the immediate effects of our 'good deeds', because our efficient use of aquifers in farming or decision to compost food scraps instead of throwing them into a landfill ultimately benefit future generations.

As Professor Plakias further adds, most of the ethics our society has grown up on are not fit for facing the issues of today. The US, for instance, was established on the political thoughts of Enlightenment thinkers, such as John Locke, who stated that you could take as many resources as you wanted, as long as you left behind 'enough and as good' as was available before.[6] This line of thinking was established during a period when natural resources – though not something early settlers should have abused – were plentiful and the population level relatively low. But in America today, our past generations' failure to leave behind 'enough and as good' as what they took has resulted in the growing limitation of natural resources. Moreover, our current generation is now responsible for figuring out how to address environmental issues, such as water scarcity and soil erosion from fertilizer overuse. How then do we get these ideas to resonate more with our society? Perhaps it's a matter of forming a memorable image of food waste.

~

When it comes to other environmental or food issues, we have a distinct image to attach to the problem. For instance, when you hear about the modern poultry industry, a gruesome image of thousands of chickens tightly imprisoned in battery cages might automatically come to mind. Or, when you hear about monoculture farming, you might imagine endless fields of wheat or corn. People seem to react viscerally to these images. But is there a way we can create that same sort of instinctive, emotional reaction to act on what we're seeing with an issue as complex as food waste?

Ryan Sutyla, student coordinator of HAVOC's food salving program, assuredly told me that guilt was not the way to go. 'I'm not a fan of getting kids more aware of food waste by weighing their food after dinner or lunch. I don't think it sends a good message. I think people get turned off by [these tactics] and don't internalize [anything transmitted this way].' He added, 'I don't think putting anything on one of these things,' picking up one of the clear plastic card-holders placed on every dining table, 'is gonna change anything either. It's like with recycling campaigns, if people want to recycle, they'll recycle'.

And when I asked about potential solutions, he responded, 'Food waste is not an issue that most Hamilton kids think about, for better or for worse. I don't think you're going to change that culture here or at any college campus. I think your best bet is to control it from a more Bon Appétit level, reusing food, thinking about how much they make, planning portions. I think the better way to go about it is to reduce the amount of food that's inherently in the dining halls at Hamilton or at any other college.'

In contrast to Ryan's belief, however, one faculty member insisted that guilt was, in fact, a very effective way to encourage others to reduce food waste. 'At home, I make sure to separate all of our recyclables,' she declared. 'But when my husband throws away something into the wrong bin, I feel very guilty because that product can eventually be recycled and used for something else. That guilt encourages me to continue making the right choices. And this same sort of feeling can help influence people's decisions to waste less food.'

But if guilt only temporarily sways our emotions or opinions, would assessing this issue through our personal values more effectively influence our attitudes toward food waste? Kirsten Kampmeier, former student manager of the Hamilton Community Farm, believes that it might.

Unlike most people I interviewed, Kirsten understands that food waste is a big enviro-ethical issue. As she states, 'It's bad to waste food because it's disrespectful to the people who helped grow your food, get it to you and cook it for you.' And if we're only in a position where we're going to consume this food, we ought to at least recognize and respect all the work that's put into this process. For Kirsten, she feels that it's difficult for people to become invested in an issue if they can't find something that compels them to act. 'For me, I know that I value the people in my life, food and soil, for instance,' she listed. 'Soil is, in many ways, the base of our existence – it gives us a place to stand and it grows the food that keeps us alive. Without healthy soil, we can't survive as humans.

'Knowing my own life ethics, and sticking to it, helps guide my life choices. Not everyone is going to value something, like soil, as I do. But, I think if people can find what they value – like people, for example, because everyone values their family and friends – and get behind that and consider how their choices can affect *their* people, maybe they'll become encouraged to care for the environment, waste less food or care about any other social issue that needs attention.'

There's no definite answer for how to waste less food and motivate others to be mindful of their consumption and waste management habits. Institutions, companies, organizations and even political bodies have a responsibility to find and establish solutions that work best for them. But no matter what these policies or programs are, the success of these resolutions will also depend on our personal receptiveness to this problem, because we all hold different values and come from diverse backgrounds. The most effective way for our campus, regional, national and global communities to reduce food waste, then, will come from our own initiative and investment, while the foundation for larger waste reduction practices are also in place.

Different groups and individuals across the Hamilton College community are already doing their part to minimize the food waste generated in Commons and McEwen, following the solutions for waste management suggested by most studies.[7] Student volunteer organizations pack, freeze and deliver edible leftovers to local senior centres and food banks. Moreover, Bon Appétit and Physical Plant workers collect pre- and post-consumer waste from the kitchens and dish rooms of both dining halls and transport it to a local farm for composting.

On the Bon Appétit level, employees have also taken additional measures to reduce the amount of excess food by cooking in smaller batches and eliminating all the trays in the dining halls. Studies have shown that people take less food when they don't have trays to pile food on top of in all-you-can-eat settings, such as school cafeterias.[8] And from what Chef Derek Roy has seen over the years, our school has been able to cut losses on both food and water used for cleaning trays. Other strategies include freezing in-season fruit to use during later months and pressing blemished, overripe or leftover fruits and vegetables for juices in McEwen as part of their participation in the corporation's national Imperfectly Delicious Produce program.[9]

Upon hearing this, you might consider Hamilton to be doing a remarkable job at managing its leftovers and food scraps. And you might be right. Not every school, organization or business in America can boast of having such programs. But even with these food salvaging and composting initiatives in place, we shouldn't rely on these structures and the 'hidden' post-consumer labour of Bon Appétit and Physical Plant as the only solutions to food waste. That is, we ought not to think that wasting food is acceptable because there are alternative uses for food scraps, or other measures for getting leftover food consumed. Therefore, in addition to setting up food donating and composting systems, reducing food waste more efficiently at Hamilton College will rely on the individual motivation, dedication, care and understanding of each college community member, and especially those that eat in the cafeterias.

Developing a habit takes a lot of self-determination. If you're not accustomed to cleaning your plate, or feeling compelled to do so, wasting less food as you consume can take a lot of effort. However, we ought to try and eat, to the best of our abilities, as much of what is on our plates as possible. We ought to take only as much as we can finish and ask for smaller portions. We ought to handle food more carefully and drop less food (on the counters and floor) as we make our way through the buffets. We ought to prepare less food in the first place. We ought to promote less wasteful and irresponsible behaviour by raising more awareness about not only the magnitude of the social, environmental and ethical implications of wasting food, but also the types of food waste management practices that exist on campus. In doing so, people can then become invested in food recovery or composting projects if they so choose. Finally, we ought to encourage more conversations about food waste and teach more students to value food or each component of the food cycle. If we can inspire people throughout the community to think before and after they eat, we might be able to change our campus attitude towards food waste, one person at a time.

Although I, as well as those interviewed for this research, may have become more cognizant of the problems and solutions surrounding food waste at Hamilton, I strongly believe that the information gathered for this particular project is just a starting point for adding more to the multifaceted story of food waste on our campus. Reaching 'zero waste' is a lofty goal that we, as a community, will never reach. But, as I step away from this project, looking at my own eating and waste reducing habits, I cannot help but now think in terms of 'ought'. I only hope that others will begin to think this way as they continue their lives at and away from Hamilton College.

Acknowledgements

Thank you to Franklin Sciacca, Lucas Phillips, Naomi Guttman and Carolyn Dash for reviewing portions of this manuscript. Appreciation also goes to Alexandra Plakias, Kirsten Kampmeier, Victoria Blumenfeld, Don Croft, Derek Roy, Tim Gadziala, Ryan Sutyla and my other anonymous interviewees for providing me with information for this paper.

Notes

1. K.D. Hall, J. Guo, M. Dore and C.C. Chow, 'The Progressive Increase of Food Waste in America and Its Environmental Impact', *PLoS One*, 4.11, e7940 (2009) <http://dx.doi.org/ 10.1371/journal.pone.0007940> [accessed 12 October 2015].
2. Soper Commons Café and the Green Café at McEwen dining halls are more colloquially known as 'Commons' and 'McEwen', respectively.
3. Physical Plant keeps a record of how much waste they manage, but only the data from fiscal years (FY) from 2013 to 2015 contain information on composting. The data from these three periods are used to calculate an approximation of how much food the school typically composts annually. Hamilton composted 131.0 tonnes of organic food waste during FY 2013, 131.4 tonnes in FY 2014 and 108.2 tonnes in FY 2015; these figures average to 123.5 tonnes.
4. This waste audit focuses on waste solely from Commons, because, as the largest dining hall on campus, it provides the most representative information about how much food is typically wasted during dinnertime, the busiest meal period, according to Chef Derek Roy.
5. These results do not reflect whether all of the people who swiped into Commons actually stayed in the dining hall to eat their meal. Some students may have entered Commons to pick up food and leave immediately. Additionally, these numbers do not reveal if students re-swiped their cards to eat at Commons a second time, the maximum number of times students can re-enter a dining hall during

one meal period.
6. Alex Tuckness, 'Locke's Political Philosophy', in *The Stanford Encyclopedia of Philosophy*, ed. Edward N. Zalta <http://plato.stanford.edu/entries/locke-political/> [accessed 31 March 2016].
7. For an extensive list of waste reducing strategies, refer to: Dana Gunders, 'Wasted: How America Is Losing Up to 40 Percent of Its Food from Farm to Fork to Landfill', Natural Resources Defense Council (2012) < https://www.nrdc.org/sites/default/files/wasted-food-IP.pdf> [accessed 31 March 2016].
8. Jonathan Bloom, *American Wasteland* (Cambridge, MA: Perseus Books Group, 2010), p. 241.
9. In May 2014, Bon Appétit Management Company's Vice President of Strategy Maisie Ganzler launched the company's national Imperfectly Delicious Produce program to save 'cosmetically challenged produce from going to waste'. Hamilton's Bon Appétit staffs at McEwen use blemished, overripe or leftover produce in pressed juices as a way to participate in this program ('Imperfectly Delicious Produce', Bon Appétit Management Company <http://www.bamco.com/timeline/imperfectly-delicious-produce/> [accessed 7 October 2015]).

Pig, Pork, Prep, Print: Cochon555 and Whole Animal Cookery Discourse

Robert McKeown

The pig is getting a tattoo. It's true: a three hundred-pound, Florida-raised Black Hoof is in the middle of being inked. Armed with his needle, the artist assigned to the specimen slowly works his way into the flap of meat on the side of the pork belly. A clutch of almost one hundred people – some eyeing the beast, others concentrating on glasses of pinot noir or toothpicked slices of blood sausage – peer on with a mix of curiosity and amazement. With a name like a gang (or perhaps a blues band), a team of butchers known as the Miami Smokers wait in a semi-circle just behind the beast, taking turns with hack saws and cleavers. They're all bearded and tattooed themselves. On a stage behind them a group of bartenders are busy crafting a series of cocktail punches. All are there to offer their creative culinary services up in honour of the very animal at the centre of it all.

This is just a moment of the action at the Miami version of Cochon555. In nine years, it has gone from being a curious upstart to one of North America's most thoughtfully staged and rightfully popular culinary events. It's breadth of competing stars – who are clustered in groups of five in parallel competitions – culled from across the spectrum of food, wine, cocktail and farming communities rivals some of the biggest events in the country. But unlike other celebrity-mad events in its category, Cochon555 has gotten deeper as it has gotten older, not just more famous. As Cochon555 founder Brady Lowe likes to say, it has moved into a romantic phase with an emphasis on education.

The concept is simple. Chefs apply in every city, usually by the dozens. Five are eventually chosen based on their acumen, marketability and gastro-potential to make things, well, deep – to form their own opinions and, through their food, to re-shape and inspire those of tens of thousands of others. One week before the event, an in-state (often in-county) farmer delivers a roughly two hundred-pound heritage pig to the doorstep of the chosen chef. Beginning then, they have a week to come up with five to six dishes using the whole animal. First they must serve a composed plate to twenty-four judges during an eight-minute window. Then they must deliver 450 portions to a crowd numbering between five and six hundred guests.

Butchery is the least of their worries. What if the blood is not set and the pig is not as clean as they like? What if it has high water content, eliminating certain preferred cooking methods? Will that cost them a day – or three? Where to store such a carcass, especially in small restaurants with smaller walk-in fridges and cutting tables, if they have them at all? Odd bits may be popular, but there's just one tail, two ears, one tongue and two cheeks to go around – what to serve to whom? And when…and how? Some breeds have copious fat; others are leaner. The coming days are a hectic combination of logistics, creativity, instinct and reaction and problem-solving, all of which hopefully lead to a winning combination.

Event creator/owner Brady Lowe planned it precisely so. Like a film director, Lowe has a commanding presence, eyes that heat-seek onto details others don't see – plates that are not bio-degradable, ice cut in the wrong shape – and a scholar's knowledge about the context of his chosen field. He throws words like romance, discourse, education and cutting pig out there in humble, symbolic piles that then grow different meanings for different members of his audience. Raised in Iowa, he's at ease with pig farmers. Forged and shaped by the big personalities of the Atlanta corporate and hospitality worlds, he's also adept at commanding a room full of gastronomical alpha figures. He talks early hip-hop history with his foodie DJs and has a familial warmth about him that is, in many ways, the fuel for the cohesive core that keeps Cochon555 from becoming another sprawling, liquor-juiced fraternity party for the gourmet classes.

For Lowe and his participants, the event is more a process and hyper-local expression than it is a yearly happening for the dine-out set in sixteen cities. Interested in the meaning and the message, he hopes Cochon555 remains larger than him and its kitchen talents as the brand gains reflexive fame in the greater media world. It's as much about going backwards to a more honest, rural approach as it is about leveraging the shiny, happy, adolescent stage glamour and chic of the Americana culinary scene. His charity, Piggy Bank, provides farmers with heritage breed piglets in exchange for posting their business plans online. Ask him about the Iowa farm he is developing to raise them on, and it sounds like an elite boarding school for animals, trumpeting its credentials, diversity and idealism.

The Cochon555 process demands that chefs – and diners – stop and think. It forces them to confront how each animal demands certain preparations over others; how certain breeds take better to regional climates than others; how the shape and size and genetics of a certain might force conceptual forks in the road – emphasize fat or muscle, cut with acid or extend with sweetness – when they least expect it. As much as chefs like to play the unflappable master of their domain, any one who has ever worked in a professional kitchen will tell you they are just as much at the hands of suppliers, the air-conditioned mega-market aisles and neon-lit landscapes of pre-packaged commodity cuts and specials as a budget shopper. Mom, after all, doesn't worry quite as much as being put on COD or having the electricity turned off if she comes in 3% under budget.

My own personal history with offal goes back as far as my first memories in Montreal, at age four, when in protest I would not come down if my parents cooked beef liver. All the parts of the pig staring back at me in Mafia-owned, pork-centric butcher shops in New Jersey was a sort of bridge towards everyday embrace of their dizzying range of textures and flavours. I first remember the actual word offal when it appeared as its own category on the mid-90s menus of chef Lydia Shire's Biba in Boston. In a city known for staid, Catholic palates, she championed hearts (veal and duck) and minds (pigs and veal brains) and sold them out nightly.

Still, I didn't work offal into my regular consumption rotation until I discovered late-night Taiwanese cooking in Boston's Chinatown a year or two later – steaming soups of intestines and crispy ears laced with bracing hits of chilli and black vinegar and, my favourite, duck tongues. With the budget of a cook/writer, the price of the odd bits was definitely right. If Boston demystified the idea of eating the whole pig, living in Bangkok normalized and elevated it for me. One of my weekly indulgences was kway chap, a black pepper-singed broth where you chose the pig parts of choice – tongue, ear, blood and intestines for me – and the vendor mixed them with shocked white, hand-rolled rice noodles. Careful doses of chilli vinegar punched it up even more, while white rice served as an alternate canvas for the palate, focusing the pops and chews and mineral-y undertones of the offal-packed soup.

Image wise, to this day whenever I think of whole animal eating, I also think about a setting naturally suited to theatrical cooks and serving stations, raised central platforms for animal display and finishing flourishes courtesy of a chef/whole animal auteur. A few that come to mind: the braised lamb's head that is the piece de resistance of the Jemaa El Fnaa in Morocco, where each cook seemingly anoints the face section of your choice with a careful spoon caress, smoke mingling with the glare of the exposed neon overhead, and the odd but addictive combo of fresh, acid-sweet orange juice cutting animal fat in one's mouth. In Bangkok, my favourite kway chap vendor set up in front of an Old Deco theatre and served from a podium he set up for himself. He always seemed to unravel his smile broader and brighter the more adventurous parts one chose. Like Christmas memories in the mind's eye of a child, these images danced in my head as I followed Cochon555 online in the last half of the decade I lived abroad.

So when I saw the elegant, curvaceous letters that form the word offal load onto the Oxford Symposium website as the theme for 2016, I knew I had to find a way to make it my object of study. What Cochon555 represents is a perfect storm of diner interest, media attention, chef platforms, idealism and event-driven opinion shaping that is why North America has become such an incubator for global dining trends – even ones they don't necessarily start. My personal research resides at the intersection of food, communication and culture. More precisely, I am as interested in the power of food to bring people together in the name of culture as I am in the crucial power of food journalism and media to exponentially multiply the power of dining and diners. Early food writing was as much about personal experience as anything. In the 70s and 80s and early 90s, the role of food critics brought the restaurant into full view as a social institution. Nowadays, it's not just about experience, but also about narratives. Who shapes the story? How do they shape it? In what way do audience reactions compound or deliver a multiplier effect? And at what point and in what way do the actual experiences of consumption sites (restaurants) and happenings (Cochon555) bring these disparate strands together to further shape opinion? Most of all, does it matter?

I hope that this paper can bring to bear what I've gained in time spent across some pretty vast parts of the world and the food cultures they represent. I hope the focus on experience and on certain opinion-makers, thrust into high-pressure setting of improvisation, will provide a fun and original way to inquire into how the pig in particular has taken up a powerful spot in the American culinary imagination. I hope to challenge how valuable chefs are to any process of education or evolution in our food world, but also how important it is to challenge them back – what can they learn? What about the normally glossed mistakes they inevitably make in a live setting like Cochon555? The idea is not to criticize. It is instead to examine ourselves as crucial players in the greater process of building knowledge and a better community with it in hand.

The Why – Events, Guests, Chefs and Meaning-Making

Cochon555 is more than just a space where food is consumed. It is also wholly unlike the celebritized food-and-wine bashes where thousands of people wait in interminable lines for sexed-up burgers and a chef selfie – they stay within the scripted eat-ogle-sip-leave confines of event-dom. Cochon555 is a site of both meaning-making and world-making, and every event also sets the stage for the construction of the producer-to-guest relationship differently. In each city, Cochon555 re-invents itself in ways that are hyper-local. New farmers – and thus specific breeds befitting the locale's climate – are engaged. Narratives and storylines produced by the character of each city bubble up from below and take the form of culinary influences or cocktail flavour profiles. Regional producers (cheesemakers, distillers) work across lines of kitchen and bar to help best express the terroir of their given swath of agricultural sites.

The process of gastronomic inclusion or exclusion dictates the what and the how of dishes served to Cochon555 guests, whether pig parts, heirloom vegetables or native spices. From menu language and graphical layout to plating standards and textures, each producer must make conscious choices about where to get what ingredients, how to prep, cook and present them and what stories and narratives to ultimately use to connect with guests. In the larger foodscape, this applies not just to those present on the floor the day of the competition, but to potential or virtual guests who read about such experiences by seeing online videos or Instagram posts featuring chefs or sommeliers as they contribute – in just one of many forums – to building a reflected reputation not just in person, but in persona.

The How – Cuisine as Relation + Other Theoretical Works

Through exploration and discussion of the aforementioned players, I would like to engage an idea from the academic discipline of literary studies. I should note that, while I have worked as a writer and journalist, I have never formally studied this discipline. Which is why this theory appeals to me: I think it is readily understood and approachable. I first encountered the idea in question in an essay by Shu-Mei Shih (2013) proposing a way of investigating the cultural forces behind different works in the same genre, one she terms Comparison as Relation. While comparative literature about former Colonial subjects is the object of Shih's arguments (79), in the pages that follow comparative cuisine as it relates to whole pig cookery – or Relational Cooking – will be explored within both the content of individual events and, through comparison, with events over a period of roughly five years. In her essay, Shih uses what she terms an integrative world historical lens to help tease out the connections between Colonial subjects in geographically and culturally different scenarios. Her essay takes in a broad sweep of European, Asian and Caribbean history and fictional literature using these locations to examine the lives of the characters lies at the core of her discussions. In contrast, this paper will develop its own act of Relational Cooking based upon the working chefs, sommeliers and bartenders who interact with the diners of different markets and engage them as hosts, creators and personalities. While Shih takes as her concern Colonial and national histories and unites them through comparison, we will examine the journeys of our chef/creators as they relate to the pig as an animal and provider of cooking context and subject in relation to their own set of geographic and gastronomic circumstances.

There is a geographic and cultural specificity in the way the chefs and creators of Cochon555 work – in each case, very differently in each city with a pig as common canvas. This must be considered on two levels. First, how does the chef serve as a translator of an agricultural product – in this case, the pig? What narratives does he attempt to create and what stories does he tell? Is this a one-off for the event? Is it connected to their restaurant brand, or on a broader scale to their city or culture of origin? Second, how far can we take the comparison of the various creators and competitors of Cochon555 – and event director Brady Lowe – to the film studies idea of the director as auteur, or someone who carries out a vision by capitalizing on their ability to control almost all crucial aspects of the process of creation? Another important aspect of Cochon555 is that, unlike Shih's authors, all the subjects at hand for this paper are creatively active on a daily basis, translating fresh product into plated cuisine and representing their own personal philosophies and experiences for thousands of diners a week. Even if food is relational, it is also always in process.

Like toasting spices for to enhance and deepen their flavour, various aspects of other theoretical works will be used in order to attend to the particular approach and construction taken by Cochon555 chef-competitors in relation to whole pig cookery. Ulf Hannerz's interview on transnational cosmopolitanism (Rantanen 2005) will be drawn upon to bolster the idea of chefs as culinary cosmopolitans. Philosopher Kwame Anthony Appiah's essays promoting cosmopolitan acts as noble and with respect to cultural interests and beliefs, while recognizing 'the practices and beliefs that lend them significance' (2006: XV), provide an idealist and humanist way of looking at the world at large. I will also consider the inter-connected roles of diners; the farmers who raise the animals they ingest; the opinion-shaping events and social media platforms through which they are textualized; and the social imaginaries they create surrounding modern North American food culture. Events and dining rooms are, after all, wholly social and modern arenas. Priscilla Parkhurst Ferguson, in her book on the importance and persistence of food talk, illuminates the binary nature of culinary experiences:

> When we ask ourselves [...] where this food world is headed, we come up against the persistence of the fundamental oppositions [...] cooking versus chef-ing, formality versus informality, tradition versus invention, culinary individualism versus conspicuous production, haute cuisine versus haute food, gluttony versus gastronomy, the virtual food of talk versus the material food in the oven or on the plate. (2014: 195)

The What – Menus + Narratives

Besides the daily acts of eating and cooking, the most important form that food experiences take is when they are recorded in texts. Seemingly simple, when put into print a dish or a meal is inscribed and given permanence in a way that allows vast audiences to then engage with it over and over, one modifying the other in meaning through each encounter or related act of commentary. By recording their creator's intention, printed menus, articles and blog or social media posts serve as reference points – signposts really, leading to the next culinary step – in the consumption process. Readers, diners, guests or anyone interested in eating can interact with and join a broader discussion on, say, a chef's representation of their cuisine – at least the way they see or describe it. It is here where the ideas of an event like Cochon555 take shape, perhaps innocently during the event, but gaining dimension beyond just being food talk and taking on discursive elements in their relation to agriculture, farmers or the culinary nature of a certain city at a certain time.

Like a semiotician's map, menus also provide sets of signs and symbols that help guide and influence customers and cue those serving or cooking them. Linguist Dan Jurafsky contextualizes the menu as such: 'every time you read a description of a dish on a menu you are looking at all sorts of linguistic clues' (2014: 9). For example, what if a Cochon555 chef chooses to write his menu notepad-style rather than use printed fonts, resulting in something proprietary: slightly slanted, maybe chunky lettering, seemingly screaming 'Hey, relax, this is Everyday Stuff you're eating. You'll like it!' Such a mix of anglicized direct or shorthand descriptions can also operate on multiple textual and symbolic levels. Dish names are in all-upper case and bold print, while dish descriptions are in lighter block lettering. When guests approach the tables, they are also able to use the printed menu as a jumping-in point for initiating conversation, asking, for example, for further explanation from sommeliers of cooks as to whether dishes have certain flavour profiles, origins, ties to authenticity or connections to the creator's past or current body of work.

Pig x City x Year – A Framework for Analysis

By challenging each chef to stay within the same technical format and to use the same animal, Cochon555 actually represents an ideal set of conditions for comparison. That's because it is a fairly controlled setting – the same product, time frame for preparation, eight-minute window for serving to judges. Further, by returning to the same cities in different years, there are also grounds for a relational exploration of when Cochon555 was held and how it has evolved throughout the years. Though the chefs are different, by working in the same city, they are exposed to the same types of ideas – and often form similar habits – as their peers. Cooking communities always imitate. There are finite pools of talent to hire from and limited places (culinary schools, prominent restaurants) in which cooks can be trained. The same few thousand diners form the base of regulars that very much define not just the reservation books of Cochon555's pool of restaurants, but the chatter surrounding food that so often shapes culinary scenes.

Assuming the above context, I did a quantitative content analysis of Cochon555 menus from the years 2011 to 2016. The goal was to see how the chef-community learned and adapted throughout the years. Here are some of the things I looked for: What parts of the pig tended to show up more or less than others? Did the chefs cook in the same style as they do at their restaurants? How was the locale of the event reflected in the content or gastronomical story told (or not) through the menus? Did any cultures dominate over others? Were the menus organic in their approach or a curated mix of cultural, personal or narrative approaches? By considering chefs as translators and/or auteurs, the way these ideas are represented (or not) on menus goes a long way towards measuring how Cochon555 has evolved – elevating the conversation around whole animal cookery, heritage breeds and safer, more honest farming.

Cochon555 Coded: Menus 2011 to 2016

Cultural Context
Did the chefs establish a connection to some type of greater food culture in the body of their pig cookery at Cochon555?

Restaurant Connection
Was the food the chef at issue cooked connected to or an obvious extension of the style presented by their restaurants in day-to-day menus?

Storyline
Did the Cochon555 menu of the chef in question show an obvious storyline connecting at least four of the five dishes? One dish was discounted as, in some cases, desserts tended to get off message.

Urban Relations

In style or references, did at least three of the five dishes on the menu exhibit a link to the culinary lifeblood of the city? This could be historic, signature dish-related or exemplary of a greater style of cooking the hub in question is known for.

Below, the results are shown in a series of graphs. Note the across-the-board rise in all categories over a five-year period.

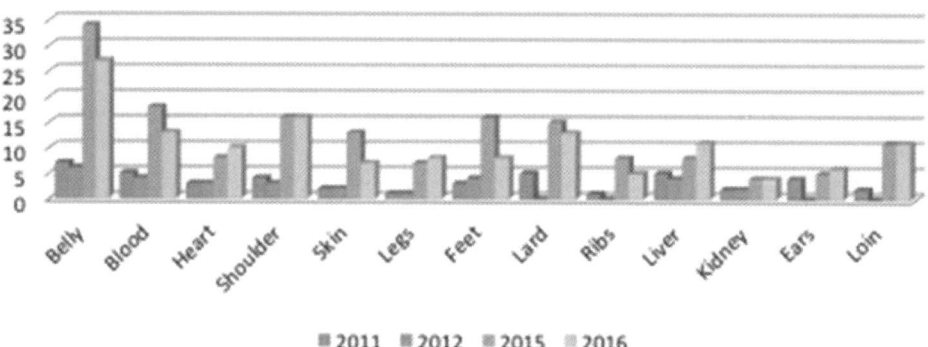

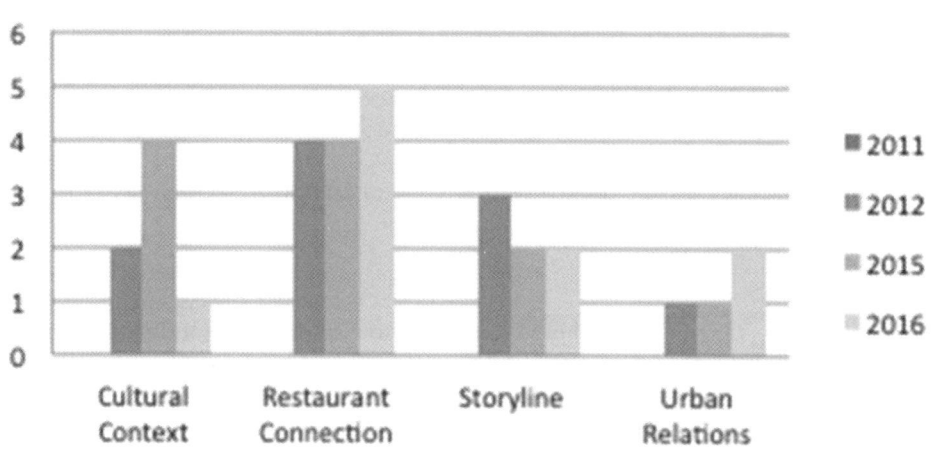

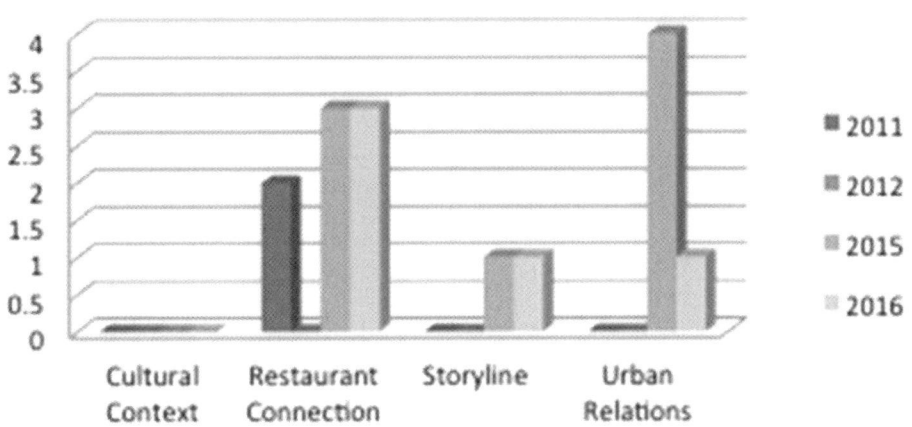

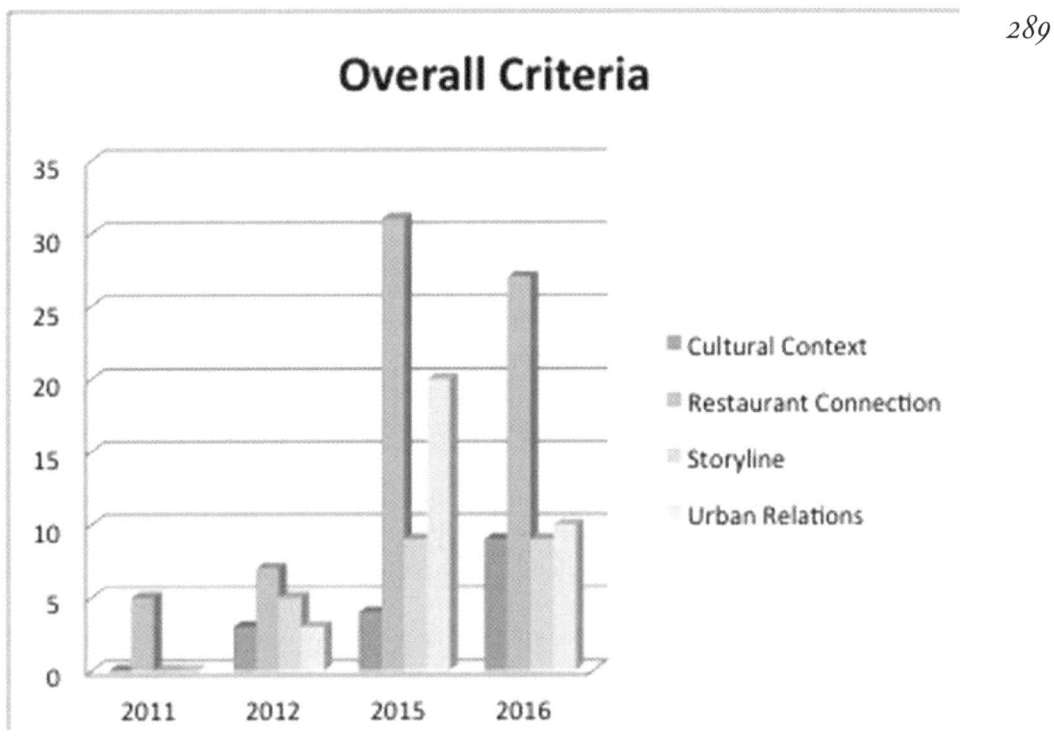

Offal: Rejected and Reclaimed Food

To Connect and To Frame

With its amplification of restaurant industry power and attachment to the pork-centric ways of chefs in the past decade, Cochon555 may at first seem like just another hip event. But that is not the case – it goes way beyond that identification in content and in meaning. By challenging chefs to combine an understanding of technical cooking, butchery, sourcing and thoughtful creation, the event operates at the junction of the personal and the cultural. To perform well, each chef must exhibit an understanding of the social conditioning that's made cooking pig a must for any restaurant kitchen. To win, they must go deeper than this, attaching themselves to geography and narratives that connect their day-to-day cooking with concerns surrounding locality, food cultures and whole-animal utilization.

By analyzing the frames which Cochon555 chefs applied to give their body of cooking salience and comparing them across a gap of time that could be measured in notable changes in restaurant concerns and trends, it is possible to see meaningful changes in how cooking is approached. This evolution is also reinforced by the food talk surrounding such menus at the event and in online and social media forms. Culture, narratives, concerns of sourcing, connection to the urban or regional environment – the menu content study shows generally rising concerns across-the-board in every category that was coded for.

In 2012 New City, for example, the menus revealed nothing much more than cooking for cooking's sake – not much more of an aim than tasting good. Only two of five chefs established a link to a specific food culture, and only one chef seemed to reveal the stylish and contemporary NYC way that's brought the city such dining fame. Consider the eclectic jumble of 2012 dishes from one particular chef (theme in parentheses): pig's head pastrami (Jewish deli), raw taylor bay scallop with trotter ragout (upscale Southern-tinged comfort), *puerco en salsa verde* (vaguely Latin). Now compare that to the red thread of dedicated food and taste cultures running through the 2015 presentations. Danji offered an Urban Manhattan take on Korean: classic head cheese with Chinese mustard and cucumber kimchi and pig trotters texturally counterpointed by cabbage salad and radish Kimchi. Or the cheeky gastronomic dive into the all-day breakfast culture espoused by New York's diners and delis, given porky dimension by the Cannibal Inn: a bread basket with pan au chocolate au bacon or a Cotechino 'McMuffin', an offal-stuffed breakfast sausage sandwich with an 'haute' bordelaise twist on ketchup.

Almost a decade into existence, Cochon555 chefs know that to find a way to strongly represent their brand of food means they must use each individual plate to establish connections well beyond their kitchens – to the nature of each heritage breed pig, to their agricultural region, to dining culture, even to the flavours of other countries. Taken individually, the best among them are able to tell a personal tale that illuminates their own version of cultural translation, culinary authenticity and chef-identity that is in constant interaction with the dining public and on-going concerns around the nature and importance of food, products and cuisine. Whether by city or by chef (or winemaker…or barkeep…or sommelier), each Cochon555 creator must be evaluated relationally – their cuisine's context a function of time and space in relation to other chefs, near and far. By choosing a particular culture from which to draw inspiration – New York breakfast culture, high-altitude Italian white wine varietals – and then applying it to let the taste and nature of heritage breed pigs shine brightest, they join a process that is larger than any one person or plate at any one time.

In the Name of Amplification – Audiences and Mediation

While love of food and pork may be the obvious features of the Cochon555 audience, every city produces a unique relationship between their local product, their chefs and their diners. There are five to six hundred guests at most events, twelve hundred at others, throughout sixteen to twenty cities a year. Thirty per cent of those involved come from industry, meaning over a hundred chefs, cooks and restaurant owners bolster the potential for influencing at each event due to their outsize demographic ability to hold sway over others. But these numbers pale in relation to the virtual community of social media followers and message-producers – a true gastronomic public - who are, in the week of each event, hyper-active in the blogosphere. Any given competing chef, farmer or winemaker averages in the tens of thousands of social media followers, as does Cochon555 itself. Hundreds, often thousands, of likes and posts are made the day of the event. With each passing year – and every Cochon555 tour cycle – the messages that are the object of consumption by the virtual foodie classes become more specific in their content and more informed by research, culture and community.

Initially fed by the ideas of historically and agriculturally concerned writers such as Michael Pollan, Wendell Berry, Amy Trubek and Mark Kurlansky, the conversation in even popular food and cooking magazines has now transferred its focus from chefs and trends to farmers, agriculture, foodways and meaning. While it is important to note that events such as Cochon555 and the restaurants they promote are still wholly upper middle-class sites for engagement and experience, this does and should not discount the way they seek to empower and valorize ideas that are not just about marking difference, but making one in profound ways. These include demands to know where food comes from and where and how it is raised, ideas about and emphasis on local sourcing, the desire for heritage breed animals, the promotion and execution of whole animal cookery and the greater issue of protecting and producing all these ideas in relation to a safer and more open food system in the future.

As a universal form of consumption, eating is a mandatory act for human survival, at once highly pleasurable as an endeavour and also an integral part of a larger, globalized socio-cultural system with a political economy all its own. As a way of meaning-making, the study of food represents a way in which people created worlds of their own where foodways become, as Lucy Long writes, 'a network of activities and systems – physical, social, cultural, economic, spiritual and aesthetic' (2004: 23). Given the results of the quantitative and framing analysis in this paper, it can be argued that the pursuit of flavour and a desire to connect emotionally – and for some intellectually – are common concerns uniting diners and chefs. How they go about establishing, digesting (in the mind and the body) and reacting to such connection points, however, is where the ultimate power to influence thinking about heritage breed farming and whole pig cookery movement lies.

Theorists such as James Clifford (1997) have promoted the idea of using chronotopes –settings in which human subjects can be examined in similar social conditions. In this vein, this paper has cast Cochon555 as a culinary arena in which socio-cultural meaning and related ideas are consumed, experienced and even produced, in reality and symbolically. Given limited space, this paper used a combination of ethnographic observation, content analysis and framing analysis. The way cooking was conducted in relation to the Cochon555 challenge – cook a whole pig in six dishes in one week for at least four hundred and fifty people – provided a meaningful entry point for larger discussions about what eating and drinking a certain way means to us as humans. Food and menus, then, can function as 'texts' and are themselves sites for cross-cultural engagement and mediation. Given the intensely personal nature of dining, they also allow for a particular relationship with each individual eater and/or reader. James Carey, in his treatise *Communication as Culture*, sums up the layered dynamics behind the human relationship to communication forms: 'To study communication is to examine the actual social process wherein significant symbolic forms are created, apprehended, and used […]. We create, express, and convey our knowledge through the construction of a variety of symbol systems: art, science, journalism, religion, common sense, mythology' (1992: 30).

Given the limited space in this essay, one focus could have been more deeply addressed is the dynamic between culinary identity and the concepts of distance and landscape. How far is the consumer from the place where the product is raised? Not just literally, but in terms of the process of rendering and production? How direct is the relationship between the person who cooks the food and when and how the guests eat it? What kind of relationship exists between the area's foodways and land? Finally, can those in a position of power to produce or shape discourse and address such gaps and distances meet their responsibilities? These are all concerns that must be further explored, and it is it is at events like Cochon555 where those on a larger culinary stage have an opportunity to meet the challenges ahead of them, engaging their audiences and circulating ideas in the same way their food does flavours.

Bibiolography

Appiah, Kwame Anthony (2006). *Cosmopolitanism: Ethics in A World of Strangers* (New York: Norton).
Carey, James (1992). *Communication as Culture* (New York: Routledge).
Clifford, James (1997). *Routes: Travel and Translation in the Late 20th Century* (Cambridge, MA: Harvard

University Press).
Jurafsky, Dan (2014). *The Language of Food: A Linguist Reads The Menu* (New York: W.W. Norton).
Long, Lucy (2004). 'Culinary Tourism: A Folkloristic Perspective on Eating and Otherness', in Lucy Long (ed.), *Culinary Tourism* (Lexington, KY: University of Kentucky Press), pp. 20-50.
Parkhurst Ferguson, Priscilla (2014). *Word of Mouth: What We Talk About When We Talk About Food* (Oakland, CA: University of California Press).
Rantanen, Terhi (2007). 'A Transnational Cosmopolitan: An Interview with Ulf Hannerz', *Global Media and Communication*, 3.1: 11-27.

Blood, Not So Simple

Jennifer McLagan

Blood! The mere mention of it is more likely to trigger images of vampires and horror films than delicious nourishing meals or must-try recipes. Made stylish and sexy by the vampires on television and the big screen, this fascination for blood has not translated into the dining room. On the plate blood evokes disgust, even fear, and not only from vegetarians or those holding certain religious beliefs. In fact many food lovers recoil from the idea of eating blood, and even those who enjoy a good blood sausage rarely consider cooking with blood. Of all the animal offal, blood is the most contentious and divisive, weighed down by religion, taboo, fear and revulsion. How did this excellent source of protein become so abhorred? Taking an animal's life was, and should remain, a significant event, and as a result blood became central to many religions and rituals. Animals were sacrificed with their blood integrated into the following ceremony or celebration. One of the earliest literary descriptions of a blood pudding appears in Homer's *Odyssey*. It tells how Ulysses and his men ate a blood pudding to celebrate their victory:

> 'listen to me,' says Antinous, 'there are some goats' paunches down at the fire, which we have filled with blood and fat, and set aside for supper; he who is victorious and proves himself to be the better man shall have his pick of the lot' (Book XVIII).

Blood pudding was a reward for bravery and success. The Nordic people shared this positive attitude to blood, believing that by drinking an animal's blood they would acquire its qualities and strengths. In the twelfth-century Danish tale *Gesta Danorum*, the great warrior Bjarke kills a giant bear, then offers its blood to the younger, less confident fighter Hjalte. Once the youth drinks the bear's blood he is filled with the animal's strength and fighting spirit.[1]

However, blood was not universally embraced. In the Jewish faith blood represents life, and religious law strictly forbids the consumption of meat containing blood. So when animals are slaughtered their blood is discarded, and the meat is salted, or brined, to remove any remaining traces of blood before it is eaten. While Saint Paul (Romans 14:14) wrote that no foods were forbidden to Christians, many of his early followers adopted this blood taboo. For Jews and Christians, the ban against blood was seen as a rejection of pagan sacrifices and a means of setting themselves apart. Muslim halal laws also forbid eating blood, not because blood represents life, but instead because Muslims believe it to be dangerous and harmful. A possible reason behind this tradition could be the fact that if animals are not correctly bled at slaughter, their meat discolours and does not keep well. Aside from religious groups, others, such as vegetarians and vegans, do not consume blood for ethical reasons.

Our attitude towards blood is inherently linked to our culture and social identity. Although we know rationally that blood is just another animal product, there is no denying that it evokes a strong emotional response. Even if we are not subject to religious or ethical taboos, blood is often associated with pain and represents life and death. Our food choices are enmeshed in a complicated of web of conventions and education. Paul Rozin has pointed out that our rejection of certain foods is more likely to stem from our cultural rather than our personal experience.[2] So, it is not the actual eating of blood that is disgusting, it is the idea of eating it that repulses us. The Spanish chef Andoni Luis Mugaritz pointed out, 'you can enjoy something without being conscious of what you're eating, still once you know, you either choose to enjoy it or the opposite.'[3] Added to the religious and cultural prejudices against blood there is the element of fear with many of us believing that blood is harmful, possibly even deadly. Blood is carrying a lot of baggage.

Vegetarians are against the killing of animals but like milk, consuming animal blood does not always result in the death of the animal. In rural communities, when other food sources were scarce, animals were bled. This practice dates back at least 2500 BCE and, according to C. Anne Wilson, continued up until eighteenth century in Scotland.[4] For many in extreme conditions, like the soldiers in Mongol armies of the thirteenth century and early North American explorers and trappers, blood was an emergency food. These groups bled their horses to sustain themselves and keep their means of transport. A well-nourished beast is a good source of blood: 310 millilitres can be taken from a horse every ten days without damaging its health or strength, while a cow can provide four litres of blood every two weeks with no ill effects.[5] If you bleed a cow for a period of two and a half years, you obtain about the same amount of protein as if you had waited the identical length of time and slaughtered it.[6] Many nomadic peoples continue bleed their animals today as it provides them with a dependable food source. In Tanzania and Kenya, Masai herders travel long distances in search of pasture for their animals, and during this time they live almost exclusively on a diet of blood and milk. To remove the blood, they use a specially designed arrow that does not penetrate the animal's neck too deeply. They drain between two and four litres of blood from the animal's jugular vein before sealing the wound. The blood is drunk straight, or mixed with the animal's milk.[7] In a hot climate meat doesn't keep well, consequently an animal is only killed for special occasions when all of it can be consumed quickly. Other African tribes bled their animals and coagulated the blood by boiling it and turning it into cakes of solidified blood.[8] This preserved the blood and made it easy to transport. Berber tribes drank a mixture of raw blood and milk to relieve their thirst when water wasn't available.

Animal blood is a good source of iron and has all the essential amino acids. While some amino acids are only present in small amounts, mixing the blood with milk, or grain, improves the ratio to make it an excellent food. Blood is a practical, nourishing food, and some have even promoted its medicinal benefits. An engraving published in 1890 edition of the French journal *Le Monde Illustré* depicts young women gathered outside an abattoir.[9] Why? They were there to drink the fresh blood. They believed it would protect them against tuberculosis; it didn't of course, yet it did boost those Belle Epoch ladies' iron levels. Blood is rich in easily absorbed heme iron, which makes it useful in combating iron deficiency.

Until recently, animals were slaughtered in small local abattoirs or at home. My 1978 edition of *Joy of Cooking* explains, in detail, how to deal with the blood from a freshly killed animal or bird. Cooking with blood was part of our food culture. Today, we have no idea where or how the animals we eat are slaughtered, and most of us don't want to know. We would rather forget that our steak requires the death of an animal. Industrial farming has provided us with vast amounts of cheap meat. Yet, in spite of the large numbers of animals being killed and the litres of blood produced, blood remains hard to get. You won't find it in the supermarket, or even the local butcher, and as a result very little, if any, makes it into our kitchens.

Blood only turns up on our plate when we cut into a piece of rare meat, or so we think. People who like their meat rare believe they are fans of blood; however it is not blood that oozes out; it is a mixture of water and myoglobin. Myoglobin is a red coloured protein that carries iron and oxygen to the muscles. The more active the muscle, the more oxygen it needs and the more myoglobin it has, making it darker in colour. The less exercised muscles have less myoglobin and consequently are paler. Myoglobin, like blood, changes from red to brown when it is heated.

Blood also delivers nutrients and oxygen to the animal, but it circulates through veins and arteries. A mixture of water, cells, proteins and enzymes, blood can be broken into two parts: the plasma and the cells. The plasma is a straw-coloured liquid that is mostly water with six to eight per cent protein. The cellular part is made up of red cells that carry oxygen and give blood its colour, the white cells that fight infection, and the platelets. The composition of animal blood is relatively constant. The species, its age and how and where the animal is raised are factors that modify the composition of its blood and lead to minor differences and variations in taste. Blood makes up three to five per cent of an animal's live weight: an average yield from a cow is ten to twelve litres containing 45 milligrams of iron per 100 millilitres, and from a pig it is three litres with 42 milligrams of iron per 100 millilitres.[10] Blood is 18 per cent protein, 50 per cent of which is in the red blood cells, representing 60 per cent of the total protein available from the by-products of an animal.[11]

In January 2016, 9.74 million pigs were slaughtered in the United States alone, which yields roughly 29 million litres of blood.[12] When we add in the blood from all the other animals slaughtered in the USA and then the rest of the world, it becomes apparent that we are awash in this excellent source of protein and iron. Unfortunately much of this blood is discarded, which if handled incorrectly overwhelms standard water treatment systems, becoming a serious pollutant. Blood dumped into rivers and lakes increases their nitrogen levels, promoting the growth of algae that clogs water systems and kills off aquatic life. By creating a demand for blood we could reduce blood dumping and the pollution problems it causes. Despite fears that animal blood is dangerous and carries BSE (bovine spongiform encephalopathy), commonly called mad cow disease, it poses no greater risk to humans than any other animal product. A healthy animal's blood is sterile, but it is very susceptible to bacteria and care must be taken that it is not contaminated in the abattoirs.[13] The easiest blood to collect and process is from pigs and cattle. Sheep's blood risks contamination from the wool and chicken from feathers. In the past blood was collected in an open vat system, with the animals passing overhead on the line, making the blood vulnerable to contamination. All the blood was mixed together, so if a problem was discovered with a single animal it meant destroying the entire batch. The best way to collect blood for human consumption is with a closed system where there is no exposure to the air so the blood remains sterile during the whole process. The animal is stunned, and then stuck with a hollow knife that injects an anticoagulant into the blood, which is drained via gravity, or with a pump, and transferred to refrigerated tanks. The blood from each, or small groups of animals, is tracked. If one animal fails to pass inspection, only a small amount of blood has to be rejected. Blood can be stored for four days at 2°C and up to six days at 0°C.[14] Animal blood can also be frozen or dried. As disposing of blood without causing an environmental problem is costly, investing in the collection of the blood from animal slaughter makes economic sense, especially for large-scale abattoirs. Expanding the market for blood would encourage the use of high tech blood collection systems and reduce costs.

The food industry has realized the value of blood as a cheap, high quality protein source, and they use about a third of the blood produced, with the meat industry being the biggest consumer. Blood is in blood sausages, of course, and in many other meat products to bind them and to add colour and protein. It acts as a filler, an emulsifier replaces fat and is even in gelatine. Blood's protein and water content resembles eggs making it a good it replacement for them.[15] The resulting products, especially baked goods, are cheaper and can be eaten by those with an egg allergy. However, blood's dark colour and distinctive taste restricts its usefulness for the food industry. They prefer to only use the plasma portion which can be added to a wider range of products. Blood plasma binds imitation crab and improves the protein content of flour, allowing pasta to be made with cheaper flour, and it even fortifies sports supplements. Blood is often where you least expect it. Scientists are now studying the bioactive peptides found in blood. These act as antioxidants that fight bacteria and have been shown to lower cholesterol and blood pressure levels. Current thinking is that these peptides could be added to foods to make them 'healthier'.[16] So blood may become a health drink once again! There is also a demand for high quality protein in developing countries that blood can fill. Apart from the food industry, blood finds its way into medical, pharmaceutical and paper products, as well as fertilizer, animal and pet food. Fido has better access to blood, and indeed most offal, than we do.

One of the more curious non-food uses of blood is in mortar. In the past, blood was added to mortar to make it water repellent and help it cure quickly. Today blood is added when repairing the mortar in historical buildings, and modern concrete buildings can also benefit from the addition of blood to the mix. As well as repelling water, blood makes concrete stronger and more resistant to salt, increasing its life span.[17] Despite all of these varied uses for blood, much of it is still discarded.

Leaving aside those who don't consume blood for religious and ethical reasons, how do we convince the rest of the population that they should consider cooking with blood? We can make a logical, objective case for eating this important, cheap protein source by arguing that it makes economic sense. We can invoke the moral case for eating the whole animal, including its blood. However, we would be well advised to remember the legend of Dionysius, King of the Greek colony of Sicily, who imported a Spartan cook to make him the famous Spartan speciality *melas zomos,* or black soup, made with blood. Dionysius didn't like the taste of the soup and complained vehemently to the cook who simply explained that the soup was missing two key ingredients that made it delicious – hunger and thirst.[18] We need to make blood appetizing.

It is often argued that the problem is blood's colour, taste and odour. True, blood is dark, almost black, when cooked, which can limit its use. Blood has a distinctive, metallic taste, with a touch of liver, but you can modify this flavour with the addition of other ingredients. As for its smell, fresh blood is clean and neutral, not at all offensive. Even so, if we want to get blood into the kitchens of the western world we must realize, to quote Frank Muir, 'Nobody can be expected to affect academic detachment about something he puts into his mouth and swallows.'[19] What we have to change is our attitude to blood to make it more palatable. We need a practical plan to encourage cooking with blood. The first step is to remove its association with Halloween and vampires and to stop characterizing it as a bizarre, weird food. The desire to shock with blood is obvious, and I fear too tempting, especially for some younger chefs. We need to promote blood as simply another form of animal protein just like a steak or eggs. Eggs are an odd food if you think about them, but we don't. Eggs are simply eggs, a useful and very normal ingredient that we all cook with. Once we normalize blood and reassure people that it is safe to eat, we need to make it readily available. This is a chicken and egg problem: if people can't get blood they won't use it, and if they don't demand blood there will be no supply. Promote an ingredient well, and it will be available everywhere – just look what happened with kale.

To encourage cooking with blood, we must give people recipes. There already exists a good repertory that an experienced cook can turn to, the most familiar to Europeans being the numerous varieties of blood sausage. This includes British black pudding, Irish *drisheen*, the different French *boudin noirs*, Spanish *morcilla* and even *blodpølse,* a sweet version from Norway. While there are devotees of all these forms of blood sausage, we could broaden their appeal and persuade the less enthusiastic by modernizing blood sausage's presentation. Instead of just adding slices to a fry up, or serving it with traditional apples and potatoes, try matching it with rhubarb, broad beans or pairing it with scallops, which would update its image. We can explain that blood can be added to numerous soups and stews to enrich and thicken them. Anyone who has eaten the French game dish *lièvre royale* knows just how brilliantly this recipe uses the taste, richness and thickening power of blood. There is *czarnina*, a duck's blood soup from Poland, the French *civets* and *coq au vin* – although you rarely see a rooster, let alone its blood, in the later. Or the Filipino *dinuguan*, a stew of pork offal known as chocolate meat thanks to colour it turns when thickened with blood. Coagulated blood is popular in Asia where it is sold as a snack and added to soups. Nonetheless all these recipes for stews, soups and sausages, while delicious, are problematic for a population that increasingly avoids strong tasting foods. Reworking them for current tastes might be one way to make them more approachable. Italian and Scandinavian recipes often mix blood and flour to create dishes where the blood is less noticeable. Surely we can tempt people into trying blood with interesting blood pasta, crisp blood crackers and hearty breads or pancakes topped with ligonberry jam.

In today's food world most trends filter down from the top via food writers, chefs, restaurants and television personalities. Some well-known names have already promoted blood: Brad Farmerie in New York City has given classes on cooking with blood to chefs. Andy Richer serves *Laap Meuang*, a northern Thai salad that includes fresh blood, in his restaurant Pok Pok in Portland, and Fergus Henderson is cooking blood cake at St John in London. In April 2014 the *Guardian* put cooking with blood at the top of their annual guide to the best cooking, eating and drinking, and in February 2015 the *San Francisco Chronicle* had a cover story on blood in their food section. Despite all this promotion, blood has yet to break through into the main stream; it remains a niche ingredient. Perhaps we have not been promoting blood in the right way?

Surely it was inevitable that the Scandinavians with their long history of cooking with blood would turn their attention to blood as an ingredient. Noma, the world-renowned restaurant in Copenhagen, set up The Food Lab in 2008 'to explore the edible potential of the Nordic region – the flavours that say something about us and imbue the foods we eat with a connection to this place and this time'.[20] Preoccupied with the taste of blood, they devoted a lot of time and effort to masking its flavour. Cocoa powder and spices like cloves and cinnamon have traditionally been added to mute blood's taste. The cooks at the Food Lab found that koji (a fungus used in fermenting soy and rice) and woodruff worked well too. Interestingly they discovered that adding acidic ingredients reduces blood's metallic flavour. They tried a wide range of blood recipes including mixing blood with kefir, and created a drink called a Red Russian, a mixture of vodka and blood, but neither was successful. More productive were the recipes where they substituted blood for eggs.[21] Not only do blood and eggs have similar protein compositions, useful for those who have an allergy to eggs, but another advantage is that blood has half the calories of eggs. Blood's resemblance to eggs is its most useful quality for cooks. It allows us to think more creatively about using blood. Anywhere you use an egg you can substitute blood – to make custard, an emulsion or foams. When whipped, blood produces a very fine foam for baking that is more stable than egg foam. Chefs I know have made everything from savoury custards to blood hollandaise, all good, yet these may not the best recipes to expand blood's general appeal. A Toronto chef of Italian heritage, Rob Gentile, makes a delicious blood gelato and an amazing *torta di sanguinaccio* that he serves with figs steeped in grappa and creamy custard; both these dishes tempt diners to try blood for the first time. In my book *Odd Bits* there is a recipe for chocolate blood ice cream based on a traditional Italian recipe for *sanguinaccio*, a sweet blood dessert, and chef Mugaritz has created a blood macaroon. Surely these recipes would make blood more popular, at least in restaurants and for adventurous cooks. Switching blood's focus from the more traditional savoury to sweet could be the best way to win over palates and minds. Yet home cooks might still find these dishes too challenging. To interest them in cooking with blood, we must seduce them with straightforward desserts that taste good. While this sounds obvious, it is often overlooked. Developing recipes for pancakes, meringue, cakes, brownies and cookies that include blood may be the answer.

Will blood become an everyday ingredient? Why not? Blood is cheap, a good source of protein, safe and versatile. It makes economic, environmental and nutritional sense to use it. Remember blood is already in many food products and is easily added to breads, pastas, crackers and ice cream, pastries and cakes. Becoming a regular ingredient on restaurant menus would normalize blood and make it more acceptable. Availability is key, so blood must be in butchers' shops and supermarkets. We know food preferences are learned and can be changed with exposure to new foods. By giving blood cachet with good, positive publicity and following it up with consumer education we can overcome prejudices and change attitudes to blood. Everyone interested in food and sustainability should be actively looking for ways to promote blood as an ingredient. Then, and only then, will blood finally make it back into our kitchens. As Ms Siesby noted back in 1980, 'It simply is not decent to throw away such a valuable food.'[22]

Notes

1. Brigit Siesby. 'Blood Is Food', *Petits Propos Culinaires* 4 (February 1980), 42.
2. Paul Rozin, 'Acquisition of Stable Food Preferences', *Nutrition Reviews* 48.2 (February 1990), 107.
3. Michael Paterniti, 'The Most Adventurous Restaurant in the World Is on a Small Hilltop in Spain', *GQ Magazine,* May 2014, p. 10.
4. C. Anne Wilson, *Food and Drink in Britain from the Stone Age to Recent Times* (Chicago: Academy Chicago Publishers, 1991), p. 63.

5. Jennifer McLagan, *Odd Bits: How to Cook the Rest of the Animal* (Berkeley: Ten Speed, 2011), p. 216.
6. Siesby, p. 44.
7. McLagan, p. 216.
8. Reay Tannahill, *Food in History* (New York: Stein and Day, 1973), p. 131.
9. M. Louis Bombled, '*Aux Abattoirs*', *Le Monde Ilustré*, 1 March 1890 <http://gallica.bnf.fr/ark:/12148/bpt6k6228890w/f5.item.zoom> [accessed 15 May 2016].
10. Jack A .Ofori and Yun-Hwa P. Hsieh, 'Issues Related to the Use of Blood in Food and Animal Feed' *Critical Reviews in Food Science and Nutrition* 54.5 (2014), 687; Quality Meat Scotland, 'Topic 7 – Blood', *Adding Value to Scottish Read Meat Supply Chain*, p. 1.
11. Ofori and Hsieh, p. 688; Quality Meat Scotland, p. 1.
12. USDA National Agricultural Statistics Service, *Livestock Slaughter*, 2016, p. 5.
13. Ofori and Hsieh, p. 690.
14. John Sjöberg, *Animal Blood Recovery for Edible Purposes* (Sweden: Anitec, [n.d.]), p. 6.
15. Ofori and Hsieh, pp. 229, 231, 235, 238.
16. Clara S. F. Bah and others, 'Slaughterhouse Blood: An Emerging Source of Bioactive Compounds', *Comprehensive Reviews in Food Science and Food Safety*, 12 (2013), 319.
17. J. G. Xu and others, 'Influence of Ox Blood on Water Absorption of and Chloride Penetration into Concrete', *Advanced Materials Research*, 261-263, 1.
18. William Kitchiner, *The Cooks Oracle: Containing Receipts for Plain Cookery* (New York: Evert Duyckinck, George Long, E. Bliss and E. White, 1825), p. 23.
19. Frank Muir, *The Frank Muir Book* (London: Heinemann, 1976), p. 279.
20. Nordic Food Lab, 'Who We Are', *Nordic Food Lab* <http://nordicfoodlab.org/whoweare/> [accessed 15 May 2016].
21. Elizabeth Paul, 'Blood and Egg', *Nordic Food Lab*, 7 January 2014 <http://nordicfoodlab.org/blog/2013/9/blood-and-egg?rq=blood%20ice%20cream> [accessed 15 May 2016].
22. Siesby, p. 49.

Frikandel, the Most Popular Dutch Snack: Wasteful or Sustainable?

Lenno Munnikes

Introduction

This study examines the *frikandel*, the most popular snack in the Netherlands. Rather than analyzing its popularity, though, this paper attempts to trigger a sociological discussion about this snack regarding sustainability, social identity and the historical role snacks have played in the creation of Dutch food culture and cuisine, which has been largely ignored in academic literature.

The *frikandel* is a typical Dutch snack: it is easy to prepare, it can be eaten quickly on the go, and it is filling and cheap. While it includes some exotic spices that potentially remind Dutch people of the Dutch Indies, its other ingredients have been considered controversial for a long time. Rumours held that the main ingredients were brains, feet, ears, eyes, cat meat and the like: food stuffs which are considered offal or waste meat in the Netherlands. Contrary to popular belief, however, the meat used in the *frikandel* is not controversial, though the processing techniques may be questionable.

Nowadays, in our need for sustainability and animal-friendly meat production, the *frikandel* can also be seen as a good example of this trend, since the meat of the whole animal is used for the production of the *frikandel*. But this begs the question: does meat ever exist as waste? Or can killing an animal and letting it go to 'waste' ever be considered ethical at all?[1] It is not unthinkable that, by using local ingredients and more animal-friendly meat, the *frikandel* can become a ethical snack.

This paper commences with a short historical overview of the place of snacks in Dutch food history and culture. Snacks have played an important role in Dutch households and in forming Dutch cuisine, food culture and food history. From a sociological perspective, the importance of snacks in the Netherlands is an interesting subject for examining Dutch social identity, following the popular saying 'you are what you eat' or in this case 'you are what you snack'.

Subsequently, the discussion focuses on the *frikandel* itself: its origin, ingredients and production. The end of this paper discusses how it is possible that a snack with such a dubious image can be so popular, and also whether it is possible to consider the *frikandel* as a sustainable, instead of wasteful, snack due to its production from the entire bodies of animals, except the carcass. Finally, this study highlights the snack's importance as a socio-historical research topic and shows that it can offer cultural insights into eating habits and the food history of the Netherlands.

Frikandel: Wasteful or Sustainable?

The Rise of the Snack

In the Netherlands, there is a long tradition of selling and consuming snacks. Since the end of the 1970s, snacks have been mostly deep-fried and sold in so-called 'snackbars'. The snackbar, a typically Dutch eating place, has a long history, dating back over a century. An important moment at the beginning of this tradition of selling and consuming snacks happened around 1900 when Herman Kwekkeboom started to sell croquettes in his pastry shop on the Rapenburg in the old centre of Amsterdam.[2] Nowadays Kwekkeboom croquettes are still very popular because of their taste and also their name and tradition. Like Kwekkeboom, there are a couple other brands with a long tradition and a high culinary status, and these brands also have their origin in pastry shops run by famous confectioners. Another famous example in Amsterdam is Febo, named after Ferdinand Bolstraat, a street in southwest Amsterdam. Today Febo is a snackbar chain that has played an important role in the history of the '*automatiek*', a kind of food wall described later.[3]

This was an important moment in the history of creating the Dutch way of eating out and establishing the role of small snacks in Dutch food culture. In the 1920s and 1930s, it became popular in the Netherlands to eat small snacks outside in a new kind of eating place. Probably due to this popularity, businesses selling these small snacks spread rapidly. Local butchers, pastry shops and bakeries started to sell different homemade snacks, such as croquettes, sandwiches, salads, meatballs and so on. These places began to be called lunchrooms, like their counterparts in the United States. But sociologically it is more interesting that these lunchrooms were not exclusive to one class in society, but accessible for people from all social echelons, probably because these places were a comfortable place for not just a quick lunch, but also for snacking before or after the theatre.[4]

During the economic crisis of the 1930s, however, these lunchrooms decreased in popularity and changed into more simplified and less expensive versions, soon to be called 'cafeterias'. The cafeterias supplied food and drinks that were cheaper and mostly sold in a self-service form.[5] The cafeterias were especially common in cities, and they also became a place for eating out for every class in society. However, it is still unknown whether there were differences between the food items consumed by the different classes of Dutch urban inhabitants.[6]

After World War II the cafeterias became even more popular due to a new trend: French fries. French fries became very popular in the 1960s and 1970s.[7] It is probably during those decades that the cafeterias started to be called snackbars. At the same time, industrialized production of food items like snacks also supported the development of these 'new' snackbars. One significant difference between the cafeterias and snackbars was that snackbars were more suitable for quick meals and for take-away.

Moreover, at the same point in history, the *automatiek* became a common sight in the centre of cities in the Netherlands. The *automatiek* has been considered typically Dutch, but from the 1930s onwards these food walls were also present on the streets of

New York City, around the same time they started in the Netherlands.⁸ But the food walls largely disappeared everywhere except in the Netherlands. An *automatiek* is a glass wall with small compartments, which can be filled from behind and from the front side, and are situated mostly on sidewalks. One can simply insert coins and take a snack of one's choice. Even nowadays, the *automatiek* is part of snack culture in the Netherlands. As such, the rise of the snackbar and also the *automatiek* reveal that more anonymous and take-away characteristics became more popular over time.

During this period, the modern *frikandel*, as it is known today, made its appearance in Dutch cuisine. Remarkably, it took quite long, particularly compared to most Western countries, for new snacks from the US, especially hamburgers, to become popular in the Netherlands: it was only in the late 1970s that this new trend really developed. It seems that Dutch people preferred eating their own 'traditional' snacks over experimenting with new ones. Also interesting is that snacks with some connection to the Dutch Indies have become very popular, such as lumpia and satays. Similar to the *frikandel*, these snacks are retrieved from an *automatiek* or deep-fried and eaten at home.

The Story of the *Frikandel*

In the Netherlands, it is widely known that the modern *frikandel* was introduced in the 1950s. This was the time that snacks became the most popular food items eaten outside of the home.

However, there is significant controversy about the origins of its name. *Frikandel* should not be confused with '*Frikadel*', a flat meatball of German origin. The best description of the *frikandel* in English is a minced-meat hot dog or sausage stick. For many years, the *frikandel* has been the most popular snack in the Netherlands. Millions of them are sold in snackbars, but also in sports canteens and deep-frozen in supermarkets for frying at home. It is still significantly more popular than the croquette or the famous '*bitterballen*' [fried mini-croquettes].

But the history of the *frikandel* is not easily examined: different sources offer different stories about its origins. Some Dutch food writers and scholars recognize the original *frikandel* in a recipe published in *De Nieuwe, Welervarene Utrechtse Keukenmeid*, a cookbook written in 1771. This book aimed to help kitchen maids improve their cooking during the eighteenth century. One of the recipes is for '*Frikadellen*', translated here:

> You need 500 grams veal meat, finely chopped. Mix the meat with one egg and two egg yolks and some white bread. Add some pepper, nutmeg and cloves. Then make *frikadellen* out of it [probably that is more the form than the product] and bake them in butter.

In this recipe, they interestingly distinguish between whether the cook wants to roast the *frikadellen* on the spit or bake them in butter. When roasting on a spit, mace instead of nutmeg must be used and the cloves are not added anymore. Then one forms the meat into an oblong ball, wraps it in veal caul and roasts it.[9]

There are some very remarkable differences in the recipe, which are probably due to the fact that some items will burn when roasted and not when baked in butter. But I don't know if it is up to me to doubt whether the modern *frikandel* has something to do with the eighteenth century *frikadel*, but there is an important difference is in the name: since the 1950s, *frikandel* is written with a 'n'. There are also a lot of differences between the ingredients.[10] The most important ingredient in the historical dish is veal meat, which is not used in the modern version. In the next section I will describe the ingredients and production of the modern *frikandel*, and you can draw your own conclusion.

More information on the history of the *frikandel* can be found online and in the stories presented on *frikandel* packaging. One of the most popular origin stories involves Jan Bekkers, who later formed Beckers, the largest producer of modern *frikandel*. Jan Bekkers was the son of a butcher family, and, after he went to the US several times to explore the modern snack culture there, he established his own snack factory in Deurne in the 1950s. According to the story, Bekkers liked the small hot dog sausages in the US, but found that they were not suitable for deep-frying.[11] So he designed one without casing that was suitable for deep-frying. Though there are various marketing stories concerning the origins of the *frikandel*, the verity of these anecdotes is not the subject of this paper. However, the potential history of the modern *frikandel* can be gleaned through these narratives. There is no patent on the *frikandel*, which explains the different claims of different producers. It is not a niche product in the Netherlands, but an object of mass production and consumption.

Generally, the history of snacks that date back to the eighteenth century can excite warm, traditional feelings in consumers, but that is not really the case for *frikandel*. Though most rumours seem unfounded, *frikandel* has long been and still is surrounded by dubious stories about its production, stories that can be seen as our national horror stories, as a kind of a national fairy tale.

The alleged production process of the *frikandel* and its ingredients has led to a long tradition of popular facts and scary stories. As such, the ingredients of *frikandel* have been considered controversial for a long time. Sheep eyes, pigs' brains and even cat meat were rumoured to be the main ingredients. Clearly these stories are fictitious, but its ingredients are still dubious. *Frikandel* is made of '*separator vlees*', which translated means something like 'mechanically separated meat', or meat that is scraped or hosed under high pressure off the bones of chickens, pigs and even horses. In most industrially produced meat, these parts are considered inedible and discarded. In light of contemporary sustainability concerns, the question arises whether the *frikandel* is a wasteful or a sustainable snack.

It is important to summarize the ingredients to better understand the *frikandel* without scaling these ingredients on some normative standard. The main ingredients given here are of the Beckers variant; however, there are a lot of other brands with similar but different ingredients: '58% chicken (separator meat), water, 15% pork lard, bread crumbs, salt, seasonings, onion powder, E621, E316, E331, dextrose, E450, E451, Soya'.[12] The main ingredient is the 'separator' meat, which in the case of Beckers comes from chicken and pork. As can be seen, no particularly strange ingredients are included. No controversies can be found here except that separator meat has had a bad name, as such meat is mostly considered as waste or offal.

Scope and Discussion

The search for a culinary culture in the Netherlands is a highly popular contemporary topic. As in most Western countries, local, authentic, healthy and organic are also rising stars in the Dutch food world. At the same time, there is also a growing need and desire for meat raised and produced in more animal-friendly ways.

As such, it might seem strange that the number one snack in the Netherlands is the *frikandel*, a stick made of mechanically separated meat, which seems to embody the opposite characteristics of popular culinary demands, except perhaps authenticity. With six hundred million *frikandellen* are consumed each year in the Netherlands by seventeen million inhabitants, the popularity of the *frikandel* is indisputable.[13] What makes it so popular, however, is not its culinary excellence. Perhaps, then, its fame is due to its simple no-nonsense character, particularly when it is consumed in a white bun with copious mayonnaise applied on top of it.

Regardless, the *frikandel* can now be considered a traditional Dutch food. There are some food items and eating habits that can be considered 'authentically' Dutch. Without resorting to politics, some of these evoke comforting, nationalistic feelings. In this sense, ethnic origin is irrelevant, as everyone eats '*oliebollen*', deep-fried beignets, on New Year's Eve.[14] But it seems unlikely that these feelings are the only explanation for the great amount of *frikandellen* consumed in the Netherlands, since the *frikandel* has the image of a low status snack among Dutch national foods. Instead, its popularity may be due to the marketing strategies of the *frikandel* producers who are trying to uplift the culinary image of this snack.

Generally, the Netherlands does not have a history of easily adopting new or exotic foods; Dutch cuisine generally consists of plain, simple fare.[15] The *frikandel* is a perfect example: no-nonsense, cheap and easy. This follows the creed of a famous saying in the Netherlands: '*doe maar normaal, dan doe je al gek genoeg*' [you better act normally, since you are already crazy enough].

In her theory of 'Ethical Gourmandism', Carolyn Korsmeyer offers five points about the nature of taste sensations:

1. Taste is a sense whose natural affinities are culturally developed
2. Flavour-taste properties manifest in experience
3. Cultivating and refining taste always requires knowing what one is eating

4. Tastes possess aesthetic characteristics
5. If one finds a food delicious, then one tacitly recognizes it as good to eat.[16]

Considering the *frikandel* through these five points reveals some distinguishing features of this snack. There is not much wrong with the taste of the *frikandel*, as it is quite comparable in taste and texture to a spicy meatball. However, points three and five seem to challenge the popularity of the *frikandel*. It is difficult to recognize the ingredients of the *frikandel* by eating it. Probably this difficulty is the origin of the fictitious stories surrounding the *frikandel*.

However, the snack's dubious image does not correspond with the exponential amounts of *frikandellen* eaten in the Netherlands. Given this vast amount, there must be something good in the taste of the *frikandel*. But to assume that the taste of the *frikandel* is cultivated, like chilli peppers or coffee, would also be a wrong conclusion.[17] Despite the accessible taste, in the 1980s and 1990s an idea developed that something is wrong with eating sausages and other prepared meat snacks unless one knew exactly what one was consuming. That discussion expanded in the 1990s and 2000s, when we saw an increasing attention to the link between food and health and a corresponding increase in the popularity of organic, vegetarian and animal-friendly food. Those trends may explain why the popularity of the *frikandel* has decreased slightly since those decades – although the dried sausages that are so trendy right now in the Netherlands also have ingredients that are not easily recognizable recognizable by taste.[18]

The important fact to consider about whether the *frikandel* is wasteful or sustainable is that, during the production process, the meat of the whole animal is used. Thus, in terms of sustainability, this process may seem more ethical than killing an animal merely for certain parts, like fillets. This fact may make the *frikandel* a good example in terms of animal welfare.

While *frikandellen* are consumed in much larger quantities by the masses than by the elite, it seems clear that the producers intend to conquer the elite as well.[19] But perhaps there is no difference anymore between the elite and the masses if one considers the massive consumption rates of the *frikandel*: it may just be that the elite do not want to publicly admit they also eat (a lot of) *frikandellen*. A suggestion would be to produce a gentrified variant made of locally raised organic meat, recognizable ingredients and so on, similar to the changes seen in dried sausages over the last five years. At the same time, separator meat could still be used, perhaps identified in a more recognizable way. And, if we could also find a solution for the high amount of salt, saturated fat and iron and prepare in a more healthful way, we could create a future-proof snack.

Conclusion

This paper presents a historical overview of the most popular snack of the Netherlands, but it also offers psychological and sociological insights into the ethical choices behind the consumption of the *frikandel*. As such, this paper embodies a multi-disciplinary scope, as there are no strictly scientific articles about the *frikandel*.

Furthermore, while the paper considers the seeming contradiction of the *frikandel*'s production process – this kind of meat is often considered inedible, and yet so many *frikandellen* are consumed each year – but it does not discuss the unhealthy aspects of eating the *frikandel* or other snacks. Much can be said, though, about the health risks of eating a lot of *frikandellen*, particularly concerning the excessive intake of saturated fats and iron. The Dutch council on food health (Voedingscentrum) has declared processed meat to be a high-risk food, pointing to a possible connection between fabricated meat and heart failure and even bowel cancer.[20] Despite the fact that the unhealthy effects of snacks are well known, millions are still consumed every year.

The rise of snacks and the start of the eating places that sell them comprise a lacuna in the study of Dutch food history. This form of dining and the important role of snacks are seriously underestimated in the development of Dutch food culture. Writing about food history and food culture is a trend in the Netherlands, and books about reinventing traditional cooking methods, such as fermenting, are currently very popular. Maybe there is not much honour to be gained from writing about snacks: snacks, and especially the *frikandel*, have suffered a bad image as unhealthy. Of course it is important to advise people about the risk factors of eating (too many) snacks, but it is also important to recognize the significance, on the economic and also cultural levels, of the production and consumption of snacks, and particularly the *frikandel*. As such, this paper has shed much needed light on the importance of snacks in creating Dutch food culture and Dutch culinary history.

Afterword

When I told my friends, family and colleagues that I was writing a paper about the *frikandel* almost everyone looked at me if I had lost my mind. Some started to call me Mr Frikandel, but I believe this paper helps reveal deeper layers of this particular snack. When I wrote my master's thesis about food cultures at the University of Amsterdam, my examiner was Anneke van Otterloo, then one of the few Dutch scholars studying food.[21] She maintained that the role of snacks in the Netherlands should be examined more, and this paper can be considered a first step in this direction.

Notes

1. D. Wicks, 'Humans, Food and Other Animals: The Vegetarian Option', in *A Sociology of Food and Nutrition: The Social Appetite*, ed. by J. Germov and L. Williams (Oxford: Oxford University Press, 2013), pp. 281-83.
2. The *kwekkeboom* croquette is a snack with a long history and a high culinary status (<https://www.kwekkeboom.nl> [accessed 22 May 2016]).
3. Febo is of one of the oldest snackbars of the Netherlands (<www.febo.nl> [accessed 22 May 2016]).
4. A. H. van Otterloo and A. A. de la Bruheze, '*Snacks, snackcultuur en buitenshuis eten in Nederland,*

1920-1980', *Spiegel Historiael*, 3-4 (2003) <http://www.isgeschiedenis.nl/archiefstukken/snacks_snack-cultuur_en_buitenshuis_eten_in_nederland_1920_1980/> [accessed 22 May 2016].
5. van Otterloo and de la Bruheze.
6. A. Warde, *Consumption, Food and Taste: Culinary Antinomies and Commodity Culture* (London: Sage, 1997), pp. 109.
7. van Otterloo and de la Bruheze.
8. Febo, '*Geschiedenis: Onze Historie*' Febo <http://www.febo.nl/over-ons/historie/> [accessed 22 May 2016]. On the *automatiek* in New York, see Laura Shapiro and Rebecca Federman, '"Let's all go eat at the Automat": Machines and Miracles in New York City', in *Food and Material Culture: Proceedings of the 2013 Oxford Symposium on Food and Cookery*, ed. by Mark McWilliams (Totnes, Devon: Prospect Books, 2014), pp. 272-280
9. Onbekend (red. P. M. van Weert-Landwehr), *De Nieuwe Welervarene Utrechtse Keuken-meid.* (Utrecht: Begijnekade 18 Uitgevers, 2007), pp. 35.
10. Onbekend; 'Frikandellen (Beckers)', Calorielijst.nl, 2017 <http://www.calorielijst.nl/product/?calorie=6515> [accessed 22 May 2016].
11. Deurnewiki Contributors, 'Johannes Jacobus Franciscus Bekkers (1920-2003)', *Deurnewiki*, Heemkundekring H.N. Ouwerling, 2015 <http://www.deurnewiki.nl/wiki/index.php?title=Johannes_Jacobus_Franciscus_Bekkers_(1920-2003)> [accessed 22 May 2016].
12. 'Frikandellen (Beckers)'.
13. Thuisbezorgd, a website for online food ordering, shows statistics of the most eaten snacks: Jalena, 'Top 20 *meest bestelde snacks* 2015', *Thuisbezorgd.nl* <https://www.thuisbezorgd.nl/blog/meest-bestelde-snacks/> [accessed 22 May 2016].
14. J. Leerssen, *Elementaire Deeltjes 23 – Nationalisme*, (Amsterdam: Amsterdam University Press, 2015), pp. 33-34.
15. S. Mennell, 'Culinary Cultures of Europe', in Germov and Williams, pp. 248-53.
16. C. Korsmeyer, 'Ethical Gourmandism', in *The Philosophy of Food*, ed. by D. M. Kaplan (London: University of California Press, 2012), pp. 89.
17. Korsmeyer, p. 93.
18. Jalena.
19. P. Bourdieu, *Distinction: A Social Critique of the Judgement of Taste* (London: Routledge, 1984).
20. Vodingscentrum, '*Vlees*', *Vodingscentrum* <http://www.voedingscentrum.nl/encyclopedie/vlees.aspx> [accessed 22 May 2016].
21. A. H. van Otterloo, *Eten en Eetlust in Nederland (1840-1990). Een historisch-sociologische studie* (Amsterdam: Bert Bakker, 1990).

Offal and Extremities in Art

Gillian Riley

Introduction

In societies where nothing is wasted, every part of a slaughtered animal has its value. What we think of today as prime cuts were a small proportion of what was once eaten and enjoyed. Recipe books and other sources tell us a lot about these parts, from internal organs like brains, livers, lungs, tongue, spleen, stomach, intestines, heart and various glands to extremities like trotters, snouts, ears, eyes, tails, testicles and nipples. This paper explores how the visual representation of some of these might help us understand their gastronomic status. Sausages are not strictly speaking offal, but they often contained a fair amount, and pies throughout history are receptacles for edible parts that might not have been very appealing on their own. A seventeenth-century Dutch kitchen scene shows a fearsome young woman chopping up offal, perhaps for sausages or brawn.

    The painter Jan Steen got to know his second wife as he stopped off at her market stall for a snack of home-cooked sheep's trotters. They can be seen in still lifes by his contemporaries, for example a still life by Jacob van Hulsdonck, alongside tongue and ham. Sixteenth-century Antwerp had a flourishing butchers' guild, and historians have shown how Aertsen's version of a butcher's stall tells us as much about local politics as the vivid display of animal parts, including a striking selection of offal. Painters often exploit the decorative sight of lights and associated organs as part of an eye-catching display. The butchers of Bologna were political animals, as portrayed by Annibale Carracci, operating a dignified trade in a prosperous city. In Florence Empoli's gluttonous kitchens and larders include sightings of offal, and going back several centuries we have the detailed illustrations to the *Tacuinum Sanitatis* which have medical rather than political messages. At the Symposium, my presentation showed a selection from the surprising number of works of art with offal in them from the seventeenth and eighteenth centuries.

Looking at images of offal in art we might ask 'Why paint offal?' and not come up with an answer, but we can learn a fair amount about the esteem in which it was held from how it was presented by a painter for his clients. These images mitigate what we consider to be gruesome aspects and emphasize the deliciousness or decorative qualities of offal. Some still life paintings from the Low Countries show a tongue and trotters alongside luxury items like hothouse fruit, lemons, a whole ham and a pile-up of cheeses, with costly Chinese porcelain and exquisite glass goblets. Is there some irony here? Perhaps a reminder of the humble snacks of a successful merchant's early days. Other paintings show offal in a pantry or larder, a kitchen, or a market stall or shop.

Offal was enjoyed in the past by all classes, not so much avoiding waste, or dealing with the dodgy stuff, but with a relish for special ingredients, a tasty way of eating both organs and extremities. You got plenty of chops from a pig, but only one tail and snout, two ears and four trotters, which were prized, not despised, as well as a lot of organs. The abundance of contemporary recipes seems to suggest that the trouble taken to deal with these extremities was worth the effort. Most of the images discussed here are from the sixteenth and seventeenth centuries, when Bartolomeo Scappi's *Opera* of 1570 was still in use, and Robert May's *Accomplisht Cook* of 1665 reflects his experiences in Europe as well as English cooking.[1] Scappi has nine recipes for dealing with the heads of various animals, and four for tongues, while May has almost thirty for tongues, sixteen for heads and over ten for 'neats feet'. They both go into considerable detail, with delicious and imaginative seasonings, dealing with just about every organ and extremity imaginable, which indicates that offal was not inferior food, but a much appreciated and enjoyable ingredient.

Most offal goes off quickly, so it is a treat to enjoy liver, brains, sweetbreads and of course blood, in profusion, immediately after slaughter. We get a sense of this from the *Tacuinum Sanitatis,* where families can be seen cooking and eating offal of different kinds. In the various versions of this work, offal from several animals is shown in a contemporary (late fourteenth-century) setting, often in the process of being cooked and served in a family setting. The *Tacuinum Sanitatis* was the Late Medieval equivalent of a coffee table book, art directed by Giovannino de' Grassi in his studio in Milan, with a fairly perfunctory treatment of the text along with a full page illustration of each topic, charmingly idealistic scenes from everyday life, with decorative gentry disporting themselves while picturesque peasants get on with the work. We can compare the information in these with medieval and renaissance recipes and health handbooks.

The most haunting image from the Low Countries is a mysterious kitchen scene by Willem van Odekerken who was working in The Hague during the mid-seventeenth century. A solemn young woman wields a cleaver over a shallow tub of what looks like liver, lungs complete with windpipe and possibly spleen and other organs. Her demeanour mitigates what might have been a messy procedure; her blue robe and the immaculate white shawl over her head imply purity, a contrast to the red curtain that swings down from the left. Other kitchen scenes by the same artist are pleasant but rather banal. You might enjoy hanging them on your wall, if you appreciate the reassuring calm of humdrum domesticity, like the servant maid with a bowl of fruit and a goose or swan and a pig's head, scalded and scrubbed and ready to cook, sitting on a plate. But this particular painting is numinous and somehow scary. It is impossible to tell who might have owned it, and what they saw in it. Probably not offal. Perhaps a reference to sacrificial slaughter, or to woman as priestess in her temple the kitchen. Nevertheless offal is here being chopped up with a massive cleaver, for some down-to-earth purpose. It is hard to tell if it is raw or cooked. Some items are not too difficult to chop, but raw liver is a struggle. Bartolomeo Scappi, in his *Opera* of 1570, instructs us to give it a boil until firmed up, then grate it as you would cheese. So does Robert May, in *The Accomplisht Cook* of 1665, who has many recipes for 'Haggas Puddings' which include offal, some with oatmeal, others with breadcrumbs, all seasoned imaginatively with herbs and spices. One has 'calves panch, calves chaldrons, or muggets, being clenged', cooked, then chopped fine, mixed with breadcrumbs, herbs and spices, currants and dates, and seasoned with salt and sugar, boiled in a cloth or calf's stomach, and served decorated with sliced almonds and doused with melted butter. It is now accepted that although this 'pudding' with its various fillings is considered to be Scotland's national dish, it was not invented there, but flourished wherever conditions created a taste for these frugal but tasty dishes, using a mixture of fat and cereals, well-seasoned, with perhaps the added luxury of dried fruit and spices.

For recipes contemporary with paintings from the seventeenth-century Low Countries we turn to *De Verstandige Kock*, published as part of a bigger treatise on household and estate management in 1667. The title is usually translated as *The Sensible Cook*, which is perhaps somewhat banal, compared with Robert May's more inspiring title, *The Accomplisht Cook*. Sensible, prudent and knowledgeable (all possible translations of *verstandige*), our Dutch housewife was given instructions for making use of *afval* in various ways; brawn from head meat, tripe, trotters and three kinds of *beulingen*, pudding or haggis to us, one of which is made of cooked and grated pig's liver, with white bread soaked in milk, eggs, spices and pork fat. It is possible that the young woman in the Van Odekerken painting is preparing something on these lines.

Dorothy Hartley wrote of offal as prepared in the last century with a drawing of a pot of sheep's pluck on the fire, with the windpipe hanging out to 'drain off impurities'.[2] To make haggis the various organs were cooked whole, then chopped with some fat or suet, and augmented with bread or grains, with appropriate seasonings. One looks in vain for these cooked offal dishes in paintings, but there is one sighting in a seventeenth-century work by Tomás Hiepes in the Prado, where, bottom right, are some sausages, possibly a kidney in its fat, or a lump of fatty bacon, and a neat pudding, tied firmly at both ends, which resembles a haggis.

Van Odekerken's sinister young woman and glimpses of raw pluck and other material are the best evidence we have of the actual preparation of offal. But the sight of raw livers and lights and related body parts had a savage beauty; the cascade of red and brownish organs, often suspended in the background of a genre scene, was a familiar sight. We see them hanging among joints of meat in Aertsen's Butcher's Shop where the decorative qualities of the meat, the brilliant reds and browns, perhaps reinforce the complex messages within the painting. The local politics of the Butchers' Guild and entrepreneurial property developers vie with religious symbolism in this complex work, which mattered enough to the painter and his clients to exist in several versions.[3]

Offal and Extremities in Art

Liver and lights appear in more sombre colours in two later paintings of butchers at work by Annibale Carracci. In the smaller version, in the Kimbell Art Museum at Fort Worth, the offal is cascading from the body of a beef carcass hung up for sale. According to C. D. Dickerson, the rapid, fluent brushstrokes seem to show that it might have been painted on the spot, out of doors, in the meat market of Bologna. He argues persuasively that this painting and the much larger version, in Christ Church Oxford, are not picturesque views of humble proletarian activities, like the leering comic characters of Passarotti's butcher's shop, but sensitive portraits of respected citizens going about their skilled craft with dignity and self respect. This representation of the butchers' profession is part of a political statement as potent as that of Aertsen, and indirectly illustrates the standing of offal as a desirable foodstuff.[4]

No politics in the striking image of a hen and the pluck of a sheep or pig in the painting by Abraham van Beyeren done in 1664: they are presented as ingredients for a meal, but with what possible hidden meanings we can only guess. The featherless hen is drab and lifeless, the offal glows with bright tones that match the bitter orange ready to squeeze over some oysters.

Many other kitchen and pantry scenes show pluck suspended in the background, alongside prime cuts of meat, indicating that it had considerable gastronomic significance.

Chicken livers and gizzards were too good to discard when preparing a roast; they are often represented tucked under the wing of a fowl as it is secured on a spit, or ready to eat on a cooked bird dished up for a banquet. The creature would have been trussed 'with his head tucked underneath his arm' as the old song goes, as a way of fixing it onto the spit, or the skewers used to secure it there. Ivan Day demonstrates this in his hands-on historic cookery classes, offering a nice example of how paintings can tell us things about preparing food that are not made clear in cookery texts.

Tripe, the stomach linings of various ruminant animals, is listed in the *Tacuinum Sanitatis* where cooking and enjoying it is pictured, without giving details of the four different kinds and their preparation.

The definition of offal can be broad enough to include heads and their contents, feet and trotters as well as internal organs. Brains and tongues are perhaps the more prestigious head organs. The nearest we can get to brains is maybe the creepy reminder of their resemblance to the interior of roasted chestnuts in a painting by Adriaen Coorte. Tongues appear in several still lifes from the Low Countries. Peter Benoit shows us a tongue among a display of luxury foods, with oranges and lemons, a pomegranate, a dish of pickled cucumbers with sprig of dill, a mature cheese, a soft cheese decorated with a rosebud and a chicken, studded with cloves and roasted to perfection with its liver tucked under a wing as described above. We also see them in several versions of a table spread with luxury items by Jacob van Hulsdonck, who was working in Antwerp in the seventeenth century, where a dish of cooked sheep's trotters and a bright pink tongue on a dish lined with fresh green leaves might indicate how they were enjoyed alongside a fine ham, hothouse fruit and expensive imported oranges and lemons. The overall impression of luxury is perhaps made more piquant by the contrast with the less prestigious items. The artist made several versions of this colourful mix of foodstuffs. Biographies of Jan Steen tell how he met his second wife by frequenting the market stall where she sold sheep's' feet. Cheap tasty street food, like pickled herrings and trotters, although delicious in their own right, were also valued as symbols of the robust simple fare that nurtured the great trading nation that the Low Countries had become, and so fit comfortably into a spread of fine food.

Looking back to Scappi's banquet menus, in Papal Rome, a century before the Protestant Dutch Republic, we see how time and time again offal dishes are listed alongside luxuries. Calves' feet in a garlic sauce, sweetbreads and ham in pasties, pigs' snouts and ears in a jelly, a blood pudding flavoured with marjoram, kids' heads boned and stuffed and served decorated with parsley and borage flowers, calves' heads cooked then gilded (coated in a mixture of egg, breadcrumbs, herbs and spices, then fried golden), with egg, tarts of cows' and pigs' udders, salt tongue, cooked and sliced, a salad of calves' feet set in jelly, stewed kids' heads, gilded and decorated with lemon slices and seasoned with sugar and cinnamon, and much more. It appears from the context and the subtlety of the recipes that offal was not then considered inferior to the nobler cuts of meat.

Other organs are rarely seen in art: we glimpse testicles and sweetbreads in the bottom left corner of a seventeeth-century work by Francisco Barrera illustrating the month of April, presumably from the slaughtered sheep, whose head is displayed along with the rest of the animal.

Heads have quite an impact in a whole range of genre and still life paintings, not just as ingredients but also as living creatures we have slaughtered on order to eat. The flayed ox head in Aertsen's butcher's stall is decorative as well as shocking, and if the reproachful eyes lose some of their impact, there is melodrama in the head of a calf in a still life by Boselli, but the raw violence of Goya's meat stall is shattering: his treatment of the head reminds us of the dread and suffering of the murdered animal, not the tasty party dish Robert May, in his *Accomplisht Cook* of 1665, served forth garnished with sprigs of parsley and pretty blue borage flowers. Carlo Magini's calf's head is so sanitized, placid, that it seems acceptable as a dish rather than an animal, not at all disturbing. Scappi and Robert May have several recipes for calves' heads, often cooked whole and carefully coated in breadcrumbs and fried to a golden that is then decorated with flowers. But the head is usually butchered to release the various parts, the brains removed for a more prestigious dish, the tongue a separate organ, and the cheeks or jowl prepared in different ways, then what is left cooked until the flesh can be removed and dealt with in various ways, like brawn in its jelly, or salted and cured. Rarely does a painting tell us anything about these procedures; we have just one image, by Mateo Cerezo in 1664, of a flayed head split down the middle as in some of the recipes. So information we get in art about offal seems to be limited to what is visually satisfying. A painting like Frans Snijders's 'Butcher's Shop' of 1630 shows much offal along with game and other meat. A basket of heads, more than five of them, is gruesomely realistic, and the flayed head of an ox is equally disturbing. The butcher himself is carefully removing the caul fat from the carcass of a pig or sheep, his skill and precision contrasting with the massive brutality of the huge ox in the background and the dark meat of a wild boar hanging on the left. A glistening cluster of pluck hangs from a hook on the left. Fewer hidden messages, a more sophisticated baroque realism.

In Florence, Jacopo Chimenti da Empoli produced many religious works and some crowded scenes of food suspended in kitchen or larder, with a greedy pile-up of ingredients, expensive props which contemporary gossip said he and his studio devoured with glee once the painting was done. Heads and trotters abound. One larder scene of 1624, in the Uffizi, has a pig's head in one corner, and a calf's in the other, alongside a calf's foot, almost indiscernible among the decorative fowl and joints of meat. Another larder displays various cured meats, salami, and the head of what looks like a goat on a platter, dwarfed by the massive ox's foot hanging alongside some sides of bacon. The bread, cheeses, hard-boiled eggs, cherries and fresh young vegetables imply a studio snack of considerable proportions. Giacomo Legi in Genoa has a more disturbing larder with a sheep's head towering over a table of fowl, some dead, some alive.

In conclusion, it looks as if offal as seen in art reinforces the possibility that it was a respected ingredient rather than an inferior commodity, both *cucina povera* and posh gastronomy, delicious when prepared with care, as many recipes attest, and so worthy of inclusion in genre and still life paintings, whatever complexities of meaning they might also contain.

Notes

1. Bartolomeo Scappi, *The Opera of Bartolomeo Scappi (1570): L'arte et prudenza d'un maestro Cuoco (The Art and Craft of a Master Cook)* (Toronto: University of Toronto Press, 2011); Robert May, *The Accomplisht Cook; Or, the Art and Mystery of Cookery* (Gloucester: Dodo Press, 2010).
2. Dorothy Hartley, *Food in England: A Complete Guide to the Food that Makes Us Who We Are* (London: Piatkus, 2009), p. 148.
3. This has been explained in detail by Charlotte Houghton in 'This Was Tomorrow: Pieter Aertsen's "Meat Stall" as Contemporary Art', *The Art Bulletin* 86.2 (June 2004), 277-300.
4. C.D. Dickerson III, *Raw Painting, the Butcher's Shop by Annibale Carracci* (Fort Worth, TX: Kimball Art Museum, 2010).

'A Sentimental Passion of a Vegetable Fashion': How American Culture, Politics and Commercial Agriculture Reflect and Influence Shifting Opinions of Fruit and Vegetable Offal

Charity Robey

Why are large, misshapen or irregular fruits and vegetables accepted and even celebrated at some times but considered disgusting or freakish at others? What do our reactions to 'abnormal' fruits and vegetables tell us about our food preferences and prejudices? How does the current interest in curbing food waste fit into contemporary beliefs about the wholesomeness, nutrition and deliciousness of vegetable offal?

In this paper, I'll show that the acceptance and celebration of the naturally diverse shapes and sizes of things Americans grew and consumed in the pre-Industrial period gave way to a preference for uniformity and perfection according to a set of standards based on size and shape rather than taste or nutrition. I'll describe how the farm-to-table movement has been an important catalyst in the shift back to consumers' embrace of non-standard produce, and how recent interest in reducing food waste is elevating the 'ugly vegetable' from the scrap heap to the grocery aisle and even to the white-cloth-covered tables of the elite.

Giant Peaches, a Huge Turnip and a Sweet Potato that Fed Florida

American culture, folk-tales and children's literature from the 'old world' abound with tales of giant fruits and vegetables. These stories are symptomatic of the fascination with vegetative enormity that is part of the world's cultural heritage and has, in turn, informed the cultural tapestry of American tastes.

Perhaps because in the new world these giant fruits and vegetables are associated with whimsy, as well as plenty and abundance, they were a mainstay of American marketing in the twentieth century as commercial growers sought a national audience for their brands.

There is something magical about a giant peach, a fact that lies at the centre of two very different children's stories, the Japanese folk-tale of Momotarō, or Peach Boy, and the 1961 book *James and the Giant Peach*, by the British author Roald Dahl, a story that has become so much a part of the American imagination that it is not perceived as a foreign story.[1] In the Japanese tale, a giant peach floating down a river brings a cherished son to a childless couple, and in Dahl's story an enormous peach saves the orphan James from a grim existence and transports him to a life of adventure.[2]

'The Giant Turnip' is a tale of a root that grows so large that it takes three generations of a family plus all the household animals lined up one behind the other to pull it out of the earth. A Russian folk-tale that has been reused and repurposed in songs and literary works, the turnip always serves as an out-sized symbol of well-being and abundance. Aleksey Tolstoy popularized the Giant Turnip as a children's story, entitled *The Gigantic Turnip*, and there are versions in Russian, Swedish, Lithuanian, Ukrainian and Spanish.[3]

The popularity of *The Gigantic Turnip* in America speaks to the old world and immigrant experience that celebrates a life of prosperity and plenty. Ebi Kondo, Senior Horticulturist at the Denver Botanic Garden, wrote that the American practice of carving a large pumpkin at Halloween began after nineteenth-century immigrants from Ireland and Scotland, with a tradition of carving large turnips at Halloween, brought the practice over and adapted it to American native pumpkins, large fall vegetables that serve as a symbol of plenty.[4]

The author Zora Neale Hurston, a collector of African American folklore, recorded scores of tall tales and legends told by ordinary people describing giant pumpkins, cabbages, corn, cucumbers and watermelons – stories of fruits and vegetables that were often an expression of collective well-being. An example is this bit of Florida folklore told to her by James Presley: 'My daddy raised uh sweet potato so big they had to make a sawmill job out of it, an' all de houses was made outa tater slabs an whut you reckon they did wid all dat sawdust? Made tater puddin.'[5]

Figure 1
Like the giant sweet potato in James Presley's tall tale, this one, grown at Sylvester Manor in Shelter Island, NY was made into 'tater puddin'. Charity Robey. photographer.

Images of giant fruits and vegetables have long been used in marketing directed at children, depicting vegetables as fun, silly and wholesome, an appeal based on American tall tales and larger-than-life stories such as those by Paul Bunyan and Mark Twain. In 1933 the Washington-Oregon Pear Bureau produced a pamphlet to convince children and their families to eat more pears. The pamphlet featured a giant pear that served as a house.

Figure 2
This pamphlet featured a giant pear, the central illustration of the Washington Oregon Pear Bureau's appeal to children and their families to eat more pears. Charity Robey, photographer.

In the early twentieth century, the Minnesota Valley Company began to sell a very large variety of pea called the Prince of Wales using a spokesman named the Jolly Green Giant, a grass-coloured cousin of the mythical Paul Bunyan. Lumbering onto the scene carrying a peapod the size of a canoe, the giant promised mothers that 'every day that's Green Giant Day at your house is 'treat' day – with plates scraped clean'.[6] This guarantee of wholesome abundance and safety from hunger no doubt appealed to the American consumer with its reassuring message.

Thomas Jefferson, James Madison and the Founding Cucumbers

The previous section looked at size from the perspective of how our immigrant experience, rural roots and our national narratives inform the popular imagination and have been tapped into by commercial markets. There is an important historical and political perspective on how fresh produce plays a role in forming national identity and even contributes to the idea of American exceptionalism, and it starts with the founders of the United States.

In pre-Industrial America, large fruits and vegetables were considered attractive, desirable and healthful. Before fruits and vegetables were grown commercially and shipped long distances, there was little uniformity to their appearance, and people consumed what we would today call 'ugly vegetables'. Uniformity was not necessarily even a desirable characteristic of produce.

Thomas Jefferson and James Madison were early proponents of the virtues of very large American fruits and vegetables, which they felt would demonstrate American farmers' agricultural superiority to their European counterparts. In *Founding Gardeners*, Andrea Wulf writes that Madison grew 'giant beetroot species from France' at Montpelier, his home and farm in Virginia.[7]

Shifting Opinions of Fruit and Vegetable Offal

In Jefferson's 1785 *Notes on the State of Virginia*, he catalogued the grains, vegetables and fruits – native and imported – that the founding farmers grew:

> Tobacco, Maize, Round potatoes, Pumpkins, Cymling, Squashes [...]. Besides these plants, which are native, our farms produce wheat, rye barley oats buck wheat broomcorn and Indian corn. We cultivate also potatoes both the long and the round, turnips carrots parsneps. Pumpkins and ground nuts.[8]

Jefferson deplored the ruin that he saw brought down on Virginia farmers who grew tobacco; he said that when farmers were forced to abandon tobacco, 'a happy obligation for them it will be. It is a culture productive of infinite wretchedness'.[9] He warned against farmers who over-extended themselves financially and exhausted their soil to grow a crop that was unwholesome and inedible. Jefferson's first-hand experience farming tobacco led him to convert his own land at Monticello from tobacco to grains starting in 1793.[10] He wrote that American farmers should grow food: by planting the right seeds and plants, and following careful farming practices, they could and should grow the largest vegetables possible.[11]

American exceptionalism may have had its first flowering in the realm of cucumbers. In 1825 Jefferson, then in his eighties, read in the *Cleveland Herald* that an Ohio farmer had grown cucumbers well over a metre long. Jefferson wrote to the governor of Ohio, 'although giants do not always beget giants, yet I should count on their improving the breed', and he asked for some seeds.[12] He distributed them before his death a few months later, and his efforts to establish the enormous cucumber met with apparent success. Peter Hatch writes in *A Rich Spot of Earth*, 'The rector of Charlottesville's Christ Church Frederick Hatch reportedly produced an eighty-eight inch [2.2 metre] long cucumber from the Monticello stash of seeds a few years after Jefferson's death.'[13]

Figure 3
'The rector of Charlottesville's Christ Church Frederick Hatch reportedly produced an eighty-eight inch long cucumber from the Monticello stash of seeds a few years after Jefferson's death' (Peter Hatch, A Rich Spot of Earth (Yale University Press, 2012), Figure 6.7, p. 132). Reprinted with permission of Yale University Press.

American State Fairs and the Beautiful, Ugly Vegetable

As the Industrial Revolution in America took place, attitudes towards fresh produce evolved. Very large and irregularly shaped fruits and vegetables were still exciting, but as manufacturing methods created the expectation of uniformity and as shipping methods became more sophisticated, Americans grew less interested in eating them.

Starting in the mid-twentieth century, agricultural festivals and state fairs across the United States began to give prizes for the largest vegetables and fruits, thus celebrating the achievements of the growers but also fuelling the shift in perceptions of produce. The people who crowded the harvest-time agricultural exhibits of these enormous fruits and vegetables considered them freaks of nature or the result of extreme farming. The implicit assumption was that these agricultural exemplars were unlikely to be good food.

The New York State Fair, held every year since 1841, is the oldest in the country, and the Minnesota State Fair, in operation since 1859, is the country's largest.[14] Both fairs feature agricultural awards for the largest pumpkins, squash and cabbage and have a separate category of awards for 'best' fruits and vegetables for the smaller, more regular, 'perfect' specimens.

The largest state of the union, Alaska, also has the shortest growing season, yet it claims the distinction of raising the largest specimens of cabbage, pumpkin, squash, leek and other vegetables thanks to rich soil and nearly twenty-four-hour sunlight in the summer months. Professor Stephen Brown of the University of Alaska, a district agriculture agent, advises farmers who are looking to grow giants. His unqualified enthusiasm for his state's monster produce has included these words of praise for Alaskan cabbage: 'The most commonly grown giant vegetables in Alaska are Northern Giant variety cabbage and O/S Cross variety cabbage […]. To me, they are the most delicious cabbage I've ever had. It is my understanding they are just as nutritious too. A fifty-pound giant cabbage will feed 250 people.'[15]

Most of the giants grown in Alaska end up in competition at the Alaska State Fair and are then donated to the Alaska Wildlife Conservation Center to be fed to injured or orphaned moose, grizzly bears and wood bison.

The USDA and the Codification of Fruit and Vegetable Aesthetics

The creation of national standards for grading and marketing food marked a fundamental shift in thought about what characteristics make American produce desirable as food.

Standards for crops such as cotton and tobacco were in place in the very early history of the United States, but the first grading of food crops began when wheat standards were proposed by the Chicago Board of Trade in 1856 to address the problem of sellers mixing grain from different producers in the same bin. William Cronon described the effect of this turning point in his book *Nature's Metropolis*: 'The grading system allowed elevators to sever the link between ownership rights and physical grain, with a host of unanticipated consequences.'[16]

The United States Department of Agriculture (USDA) was created by President

Lincoln in 1862; by the twentieth century it issued quality guidelines for virtually every kind of fruit or vegetable raised on American farms. Although USDA standards are completely voluntary, they play a profound role in establishing the physical characteristics of ideal fruits and vegetables for commercial growers, and these desired features in turn shape Americans' views of what constitutes vegetable perfection. Produce that does not conform to the highest standards described by the USDA rarely makes it to market: retailers reason that if consumers will not buy it, neither will they.

Figure 4
Apples that do not conform to the highest standards described by the USDA, rarely make it to market. USDA <https://www.ams.usda.gov/sites/default/files/media/Apple_Visual_Aid%5B1%5D.pdf>.

On its website, the USDA describes these quality grades as 'a "language" among traders. They make business transactions easier whether they are local or made over long distances. Consumers, as well as those involved in the marketing of agricultural products, benefit from the greater efficiency permitted by the availability and application of grade standards.'[17]

The produce that gets to grocery stores is generally 'Grade 1' or 'Fancy', even though the standards for Grade 2 and lower do not compromise nutrition or safety, just aesthetic standards, and subjective ones at that. The quality grades do not touch upon taste, flavour or sweetness.

The standard for 'US Fancy' peaches is an example of the USDA definition of peach beauty. It specifies that the fruit should be 'mature but not soft or overripe [...] free from damage caused by bruises, dirt or other foreign material, other disease, insects or mechanical or other means. In addition to the above requirements, each peach shall have not less than one-third of its surface showing blushed, pink or red color'.[18]

In spite of the fact that the USDA standards are voluntary, farmers, grocers and the people who market fruits and vegetables watch them closely in order to sell produce. For a look at how these standards affect the supply chain, we can start with a farm in

Florida. Carl Grooms and his wife DeeDee are part of a family that has raised a number of crops, now mainly strawberries, on about three hundred acres (1.21 square kilometres) at their Plant City, Florida, property for three generations. During a visit to the farm on one of the last days of the March harvest, Carl Grooms told me that strawberries are one of the only commercially grown fruits picked and packed by hand directly in the field at the height of ripeness, and they do not continue to ripen after they are picked.

Grooms adheres to USDA standards because he has to. The wholesaler he sells to can and will reject any pallet of berries that falls short. And because the USDA standards do not touch on flavour or sweetness, the wholesaler to whom he sells 'juicers' (berries that are processed on the farm and sold sliced for juice) includes a clause in the contract specifying a minimum sweetness as assessed by a Brix test, which measures the sugar content in the juice of a fruit or vegetable.[19]

The unintended consequences of the USDA standards, which define quality by size, shape and appearance rather than flavour and nutrition, are not only that food goes to waste if it doesn't quite conform. The standards actually deform agricultural practices, seed development and the entire commercial agricultural supply chain.[20]

Figure 5
Packed by hand directly in the field, strawberries do not continue to ripen after they are picked. Charity Robey, photographer.

Shifting Opinions of Fruit and Vegetable Offal

The Rise of Farmers Markets Stimulates Consumers' Growing Embrace of Nonstandard and Tiny Produce.

In the twenty-first century, the rise of farmers markets and the popularity of organically grown produce brought Americans in closer contact with fruits and vegetables that do not conform to the highest USDA standards, increasing awareness and acceptance of produce diversity.

For example, although the USDA #1 standard for strawberries specifies that berries must have a minimum diameter of three-fourths of an inch (about two centimetres), many strawberries purchased directly from farmers are much smaller. In fact, the superior taste and flavour of farm-stand berries, which have more to do with freshness and ripeness than with size, have made farm-stand strawberries a luxury food item which most consumers consider superior to berries purchased in a grocery store.

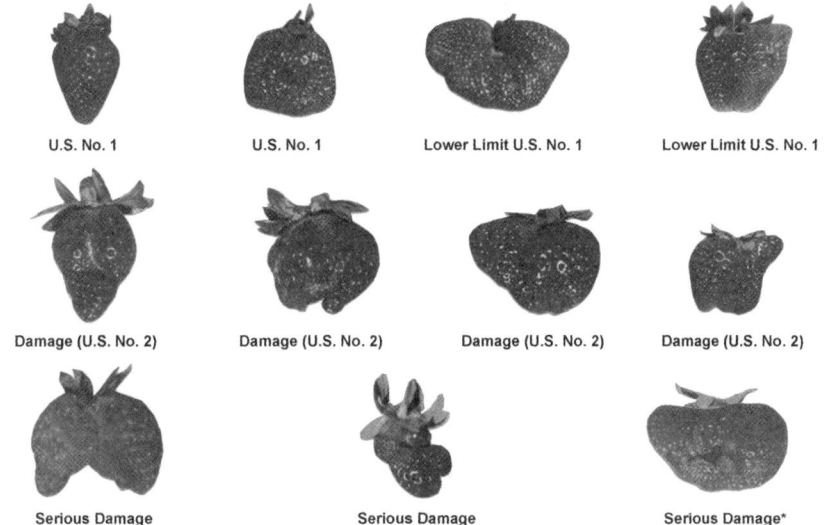

Figure 6
USDA standards, which define strawberry quality by size, shape and appearance rather than flavor and nutrition. USDA <https://www.ams.usda.gov/grades-standards/strawberries-grades-and-standards>.

Offal: Rejected and Reclaimed Food

A decided shift in consumer preferences began in the latter part of the twentieth century as many Americans began to regard tiny fruits and vegetables (e.g. strawberries, mini-watermelons, mini-carrots, cherry tomatoes and micro greens) as luxury items, preferable to 'normal' sized and large ones. This preference is based largely on the idea that small means tender, sweet and easy to process, while large means fibrous, heavy, bland or woody. Stephen Forbes, the director of the Botanic Gardens of South Australia and an expert in the cultural history of plants, has commented on these changing tastes:

> The modern technology of crop production, storage and distribution has also changed how we perceive plants as luxury foods. Many fresh fruits that were seasonal luxuries, such as apples, strawberries and tomatoes, are now considered all season commodities. Neoteny in vegetables and salads represents another manifestation of changes in crop technology that sees baby peas, baby carrots, broccoli shoots, baby salad greens and so on reaching our tables in recent decades.[21]

Figure 7
Carl Grooms holds a perfect strawberry that meets the USDA standard with a minimum diameter of about two centimetres. Charity Robey, photographer.

Farmer Megan Kent of Kent Family Growers encounters these preferences every time she interacts directly with her customers at the market, or when the Community Supported Agriculture customers pick up their shares. 'Most people don't want large anything', she said. 'Huge cabbages, squash, lettuces, peas, beans, cucumbers and root

Figure 8
Many consumers prefer small fruits and vegetables, such as these mini-watermelons, to 'normal' sized and large ones. Charity Robey, photographer.

Figure 9
Megan Kent of Kent Family Growers holds an enormous, but perfectly ripe and delicious strawberry grown on her farm. Daniel Kent, photographer.

vegetables seem to instill distrust or even outright aversion.'[22]

Clark McCombe, the owner of Briermere Farm in Riverhead, New York, said he stopped growing the Jersey Queen variety of peach in part because the fruit was so large that customers avoided it: 'We actually grew one that was six pounds, so big it didn't fit in our usual containers. I had no idea how to price it because we sell by the pound, and one peach would be over ten dollars.'[23]

Waste, Food Policy and the Glamorous, Ugly Vegetable

As food waste emerged as an international issue in the twenty-first century, attitudes towards non-standard fruits and vegetables became political. The farm-to-table movement, which emerged in the seventies, has grown even more dramatically in the last ten years to create a supply chain that puts cookers and eaters in ever-closer communication with the people who grow their food. The increasing role of farmers as educators and policy advisers to consumers, industry and government has led to more use of ugly fruits and vegetables as food.

As Megan Kent has explained, 'I think many people are simply confused about how their food is grown or produced and have never been taught to recognize varieties, ripeness level and freshness. This is a learned process obviously – not an innate one.'[24]

The identification of food waste as a global problem was highlighted by the European Union announcement that 2014 was the 'Year against Food Waste'. This increased awareness has resulted in retail initiatives in Europe and North America to curb food waste by selling vegetable offal through retail outlets in England (Waitrose and Tesco), Austria (Billa), France, (Intermarché), Italy, Portugal (Fruta Feia), Canada (Loblaw) and the United States (Whole Foods, Imperfect Produce, Trader Joe's).

We are beginning to see the first American wholesale giants take up the fight against food waste with the announcement that a large produce distributor in the Northeast, Baldor, will completely eliminate food waste in their own operations through a combination of selling 'ugly vegetables', using overripe and spoiled produce as feed for pigs at certain New York area farms, and creating a 'veggie blend', a powder made of twenty types of vegetables that may be used as a flavouring.[25]

Ending food waste has become a trending cause célèbre, with food world luminaries such as Dan Barber and celebrities such as Beyoncé joining the movement to end food waste by finding stylish and creative ways to distribute and consume unwanted produce.[26]

Combating food waste by consuming vegetable offal has also become a political statement. At a United Nations luncheon of leftover and discarded vegetables in 2015, former White House Chef Sam Kass and Dan Barber created a menu featuring a 'Landfill Salad', and on 10 May 2016, an event in New York City called Feeding the 5000, organized by Feedback (a British nonprofit working to end food waste), provided a free meal of ratatouille and vegetable torte to thousands of New Yorkers, feeding them potatoes, onions, eggplants, carrots, spinach and other vegetables that would otherwise have been wasted. Both events involved the farm-to-table advocate and chef Dan Barber, who was quoted as saying of the movement towards acceptance of vegetable offal, 'You don't do that by lecturing – you do that by hedonism.'[27]

Hedonism may work since it draws on our natural impulse to enjoy food, and as folk-tales about enormous fruits and vegetables suggest, the wonder and admiration humans have for the diversity of edible things is also in our nature.

The moral of the story of the giant turnip provides guidance in solving very big problems, such as food waste. When the grandfather, grandmother, granddaughter, dog, cat and mouse all line up to harvest a turnip the size of their house, they achieve something great by working together, 'Because on a farm, everyone helps.'[28]

Conclusion

Ever since Eve handed Adam the apple, fruits and vegetables have symbolized more than sustenance. This paper has shown how American attitudes about fruits and vegetables are influenced by culture and folklore, especially in the pre-Industrial era, by standardization and commodification in the modern world, and by global political issues today.

Children's stories such as *The Gigantic Turnip* and African American folk-tales of enormous sweet potatoes are evidence of a very human fascination with large vegetables and their association with abundance. Thomas Jefferson exalted the role of the farmer as a grower of food, and his fascination and celebration of large and vigorous produce was part of his view of America's potential to develop superiority as a nation.

American state fairs, starting in the nineteenth century and continuing to this day, celebrate the extreme farming resulting in enormous fruits and vegetables, even as commodification caused consumers to question the wholesomeness of this produce as food.

Fuelling distrust of non-standard produce, the grading of fruits and vegetables, even according to voluntary standards such as those of the USDA, has unintended consequences. When farmers adopt agricultural practices and make decisions about seed and pesticide use in an effort to avoid non-conforming crops, they rule out growing produce they fear they won't be able to sell to consumers, who then in turn rarely encounter non-symmetrical strawberries, for example, and avoid eating them when they do.

Today's American consumers are finally beginning to develop a more nuanced appreciation of vegetable beauty, similar in many ways to the pre-Industrial attitudes toward fruits and vegetables. Farmers and the people they feed are in closer contact, and growers are better able to educate and advise consumers, leading to more use of ugly fruits and vegetables as food.

Notes

1. Florence Sakade, *Peach Boy and Other Japanese Children's Favorite Stories* (Tuttle Publishing, 2008).

Offal: Rejected and Reclaimed Food

2. Roald Dahl, *James and the Giant Peach* (New York: Knopf, 1961).
3. Aleksey Tolstoy, *The Gigantic Turnip* (New York: Barefoot Books, 1998).
4. Ebi Kondo, 'The Turnip and Halloween: A Surprising Pair', Denver Botanic Gardens, 27 October 2015 <http://www.botanicgardens.org/blog/turnip-and-halloween-surprising-pair> [accessed 26 October 2016].
5. Zora Neale Hurston, *Every Tongue Got to Confess: Negro Folk Tales from the Gulf States* (New York: Harper Collins, 2001), p. 130.
6. 'Jolly Green Giant', pamphlet, Cecily Brownstone Collection, New York University.
7. Andrea Wulf, *Founding Gardeners* (New York: Vintage, 2011), p. 192.
8. Thomas Jefferson, *Writings: Notes on the State of Virginia* (New York: The Library of America, 1984), p 164.
9. Jefferson, p. 293.
10. 'Crops at Monticello', *Monticello.org*, Thomas Jefferson Foundation, Inc. <https://www.monticello.org/site/plantation-and-slavery/crops-monticello> [accessed 27 May 2016].
11. Jefferson, p. 164.
12. Letter by Thomas Jefferson to Thomas Worthington, 29 November 1825, Founders Online, United States National Archives < https://founders.archives.gov/documents/Jefferson/98-01-02-5695> [accessed 27 May 2016].
13. Peter J. Hatch, *A Rich Spot of Earth: Thomas Jefferson's Revolutionary Garden at Monticello* (New Haven: Yale University Press, 2012), pp. 132, 133.
14. New York State Fair <http://nysfair.ny.gov/about/fair-history/> [accessed 24 May 2016]; Minnesota State Fair <http://www.mnstatefair.org/general_info/fair_history.html> [accessed 24 May 2016].
15. Interview with Stephen C. Brown, Ph.D., Professor, District Agriculture Agent, Cooperative Extension Service, University of Alaska, Fairbanks.
16. William Cronon, *Nature's Metropolis: Chicago and the Great West* (New York: WW Norton, 1992), p. 116.
17. USDA Standards <www.ams.usda.gov/grades-standards/fruits> [accessed 22 May 2016].
18. New York State Fair.
19. Interview with Carl and DeeDee Grooms, Fancy Farms, Plant City, FL, 15 March 2016.
20. Rochelle Bilow, 'Are Beauty Standards for Fruits and Vegetables Unfair?', *Bon Appétit*, 29 July 2014 <http://www.bonappetit.com/entertaining-style/trends-news/article/fruit-vegetable-beauty-standards> [accessed 22 May 2016].
21. Stephen Forbes, 'White bread and Densuke Melons', *Greenspace: Beauty & Truth – The Relationship Between People and Plants*, 29 March 2016 <https://stephenjforbes.wordpress.com/2016/03/29/white-bread-and-densuke-melons-plants-as-luxury-foods/> [accessed 22 May 2016].
22. Megan Kent, Kent Family Farm, Canton, NY, email to the author, 19 January 2016.
23. Interview with Clark McCombe, Briermere Farm, Riverhead, NY, 5 May 2016.
24. USDA Standards.
25. Jesse Hirsch, 'One Massive Producer Is Reinventing Its Approach to Food Waste', *Edible Manhattan* (April/May), 18 April 2016 <http://www.ediblemanhattan.com/foodshed-2/food-waste-baldor/> [accessed 22 May 2016].
26. Brooke Bobb, 'Why You Should Buy Ugly Fruits and Vegetables', *Vogue*, 28 March 2016 <http://www.vogue.com/article/ugly-produce-fruits-vegetables-food-waste-cooking> [accessed 22 May 2016].
27. Peter Holley, 'Why World Leaders Dined on Trash at the U.N.', *The Washington Post*, 28 September 2015 <https://www.washingtonpost.com/news/morning-mix/wp/2015/09/28/why-world-leaders-dined-on-trash-at-the-u-n/?utm_term=.ab8119ae3e32> [accessed 22 May 2016].
28. Janice M. Del Negro, *Folktales Aloud: Practical Advice for Playful Storytelling* (Chicago: American Library Association Editions, 2 December 2013), p. 19.

Gone and Forgotten: Hook Steaks, Trash Bags and Other Vanished Icelandic Offal Dishes

Nanna Rögnvaldardóttir

We Icelanders have a curious kind of relationship to what we consider as our traditional food, which happens to be partly offal-based. We are not really proud of it, and some of it may disgust us, especially younger people – but we still like to talk about it, describe it to tourists; we talk about how it is prepared and eaten, and often embellish the stories with some dubious 'facts'. We talk about sheep heads, ram testicles, black pudding and so on. Sometimes we serve this to unsuspecting tourists and snigger a little when they find it disgusting.

Many Icelanders seem to think that no one else eats anything similar, and most people sincerely believe that this is, more or less, what our ancestors ate all the time: that Icelandic cuisine remained almost unchanged from the Settlement of Iceland over 1100 years ago until the early twentieth century.

What they do not realize is that their ancestors cooked and ate things that would shock and disgust the average Icelander exactly as descriptions of the 'accepted' traditional food does tourists.

Many of those dishes have vanished from memory and can only be found in written sources or old tales and poems. No living person has ever tasted them. Some disappeared because people were marginally better off than before. Others slowly faded away, sometimes because they were fiddly and time-consuming to make, sometimes because ingredients were hard to get or because of changing tastes. And some have perhaps disappeared simply because they were not included in the limited collection of dishes commonly served at *þorrablót*, the Icelandic winter feast that celebrates traditional cuisine.

But even the *þorrablót* has changed. The current model was invented by a Reykjavík restaurant around 1960. The first *þorrablót* in my home region of Skagafjörður was held in 1897 and was described thus:

> Everyone brought food in containers of some sort and this was then arranged in a huge trough that had been specially made for this. Then people gathered around the trough with knives and other utensils and dived in. There were all sorts of Icelandic delicacies: smoked lamb, fermented shark, all kinds of whey-preserved food such as seal flippers, hook steak, cattle and sheep feet, lamb neck fat, and other common food.[1]

Offal: Rejected and Reclaimed Food

Of the dishes mentioned, only the smoked lamb and the shark would be found at a regular þorrablót now, and some have completely disappeared.

Many of those dishes were made from animal parts that are not now used for human food. Others were made from parts that are still used, and may even be highly prized, but the cooking and preservation methods, and the dishes themselves, were vastly different from modern dishes. Almost anything that could remotely be considered edible was used, along with several things that might not be.

This is of course not unique to Iceland. Still, there were special conditions that made offal perhaps even more important in Iceland than elsewhere. To understand this, we should look at the background that shaped Icelandic cuisine.

Iceland was for many centuries probably the poorest country in Western Europe, at least. It was always somewhere north of life: the climate was harsh and unforgiving, and the resources were limited. After the fifteenth century, no grain was grown, no vegetables were cultivated; there was no fruit except a few types of berries, no nuts, very few wild things to be picked. Some grain was imported but it was used for ale or porridges rather than bread, which was rare.

Instead, we had fish, mostly eaten dried; we had lamb and mutton and some beef but no pork or chicken; we had milk and dairy products, seals and whales and seabirds. But all of this was very dependent on the whims of nature – a harsh winter with lots of snow and icebergs in the fjords could mean that the farmers lost part of their livestock because they ran out of hay for feed; a volcanic eruption could mean that most of the livestock perished because of volcanic ash and poisonous gases.

On top of this, Icelandic farmers faced an additional challenge, which was preservation, especially important because most of whatever food people could raise or hunt or gather was very seasonal. Animals were usually slaughtered during a short period in the autumn, after being driven down from the mountains where they had spent the summer. Then the meat and the offal had to be preserved throughout the year. Most of the fish was caught during the late winter and spring, and also had to be preserved.

One of the things Icelanders lacked was salt, which had to be imported and was expensive. Another thing that was scarce was firewood, which meant smoking was not always an option, but much of the meat was smoked, and the fish was mostly dried. That left the problem of storing the offal.

During the short summer, the cows and ewes produced a lot of milk; most of it was made into *skyr* and butter and stored for a long time, and the by-product of this practice was whey, which could be fermented and used to preserve food. This is one of the things that makes Icelandic offal dishes special – so many of them are whey-preserved, or soured, as we say. That goes for much of the surviving traditional stuff, like black pudding and ram's testicles, but also for a vast number of vanished dishes.

Watching Dishes Vanish

I grew up on a farm in northern Iceland in the 1960s. My family has lived on this farm since 1733, and many of our old food traditions still survived. Several of the dishes that I grew up with and watched being made or helped make are now more or less unknown. My interest in this type of food stems partly from the fact that I feel as if I literally watched some of it disappear from Icelandic food culture.

One of my favourite times of the year used to be 'slaughter time' in the autumn. I was very young when I realized how important it was to process the offal quickly, as it would spoil long before the meat, and to stir the blood so it wouldn't coagulate. Everyone was very busy preparing and preserving food; stomachs and large intestines were emptied and the intestinal fat wrapped up in bundles called *mörvar*; then everything was brought into the kitchen, where my mother would wash and scrape the stomachs and colons, and we children had the job of plucking away any fat adhering to the colon and cutting or tearing glands from the intestinal fat.

Almost nothing was thrown away. My mother made it all into food, if not for the family, then for the animals. There were a couple of huge barrels in the larder, filled with fermented whey and lots of food, almost all of it made from offal, but in another room, where the dogs slept, there was still another whey barrel filled with food for them, for instance lungs and cow and sheep udders. Lungs had earlier sometimes been made into sausages and udders were often lightly salted, then smoked, but mostly this was just boiled and whey-preserved. Sometimes the old men on the farm, my grandfather and his brothers, had a craving for something they had eaten in their childhood and got some from the dog barrel. Of course I got a taste too.

All parts of the stomachs of sheep and cattle were used, mostly cut up, sewn into pouches and stuffed with various things, except maybe the omasum, because with all its folds it was so difficult to clean well. Still, it was eaten in some parts of the country until the beginning of the twentieth century, usually stuffed with lamb suet.

But this was one of the dishes that I only heard about, probably because by this time people could afford not to eat such things as *ruslakeppur* or trash bag, which was a method to use up all the odds and ends from the carcass: cut-offs from tripe, liver and lungs, veins, the uterus, glands, just about anything, mixed with chopped suet, sewn into a piece of lamb stomach and boiled. This was eaten by the poor in earlier times but by the late nineteenth century usually reserved for dogs. *Kirtlabaggi*, gland bag, was glands from the lamb, stuffed into the large intestine with some fat, boiled and smoked or preserved in whey.[2]

Krókasteik, hook steak, was the uterus of a cow or ewe, cut up and scraped, either boiled whole and preserved in whey or cut up and used in black pudding – or added to the trash bag. *Krókasteik* is a very old term, mentioned in a rhyme dated to the fourteenth century.[3]

The small intestines of a sheep were cleaned and washed. In the south and west of Iceland they were usually braided and boiled. This was called *vil* and survived into the twentieth century but in later years usually as dog food.[4] In other regions it was customary to wrap the intestines around meat, sometimes a piece of *magáll*, which is a sort of smoked lamb bacon, but sometimes the esophagus or the windpipe of the animal was used. The bundle was boiled, preserved in whey, and served in slices. This was called *garnabaggi*, intestine wrap.⁵

Offal Treats

But many of the vanished offal dishes were not simply food for the poor and starving, they were considered delicacies and held in high regard. *Gollur* is mentioned in a nursery rhyme that every Icelandic child has heard many times, yet almost none of them know that it is stuffed lamb's pericardium, a dish that was well known up until the mid-twentieth century. The heart was removed from the pericardium, which was then inverted so the fat was on the inside and stuffed, sometimes with slices of the heart itself, sometimes fat or fatty meat, kidneys, even lamb tenderloin. It was then boiled and often served to children or others as a treat or prize. In some places, it was customary to give a special treat to the shepherd at Michaelmas, sometimes *gollur* from the fattest sheep slaughtered that autumn; this was called *smalagollur,* shepherd's pericardium.⁶

Lamb's liver is now mostly used for *lifrarpylsa*, somewhat similar to haggis. It is still popular, and most Icelanders think it is an ancient dish that has remained unchanged since the Settlement, but in fact there is no evidence of it earlier than the nineteenth century. Before that, livers were usually just boiled and preserved in whey, and often served with melted sheep tallow with cracklings.

The blood of lambs and other animals was used for several dishes and seems always to have been highly prized. We have a description written by a man who was hunting wild sheep in the mountains of southwestern Iceland. He was unable to drive the animals he caught back home so he had to slaughter them and if he had nothing else, he bled them into his hat, then he removed the stomach, cleaned it, and poured the blood into it to carry it home. Once he forgot to wash his blood-soaked hat before he put it back on his head and frightened the life out of the people he met.⁷

Most of the lamb's blood was used for black pudding, still popular in Iceland. But there was another dish that was also made from cattle blood, and may have been more common when flour was scarce. This was called *steinblóð*, stone blood. The blood was not stirred while cooling, but left to coagulate. Then it was cut into pieces, boiled briefly, and placed in fermented whey.⁸

Another method was to mix rye flour with cattle blood, put the mixture into a bag, and boil it. Then it was cut into cubes, fried in tallow, and eaten hot, strewn with sugar. Horse blood was sometimes used for blood sausage and other blood-based dishes, but it was thought inferior to lamb and veal blood.

My favourite childhood dessert was a sort of pudding made from the blood of a milk calf, usually a few days old. We called this *blóðkássa*, blood stew – not a very dessert-like name, I admit – but it also had strange names like *villibráð* (wild game) or *kálfadans* (calves dance). It was made from milk, flour, butter and blood, and sometimes raisins or caraway seeds, cooked into a thick sauce that would set when it cooled. Then it was eaten with liberal amounts of cinnamon sugar. One writer described the dish, made with sugar and raisins, as 'living honey'.⁹

Large bones and heads of cattle and sometimes horses were often made into a special treat called *hraun*, meaning lava or craggy rocks. They were hung in a shed to ferment, or smoked, then boiled. No one makes this anymore, but there is a description written in 1972, when an old man made it to show how it had been done: A piece of the backbone of a cow, with some meat attached, was hung in the cow shed, at the dampest place in the back. When it had become slimy and greenish, it was wrapped tightly in a cloth and placed in the corner of the cowshed, covered with hay if the weather was cold, for about a week. Then the *hraun* was boiled and eaten.¹⁰

Cattle bones were boiled and preserved in whey for a long time until they begin to soften slightly. Then they were scraped and the scrapings were stirred into melted tallow, poured into a jar, and used as a spread for bread.

Lamb's heads are still popular in Iceland. But the brains are no longer used: in fact it is illegal to sell them because of scrapie, a disease related to mad cow disease. They were used in a few dishes but had almost disappeared before scrapie became a problem. They were often kneaded with rye flour and made into patties that were boiled with the lamb's head or baked on embers.

Lamb's head is always cooked and eaten whole; the cheeks are not sold separately, neither are the eyes or ears, nor the tongue, although all are eaten. But the tongues of other animals were treated separately. My favourite sandwich filling when I was a child was smoked foal tongue. That is another vanished treat – or almost vanished; it has never been sold in any shop, and almost no one knows of it. But to my great delight, I discovered a few years ago that a cousin of mine still makes it.

Wild Offal

The only land mammal in Iceland that is hunted as game is the reindeer, a late eighteenth century import from Norway, but there were geese, ducks and seabirds. Seals were hunted and sometimes whales beached themselves. *Hvalreki* – the beaching of a whale – is a term still used in Icelandic when something extremely fortunate and unexpected happens. The meat and blubber of a whale could save many lives in times of famine.

In the spring of 1882, when people in northern Iceland were starving, several large whales were beached, probably saving many from hunger and even death, and a description of this incident reveals a forgotten dish that other sources indicate was known back in the thirteenth century. It also shows both the extreme poverty of Icelandic peasants, and the problems of keeping and preserving what little they had: 'Some people kept the blubber in dark, damp houses; others buried it but took care that it wasn't touched by earth, and kept it thus for a long time, even up to four years. This was called *myrkurhvalur* (whale of darkness) and tasted reasonably good, even though it had become quite disgusting to look at'.¹¹ The very best blubber was said to be the bit surrounding the blowhole. It was hung to dry and ferment for a few months before it was eaten. That is not done any more, but whey-preserved whale blubber is still eaten in Iceland.

The tail of the whale was cooked separately before being placed in fermented whey; it was said that the tail of a fin whale needed to be boiled for a whole day. The tail and flippers of the small harbour porpoise were boiled, then chopped and made into flipper jam. The smoked tongue of a whale, especially a calf, was considered a real treat. Well cleaned, boiled and whey-preserved whale intestines were 'edible' according to a eighteenth-century writer who also says that whale penises give strength and power to those who eat them. He doesn't give a recipe, though.[12]

Seal blood was sometimes used for a sort of porridge or pudding, but sources indicate that this was a rather unpopular dish.[13] But the head and flippers were considered very good; they were usually singed by fire and boiled. Singed seal flippers are in fact still served at certain midwinter feasts.

Seal blubber was cooked separately from the meat, usually salted, then dried, but Eggert Ólafsson, who wrote about it in the eighteenth century, says the best method is to preserve it in ash from burned seaweed.[14] Well-cured seal blubber should be green throughout. It was usually eaten with dried or half-dried fish. *Selavafningur*, seal braid, was made from two strands of cleaned seal intestines and one of seal blubber that were braided together, then smoked and boiled, or boiled and preserved in whey.

Game birds were widely used, especially seabirds like puffin and guillemot. Two other popular seabirds were the large gannet and the fatty and foul-smelling fulmar. Sources from Mýrdalur and the Westman Islands describe how every scrap of those birds was used. The wings, legs, head, and neck of the gannets were scorched by fire, then boiled and eaten. Gannet pudding was made from gannet liver, rye flour, lamb suet, and raisins, stuffed into the neck of a gannet and boiled. The internal fat of a large gannet could weigh up to half a pound; it was rendered and used as a spread for bread and dried fish.[15]

The fulmar was often so fatty that it was difficult to pluck it without the half-liquid fat running out of the bird's neck. *Fýlafeitarbræðingur*, a mixture of fulmar fat and sheep tallow, was the main spread for bread and dried fish in the Westman Islands in the nineteenth century. Fulmar and gannet skin was also eaten; it is very fatty, and, while some couldn't stomach it, others loved it. Fulmar heads were eaten separately and considered very tasty but fiddly to prepare.[16]

Stretching the Catch

Fish, fresh and especially dried, has always been one of the mainstays of the Icelandic diet, and of course fish offal was used in many imaginative ways. I will not talk about fish cheeks or tongues – or, rather, throat muscles – because you can get them in many restaurants in Iceland. But I do want to include whole cod's heads, even though a young innovative chef, Gísli Matthías Auðunsson, has single-handedly brought them

Vanished Icelandic Offal Dishes

back from oblivion in a new guise. He serves a fresh cod's head boiled in broth; it is brought whole to the table and the guests at his restaurant share all the delightful tidbits between them.

And there are many. In his great five-volume work Íslenskir sjávarhættir, Lúðvík Kristjánsson lists no fewer than 363 names for various parts of a cod's head: bones, cartilage, membranes, muscles and skin. The book devotes fourteen pages to descriptions of the proper techniques of tearing up a dried cod's head, naming every single bone, every part of the gills, every small muscle, along with a description of how they were eaten or utilized.[17] Even the dried gills from the fish head were eaten, usually either boiled or grilled on an open fire and served with lots of seal or whale blubber or melted sheep fat, or they were soured in *skyr* or whey.

When fish heads were eaten fresh, the gills were removed and then the head was either boiled and served whole, often stuffed with fish liver, or boiled until it began to fall apart, then all bones were removed and the fish from the head was mashed with melted tallow or butter.

Bjarni Sæmundsson, Iceland's first ichthyologist, wrote in 1924:

> A big, fat head of a cod or ling is almost a full meal for the average man and the same goes for a couple of ocean catfish heads; there is a lot of food to be found in the head of a large tusk and everyone knows how delicious and full of fat the head of a halibut is. There is some very fine fat in the brain cavity of an ocean perch. To make the heads even better, some of them, such as large cod and ocean catfish heads, can be fried.[18]

The rest of the bones were used too. *Beinfeiti* or bone fat was made from the bones of small halibuts that had been filleted. They were buried in gravel for two or three days, then washed and hung to dry until they had taken on a red hue. This was then boiled and eaten and was considered a treat.[19] A poem from the seventeenth century describes it as 'very good for the stomach'.[20]

Fish bones, fins and tails, along with some fish skins, were often preserved in fermented whey for a good while, then boiled or steamed for several hours, until they began to soften somewhat – but not quite, as the name of this dish was *bruðningur*, crunch.[21] This, and a similar dish called *beinastrjúgur*, where the bones were preserved in *skyr*, was also made from bones of sheep, seabirds and cattle.[22] It was not exactly popular, as this old rhyme shows:

> *Guði sé lof fyrir skráp og skinn*
> *skorpið roðið og bruðninginn*
> *engan máta ég að því finn*
> *því ómatvönd eru harðindin.*

[Thank God for shark skin, the wrinkly fish skins, and the crunchy bones; I'm not complaining about this because one can't have dislikes in times of famine.]

Shark fins and tails were dried and grilled until the skin began to fall off, then beaten with a mallet, cut up and placed in well fermented whey. The fins of the halibut were mostly eaten fresh but also cut into long shreds, salted and dried. The skin of dried and salted fish was fried and eaten with butter or *bræðingur*, a mixture of sheep tallow and fish oil. Dried fish skins were also preserved in sour *skyr*. Ocean catfish skins were sometimes soaked in hot broth from smoked lamb and then eaten with fat skimmed from the broth. This was considered a great delicacy.

Lumpfish jam or *rauðmagasulta* was made by taking freshly boiled *hvelja*, the jelly-like fat layer and skin of a male lumpfish, and pouring some vinegar over it while warm. The *hvelja* then coagulated when it cooled and was eaten with potatoes or spread on rye bread.[23] Another way to use the *hvelja* was to hang it in a shed in the spring and leave it until ewe's milk was available in late June. Then it was scalded, scraped and placed in a bowl of milk to coagulate. Then it was sliced, preserved in fermented whey and later eaten mixed with porridge and sour milk. In the Strandir region, the *hvelja* was sometimes fried and eaten with *bræðingur*.

Rotten Icelandic shark often shows up on lists of the most disgusting foods in the world, and some still eat *hákarlsstappa*, boiled fermented shark, mashed with fermented tallow or butter. But there was an older and even more potent version, involving shark cartilage, which was cut up, mixed with some shark meat, put in a bag, and fermented, usually in the cowshed, for one to five weeks, depending on the desired potency. All the yellow stuff was washed off, and then it was boiled. The pot had to be skimmed frequently because the smell was terrible. After draining, the cartilage and shark meat was mixed with fermented sheep fat. This was stirred for quite a while and either eaten hot with bread or dried fish, or cooled, then sliced and eaten on bread.[24] Strange as it may seem, this dish was much prized by many, as evident by this old rhyme:

Hákarlsstöppu heita fékk
hennar kenndi góðan smekk.
Ekki nennti ég í það sinn
allan lesa borðsálminn.[25]

[I was served hot *hákarlsstappa*, it tasted so good that I couldn't be bothered to finish reading the table graces.]

The stomach of several types of fish, called *kútmagi*, was cleaned and either dried, then boiled and preserved in whey, or stuffed with fish liver (*lifrarmagi*) or a mixture of liver and rye flour (*mjölmagi*). Actually, *kútmagi* is not quite forgotten, as some male clubs serve it at special functions. Stuffed stomachs were usually just boiled but a large cod stomach stuffed with liver was sometimes parboiled, then roasted on a spit. This was called *steikimagi*.

Vanished Icelandic Offal Dishes

The stomach of a skate, called *pjanka*, was cleaned, brined but not stuffed, just boiled and preserved in whey. It was often eaten with whipped milk. Dried halibut stomachs were parboiled, and then preserved in *skyr* or buttermilk. Dried stomachs of blue ling were sometimes cut open and cleaned. Several stomachs were sewn together and used to wrap around butter slabs.[26]

Swim bladders were boiled and preserved in whey or in some *skyr*. They are a rich source of isinglass, and if a bladder was parboiled briefly, then put into a bowl of *skyr* while still hot, the *skyr* coagulated and could be cut into slices. *Sundmagaskyr* was considered a delicacy.[27]

Although isinglass was widely used in jellies and desserts before gelatine became popular, I'm not sure if swim bladders were ever used as a dessert by themselves anywhere else – but there are Icelandic recipes for whey-preserved swim bladders, cut up small, caramelized in sugar, and served with whipped cream.[28]

Dried swim bladders could be soaked in salted lamb broth overnight, then cooked in butter. Milk was added, along with some flour, to make a gluey mass, called *sundmagasteik*, swim bladder steak. One source tells of a woman who made what she called swim bladder cheese by cooking a large amount of barley porridge and arranging it in a barrel in layers, alternating with swim bladders.[29]

Shark's intestines were usually cleaned, soaked overnight and then either boiled and preserved in whey or cut into segments which were then stuffed with a mixture of rye flour, lamb suet and yarrow, boiled and eaten fresh or whey-preserved.

A female shark often carries hundreds of eggs, sometimes enough to fill a barrel. They were eaten fresh or boiled and placed in fermented whey. The eggs are said to have tasted rather nasty but were eaten anyway. One source even says they were used for baking.[30]

Fish roe, fresh or lightly smoked, is still used; it is simply boiled, frequently with the liver, and eaten warm with potatoes and butter. Earlier the broth was often mixed with fermented whey and eaten as a soup, sometimes with dried yarrow added. Roe soup was not very popular, as evident by an old saying: 'This looks like it is turning into roe soup,' meaning 'Here we have another fine mess'.[31]

Hrognakökur, roe cakes, were made from roe kneaded with rye and shaped into thin flatbreads that were fried in fat, or into thicker cakes boiled in a mixture of whey and water. Those breads seem to have been rather unpopular. They were very dry and needed a lot of fat.[32]

Raw lumpfish roe was crushed, sieved, and stirred into hot milk, which then coagulated. This was called *hrognaystingur* or *hrognadrafli*. It was cut into slices when cold and eaten with whipped milk. *Hrognaostur*, roe cheese, was made by weighing lumpfish roe down in a barrel. Then it was cut into pieces and preserved in whey.

It was not just the roe that was eaten. *Svil*, or cod's testicles with semen (*milt*), was usually either buried in earth and fermented, or boiled and then preserved in whey. It could also be smoked or hung in an airy place and half-dried before cooking. Some made *sviljaostur*, milt cheese. Fresh *svil* were boiled, churned, stirred into fresh milk and finally some fermented whey was added, and this was drained in a cheesecloth. The texture is said to have been fairly similar to milk cheese but more crumbly.[33]

Conclusion

These are just some of the disappeared offal dishes that most living Icelanders have never known. In summary, it can safely be said that my countrymen became quite good at using every scrap of the meagre resources they had. Other nations did this too, but some of the methods and recipes used in Iceland may have been rather unique.

Notes

1. Björn Jónsson, 'Þorrablót á Hólum', *Ýmsir þættir og greinar*, HSk. 2146, 4to. XVII.
2. Hallgerður Gísladóttir, *Íslensk matarhefð* (Reykjavík: Mál og menning, Þjóðminjasafn Íslands, 1999), p. 135.
3. *Den norsk-islandske skjaldedigtning*, B (Copenhagen: Gyldendalske boghandel – Nordisk forlag, 1915), p. 416.
4. Kristleifur Þorsteinsson, *Úr byggðum Borgarfjarðar II* (Reykjavík: Ísafoldarprentsmiðja, 1972), p. 60.
5. Finnur Jónsson, *Þjóðhættir og ævisögur frá 19. öld* (Akureyri: Bókaútgáfa Pálma H. Jónssonar, 1945), p. 371.
6. 'Smalagollur', *Vikan* 37 (1943), pp. 13-14.
7. 'Um villifé á Núpsstað'. *Blanda* 7-10 (1924), 92.
8. Gísladóttir, pp. 101-02.
9. Friðrik Eggerz, *Úr fylgsnum fyrri aldar I* (Reykjavík: Iðunn, 1950), p. 149.
10. Gísladóttir, pp. 119-21.
11. Jón L. Hansson, 'Harðindin í Húnavatnssýslu vorið 1882 og hvalrekinn á Ánastöðum', *Lesbók Morgunblaðsins* 6 (1939), 42.
12. Lúðvík Kristjánsson, *Íslenskir sjávarhættir*, 5 vols (Reykjavík: Menningarsjóður, 1983-86), V, p. 71.
13. Jónas Jónasson, *Íslenskir þjóðhættir* (Reykjavík: Ísafoldarprentsmiðja, 1934), p. 44.
14. Eggert Ólafsson and Bjarni Pálsson, *Ferðabók Eggerts Ólafssonar og Bjarna Pálssonar um ferðir þeirra á Íslandi árin 1752–1757 I* (Reykjavík: Örn og Örlygur, 1974), p. 286.
15. Sigfús M. Johnsen, *Saga Vestmannaeyja* II (Reykjavík: Ísafold, 1946), p. 39.
16. Johnsen, p. 49.
17. Lúðvík Kristjánsson, *Íslenskir sjávarhættir*, 5 vols (Reykjavík: Menningarsjóður, 1983-86), III, p. 294.
18. Bjarni Sæmundsson, 'Hugleiðingar um hagnýtingu á fiskúrgangi', *Ægir* 11 (1923), 169.
19. Þórleifur Bjarnason. *Hornstrendingabók* (Akureyri: Þorsteinn M. Jónsson, 1943), p. 212.
20. Kristjánsson, III, p. 292.
21. Jónasson, p. 42.
22. Bjarni Pálsson, 'Um íslenzk matvæli', *Tímarit hins íslenzka bókmenntafélags* 2 (1881), 68.
23. Gísladóttir, p. 174.
24. Kristjánsson, III, p. 387.
25. Sæmundur Dúason, *Einu sinni var* II (Akureyri: Prentverk Odds Björnssonar, 1967), p. 234.
26. Lúðvík Kristjánsson, *Íslenskir sjávarhættir*, 5 vols (Reykjavík: Menningarsjóður, 1983-86), IV, p. 352.
27. Kristjánsson, V, p. 437.
28. Gísladóttir, p. 187.
29. Kristjánsson, V, p. 437
30. Guðni Einarsson, 'Góði hirðirinn á Krossi', *Morgunblaðið*, 27 February 1994, p. B5.
31. Jón Thorarensen, *Svalheimamenn* (Reykjavík: Nesjaútgáfan, 1977), p. 361.
32. Pálsson, p. 68.
33. Kristjánsson, IV, p. 441.

Outlaw Offal: The Curious Cases of *Tête de Veau* and *Foie Gras*

Richard Warren Shepro

Offal may be privately shunned based on squeamishness, or popular views, or medical advice. What makes any particular kind of offal so odious – so awful – that its use for human consumption should be prohibited by governmental action? Who should decide these issues, and why? When is it appropriate for a single rule about a particular food to apply to all citizens?

It is one thing to dislike a dish, or disapprove of it, or believe that others need to be warned about it, or to regulate it to ensure purity or safety. But actually to ban a dish and prohibit others from choosing to eat it is a drastic step and one that, historically, has been rare. Madeleine Ferrières's monumental study of food fears, *Histoire des peurs alimentaires du Moyen* Âge *à l'aube du XXme siècle*, translated inventively as *Sacred Cow, Mad Cow: A History of Food Fears*, does not describe a single product from the Middle Ages on that was actually prohibited.[1] The focus instead was on adulteration, purity and public safety.

Consider the following meal that would be prohibited by law under some recent statutes: Two French and one US lawyer have a matter to discuss, and meet for lunch in Paris near their offices, at Apicius, a calm, refined restaurant with a celebrated chef in the 8th arrondissement. After brief introductions, they sit on a terrace overlooking a walled-in garden and examine the menus. Three of the nine starters are *foie gras* preparations; the main selections include five offal dishes.[2] Each chooses the *foie gras de canard froid* to be followed by *tête de veau*.[3] After discussion with the sommelier they select a serious red Burgundy, and the three proceed to a dining room, where the well-dressed patrons speak quietly, intent on their conversations and their food and wine.

In this milieu, this is a normal (admittedly somewhat spectacular) business lunch. It is not an illicit venture into forbidden pleasure or exotica – no secret den for eating monkey brains – and the two dishes seem familiar, delicious and old-fashioned in a comforting, *Franco-Français* way.

By contrast, serving *foie gras* was illegal in Chicago from 2006 to 2008 and in California from 2012 to 2015. California's efforts to ban the product continue in the lawsuit of *Kamala D. Harris, Attorney General of California v. Association des* Éleveurs *de Canards et d'Oies du Quebec et al.* (U.S. Court of Appeals for the Ninth Circuit, pending). And in a novel, separate effort, animal rights groups are attempting through US courts to force the US Department of Agriculture (USDA) to create a nationwide ban through *Animal Legal Defense Fund* v. *United States Department of Agriculture*, No. CV12-04028 ODW (Central District of Calif. Pending).

In the 1990s, worry emerged that the epidemic of bovine spongiform encephalopathy (BSE in English, ESB in French or, popularly, 'mad cow disease' or *'vache folle'*) could cross the species barrier and lead to variant Creuzfeldt-Jakob disease (vCJD), another prion-related disease that would destroy the brains of affected humans. As a result, in 1996, selling or serving bovine brain (and therefore *tête de veau*) became illegal in France.[4] This prohibition was short-lived as to veal, although bans on other veal offal products came and largely went in the ensuing years.

*Foie gra*s and *tête de veau* have strong cultural significance in some locales but seem strange, mysterious or abhorrent to some people in others. Both are part of what France considers its 'patrimony'. In 2005, the French Assemblée Nationale added to the French agricultural code a declaration that as a matter of French law, '*Le foie gras fait partie du patrimoine culturel et gastronomique protégé en France*' [*Foie gras* makes up part of the cultural and gastronomic patrimony protected in France].[5] These are not just pretty precatory words making a cultural statement; enacting them into law was a crucial defensive act by a national parliament worried about a European Union (EU) treaty (the 'Council of Europe Convention for the protection of animals kept for farming purposes') that prohibits *foie gras* production (but not sales or consumption) except where it is a traditional product. Enshrining *foie gras* within French law could establish a cultural exception to allow France to avoid EU interference from Brussels. The formal commentary to the French law is defiant and definitive, declaring that the French government has determined, after investigation and concern for the well-being of animals, that objective standards established *foie gras* to be vital to the French model of gastronomy.

By contrast, in 1996, early in the mad-cow crisis, France had been willing to abandon *tête de veau*, equally part of the *patrimoine*. Even without a law to support it, *tête de veau* held a considerable cultural position. The dish was said to be the favourite food of Jacques Chirac, President of France at the time. Nine recipes for *tête de veau* grace Alexandre Dumas's *Grande Dictionnaire de cuisine* (1873), with seven more for just the constituent part, veal brain. The French government, defender of *foie gras*, appears to have otherwise been consistently more strict in its regulation of offal than European Union regulations require, sometimes (as with sweetbreads) imposing bans that France's own courts later determined to be overzealous and improper.

Reasons for Bans

Banning particular foods was not, in the past, part of the legislative repertoire. For many centuries, governmental food regulation has focused only on protecting consumers against fraud in the marketplace, ensuring purity (or at least prohibiting adulteration) and providing a balance between perceived public safety, on the one hand, and prevention of economic harm to those who make their living from raising, growing or otherwise producing the food, on the other.[6]

More recently, views about when a government should enforce food preferences has changed. As Elizabeth M. Williams and Stephanie Jane Carter note, 'Beliefs about proper eating can rise to the level of pious cult, complete with the need to proselytize and convert others, and to impose beliefs on others by […] the force of law.'[7] A deep fear of serious human health issues (whether proven or not) and views about animal rights led to the legal prohibitions on *tête de veau* and *foie gras*.[8] By contrast, *foie gras* receives support from a different trend, the creation of legal rules to preserve culinary traditions.[9]

Mechanics of Bans

Banning a food requires either a law passed by a legislature or other parliamentary body, or an action by an administrative agency that has had authority delegated to it by a parliamentary body.[10] In addition, citizens can bring lawsuits arguing that somehow existing law or regulations already prohibit or should prohibit a substance.

Most legal systems allow laws and actions by administrative agencies to be challenged in court, recognizing that banning a food interferes with personal liberty. However, governments have broad discretion ('police powers') to promote the general welfare through legislation regulating behaviour. In the US, the famous rule that most such laws, if non-discriminatory, need only be 'rationally related' to a 'legitimate' government interest actually stems from a Supreme Court decision upholding a ban on 'filled milk' (skim milk emulsified with non-dairy fats), *United States v. Carolene Products Company*, 304 U.S. 144 (1938).

Nevertheless, challengers may argue that a ban violates rights guaranteed by some higher authority, such as the country's constitution or, as in the European Union, by a supervening treaty or action by a multi-national body, or that the ban is preempted by action of a different governmental body. Bans by a rule-making authority that is not a legislature can usually be challenged on the grounds that the agency exceeded its authority, abused its discretion or acted capriciously.

The nuances of food regulation are complex and confusing. In the US, for example, the USDA and the Food & Drug Administration (FDA) share jurisdiction over meat and poultry products. The USDA has exclusive jurisdiction over slaughter and processing. Where not preempted, each state or municipality can have its own rules.

A crucial legal issue as to who (besides the legislature) gets to decide what foods are banned is the concept of 'standing': only someone who has suffered an injury in fact can pursue a lawsuit. By what right, judges may (and do) ask, is the Animal Legal Defense Fund entitled to argue that *foie gras* should be banned by the USDA because it harms humans, if their members already avoid eating it voluntarily? And who legitimately speaks for animal welfare, the legislature or animal rights groups?

In the European Union, there is complex national law and regulation in each country, and supervening EU law on top of that. EU rules were mainly designed originally to promote free trade within the EU, ensuring easy and tariff-free passage of goods from country to country. However, '[t]he heyday of market-oriented food law [...] ended in tears' after a series of traumatic health crises in the 1990s, including the BSE crisis, and as a result EU food law was essentially reworked in favour of a system focused more on food safety for consumers.[11] Now the overriding EU principle, embodied in Article 14(l) of Regulation 178/2002, is that food shall not be placed on the market if it is unsafe. The ultimate regulatory weapon is the 'precautionary principle'. Derived from EU treaties, the precautionary principle applies if a scientific evaluation of a product or process discloses a dangerous effect, but there is no clear evidence of the magnitude of risk. When invoked, as it was during the mad cow crisis, the precautionary principle shifts the burden of proof dramatically. Instead of the government or a complaining litigant needing to demonstrate a risk, the producer of the product is required to demonstrate that it is not harmful.[12]

Foie Gras

Foie gras has a long and mythic history dating to ancient Egypt, when birds were first force fed to enlarge their livers. Part of everyday life in France, particularly in the southwest, and *de rigeur* for holiday meals, *foie gras* is exotic or unknown in other areas. For US gastronomes travelling in the 1970s and the early 1980s, when fresh *foie gras* was unavailable in the US, *foie gras* dishes in France had an irresistible allure. Once *foie gras* began to be produced in the US in the 1980s – an exciting gastronomic moment for many – the *gavage*, the force-feeding near the end of the duck's life that enlarges its liver, creating the *foie gras*, became a focus of criticism by animal rights advocates.[13]

The positions are well known.[14] 'Ethics' is constantly mentioned in discussions of *foie gras* in the United States and England; rarely in France. In France, the food has long been described as a 'guilty pleasure' because it is a caloric, expensive food. It was a small step for US critics to alter the meaning of that phrase by suggesting consumers feel guilty about the *gavage*.[15]

In 2007, Paul Levy prepared to write at length about the morality of *foie gras* and then decided he need not:

> The more I looked into it and reflected (and I've actually witnessed the gavage, the 'force-feeding' at first hand – in which the ducks waddled up, with every appearance of eager greed, to swallow the flexible feeding tube), the more convinced I became that there is almost no ethical problem about the normal, non-industrial production of *foie gras*.[16]

The best publicized opponent, and lobbyist for laws prohibiting *foie gras*, has been PETA (People for the Ethical Treatment of Animals), founded in 1980, whose descriptions describe what Paul Levy saw as a happy waddle in rather different terms: 'workers ram pipes down the throats of male ducks'. In its lobbying efforts, PETA has often distorted what the law is in other places.[17] A peer-reviewed analysis prepared by the American Veterinary Medical Association Animal Welfare Division did not share PETA's view that ducks raised for *foie gras* are treated poorly compared to other fowl.[18]

What you think about the movement to ban *foie gras* depends a lot on your feelings about other foods. PETA and its allies oppose all use of animal products for food. Elizabeth Williams has noted that beef and chicken 'are so basic to the American diet that [...] it is unlikely that [public concern] will result in the ban of beef and chicken'.[19] *Foie gras* became an easy target, obscure, produced at only a handful of farms in the US, and – unlike veal – with no big agribusiness supporter to oppose a ban.

Cathy K. Kaufman, examining the ethics topic in 2007, reasoned that *foie gras* is unexceptional if you start 'from the premise that killing animals for food is morally acceptable provided that animals not suffer unnecessarily in their rearing or slaughtering', and suggested another reason opponents focused on *foie gras*: '[c]ontrary to the conclusory declarations of the animal rights activists, the fact that foie gras is an expensive, elitist luxury alone does not render it morally objectionable.'[20] Or, as the American chef David Chang wrote after investigating a US producer, 'I don't think I'd want to be an animal that was raised for meat, but as far as farm animals go, they seemed to be pretty cool with things.'[21]

A different ethical analysis against demonizing *foie gras* is provided by the law professor and animal rights theorist Gary Francione, a vegan who opposes *foie gras* bans and the violence encouraged by many *foie gras* opponents, such as the death threats issued in February 2016 to a pub in Norfolk, England, after advertising a Valentine's Day special dinner including *foie gras*.[22] Francione abhors 'reformist', 'single-issue' lobbying campaigns that 'tell people that foie gras is worse than other animal products'. In his view, 'there is no morally coherent distinction between foie gras and [...] steak, chicken, fish, ice cream, cheese, etc'. Singling out *foie gras* just makes 'people feel better about eating a hamburger instead'.[23]

Meanwhile, in France, as Christmas and New Year's approach, the media is full of articles with hidden assumptions of good cheer, such as '*Réveillon de Noël: quel foie gras choisir?*' which asks, 'What *foie gras* preparation will you serve?', taking for granted that you will serve *foie gras*. Concurrent with the emergence of *foie gras* controversies in other countries, the celebrated French food writer Christian Millau published a comprehensive dictionary of [French] gastronomy that included a nine-page *foie gras* entry that raised a few serious questions:

> In 1898, was Hungarian *foie gras* better than French?
> Are new cooking methods ('*mi-cuit*,' '*sous-vide*') advances or not?
> What is the role of '*terroir*' and authenticity in the raising of *foie gras*?
> Is the more plentiful duck *foie gras* ever equal to the best goose *foie gras*?

Morality or criticism of *foie gras* in general? Not mentioned at all.[24] I know one French woman, otherwise a strict vegetarian, who makes one exception to her diet: she adores *foie gras*.

In 2004, California passed a prospective prohibition aimed at *foie gras* production and sales, with a deadline, in the style of prospective auto emissions rules: find a method of production by 2012 that does not require force feeding, or *foie gras* will become illegal. Chicago's city council banned restaurant sales of *foie gras* in 2006 by a vote of 48 to 1. A whole series of legal arguments aimed at overturning the ban failed, but in 2008 it was repealed by the same body that had enacted the ban, by a vote of 37 to 6.

When no *gavage*-free *foie gras* emerged, the California law went into effect as anticipated. One part bans force feeding a bird in California for the purpose of enlarging its liver; the other bans sales in California of products that are 'the result of force feeding a bird for the purpose of enlarging the bird's liver beyond normal size'.[25] Two *foie gras* producers and a restaurant brought a lawsuit arguing that the sales ban violated US federal law and the US Constitution. When they attempted to enjoin the ban while their lawsuit was considered, the Federal trial judge hearing the case, Stephen V. Wilson, in Los Angeles, turned them down on the grounds that they were unlikely to win their case. They appealed. The Court of Appeals turned them down too, rejecting the ideas that the statute was 'void for vagueness' or discriminated against or impermissibly regulated interstate commerce.[26]

The plaintiffs amended and resubmitted their complaint twice. On the second try they found an argument Judge Wilson would accept, and in January 2015 he struck down the part of the law that prohibits sales because it conflicts with the USDA's exclusive authority to regulate poultry ingredients. He found the sales ban to be a disguised ingredient restriction trying to bypass federal standards by 'creatively phrasing its law' in terms of the production method by which the ingredient (liver of a force-fed duck or goose) was produced.[27]

This is the decision being appealed by the State of California. The technical question on appeal is whether California impermissibly introduced an 'ingredient requirement', requiring only *gavage*-free, non-force-fed poultry livers, which would be inconsistent with USDA standards.[28] The lawyer defending the overturning of the sales ban notes repeated accords over recent decades between the French government and the US to follow French standards and definitions for *foie gras*.[29]

In both Chicago and California, restaurants imagined and employed a curiously optimistic legal loophole. More than a few restaurants claimed they could give free *foie gras* to customers who were paying for other items. Some sold toast or brioche at prices inflated to cover the free *foie gras*. That this strategy for the most part succeeded is more an indication that local authorities had little interest in enforcing the bans than that this jailhouse-lawyer type of legal argument was sound. Animal rights organizations did sue at least two California restaurants over this practice but the suits were suspended after the ban on sales in California was overturned.

The myriad of court decisions can confuse people who have a deep interest in the key substantive arguments about the product. Often, the courts focus on – some might say get bogged down in – complex procedural issues, edgy questions about the technical wording of the statute (might it inadvertently ban down jackets made from ducks raised for *foie gras*?), or strange, fanciful issues ('The court assumes, but does not decide, that *foie gras* may be produced without force-feeding birds to enlarge their livers.'[30]).

Animal cruelty arguments are not even mentioned in the State of California's appellate briefs, which exclusively focus on whether California is preempted from acting based on Federal law.[31] However, in the separate *USDA* case (confusingly, also proceeding in California), *foie gras* opponents are attempting to force the USDA to prohibit the sale of *foie gras*. The plaintiffs repeat an old claim that *foie gras* is the product of 'dead, dying, disabled, or diseased poultry', and present a new argument that it is toxic to humans, carrying serious risks for humans, leading to arthritis and Alzheimer's disease. The lawsuit seeks a ban over the entire US, not just California.

The US Attorney General's office represents the USDA and directly addresses these claims, arguing *foie gras* liver is temporarily enlarged but not diseased, calling the plaintiff's evidence 'questionable' and noting that *foie gras* has been safely consumed by humans 'for more than 5,000 years'.[32]

A weak point for the opponents of *foie gras* in the *USDA* case is the doctrine of standing: if those seeking the ban already avoid *foie gras*, how are they harmed and why are they entitled to bring the lawsuit? In November 2015 in an appellate argument in Los Angeles, their lawyer asserted their right to ban *foie gras* stems from its having become unavoidable at social gatherings: guests can't know whether the *foie gras* served is produced by force-feeding or a safe, 'cruelty-free' *foie gras*, so the 'toxic substance' might inadvertently be ingested by its opponents. The three judges hearing the matter appeared confused that people upset by the force-feeding of ducks believe they are being force-fed themselves.[33]

There is an anti-*foie gras* movement in France, but it is only occasionally taken seriously. The French press ridiculed the *foie gras* bans in Chicago and California and compared them to Prohibition in the US.[34] Nevertheless, a private criminal proceeding was brought against a particular *foie gras* producer, Ernest Soulard, in 2014. Under a system that is distinctly different from Anglo-American jurisprudence, France allows criminal charges to be initiated by a private plaintiff, in this case an animal rights organization called L214, which prosecuted Soulard for illegal 'serious animal cruelty'. A government public prosecutor then investigates and tries the case alongside the plaintiff. L214 argued that the *gavage* itself was *per se* illegally cruel. Eventually, the public prosecutor disagreed. In January 2015 the prosecutor asked the court to drop the charges, arguing that the animal rights group was trying to use the case improperly to put the *gavage,* an accepted practice, on trial. The court did not allow the question of whether *foie gras* production is always illegally cruel to be considered, found that Soulard had not committed animal cruelty and required the losing party, L214, to pay

Soulard's court costs.[35]

Tête de Veau, Cannibals and the Sweetbreads Error

Predictions of the epidemic spread of a newly discovered disease are unreliable even when the causes are known. When causation is murky, regulators face difficult judgements. For variant Creuzfeldt-Jakob disease, predictive models prepared in the 1990s at the Wellcome Trust Centre for the Epidemiology for Infectious Disease at Oxford predicted the BSE epidemic would lead to 500,000 human victims or more. Faced with such dire predictions, and beset by charges they had acted slowly and deliberately hid problems, governments took strong action against offal. Invoking the precautionary principle, individual European countries and then the European Commission began to define certain offal (mainly spinal cords, brain tissue, spleens, sweetbreads and eyes) as 'Specified Risk Materials', and to regulate or prohibit their use both in animal feed and as human food.[36] In a combination of public health measure and protectionism, import restrictions were also imposed on beef based on the country of origin.

However, fewer than 100 vCJD cases ultimately ensued, almost all in Britain, where BSE cows were most prevalent, and consumption of offal by humans was never specifically implicated. In 2014, Stanley Prusiner, the biologist who won a Nobel Prize in 1997 for discovering prions, wrote, 'The only risk factor for vCJD' yet identified 'was the consumption of hamburgers in Great Britain more than two times per week.'[37]

One reason medical experts were so worried mad cow disease would lead to a human epidemic of encephalopathy was the discovery that kuru (an incurable disease of the central nervous system among the Fore people of Papua New Guinea), scapie (a similar disease affecting the brains of sheep), BSE and vCJD were all related diseases associated with the mysterious pathogens that Prusiner discovered and named 'prions'.

The kuru epidemic was the most curious, and certainly the most exotic. Research in the 1950s suggested the epidemic was spread through ingestion of inner organs of infected departed kin ('funerary' or 'mortuary' endocannibalism) in order to perpetuate their spirit. The practice, and within a few years the epidemic, is said to have ended because cannibalism was outlawed or at least discouraged by the government of Australia, which had jurisdiction over Papua New Guinea at the time.

Evidence about transmission of vCJD to humans through eating bovine offal or other beef is still unclear. The offal bans were motivated largely by extrapolation from experiments in which brain tissue from kuru victims and from scapie-infected sheep brains were injected into the brains of chimpanzees, or in some (scapie) cases fed to them. Many chimpanzees then developed encephalopathies after a period of months or years. The long incubation periods added to the public alarm: might savouring a piece of beef lead to the destruction of your brain many years later? Brain tissue was mainly used in the experiments because the disease was in the brain, although in the quest to discover the agent of infection other experiments were done. Only infected tissue was injected. Offal products were not viewed as dangerous unless they came from diseased animals.

Outlaw Offal

Gradually, many bans on offal have been eliminated. Veal offal was the first to be exonerated, but in fits and starts. France banned all beef and veal offal close to the spinal cord in May 1996. Most veal offal from French animals under six months old was allowed back in French markets by the end of July 1996. In 2000 France abruptly banned veal sweetbreads (*ris de veau* [thymus gland]), and then just as abruptly allowed them to be sold two years later. The *fraise de veau*, a membrane connecting parts of the intestine that is essential to some traditional sausages, returned to commerce only in 2015.

Why, during a period when there was so much uncertainty and speculation about how humans could develop food-related encephalopathy, were the French officials sure enough to excuse veal so quickly? Although the original cause of BSE was not known (it can arise spontaneously) the epidemic was thought to be spread through contaminated animal feed, particularly meat-and-bone meal, a product of the rendering industry made from offal and other slaughterhouse waste.[38] After feed laws changed but the epidemic continued, it was discovered that the food supply in some countries was not secure and the new feed laws were not being followed.

Veal, however, has a different feed supply, and BSE has not been found in calves. In France, veal is generally slaughtered at two to five months, having been fed only on milk or on specialized feed made from (highly subsidized) milk powder and digestible fibre. In other countries the animals may be somewhat older and may be partially fed on grass or even with animal protein.[39] So veal brains from young French calves could make a quick return to the market, and *tête de veau* came back to restaurant lists. The chef at Apicius, Jean-Pierre Vigato, has since said it is the one dish that will never leave his menu 'for just one reason: its principal gourmand and consumer is me!'[40] The return of *tête de veau* was quiet, though. There were no celebrations or ceremonies of the sort that in Italy later accompanied the return of *bistecca alla Fiorentina,* dear to Tuscan tradition, which includes a portion of spinal cord and was therefore legally prohibited from 2001 to 2005 (though never hard to find if you knew where to ask).[41]

Cannibalism dances about at several points in this story. Quite aside from the macabre kuru stories, there is now a rather popular belief that the cause of the mad cow epidemic was our industrial agriculture infrastructure's forcing cattle to become cannibals – against the laws of nature – beginning in the early 1980s–by feeding them meat-and-bone meal.[42] However, this explanation is not quite right. It is certainly true that outlawing animal-based feed for cattle in the EU and certain offal-based feed in other areas has coincided with a decline in BSE. But any natural law protecting cows from cannibalism had been broken long before. Meat-and-bone meal has been fed to cattle since at least the nineteenth century. Researchers associate the BSE epidemic not with cannibalism but with a new meat-and-bone meal production method adopted in the UK in the early 1980s to reduce energy costs and be environmentally sound. The rendering temperature was lowered, use of hexane to extract fat was eliminated and more protein was recovered from offal, but apparently the process left deadly prions intact.[43]

Legal decisions about health issues should be based on science, but cultural attitudes affect what questions get investigated. Once cannibalism is mentioned it tends to dominate the discussion. Recent research has altered the assurance that we know the kuru/cannibalism story: we seem to know less about the eating practices and more about how genetics shapes people's susceptibility to the disease. Some anthropologists now, controversially, question whether cannibalism ever took place, even though not so long ago writers were confidently providing detailed second-hand descriptions of the ways the Fore prepared and ate human flesh.[44]

It is now known that some people are genetically more susceptible to prion diseases than others, and some people are essentially immune. Researchers continuing to work on kuru have discovered rapid human evolution in favour of a genetic mutation (an 'acquired prion-disease resistance factor') that has made many members of the Fore tribe less susceptible to kuru, and the incidence of the disease might have dropped dramatically even if cannibalism had continued (which some believe it has).[45] More recently it has been demonstrated that in transgenic mice this gene provides protection not only against kuru but also vCJD.[46]

The mysterious ban on veal sweetbreads was put in place by the French Minister of Agriculture in 2000, more than four years after *tête de veau* was brought back, and now seems generally agreed to have been a mistake. It led to a rare successful challenge to a government operating under the strong protection of the precautionary principal. Dozens of producers of sweetbreads successfully sued the French government over this ban and won. In 2010, after years of appeals by the government, the producers won final judgements from the Conseil d'Etat, France's highest administrative court.

The French government exonerated sweetbreads in stages based on their diet and certification. The order of 28 March 2002 allowed thymus glands from cattle born after 1 January 2002 in France or in an EU member state, if accompanied by a health certificate stating that the calf was fed with food not incorporating ruminant material other than milk and materials derived from milk; then under the decree of 26 September 2002, the Minister authorized selling the thymus of all young French calves, without any certificate.

The argument by which the producers won is in some ways similar to the preemption argument that the *foie gras* producers used in California. The court did not directly address whether there was evidence that sweetbreads were harmful, but rather that actions by the EU Commission and the European Parliament had already defined the list of products that were risky (which actually included sweetbreads from the UK and Portugal, but not from France) and that to expand this list the French authorities would have needed to present evidence of potential harm that had not been known to the EU agencies. Failing that, they had misapplied scientific evidence, grossly abused their discretion, their action was to be condemned, and the French state would have to compensate sweetbreads producers for millions of Euros in lost profits.

However, unlike the California *foie gras* law, the sweetbreads ban came during an international public health crisis concerning the possibility of widespread BSE and vCJD. Did the Conseil d'Etat forget about the precautionary principle? The Minister of Agriculture at the time, Jean Glavany, had made his decision based on an opinion of the French Food Safety Agency (AFSSA), which felt it applied that principle correctly.[47]

Although it is not cited in the court decision (the decision focused more on procedure than on medical substance), mid-way through the sweetbread ban, the leading French researchers had already found the ban to be pointless, noting that no one has succeeded in infecting any other animal with tissue taken from a diseased calf thymus even by direct inoculation in the brain.[48]

Did the French authorities overreact about vCJF, given what was known and predicted at the time, or were they simply overzealous regarding sweetbreads? It may too soon to tell. Over what time period is the work of regulators to be judged? It has been long enough for judges but perhaps not long enough for historians. Offal seems to have made a complete legal comeback in France, with *tripiers* back in style and thriving organizations that celebrate offal such as the *Académie des Abats*, and quite a few *Clubs de la Tête de Veau* and *Confréries du foie gras* in different parts of the country.

In January 2016, in response to an outbreak of avian flu A5N1 in duck farms in Southwestern France, the French government prohibited newly hatched ducks from being brought to any farms not free of bird flu. In May 2016 a four-month temporary prohibition on slaughtering ducks or producing *foie gras* began in the areas most affected. The government announced it would compensate producers for their loss. Although English-language headline writers loved being able to tease their readers by writing 'France Bans Foie Gras,' *Le Figaro* called it a brutal measure necessary to protect the '*fleuron*' of French gastronomy.[49] Four months later the *gavage* and production of *foie gras* resumed amidst cautious optimism that the bird flu had abated.[50]

As of December 2016, human consumption of *foie gras* and *tête de veau* was permissible everywhere.[51]

Notes

1. *Histoire des peurs alimentaires du Moyen Âge à l'aube du XXme siècle* (Paris: Éditions du Seuil, 2002); *Sacred Cow, Mad Cow: A History of Food Fear* (New York: Columbia, 2006).
2. *Le pied d'un cochon noir de bigorre en galette croustillante; la tête d'un veau de lait, langue et cervelle ravigotées; la pomme de ris de veau cuite au sautoir;* a fourth *foie gras* dish with duck meat, *la tourte Apicius façon grande cuisine classique.*
3. Although American judges seem to think *foie gras* is liver made into a paté, it is rarely combined with other ingredients. Instead, whole *foie gras* is placed in a terrine or wrapped in a towel to form a sausage shape (*foie gras à la torchon*), cooked at a low temperature and aged before serving or, more common outside France, very quickly sautéed in slices from a raw state – very quickly indeed because it will melt into nothingness. *Pâté de foie gras* and *mousse de foie gras,* under French law, are allowed to have as little as fifty per cent *foie gras*. Usually sold in tins, they are not the products that excite lovers of *foie gras*. *Tête de veau* (veal head) is not a 'head cheese paté' as is produced in some countries but rather a sort of *pot au feu* including braised brain, tongue and cheek meat, with small vegetables, served with *sauce*

ravigote, sometimes topped with crispy slices of ear.
4. *Journal official No 150. Arrêté du 29 juin 1996.*
5. *Loi d'orientation agricole no.2341, article L.654-27-1 du code rural*, effective 5 January 2006.
6. See, for example, the classic article explaining the history of food regulation by Peter Barton Hutt, 'Government Regulation of the Integrity of the Food Supply', *Annual Review of Nutrition* 4 (1984): 1-21, or the essay by the founder of the 'food freedom' organization Keep Food Legal, Baylen Linnekin, 'Bans', in, *The Oxford Encyclopedia of Food and Drink in America*, ed. by Andrew Smith and Bruce Kraig (Oxford: Oxford University Press 2012), pp. 115-20.
7. *The A-Z Encyclopedia of Food Controversies and the Law* (Santa Barbara, CA: Greenwood 2011), p. xxv. Legal rules to ban transfats or enforce portion sizes are examples.
8. Religious taboos are another common reason for shunning foods, but even in countries dominated by one religion, religious prohibitions rarely are reinforced by law. In India, the beef question is left to individual states. Slaughtering beef is generally prohibited while serving beef products legally slaughtered elsewhere is often legal.
9. Protection of culinary tradition takes many forms, including protectionist labelling legislation (*Champagne, pizza Napoletana*, and so on) and purity laws (the Bavarian *Reinheitsgebot* beer purity law of 1516) that can also be viewed as protectionist. The Yu'pik people of Alaska have special rights to fish for salmon in the Yukon river; certain groups deemed 'aboriginal' are afforded special rights under the International Whaling Convention. Other traditions have fared less well. The USDA's ban on lungs, enacted in 1971 without much attention, has no basis in medicine according to experts I have consulted, and inadvertently outlaws traditional versions of the Scottish dish haggis. See Alex Massie, 'Mr Obama, Tear Down This Offal Wall', *The Spectator*, 25 January 2013 <http://blogs.spectator.co.uk/2013/01/mr-obama-tear-down-this-offal-wall/> [accessed 15 May 2016].
10. There are also imaginary bans on offal. Some types of offal are apparently considered sufficiently odd or repugnant that myths arise about their illegality even when they are perfectly legal. Many press accounts mention the illegality of selling animal blood for human consumption (pig's blood is essential to much charcuterie) and animal bladders as a cooking implement (*poularde en vessie*) but they do not appear actually to be illegal anywhere.
11. Bernd van der Meulen, *EU Food Law Handbook* (The Netherlands: Wageningen Academic Publishers 2014), p. 208.
12. See 'Communication from the Commission on the precautionary principle,' COM/2000/0001 final (2000).
13. Since the 1950s, most *foie gras* has been produced from ducks, not geese.
14. Mark Caro provides commentary on the arguments so even-handed that *The Foie Gras Wars* (New York: Simon & Schuster 2009) is quoted by people on both sides of the controversy.
15. By contrast, in France, feeling guilty about the bird is considered an essential part of the experience when eating an ortolan.
16. Paul Levy, 'Can Foie Gras Be Produced Ethically?' *The Guardian*, 28 June 2007.
17. Richard Shepro, 'A Foie Pas', Letter to the Editor, *The Chicago Tribune*, 24 June 2007.
18. American Veterinary Medical Association, 'Literature Review on the Welfare Implications of Foie Gras Production' (7 May 2014).
19. Williams, p xxviii.
20. 'The Foie Gras Fracas: Sumptuary Law as Animal Welfare?', in *Food & Morality: Proceedings of the Oxford Symposium on Food and Cookery 2007*, ed. by Susan R. Friedland (Totnes, UK: Prospect Books 2008), p. 125.
21. David Chang and Peter Meehan, *Momofuku* (New York: Clarkson Potter 2009), pp. 265, 262-71.
22. '"Death Threats" Pub Removes Foie Gras from Valentine's Menu, BBC News, 10 February 2016 <http://www.bbc.com/news/uk-england-norfolk-35540336> [accessed 15 May 2016].
23. Facebook posts, 4 & 8 January 2015, 13 February 2016, in Gary L. Francione and Anna Charlton, *The Abolitionist Approach to Animal Rights* ([n.p.]: Exempla, 2015).

24. *Dictionnaire Amoureux de la Gastronomie* (Paris: Plon 2008), pp. 342-50.
25. California Health and Safety Code, Section 25981; Section 25982.
26. *Association des Éleveurs de Canards et d'Oies du Quebec* v. *Harris*, 729 F.3d 937 (9th Cir. 2013).
27. *Association des Éleveurs de Canards et d'Oies du Quebec* v. *Harris* (Central District of California, 17 January 2015). There are multiple court decisions with the same or similar names.
28. Ducks and geese do gorge themselves naturally, and to some extent this can be encouraged by breeders, so from time to time someone does announce the production of 'cruelty-free *foie gras*,' but none of these have gone into production of any significant scale, and the livers are small, compared to *foie gras* livers, and do not fit the USDA definition of *foie gras*. See, for example, Dan Barber, 'The Farmer Who Makes "Ethical" Foie Gras', *The Guardian*, 18 January 2015 <http://www.theguardian.com/world/2015/jan/18/the-farmer-who-makes-ethical-foie-gras> [accessed 15 May 2016].
29. *Association des Éleveurs de Canards*, Answering Brief of Appellees, 2 November 2015, pp. 29-33.
30. *Association des Éleveurs de Canards* (Central District of California) 7 January 2015, fn. 8.
31. *Association des Éleveurs de Canards*, Appellant's Opening Brief, 24 August 2015. Appellant's Reply Brief, 16 December 2015 (Central District of California).
32. Brief of US Attorney General's office on behalf of the USDA, submitted April 22, 2016 for oral argument July 19, 2016.
33. Oral argument in *Animal Legal Defense Fund* v. *United States Department of Agriculture*, No. 13-55868, 4 November 2015 <http://www.ca9.uscourts.gov/media/view_video.php?pk_vid=0000008497>. See discussion beginning at 4 minutes and 12 seconds.
34. '*Je n'irai pas jusqu'à dire que ça créera un nouveau Al Capone, mais c'est tout comme*', *Paris Match*, 30 June 2012.
35. The case is fairly well described in a detailed press release put out by the French *foie gras* association, and in French newspapers during the process of trial, 2014-2105. 'LA FILIERE FRANÇAISE DU FOIE GRAS SALUE LA DECISION DE JUSTICE DANS LE CADRE DU PROCES INTENTE PAR L214 A L'UN DE SES ADHERENTS' <http://www.eurofoiegras.com/docs/Com.%20presse%20CIFOG.pdf>[accessed 15 May 2016]. A good English-language article is 'French Foie Gras Producer Acquitted in Animal Cruelty Trial', *RFI*, 19 March 2015 <http://en.rfi.fr/visiting-france/20150319-french-foie-gras-producer-goes-trial-over-extreme-cruaulty-against-animals> [accessed 15 May 2016].
36. '*Matériels à Risques Specifiés: cervelle, yeux, amygdales, moelle* épinière*, rate, intestins, colonne vertébrale*'; Currently, these categories apply only to animals older than 12 -14 months, except for *amygdales, intestins* and (for sheep and goats), *rate* (spleen), which are included regardless of age.
37. *Madness and Memory* (New Haven: Yale University Press, 2014), p. 297. Other sources give higher numbers (still below two hundred) but include transmission of vCJD in other ways, such as through transplants of corneas from infected persons.
38. 'Meat and Bone Meal', *Feedipedia*, 2016 <http://www.feedipedia.org/node/222> [accessed 15 May 2016].
39. John Webster, *Management and Welfare of Farm Animals* (New York: John Wiley, 2011), p. 132.
40. '*Le seul plat qui n'ait jamais quitté la carte d'Apicius. Pour une seule raison: le principal gourmand et consommateur, c'est moi*!' (Vigato: *Mon carnet de recettes* (Paris: Éditions de la Martinière, 2011), p. 128).
41. Giorgio Locatelli, 'Time to Savour Fiorentina,' *The Guardian*, 20 January 2006.
42. For example, 'Mad Cow Found in California...Because Cows Are Being Fed Blood, Animal Parts and Feces', *WashingtonsBlog*, 26 April 2012 <http://www.washingtonsblog.com/2012/04/mad-cow-found-in-california-because-cows-are-being-fed-blood-animal-parts-and-feces.html> [accessed 15 May 2016]; Dick Ziggers, 'Meat and Bone Meal Back into Feed', *All About Feed*, 12 January 2010 <http://www.allaboutfeed.net/Home/General/2010/1/Meat-and-bone-meal-back-into-feed-AAF004005W/> [accessed 15 May 2016].
43. Jean-Philippe Deslys and André Picot, *La vache folle* (Paris: Flammarion, 2001), translated as *Mad Cow Disease* (Paris: Flammarion, 2002).
44. For example, William Arens, 'Rethinking Anthropophagy,' in *Cannibalism and the Colonial World*

(Cambridge: Cambridge University Press, 1998), pp. 50-51; Richard Rhodes combines the precision of Julia Child with the imagination of a pornographer in his description of the Fore funerary customs in *Deadly Feasts: The 'Prion' Controversy and the Public's Health* (New York: Simon & Schuster, 1998), pp. 21-26.
45. Simon Mead and others, 'A Novel Protective Prion Protein Variant that Colocalizes with Kuru Exposure', *New England Journal of Medicine* 361 (2009): 2056-65.
46. Emmanuele Asante and others, 'A Naturally Occurring Variant of the Human Prion Protein Completely Prevents Prion Disease', *Nature* 522 (2015): 478-81.
47. CE, 5 juil. 2010, n°309634, Prodal, Recueil Lebon (inédit).
48. Deslys, pp. 82, 97.
49. Eric de la Chenais, '*Les usines de foie gras au point mort pendant 4 mois*', *Le Figaro*, 2 May 2016.
50. '*Landes : après la grippe aviaire, le retour du foie gras mais avec la peur au ventre*', *Sud-ouest*, 3 September 2016.
51. Except, of course, in jurisdictions where consumption of all bovine products is prohibited.

Mocotó Jam: Children's Food

Marcella Sulis and Myriam Melchior

Introduction
Made of cooked ox foot, a bovine part usually rejected in Brazilian gastronomy, the *Geléia de Mocotó* is a popular sweet treat. Because it is particularly recommended for infants' nourishment, this jam has become linked with childhood in the memory of many Brazilians. Nowadays, however, due to agendas that restrict the use of sugar or reject the consumption of animal food, this jam is very seldom prepared as a craftsman product. A study of these agendas brings to light socio-cultural and historical factors behind this jam's preparation: sugar, associated with the founding of Brazil, and bovine waste products, central to the cooking practices of enslaved Africans and their descendants. By discussing some historical and social sources and considering the present production of *Geléia de Mocotó*, this paper aims to show the jam's cultural importance in Brazil and to restore it as a culinary technique in Brazilian confectionary arts.

Some Considerations about the Origins of *Mocotó*
In Brazil, the largest part of animal food consumption is of bovine cattle. Not native to the country, bovines were brought by the Portuguese and Dutch during the time of the Great Navigations and spread inland from the coast. These cattle helped occupy the vast Brazilian territory, being used for transport, as a source of power for building and agriculture and as food.[1] In this respect, the Portuguese introduced the consumption of cattle and established the culinary use of a variety of meat cuts, including the shinbones and feet.

According to Raul Lody, in Portugal the dish called *mãos de vaca* (cow's hands), prepared with bovine shinbones, was traditional in Ribatejo, a province of medieval origin situated alongside the Tagus River.[2] There, chickpea was added to the broth. During colonial times, this dish was made without chickpea, especially in the north and south, and called *Caldo de Mocotó*. The term *Mocotó* has become a synonym for the ox marrow from the shinbones and feet, and can also be used to name those cuts. It is the popular name used for the dish, the cut and culinary products derived from the ox marrow, like the broth and the *Geléia de Mocotó*.

Mocotó's cultural significance, and more specifically that of the *Geléia de Mocotó* itself, lies in its ambiguous association with parts of the ox usually rejected as food. Although the broth and the jam are popular, traditional products in Brazil, the ox parts from which they are made are not often consumed. It is not common to find them in supermarkets or to find them prepared in restaurants. Foot and shinbone cuts are usually disdained and left behind. Consequently, these parts have low economic value, and are often used industrially for products like cosmetics, gelatin, jelly and, of course, commercially made *Geléia de Mocotó*.

Nevertheless, like the broth, the jam has an old history that long preceeds its use by industry. Old sources reveal some of the contempt for these ox parts, especially when we consider the name of the old Portuguese *mãos de vaca*. If in Portugal *mãos de vaca* straightforwardly indicates which part of the animal is being used, Brazilian name for this dish name famously refers instead to someone who does not waste resources, but with a negative connotation, as in someone who is a miser.

Such characterization may have contributed towards a negative conception of the consumption of ox feet. For example, while one of the most important Brazilian food historians, Câmara Cascudo, states that eating *Mocotó* developed as a way of using devalued cattle shinbones and feet after slaughter, we noticed kind of avarice in his description, as if economics superseded taste and customs to find a use for waste in cattle-raising regions and urban slaughterhouses.[3] Perhaps that might not have been the case: it is possible that Portuguese noblemen may have stopped eating feet and shinbones as these parts became food for more impoverished people.

The etymology of *Mocotó* is also important here: it has its roots in the indigenous Tupi language, from the word *mo-cotog*, as well as in the junction of the indigenous Tupi and Guarani languages, from the term *mo-coto*, which translates as: 'make it toss, make it tremble'.[4] This meaning is certainly different from the name used in Portugal. At the same time it is important to remember, as explained by the anthropologist Eduardo Viveiros de Castro, that the indigenous people of the region bond with their food differently than in Western culture: in their perspective, animals and food are, by their own nature, understood to be like human beings and thus neither as objects nor as a decayed nature.[5]

The indigenous people of the State of Bahia started making *Mocotó jam* using the capybara feet, of *Capivara de Cara Roxa* (*Rochildes capivarium*), which was documented by the Jesuit priest Martinho D'Anchieta in 1682.[6] While this practice may indicate indigenous assimilation of Portuguese culinary practices, it may mean instead that these people already had a use for animal shinbones and feet before the arrival of the Portuguese.

One way or the other, it is interesting that the origins of *Mocotó* are ambiguous. For example, the indigenous use of *Capivara* feet to make *Mocotó* did not take root: in Brazilian culture only bovine feet are used for such purpose. However, it was the indigenous term *Mocotó* that became common. Besides, in Brazil the use of the cow's shinbones for the nourishment of common citizens comes from neither the indigenous people nor the Portuguese, but mainly from the descendants of enslaved Africans, who passed on the *Mocotó* tradition in our culinary culture. During the colonial period, enslaved people survived by cooking and eating foods despised by sugar cane mill owners and Portuguese noblemen. Since then, due to its low cost, these rejected bovine cuts have become good for providing affordable protein and valuable nutrients.

While *Geléia de Mocotó* shares its origins with the *Caldo de Mocotó*, which is popularly believed to have reinvigorating and even aphrodisiac effects, the jam is symbolically connected to Brazilian confectionary and its history. Indeed, *Geléia de Mocotó* is an icon of Brazilian sweet food's art, but it has also benifitted from publicity, especially since 1960, as a nutritious and tasty food for children. This juxtaposition of the jam's ambiguous association with rejected bovine parts and its purified link to food for children creates a complex cultural field

A Brief History of the Brazilian Sweet Food's Art

Brazil has long been one of the largest worldwide sugar producers. In effect, the process of colonization resulted from the establishment of the sugar cane mills. The renowned Brazilian sociologist Gilberto Freyre designated Brazil as a 'Sugar Civilization'.[7]

Perhaps as a result, Brazilians stand out for their love of sweet culinary dishes; traditional recipes containing sugar have been passed along from generation to generation. These recipes have their roots in the traditional of both the Portuguese and the Africans who, after arriving in Brazil as slaves, often found in sugar their only source of economic subsistence. The researcher Cláudia Lima reminds us that 'the black slave women that arrived in Brazil, since the first African batches, during the XVI century, were already cooks, no matter from what region they were pulled away'.[8] Although not common in the foods of the African regions where these women learned to cook, the enslaved population necessarily adopted the use of sugar in recipes that developed under the influence of the Portuguese confectionary art and with the use of native Brazilian ingredients.

Thanks to the large amounts of sugar used in their preparation, sweet dishes usually last much longer, which favours their commercialization and trade. Using sugar for food conservation is a very old art, inherited from the Moors and Portuguese. As Leila Algranti reminds us, over time the method of preserving foods, whether using sugar or salt, shapes both culinary culture and the tastes of those who consume these foods.[9]

Sugar-based preservation used for the long voyages to and from Portugal as well as throughout the Brazilian territory undoubtedly affected the region's cuisine. During the first colonial phase, associated with the sugar mills, enslaved women made use of the coarse, brown sugar leftovers, which were mixed with manioc flour or maize. These leftovers also contributed to the production of the famous Brazilian alcoholic liquor *cachaça*.[10]

In a similar manner, the use of rejected meat also helped to elaborate the national Brazilian stewed black beans dish: *feijoada*. Apparently, combining these leftovers from sugar and bovine processing may also have created *Geléia de Mocotó*.

When the sugar economic cycle was replaced by the gold cycle, a large number of slaves from the northeast were sold inland, to the cities of today's State of Minas

Gerais, and to the cities of the southeast, like Rio de Janeiro.[11] Food commerce in those regions was mainly the work of enslaved or recently freed black women, who worked as retail dealers. They worked in alleys, street corners, villa sidewalks and within or outside farms; they usually had to split their profit with the farm owners or to bring their masters food from the places of sale, called *Secos e Molhados* (grocery), also named *Quitandas*.[12]

This last designation refers directly to the black women who undertook the sale of food items: the *quitandeiras*. *Quitanda* derives from '*ki'tana*', from the Quibundo Angolan language, and means open-air market, public square and *Secos e Molhados*. These other meanings may be why women who sold their products on the street stopped being called *Quitandeiras* and were identified instead as *Negras de Tabuleiro* [Black Women with Their Trays]. They would sell *doces* [sweets] and *quitutes* [delicacies], though there may have been little difference in the use of *doces* and *quitutes*. Roberto Moura treats '"*doces*" ou "*quitutes*"' as synonyms to emphasize 'the sweets of the street, made by black women', which according to him would include: '*mocotós, vatapás, mingaus, pamonhas, canjicas, acaçás, abarás, arroz de coco, feijão de coco, angus, pão-de-ló de arroz, pão-de-ló de milho, rolete de cana, queimados, isto é, rebuçados* etc.'[13]

Some of these sweets or delicacies were decorated with coloured paper trimmings, either in blue or carmine. Apparently, they all included sugar in their recipes. Thus, we may guess that Moura's reference to *Mocotó* would, in fact, be to *Mocotó* jam or to a sweet made of *Mocotó*, a more consistent version of its manufacture.

The sale of sweet and salty food on the streets represented a source of subsistence and liberty, and Brazilian sweets culture still bears this symbolic character. Also, according to Almir El-Kareh and Héctor Bruit, the cuisine of the colonial period was and still is present in street foods, which serve as accessible, tasty and nutritious alternatives for the low-income population.[14]

Mocotó jam's movement to a food for the middle classes and the urban elite is documented by the end of the nineteenth century. By then coffee drove the economy, and pastry shops and coffeehouses prospered among the urban classes of Rio de Janeiro.[15] Among them, one stands out, the *Confeitaria Colombo*. (The name *Confeitaria* can be used for pastry shops, tea rooms, delicatessen, breakfast and lunch services, cafeterias, etc.)

The *Confeitaria Colombo* was founded in 1894 by Manoel Lebrão and Joaquim Borges de Meirelles, who came from Portugal. This luxurious confectionary, inspired by the French *Belle Époque* architecture, remained a city icon for more than a century; since 1990 it has become a Listed building due to its importance to the city. One of the café's secrets has been its recipes for sweets and delicacies, not only Portuguese but also Brazilian specialties. Among these, its *Mocotó* jam has become well known as the *Geléia de Mocotó Colombo*.

At the end of 1980, *Confeitaria Colombo* went through a financial crisis and was acquired, in 1992, by the Dutch multinational food enterprise Arisco. Ever since, the name of this establishment has become associated with the largest producer of the *Mocotó* jams in Brazil, as Arisco has invested in the manufacture of the *Geléia de Mocotó Colombo*.[16]

Antônio Rodrigues and Renato Freire note that the association of the jam and the *Confeitaria Colombo* led consumers to want to keep a glass cup of the jam as a sort of souvenir, which became almost a cultural commonplace in Rio de Janeiro: all homes seemed to have a cup of the *Colombo* jam like as a personal utensil or an item of recollection. In this respect, the glass came to embody childhood memories, linking a given meal with parents or an encounter with cherished relatives at the *Confeitaria Colombo*. The jam has become a symbol of the culinary identity of Rio de Janeiro.

The Culinary Industry and the Promotion of the *Geléia de Mocotó*

Many Brazilians still experience the taste of the *Geléia de Mocotó* as linked to memories of childhood nourishment and comfort. To a great extent, this linkage goes back to the 1960s and 70s, when the food industry began massive publicity campaigns. This process accompanied the growth of the cities: city spaces disaggregated and extended to the suburbs as highways replaced nets of railway transportation.

The food industries established on the main access roads to large metropolitan centres started to commercially produce food for every corner of the country. At the same time, supermarkets replaced the old *quitandas*, and the urban population, affected by massive TV advertising for industrialized food, became detached from traditional food manufacture. Many people have never seen a bovine slaughterhouse, and each generation seems to have less contact with culinary methods and basic ingredients, like the feet and shinbones used to manufacture *Mocotó* sweets.

This estrangement from traditional cooking provided the context for the advertising adopted by industry to promote *Mocotó* jams. For example, before acquiring the *Colombo* trademark, Arisco made *Inbasa* instead. During the 1970s, their advertisements for this jam emphasized that the product was rich in vitamins and proteins needed by children. Such a proposition corroborated people's already established understanding of this food as a source of nutrients and subsistence rooted within popular culture. In addition, advertisements played on Brazilian sweets culture's association with maternal affection and tenderness.

That cultural bond is reflected in and reinforced by one of the most popular books about raising children in Brazil: *A Vida do Bebê* [*The Life of the Baby*], by professor and pedriatician Rinaldo De Lamare, appeared for the first time in 1941 and has been republished 43 times.[17] A manual with practical advice regarding several aspects of a child's development, the book has long been a reference for many Brazilian mothers. In the last edition, of 2014, under the chapter on *Seasoning and Condiments*, we still find De Lamare's recommendation that cinnamon can be added to 'the traditional puddings and sweets' served to babies. This shows that, in spite of the new health alimentary principles for sugar control, sweets still retain their cultural strength in Brazil.

The jam's popularity has led to another important cultural development: the widespread use of the glass cups in which the industrially produced jam is sold. The cups, nicknamed *copos de geléia* [jam cups], are disconnected from their original use and added to the domestic utensils of many among the impoverished population who cannot afford to buy a more expensive set of glasses. The cups are often used for drinking coffee, a common habit in Brazilian culture. There are people who would rather drink their coffee in glass jam cups than in porcelain cups, alleging that doing so improves the flavour of coffee and makes it special.

Despite of all the ways in which *Geléia de Mocotó* is wrapped up in Brazilian culinary identity, new nourishment standards and a sort of new consciousness about the origin of food are raising obstacles to its traditional popularity. One of them, as we already stated, is restricting sugar consumption for health reasons. The other is the outburst of new adepts to the different types of vegetarianism. Of course vegetarians, whose number increases everyday in Brazil, reject the *Geléia de Mocotó* due to its animal origin.

Yet more interesting than these may be the taboo concerning animal parts that are culturally rejected. As Mabel Gracia and Jesús Contreras state, 'the incorporation of aliments supposes the incorporation of its moral and behavioral qualities.'[18] Therefore, the *mãos de vaca* remains rejected, even by those who ingest many other meat cuts every day. Blog comments and social networks post often show that people are surprised to learn that *Geléia de Mocotó* is made from bovine feet. This shows us a very interesting example of *offal* food: one with a paradoxical mixture of the feeling of comfort, confidence and motherly affection and the feeling of repugnance or repulsion that blur its memory and experimentation.

Consumers unaware of the jam's ingredients also seem to ignore its history and socio-cultural importance. For this reason, this work aims at resisting the power of the trends that jeopardize the cultural importance of *Geléia de Mocotó*.

Geléia de Mocotó as a Tradition

As we have tried to demonstrate, *Geléia de Mocotó* is densely structured within Brazil's culinary culture. We mentioned nets of reciprocal relationships determined by cultural traces, by its influences and hybridism. Furthermore, even though *Mocotó* may still be a sort of food considered inappropriate for consumption by some social groups, we have tried to point out different cycles through which this food has been redefined. Summarizing, these cycles would be delineated as follows: a traditional Portuguese food, assimilated in various regions of the country, became a devaluated food fit only for the indigenous and slaves, according to the colonizers. Later the jam was raised to a means of subsistence and resistance by the descendants of the enslaved Africans. Then the jam turned into a popular street food, and in the twentieth century it emerged as a luxury product in the Brazilian *Confeitarias*. Finally, industrialized for the crowd, we arrived in time to recover its patrimony.

Proposing *Mocotó* jam as culture and identity, we conducted an interview with Dona

Mocotó Jam: Children's Food

Maria, (*Dona* being the polite form of address for an older woman), who told us about her home recipe for the jam that she has sold for the last fourteen years at the famous *Feira de São Cristóvão* in Rio de Janeiro.[19]

The sweet products she sells include a great variety of traditional Brazilian items, including *cocada* [coconut confection], *pé-de-moleque* [peanut brittle], *quebra-queixo*, [jawbreakers], *rapadura* [hard squares of raw brown sugar], *doce de leite* [condensed milk sweet], *doce de jaca* [jackfruit marmalade], among others. A common characteristic of these traditional sweets is the long time needed for their preparation, as well as demanding knowledge and specific techniques of the Brazilian confectionary.

Dona Maria tells us that the preparation of *Geléia de Mocotó* starts with the right stirring time and the right amount of sugar needed to achieve the desired jam consistency.

Prepared with cinnamon, sugar, ox foot and shinbone, *Geléia de Mocotó* is thickened by the main ingredient itself, the bone marrow, which together with sugar reaches a gelatinous and mushy consistency. After being cooked, the mixture is beaten until it reaches the point of being cut, that is, the stage when the jam can be sliced. There are many recipes that use orange and lemon for a special flavour. Others make use of pineapple, milk or coconut among their ingredients. In the State of Minas Gerais, this jam is more rigid, because milk and more sugar are added to it, according to Dona Maria. Her recipe goes as follows:

1 ox foot
1 cup of honey, molasses or grated raw brown sugar hard square
50 g of fennel
10g of clove
20g of cinnamon

Boil the *ox foot* for about two hours with sufficient water to cover it. Drain the cooked portion and take the broth to the refrigerator. When cold, remove the upper fat layer. Now boil the broth at low temperature to soften it. Prepare a sort of tea with the rest of the ingredients, adding it to the *Mocotó*. Pour into glass cups and take to the fridge.

For Dona Maria, the jam is a symbol of childhood, health and '*sustância*', a popular name used to refer to vigorous food. Considering the benefits derived from *Mocotó* jam's consumption, she repeats the popular wisdom associating the jam with childhood: 'children grow strong and healthy, it helps the boy to turn unto a lad'.

Having worked for forty years at the *Feira de São Cristóvão*, Dona Maria started with her husband's help when this open-air market was not yet part of the present pavilion. She used to prepare sweets at home, selling them on Sundays, and told us that thanks to this work she raised her son and was able to buy a home. Nowadays, she rents three tents, two of them for producing her sweets and the other to sell them. Her son and brother help her with the artisanal manufacture of her products.

We also learned from her that, at present, not many people make *Geléia de Mocotó*, because its home production is long and tiring. Instead they buy it in a supermarket. She still produces it, however, explaining, 'In order to guarantee its quality, I always make it in the same manner. The jam must follow the rules, each stage to the letter. So, the *Mocotó* is fresh, not so sweet. As you can see, I've been doing it during all my life.'

During our interview, the confectioner emphasized the importance of passing on the knowledge about the skill needed to make the jam, an activity that involves family and friends and maintains relationships of proximity.

Even those who do not take part in the manufacturing process are able to redeem the tradition and transmit it to their children, relatives or friends, according to Roberto Benjamin, a researcher of culinary studies. Sharing the tradition ensures that the family bond of the Brazilian confectionary stays alive.[20]

This bond is demonstrated by Dona Maria, who says, 'I learned to make *Mocotó jam* with my aunt; my son and brother are the ones who help me in the manufacture of sweets today.'

Traditional sweetmeats, like Dona Maria's jam, are not available at commercial shops or grocery stores. They are found in free markets and informal trade places. Artesianal jams are special products usually of a higher quality.

Sweet food reinvented by confectioners offers a way to resist the changes caused by the industrialization of these traditional products. Using Eric Hobsbawm concept of the 'invented tradition', we can say that Dona Maria avails herself of tradition and innovation to adapt to new challenges.[21] According to her, it is a question of 'a tradition that cannot fall into oblivion'.

It goes without saying, for us, that the dialogue between tradition and innovation seems to be clearly present when she makes *Geléia de Mocotó*. So, if nowadays her work is almost a rarity, to insist on making this jam is an act of resistance towards the immediacy of today's food, a rejection of the hegemonic models and the homogenized offrings of the food industry.

Final Considerations

This article sought to demonstrate that the *Mocotó jam* tradition endures in Brazil through the knowhow of confectioners and handicraft producers; its manufacture has provided an important source of income since colonial times. Furthermore, the traditions of the jam are maintained by informal networks like the family and by embracing the importance of sugar's cultural traditions in Brazil.

These informal ties have supported the industrial production of the jam, not the other way around, since the formal system – the industrial system – has shown itself unable to maintain the social and cultural ties that structure the jam's tradition. For this reason, we emphasize the importance of artisanal practices for Brazilian confectionary. These practices ensure that sweet food and recipes from colonial times can reach our present time. Making jams and selling them, in addition to providing work and a source of income, is a practice that refers to cultural memory and valorizes the ethnic contributions that constructed Brazil's culinary identity. *Geléia de Mocotó* survives as a particular mode of resistance to the forces of industrialization.

Notes

1. Marcelo Correa da Silva, Vanda Maria Boaventura and Maria Clorinda S. Fioravanti, 'História do Povoamento Bovino no Brasil Central', Dossiê Pecuária, *Revista UFG*, 13 (2012), 34-41 <http://www.proec.ufg.br/revista_ufg/dezembro2012/arquivos_pdf/05.pdf> [accessed 11 May 2016].
2. Raul Lody, *Brasil Bom de Boca: Temas da Antropologia da Alimentação* (São Paulo: Senac São Paulo, 2008).
3. Luiz Câmara Cascudo, *História da Alimentação no Brasil*, 3rd edn (São Paulo: Editora Global, 2004).
4. Clovis Chiarada, *Dicionário de Palavras Brasileiras de Origem Indígena* (São Paulo: Limiar, 2008).
5. Eduardo Viveiros de Castro, *A Inconstância da Alma Selvagem*, 5th edn (São Paulo: Cosac Naify, 2002).
6. Álvaro Andrade, 'Geléia de Mocotó: uma História de Sucesso', *Recanto das Letras* (2007) <http://www.recantodasletras.com.br/humor/688964> [accessed 9 May 2016].
7. Gilberto Freyre, *Açúcar: uma Sociologia do Doce, com Receitas de Bolos e Doces do Nordeste do Brasil* (São Paulo: Editora Global, 2007).
8. Cláudia Lima, *Tachos e Panelas: Historiografia da Alimentação Brasileira* (Recife: Raízes Brasileiras, 2009), p. 105.
9. Leila Mezan Algranti, 'Doces de Ovos, Doces de Freiras: a Doçaria dos Conventos Portugueses no Livro de Receitas da Irmã Maria Leocádia do Monte do Carmo, 1729', in *Cadernos Pagu*, 17-8 (2002), <http://www.scielo.br/scielo.php?script=sci_arttext&pid=S0104-83332002000100017> [accessed 10 march 2015].
10. Maria Letícia M. Cavalcanti, *O Negro Açúcar* (Recife: Edições Bagaço, 2008).
11. Roberto Moura states that 'between 1872 and 1876, coming from the North and Northeast, 25,711 slaves arrived in Rio de Janeiro' (*Tia Ciata e a Pequena África no Rio de Janeiro*. 32 vols (Rio de Janeiro: Coleção Biblioteca Brasileira, 1995), p. 35).
12. Antônio Geraldo da Cunha, *Dicionário Etimológico da Língua Portuguesa*, 4th edn (Rio de Janeiro: Lexicon, 2010).
13. Roberto Moura, *Tia Ciata e a Pequena África no Rio de Janeiro*, 32 vols (Rio de Janeiro: Coleção Biblioteca Brasileira, 1995), p. 46.
14. Almir Chabain El-Kareh and Héctor Hernán Bruit, 'Cozinha e Comer, em Casa e na Rua: Culinária e Gastronomia na Corte do Império do Brasil', no. 33 (Rio de Janeiro: Estudos históricos, 2004), pp. 76-96.
15. Antônio Edmilson M. Rodrigues, *João do Rio. A Cidade e o Poeta. O Olhar do Flâneur na Belle Époque Tropical* (Rio de Janeiro: Editora FGV, 2000).
16. Antônio Edmilson M. Rodrigues and Renato Freire, *Confeitaria Colombo: Sabores de uma Cidade* (Rio de Janeiro: Casa da Palavra, 2013).
17. Rinaldo De LaMare, *A Vida do Bebê*, 43rd edn (Rio de Janeiro: Agir, 2014), p. 70.
18. Mabel Gracia and Jesús Contreras, *Alimentação Sociedade e Cultura* (Rio de Janeiro: Fiocruz, 2011), p. 128.
19. The São Cristóvão open-air market has existed since 1945, and is the largest *'nordestino'* (pertaining to northeastern Brazil) market outside its originating region. Besides being an important commercial nucleus and representative of the northeastern community in our city. Today, this market has also become a tourist attraction and place for cultural leisure in Rio de Janeiro.
20. Roberto Benjamin, *Doçaria e Civilização: a Preservação do Fazer*, ed. by the Seminário Gastronomia em Gilberto Freyre (Recife: Fundação Gilberto Freyre, 2005), pp. 37-41.
21. Eric Hobsbawn and Terence Ranger, *A Invenção das Tradições* (Rio de Janeiro: Imago, 1997).

The Tradition of Offal in the Greek World: From Classical Antiquity to (Post-) Byzantine Times

Stephanos Tanis[1]

Ἀντίνοος δ' ἄρα οἱ μεγάλην παρὰ γαστέρα θῆκεν, ἐμπλείην κνίσης τε καὶ αἵματος

[Antinoos then placed for him a great stomach, filled with fat as well as blood.]

Odyssey 18. 118-9

'φάε τοῦ σκάρου τὸ σκατό,
τῆς συναγρίδας μέση
καὶ τοῦ ροφοῦ τῇ κεφαλή
νὰ δεῖς ποιὸ θὰ σ'ἀρέσει.'

['eat skaros' shit,
the middle part of a common dentex and
a grouper's head, so to see what you like the most.]

Greek folk saying

'Πρὸς τούτοισιν δὲ παρέσται σοι θύννου τέμαχος κρέα δελφακίων, χορδαί τ' ἐρίφων, ἧπαρ τε κάπρου κριοῦ τ' ὄρχεις χόλικές τε βοὸς κρανία τ' ἀρνῶν νῆστις τ' ἐρίφου γαστὴρ τε λαγώ, φύσκη, χορδή, πνεύμων ἀλλᾶς τε.'

[Next to these there will be for you a tuna's piece, meats of piglets and intestine-cords of kids, and liver of boar and ram's testicles and the (large) intestines of an ox and heads of lambs and the jejunum intestine of a goat, the belly of a hare, tripe, a cord, lung and sausage.]

Deipnosophists VII. 140

Here we have three texts of Greek from three different periods, three invitations to food, three appraisals of fine cookery, i.e. offal from domesticated animals, game and fish.

The first text is Homer. The scene takes place during a banquet at Odysseus's palace in Ithaca, where Penelope's suitors live shamelessly extravagantly at the expense of the absent king. Antinoos, a prominent suitor, offers to a *xenos* [guest], the unrecognizably disguised Odysseus, a fine piece of meat: not goat or lamb, nor suckling piglet, game or beef, but the finest blood and guts; blood and guts was also the share of the gods during blood sacrifices in the ancient Greek world. Could the wise gods of Greece be thus deceived? And Odysseus, the man of many devices?

The second piece comes millennia after Homer's epics that are full of guts and blood and death of many great heroes such as divine Achilles. It is a piece of Greek folk wisdom about the finest of the sea: dentex belly, grouper's head and the entire offal of a wrasse! 'What then you think you'd like the most?' asks the man in the know. I shall come back to wrasses later on.

The third text from Athenaios's *Deipnosophists* is the main dish here, '*Greek offal traditions from classical antiquity to Byzantine times*'. I say 'main dish' also because in Athenaios's passage we come across some intriguing terms on offal, which are most often unsatisfactorily translated and interpreted. Let us go through one translation I picked up randomly, D. C. Yonge in 1854:

> Besides this you now shall have a slice of tunny, a slice of pork, some paunch of kid, some liver of goat, some ram, the entrails of an ox, a lamb's head and a kid's intestines; the belly of a hare, a pudding, some tripe, and a sausage.

Comparing this mid-eighteenth century translation to the one I give above, the differences are striking. Differences regard, principally, the manner in which most terms about offal are treated. Yonge's translation makes no distinction whatsoever between types of intestines and tripe: for the χορδαὶ τ' ἐρίφων we are given 'some paunch of kid', the χόλικές τε βοὸς are just 'the entrails of an ox' and the νῆστις τ' ἐρίφου are only 'kid's intestines' without any further explanation so it is absolutely impossible for the reader to comprehend the passage with any specificity. I surpass this kind of carelessness on the ground that Yonge had not translated the *Deipnosophists* for offal purposes, although, surely, he could have given us something better than, say, regarding animals, where a male wild boar's liver, ἧπαρ τε κάπρου, becomes goat liver! Next it is 'testicles' as food. For κριοῦ τ' ὄρχεις Yonge presents us only 'some ram' instead of 'ram's testicles or even fries'. Is it just Victorianism or personal disgust for such pieces? Or perhaps gentleman Yonge could not even possibly think that the great and all-elegant ancient Greeks could have been ever interested in such repulsive dishes. Whatever the case, the point is that few translations, particularly the old ones and especially when dealing with matters of guts and blood (as well as sex), serve sufficiently the modern reader. Yonge's translation offers a good example of how arid and wide of the mark a translation can be; how often the inexperienced eye in Greek and Latin is misled when in search of information of this sort in old translations this I shall not discuss here; pointing it out is more than enough.

The truth is that snouts and trotters, let alone eyeballs, testicles or wombs, are not foods for all. Featuring in the cooking and eating habits of almost all omnivorous (even anthropophagic) cultures, past and present, offal has always been one of the most controversial ingredients in world food history for various reasons, social and religious, culinary and hygienic. It has always been a food with great enemies and even greater defenders; the polemic still goes on among Greeks and Italians, French and British, Near, Middle and Far Easterners and many other cultures beyond the great oceans. Going through our surviving sources from classical antiquity the picture seems to be no different at all. Pythagoras, allegedly, hated not only broad beans but also brains and perhaps all internal organs, too; in comedy also, offal is mentioned here positively as a delicacy and there contemptuously; Homer has it 'royal'; Athenaios speaks highly of it through many of his references to older Greek works; the same with Archestratos's *Hedupatheia* (*Pleasant Living*) in several passages, e.g. Fr. 60 on stomach/tripe-sausage and stewed sow's womb with spices and in Fr. 19 on conger eel heads; the Roman *Apicius* also celebrates offal dishes (II. 3. 1 *Vulvulae botelli* i.e. sow's matrix); and medical doctors and dieticians had written extensively on the properties of offal parts.

Guts and blood was also the fair share of the gods (Figure 1): for their blood sacrifices in honour of their gods the Greeks were carefully selecting the proper animal, slaughtering it accordingly, then placing certain cuts to the altar to be burned; the smell of the burned meat enjoyed a special term, '*knisē/knisa/knissē*' (after an homonymous kind of fat often similar to δημός/*dēmos*, c.f. LSJ s.v.: πιμελῆ/*pimelē*, στέαρ/*stear*), a still existing term in Greek; finally the meat was distributed among the attendants. The smell and the spectacle of the flowing blood, especially during mass sacrifices, the so-called *hecatombs*/one hundred victims, must surely have been a strong experience for all participants, as the priesthood intended. Heart and stomach were often removed first

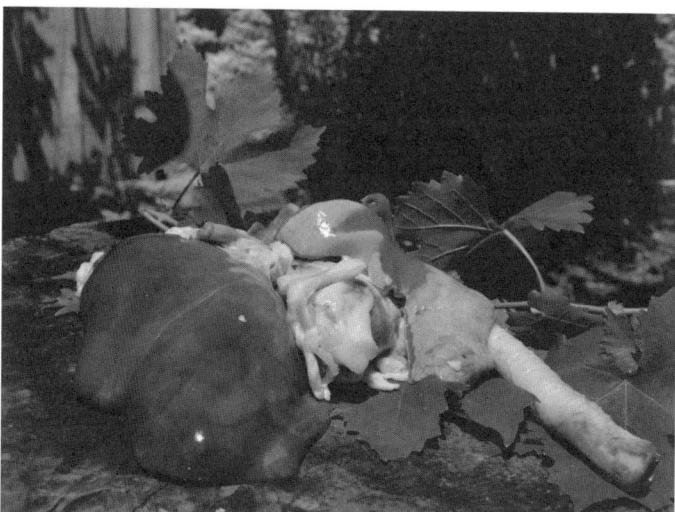

Figure 1.
Fresh entrails of a goat, except the intestines and tripe, for traditional Greek Pascha dishes. In splachnoscopy the animal's cavity was emptied carefully, the offal was inspected by experts and then it was consumed first among all sacrificial offerings.

The Tradition of Offal in the Greek World

from the cavity after the animal's sacrifice; the fresh, still warm offal was inspected and 'read' by experts. *Splachnoscopy*, e.g. *hepatoscopy*/liver-reading as well as *osteomanteia*/bone-reading were common practices in the ancient Mediterranean; the Etruscans were known for their haruspicy and human sacrifices; the latter were also practiced by Greeks on special occasions during prehistoric times (e.g. the myth of Iphigeneia's sacrifice). To what extend the Minoan and Mycenaean cultures were familiar with occasional ritual anthropophagy and under what conditions is no less clear than whether human offal parts or blood were also ceremonially consumed. Herodotos (III. 12) reports a unique incident of frantic cannibalism practiced by Greek mercenaries fighting in Egypt in *c.* 525 BC just before the battle, the inflamed Greeks killed some of their captives and used their blood in a wine and blood cocktail, apparently to take heart – a unique example, whether real or literary, of anthropophagy in the record of Greek history.

In another passage (II.39), fifth century BC Herodotos reports that (contemporary?) Egyptians avoided consuming animal heads and were selling them to the Greek tradesmen and mercenaries in Egypt, who apparently loved such pieces of meat; exactly what reasons (e.g. fasting period) lay behind Herodotos's Greek-Egyptian contrast we cannot know, but archaeological evidence shows that animal heads were included in the ancient Egyptian diet.[2]

Going through our sources, we come across classic Greek and Roman offal delicacies; many were inherited by the Byzantines, and some have survived until our day only slightly altered. These included finely spiced sausages, both fresh and cured, boiled tripe and heads in garlic-vinegar sauce, grilled or braised tongues, as well as the now extinct extravagant dish with a sow's womb with the best quality of it being, in Andrew Dalby's words, 'the womb of a sow that had just miscarried'; and of course sea food both raw and cooked.[3] Among all offal foods of classical antiquity, two were the most talked about. The first was the *garos*, a fish sauce made of fermented fish guts flavoured with herbs and spices, often enriched with olive oil (*elaiogaros*), wine (*oinogaros*), vinegar (*oxugaros*) or diluted and softened by water (*hudrogaros*). The *garos*, L. *garum*/*liquamen*, was not just a gentlemen's relish, only for few, but something for all regardless of socio-economic status; it was the staple sauce to spread on bread, to pour over vegetables and meats and to use as a marinade for meats and fishes, often instead of salt.

Next is the *melas zômos*, the most famous ancient Greek dish of all; its fame echoes until today. In fact it was not a food for all Greeks, for, as Plutarch notes, only the fearless Spartans could 'enjoy' it (*Lykourgos* 12). The legendary, terrifying and repulsive for all 'except' Spartans *melas zômos* was a simple black broth made of boiled pork, miserably spiced up with vinegar but with a generous dose of pork blood. Raw or cooked blood we simply do not know: no Laconian cookbook, even a short one, has ever been found, and Spartans were always laconic about monstrosities attributed to them. Without anyone being ever interested in that sort of gruesome cuisine, the special *melas zômos* died out along with Spartan power; forgotten as an edible dish, it was remembered rather as a joke or, at best, as the fuel that once propelled Sparta. A Sybarite once commented on it thus: 'of course Spartans are the bravest in the world; anyone logical would rather die ten thousand times than have such a pitiful diet' (Athenaios 138d).

Spartans rarely, if ever, had the chance to enjoy the renowned *sukôton/sesukasmenon*, the ancient Greek version of *foie gras* made of domesticated birds' hypertrophic, owing to excessive forced fig-feeding, livers; the Greeks named their luxurious liver dish *sukôton/sesukasmenon*, i.e. 'figed' after the *sukon*/fig fruit, which gradually changed the word for liver from *hepar* to *sukôti*. The Byzantines used both words and loved 'figed'-livers as much as their Greek and Roman ancestors (fourth century AD Oreibasios, *Medical Collections* II. 107-8, *sukôton hepar*, i.e. from fig-fed goose liver).

The Offal Delicacies of Byzantium

The Byzantines were the flag bearers of the classical world not only in terms of politics, philosophy, art, science and the art of war, but also regarding the pleasures of life and food. They loved and knew well how to organize magnificent banquets, and their everyday diet was based on the ancient Greek and Roman diet based on grains, vegetables, fruits and wine; in fact, their diet was not much different from today's Mediterranean diet.[4] Meat remained a luxury for the majority as well as a forbidden food for all during the exhausting fasting periods demanded by the church.[5] Further, the Byzantines were the last Mediterranean Europeans to produce and enjoy the *garos*.

In short, foodwise, they were true Greeks and Romans. Perhaps they never produced highly sophisticated treatises on the art of cooking and banqueting such as the classical Greek Archestratos's *Hedupatheia* and Athenaios's *Deipnosophists*, but from their literature they appear to have been no less interested in the importance, properties, production and taste of all the foods available in their lands and markets, whether local or imported. Fourth-century AD Greek Oreibaseios and eleventh-century AD Byzantine Jew Symeon Seth both wrote extensively on the properties of foods; the *Geoponika*, among other works, impressively handled a huge range of agricultural matters, including food production. There is also a great body of works, including poetry, on everyday secular and church life. In this category, the *Ptôchoprodromos* is a great source with ample information on food matters, including offal. In general, byzantine references to offal are no less frequent than those in the works of the classical Greek and Roman past. Medical works are no exception: from the period's dietary manuals we get a complex picture of offal matters: nutritious, nourishing (on heads), emetic (for brain), slow in digestion (on liver, which, nevertheless, is also nutritious) or productive of bad humours and/or of phlegmatic blood; heads are heavy whereas feet, trotters, snouts and ears are light; udders are described as cold, just as tripe and intestines, unlike liver which is described as hot, according to the byzantine tradition of categorizing foods in 'hot and cold' terms (*On the Properties of Foods*; *On Foods from Animals*). Medical advice, expectedly, was not always happily received, and no medical compendium could make the Byzantines stop enjoying their favourite dish, be it vegetable, fish, meat or offal. Only church regulations regarding blood consumption and blood sacrifices had effect; within the territories of the Empire of Christ, there was no space for practices so strongly associated to the old religion and the ancient gods: splachnoscopy/haruspicy/hepatoscopy were for the Church totally sinful and sacrilegious, disgustingly and dangerously 'Hellenic' and barbaric and as such should be brought to extinction. It was during the byzantine period that dishes with blood were for the first time in Greek history officially strictly forbidden: the Second and Sixth Ecumenical Councils/Synods (553 and 680-681 AD, respectively) issued canons against blood consumption, according to which 'the clergy man who eats blood is to be deposed and the layperson to be excommunicated'. Further strict laws against blood consumption were issued during the reign of Leo VI the Wise (886-912 AD), following mass food poisoning.

Were these laws effective? Practically they were: blood sacrifices were terminated, and blood foods were gradually abandoned – though not effortlessly and definitely not forever. Byzantine reports on blood consumption come as late as the fifteenth century, and there is too little to say on blood sacrifices and haruspicy in Greece today.[6] However, whereas certain foodstuffs such as blood sausages, αἱμάτια/*haimatia*, vanished from the Greek table, some othes, such as the famous αἱματία/*haimatia* did not cease but continued to exist in a bloodless fashion until today.

The special αἱματία/*haimatia* we often come across in classical texts (e.g. *Odyssey* 20. 25-8) is today known as *omatia*/*giomatia*, a type of fresh uncured sausage made of the pig's imagabomasum (gastrointestinal tract) and/or the omasum (third stomach) stuffed with chopped internal organs, caul fat, cracked wheat (μετά πιμελῆς καὶ ἀλφίτων, *Schol*. Aristophanes, *Knights* 198) and blood, as well as onion, garlic, aromatic greens, herbs and spices; after its stewing or roasting the *haimatia*/*omatia* is served hot and it is not for keeping.[7] Very similar to the *haimatia* but less sophisticated in terms of ingredients was the *boulntouna*, a simple blood sausage.[8] By contrast, 'proper' blood-free sausages (often mentioned as ἀλλάντια/*allantia*, i.e. salted and cured) that were particularly popular among ancient Greeks, Romans and Byzantines escaped the wrath of the church; without blood there was apparently nothing wrong.

Not all sausages were cured; the Greeks have always been fond of things fresh. In the category of fresh sausages, we can possibly add the still popular spleen sausage, the *splēnantero* (see Figure 2 overleaf). If this unusual sausage was indeed known in byzantine times, I would propose for it, albeit with some reservations, the byzantine term *sukôtokoila*, meaning 'liver-ed' stomach, as liver is the standard term for heart, spleen and lungs in modern Greek and it seems also in Byzantine Greek, considering the period's similar terms *sukôtophleggouna* and *hepatopneumona*, where liver seems to have been the most important ingredient and defining organ, c.f. modern Gr., *sukôtia*/*sukôtaria*, the generic term for all internal organs except tripe and intestines; cf. Byz. *enterokoila*, *hordokoila* and *hordokoilitsin* in which intestines (*entero*-; *hordo*-) come first as in the case of *enterokardiosukôtophlegmona* and *hourdoubelia*/intestine-skewer, both fine descriptions in my view of the modern *kokoretsi*.[9] Another food involving intestines was the *kolix to gardoumion* or *gardoumenon*, which corresponds perfectly to the

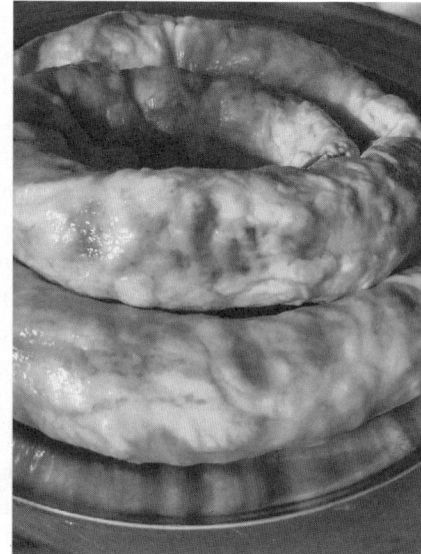

Figure 2. Fresh spleen sausage, splēnantero, made from goat large intestine.

Figure 3. The gardoubes (the gardoumion/ gardoumenon of the Byzantines), a popular offal dish often included in the Greek Pascha menu.

gardoubes (Figure 3) and less likely the *kokoretsi*, both traditional Greek Pascha offal dishes with the latter still popular also in the Balkans and Turkey; intestines were eaten on their own, often plaited (Byz. *plektē*; *plexoudes* in modern Greek), and then grilled, fried or boiled.

Offal dishes and tripe soups were not only foods to be consumed at home; citizens could also enjoy their offal in taverns, in their city's market places/*agoras*, and in inns while travelling. Places of this kind were usually cheap, seamy and even suspicious foodwise. Owners could be women, often retired prostitutes; a term for the female owner was *hordokoilistra*, intestine stomach maker. The dirty job of washing all the stuff for cooking was done by the *enterohordoplutēs*, also a contemptuous term, meaning 'he who cleans intestines'.

Such places offered *Ptôchoprodromos*, grilled, fried or boiled intestines (*hordai/hordia*); boiled *koiliohorda* (also *hordokoila, soiligourda, enterokoila*), a soup or stew of tripe and intestines; hoofs and heads (*podokephala*) in soups served with garlic-vinegar sauce (*oxista* cf. modern *skordostoubi/skordalmi*); tripe soups usually with all the compartments of the stomach/*koilia*, again served with garlic-flavoured wine vinegar; udders cooked in a style often referred to as *mastomagereia*, a compound word usually indicating boiling; internal organs (liver, heart, spleen, lungs, sweetbreads, kidneys, wombs and more) cooked in various ways, some of which were similar to the traditional Greek Easter soup *mageiritsa*; and all kinds of sausages, secretly even blood sausages, as well as more sophisticated recipes such as *koilia monthuleutē, staphidoxnoton lapara* and *monokuthron*.

Along with poultry and game offal, both popular, seafood, raw or cooked, had always been a great treat; it seems sea food recipes and fish dishes with tuna, sardines, mullets, wrasses and other fish followed the ancient Greek and Roman traditions. Nevertheless, influences from abroad, particularly the East, seem to have been common and popular regarding several dishes, principally meat dishes, since Byzantium was the ultimate cosmopolitan empire. Fish roe and caviar (*haviarin/haviaritsin*) was abundant, even black caviar; a caviar type termed as *sahaltikin* appears to be of premium quality. Caviar was the business of the *haviaropoulēs*/caviar seller, who displayed his fish roe and caviar in jars and barrels for people to see; from the hilarious term *haviarokatalutēs*, 'caviar eater' or, more accurately, 'caviar catalyst', it seems caviar was extremely popular and also much cheaper than it is today (e.g. 'you're not a child of a respected man, nor of a palace manager, you're a child of a grocer, of a caviar eater' (*Ptôchoprodromos* IV. 103-4)).

As for the *garos/garum/liquamen*, the beloved fish sauce of ancient Greeks and Romans, this continued to spice up many dishes of the period to such an extent that even the haute cuisine of the byzantine imperial palaces was more than once described by western European guests as unpalatable. The tenth century Liutprand of Cremona was totally disgusted by a *garos*-seasoned meat dish specially prepared for him by the Constantinopolitan royal kitchens – or it was his reaction caused by his maliciousness toward the Byzantines? Whatever the case, what is important here is that by the tenth century the *garos/garum* was long forgotten by the western Roman world. Dalby managed to dig out a sixteenth century report on *garos* from a Frenchman in Constantinople.[10] Such was the Byzantines's fondness for their traditional fish sauce that a version of it called *haimation*, i.e. with blood, is mentioned as the best *garos* by the *Geoponika*, a tenth-century compilation of old Greek and Roman works; fish blood sauce seems not to had troubled the church as much as animal blood, or perhaps it was simply too irresistible even for the clergy.

Offal: Rejected and Reclaimed Food

A Short Precis on the Current Status of Offal in Greece

Despite the recent advance of 'steak culture' and growing preference for 'cleaner' cuts, and even with the still on-going controversy about offal health and safety issues, traditional offal foodstuffs remain popular among Greeks and still form an important chapter in the record of Greek cuisine. Further, unlike other vegetable, fish or meat dishes, traditional Greek offal dishes have remained virtually the same: culinary fossils, they seem to be very close to their byzantine predecessors in terms of ingredients and cooking methods. Of course, several ingredients and cooking methods have inevitably changed, but not considerably. Our available sources on the matter attest to this view. For example, differentiations as in the case of the blood-containing *haimatia/omatia* took place only because of religious prohibitions against the use of blood. Greek offal dishes, in my view, have no significant changes to exhibit, or at least not changes to the degree other foods, stews and roasts in particular, went through in time. The main reason is that offal cooking, in spite all the praises it has been enjoying for centuries, has basically remained an 'unrefined' simple home and tavern food and not, at least so far, an area for chefs interested in high cuisine.

I have left for the end a uniquely extravagant 'recipe' for fish offal, not processed or fermented and turned to *garos/garum*, but fresh right from the cavity of the fish. This interesting technique is used only with a certain fish species, the *skaros* (*sparisoma cretense*, family *caridae/Labridae*), a kind of parrot wrasse of the Greek seas, particularly the Aegean. Fish here should be very fresh, catch of the day, or more precisely, catch of the early morning before the omnivorous *skaros* starts feeding on its favourite sea weed and creatures. How is the fish prepared? After carefully extracting the bitter gallbladder by an incision next to the right pectoral fin, the fish is sprinkled with rock sea salt and then falls on the grill as it is, fresh, unscaled, ungutted. The result is surprising: despite containing the bolus and chymus, the *skaros* offal does not smell unpleasant; on the contrary it is perfectly edible, exquisitely delicate and well balanced in taste. Those few in the know prefer the *skaros* on May-June, hence the old saying in rhyme, "έλα το Μάη στο γιαλό, φάε του σκάρου το σκατό', ['come on May on the shore, and eat skaros' shit'] (see Figure 4 opposite).

I think we might have a hint how old this recipe is. It comes from Athenaios, *Deipnosophists* VII. 113a-c, not in the recipe quoted from Archestratos' famous *Hedupatheia* that celebrates culinary art and pleasure in verse, but from another quotation dating sixth or fifth century BC.[11] Here I quote the crucial part and translate:

> Ἁλιεύομεν σπάρους καὶ σκάρους, τῶν οὐδὲ τὸ σκᾶρ θεμιτὸν ἐκβαλεῖν θεοῖς.

> [We fish breams and parrot wrasses, of which even the shit is not righteous for the gods to throw out OR of which the shit not even the gods throw out.]

The Tradition of Offal in the Greek World

*Figure 4.
A 720 gr. grey
skaros caught early
morning and ready
for grilling as it is:
unscaled, ungutted,
with everything in it!
Corinthian Gulf
17 September 2016.*

This passage is crystal clear and does not allow any misinterpretations wherever we place the οὐδὲ. It seems thus quite clear that ancient Greeks, at least fishermen and lovers of bizarre tastes, were not discarding the obvious from their fresh wrasse but were enjoying the whole *skaros* fish as it is, ungutted, with all the entrails. 'Not even the gods would throw it away' says Athenaios, quoting sixth and fifth century BC dramatist and thinker Epicharmos from his *Wedding of Hebe*. Greek and Roman sources often mention the popular *skaros* as ἄριστος/*aristos*, i.e. very best (e.g. Oreibasios, *Medical Collections* II. 113, 1-2). 'Come on May on the shore [...]', say modern Greeks, whose anthology on the graceful *wrasse* seem to be not only timeless but also limitless: 'σκάρο με λένε, πιάσε με, και το σκατό μου φάε', 'skaros they call me, catch me, and eat my shit' and in another regional version 'σκάρος είμαι, ψήσε με, λάδι και ξύδι ρίξε με, και το σκατό μου φάε', 'skaros I am, grill me, olive oil and vinegar pour over me, and eat my shit'! Another example of such eating habits is with game: un-gutted woodcock on the grill, which is not done with any other bird, just woodcock.

As highly gastrimargic (and indirectly coprophagic), the Greeks, ancient and modern, had always a taste for internal organs. The list is limitless: raw sea food (urchins, sea squirts and cucumbers as well as numerous kinds of seashells); whole crustaceans, molluscs and cephalopods (for their ink sacks, gonad, eggs, testicles); whole fish whitebait style (*marida*/fry, *atherina*/smelt, little red mullets, etc.); fish roe and fish liver from many types of salt- and freshwater fish; snails, too, have always been popular; last but not least, liver, spleen, heart, lungs, kidneys – along with, of course, all the offal from domesticated animals and often wild animals (deer, boar, hare, wild rabbit, including, hedgehogs and badgers), including heads (cheeks, eyeballs, tongues), hoofs and trotters, tails, bone marrow, large and small intestines, testicles, wombs and all the stomach compartments (reticulum, rumen, omasum, abomasum). Some animals were never offal sources for any proper Greek table, including dolphins, seals, reptiles, insects, rodents, canines, cats and horses (although many of these have undoubtedly been tried under extreme conditions, in difficult times or as part of special therapeutic diets); generally Greek culture avoids such meats, unlike in other culinary spheres outside the Mediterranean, where many of these animals are perfectly edible, including some or all of their internal organs.

Traditional Greek offal cooking certainly lacks the complex, multi-coloured and multi-flavoured dishes of, say, Asia; nor is it presentable as international haute cuisine. However, even if in a primitive manner, it does focus on each particular ingredient. Quality and simplicity is the principal rule in Greek food: e.g. fresh *wrasse* with everything in it or fresh sweetbreads, grilled with only rock salt. Tripe soups are also a great example; they have remained astonishingly the same since antiquity, including only tripe, water, olive oil and little seasoning with, in pure pre-Colombian Mediterranean style, no tomatoes. In short, Greek offal cooking is, above all, impressively simple. It is Mediterranean and can be healthy if the meat-source is well checked. It is also important in terms of food history.

Notes

1. I must thank Mark McWilliams for his useful suggestions in the early stage of my work and Andrew Dalby for his kindness and encouraging comments during the Oxford Symposium on Food and Cookery in July 2016.
2. S. Ikram, 'Meat Processing', in *Ancient Egyptian Materials and Technology*, ed. by P. T. Nicholson and I. Shaw (Cambridge: Cambridge University Press, 2000), pp. 656-71.
3. On cooking pots, plates and utensils in classical Greece, see S. Tanis, 'The Material Culture of the Classical Greek Banquet', in *Food and Material Culture: Proceedings of the 2013 Oxford Symposium on Food and Cookery*, ed. by Mark McWilliams (Totnes, Devon: Prospect Books, 2014), pp. 326-31; A. Dalby, *Siren Feasts. A History of Food and Gastronomy in Greece* (London: Routledge, 1996), p. 61.
4. Ph. Koukoules, *Buzantinon Bios kai Politismos, Vol. V.* (Athens 1952), 137-205. Subsequent citations refer to this source as Koukoules 1952.
5. Koukoules, pp. 9-205; A. Dalby, *Tastes of Byzantium. The Cuisine of a Legendary Empire.* (London, I.B. Tauris, 2010), pp. 93-94; W. Mayer and S. Trzecionka, *Feast, Fast Or Famine. Food and Drink in Byzantium*, Byzantina Australiensia 15 (Brisbane: Australian Association for Byzantine Studies, 2005).
6. In few certain communities there is still the tradition of blood sacrifices, involving the slaughter of a fine bull; the ritual is completed secretly without any leaks. What remains today from this ancient culture is the so-called reading of the scapula/*osteomanteia* (a rare practice) and liver/*hepatoscopy* (even rarer) in few places mostly among herdsmen.
7. The very special *omatia* is usually prepared after the *hoirosphagia* (ceremonial pig slaughter) on special

days or during religious festivals.
8. Koukoules compares *boulntouna* with the Venetian *boldon* (p. 59).
9. Unless Ptôchoprodromos's *enterokardiosukôtophlegmona* was invented to playfully compete, nevertheless unsuccessfully, Aristophanes's 171-letter ridiculously long (in Greek) in *The Assemblywomen*: *lopadotemachoselachogaleokranioleipsanodrimupotrimmatosilphiokarabomelitokatakechumenokichlepikossuphophattoperisteralectryoptokephalliokigklopeleiolagôosiraiobaphētraganopterugôn*, which also refers to certain offal parts such as heads of fish and birds.
10. Dalby, *Tastes*, p. 68.
11. Unfortunately, all details in Archestratos's Fr. 14 concern ingredients and not the treating of the fish itself; only the washing of the fish is mentioned, unless we take the πλύνας εὖ as an indication of washing the fish un-gutted.

Axolotl: Pre-Hispanic Delicacy, Rejected Monster and Reclaimed Wonder of Science and Literature

Fernando Valerio-Holguín

Translated by Eva Ennis

Introduction: The *Axolotls* in the Kitchen and in the Culture

The pre-Hispanic Mexican kitchen is one of extraordinary richness and complexity. Among the foods that are appreciated today by some and rejected by others, there are more than five hundred species of animals, as well as plants. Among the former, a small batrachian called *axolotl* deserves special attention. Its habitat is Lake Xochimilco, south of the City of México.1 For the Aztecs, *axolotls* constituted an exquisite delicacy with stimulant and aphrodisiac properties, and they were also believed to possess mystical qualities. Considered a food for the gods, *axolotls* were prepared in broths, stews, *tamales* and served in banquets for royalty. Even today, in addition to their medicinal use for the treatment of asthma and bronchitis, *axolotls*, because of their protected-species status, are prepared occasionally in such dishes as Xochimilco-style fried *axolotl*, with yellow chilli sauce, *axolotl tamal* and Puebla-style *axolotl* soup.

The purpose of this essay is to analyze how the *axolotl*, a delicacy of pre-Hispanic and modern cuisines, but rejected as food by many contemporary diners, has been reclaimed as an object of scientific study and literary imagination. I am also interested in analyzing why this biologically complex amphibian has attracted much attention from various areas of knowledge. The *axolotl* is a unique animal, because it is an object of culinary, mythical, scientific and literary significance. My research scope includes the cultural importance that this batrachian had for the Aztecs' ingestion and social practices of consumption, as well as its presence in contemporary culture through recipes and forms of preparation. Moreover, this study investigates the *axolotl's* presence in scientific research and in the literary imagination. Although there are many studies on the *axolotls*, this essay aims to build a bridge between various disciplines that have taken it as an object of study.

For the Aztecs, the *axolotls* were divine creatures, since they represented the god Xólotl, who escaped sacrifice by transforming first into a maguey plant and then into the amphibian *axolotl*, to be finally caught and killed. Currently, the *axolotl* is used in research on the regeneration of tissues, as well as in neotenic experiments, since this animal maintains, in its adult stage, characteristics of young tissue. If science has recovered the *axolotl*, so has the literary imagination.[2] In Latin American literature, Julio Cortázar wrote '*Axolotl*', a short story that tells the story of a man who, fascinated by the *axolotls*, goes to the aquarium daily to observe them, eventually becoming one. In 1971, Mexican writer Salvador Elizondo acquired two samples of *axolotls* to study them and, mentored by the geneticist Leon de Garay, carried out experiments to stimulate their metamorphosis. As a result of his experiments, described by the author as 'fantastic biology', he wrote '*Ambystoma trigrinum*', a text that is part of the book *El grafógrafo* [*The Graphographer*]. Other writers who have reclaimed the *axolotls* in their works are Juan José Arreola, who wrote '*El ajolote*' [*The Axolotl*] that later would be included in his *Bestiario* [*Bestiary*], while Octavio Paz retrieves this animal's mythological resonance in *Salamandra* [*Salamander*], as does José Emilio Pacheco in *El reposo del fuego* [*The Rest of Fire*].

The Changing Status of Pre-Hispanic Gastronomy: The *Axolotls*, Offal or Delicacy?

Although offal refers to the internal organs of an animal slaughtered for food consumption, in a broad sense it also means crumbly, exaggerated or by-products that are discarded or rejected in the course of food processing.[3] The Aztecs' pre-Hispanic gastronomy is now considered as offal by certain gastronomic communities in México and only reclaimed by the curious, the foodies and the gourmands.[4] Along with some of the offal dishes, insect larvae, armadillos, frogs, turtles, a type of dog, *tuzas*, opossums, *axolotls*, salamanders, *iguanas* and snakes were used. Also, among the Aztecs, the consumption of *charales*, *juiles*, *mexclapiques*, *acociles* and *meliponas* was common. Preparation of these foods includes the use of a wide variety of hot chilli peppers. A partial listing of these types of dishes includes frogs in chilli sauce, *axolotls* in yellow chilli, Puebla-style *axolotls* and *mextlapique*, or *axolotl tamal*.

The king of the edible animals in pre-Hispanic México, and one of the most likely considered to be offal, is the *axolotl*. The word comes from the Náhuatl '*Axolotl*', which means 'monster of the water', and, in turn, the god Xólotl. Also known popularly as 'the fish that walks', due to its amphibian characteristics, the *axolotl* has an ugly appearance, which is in part why its use in cooking is usually rejected. Of Pleistocene origin, the *axolotl* is the larva of the *urodela* salamander that belongs to the *Ambystomatidae* family (Greek *stoma*, snout; and *amblys*, acute), of which thirty species are known. The *axolotl* is the *Ambystomatidae mexicanum*.[5] It measures approximately thirty centimetres, has four limbs, very long gills and a thin, short tail. In its natural habitat, it can live up to three years, and under controlled laboratory conditions, up to twenty-five. The female *axolotl* reaches its adult stage between the ages of twelve and eighteen months; it can then lay up to four hundred eggs.[6] The most remarkable feature of the axolotl is that it remains in its larval immature stage during its entire life. Its transformation to maturity can be induced while in captivity through the use of hormones. Hence, it is of interest to the scientific research community engaged in tissue regeneration and cloning. Currently, the *axolotl* lives in the waters Xochimilco and Chalco-Tláhuac lakes in the State of México. The *axolotl* may be considered what Richard Goldschmidt called 'a hopeful monster' and though it is not a mutant, its monstrosity is a result of its physical abnormality.[7] The word 'hopeful' stems from its unique neotenic characteristic, and from the taste of its meat as a 'dish for a prince'. After the arrival of the Spaniards in México, the first to report about the god Xólotl was Fray Bernardino de Sahagún. Xólotl was Quetzalcóatl's twin brother (or his double), but unlike him Xólotl was deformed and monstrous: 'he was considered the god of the twins and the abnormal.' If Quetzalcóatl was 'the feathered serpent', Xólotl was 'the monster of water'. Moreover Xólotl was associated with the sun, twilight, fire and lightning. When the gods decided to throw themselves into a fire so the Fifth Sun would move, the only exception was Xólotl, who escaped and turned into a corn plant. However, after being discovered, he first turned into a maguey plant, his last metamorphosis being an *axolotl*.[8]

For the Aztecs, and for certain contemporary gastronomic communities in México, ingestion of the *axolotl* has symbolic significance because the amphibian represents cosmic force and eternal youth.[9] Consuming food involves several organs, the mouth being the principal one. Food consumption is preceded by use of the nose, eyes and fingers, which are involved with sensory perception of the food. Both sight and hearing are kinds of long-distance perception. Smell and taste require contact with the object – especially taste, because of the tongue's taste buds.

Animal meat can be introduced to the senses in two ways. On the one hand, the meat is covered with sauces to hide its appearance and, on the other, meat is served 'as is', without garnishment. In the first case, there is a pornographic aspect in the depiction of the meat dish where it may appear, according to Magee, as 'glossily lush and voluptuous and sinful'.[10] In the latter case, a dish is depicted in a simple and realistic way, and its primary attraction is its flavour. Barthes qualifies the visual adornment of food as 'concealing the nature of the food' and argues that:

> Ornamentation proceeds in two contradictory ways, which we shall briefly see dialectically reconciled: on the one hand, fleeing from nature thanks to a kind of frenzied baroque (sticking shrimps in a lemon, making a chicken look pink, serving grapefruit hot), and on the other hand, trying to reconstitute it through an incongruous artifice (strewing meringue mushrooms and holly leaves on a traditional log-shaped Christmas cake, replacing the heads of crayfish around the sophisticated *bechamel* which hides their bodies.[11]

The pornographic makeover of the food, so frequent in haute cuisine, has gazing as its object. Simple food with without garnish, however, centres on taste. According to Ming-Yeh T. Rawnsley, the Chinese prefer taste with regards to food.[12] Mexicans also show this preference. Regarding the *axolotl*, Fray Bernardino de Sahagún says that 'it is mainly lean meat, good for a vigil, yet it alters mood and it is bad for continence'.[13] Mexican chef and researcher Eduardo Plascencia, somewhat like Sahagún, describes *axolotl* meat as 'delicate and with a gelatinous texture'.[14]

Many Mexican dishes, like Chinese food, are focused on flavour, not appearance. In some Mexican gastronomic communities, offal food such as ants, grasshoppers and brains, which are perceived as ugly and unpleasant in appearance, are considered to be a delicacy in the kitchen.[15] This is the case with the *axolotl*: disgusting, it becomes 'a food for princes' when prepared in various dishes. Dishes prepared with *axolotls* may be presented ungarnished as well as covered with sauce. In the Puebla-style *axolotl* soup, for example, the *axolotl* appears to swim; in Xochimilco-style fried *axolotl*, the batrachian is served as if it were a burnt corpse. Among the *axolotl* recipes, the *tlapique* deserves attention because of its pre-Hispanic-origin cooking process. *Tlapique* or *mextlapique means* in Náhuatl 'thing wrapped in corn leaves, as well as *tamalli*'. From this last word comes the Spanish word *tamal*. Unlike the latter, *tlapique* contains no corn flour, nor is it steamed. It consists of frogs, tadpoles, small fish and *axolotls* placed on three layers of corn husks. Wrapped carefully, it is heated on a griddle until it stops dripping. It includes vegetables, herbs (*epazote, vinagrera*), prickly pears and dried chillies. In other dishes, the *axolotl* is lightly covered with sauce as, for example, *axolotl* in yellow and green chilli peppers, *axolotl* in red broth and *axolotl* stewed with coconut oil.

Currently, the *axolotl* is used for medicinal and ritual purposes, or as a pet in home aquariums, whereas the consumption of *axolotl* is limited to dishes of certain Mexican communities. It is popular in the market of Puebla, which indicates of the *axolotl* in this sector of society.[16] (I suspect that the Mexican middle class and cosmopolitan elites reject this type of food, considering it disgusting and primitive). The *axolotl* is endangered, and is therefore protected by the Mexican Department of Agriculture, Livestock, Rural Development, Fisheries and Food (SAGARPA), whose objective is to 'reverse the deterioration of ecosystems, through actions of water, soil and biodiversity conservation'.[17] The *axolotl*'s eventual extinction is being blamed on Xochimilco's pollution, urban expansion, tourism and the introduction of other species, such as common carp and tilapia. A report in *El Comercio,* a Peruvian newspaper, gives this account: 'In 2013, during a six-month period, the first part of a census on axolotls was conducted, and none was found. Biologist Luis Zambrano said that the amphibian was 'on the brink of extinction;' even though he clarified that another census will be taken this year since the rainfall season might have affected the count. In 1998, there were 6000 axolotls per square kilometre, according to the Mexican Academy of Sciences.'[18] Statistics indicate that axolotl is on the brink of extinction.

In spite of the ban on its consumption, the *axolotl* continues to be used in the kitchen, both legally and illegally. *Axolotl* is being grown by individual breeders, especially in the area of Xochimilco, and it can be found on the black market, sold for medicinal purposes and religious rituals as well as for use as pets and food. In México City, it can be found in the Lázaro Cardenas markets in the Morelos neighbourhoods, Nuevo San Lázaro in Mixhuca (known as the fish market), in La Merced and the Sonora Market. In 2015, a white or 'albino' *axolotl* could be bought for five hundred pesos (about US$29.00), and a black one for three hundred pesos (about US$17.00).[19] The *axolotls* can be purchased legally in the centre of Biological Research and Aquaculture of Cuemanco, the UAM-Xochimilco, or in the UMA (Management Unit for the Wild Life Conservation), a unit of the Department of Environment and Natural Resources (SEMARNAT).

Essence, Principle of Incorporation, the Body

If for the Mexican gastronomic community consumption of the *axolotl* is linked to cultural identity, it should not be attributed solely to nostalgia, which seems to be the view of some critics.[20] *Axolotl* seems to express what is perceived as the essence of Mexican identity. Barthes's musings on food and French nationalism facilitate understanding the link between food and the construction of the nation. In 'Wine and Milk' and 'Steak and Chips' from *Mythologies*, Roland Barthes exposes the essentialism of French culture, noting the 'Frenchness' of these products, from the perspective of a semiology of taste. Wine is French, as milk is American: 'But milk remains an exotic substance; it is wine which is part of the nation.' Both French wine and steak share the characteristic of blood, but what is truly French are fried potatoes (known in English as 'French fries'): '*la* frite, chips, are the alimentary sign of Frenchness.'[21] Each country finds its cultural essence in a particular food.

Food is important to the construction of cultural identity, but another factor that needs to be taken into account is the 'incorporation principle' that allows communication between the body and the outside world through the mouth. Claude Fischler argues that 'incorporation is [...] the basis of collective identity and, by the same token, of otherness. Food and cuisine are a central component of the sense of collective belonging'.[22] Thus, the incorporation of food carries the sense of essence in a particular culture. Unlike Baudrillard, for whom the human body is an allegory of the microcosm, George Yúdice observes that 'the body is not simply the screen on which the rampant exchange of information and images is captured, it is rather the battleground on which subjects are constituted, contradictorily desiring and rejecting prescribed representations'. By the same token, for the Mexican gastronomic community, *axolotl* intake constitutes not only a cultural sign, but also a social act that connects two or more people of Mexican background and mediates the cultural meanings between them.[23]

Food, then, constructs subjectivity in relation to social spaces. If we take into account the 'incorporation principle' as a key concept to understanding the nature of the process of food incorporation in its relationship with the representations, the Mexican gastronomic community consuming *axolotls* does not view the dish as offal or exotic, but as an animal and a totemic meal.[24] The spirit of Xólotl, the twin god, is in the *axolotl*, and its incorporation into the body constitutes a symbolic, whether conscious or unconscious, transubstantiation of the qualities of the god: his sacrifice, his ability to morph, his eternal youth, his sexual vigour and his curative properties.[25] The *axolotl*, radiating a mythology, is consumed in various forms for various purposes: as an aphrodisiac and to treat cough, asthma, bronchitis and skin afflictions.

The Mexicanness of the *Axolotl*: Mexican Writers and Their Culture

Unlike natural species, which according to Claude Lévi-Strauss were not good to eat but good for thinking, the *axolotl* is good for both.[26] Among those Mexican writers who have thought about the axolotl in their works — though perhaps never tasted it — are Juan José Arreola, José Emilio Pacheco, Octavio Paz, Salvador Elizondo and Roger Bartra. In order to think about the nation through the *axolotl*, 1990 Nobel Literature Laureate Octavio Paz devotes some stanzas to it in his poem '*Salamandra*' ['Salamander']. He refers to Xólotl as the god who refuses to sacrifice, then undergoes different metamorphoses — corn, maguey and *axolotl*:

> Not beating the sun nailed in the middle of the sky
> Not breathing
> Do not begin the life without the blood
> Without the ember of the sacrifice
> Do not move the wheel of days
> Xólotl refuses to be consumed
> Hid in the maize but was found
> Hid in the maguey was found
> Fell in the water and became the *axólotl* fish
> The two-beings
> And 'then they killed him'.[27]

For Paz, the Xólotl god is essential, since without his forced sacrifice ('then they killed him'), the sun would be static, and therefore the cycle of nature would not exist: 'The wheel of the days'. The Salamander is the representation of the fish god which gives rise not only to the Mexican nation, but also to the world.

In his poem '*El reposo del fuego*' [*The Rest of Fire*], José Emilio Pacheco follows Paz's line of the argument by reflecting on *axolotl* in terms of the nation. However, this time, Pacheco emphasizes the *axolotl*, not the god:

> The *axolotl* is our emblem: it embodies
> the fear of being nobody and losing oneself
> at incessant night where the gods
> rot under the lake and their silence

is gold, like Cuauhtémoc's gold invented by Cortes.[28]

If for Paz, the Xólotl god is the origin of the life in the Mexican nation through voluntary/involuntary sacrifice, for Pacheco, the *axolotl* points toward a reflection about the identity of the contemporary Mexicans. It expresses 'the fear of being nobody', and bespeaks the risk of 'getting lost' in the mythical past ('the gods / rot under the lake'). Moreover, the *axolotl* represents the illusion of richness that was just a promise and that has brought so many historical calamities to the Mexican nation.

For Juan José Arreola, the *axolotl* is both an 'emblem' of the nation and an allegory, from a scientific and philosophical perspective. In '*El ajolote*' [*The Axolotl*] included in *Bestiario*, Arreola sees this amphibian from a historical, philosophical and scientific perspective. In his text, the *axolotl* shares male and female traits. At the same time, it is considered a phallic symbol ('the axolotl is a *limgam*') with the capability of getting women pregnant in river waters.[29] The narrator divulges that his mother met a woman who was impregnated by an *axolotl*. Referring to the origin of the *axolotl*, Arreola quotes the Spanish priest Bernardino de Sahagún who stated that a woman, who was raped and then washed in the Axotitla lagoon, gave birth to an '*acholote*' ['*axolotl*']. Moreover, the first time the Dominican priest saw an *axolotl*, he exclaimed '¡Simillima mulieribus!' ['It looks like a woman!'].[30] Arreola also draws on scientists and philosophers, like Anton Vital'evich Nemilov (1879-1942) and Jean Rostand (1894-1977), to support his thesis that the female salamander suffers from 'catastrophic' menstrual periods.[31] The text ends with a *boutade* that, while interpreted as humorous, is also misogynistic: 'The three [animals] remaining are a female bat, the women, and an anthropoid monkey.'[32] Although Mexicanness is constructed as male, femininity also forms a part of it.

In *El grafógrafo* [*The Graphographer*], Salvador Elizondo includes a chapter on the axolotls, '*Ambystoma trigrinum*'. He begins his essay with the definition offered by the Spanish Royal Academy. Then he expands it, in random fashion, with scientific, literary, daily and impressionist observations about the batrachian. Moving between science and literature, Elizondo calls his project a 'fantastic biology experiment'.[33] Elizondo proposes to think of the *axolotl* as a space of scientific, artistic and cultural representation and admits that he 'dream[s] while contemplating [it]'.[34] He also acknowledges his aesthetic fascination with the animal: 'the *axolotl* is without a doubt, if not the most beautiful or the most useful, the most interesting of the contributions of Mexican nature to the greatest confusion of the sciences, and the greatest wealth of literature and the arts'.[35] For Elizondo, the fascination with the *axolotl* becomes an impulse for writing.

Like Arreola and others in the area of science or historiography, an aspect that attracts Elizondo to the *axolotl* is its hybrid nature, and especially its sexual ambiguity: 'The ideal inhabitant of an ambiguous habitat: mud, which is neither liquid or solid, as the *axolotl* is neither terrestrial nor aquatic; nor fully branchial nor totally pulmonary, but both or none at once'. Its sexual indeterminacy is further emphasized by the fact that it also belongs to both water (as *axolotl*) and fire (as salamander). With regard to gender, Elizondo notes that axolotls' 'vaginas are similar to those of women as they shed blood every 28 days'. Like Arreola, he believes that the morphology of the *axolotl* is paradoxically phallic. Male/female, the salamander is to Elizondo 'a connubial figure' and 'a live phallic symbol'. Elizondo proposes to examine this phenomenon from a scientific, literary and cultural viewpoint. From the latter viewpoint, he proposes an *axolotl* culture that takes place in an imaginary town: *Axolotitlán*: 'a city founded for its population by genetically mutant beings'.[36] This utopia is built on the difficulties of Mexican social and cultural realities.

The approach of Roger Bartra to the amphibian in *La jaula de la melancolía (The Cage of Melancholy)* is quite different from that of previous writers. He intends to demystify the interpretations that Mexican writers have made about their culture. To achieve this objective, he proposes, paradoxically, twenty-two vignettes on the *axolotls*, followed by respective chapters where he addresses the issue raised in the prior vignette. Bartra is not interested in reflecting on the relationship between the biological and the social, i.e., in social Darwinism. Rather, he explores the counterpoint between the vignettes and the chapters. According to him, they 'play with the information in such a way that the criticism is merged in a natural way with the analysis'.[37] This method of writing results in a hybrid text that, while it discusses various interpretations of Mexican culture, also reflects on his own writing.

Paz, Pacheco, Arreola, Elizondo and Bartra seek to interpret their culture in the mythical and archaic space of the *axolotl* androgynous figure. To them, the *axolotl* is the symbol of Mexicanness that they intend to question. Bartra offers the best definition of what the *axolotl* means to Mexican intellectuals: 'Xólotl is a *numen* linked to death and *transformations*, a mutation in various strange ways, a flight from death, to find it as *axolotl* in the water. There is a common element in this: *a constant struggle against fate, a permanent flight from it*. And this is done exclusively through transformations.'[38] As *numen*, the *axolotl* aims in multiple directions. On the one hand, it expresses the contradiction of offal and delicacy; on the other hand, it serves as scientific and artistic inspiration. In Mexican cultural identity, the *axolotl* awakens the desire for incorporation of one of these aspects, or of all at once. In the Spanish verbs 'to savour,' 'to observe', 'to think', 'to hypothesize' and 'to test', we can witness these different directions.

Conclusion

During the era of the Aztecs, the *axolotl* was regarded as an exquisite dish worthy of kings. During colonial times, it was demonized by the Catholic Church for its unattractive aspect, which was associated with the devil.[39] The rejection of the *axolotl* also had to do with a rejection of indigenous culture as primitive, and with a reaffirmation of Hispanic values. Then the *axolotl* was recovered and incorporated as both 'real' and 'imaginary' by Mexican culinary communities. The 'real' incorporation through its consumption highlighted the exquisite taste of its meat and medicinal properties. As to the 'imaginary' incorporation, the *axolotl* had – and has – meant a transubstantiation of Mexicanness as a reaffirmation of the collective. A 'symbolic' incorporation by writers has to be included, from myth to the search for 'Mexicanness'. Ingested, studied, painted, included in poetry, the *axolotl* is the Mexican intellectuals' 'Aleph', which contains all Mexican culture.[40]

Notes

1. Adriana Pérez de Legaspi, *La gastronomía prehispánica, saberes y sabores de nuestros antepasados* (Mexico City: Mexicanísimo, 2011), pp. 19-25.
2. Other writers who have written on the *axolotl* are Frank Herbert who invented a technology called 'axolotl tanks' in his novel *Dune Universe and Destination: Void* (New York: Berkley Publishing Corporation, 1966); the Polish writer Jacek Dukaj who wrote the novel *The Old Axolotl* (Warsaw: Allegro 2015). Two childrens' books are Fre Chevere's *Axolotl: The Water Dragon and Princess Yolotli* (Bloomington, IN: Xlibris, 2015) and Susan Hood's *Spike: The Mixed-up Monster* (New York, N. Y.: Paula Wiseman Books, 2012).
3. According to *Merriam-Webster*, the word offal, which originated in the Middle English during the fourteenth century, comes from the combination of the words off + fall: 'In its original sense, *offal* refers to something that has fallen or been cast away from some process of preparation or manufacture, and it has been used to describe such things as the stalks and dust from tobacco leaves, the less valuable portions of an animal hide, the by-products of milling grain, and the viscera and trimmings of a butchered animal. The word *offal*, however, is not an etymological cast-off, but is an English original that arose in the late fourteenth century as a combination of *of* (the Middle English spelling of 'off') and *fall*, aptly naming that which 'falls off' or is cast aside from something else. Since the late sixteenth century, *offal* has also been used as a synonym for *trash, garbage and rubbish*' <http://www.merriam-webster.com/dictionary/offal/> [accessed 30 April 2016].
4. I call 'gastronomic community' a group of people that, in space and time, shares the same foods and identity.
5. Alejandro Molina Vásquez, 'El ajolote de Xochimilco', *Ciencias*, 98 (2010), 55.
6. Molina Vásquez, p. 57.
7. Jean Gayon, 'Los monstruos prometedores: Evolución y teratología', in *Monstruos y grotescos. Aproximaciones desde la literatura y la filosofía*, ed. by Cármen Alvarado Lobato (Mexico City: Universidad Autónoma del Estado de México, 2014), p. 17.
8. *Axolotiada*, ed. by Roger Bartra, (Mexico City: Fondo de Cultura Económica, 2011), p. 35.
9. *Axolotl* consumption is limited to the geographical areas of the states of México and Puebla. This batrachian is not even known in many other states of México.
10. Richard M. Magee, 'Food Puritanism and Food Pornography: The Gourmet Semiotics of Martha and Nigella', *Americana: The Journal of American Popular Culture*, 6.2 (2007), p. 1. <http://www.americanpopularculture.com/journal/articles/fall_2007/magee.htm/> [accessed 19 April 2016].
11. Roland Barthes, *Mythologies*, trans. by Annette Lavers (New York: The Noonday Press, 1991), pp. 131, 79.
12. Ming-Yeh T. Rawnsley, 'Food for Thought: Cultural Representation of Taste in Ang Lee's *Eat Drink, Man, Woman*', in *Food for Thought: Essays on Eating and Culture*, ed. by Lawrence C. Rubin (Jefferson, NC: McFarland, 2008), p. 225.
13. Juan José Arreola, 'El ajolote', in *Bestiario* (Mexico City: Joaquín Mortiz, 1972), p. 40.
14. Eduardo Plascencia, '*Ajolotada, el escurridizo platillo poblano*', *Animal Gourmet* <http://www.animalgourmet.com/2013/10/16/ajolotada-el-escurridizo-platillo-poblano/> [accessed 1 February 2016].
15. One of the most 'offal' food consumed by the Aztecs was human flesh. According to Luis Alfonso

Ramírez Vidal, 'The pozole, a preparation with human flesh of victims of war or as part of the offering to the gods had, among other ingredients, corn and chillies' ('*Comidas y etnicidades: africanos e indígenas en la olla del misionero*', in *Cocinando en el fogón de las identidades; comidas, saberes y regiones. Cátedra abierta. Universidad, Cultura y Sociedad* (Antioquia, Colombia: Universidad de Antioquia, 2010), pp. 37-49 (42).

16. Plascencia recounts the experience in finding *axolotls* in the *Mercado de Puebla* [Market of Puebla]. He discovers that a very quiet and discreet lady had some live *axolotls* for the preparation of the dish '*ajolotada poblana*' [Puebla-style axolotls].
17. Chema Gómez, 'La extinción del ajolote y su vida en el mercado negro', *Vice* <http://www.vice.com/es_mx/read/la-extincion-de-ajolote-y-su-vida-en-el-mercado-negro> [accessed 7 April 2016].
18. '*El ajolote desaparece de canales en México D.F.*', *El Comercio*. 28 January 2014 <http://elcomercio.pe/ciencias/planeta/ajolote-desaparece-canales-México-df-noticia-1705838> [accessed 7 April 2016].
19. Gómez.
20. Jopi Nyman, 'Cultural Contact and the Contemporary Culinary Memoir: Home, Memory and Identity in Madhur Jaffrey and Diana Abu-Jaber', *Autobiographical Studies,* 24.2 (2009), 282.
21. Barthes, pp. 61, 63-64.
22. Claude Fischler, 'Food, Self and Identity', *Social Sciences Information,* 27 (1998), 276-78.
23. George Yúdice, 'Feeding the Trascendent Body', in *Essays in Post Modern Culture*, ed. by Eyal Amiran and John Unsworth (Oxford: Oxford University Press, 1993), pp. 81, 20.
24. The characteristics of the *totem* animal are transferred to people who consume it. In the case of *axolotls*, the characteristics are their ability to survive and their eternal youth.
25. With regard to wine as a *totem* beverage, Barthes declares that 'as all live totem, wine supports a varied mythology that is not disturbed with contradictions' (p. 75). The same could be said about the *axolotls*.
26. Bartra, p. 19.
27. Octavio Paz, *Salamandra* (Mexico City: Joaquín Mortiz, 1990), p. 95 (my translation).
28. José Emilio Pacheco, *El reposo del fuego* (Mexico City: Ediciones Era, 1984), p. 48 (my translation). 29 *Lingam* is a phallic symbol representing the Hindu goddess Shiva.
30. Arreola, p. 40.
31. Anton Vital'evich Nemilov (1879-1942) was a Russian scientist specializing in animal science; Jean Rostand (1894-1977) was a French philosopher and biologist specializing in amphibian embryology, parthenogenesis and teratology.
32. Arreola, p. 41.
33. Claudia L. Gutiérrez Piña, '"*Ambystoma Trigrinum*" de Salvador Elizondo: Escritura en metamorfosis', in *Monstruos y grotescos. Aproximaciones desde la literatura y la filosofía*, ed. by Cármen Alvarado Lobato (Mexico City: Universidad Autónoma del Estado de México, 2014), p. 297.
34. Salvador Elizondo, '*Ambystoma Trigrinum*', in *El grafógrafo* (Mexico City: Joaquín Mortiz, 1972), p. 22.
35. Gutierrez Piña, p. 298.
36. Elizondo, pp. 18, 19, 20, 23.
37. Roger Bartra, *La jaula de la melancolía* (Mexico City: Tidisa S. A., 1997), p. 21.
38. Bartra, *Axolotiada*, p. 37.
39. Personal communication with Eduardo Plascencia.
40. In Jorge Luis Borges's short story 'The Aleph', the narrator finds, in the basement of an old house, the aleph, a point that contains 'all points of the universe' (*Ficciones, El Aleph, El informe de Brodie* (Caracas, Venezuela: Ediciones Ayacucho, 1993), p. 172).

Abjecting Crab Brain: Offal Eating and Ethnic Identity in *The Joy Luck Club*

Jiachen Zhang

Ever since the first group of Chinese labourers were summoned to work in a sugar mill on the island of Hawaii in 1835, a development which quickly led, only ten years later, to the famous reliance on Coolie labour to build the American railroads, Chinese Americans were routinely depicted by U.S dominant culture as indiscriminate consumers of disease-ridden animals, animal offal and other unmentionables. A few months after the Centennial Exhibition opened in Philadelphia on 10 May 1876, *Harper's Weekly* published a sketch by Walter Brown named 'Our Artist's Dream of the Centennial Restaurants', which was dedicated to the grand opening of the fair and its celebration of the hundredth anniversary of American independence.[1] Brown's sketch depicted a cluster of restaurants and stalls on a hill with various signs advertising the food they offered. In between the German, Russian and Mexican stalls among other purveyors of wholesome or acceptable ethnic cuisines, the Chinese outlet stands out, alone advertising such unpleasant dishes as 'Rat Pie' and 'Hashed Cat'. While both dishes highlighted the American depiction of Chinese eating unpromising animals, Brown lists catsup, a word used as a referent for tomato ketchup in the 1800s. Yet more than coincidentally, Brown deforms the word into 'Cat Sup', reminding people of the eccentric soup made of cat meats rather than the common condiment.[2]

Andrew Haley might be right to see the cartoon as a manifestation of a general American 'fear about foreign cuisine'. He further observes that 'in the United States in 1876, French food was recognized as the world's only great cuisine, and neither American nor ethnic dishes had many defenders [...]. America was not ready to experience the diversity of the world's cuisine'.[3] Yet we could not neglect Brown's ridiculing Chinese cuisine as the most uninviting food in his biased representation of foreign cuisines, and the cartoon clearly bespeaks the discriminating treatment that Chinese food and people suffered during the anti-Chinese sentiment that began in the late nineteenth century and reached a high point of dogmatism in the early 1930s. Just seven years after the publication of Brown's cartoon, *The New York Times* consolidated the link between Chinese coolies and their habits of eating rats:

> Do the Chinese eat rats? This has always been a mooted question. Geographers contain the assertion that they do, and an old wood-cut of a Chinaman peddling rodents, strung by the tails to a rack which he carried over his shoulders, is a standard illustration of the common school atlases of 10 years ago.[4]

Offal Eating and Ethnic Identity in *The Joy Luck Club*

Nor was the American disavowal of Chinese food limited to the belief that it was somehow more 'ethnic' and less open to assimilation into mainstream US dining than Italian or German foodways, as suggested by Lisa Heldke.[5] US culture also started to associate Chinese culture with offal and other rejected foods, portraying the Chinese not only as a despicable and barbaric people who misuse pets for food, but also as an origin of that epidemics that animal offal and rejected animals might carry. The American public health department blamed the Chinese as the ultimate reason for the severe epidemic of smallpox that hit San Francisco in the summer of 1876. Dr Hohn Meares, the newly appointed city health officer, claimed that the spread of 'the typical Oriental disease' originated among the 30,000 'unscrupulous, lying and treacherous Chinamen' living in the heart of the city, who infamously raised cats and rats for their food.[6]

Inseparable from this Orientalizing of Chinese food and people, to use Edward Said's term, was a silencing of the voices of actual Chinese cooks and consumers who clearly suffered from cultural and linguistic differences and nevertheless were portrayed as people who conspicuously valued 'stealth and secretiveness'.[7] Yet the invisibility of the Chinese presence in US cultural representations ran counter to the historical fact that shortly after the 1860s Chinese waiters and cooks replaced African American servicemen to become the largest group in the California service sector. Notably, Chinese cooks were considered to be reliable helpers, but they were almost invariably forbidden to cook Chinese food for their white employers.[8] US culture's stigmatization of Chinese food and their reliance on Chinese restaurant workers clearly placed the Chinese as the ones considered best fit to fill the jobs shunned by whites. One might even suggest that W. E. B. Du Bois' famous description of the African American cooks and waiters as the 'unskilled offal of a millionaire industrial system' in his political autobiography *Darkwater* (1920) could be no less readily applied to Chinese labourers in this period.[9]

This depressing relegation of Chinese food and workers to offal seemed to be quickly forgotten by America's dominant culture shortly after the breakout of the Second World War. It is particularly interesting to see the reinvigoration of offal eating scenes in Chinese American literature emerging in the past fifty years. This process is apparent even in the pioneering work of Maxine Hong Kingston, the writer who first established Asian American literature as a serious and distinctive literary field in the 1970s. In *The Woman Warrior* (1976), a collection of Chinese folklore and memoir, Kingston grows up with a mother who turns the most unlikely creatures into food. Thanks to her mother's efforts, the second-generation immigrant is fed with 'racoons, skunks, hawks, city pigeons, wild ducks, wild geese, black-skinned bantams, snakes, garden snails, turtles that crawled about the pantry floor and escaped under refrigerator or stove, catfish that swam in the bathtub'.[10] Kingston relates her mother's superior cooking and eating ability to her mother's triumph over the 'sitting ghost', thus placing Brave Orchid as one of the Chinese heroic heroes who battle against ghosts and monsters. Yet Kingston's inclusion of racoons and skunks, which are not native to China at all, in the mother's cooking list reinforces Brave Orchid's image as one of the Chinese immigrants who successfully transform American animals into nutritious food and strive to survive unfavourable treatment as a racial minority, both physically and psychologically.

The difference here is that the psychological strength of offal eating is dismissed not by dominant white US culture, but by Kingston's own second-generation American-born children, who are always confronting their struggle to create an identity as both ethnic and American characters. Brave Orchid's children hold candy over their noses to mask the smell of the skunk being dismembered in the kitchen. They would rather 'live on plastic' than eat offal, which they regard as a symbol of Asian primitiveness and an affront to American standards and food taboos.[11]

Amy Tan follows Kingston's lead, likewise making use of offal to scrutinize the dynamic of Othering and ethnicity within American-born Chinese immigrants' troubled sense of identity in the award-winning novel *The Joy Luck Club* (1989). Yet while American cultural representations of Chinese offal eating seems to reinforce dichotomies of whites versus Chinese, civilized versus barbarous, superior versus inferior, I will suggest that Tan moves further to unveil implicit yet inherent instabilities of the mechanism behind the consumption of offal. Using Julia Kristeva's understanding of abjection, such instabilities notably originate in the way that animal offal and rejected animals blur boundaries, and they significantly manifest in Tan's novel as clues to foreshadow Chinese American heroines' ultimate failure to submit to the American characters.

The Joy Luck Club is well-known for its vivid depiction of intergenerational conflicts between four pairs of Chinese-born mothers and American-born daughters. As the author attempts to describe from the novel's first page, it seems that running away from chaotic Chinese mothers and ethnicity into the shelter of what seem to be reasonable and orderly American characters is an underlying impulse for all the American daughters in their youth and adulthood. After many of the daughters' efforts prove to be in vain, their rejection of Chinese identity seems to work by refusing to accept the mothers' cooking. As one of the pivotal activities in *The Joy Luck Club*, eating is used by the American daughters as a way to refuse their Chinese mothers' attempts to manipulate the development of their American characters. For the Chinese mothers, 'joy luck' simply does not exist to 'those American-born minds' when their daughters cannot relate themselves to 'the excellent dishes their mothers cooked'.[12]

The American daughters' rejection of Chinese cooking culminates in the narration of a typical Chinese feast for the celebration of Chinese New Year, featuring its prolonged depiction of what is to them loathsome Chinese eating. Notably, the feast crosses national and ethnic boundaries through the attendance of newly wed American son-in-law Rich and some Chinese American grandchildren. Although Waverley Jong, one of the American daughters, states that 'crab isn't Chinese', the new-comers are surely not well aware of how to eat the crabs served at the feast.[13] Chances seem high that some guests will believe American daughter Jing-mei Woo when she tells them that Americans regard crabs as domestic animals, as pets not suitable for cooking.[14] To make

Offal Eating and Ethnic Identity in *The Joy Luck Club*

things worse, the Chinese mother not only cooks the crabs, but then teaches her guests how to eat its best part, as Jing-mei Woo describes:

> Then [Lindo Jong] turned to Rich and said with much authority, 'Why are you not eating the best part?' And I saw Rich smiling back, with amusement, and not humility, showing in his face. He had the same coloring as the crab on his plate: reddish hair, pale cream skin, and large dots of orange freckles. While he smirked, Auntie Lindo demonstrated the proper technique, poking her chopstick into the orange spongy part: 'You have to dig in here, get this out. The brain is most tastiest, you try.' Waverly and Rich grimace at each other, united in disgust. I heard Vincent and Lisa whisper to each other, 'Gross,' and then they snickered too.[15]

The Chinese mother's imparting of Chinese culinary knowledge naturally leads to the American children's physical and psychological reinforcement of the obvious American food taboos. Yet the uncanny physical resemblance between the crab and Rich turns my attention to Julia Kristeva's famous theory of the abject. Kristeva develops her theory from the cultural anthropologist Mary Douglas's belief in the threatening position that 'matter out of margin' claims in society. Douglas writes:

> all margins are dangerous [...]. Matter issuing from them is marginal stuff of the most obvious kind. Spittle, blood, milk, urine, faces or tears by simply issuing forth have traversed the boundary of the body [...]. The mistake is to treat bodily margins in isolation from all other margins.[16]

Kristeva continues to attach great importance to the skin on milk, for example, suggesting it is abject because it is neither liquid nor solid but exists in the indeterminable space between both. The abject, then, is something located on the border but that also disrespects the border. Kristeva writes, 'It is thus not lack of cleanliness or health that causes abjection but what disturbs identity, system, order. What does not respect borders, positions, rules. The in-between, the ambiguous, the composite.'[17] Kristeva suggests here that. when a food such as the crab brain, the offal which reminds people of their own brain, breaches the categories between important organs and disposable food, the abject is formed.

This imagery of abject formation reappears when Tan depicts a fishmonger and a café in San Francisco's Chinatown:

> Farther down the street was Ping Yuen Fish Market. The front window displayed a tank crowded with doomed fish and turtles struggling to gain footing on the slimy green-tiled sides. A hand-written sign informed tourists: 'Within this store, is all for food, not for pet.' [...] At the corner of the alley was Hong Sing's [...]. A Caucasian man with a big camera once posed me and my playmates in front of the restaurant. He had us move to the side of the picture window so the photo

would capture the roasted duck with its head dangling from a juice-covered rope. After he took the picture, I told him he should go into Hong Sing's and eat dinner. When he smiled and asked what they served, I shouted, 'Guts and duck's feet and octopus gizzards.'[18]

Slaughtering the animals on-site, killing what were, presumably, 'pets', and displaying their corpses for window-shopping: all of these actions here seem to typify Chinese food in general in the mind of the young protagonist. Sau-ling Wong insightfully links the image of eating unlikely animals to 'quasi-cannibalism', a notion that cruelly intrudes on humanity and contemporary social orders.[19] Clearly Wong's claim of quasi-cannibalism is built upon the similarities between animals and human flesh, and echoes with the western world's long history of rendering consumption of animals as barbaric and inhuman acts. The ancient Greek writer Plutarch wrote an essay entitled 'Flesh-eating' in which he relates meat to embalmed human flesh.[20] Since meat is by nature the product of the dead animals, it reminds people frequently of violence, aggression, the spilling of blood and pain. In other words, it constantly trembles on the borders between clean / dirty and purity / contamination, where Kristeva sees the production of the abject.

Tan's depiction of San Francisco's Chinatown frequently reminds the 'predominantly white and female [American] readers' of the violence that precedes the consumption of offal and rejected animals.[21] It orients attention towards the blood-stained smocks on the butchers as well as the temporary liveliness and doomed deaths of the living animals on the food stalls. Tan's semiotics of disgust in Chinese cooking extends to their way of eating in one of the Chinese mother Ying-ying's childhood memories. She speaks of the adults eating living animals:

> I raced to the pavilion and found aunts and uncles laughing as they used chopsticks to pick up dancing shrimp, still squirming in their shells, their tiny legs bristling. So this was what the mesh cage beneath the water had contained, freshwater shrimp, which my father was now dipping into a spicy bean-curd sauce and popping into his mouth with two bites and a swallow.[22]

The savage eating of living animals recalls the pioneering anthropologist Claude Levi-Strauss' famous belief in cooking as a moral process. In his mind, cooking transfers raw matter from 'nature' to the state of 'culture'. Treating food practices as a system of language, the anthropologist identifies 'nature', 'culture' and 'rotten' as the culinary triangle. Culture is regarded as the most complex of those food practices, which distinguish humans from the primitive humans or animals.[23] Read in this context, Tan's description of eating living animals invokes the historic negative assumptions about Chinese food that have situated this cuisine outside the orbit of human civilization.

Tan's uncanny return to Chinese primitiveness both in eating and cooking contradicts the semiotics long held in the western thought: here meat is not dead, as it was to Plutarch, but alive. On the surface, such oppositions to western tradition justify the American daughters' loathing of Chinese ways of eating. Their clear division of food practices into either disgusting or delectable grows out of their need to stand with the American social order: their actions reinforce American taboos about eating offal and rejected animals that stigmatize Chinese food as filth, as outside the civilized social order. This thought is famously explained by Mary Douglas in *Purity and Danger* (1966):

> Ideas about separating, purifying, demarcating and punishing transgressions have as their main function to impose system on an inherently untidy experience. It is only by exaggerating the difference between within and without, above and below, male and female, with and against, that a semblance of order is created.[24]

In Douglas's view, designating polluted food maintains the social order. As I attempt to explore in the opening of the paper, it fits the US culture's interest to view the Chinese ethnic food as primitive, as savage Other, constructing an effective semiotics of multicultural salad-bowl America. Using food metaphors to depict the role of ethnicity in the whites' imaginations, bell hooks points out in her famous essay 'Eating the Other' that 'ethnicity becomes spice, seasoning that can liven up the dull dish that is mainstream white culture'. She further argues that imbibing what Others eat (allowing Chinese Americans to practice their own eating in Chinatown in this context) is to ingest that Other. She claims in the end of the essay that 'the overriding fear is that cultural, ethnic, and racial differences will be continually commodified and offered up as new dishes to enhance the white palate – that the Other will be eaten, consumed, and forgotten'.[25] For example, the 'Caucasian' American in Tan's scene takes a photograph 'that would capture the roasted duck with its head dangling from a juice-covered rope', clearly showing his fascination with and desire of the ingestion of the Other.[26] By telling him about the unclean food items for sale in the Chinese cafeteria, Waverley joins the Americans' need to consume the Chinese ethnic inferiority. In other words, the American daughters' loathing of Chinese food does not stop at the simple rejection of their own Chinese culture and ethnic roots; they believe that their hatred of Chinese food strengthens their affiliation with a white majority US culture they now regard as exclusive and superior.

Yet the Othering of Chinese offal and rejected animal eating could never amount to a complete exclusion. After all, what lies behind the American taboo against offal eating – and the racial discrimination such taboos reinforce – is based on the abjectness of offal itself. The historical coupling of rat eating and filth to characterize the Chinese race, described in the beginning of this paper, grants us an opportunity to observe the incomplete exclusion of rats from American modernity. Rats are believed to blur the boundary between civilized and foreign. David Sibly observes that rats have 'a particular place in the racist bestiary because all are associated with residues – food waste, human waste – and in the case of rats there is an association with spaces which border civilized society, particularly subterranean spaces like sewers, which also channel residues and from which rats occasionally emerge to transgress the boundaries of society'.²⁷ Maud Ellmann reaffirms the rats' defiance of such a boundary, and points out what it means to the social minorities:

> Literally gnawing through the walls of man-made structures, rats in modernism augur the collapse of boundaries, especially the boundaries of meaning [...]. Associated with migration, it eats away the bounds of countries and cultural traditions with the rapacity of a multinational company [...]. Within the multicultural city, rats continue to invade the heart of domesticity, blurring the distinction between inside and outside, tame and wild, *heimlich* and *unheimlich*. Rats are therefore abject, in the sense that Julia Kristeva employs the term: they represent 'the in-between, the ambiguous, the composite.²⁸

In this light, the choice of rats to denigrate Chinese American foodways and immigrants no longer serves to strengthen American mainstream culture as bell hooks and the American daughters in the novel believe; instead, it foreshadows the failure of the ritual to cast Chinese eating away. Ellmann continues, developing Kristeva's theory of abjection in this new direction:

> The abject is that which a culture casts away (ab-jects) in order to determine what is not itself, through rituals such as burning, burial, and exorcism. The resilience of the rat, however, demonstrates the failure of these rituals, for the abject always pops back up again, adapting itself to each new persecution [...]. The rat is a gnawing reminder of this inability [to exclude the abject thing].²⁹

Significantly, the inability to exclude the abject food is evident in the American daughters' seemingly strict loathing of Chinese food. Even though young Waverley despises the Chinese eating in Chinatown, she grows up with 'three five-course meals every day, beginning with a soup full of mysterious things [she] didn't want to know the names of'.³⁰ Likewise, Waverley's and Rich's apparent rejection of eating crabs as gross turns out to be in vain. They finish eating the crabs and leave behind a table full of 'crab carcasses'.³¹ A crab shell is even placed between Waverley and Rich as an ashtray for their cigarettes. To some extent, they have unconsciously joined the group of cruel eaters of the animals, which partly indicates the nature of the abject.

To make things worse, the relation of such abject food to the subject formation of the individual has been complicated in Ying-ying's childhood memory, which remains unknown to the American daughters. In the mysterious narration of 'The Moon Lady', the four-year-old protagonist runs into another scene in which fishermen kill river animals for food:

> I turned around and a sullen woman was now squatting in front of the bucket of

fish. I watched as she took out a sharp, thin knife and began to slice open the fish bellies, pulling out the red slippery insides and throwing them over her shoulder into the lake. I saw her scrape off the fish scales, which flew in the air like shards of glass. And then there were two chickens that no longer gurgled after their heads were chopped off. And a big snapping turtle that stretched out its neck to bite a stick, and – whuck! – off fell its head [...]. It was not until then, too late, that I saw my new clothes – and the spots of bloods, flecks of fish scales, bits of feather and mud.[32]

This sensational paragraph foregrounds many of the abject effects that Kristeva envisions, including human interaction with fish and animal blood. In 'Semiotics of Biblical Abomination', Kristeva argues that biblical prohibitions follow similar logic of separation. When she touches upon food taboos, one of the three categories of abomination, Kristeva maintains that these designate the semantic area of those foods that 'imply the pure / impure distinction'. For example, the blood of animals is not appropriate to be eaten since it suggests to the eaters their animal instincts and reminds them of forbidden cannibalism. To mix blood and animal flesh together is to mix death and birth, violence and food, fuelling feelings of abjection. Many river animals are also impure since they suggest a movement between land and sea as well as a worrying proximity to humanity that further suggests admixture and confusion.[33] In this light, Tan can be seen as complicating Kristeva's thought on food taboos since Ying-ying meets with a lot of trouble after she mistakenly mixes animal blood with her body. She is seen not as human any more but as 'an apparition covered with blood'. Her bodily abjectness finally turns out to be her lost identity in the society, which leads to her traumatic life afterwards.

From this perspective, it is important to see the harm of the daughters' refusal to recognize their mothers' pasts. Without knowing Ying-ying's tragic story, they cannot hold themselves against the revulsion and fascination of the abject. It reminds us to see the importance of learning the mothers' Chinese narratives for their Chinese daughters. The importance lies not only in the sustenance of the Chinese ethnic roots in the joy luck club, but also in how they attempt to educate their daughters. As Ying-ying says, 'All her life, I have watched her as though from another shore. And now I must tell her everything about my past. It is the only way to penetrate her skin and pull her to where she can be saved.'[34] Learning their mothers' pasts thus is an important way for the daughters to survive in American society. The daughters' rejection of their mothers' stories, to some extent, has trapped them in the ethnic abject under the dominant US culture.

The implicit foreshadowing of the daughters' troubled subjectivity comes to fruition in Tan's narration of their failure to assimilate with the American characters throughout the novel. For instance, despite her education at UC Berkeley, Waverley Jong is still regarded as 'oriental' and unfit to marry a white American citizen. Deluded by her faith in American promises of opportunity and advancement, she soon becomes a subject of what Lauren Berlant has called 'cruel optimism'.[35] Whereas the heroines' lives abound with the depressing side-effects of American freedom – leaving them with many choices but the catch that it is 'easy to get confused and pick the wrong thing' – the American culinary Othering of Chinese food fails their expectations and deteriorates their American identity as well.[36]

Exploring instabilities within Chinese offal consumption in *The Joy Luck Club* clearly argues against the simplistic dichotomies lying behind the cultural representation of American racism. In *Black Hunger* (1999), Doris Witt pays a special attention to chitterlings as representative of African American soul food and regards it as an ideal site to reflect 'a far more intricate dynamic of [white's] attraction and repulsion, of inexpressible envy and desire'.[37] The juxtaposition of Chinese offal and ethnic identity in Amy Tan's narrative similarly shows Chinese food blurring the presumably solid boundary between Chinese primitiveness and American civilization – a blurred boundary that partly results in the confused ethnic identities of the Chinese American subjects. Since such difference seems to reflect dissimilarities in how food operates in the construction of divergent ethnic identities, we need more comparative work on cross-cultural practices of culinary Othering in the future.

Notes

1. See 'Centennial Exhibition 1876 Philadelphia Scrapbook', *Free Library of Philadelphia* <http://libwww.freelibrary.org/diglib/ecw.cfm?ItemID=c180220>.
2. It is worth noting that the word Catsup originated as 'ketsiap', a pickled Salmon sauce. It gradually went through various changes, with addition of tomato sauce in particular. 'Catsup' remained as the most popular word describing the sauce until Heinz invented the word 'ketchup', which later became more acceptable to American consumers. The word 'catsup' is still a recognized version of the word indicating ketchup now.
3. Andrew P. Haley, *Turning the Tables: Restaurants and the Rise of the American Middle Class, 1880-1920* (Chapel Hill: University of North Carolina Press, 2011), p. 94.
4. 'Mott-Street Chinamen Angry: They Deny That They Eat Rats – Chung Kee, Threatens a Slander Suit', *New York Times* (1857-1922) 1 August 1883, p. 8.
5. Lisa Heldke, *Exotic Appetites: Ruminations of a Food Adventurer* (London: Routledge, 2003), p. 51.
6. Nayan Shah, *Contagious Divides: Epidemics and Race in San Francisco's Chinatown* (Berkeley: University of California Press, 2001), p. 1.
7. Jacob Riis, *How the Other Half Lives: Studies among the Tenements of New York* (Stillwell: Digireads.com Publishing, 2005), p. 48.
8. Yong Chen, *Chop Suey, USA: The Story of Chinese Food in America* (New York: Columbia University Press, 2014), pp. 44-70.
9. W. E. B. Du Bois, *Darkwater: Voices From Within the Veil* (Massachusetts: Courier Corporations, 1920), p. 67.
10. Maxine Hong Kingston, *The Woman Warrior: A Memoir of a Girlhood among Ghosts* (London: Pan, 1977), p. 85.
11. Kingston, p. 87

12. Amy Tan, *The Joy Luck Club* (London: Vintage, 1989), pp. 41, 40.
13. Tan, p. 203.
14. Pages before the crab feast, Su-yuan's steaming the living crabs evokes Jing-mei's childhood memory of her mothers' cooking crabs, which she treats as her new playmate. Significantly, she equals the imaginary scream of the crab with her own scream for help to break out from the maternal cruelty: 'To this day, I remember that crab screaming as he thrust one bright red claw out over the side of the bubbling pot. It must have been my own voice, because now I know, of course, that crabs have no vocal cords' (Tan, p. 201).
15. Tan, pp. 31-32.
16. Mary Douglas, *Purity and Danger: An Analysis of Concept of Pollution and Taboo* (London: Routledge, 2006), p. 150.
17. Julia Kristeva, *Power of Horror, an Essay on Abjection* (New York: Columbia University Press, 1982), p. 4.
18. Tan, pp. 90-91.
19. Sau-ling Wong, *Reading Asian American Literature: From Necessity to Extravagance*, (Princeton: Princeton University Press, 1993), p. 31.
20. Deborah Lupton, *Food, the Body and the Self* (London: Sage Publications, 1996), p. 117.
21. Sau-ling Wong, '"Sugar Sisterhood": Situating the Amy Tan Phenomenon'. *Amy Tan*, ed. by Harold Bloom (New York: Chelsea House Publishers, 2009), p. 54.
22. Tan, p. 75.
23. In discussing the difference between the roasted food and the boiled food, Levi-Strauss regards boiled food as a cultural object since humans distance their food from direct contact with fire and try to meditate the relations between them and the world through water (Claude Levi-Strauss, 'The Culinary Triangle', *Food and Culture: A Reader*, ed. by Carole Counihan and Penny Van Esterik (London: Routledge, 1997), pp. 20-27).
24. Douglas, p. 5.
25. bell hooks, 'Eating the Other: Desire and Resistance', *Eating Culture*, ed. by Ron Scapp and Brian Seitz (Albany: State University of New York Press, 1998), pp. 181, 200.
26. Tan, p. 91.
27. David Sibly, qtd. in Nayan Shah, p. 27.
28. Maud Ellmann, 'Writing like a Rat', *Critical Quarterly*, 46.4 (2004), 62.
29. Ellmann, p. 62.
30. Tan, p. 89.
31. Tan, p. 206.
32. Tan, p. 76.
33. Kristeva, pp. 90-112; Kelly Oliver, 'Nourishing the Speaking Subject: a Psychoanalytic Approach to Abominable Food and Women', *Cooking, Eating, Thinking: Transformative Philosophies of Food*, ed. by Deane W. Curtin and Lisa M. Heldke (Bloomington: Indiana University Press, 1992), p. 73.
34. Tan, p. 251.
35. As Lauren Berlant puts it, 'cruel optimism' becomes apparent whenever you find that 'something you desire is actually an obstacle to your flourishing', a predicament based on the condition of a person's 'maintaining an attempt to [reach] a problematic object in advance of its loss' (*Cruel Optimism* (Durham, NC: Duke University Press, 2011), p. 2).
36. Tan, p. 191.
37. Doris Witt, *Black Hunger: Food and the Politics of US Identity* (Oxford: Oxford University Press, 1999), p. 79.

The Lore of Tripe: Middle East and Beyond

Sami Zubaida

In Baghdad, where I grew up, *Pacha* had great resonance. Many Iraqis, then and now, held it as a national dish, combining a populist appeal with delicious richness. *Pacha* designated various combinations of basic ingredients: tripe, intestines, head and feet, usually of sheep. The most common was a soup or stew combining all the elements with chick-peas or split peas. Seasoning may include dried limes, *loumi basra* (known in Persian as *limou omani*), which gives it a spicy acidity. Bread, typically dry or stale, is broken into the broth (making it a *tashreeb*), and various condiments can be used in serving, such as garlic, hot pepper and vinegar. This was typical street food, served from cook-shops, usually in the corners of market districts, catering for workers and market people. Some of the more renowned of these establishments became restaurants. Shops and households would send servants for take-aways. The dish was considered as most suitable for breakfast, or, similarly as a late-night/early-morning cure for drinkers and revellers.

In my family home there was a different concept of *pacha*. We did not partake in the market take-away because we kept a Kasher house, and in any case thought the market version much inferior to our *pacha*, more elaborate and delicious. The tripe, different stomach compartments of the sheep, was fashioned into pouches with scissors, needle and thread, and stuffed with rice, chopped meat and offal (liver and heart), seasoned with salt, black pepper and *baharat*, a mixture of aromatics. Intestines would be similarly stuffed, like a sausage, and indeed labelled in our household as *sujuq*, which means sausage. These would then be poached in a broth, comprising the feet and tongues, sometimes other bits of the head, but not the brains, which were cooked separately. These would then be cooked slowly, the pot placed over a gentle wood fire, overnight. Some Jewish households, like ours, would typically serve this as a Sabbath lunch on special occasions, to replace the usual stuffed chicken, known as *tebit* (overnight). The special occasions were feasts or family gatherings at which a lamb would be slaughtered and butchered in the house. Women and servants would then engage in the intensive labour of washing and cleaning the tripe and intestines, including scraping them with razor blades, then soaking them in aromatic marinades, including citrus peel and vinegar. There follows the fashioning into pouches, with scissors, needle and thread, then stuffed and sown up as parcels and sausages. There was a festive atmosphere around these preparations, and the meal certainly worth the effort, served in portions of the parcels, supplemented with one or two feet and slices of tongue on each plate, with pickles and relishes on the side. I could never understand,

The Lore of Tripe: Middle East and Beyond

then, what I discovered subsequently in my English life, of the disdain and disgust in which tripe and offal were held.

The stuffed tripe at that time seemed to us to be peculiar to Jews, as against the tripe soup common to the Baghdad markets and populace. My subsequent discoveries and education in Middle East cultures revealed many other examples. Iran and Anatolia, including northern Iraq and the Arab Levant, all have versions of stuffed tripe. It also has an ancient ancestry in Medieval Arab cookery. The fourteenth-century manuscript *The Description of Familiar Foods* contains three recipes for stuffed tripe cooked overnight, labelled *Sukhtur* or *Kiba*, an Arabization of the Persian *sukhtu* and *kipa*.[1] The prescribed preparation of the gut is similar to that followed in our home: thorough washing (but with soap!) and scraping, then marinating in citrus, vinegar and aromatics, followed by stuffing with meat, fat, rice and chickpeas, topped with water in a sealed pot, then placed in a *tannur* till morning. The second recipe is more extravagant and includes a sheep's head, chicken, pigeon and much else, also cooked overnight in a *tannur*. The third is more basic. Unlike our modern preparations these recipes do not include trotters, but there are separate recipes for those, called *akari`*, similar to modern Arabic usage *kawari`*.

It is interesting to note a parallel dish in French Provencal cookery: *pied-et-paquet*, sheep's foot with a 'packet' of sheep's tripe stuffed with bits of meat and herbs. I first came across this dish during a two-month stay in Aix-en-Provence in the late 1980s. At the institute to which I was attached there was a colleague of Syrian origin married to a French woman. We discovered a lot in common in our backgrounds: school life, music and songs and food. His family repertoire also featured stuffed tripe with head and feet, and we decided to recreate the dish. He ordered the *pied-et-paquet* ingredients from his butcher one fine Saturday. We sat in the kitchen with his wife and another colleague, with scissors, needle and thread, making tripe pouches and stuffing them with rice, ground meat and herbs, then into a pressure cooker, with feet, covered in stock. We left it cooking and went for a swim, returning to a sumptuous lunch.

Later, in London, reminiscing on the joys of tripe with Iranian friends, they decided that we must have a dinner party around the dish, in my kitchen. One particularly enterprising member was in charge of procurement, from Turkish and Pakistani butchers in Dalston and Hackney. There followed a long session of preparation, then cooking in an enormous cauldron I had acquired as a curiosity. Stuffed tripe pouches, feet and heads were stewed in stock with aromatics, including the dried limes much favoured in Iran. It was washed down with iced vodka.

Vocabularies

Before proceeding further, let us consider the vocabularies of tripe and offal in the Middle Eastern regions and former Ottoman lands.

In Iran and parts of Anatolia, similar parcels of stuffed tripe are cooked in a soup with the feet and parts of the head. The parcels are called *kipa* or *sukhtu*, and the soup *kalla pacha* (head and foot), in both Persian and Turkish. The word *pacha* means feet (*paicha*, Persian diminutive of *pai*, foot). In Iraq *pacha* came to designate the whole caboodle, and, curiously, in Greece, where *patsas* covers all the elements in a soup. In Iran, Turkey, the Caucasus, parts of the Balkans and Central Asia, a distinction is made between tripe soup or stew, *iskembe* in Turkish and Persian, and *kalla pacha*, the head and feet soup. Iraq shares in elements of Turko-Iranian culture more than other Arab lands. There is a parallel Arabic vocabulary of offal. Tripe is variously designated as *kirsha/kurush*; bellies, *fawaregh*, 'empties'. Feet are variously *kawari`* or *maqadim*. Head is *ras*. Interestingly, there is a generic Arabic word, *sakatat*, equivalent to the English 'offal', and the French *abats*, to mean 'fallen things'. It is used to designate organ meats as well as tripe. In Turkish usage it has come to designate the pluck of attached lungs, liver and heart.

Stuffed intestines are also common throughout the region, most commonly called *bumbar/mumbar*, found in restaurants and street stalls, mostly in market areas. I recall one occasion in downtown Cairo, coming across a popular restaurant displaying coils of *bumbar* at the front. I hesitated, given the apparent standards of hygiene and flies, but temptation got the better of me when I noticed the serving: pieces were cut with scissors, then fried in hot oil to order, a process which would kill the germs. It was delicious, though I avoided salad! Significantly, the restaurant was called Antepli, after the Anatolian city of Gaziantep. The other occasion I came across it in Egypt it was prepared by the cook of an upper class household, attributed to the Ottoman past. In modern Turkey, *bumbar* is associated with east and south Anatolia, notably the Kurdish city of Diyarbakir.

Kokorec is another preparation of intestines and offal meats, found in Turkey, Greece, Albania, parts of the Caucasus and Central Asia. It is a sausage made from intestines/chitterlings platted together, often over bits of offal meats (liver, sweetbreads, etc.), and grilled over an open fire. It has a family resemblance to the French *Andouillette*, the French chitterling sausage, also platted chitterlings around various bits of meat, beloved by its connoisseurs, detested by detractors. Grilled *kokorec* in sandwiches and wraps is common street food in Istanbul and other cities. In Greece and Cyprus, where it is *Kokoretsi*, it tends to be reserved for Easter feasts, when young lambs ad goats are slaughtered, and their fresh innards cooked. Another Easter dish is *Magiritsa*, a soup of innards and offal meats with lettuce and dill, often finished with *Avgolemono* (egg yolk and lemon) sauce. This sauce also features in Aegean Turkey (known as *Terbeyeli*) for tripe dishes, among others.

Heads are part of this repertoire, either boiled, whole or in part, with feet (*kelle pacha*), or cooked whole and served with garnish. Typically, around the Middle East and the Mediterranean, they are cut in half symmetrically, then baked over a small amount of water or stock, with aromatics and maybe vinegar. They can also be roasted on a spit. Maghrebi butchers in the markets of Barbes and other parts of Paris feature rotisseries of sheep heads instead of the usual chicken.

The Lore of Tripe: Middle East and Beyond

The last time I enjoyed a head of lamb, however, was in London at a Sicilian themed lunch. The well known Bocca di Lupo restaurant held a series of lunches based on the gastronomic episodes of the Inspector Montalbano novels by Camelieri. The one I attended featured roasted sheep's head as one of the courses. This was served to communal tables, and I had to 'carve' and distribute morsels at my table. I ended up eating most of it!

Brains are eaten as part of the whole head, but more usually cooked by themselves as a delicacy. The variety of recipes will be familiar to foodies. Curiously, brains don't seem to be classified as offal in Western convention. In Egypt, however, there are specialized stalls and cook shops offering *kibda wa-mukh*, liver and brain.

There are many recipes for sheep's tongues. Typically, in my household of origin and many parts of the Middle East, they are stewed in a sauce, often with tomato paste, with chickpeas or split peas, with aromatics, including dried lime. Another common recipe is to poach the tongues after marinating, then serve cold with salads and dips.

Caul fat is the thin membrane, a large web of fat, which surrounds the intestines of sheep and pigs. It is used in many parts of the world as a rich wrap for various meats. The British faggot and the French *crepinette*, the first containing minced organ meats, the second seasoned forcemeat, are both examples of meat enriched by a wrap of pork fat. In the Middle East it is usually lamb caul. The best known such item, now in the global kitchen, is the Cypriot *sheftalia*, pork or lamb seasoned forcemeat made into a sausage-like parcel coated in caul, usually grilled over charcoal as a kebab. People have puzzled over the derivation of the word *sheftalia*: some have guessed, wrongly, that it derives from the Turkish *sheftali*, for 'peach', which seems odd as it has no connection or resemblance to the fruit. The most likely sense is that it is a compound of '*shish kofta*', becoming *shefta*, an actual usage in parts of the Arab world, with the 'lia' as the Greek suffix. I found a similar kebab, of ground meat in caul wrapping, in a traditional market eatery in Cairo, called *tarb kebab*, *tarb* being an Arabic word for caul.

Caul also features as a wrap for liver, and also for rice. In the culinary area of south Anatolia, the Arab Levant and parts of Iran, you have various combinations of liver and caul, the simplest just wrapping the liver tightly in the lacy fat and grilling it. A variation is to thread pieces of liver on a skewer, as a kebab, then drape it in caul and grill. The liver can also be stuffed with onions and aromatics. I recently came across a similar recipe from Italy, in which the liver is stuffed with ham and mushrooms, wrapped in caul and fried.

In Aegean Turkey I came across a rice dish covered in caul, called *gomlek pilaf*, *gomlek*, meaning shirt, being the word for caul. The rice was what is called *ic pilaf*, stuffing rice, which is rice fried with chopped meats, aromatics and pine nuts, used for stuffing chickens and other meats, but in this case, covered with a layer of caul fat and finished in the oven, a sumptuous dish.

We should note that many of these dishes are now rare, to be found in traditional eateries and cook shops, typically in the markets of Anatolian and Levantine cities.

However, like many other such dishes, they may very well come back in the global kitchen as they are 'discovered' in the endless search for both novelty and tradition.

Tripe Soup and Drink

Folklore regarding the efficacy of tripe/offal soup as a remedy for hangovers, after a night of drinking, is widespread. As noted above, these soups/stews are generally considered appropriate for breakfast, providing nourishment and strength for the day ahead. As such, it was (and still is, to a lesser extent) offered as a breakfast item in specialized eateries in markets and busy centres. In Istanbul and other Turkish cities, markets and busy centres feature *Iskembe Salonu*, tripe saloons, offering tripe and *kelle pacha* soups, and maybe a lentil soup, plus a few other meat items, including organ meats, all served with bread and sauces, usually of vinegar, garlic and paprika flakes (*pul biber*). Historically, drinkers and revellers would join early morning workers partaking of the fare, believing it to be a prevention or cure for a hangover. The Istanbul establishments, however, do not themselves provide drink: they are 'dry'. There are equivalent institutions, beliefs and practices in many cities over a wide area of Arab world, including Iran, the Balkans and the Caucasus. I came across tripe joints in the Athens Omonia central market, offering *patsas* soup, also believed to be a hangover cure. There are many neighbouring *ouzerias* to provide the need for the cure. In Iraq there were folk tales and jokes about tripe shops/stalls and drink. One is about a drunken brawl beside a street tripe stall with a steaming cauldron of the stuff. As the protagonists are being separated, one of them throws his slipper at the other, it misses and lands in the cauldron. Subsequently, the man asks the tripe cook for his slipper back, and the latter fishes it out, and the man says 'no, this is not mine'!

From drink to piety: tripe and offal dishes also featured as pre-fasting breakfast, *suhur*, during Ramadan. Market shops and stalls would open before daybreak for workers and worshippers. It would set you up for the rigours of the day to come.

The early morning tripe soup was also a feature of Les Halles market in Paris. Stalls and restaurants offered onion soup and tripe soup to the market workers, and they were joined by late night revellers concluding their drinking sessions. Traces of this trade persisted in the location after the dismantling of the market in 1971. Some notable restaurants in the Les Halles area have tripe and offal specialties. Most famous is Pied de Cochon; another is Pharamond, dating back to the 1870s, which used to have a Michelin rosette. I ate in the latter many years ago, and was served a memorable *tripe a la mode de Caen*, which came to the table in a bubbling pot placed over a mini-brazier with glowing embers to keep the pot bubbling till served some minutes later. The pot combines different cuts of tripe with a calf foot, cooked slowly with aromatics in sauce that may include ham, cream, cider and Calvados, in accordance with the Normandy provenance.

The Lore of Tripe: Middle East and Beyond

Tripe and Offal in the Global Kitchen

The fortunes of these foods, we see, have varied widely over time and place. Much loved and appreciated in one context, gracing family and banquet tables, while deprecated as unpalatable or even disgusting poor foods in others. In most places, however, they have become unusual and scarce for various reasons: the decline of traditional markets and their venues, the increasing prevalence of muscle meat and poultry (the ubiquitous chicken), the spread of global cheap convenience foods, such as pizza and fried chicken, and the spread of Western habits and notions, which rejected offal foods, finding them disgusting. In recent decades, however, they are coming back, often as gourmet foods.

Food discourses and practices in the contemporary world feature an on-going quest for innovation and novelty, paradoxically paired with another quest for authenticity. Exoticism, the interest in different cultures and ethnicities, enters into both quests. There is a foodie public, avid for knowledge and practice of food trends, with an ever expanding range media outlets and blogs, cookery books, new eateries and celebrity chefs. Offal is particularly attractive in competitive 'foodism', as it involves the breaking of previous conventional barriers of taste and disgust. We note the entry of offal into the gastronomic cannon of fine dining, from, perhaps, the 1980s. An early star of this trend was Pierre Koffman's La Tante Claire, with its signature dish of pig's trotter, boned and stuffed with sweetbreads and morel mushrooms in a rich sauce. Many chefs then introduced their particular trotter recipes, and London's St John's restaurant and its chef Fergus Henderson emerged in the 1990s as beacons of innovative 'nose to tail' cookery, thus becoming a cult eatery for foodies, chefs and writers.

These trends of fashion do not seem to have hit the Middle East and the post-Ottoman world yet, nor its ethnic diasporas. It might come.

Notes

1. Charles Perry, *Medieval Arab Cookery* (Totnes, Devon: Prospect Books, 2001), pp. 368-70.